CHRISTIANITY AND SOCIAL CHANGE IN AFRICA

Essays in Honor of J.D.Y. Peel

CHRISTIANITY AND SOCIAL CHANGE IN AFRICA

Essays in Honor of J.D.Y. Peel

EDITED BY

Toyin Falola

CAROLINA ACADEMIC PRESS
Durham, North Carolina

Library of Congress Cataloging-in-Publication Data

Christianity and social change in Africa : essays in honor of J.D.Y. Peel /
edited by Toyin Falola.

    p. cm.

  Includes bibliographical references and index.

  ISBN 1-59460-135-6

  1. Church and social problems—Nigeria. 2. Church and social problems—Africa, West. 3. Social change—Nigeria. 4. Social change—Africa,
West. 5. Nigeria—Social conditions—1960– 6. Africa, West—Social conditions—1960– I. Peel, J. D. Y. (John David Yeadon), 1941– II. Falola,
Toyin. III. Title.

  HN39.N55C48 2005
  306.6'76608—dc22   2005007640

Carolina Academic Press
700 Kent St.
Durham, NC 27701
Telephone (919) 489-7486
Fax (919) 493-5668
www.cap-press.com

Printed in the United States of America

CONTENTS

LIST OF FIGURES

CONTRIBUTORS

Karen Barber is Professor of African Cultural Anthropology at the Centre of West African Studies, University of Birmingham. She specializes in Yoruba culture, and also does comparative work on oral literature and popular culture across Africa. Her most recent book is, *The Generation of Plays: Yoruba Popular Life in Theatre* (2000).

Sandra T. Barnes is Professor of Anthropology at the University of Pennsylvania, Founding Director of its African Studies Center, and in 2004–05 a fellow at the Stanford University Humanities Center. She is the editor of *Africa's Ogun: Old World and New,* an interdisciplinary collection of recently expanded and revised essays that focus on West African religious culture and its continuing vitality in the diaspora. Her book, *Patrons and Power: Creating a Political Community in Metropolitan Lagos* (1986), won the Amaury Talbot Prize for the best book on Africa. She is President of the African Studies Association, and sits on the Boards of Directors of the American Council of Learned Societies and the Foundation for the Advancement of International Medical Education and Research. She has been a visiting faculty member at Johns Hopkins University and the University of Ibadan (Nigeria). Her current research focuses on West Africa: pre-colonial social and cultural life along the Guinea Coast and post-colonial popular culture.

Lynne Brydon is Senior Lecturer in the Centre of West African Studies, University of Birmingham (UK). Among her publications are *Women in the Third World* (with Sylvia Chant) and *Adjusting Society: The World Bank, the IMF and Ghana* (with Karen Legge). She co-edits *Ghana Studies Review* (with Takyiwaa Manuh), and is a member of the Editorial Collective of the *Review of African Political Economy.*

Andrea Cornwall is a Fellow at the Institute of Development Studies at the University of Sussex, where she works on the politics of participation, gender, and governance, and sexual and reproductive rights. Her publications include *Dislocating Masculinity: Comparative Ethnographies* (edited, with Nancy Lindisfarne, 1994), *Realizing Rights: Transforming Approaches to Sexual and Repro-*

ductive Wellbeing (co-edited, with Alice Welbourn, 2002), *Readings in Gender in Africa* (James Currey, 2004), "Spending power: love, money and the re-configuration of gender relations in Ado-Odo, southwestern Nigeria" (*American Ethnologist*, 29:4, 2002), and "'To be a man is more than a day's work': Shifting ideals of manliness in Ado-Odo, southwestern Nigeria" (in Lisa Lindsay and Stephan Miescher eds., *Men and Masculinities in Modern Africa*, Heinemann, 2003).

Jane I. Guyer is Professor of Anthropology at the Johns Hopkins University. Her research has focused on social and economic change in West and Central Africa over the past century. *An African Niche Economy. Farming to Feed Ibadan 1968–88* (1997) studies a Yoruba town in the Ibadan hinterland, and *Marginal Gains: Monetary Transactions in Atlantic Africa* (2004) re-analyzes ethnographic and historical evidence from several areas, including Southern Nigeria. A co-edited book (with LaRay Denzer and Adigun Agbaje), *Money Struggles and City Life: Devaluation in Ibadan and Other Urban Centers in Southern Nigeria, 1986–1996* (2002; 2003, Ibadan) addresses some aspects of the "confusion" of her topic for this volume.

Hermione Harris is a consultant researcher with the Information Centre about Asylum and Refugees (ICAR) at King's College, London. Her publications include *The Somali Community in the UK* (2004). She has carried out extensive research on Yoruba churches in London, the subject of her doctoral thesis *The Cherubim and Seraphim: the Concept and Practice of Empowerment in an African Church in London* (2002).

Ogbu U. Kalu, formerly of the University of Nigeria, is the Henry Winters Luce Professor of World Christianity and Mission, McCormick Theological Seminary, Chicago, and Associate Director of Chicago Center for Global Ministries. His book, *Embattled Gods: Christianization of Igboland, 1841–1991* was first published in 1996, and has been republished by Africa World Press. The University of South Africa Press is publishing his collection of essays, *Clio in a Sacred Garb: Essays on Christian Presence and African Responses, 1900–2000*. He is the editor of *African Christianity: an African Story* that is forthcoming under the Perspective Series, University of Pretoria, South Africa.

Axel Klein is the Head of the International Unit at the UK-based NGO Drug Scope, working on a range of issues including drug policy, prison reform, and civil society capacity building. He has published on drug policy and the informal sector in Nigeria, and is currently editing a volume on illicit drugs in Africa with Isidore Obot. Previous publications include *Caribbean Drugs: from Criminalisation to Harm Reduction*, edited with Anthony Harriott and Marcus Day, and *Fragile Peace: State Failure, Violence and Development in Crisis Regions*, co-edited with Tobias Debiel.

Kai Kresse is a Lecturer in Social Anthropology at the University of St. Andrews. His publications include *Sagacious Reasoning: H. Odera Oruka in Memoriam* (Frankfurt/New York Peter Lang. 1997), co-edited with Anke Graness (reprinted in an Africa-edition by East African Educational Publishers, Nairobi, 1999); *Symbolisches Flanieren: Kulturphilosophische Streifzuege.* (Hannover: Wehrhahn Verlag. 2001), co-edited with Roger Behrens & Ronnie Peplow; and, as editor, *Reading Mudimbe*, to appear as a special issue of *Journal of African Cultural Studies* (in press). He is currently finalizing a book manuscript on Swahili philosophical discourse, dealing with poets, thinkers, and intellectual practice in Mombasa. Recent articles in the *Journal of Religion in Africa* (2003), and edited collections, e.g. Scott Reese (ed), *The Transmission of Learning in Islamic Africa.* (Leiden: Brill. 2004). He was awarded the Evans-Pritchard Lectureship at All Souls College, Oxford, for the academic year 2005–6. He is also part of the editorial team of the online journal *Polylog: Forum for Intercultural Philosophy.* He holds an M.A. in Philosophy from the University of Hamburg, where he also studied Swahili, and an MSc and a Ph.D. in Anthropology and African Studies from the University of London.

Matthew H. Kukah is a Catholic priest, Vicar General, Archdiocese of Kaduna, Nigeria. He studied philosophy and theology at St Augustine's Seminary, Jos, and received his MA in Peace Studies at Bradford University, and his Ph.D. at the School of African and Oriental Studies, London. He has served as the Secretary General, Catholic Secretariat of Nigeria; Member, Human Rights Violations Investigation Commission; Senior Rhodes Scholar, St Antony's College, Oxford; and the Edward Mason Fellow, Kennedy School of Government, Harvard University.

Murray Last is Professor Emeritus in the Department of Anthropology, University College London. He specializes in both the pre-colonial history of Muslim northern Nigeria and the ethnography of illness and healing. He has been working in and on northern Nigeria since 1961, researching a wide variety of subjects with colleagues in Bayero University and elsewhere; he visits Nigeria every year. In 1967 he published *The Sokoto Caliphate* (London: Longmans Green), and edited (with G.L. Chavunduka), *The Professionalisation of African Medicine* in 1986 (Manchester: Manchester University Press for International African Institute); in addition he has over seventy publications on history and on anthropology. He edited the International African Institute's journal *AFRICA* for fifteen years (1986–2001).

Carola Lentz is Professor of Social Anthropology at the Johannes Gutenberg University of Mainz, Germany, and was a fellow of the Netherland's Institute for Advanced Studies in 2000–2001. Following her doctoral research on labor migration and ethnicity in Ecuador, she has conducted research on ethnicity, elite formation, and history in North-Western Ghana. She is author of *Ethnic Unity and Local Patriotism: The Production of History in North-Western Ghana, 1870–1990* (forthcoming), as well many related articles, and co-editor of *Ethnicity in Ghana: The Limits of Invention* (2000). Further publications include the edited volumes *Les Dagara et leurs voisins: Histoire de peuplement et relations interethniques au sud-ouest du Burkina Faso* (2001), and *Histoire du peuplement et relations interethnique au Burkina Faso* (2003). Her current research focuses on mobility, land rights, and the politics of belonging in North-Western Ghana and South-Western Burkina Faso.

John M. Lonsdale is Emeritus Professor of Modern African History at the University of Cambridge, and Fellow of Trinity College, Cambridge. His published work includes *Unhappy Valley: Conflict in Kenya and Africa* (1992, with Bruce Berman), and *Mau Mau and Nationhood* (edited, with Atieno Odhiambo, 2003). He is a past general editor of the Cambridge University Press African Studies Series, past chairman of the African Studies Centre at Cambridge and past president of the African Studies Association of the United Kingdom. He is currently working on the intellectual life of Jomo Kenyatta, the British decolonization of Kenya, and the historical relationship between religion and politics in Kenya.

T. C. McCaskie is Professor of Asante History, Centre of West African Studies, University of Birmingham, U.K. He is author of *State and Society in Pre-Colonial Asante* (Cambridge University Press, 1995) and *Asante Identities: History and Modernity in an African Village 1850–1950* (Indiana and Edinburgh University Presses, 2000), as well as numerous book chapters and journal articles on Asante history and culture. Most recently, he was co-editor with A. Adu Boahen, E. Akyeampong, N. Lawler, and I. Wilks of *The History of Ashanti Kings and the whole country itself, and Other Writings by Otumfuo, Nana Agyeman Prempeh I* (Oxford University Press for the British Academy). He is presently writing a book on contemporary Asante.

Birgit Meyer is professor of *Religion and Society* in the Department of Sociology and Anthropology at the University of Amsterdam, and professor of the anthropology of religion at the Free University, Amsterdam. Her publications include *Translating the Devil. Religion and Modernity Among the Ewe in Ghana* (1999), *Globalization and Identity: Dialectics of Flow and Closure* (1999, edited with Peter Geschiere). *Magic and Modernity: Interfaces of Revelation and Concealment* (edited with Peter Pels), and *Religion, Media and the Public Sphere* (in press, edited with Annelies Moors). Her current research focuses on the interface of religion and media in Ghana.

Insa Nolte is a lecturer at the Centre of West African Studies at the University of Birmingham, UK. Her publications include "Identity and Violence: The Politics of Youth in Ijebu-Remo, Nigeria" (2004, *JMAS* 42/1), and "Chieftaincy and the State in Abacha's Nigeria: Kingship, Political Rivalry and Competing Histories in Abeokuta During the 1990s" (2002, *Africa* 72/3). She is presently writing a monograph on power, politics and Obafemi Awolowo in Ijebu-Remo.

Matthews A. Ojo completed his doctoral studies in theology at the University of London (School of Oriental and African Studies, and King's College, London) in 1987. His research interest is African Christianity with particular reference to the Pentecostal and Charismatic movements. He has published extensively in this field, and recently in the area of religion and politics in Nigeria. In 1999, he was involved in a British Academy-funded research on religion and media in Nigeria. In 2002, he was a Visiting Professor at Harvard University Divinity School and a Senior Fellow at the Centre for the Study of World Religions, Harvard University. He is presently a Professor and Head of Department of Religious Studies, Obafemi Awolowo University, Nigeria.

Stephan Palmié is Associate Professor of Anthropology at the University of Chicago. His publications include *Das Exil der Götter: Geschichte und Vorstellungswelt einer afrokubanischen Religion* (1991), *Wizards and Scientists: Explorations in Afro-Cuban Modernity and Tradition* (2002), an edited volume on *Slave Cultures and the Cultures of Slavery* (1995), and a co-edition of the original manuscript of C.G.A. Oldendorp's *History of the Mission of the Moravian Brethren in the Caribbean Islands of St. Thomas, St. Croix, and St. John* (1767–77) in four volumes (2000, 2002).

David Pratten is a lecturer in anthropology at the University of Sussex. His forthcoming publications include *The Man-Leopard Murder Mysteries: History and Society in Colonial Nigeria*, and various articles on youth, violence and vigilantism in southern Nigeria.

Miriam Rabelo teaches at the Department of Sociology and Postgraduate Program in Social Sciences of the Universidade Federal da Bahia (Brazil). She has carried out research in the field of anthropology of religion and health in Brazil, with a special focus on religious healing. Among her publications are: *Experiéncia de Doença e Narrativa* with Paulo César Alves and Iara Souza (Editora Fiocruz, 1999), and *Antropologia da Saúde: traçando identidades e explorando fronteiras* with Paulo César Alves (Editora Fiocruz, 1998).

Elisha P. Renne is an Associate Professor in the Department of Anthropology and the Center for Afro-American and African Studies, University of Michigan. Her research focuses on fertility and reproductive health, gender relations, religion, and social change, and the anthropology of cloth, specifically in Nigeria. Publications include *Population and Progress in a Yoruba Town* (Edinburgh and Michigan, 2003), *Regulating Menstruation: Beliefs, Practices, Interpretations* (with E. van de Walle; Chicago, 2001), and *Cloth That Does Not Die: The Meaning of Cloth in Bunu Social Life* (Washington, 1995). She is presently co-editing a volume (with B. Agbaje-Williams), *Yoruba Religious Textiles*, which will be published early in 2005.

Guy Thomas is Director of the Archives and Library of Mission 21 and Lecturer in African history at the University of Basel. While heading the project to set up the Presbyterian Church in Cameroon Central Archives and Library (PCCCAL), he was among the founding members of the Association of Friends of Archives and Antiquities-Cameroon (AFAAC). He is a core member of the Centre for African Studies in Basel and is on the Advisory Board of the journal *Le Fait Missionaire*. He has published several articles, and is about to produce his first book on the mediation, appropriation, and domestication of Christianity in twentieth-century anglophone Cameroon. Ongoing research covers a wide range of themes linked to the social history of Christian missions, primarily in West and West-Central Africa.

Asonzeh F.-K. Ukah is a Research Fellow at the Centre of African Studies (CAS), School of Oriental and African Studies (SOAS), University of London. His publications include, "Pentecostalism, Religious Expansion and the City: Lesson from the Nigerian Bible Belt," in: Peter Probst & Gerd Spittler (eds), *Resistance and Expansion: Explorations of Local Vitality in Africa*, Lit Münster (2004); "Advertising God: Nigerian Christian Video-Films and the Power of Consumer Culture", *JRA*, (2003); "Reklame für Gott: Religiöse Werbung in Nigeria," in Tobias Wendl (ed.), *Afrikanische Reklamekunst* (2002); "The Local and the Global in the Media and Material Culture of Nigerian Pentecostalism" (forthcoming); "Mobilities, Migration and Multiplication: The Expansion of the Religious Field of the Redeemed Christian Church of God (RCCG), Nigeria" (forthcoming). His current research interests focus on the economics of Pentecostal popular culture in Africa, African Pentecostal Video films; and African Diasporan Religions.

Gavin Williams is Fellow and Tutor in Politics at St Peter's College, Oxford, where he teaches comparative politics, political and social theories, and politics in Africa. He studied at the Universities of Stellenbosch and Oxford. He has published articles and edited books on politics and political economy and on land and agricultural policies in Africa, particularly Nigeria, and more recently South Africa, and on the discourses and practices of development and of the World Bank. He is writing a history of the South African wine industry.

Part A
Context and Personality

CHAPTER 1

INTRODUCTION

Toyin Falola

The Iyalorisa and the Pastor

African churches now dot many American and European cities, including Austin, Texas, where I am based. As part of the religious and social network, immigrants attend these churches and the post-service social events where food and drinks are generously offered. Social exchanges occur, with gifts to celebrants, and monetary donations to churches. The churches are mainly "local branches" of the main ones in Africa, reversing the established trend that religious headquarters must be based in Europe or the United States.

This chapter begins with a worship service in the Fall of 2004, in one of the "neo-Pentecostal" churches in Austin. Attending as an invited guest, I paid attention more as a researcher than as a man of faith. I was invited by a Yoruba couple—richer than me in income and of higher social position—who wanted to celebrate the ten-year anniversary of their wedding and the "dedication of their children to God." The couple was blessed with two children, and probably expected more. The couple, representative of the many successful African professionals in the city, are established members of the congregation. The usual worshippers were engaged, motivated, and attentive. Temporary guests like me appeared disengaged, hesitant, and observant. I sat at a strategic position where I could see nearly everybody.

The boundaries of participation were marked. The regular congregation was energized; maybe the expected "last day" was already revealed to one of them. The pastor was at his best. In one long sermon, he yielded the data that enabled us to locate Christianity in its cultural, transnational, and comparative contexts. But this church was not based in Nigeria, but in Austin-Texas, and the elements of an African church in the diaspora began to appear in the worship: sermon, songs, audience participation, clapping, testimonies of miracles, promises of healing, and open declaration of allegiance to Jesus. The pastor even asked sinners who sought repentance to raise their hands and seek forgiveness, there and then.

In the southern U.S., Yoruba cultures and traditions have begun to surface; the forces of pre-modern began to engage with those of modernity. Will there be some resolution of these forces? What are the compromises? Why is the pre-modern Yoruba culture surviving in the post-modern entity called the United States? I was posing questions without answering them, as I watched all the details. Data from secondary sources rushed through my head, creating a comprehensive bibliography locked in memory. Visual effects were added; and I could not ignore the value of observations.

Back to the service: The invited guests, not regular members of the congregation, were restless, and many wandered in and out of the church as if giving a signal to the pastor to stop talking. The pastor, as if to seize the opportunity of fresh recruitment presented to him, refused to stop talking: his sermon was long and tortuous, except to the passionate believers. I listened, enduring the pain, but I never prayed for the Lord to deliver me from the pastor. The sermon warned the congregation of the power of evil and witchcraft. As if standing before a diviner, the pastor asked the listeners to wish away illnesses, deny the reality of cancer, and the affliction of poverty, even if evidences to the contrary were there. The mere denial was more than magic, as the words became the talisman to ward off all evils.

Nigerian witches have traveled to Austin, without having to struggle for the difficult immigration papers or buy expensive, non-discount travel tickets. These evil-doers have crept quietly into Austin, and they are very dangerous. They are visible to those with the evangelical credentials, especially the pastor and a few church members with untainted faith in clean bodies. The satanic power is no longer in the color of blackness, as we were told back in Nigeria, unless they are among the few Black people in the city. Jesus Christ, although still not colorless or Black in the picture hanging on the Church wall which gave him a Caucasian nose and blonde hair, can move the mountains. The pastor was Yoruba, the accent of delivery was Yoruba; the tone was self-adulating. The stories to spread the message were full of Yoruba landscape, even of the Amos Tutuola-like mysteries—in one instance, the car of the pastor crashed into the valley of death, but sustained by an innocent tree put there by the all merciful God. The Yoruba who received Christianity in the nineteenth century are now transporting it back to Western societies where the religion came from, carrying the Bible with them together with the witches and the wicked agents into a luggage packed with pre-modern stuff to be unloaded in post-modern Austin, the city full of satanic creatures. We cannot say that the clock has turned back its hands—far from it—as Christianity in America reflects the reality of racism and segregation. However, we affirm, as this book shows, that Christianity is not only strong in Africa, its propagators have become confident to carry it to Europe and America which they now call the "Dark Continent."

* * *

About twenty miles from this African Pentecostal church is the center of a Yoruba religious organization headed by Iyalorisa Aina Olomo. Her followers include a notable professor of theater, Dr. Joni Jones (name-ritualized into Omi Osun) based at the University of Texas at Austin. They (*Ile*, as they are often known in a collective name) believe in the Yoruba *orisa*, perform the masquerade, hold regular religious sessions, and affirm the survival of Yoruba religious traditions. They probably do not know that the African Pentecostal church exists, even if the pastor warns his congregation to avoid the *orisa* and the Iyalorisa's congregation. Thus, we are back to the terrain of religious choices, if not of competition, but also of the "satanization" of others. The pastor who carried the witch with him to Austin is probably unaware that the *orisa* are waiting for him, not to protect the witch, but to create an alternative religious order. The Iyalorisa and his crowd cannot be the Esu that the pastor mentioned in his sermon. Like the pastor, the Iyalorisa is doing good work, although the pastor will retort: "good work does not lead to heaven!"

Austin-Texas reminds us that Christianity in Africa cannot be discussed without also talking about indigenous religions, African worldview, and even the other universal religion of Islam. American Pentecostalists have been recruited in the American fight against Islam. There is no need to convince the pastor to join in a jihad against Muslims: it is already part of his belief to conduct a "holy war." Christian statements that are not intended to be comparative can become so, made against the background of other religions or with the African cultures as the context. Africa's ancient religions have refused to let go, even following the African church from Yorubaland to Austin. I was reminded of J. D. Y. Peel's study on the Aladura movement. He poses a question: "What is the nature of Yoruba traditional religion?" He provides an answer:

> It is very loosely organized, both as an institution and as a system of thought...it is, in Weber's somewhat unhappy expression, 'magical'; that is, for the average member, it is largely concerned with easing the conditions of living in this world, through various techniques which enable the individual to communicate with those beings who are re-

garded as controlling the environment. This is not incompatible with a belief in a sovereign being who created the world, but he is usually regarded as beyond the worshippers' attentions. In this kind of religion one can often identify a syndrome of a belief in fate and a fatalistic attitude, a fondness for astrology or divination, a hierarchy of the objects of religious adoration and a 'this-worldly' emphasis in prayers, 'magical' techniques and general religious values.[1]

The stories of the Christian pastor and the Iyalorisa in Austin represent the phase of African religions in the "New World," a phase that makes it possible to talk about religious histories and trans-nationalism, social change and the power of tradition, localism and globalism. If both the Iyalorisa and *orisa* represent one face of the "future" of religions, they also symbolize one facet of its past. One of these "pasts" is the just- mentioned question and answer by John Peel. And we should always compare religions and their practices, in part to understand how traditions have been shaped. In chapter 16 by Miriam Rabelo, we see the story and interpretation of the encounters between Christianity (expressed as Pentecostalism and the Progressive Catholicism of the Ecclesial Base Communities [CEBs]) and a syncretic Afro-Brazilian religion, the *jarê*. A "confluence" emerged, altering the balance in, and within, traditions and redefining the cultural landscape. Like the Iyalorisa and the pastor, the CEBs and *jarê* acquire influence within a confluence.

This book contains within it all the aforementioned issues, the different views of the past and present, the various representations of "society," and the clues to its future. The chapters paint colorful images of Christianity and change in fluid societies. Not only do we see the dynamics of Christianity and the agencies of modernization, we are drawn to the world of cultural pluralism, the conflicts and prospects of secularism, and the challenges posed by the forces of traditions and human interactions. In arguments that are packaged in different ways, we come to the conclusion that the African religious and social landscape is rather complex. The authors place Christianity and other issues in the context of history, development, and pluralism. In this eclectic context, we see the role of Africans looming large, and the emphasis on many Africa-based ideas and institutions. External developments are not ignored, but they are carefully connected with the local: Christianity is linked to existing traditions and also to emerging ideas around globalization. Issues of adaptations to new ideas are underscored in several essays, even as we see

---

1. J. D. Y. Peel, *Aladura: A Religious Movement Among the Yoruba* (London: International African Institute and Oxford University Press, 1968), 289-90.

the tensions generated by cultural and religious pluralism. As part of adaptations, some essays reveal the process and power of reforms, while some are interested in issues of revivals. We also have to deal with "confusion," as in the case of Chapter 4 by Jane Guyer. Whether they are talking about reforms or revivals, we are confronted with continuity and change.

History and Context

> The large-scale adoption of Christianity has been one of the master themes of modern African history; and as the third millennium beckons, it may well prove to be of world historical significance too, contributing to a decisive shift in Christianity's geopolitical placement, from North to South.[2]—J. D. Y. Peel

The multiple faces of Christianity and social change in Africa that are captured in this volume remind us of many familiar features that the pastor and Iyalorisa represent. Christianity is based on written texts, with the power of the Bible manifesting itself in various ways. Africans have interpreted the Bible in multiple ways, some as intended by those who introduced it to them, but many in the context of local religions and cultures. If Christianity, in its earliest origins, is presented as "exogenous," it is no longer, as many now regard it, indigenous, not to mention the successful attempts that have been made to export it to the West. Africans have always served as the proselytizers of Christianity, although their own indigenous gods do not require them to advertise and sell religions. Without the African agents who have tirelessly worked to spread Christianity, the story would have been different and ambitious missionaries may still be searching for Prester John instead of scholars talking about John Peel.

This book opens with the Yoruba in part because Peel has contributed to our understanding of Christianity among them. There is another compelling reason: the Yoruba have profited enormously from Christianity and Western education, to the extent that they have formulated enduring notions of progress. Pause for a moment: remember the Iyalorisa who took the *orisa* from there. It is also a society that is always on the throes of change as it adapts to local and external circumstances. Peel has pioneered various aspects of what we know about Yoruba Christianity as his biographer, T. C. McCaskie, notes

---

2. J. D. Y. Peel, *Religious Encounter and the Making of the Yoruba* (Bloomington: Indiana University Press, 2000), 1.

in the next chapter. I have chosen not to set up this Introduction either as a substitute for, or in competition with, the remarks by McCaskie, an intellectual gladiator far more accomplished than this humble editor. Peel has emphasized the centrality of history and culture in the study of Christianity, an article of faith that I will follow as the First (and only) Commandment. On the other hand, as Gavin Williams shows in chapter twenty-five, we see the power of ideas drawn from towering figures—Marx, Weber, and Durkeheim. In not following the path charted by Williams, it is to avoid the transgression and punishment associated with what many may associate with the violation of the First Commandment. We are still far away from the happy days when scholars will agree on the theory and methodology to study religions. Generalizations, as Jane Guyer shows, equally carry their own risks.

Here is the "Lord's Prayer" customized for this book: I will keep a commitment to a set of dialogue: texts and their meanings; cultures and histories; peoples and actions; past and present; the present and the invention of a future. "Presentism" becomes moderated by history, and some kind of "projects" articulated by a definable elite groups. Some will wonder where I get this sense of dialogue from, but they can read chapter 16 by Miriam Rabelo for its more nuanced articulation. It shall come to pass!

* * *

History is preceded by pre-history, even when the events are part of recoverable orality: Axel Klein shows in Chapter 5 the presence of the Ewe among the coastal communities, indicating how the Yoruba deal with the incorporation of strangers. The Yoruba have not only witnessed the injection of "strange" people into their landscape, but also of Christianity and the strangers "from across the sea"—certainly not the Ewe, but the Oyinbo—that brought it. Yet, as an ancient group, Christianity did not reach them until the nineteenth century. Indeed, for most of Africa, early attempts to introduce the religion were unsuccessful. The concerns for trade in slaves dominated the Euro-African relations from the fifteenth to the nineteenth centuries. With the abolition of the slave trade and the rise of trade in produce, Euro-African relations were strengthened in some other ways, including the arrival of missionaries who represented different denominations and agencies, all strangers with a boldness to announce that their faith was superior to those of their hosts. The strangers arrived at a time of "confusion" in the Yoruba world, a situation with ideological and practical complexities that Jane Guyer tells us about in Chapter 4. The Yoruba joined the strangers, as agents to spread the religion in the second half of the nineteenth century. Small clusters of Christian communities emerged in various towns such as Badagry, Lagos, Abeokuta,

Ijaye, and Ibadan. Some broad patterns emerged: the missionaries and their Yoruba agents were committed workers who planted the seeds of a religious revolution. This is what John Peel told us with passion and "brotherly love" in *Religious Encounter*[3] where he writes as if he was one of those Yoruba agents. While the leadership was foreign-dominated, the local agents were Yoruba activists. We see their activism in the way they began to "translate" Christianity into a local milieu by contributing to the translation of the Bible into Yoruba, and by seeking the means to inject nationalism into their teachings and preaching. The nationalism that Christianity supplied them with translated into their eagerness to define their "race." The idea of a "one Yoruba" became so strong that one of them wrote the best book on the subject ever: Samuel Johnson's *The History of the Yorubas*. In an essay that will surely generate attention, Stephan Palmié wonders, in Chapter 3 whether we should even characterize Johnson as a "Yoruba" if he contributed to the emergence of this identity. Broadening his original scope, Palmié uses the evolution of identities to talk about religious syncretism in West Africa and Cuba, warning us to recognize "the mutually implicated historicity of both social life *and* the languages, descriptive or analytical, by which we represent it." Samuel Johnson knew exactly what he was representing, and its language of representation: the creation of a "new Yoruba" that is "Christian."

Africans have been able to rework Christianity to meet their varied needs. As with the introduction and expansion of Christianity, the environment was friendly in many areas. The plural settings have enabled different religions to compete. European colonialism gave support to missionary activities in various ways, including the creation of formal educational, economic and political institutions that empowered the educated Christians. The educated Christians with nationalist agenda supported the tendency toward secularism. Many among them became strong advocates for the creation of a new society, and some of the issues they addressed are dealt with in this book. Some of the secularist ideas combined with a climate of religious competition to bring about conflicts between Christianity and Islam in a number of countries. The lingering aspects of the conflicts have inspired Matthew Kukah to contribute an essay (Chapter 17) on this subject.

As the chapters in Section Three show, the Yoruba and many other African groups were not slow in domesticating Christianity and imposing local vernaculars on its messages. A tradition of religious assertiveness, beginning in what is now called "Ethiopianism," is a preface to the Aladura and Pentecostal-

---

3. Peel, *Religious Encounter and the Making of the Yoruba*.

Figure 1.1 - Sculpture of two Africans carrying a European in a hammock.

ism that receive prominent attention in this volume. African church founders and leaders emerged from the late nineteenth century, establishing churches free of mission control. With the freedom to finance themselves and create their liturgies, they began the process of borrowing from local cultures and African worldviews. The African Independent Churches, one of those labels for many Aladura, Pentecostal, Charismatic, and other forms of indigenous churches had to struggle with attacks directed at them by the mission-controlled churches, and by foreign church leaders who demonized them. Where they signaled anti-colonial nationalism, the European colonial governments were also hostile to them. They survived the criticisms and the attacks.

By the time we entered the twentieth century, a number of African Independent Churches had emerged, and the trend continues to this day. The example of the church in Austin updates the story to the present. Asonzeh F-K Ukah's Chapter 12 shows that Pentecostalism is on the rise, that its actors are prominent, and that they dominate a large religious space. In explaining the reasons, we can see how history is at work in the recreation of the religious vigor that characterized the emergence of Ethiopianism. Ukah connects the contemporary Pentecostalism with the economy; drawing on the Redeemed

Figure 1.2 - Livingstone, the missionary, in an African village close to Luabala village.

Christian Church, he analyzes its practices and doctrines as they relate to the economy, and also how the church members endure economic recession.

The religious universe of the modern Pentecostals is different from those of the pioneer church founders. The Aladura and the Pentecostals project enormous spiritual power. Their leaders are not accountable to the Pope or the Archbishop but to themselves or their African church founders. Religion thus provides the source of grassroots authority and power. This power, in turn, feeds the frenzy of religious self-assertion and nationalism. The churches and their leaders have control of their wallets, being self-financing organizations. But more importantly, they have the power to define the liturgy, enabling them to insert African values more powerfully into their messages. The worldview that nineteenth-century missionaries found strange is now embedded into religious practices. The benevolent forces associated with Christian worship can be damaged by the malevolent forces of evil if the Christian is not devout enough or careless not to sustain the intensity and regularity of prayers. Did the pastor not say that we should be careful of the *orisa* and the Iyalorisa?

The spread of the Aladura and Pentecostal churches in Africa is phenomenal. Ogbu Kalu yields new data in Chapter 15 on how the Aladura, originally Yoruba, spread among the Igbo. A concept of "frontier" becomes appropriate, although Kalu is not suggesting this. The Igbo Aladura chose to operate in cities that offered them opportunities to succeed far more than in rural settings. The commercial cities of Aba and Onitsha were attractive to the churches since they could draw membership from among the non-Igbo residents. With the Nigerian Civil War, 1967–1970, the Igbo Aladura received a boost, as those in trouble sought spiritual means to overcome them. The Aladura continued to grow, and they found a way to incorporate elements of "Igboness" into their liturgy.

The use of symbols—of words, spaces, and objects—is part of the powerful expression of religion and spirituality. Elisha P. Renne tells us in Chapter 7 of the importance of the white cloth to the Aladura. She notes the established uses of white cloth among the Yoruba to mark sacred locations, define spiritual spaces and represent some kind of religious identities. To the Cherubim & Seraphim Church, the way they use and represent white cloth represents dedication to God, their own moral position ("whiteness of heart," "unhidden, good intentions"), and their differences with Yoruba religions and other Christian churches. While Renne notes that some Pentecostal churches no longer emphasize the use of white cloth, she concludes that as an idea and practice, "the connections of white cloth with past practices, with spiritual protection and healing, and with the moral goodness wearing them implies, are benefits too powerful and precious to abandon." What the Yoruba see as positive, the Igbo to their East originally associated the use of white garment by the Aladura as a bad omen, and its members were asked to wear it only within church premises.

The use of white cloth may be part of the emphasis on rituals by the African Independent Churches. They must heal; the fingers of the leader must be "magical" enough to cure illnesses. The leaders must see visions; indeed, their missionary journey often begins with the vision they receive from angels or God. They see visions about others, visions of warning, empowerment, and progress. They can dream and interpret dreams. Because of the presence of witches, they must also possess the power of exorcism. This healing aspect is one area where the pastor and the Iyalorisa do have many things in common. Without healing powers, the credibility of African Independent Churches can be questioned. The pioneer missionaries probably did not factor healing into their strategy. In Peel's study of the Yoruba in the nineteenth century, he notes how the healing market in relation to religion was dominated by Muslim scholars who offered solutions to illnesses and even promised to be able to defer death. As Murray Last points out in Chapter 23, the Yoruba were attracted to this "practical religion" of healing, which the African Independent Churches were later to adopt. The missionary pioneers did not see themselves as miracle workers. Last is able to connect Islamic practices with the Yoruba

Figure 1.3 - African sculpture of a colonial officer and school teacher.

ones, to undertake an exercise in comparison that enables us to understand the role of religion in healing. The reactions to loss, pain, and suffering can also shape responses to religions.

The Religious Impact

Christianity is an agency of globalization. Its spread to Africa has been a historic moment in the migration of ideas across the Atlantic. This globalization is not a one-way traffic from Europe to Africa, as the case of Iyalorisa and the pastor demonstrates. David Pratten supplies us with analysis on one of the early encounters of missionaries with the Qua Iboe, but he is quick to point out in Chapter 18 that the African converts were not docile recipients of new ideas. The routes to conversion and religious practices are equally multiple. T. C. Mc-Caskie (Chapter 21) gives us the example of how the thirteenth Asante king, Agyeman Prempeh, took aspects of Anglican Christianity during his exile in Seychelles and refined them in Asante in a way that Christianity was blended with traditions. This is one example of the creative use of foreign ideas reaching compromises with the local. The importation of ideas to Africa is not going to stop. The various Pentecostal and charismatic movements of the last quarter of the twentieth century benefited from support and ideas from the United States and Europe.

The African Independent Churches, irrespective of their types, have become "global-centric," thanks in part to the large migrations of Africans to the West since the 1980s, and to the production of a second generation of migrants. The churches use the media and modern technologies to present their messages, drawing from events from various parts of the world. Those with branches in Europe and America are global organizations: the pastors travel between continents; they use European languages to communicate with their congregation; and the pastors and church members consume objects of modernity. The location of the churches in Western cities may reflect the need for access to the "market"—that is to people, which explains why a number of them are located in strip malls. The African churches in the West define their agenda in an ambitious manner: they not only want to minister to fellow migrants, their main targets, but to "remissionize" white people. Chapter 14, by Hermionne Harris, devotes itself to the phenomenon of church expansion outside of Africa. Using London as its example, the chapter provides details on the Aladura and Pentecostal Churches, notably the Cherubim and Seraphim Church which started with a humble beginning in 1965 and expanded to a congregation of over two hundred people by 1971; and the Kingsway International Christian Church with a congregation of over two thousand. The chapter shows an effective use of technology and the mastery of the media by these churches.

The idea of a "reverse-mission" is bold and creative, and already a phenomenal success in major Western cities. Africans now assert themselves outside of their boundaries in ways unimaginable to the worshippers of the indigenous gods and the pioneers who took Christianity to Africa. Perhaps, the future will reveal another "creolization" of religions: as the African churches borrow from the Western ones, new organizations and practices may emerge to extend the frontier of Christianity in directions that are harder to predict. Or, perhaps multi-ethnic and multi-national churches will emerge to break down some segregationist walls. Those in Africa, some labeled as Neo-Pentecostals, are connected to organizations in the West through the transfer of ideas and funds. Competition strategies are drawn from various sources, and spiritual warfare may be conducted in ways that do not respect national or religious boundaries. The flow of money suggests transnational connections that are cemented by religion. So also is the creation of global charity organizations.

The flow of money is equally strong within Africa itself, demonstrating the ability of church leaders to manipulate economic and political forces to their advantage. The African state and economy may be declining, but it does not necessarily parallel that of the churches which grow in infrastructures and finances. Re-imagining the role of the church and redefining relationships to the rich and powerful, many churches have been able to generate large amounts of money. With the ability to market themselves, different churches have been able to raise funds from millions of people, collecting the mites of the poor as well as from the abundance of the wealthy.

Western education and literacy are part of the companionship of Christianity and Africa. Both supply the tools to look at the societies in different ways, and to empower the beneficiaries to seek opportunities in the formal sectors. Africans could use the skills to write, and many did so, making use of the new genre of the print media. The missionaries pioneered the establishment of newspapers, but Africans were not slow in initiating their own. In the example provided by Karin Barber in Chapter 9, we see how the nationalism that originally instigated the establishment of newspapers in Lagos became transcended by other motives of creating bilingual media to reach multiple audiences. The use of the media to reach multiple readers, as in the example provided by Karin Barber, shows how the acquisition of English was put to good use to connect the Yoruba to another world.

Matthews Ojo's piece (Chapter 11) on the media covers the contemporary period, and yields valuable insights on the role of the media in reporting on religious issues. Ojo sees the media as promoters of moral and cultural values. Although dominantly political in its coverage, Ojo notices a shift to religious issues since the 1990s due in part to the prominent role of religious leaders in the civil society, and the difficulty of the military in persecuting them for their views. In addition, the increasing centrality of religion in politics, noted in such events as a series of clashes between Muslims and Christians, and various controversies over the role of the Sharia, turned matters relating to them into headlines. Ojo has limited himself to the press not controlled by religious organizations. There are areas of the media where they have successfully imposed themselves, as in cases of televangelism and radio broadcast. The extensive presentation in films and videos is yet another evidence of success. Even in videos that they do not control, Christian themes are powerful and common, as Chapter 13, by Birgit Meyer, shows in the case of Ghana. All "secular genres" that facilitate public presentations have been accepted by religious organizations.

Change inevitably comes to every society. However, its interpretations can be troubling, as we see from the essay by Andrea Cornwall where modern men now complain about the behavior of modern women (Chapter 6). As the men complain, they look back on the past that they constructed as pure, labeled *igba atijo*: "Accounts of the olden days relate to a time at the borders of remembered time, from which patterns of intimate relationships continue to impinge on the options of living commentators. From people's life stories, a more nuanced picture can be painted: one that reveals a spectrum of opportunities available to different actors and that locates the dramatic transformations in heterosexual partnerships not as sudden upheaval but as uneven and partial." Cornwall uses the narratives of complaint to formulate hypotheses on change with wider applicability. While not dismissing the narratives, he is of the view that they may represent attempts to grapple with the consequences of social change, or to resist those that bother them. Talking about the past and the changes of the present may also be a way of controlling the future to retain existing social structures. Invoking the past becomes a way to "moralize" about the present, even when the past being presented is not historically valid. There is always talk about the present and future as well, constructed via the agency of cultural modernity, as shown by Insa Nolte in his analysis of Wole Soyinka's book, *Isara*. The contest for power in *Isara* reveals the engagement with the forces of religion, modern politics, and globalization.

Even the terms of engagement between Christians and Muslims in Africa are being shaped by global events, as Matthew Kukah points out in Chapter 17. According to Kukah, Africans are told to ignore the history of the slave trade, colonialism, and neo-colonialism—as they are all past and dead—and to focus on the present: a "dialogue" between Christians and Muslims in order to attain peace. However, he argues that the historical and global forces that define both religions do complicate the dialogue between them. Kukah shows how the post-September 11 crises in world politics have complicated dialogue between Muslims and Christians in Africa, an example of the negative forces of globalization. We should not expect religion to be the force of stability in an unstable world, and the weaknesses in a "globalized world" will impact Africa negatively.

Kukah is very much aware of local forces, and he admirably locates the failure to resolve inter-religious crises in failure of the state itself to meet the minimum economic demands of the majority of the citizens, and in the failure to democratize society. The local forces identified by Kukah provide the context that shapes the transformation of religion itself, as we see in Chapter 12 by Asonzeh F-K. Ukah. A Kukah-Ukah hypothesis emerges, clearly and forcefully: political and economic decline inevitably forces Christianity to respond in some creative manner. In the Ukah expansion of the Kukah-Ukah thesis, what we see is the metamorphosis of Pentecostalism to neo-pentecostalism. Drawing his data from Nigeria, he shows how, in the last quarter of the twentieth century, military dictatorship and economic recession instigated "an increased level and diversity of religious demand by the masses." A new form of Christianity emerged:

> In the midst of legitimacy crises, social decay, state failure, massive corruption, endemic graduate-unemployment, environmental degradation, unprecedented abuse of human rights, and crippling poverty of many amidst the scandalous wealth of a few, new churches and ministries proliferated. One of the significant things about the new Pentecostalism is its leadership which is mainly made of young, university-educated men and women who demonstrate great zeal for all that is modern, particularly mass media, organization and advertising/marketing strategies. These leaders are not only religious leaders; they are also economic visionaries who creatively respond to the demands of their immediate environment. The ways in which they achieve this mix is both new and innovative. Numerous Pentecostal groups emerged about this period. Many other existing churches such as the Redeemed Christian Church of God (RCCG) transformed their social identity to conform to the cultural milieu. Of both categories, the RCCG stands out as a market leader of the pack.

* * *

Religion creates a process of interactions with people and spaces, bringing about social change, as we have seen with the role of missionaries in the creation of schools and hospitals. Changes in the larger society can also affect religion itself. A number of chapters underscore the relationship between religion and change. Kai Kresse (Chapter 26) uses the example of the *baraza*—the evening congregation of male friends and neighbors in front of Swahili houses—to talk about people's social, political and intellectual activities. What may appear as ordinary occurrences become the "texts" to understand deeper religious and philosophical phenomena. The *baraza*, like many other forms of oral discourse, tell us about various aspects of traditions, and the way and manner in which knowledge is constituted. In ways similar to written texts, we are supplied with rich materials to understand everyday practices and the ideologies that shape society. In Chapter 8 by Sandra Barnes, we see how the missionaries created sanctuaries to assist slaves seeking redemption, the poor and the powerless. Some had their freedom paid for by the missionaries, while the sanctuaries also provided the opportunity to give them education and new skills to survive in an emerging new age. Guy Thomas teaches us that land and maps entered into the calculations of some missionary organizations as they encountered Africa. In Chapter 22, Thomas analyzes how the missionaries "perceived, negotiated, reconfigured, and commonly subjected to the widespread predicament of access, use and ownership, and of notions of traditional overlordship, in the western region of present-day Anglophone Cameroon." This involved negotiations and conflicts over land, and the making of maps and boundaries. Using the Basel missionaries as his example, he argues that maps represented an essential tool for the Basel missionaries to protect and consolidate their position and prerogatives at times of heightened pressure and adversity. Thomas has not only identified an important area of study, but he has given us new dimensions to pursue: land is not only linked to the pursuit of commercial interests, as several studies have shown, but to the construction of missionary hegemonic power, as Thomas now tells us.

Lynne Brydon, in extending studies to the ignored Amedzofe women of the Volta region in Ghana (Chapter 20), not only calls for more works on gender, but she successfully reminds us that women are not subordinated to men. To her, the Amedzofe were not invisible and voiceless. Recognized as women and adults, they engaged in mutual and cooperative labor with men. The women were also receptive to Western education, creating the basis of change among some of them. Brydon brings us to the world of women and change, setting out the ways in which men took a back seat while the women were "involved with the worlds outside of their village, initially through the influences of missionaries and colonial administrations."

Christianity transformed politics in profound ways. It contributed to the origins of modern nationalism. Carola Lentz shows in Chapter 19 how the identity of the "Dagara Catholics" has emerged in Northern Ghana, "the self-understanding of the non-Catholic Dagara, and which transcends the small-scale colonial ethnic categories and the local patriotism of the 'native states,' the colonially introduced chiefdoms." As the Dagara became Catholics and received Western education, they began to reinvent themselves, defining their culture in ways different from others. Christian evangelization and ethnicity were merged in the Dagara, yet another example of the connection between Christianity and nationalism.

In Chapter 24, John Lonsdale provides yet another connection, this time between literacy and patriotism: the construction of "patriotic Christians" derived from the ability to read and being read to. The printed words made a difference to the way words were received and interpreted among the Gikuyu, enlarging the audiences and providing topics to argue about. Linked with Christianity in the kind of literature that was generated and the audience itself, Lonsdale argues that "words gained a value of their own, unconnected to their author's status." Opportunities widened:

The literate ability to tell stories from a wider stock of reference—but which resonated with the rich oral archive—and to a wider audience than their elders could reach; the new democracy of the printed word that subverted the intimidating hierarchy of wealth and status which loomed behind all public speech; the magnetic, convergent, power of the vernacular press to create a larger market of ideas and images both new and old; the networks of mission schools and denominations which divided Gikuyu afresh (if sometimes along old faultlines of lineage) but which also, like the press, united them in one polemical arena; the Christian search for reconciliation with their kin and the wider society, by associating their cultural innovations with what they believed to be inherent in their native past; the sharper clash of generations and greater concern for the disciplines of gender that came with literacy and migrant labor…

Furthermore, Christianity produced an elite with ideas drawn from within and outside Africa. It reconfigured the nature of local politics. For instance, Insa Nolte, drawing from a reading of Soyinka's *Isara*, concludes that:

the localization of the Bible in the "national" language also inspired a re-ordering of the national space, an attempt to constitute centers and reference points for the emerging nation. Shaped by the historical trajectories and political rivalries of the past, this re-ordering of space was competitive. Cultivating the localizing strategies of the mission, many of the emerging nation's intellectuals attempted to capture its essence through the historical perspectives of the polities which constituted it. At the time of writing, rival historical and cultural perspectives continue to coexist within Yorùbá nationalism, often refracted and shaped in turn by the insertion of the greater part of the Yorùbá into the colonial and postcolonial state of Nigeria.

Christianity has brought with it a way of reinterpreting power relations and generating new conflicts. Its ideas have provided Africans an opportunity to deal with a new reality of ritual order, social control, freedom, gender relations, and class differentiation. The history of Christianity in Africa is about the consequences of encounters with peoples, ethnicities and places, with Islam and indigenous religions, and with state power. As the encounters unfolded, the reality became complicated. New leaders have emerged, tapping into the organization networks made possible by Christianity. The leaders may resist, but they have no way to halt the spread of Western expansionism and globalization. What they have been able to do is to engage with its transformative changes. This book has to deal with this paradox: on one hand are Christianity and change that cannot be ignored or resisted, and on the other are the traditions and worldview that are too strong to destroy. The past and the present are connected. As Peel reminds us in his book on the Ijesha, the study of change is at the same time the study of the past:

> History provides, then, an essential key to a sociological understanding of contemporary realities....The communal identities in which the most salient interest-groups are grounded go back in time, overrunning the bounds of those historical periods which might be derived from the dominance of particular forms of production or particular phases of class formation. The communal identities which were once oriented to tap into the resource flow of the region adapted themselves to a competition for resources distributed from a single embracing state.[4]

Birgit Meyer (Chapter 13) seems to be endorsing this conclusion when she reveals that popular films in Ghana create "imaginations of tradition, either as satanic and negative, or by proudly asserting the newness and spectacular nature of what has to pose as old so as to satisfy a nostalgic longing for something authentic." Where tradition is presented as a "dark secret," the power of Pentecostal Christianity discovers the secret and conquers it to move the worshipper to a state of peace. We also see a set of similar conclusions in the chapter by Miriam Rabelo where the past and present are merged into a "confluence" and data seamlessly moves "to the histories through which different traditions came together."

The Pastor and the Iyalorisa

> The end of all our exploring
> Will be to arrive where we first started
> T. S. Eliot

It is time to close this chapter with a return to where the journey begins: Austin, Fall 2004. I want to create a "new" confluence with my encounters with Iyalorisa Aina Olomo and the pastor. In praying for the successful couple, their established marriage, and two children the pastor asked God to give them wealth, more children, long life, and good health. The list was not drawn up

---

4. J. D. Y. Peel, *Ijeshas and Nigerians: The Incorporation of a Yoruba Kingdom, 1890s-1970s*. (Cambridge: Cambridge University Press, 1983), 263.

by him, but by the long gone ancestors of the pastor. The list is the standard Yoruba "national prayer" for children and adults. Yoruba indigenous religions have been described as pragmatic and worldly, seeking the means to survive and flourish in a chaotic world. Christianity has appropriated this "worldliness," while still talking about idealism. The stress on prosperity by the Church has been noted by many authors, including Harris in this volume:

> As Peel has amply demonstrated, the thrust of Yoruba indigenous religion has always been eminently practical, addressing the needs of everyday existence rather than worrying about the life to come. Aladura followed in this tradition, their prayer and prophecy directed towards members' daily concerns. The C&S presents itself as a problem-solving church; "Without problems there would be no C&S," Elders say. The Born-Agains also deal with overcoming personal difficulties—but there is a difference in emphasis. Both Aladura and Pentecostals aim towards what Yoruba call "the good things in life," a state of well-being that embraces health, wealth, children and longevity. But whereas worker-students' attention was focused on returning safely with qualifications and family to Nigeria, the vistas offered to the contemporary diaspora stretch way beyond Britain to global horizons. Born-Again sermons abound with promises of property, employment in upper echelons and untold wealth. Money, consumer goods, successful employment and high social status are not only desirable, but indicate a right relationship with God. In what has come to be known as the prosperity gospel, a major movement within new Pentecostalism, material success has been elevated to an article of faith.

The Iyalorisa may be seeking the power of thaumaturgy, just like the pastor, so that both of them may tell their followers how to overcome obstacles and empower themselves. Dreams, miracles, revelations, and the conquest of evil exist in their worlds. The pastor may have found that it is much easier to connect the values of elitism with those of globalizations, and to borrow more effectively from the literature supplied by Wall Street. The *orisa* have told the Iyalorisa how yams can grow with work; Wall Street is telling the pastor how one can sleep and make money in ways that look like a miracle performed.

Christianity has acquired an African face: Africans have transformed the religion in their own ways, and carried it back to where it comes from in a luggage comprising the Bible and the intellectual apparatus of the *orisa*. Certainly, this interaction between the *orisa* and Christianity was there from the very beginning of the evangelization of *orisa*-minded people in *orisa*-land. We

Figure 1.4 - Dr. Diedre Badejo (left) and Iyalorisa Oloma Aina (right). Photo by Ramona LaRoche.

know with absolute certainty that the tolerance of the Iyalorisa's ancestors and their *orisa* made the adoption of Christianity a possibility. But we also know that the intolerance of the pastor and his predecessors has made the survival of *orisa* difficult if not impossible. But the Iyalorisa and pastor believe in conquest or "murder," even if their message is always about peace and salvation. Peel posed a question: "Why were people converted to Christianity and what was their Christian practice?" His answer:

> It follows from the fact that Yoruba religion was this-worldly and loosely organized that the Yoruba should be essentially tolerant towards other religious techniques which they believed promised similar benefits. Since a vague analogical thinking determined this, the fact that the Christian religion was the religion of men who, with their ships and guns, obviously had considerable this-worldly success, spoke in favour of the Christian religion....the fact that people could be converted at all means that members of both religious groups shared, to a considerable degree, a common vocabulary and mental outlook....The Yoruba have never lost confidence in their society."[5]

5. Peel, *Aladura*, pp. 290–291.

In saying that the "Yoruba have never lost confidence in their society," John Peel becomes the John the Baptist to the Iyalorisa. Peel works out the encounters between Christianity and the Yoruba more carefully in his third book, *Religious Encounter*, even telling us how ideas of modernity were constructed partly in relation to previous traditions and partly as a package of expectations. Yoruba Christianity has entangled itself in a complicated web of traditions. Some Christian organizations have built their organization and prestige around the condemnation of *heathenism*, as with the pastor making derogatory remarks on the *orisa*, but the landscape of culture is retained, thereby creating a marriage between the pastor and the Iyalorisa even if it will never be sanctified or consummated. Suppose it is? As if she were in the Church with me in Austin, Birgit Meyer, in Chapter 13, makes a statement on my observations:

> While Yoruba Christianity and Yoruba Culture were mutually constitutive of each other, and hence impossible to be disentangled in temporal terms (in the sense of the latter being "prior" to the former), Christian discourse itself produced a temporalizing dualism of "traditional religion" and Christianity, which informed, and still informs, calls for the Africanization of Christianity as much as it calls to discard African elements in favor of a more global, Pentecostal-charismatic perspective. Indeed, the dualism of Christianity and traditional religion appears to be remarkably resilient as a discursive frame through which arguments for and against African religious and cultural traditions are being made—as a set of practices and values to "return" to or "to be left behind."

The tenor and tone of the Iyalorisa Aina Olomo's message based on the *orisa* worship is more idealistic and worldly than that of the pastor, to give one example of how religions and their leaders can engage in role reversal and self-presentation. The Iyalorisa may be moving closer to the Christian Ethiopianists of the nineteenth century. The pastor is not "Afrocentric," and this I am able to confirm after listening to him on three occasions—his sermons are in no way connected with the larger concerns of the American Black churches, and the members of his congregation, mainly immigrants, may know little of the politics of W. E. B. Dubois and Martin Luther King Jr. It is even doubtful that they have ever heard the name of Molefi Asante, the guru of Afrocentricity, not to say nothing of having read him. The Afrocentricism that laid the foundation of Ethiopianism, the foundational ancestor of the pastor's church, is always missing in his sermons. Instead, what exists in large doses is a message of spiritualism blended with an intense therapeutic sermon on survival: "money will come, just say so!" The concerns about "this world" now share an equal space with the concerns about heaven. Thus the pastor may be moving closer to the *orisa* priests of old. The Iyalorisa, in her own idealism, pushes for the secularization of Yoruba in Austin by seeking the means to teach Yoruba. To globalize *orisa*, she and her Ile reject the notion of *orisa* in Yorubaland as the ideal, and that its globalization represents not just the flowering of the *orisa*, not just its survival, but its rebirth in several places in ways that make it possible to translate it into a local milieu. In the project of translation, the pastor and the Iyalorisa may be pursuing a similar ambition. The Iyalorisa is Afrocentric in that her "hidden agenda" is to find a way to create an identity not derived from Christianity, and not "Western." The pastor wants to be more "Western;" the Iyalorisa wants to be more "African." And did I remember to say that Iyalorisa is not Yoruba? In terms of organization, the setting of the Iyalorisa and Ile appears to follow some kind of nature's chaos, in ways similar to the arrangement of the Esu symbols at the crossroads. There are no fat checks to write, and no salaries to claim. On the other hand, the pastor follows a bureaucratic and corporate model. Even a church member who disagrees with his style and approach says that there is no need to tell him as he does not like critical comments. Speaking from a position of spiritual inequality, critics are sinners whose faith is still in the process of formation. In his bureaucratic model, the pastor is not doing anything unusual: many African churches now commercialize their structures and practices: faith is a commodity that has to be bought, although the pastor never tires of reminding the congregation that salvation is free. To be successful, the pastor cannot behave like the Iyalorisa: he has to operate like a profit-oriented company to thrive in a competitive environment and religious market place.

As the pastor returns to Christian idealism in the Fall of 2004, he asked the parents to move the children closer to God. This is also a standard "ethnic prayer," and the Iyalorisa says the same. In moving the children closer to God, the pastor might be thinking of heaven. The Yoruba also appease the *orisa* to be able to actualize the wish list. They also need the "heaven" as well, which is why they call again on the *orisa* to pave the way to a restful "heaven," and appeal to individuals to possess the right character if they want to enjoy excellent "human" relations in the unseen world. Perhaps, the Iyalorisa might be caught singing the famous Christian hymn "My God, I love thee not because I hope for heaven thereby...." if only to provoke the pastor to think about the layered meaning that heaven represents.

The pastor may be avoiding the *orisa*, but the worldview that makes the *orisa* relevant still supplies some philosophy to the pastor. Holding the Bible with one hand, the other hand is released to recall a past that the pastor and the Bible cannot control: the cultural past, of traditions so powerful that they have supplied the basis for the African liturgical revolution. Indigenous worldviews and various aspects of traditional values have become so resilient that Christianity has to make use of them to sustain its appeal to its followers. The Iyalorisa and the pastor believe in the power of benevolent and malevolent forces; although they differ on how to deal with them. The Iyalorisa and the pastor believe in supramundane forces and entities, but they differ on how to conquer them. The ability to predict and shape the outcome of future events is part of the ideas that Christianity has drawn from African values, another way in which the pastor and the Iyalorisa are connected. Tradition has refused to yield to modernity, even when we agree with those who say that we should not ignore the power of ruptures.

The Christian liturgical revolution is appealing and attractive. The couple in Austin being blessed by the pastor was not responding to the economic recession that fueled Pentecostalism in Nigeria, as F-K Ukah argues in his chapter. The family has moved outside the zone of poverty and hunger for the rest of their life. The entertainment after the sermon, with unfinished food and beverages, indicates the prestige associated with excesses and not the inner anguish of want. Indeed, from the looks of many members of the congregation, many wanted to be like the couple. One woman seating in front of me had a look of admiration. She next expressed the wish, when the congregation was asked to make individual prayers, that God should make her like the couple. I could not see the inner minds of any of the people to see whether the superstition about witches and sorceries resided there. But I could see the politics of identity in a segregated society. The church members were mainly Nigerians, which meant that the pastor was not converting members of the "Dark Continent," but consolidating the grip of "charismatic" Christianity on migrant believers. The couple and the successful church members might have climbed the ladder of social hierarchy, but that of the racial ones remains harder for them. They all probably need the ladder to reach heaven, which is where the words and power of the pastor resonate powerfully. As the handsome man and his elegant wife fixed their eyes on the pastor, and others gazed seductively on their sartorial white lace attire, I told myself that the genius of African Christianity and social change has been a careful and clever translation of globalization into appropriate local contexts, the retelling of "universal" tales in the vernacular of African languages, idioms, and dreams. Various manifestations of this genius are captured in the brilliant chapters that follow.

CHAPTER 2

JOHN PEEL

T.C. McCaskie

I

John David Yeadon Peel was born in Scotland in 1941. He grew up in the English Midlands where his father was Professor of Educational Psychology at Birmingham University. He attended King Edward's School before going on to Balliol College, Oxford, where he was a Higgs Scholar and took a First in Literae Humaniores in 1963. He went on to postgraduate work at the London School of Economics, doing fieldwork in Nigeria and completing a Ph.D. dissertation on "A Sociological Study of Two Independent Churches among the Yoruba" in 1966. Thereafter, he lectured at Nottingham University and LSE (1966–73); at the University of Ife, Nigeria (1973–75); at Liverpool University (1975–89), where he became Charles Booth Professor, Head of the Department of Sociology and Dean of the Faculty of Social and Environmental Studies; at the University of Chicago (1982–83), where he was Visiting Professor jointly in the Departments of Anthropology and Sociology; and latterly at the School of Oriental and African Studies, London University, where he has been Professor of Anthropology and Sociology with reference to Africa since 1989, Dean of Undergraduate Studies from 1990–94, and a member of the Governing Body since 1996.

These are the bare facts, and they alert us to something important. John Peel was trained as a classicist but went on to become an anthropologist and sociologist of Africa. Throughout his research and writing life John has brought the intellectual concerns of all three disciplines into a most productive conversation with one another. By this means he has made himself into—and I choose my terms with care—the foremost practising historical ethnographer of Africa and the leading comparativist among social scientists concerned with that continent. This has been a singular achievement and it has given us published contributions to African Studies of great range, depth, sub-

Figure 2.1 - J.D.Y. Peel (photo by Sophie Baker).

tlety and erudition. This has been recognized by John's colleagues and peers. He has twice won both the Herskovits Award of the African Studies Association of the U.S.A. (1983, 2000) and the British Royal Anthropological Institute's Amaury Talbot Prize for African Anthropology (1983, 2000). He has been Marett and Frazer Lecturer at Oxford University (1993, 2000), Rappaport Lecturer of the Society for the Anthropology of Religion in the U.S.A. (2003), and Galton Lecturer of the Galton Institute, London (2003). He was made Fellow of the British Academy in 1991, and has served as a vice-president of that body (1999–2000).

II

I know John Peel very well indeed as friend as well as Africanist, so I trust he will forgive me if I plunder our conversations over the years to flesh out the formal record of his intellectual trajectory. First, classics at Oxford. John considered a career in this field and, although this was not the road he took, there is no doubt that his training in it left an indelible stamp on him. It taught him to read texts closely and with immense care, both with and against their grain, to keep the problem being addressed firmly in his sights, to argue with economy and clarity, and to write with spare lucidity. These precepts have shaped all of John's writing. He has a highly attuned capacity to set out a question, marshal the evidence pro- and con-, drive the argument forward, and to do all this in a muscular, even lapidary prose. The enemy of this kind of writing is, of course, adjectival or adverbial decoration, failure to find the *mot juste*, and obfuscation of any kind. John, unlike many contemporary academics, will have no truck with the linguistically slack, baroque or obscure. The models he has sought to emulate, first encountered as an Oxford classicist, are Syme's *Roman Revolution* (a book at once precisely worded, trenchantly argued and of great cumulative power) and Housman's "Prefaces" (small masterworks of summary and judgement). What prevented John from becoming a classicist? Well, it used to be said in all-too-serious jest that classicists were of the party of Thucydides (empirical historians) or of Herodotus (comparative anthropologists), and 1960s Oxford was very much the domain of the first of these two exemplars. John wanted to combine both of these approaches in his research career, and so he looked beyond classics when the time came for postgraduate work.

John is a practising Anglican and had an early, strong and abiding interest in the sociology of religion. It was perhaps this that guided him to Ph.D. work at L.S.E. on independent churches among the Yoruba of southwestern Nigeria. But we should also remember that this was the 1960s. In that decade, sociology as a discipline was striving to embed and expand itself in British universities. There was an air of excitement about this project, and nowhere more so than at L.S.E.[1] This was also the decade that witnessed the triumph of African nationalism in its struggle to decolonize the continent, and in Britain much interest, excitement and goodwill attended the birth of Nigeria and other new sovereign nation states. John's research in Nigeria and his Ph.D. dissertation eventuated in *Aladura: A Religious Movement among the Yoruba* (1968).[2] This pioneering book was enthusiastically received among Africanists and the wider community of social scientists. With hindsight, we can see that *Aladura* was one of the key foundational texts of modern Yoruba studies and of the now flourishing field of comparative sociology of African religions. It was destined to become a classic and quite literally so, for in 2005 it is to be reprinted in a new edition in the International African Institute's Classics of Anthropology series. Re-reading it for present purposes, I am once again struck by its rigor and sensitivity in its interweaving together of Yoruba religion, culture, and history with much broader issues in the comparative sociology of religion. Spun-off from the Ph.D. thesis and book were a number of articles, of which "Syncretism and Religious Change" mapped out a number of ideas and themes that John would return to in his later work on the Yoruba and on comparative religious systems.[3]

III

With *Aladura* completed, John turned to a subject that was outside of his African interests in any obvious way. I refer to his research on the nineteenth-century British polymath and public intellectual Herbert Spencer (1820–1903), which resulted in the publication of *Herbert Spencer: the Evolution of a Sociologist* (1971).[4] Spencer was a towering figure in his day but fell into neglect in the twentieth century. What drew John to him? Here the personal fused together with the intellectual. "My own study of Spencer," John recalled thirty-three years after publication,

---

1. See A.H. Halsey, *A History of Sociology in Britain* (Oxford University Press, Oxford, 2004), 89–112.
2. See the attached Bibliography of the Writings of J.D.Y. Peel (hereafter B), item 1.
3. B, item 8; see further B, items 7, 9, 11, 12, 13.
4. B, item 2; see further B, items 10, 15, 32, 63.

had as one motive to recover and celebrate the achievement of easily
the most significant founder of British sociology. In this there was an
element of what might be called historical auto-anthropology, for I
was intrigued by how the Midlands provincial culture of my own
background had shaped Spencer's thought. A larger relevance came
from the attempt by Parsons and some of his disciples to revive a theory of social evolution. Of the viability of this neo-evolutionism I was
sceptical, so my historicist treatment of Spencer's theory, in showing
its intelligibility and cogency in relation to its own time, implied that
it was not a model for ours.[5]

John's intellectual biography of Spencer was a historical treatment. It sought
to understand the man in relation to his times and to explore his impact upon
sociology (thus, Durkheim's *The Rules of Sociological Method*, 1915, is really
an extended argument with Spencer, as the Frenchman bid for the methodological independence of sociology from biology). John's study was, therefore, an important contribution to the history of the social sciences. It also
proved to have staying power. Thirty years on from publication, historians
of ideas were still citing it as the best guide to Spencer's social and political
thought. [6]

John's research on Spencer led him on to fuller considerations of Durkheim
and, especially, Weber. Two strands of writing emerged from this encounter.
First, John began to focus on the issue of religious conversion (initially in conversation with Robin Horton). He was especially interested in the Christianization of the Yoruba, but also in the conditions of African religious conversion more generally. In an Africanist academic milieu then dominated by
Marxist (or more often *marxisant*) studies of materialism and modes of production, this was an unusual path to follow. As things turned out, it was also
prescient. Today, conversion to Christianity in all of its many varieties is, with
its Islamic counterpart, the most salient characteristic of many (or most)
African cultures. Over the intervening years, John has revisited and refined
his early work to emerge as a leading interpreter of the phenomenon of
African Christianity.[7] Second, John engaged with another Weberian theme,
that of the relationship between culture and development. In a series of articles he argued for the importance of cultural conditions in any approach to

5. B, item 63, 137–8.
6. See J.W. Burrow, *The Crisis of Reason: European Thought, 1848–1914* (Yale University Press, New Haven and London, 2000), 256.
7. B, items 13, 17, 18, 20, 39, 43, 46, 48, 53, 54, 57, 58, 59, 65.

African development, and explored what the concept of "development" might mean and intend among the Yoruba.[8]

IV

If John Peel had stopped writing in 1980 he would have been able to look back on an already distinguished academic career. But he did not, and in my opinion his work from about 1980 on moved up through the gears in terms of innovation, reach and authority. The earliest signal was the two-part article (1979, 1980) that outlined what John called "a conjectural history" of the Yoruba town of Ilesha.[9] This was a striking attempt to marry together ethnography and history to produce, well, ethnographic history. In part, I suspect, this was a response to what was then termed the "crisis of anthropology," a shorthand description for a discipline that was beset with self-interrogative uncertainty about its past and its future. Two responses emerged, distinct from one another but with fuzzy boundaries between them. One was a retreat from fieldwork into theorizing about fieldwork and its objects, sometimes insightful but more often degenerating into self-reference, confessional autobiography, and even parody. The other was an attempt to rethink the ethnographic project by bringing in history to illuminate cultural process. John more or less pioneered this approach in Africa (I suspect his year in Chicago in 1982–83, with Sahlins and others, enlarged and reinforced his commitment to the direction he was going in). The crowning achievement of John's turn to history was the dazzling, prize-winning *Ijeshas and Nigerians: The Incorporation of a Yoruba Kingdom, 1890s–1970s* (1983). The method used was to deploy history, anthropology and sociology in active conversation with one another to produce a temporal account of the development of the Ilesha town and its people. "For it is only through events, large or small," he declared, "with all their tiresome historicity, that social structures can be realized: events are the very empirical constitution of social structures."[10] This marriage of history and social science, so wonderfully well achieved in *Ijeshas*, was to be the leitmotif of much of John's subsequent work. It was to lead him eventually to consider the underlying questions of narrative, meaning and subjectivity that informed his understanding of Yoruba ethnographic history.

After *Ijeshas*, John's work took two forms. He was now involved (embroiled and mired might be the better terms for British university life under Thatcher

---

8. B, items 14, 16, 19.
9. B, items 22, 24; see further B, items 22, 25, 30.
10. B, item 4, page 15.

and her successors) as a senior professor, at Liverpool and then at S.O.A.S., in academic administration. So, on the one hand he produced a series of articles that spoke to his existing interests, or were written as prefaces, contributions or summaries for multi-authored works in which he found himself involved.[11] It might be added that these were the years in which he was the sole editor of *Africa*, the journal of the I.A.I., an onerous job which he carried out with time-consuming attention to detail. But on the other hand, John began to think of ways in which he might unite and give play to all of his intellectual interests and concerns in the context of Yoruba cultural history. This was to be a long-term project, and it began to crystallize when John read extensively in the wonderfully rich archive of the Church Missionary Society in Birmingham University. What he discovered was that, in truth, earlier scholars had only sampled the CMS papers on Yorubaland. John set about reading the entire archive. This took years. On his very many visits to Birmingham he used to stay with Lynne Brydon and myself, and I recall endless conversations in which John steeled himself to go on by bouncing his ideas and drafts off me. He revisited Nigeria, and began to produce seminar papers and journal articles that trailed or otherwise suggested what his book would be about. [12] He was also busily thinking through the conceptual scheme that he might employ, and to this end he occasionally engaged with fellow scholars on such issues as the meaning and use of historical narratives.[13] The writing process became a juggernaut. I have never counted, but I would guess that the finished book contains about half of the draft pages written and then endlessly rewritten in the making of it.

The book was, of course, *Religious Encounter and the Making of the Yoruba*, which appeared in 2000. As readers, reviewers, prize-givers and all the rest immediately recognized, this was a work of the very highest quality.[14] It was a quite breathtaking performance in its mastery of the evidence, in its measured argument and controlled narrative, in its range of reference, and in its lucidity of exposition. It is a big book, a masterwork, and the quality of its architecture is to be seen even in its contingent details. Thus, for example, the scene-setting chapter Two ("Yorubaland at War") is virtuoso stuff, the single best published account of the immensely complicated period of war and disruption that affected the Yoruba in the later-eighteenth and earlier-nineteenth centuries. The very long treatment of Yoruba-C.M.S. missionary interaction

---

11. B, items 27, 28, 29, 31, 32, 33, 34, 35, 37, 38, 42, 43, 44, 45, 51, 53.
12. B, items 30, 36, 39, 40, 46, 47, 48, 50, 52, 54, 55.
13. B, item 49.
14. B, item 60.

gives full weight to both sides in this dialogue, and manages to do so without ever subjugating historical nuance to fashionable social science.[15] My comments on the book were printed on its back cover. I reproduce them here, for I meant them then and mean them now: "Peel lifts the Yoruba past to a dimension of comparative seriousness that no one else has managed." I think this comparative relevance is the single greatest triumph of *Religious Encounter*. This is a book on Africa that is also a major contribution to historiography and the literature of social science.

Since the appearance of *Religious Encounter* John Peel has continued to produce challenging, thoughtful and well argued contributions to Yoruba and African studies. An article on Wole Soyinka's *Isara*, for example, manages to say something new and interesting about that famously allusive and elusive author. Another paper will soon be published on Whitehouse's influential conceptualization of "divergent modes of religiosity."[16] Recently, John has also been involved in such disparate ventures as the history of S.O.A.S. and a multi-handed study of the impact of new technologies on forms of religious expression in Nigeria.[17] In a sense, though, this is biding time. John Peel is currently thinking about another large project, on the Yoruba again, perhaps, or on the diaspora, or on African churches in Britain, or on the history of religious belief across West Africa. We must wait and see, but in the fullest confidence that whichever it is it will result in another path-breaking contribution from this most distinguished of Africanists.

V

I conclude on a short, more personal note. John Peel has been a leader in the field of African Studies for very many years. Over that time, he has given unstintingly of himself to students and colleagues. Some of these debts are repaid in the papers in this volume. This book is, in fact, a celebration of, and a recompense for, all that John has done to encourage, influence and shape the research of those who have contributed to his *Festschrift*. Having presumed to speak for everyone else, I will now take the usual privilege accorded writers of pieces like this and speak, albeit very briefly, for myself. African Stud-

---

15. Compare here J. and J.L. Comaroff, *Of Revelation and Revolution*, Vol. I, *Christianity, Colonialism and Consciousness in South Africa*, and Vol. II, *The Dialectics of Modernity on a South African Frontier* (University of Chicago Press, Chicago, 1991 and 1997).

16. B. items 57, 65.

17. B, item 61.

ies is fortunate to have such a potent scholar as John, and such a persuasive advocate of its cause. I am doubly fortunate then, as an Africanist and as an individual, to have John as an inspirational colleague and as the truest of friends. I salute and thank him on both accounts.

Bibliography of the Writings of J.D.Y. Peel

Books

1. *Aladura: A Religious Movement among the Yoruba* (London: Oxford University Press for the International African Institute, 1968; forthcoming, new edition, Munich: Lit Verlag for the I.A.I. Classics of Anthropology series, 2005), pp. 338.

2. *Herbert Spencer: the Evolution of a Sociologist* (London: Heinemann, 1971, and New York: Basic Books, 1972; reprinted by Gregg Revivals, 1992), pp. 338.

3. "Introduction", and selection of *Herbert Spencer on Social Evolution*, Heritage of Sociology series (University of Chicago Press, 1972; re-issued as a Midway Reprint, 1982), pp. li + 270.

4. *Ijeshas and Nigerians: the Incorporation of a Yoruba Kingdom, 1890s–1970s* (Cambridge: Cambridge University Press, 1983), pp. xiv + 346.

5. Co-edited [with J.F. Ade Ajayi], *People and Empires in African History: Essays in Memory of Michael Crowder* (London: Longman, 1992), pp. xxv + 254.

6. *Religious Encounter and the Making of the Yoruba* (Bloomington: Indiana University Press, 2000), pp. xi + 420.

Articles and shorter publications

7. 'Religious Change in Yorubaland', *Africa*, 37 (1967), 292–306; also reprinted in O. Pettersson ed. *Religion and Society: Papers in Cultural Anthropology* (Lund: Studentliteratur, 1970).

8. 'Syncretism and Religious Change', *Comparative Studies in Society and History*, 10 (1968), 121–141.

9. 'Understanding alien belief-systems', *British Journal of Sociology*, 20 (1969), 69–84; also reprinted and translated as "Was heisst 'fremde Glaubenssysteme verstehen'?" in H.G. Kippenberg and B. Luchesi eds. *Magie: die Sozialwissenschaftliche Kontroverse uber das Verstehen fremden Denkens* (Frankfurt-am-Main: Suhrkamp, 1978).

10. 'Spencer and the Neo-Evolutionists', *Sociology*, 3 (1969), 173–191; also reprinted in R.S. Denisoff *et al.* eds. *Theories and Paradigms in Contemporary Sociology* (Itasca, IL: Peacock, 1974).
11. 'The Aladura Movement in Western Nigeria', *Tarikh*, 3 (1969), 48–55.
12. 'Reply to Beattie's Comment', *British Journal of Sociology*, 21 (1970), 224–226.
13. 'The religious transformation of Africa in a Weberian perspective', *Acts of the 12th International Conference on the Sociology of Religion* (Lille: C.I.S.R., 1973), 337–352.
14. 'Cultural factors in the contemporary theory of development', *Archives Europeennes de Sociologie*, 14 (1973), 183–203.
15. 'Spencer, Herbert', in C.C. Gillispie ed. *Dictionary of Scientific Biography* (New York: Scribners, 1975), 569–572.
16. 'The significance of culture in development studies', *Bulletin of the Institute of Development Studies*, 8 (1976), 8–11.
17. [with Robin Horton], 'Conversion or confusion? A rejoinder on Christianity in Eastern Nigeria', *Canadian Journal of African Studies*, 10 (1978), 481–498.
18. 'Conversion and tradition in two African societies: Ijebu and Buganda', *Past and Present*, 77 (1977), 108–141.
19. '*Olaju*: a Yoruba concept of development', *Journal of Development Studies*, 14 (1978), 139–165.
20. 'Christianization of African society: some possible models', in E. Fashole-Luke *et al.* eds. *Christianity in Independent Africa* (London: Collings, 1978), 443–454.
21. 'Two cheers for empiricism: or, what is the relevance of the history of sociology to its current practice?', *Sociology*, 12 (1978), 347–359; also reprinted in M. Kajitani ed. *Approaches to the History of the Social Sciences* (Tokyo: Gakabunsha, 1982).
22. 'Kings, titles and quarters: a conjectural history of Ilesha. Part I, the traditions reviewed', *History in Africa*, 6 (1979), 109–153.
23. 'Urbanization and urban history in West Africa' (Review article), *Journal of African History*, 21 (1980), 269–277.
24. 'Kings, titles and quarters: a conjectural history of Ilesha. Part II, institutional growth', *History in Africa*, 8 (1980), 225–257.
25. 'Inequality and action: the forms of Ijesha social conflict', *Canadian Journal of African Studies*, 14 (1980), 473–502.
26. 'Editorial', *Africa*, 50 (1980), 243–247.
27. [with Paul Richards], 'Introduction: Rice and yams in West Africa', *Africa*, 51 (1981), 553–556.

28. [with T.O. Ranger], 'Introduction: Past and present in Zimbabwe', *Africa*, 52 (1982), v–viii.

29. 'Social and cultural change since 1940', in M. Crowder ed. *Cambridge History of Africa*, Vol. 8 (Cambridge: Cambridge University Press, 1984), 142–191, 827–832, 914–921.

30. 'Making history: the past in the Ijesha present', *Man*, 19 (1984), 111–132.

31. 'Introduction: Interventions of the state', *Africa*, 54 (1984), 2–4.

32. 'Herbert Spencer' and 'Auguste Comte', in A. and J. Kuper eds. *The Social Science Encyclopaedia* (London: Routledge, 1985).

33. 'History, culture and the comparative method: a West African puzzle', in L. Holy ed. *Comparative Anthropology* (Oxford: Blackwell, 1987), 88–117.

34. 'Progression and recursion in African social thought', in *African Futures*, Seminar Proceedings No. 28 (University of Edinburgh: Centre of African Studies, 1987), 275–292.

35. 'Two Northerners contrasted in their visions of Nigerian unity' (Review article), *Canadian Journal of African Studies*, 22 (1988), 144–148.

36. 'The cultural work of Yoruba ethnogenesis', in E. Tonkin *et al.* eds. *History and Ethnicity* (London: Tavistock, 1989), 198–215.

37. 'Perspectives on nationalism in Black Africa', in P.E.H. Hair ed. *Black Africa in Time Perspective* (Liverpool: Liverpool University Press, 1990), 57–75.

38. 'Against the motion', in T. Ingold ed. *The Concept of Society is Theoretically Obsolete* (University of Manchester: Group for Debates in Anthropological Theory, 1990), 11–16.

39. 'The pastor and the *babalawo*: the interaction of religions in nineteenth century Yorubaland', *Africa*, 60 (1990), 338–369.

40. 'Poverty and sacrifice in nineteenth century Yorubaland', *Journal of African History*, 31 (1990), 465–484.

41. 'Long-dead sociologists and African history', *Journal of African History*, 32 (1991), 501–506.

42. 'Maine as an ancestor of the social sciences', in A. Diamond ed. *The Victorian Achievement of Sir Henry Maine: a Centennial Appraisal* (Cambridge: Cambridge University Press, 1991), 179–185.

43. 'An Africanist revisits Magic and the Millennium', in E. Barker *et al.* eds. *Sectarianism, Secularization and Rationality: Essays in Honour of Bryan Wilson* (Oxford: Clarendon Press, 1993), 81–100.

44. 'Smith, Edwin W.' [missionary-anthropologist], in *Dictionary of National Biography, Supplementary Volume 1896–1990* (Oxford: Clarendon Press, 1993), 612–613.

45. 'Review Essay' [of A. Biersack ed. *Clio in Oceania*, and of E. Ohnuki-Tierney ed. *Culture Through Time*], *History and Theory* 32 (1993), 162–178.

46. 'Between Crowther and Ajayi: the religious origins of the Yoruba intelligentsia', in T. Falola ed. *African Historiography: Essays presented to Jacob Ade Ajayi* (Harlow and Lagos: Longman, 1993), 64–79.

47. 'Crowther, Bishop S.A.', in *Encyclopaedia of Language and Linguistics* (Oxford: Pergamon Press, 1994), vol. II, 795–796.

48. 'Historicity and pluralism in some recent studies of Yoruba religion', *Africa*, 64 (1994), 150–166.

49. 'For who hath despised the day of small things? Missionary narratives and historical anthropology', *Comparative Studies in Society and History*, 37 (1995), 581–607.

50. 'Problems and opportunities in an anthropologist's use of a missionary archive', in R.A. Bickers and Rosemary Seton eds. *Missionary Encounters: Sources and Issues* (London: Curzon Press, 1995), 70–94.

51. 'Africa, West', in *The Encyclopedia of Cultural Anthropology* (New York: Holt, 1996), vol. I, 20–24.

52. 'A comparative analysis of Ogun in pre-colonial Yorubaland', in Sandra T. Barnes ed. *Africa's Ogun: Old Worlds and New* (Bloomington: Indiana University Press, 1997), 263–289.

53. 'Prophetic Movements: Overview', in J. Middleton ed. *The Encyclopedia of Sub-Saharan Africa* (New York: Simon and Schuster, 1997), vol. III, 510–515.

54. 'Two pastors and their histories: Samuel Johnson and C.C. Reindorf', in P Jenkins ed. *The Recovery of the African Past* (Basel: Basler Afrika Bibliographien, 1998), 69–81.

55. 'Yoruba as a city-state culture', in M.H. Hansen ed. *A Comparative Study of Thirty City-State Cultures* (Copenhagen: Royal Danish Academy of Sciences and Letters, 2000), 507–517.

56. 'Adrian Hastings, 1929–2001: an appreciation', *Journal of Religion in Africa*, 31 (2001), 493–503.

57. 'Christianity and the logic of nationalist assertion in Wole Soyinka's *Isara*', in D. Maxwell ed. *Christianity and the African Imagination: Essays in Honour of Adrian Hastings* (Leiden: E.J. Brill, 2002), 127–156.

58. 'African studies, religion', in *International Encyclopedia of the Social and Behavioral Sciences* (Amsterdam and Oxford: Elsevier, 2002), vol. I, 259–263.

59. 'Gender in Yoruba religious change', *Journal of Religion in Africa*, 32 (2002), 1–31.

60. 'La reponse aux critiques' [reply to comments in review symposium of *Religious Encounter and the Making of the Yoruba*], *Politique africaine*, 87 (2002), 209–214.

61. 'The arts and humanities: between history and ethnography', in D. Arnold and C. Shackle eds. *SOAS Since the Sixties* (London: School of Oriental and African Studies, 2003), 87–108.

62. 'Nigeria', *Encyclopedia of Protestantism* (New York: Routledge, 2004), vol. III, 1401–1402.

63. 'Spencer in History: the Second Century', in G. Jones and R.A. Peel eds. *Herbert Spencer: The Intellectual Legacy* (London: The Galton Institute, 2004), 125–149.

64. 'Awolowo, Obafemi', 'MacRae, Donald Gunn', 'Monica and Godfrey Wilson', in *Oxford Dictionary of National Biography* (Oxford: Oxford University Press, 2004).

65. 'Modes of religiosity in West Africa', in H. Whitehouse and J.W. Laidlaw eds. *A New Comparative Ethnography of Religion* (Walnut Creek CA: AltaMira Press, 2004), in press.

PART B
YORUBA WORLD

CHAPTER 3

THE CULTURAL WORK OF YORUBA GLOBALIZATION

Stephan Palmié

Was the Rev. Samuel Johnson (1846–1901) a Yoruba? At first glance, and in the face of a massive scholarly consensus that Johnson's *The History of the Yorubas from the Earliest Times to the Beginning of the British Protectorate* (1921) represents both a towering achievement of colonial African indigenous historiography, and "the indispensable foundation for all historical and an- thropological work on the Yoruba," (Peel 1989:198) the question appears disin- genuous if not perverse. If Johnson has indeed been hailed as the "Thucydides of the Yoruba," (Smith 1994:168) would it make any more sense to debate his "Yorubaness" than to question the "Greekness" of the author of the *History of the Peloponnesian War*?[1] Still, and in a rather concrete sense, any historically meaningful answer to a question about what some of us today might call John- son's "ethnic identity" would demand specification not just of its object, but of its predicate as well. What was he when?

For so much is clear: at the time of his birth in Sierra Leone in 1846, or even in 1897 when he completed the manuscript of the book elaborating a sense of "Yoruba-ness" that would eventually become a critical qualifier of eth- nic allegiances in the formation of the Nigerian nation state in 1963, Johnson was not—or not in any contemporarily valid sense—a Yoruba himself. He only became so in the aftermath of processes he himself had helped set in mo- tion, and within which we—in contrast to himself—can retrospectively place

---

1. Ironically, the answer should probably be yes in both cases, for not only is the no- tion of "Greece" fundamentally a 19th century construction (Herzfeld 1982), the Athenian origins of Thucydides are set off by his Thracian connections and property interests, as well as by his sympathy for the Spartan cause.

him. Such backward-looping forms of narrative incorporation—the inevitable tendency towards "retrospective realignment" of the past, as Arthur Danto (1965) calls it—are in themselves hardly noteworthy.[2] Surely, by calling Samuel Johnson in, say, 1854, an "eight year old Yoruba child living in Sierra Leone" we are simply placing the events of his life under a description that arguably was not available to him (or anyone else for that matter) at a time when Sigismund Koelle (1854:5) famously charged that his fellow CMS missionaries,

> have very erroneously made use of the name 'in reference to the whole nation [known as Aku in Sierra Leone], supposing that the is the most powerful of the Aku tribe. But this appellation is liable to far greater objections than that of 'Aku', and ought to be forthwith abandoned; for it is, in the first place unhistorical, having never been used for the whole Aku nation by anybody, except the Missionaries; secondly it involves a twofold use of the word,' which leads to a confusion of notions, for in one instance the same word has to be understood of a whole, in another, only of part; and, thirdly, the name being thus incorrect, can never be received by he different tribes as a name for their whole nation.

History was to prove Koelle wrong. Within little more than half a century of the publication of his *Polyglotta Africana*, Christianized Aku returnees like Samuel Johnson had not just invalidated his second and third objection to the use of the term "Yoruba" among the literate elite in Lagos and some parts of its hinterland. They had also begun to project it into the past: to a point where even their mythical ancestors had come under a "Yoruba-description." But here, precisely, is where the problem lies: calling Samuel Johnson—or Oduduwa, for that matter—a "Yoruba" *avant la lettre* in any other than a metaphorical fashion locks us in the present in a way that risks obscuring precisely those historical realities it is supposed to address. Of course, to dispense with (or even only "bracket") principally inadmissible "commonsense" backwards extrapolations from twentieth century data might be to invite the ultimately sterile sort of "invention of this and that" arguments which, in denying the accessibility of any historical reality beneath discourse, amount to "nothing but the reverse of the objec-

---

2. If only because human social interaction could not be apprehended as "continuous" in the complete absence of such retrospective mechanisms.

tivism they claim to denounce," as Amselle (1993: 23) puts it. There is, however, a middle ground which, so it seems to me, ought to be defensible on both epistemological and methodological grounds. And it lies in the recognition of the mutually implicated historicity of both social life *and* the languages, descriptive or analytical, by which we represent it. Few have better illustrated this than John Peel, and it is in the spirit (though not letter) of his contributions that I would now like to return to Samuel Johnson and a number of his Atlantically dispersed "fellow-Yoruba" *in spe* to probe the limits of discourse and agency in the making of what, today, arguably is the global rubric "Yoruba."

* * *

The son of a British educated Saro who may or may not have been related to the Alafin Abiodun (as Ajayi 1994 has claimed), Johnson spent his formative years in a residually German Pietist Christian Missionary Society mission household in Ibadan in the 1860s, where, at the time, the term "Yoruba" could have held little meaning other than a Hausa epithet for the subjects of the long-since-devastated empire of Oyo. That Johnson eventually came to construct an Oyo empire he never had known into the prototype for a Christian "Yoruba nation," on the basis of his experience as a CMS catechist at Ibadan's Aremo quarter and pastor at "new Oyo," is a story unnecessary to detail here, if only because Peel (2000) has told it exhaustively. What does bear noting, however, is that even though, for the good Rev. Johnson, the term "Yoruba" may eventually have come to circumscribe a project, perhaps even a vocation, by the time of his death its referents were still a set of potentialities rather than sociological or political facts antedating the Atlantic dispersal of significant numbers of the constituency of the "Yoruba nation" Johnson dreamed of:

> In terms of a personal agenda, the *History* may be read as a resolute bid by a man who had been involuntarily torn from his roots—his parents were enslaved and became Christians in Sierra Leone, returning to by a man who had been involuntarily torn from his roots—his parents were enslaved and became Christians in Sierra Leone, returning to Yorubaland in 1858, when Samuel was eleven—to re-plant himself in his native soil; and who realized that his homeland needed to be re-imagined and re-configured in order for him to be truly at home there. The memory of Abiodun's vanished Oyo had to be connected to the new, extended category of "Yoruba" introduced by the CMS, and Christianity needed somehow to be integrated into its history. (Peel 2000:305)

To all extents and practical purposes, such a "nation" may nowadays be said to exist in the geographical ambit that once formed the southwestern part of the British West African colonial protectorate to which the name Nigeria— originally suggested by Lady Lugard—was to become permanently affixed upon independence. But just as the name "Nigeria" had not been coined when Johnson died in 1901,[3] the term "Yoruba" did not yet designate an entity that he could have claimed "instrumental" allegiance to at the time of his death.

The same could be said of one of Johnson's contemporaries—a man whose traces in the documentary record allow us to reconstruct a few tantalizing details in the life of one Remigio Herrera, but whose historical importance is encapsulated in the (patently Yoruba) name Adechina—by which he is remembered today among practitioners of the Afro-Cuban religion known as *regla de ocha* or Santería. When Ño Remigio-Adechina[4] died of senile debility at the officially listed age of 98 in his home on 31 Calle San Ciprián (later Fresneda) in the city of Regla's Third Ward in 1905, he had already acquired the stature of a living legend as the last African-born *babalawo* active in Cuba. Adechina is nowadays regarded as the *fundamento* ("foundation") of the cult of Ifá in Cuba, and hence as a crucial agent in the globalization of what the more than 700 delegates from a good score of countries to the Eighth International Orisha Congress in Havana in June of 2003 unanimously endorsed as the "religion of the twenty-first century." Yet irrespective of Ño Remigio-Adechina's African birth, the facial scarifications he proudly displayed in his only known photographic portrait,[5] his polygynous (or bigamist—depending on the frame of reference) marriage patterns,[6] and his reputation as the most formidable *babalawo* in Cuba in the late nineteenth century: if Ño Remigio-Adechina had ever heard the word "Yoruba," it would likely have been late in his life, and on the western shores of the Atlantic at that. In other words, and similar to Samuel Johnson's case, his "Yoruba-ness" is an artifact of retrospective recognition—though, again, as with Johnson, such recognition would be unthinkable were it not for the impact of

---

3. That Colonel A.B. Ellis still referred to "The Yoruba-Speaking Peoples of the Slave Coast of West Africa" in the title of his 1894 monograph was neither idiosyncratic nor accidental. This *was* how the Bight of Benin had been known to Europeans for centuries, then.

4. Contemporary priests of regla ocha tend to use the honorific "Ño" (from Spanish "señor") when speaking of Remigio Herrera.

5. Reproduced in Brown (2003: 64) Possibly indicating, as some have argued, Oyo origins.

6. Adechina's bautismal, marriage, and death certificates as well as his census-listing were kindly made available to me by Pedro Cosme Baños. Information about his prior marriage was provided by Luis Alberto Pedroso.

the very agency of these two men on the emergence of the social and discursive formations in which we now, perhaps all too rashly, tend to locate them.

Probably born around the end of the first or beginning of the second decade of the nineteenth century,[7] the man who came to be known as Ño Remigio-Adechina's enters the historical record as a youthful slave in 1833 when he was baptized in the parochial church of the Nueva Paz township of the province of La Habana. The name he received was "Remigio Lucumí," in the characteristic fashion of the time where the baptismal first name was modified with a term indicating African provenance.[8] We do not know when or how Remigio Lucumí acquired his freedom, but it is clear that upon emancipation he took the surname of his former owner, Don Miguel Antonio Herrera. By 1881 he is listed in a census of the town of Regla as the financially unencumbered owner of the house on San Ciprián. We also have the birth certificates of his daughter Josefa (1864) and son Teodoro (1866), and the list of sponsors of his (second) 1891 Catholic marriage to Francisca Burlet (the mother of his known children) leaves no doubt that by the 1870s, Remigio Herrera—a stone mason by trade—had become a socially well-connected, modestly wealthy citizen of the town of Regla. In other words, he was a moderately successful, but otherwise not overly remarkable, member of the urban "bourgeoisie of color" (Deschamps Chapeaux and Pérez de la Riva 1974) that had grown up under the shadow of the colonial state and its agro-industrial slave economy, that had largely cast its lot with the independence movements of 1868 and 1895, and was, by the time of Herrera's death, becoming increasingly embittered about their lack of inclusion into the republican Cuban national project. (Helg 1995)

More significant for our present purposes is a set of documents dating from the period of the American occupation of Cuba (1899–1902). For here, the octogenarian Remigo Herrera appears as a signatory of a petition to the Office of the Mayor of Havana and the American military government filed by José Cornelio Delgado and Francisco Roche on behalf of an association named *Sociedad de Socorros Mutuos bajo la Advocación de Santa Bárbara Perteneciente a la Nación Lucumí, sus Hijos y Descendientes*[9] which had legally registered with the Spanish colonial authorities in 1893, but now saw its privileges of performing "the African dance known by the name of *tambor* [i.e. drum]" on

---

7. According to David Brown (2003:317n2.) the documents we have on Don Remigio/Adechina variously put his birthdate at 1807, 1811, and 1816.

8. On which see below.

9. "Mutual aid association under the advocation of St. Barbara and pertaining to the Lucumí, their children, and their descendants".

public holidays unjustly curtailed by Havana's new civilian administration.[10] Like the other signatories to the petition, Ño Remigio stated his civil status as "born African, nationality Lucumí,"[11] and the attached *reglamento* (official statutes) of the association show that he had been its honorary president since at least 1893. As the text of the petition further explains, "this society was in other times a *cabildo de lucumí*," and the address of the association's meeting house in Havana's Calle San Nicolás in Havana's *barrio* Jesús María leaves room for speculation about whether it may have been identical with the famous *lucumí* cabildo Changó Tedún founded on Calle Egido in the early nineteenth century, but domiciled at San Nicolás during its waning years. What is more, with ethnographic hindsight, the roster of names on the front pages of the *reglamento* can be read as a veritable *Who Is Who* of late nineteenth– and early twentieth–century Afro-Cuban religion: as David Brown's (2003:62–112) meticulous reconstruction of initiatory genealogies in Afro-Cuban religion demonstrates, at least seven of the thirty male functionaries are identifiable as the leading *babalawos* of their time,[12] while at least two of the twenty-three female officeholders, Belén González and Margarita Armenteros, are nowadays revered as founders of important *ramas* (branches) of initiatory descent in *regla de ocha*.

Obviously, the term "*lucumí*" circumscribed significant aspects of Ño Remigio-Adechina's public identity, and it is reasonable to assume that it held personal meanings for him as well. However, what these meanings, public or private, may have been is a thorny question. To be sure, *lucumí* appears in Spanish records as a designation of the local or regional origin of African slaves as early as 1547. The term is well documented for Cuba since the beginning of the eighteenth century, and much like the Brazilian terms Nagô or Quêto, is today generally regarded as an indicator of the presence of Yoruba and / or their culture—both by scholars and practitioners of religions in which the worship of beings known as *orichas / orixas / òrìṣà* figures prominently.[13] Yet if the term

---

10. U.S. National Archive, Record Group 140, Military Government of Cuba, letters received, 1899–1902. Box 120. The petition concerned a prohibition the Mayor of Havana had placed on their use of drums – which the American Military Government upheld.

11. "[N]atura[l] de África de nacionalidad lucumí."

12. Besides Remigio Herrera/Adechina whose Ifá sign was Obara Melli, these included Eulogio Rodríguez Gaitán known as Tata Gaitán (Ogunda Fun), Pedro Pablo Pérez Rodriguez (Obé Yono), Bernabé Menocal (Baba Eyiogbe), Bonifacio Valdés (Obé Weñe), Estéban Quiñones (Ika Meli), and Luis Pacheco.

13. Law (1997:207). Although Law neglects my own (minor) contribution to unraveling the mysteries of the designation *lucumí* (Palmié 1991:479f.), his is by far the most exhaustive treatment of the question of whether it did or did not refer to any specific region

lucumí ever had any unitary or even only diachronically stable referent in the distant past, by the time Ño Remigio's name appeared on the *reglamento* of the *Sociedad de Socorros Mutuos bajo la Advocación de Santa Bárbara Perteneciente a la Nación Lucumí, sus Hijos y Descendientes*, it was undergoing rapid and portentous change. For, wittingly or not, by the turn of the twentieth century Ño Remigio-Adechina and some of his fellow members in the *Sociedad* had embarked on a project at once curiously similar to, and radically different from, the one the Rev. Samuel Johnson had been hatching in his Oyo parish at the same time. If Johnson helped to write into being the Christian hermeneutics and historiographical foundations on which a future "nation" open to "every true son of Yoruba" (Johnson 1921:642) might become "imaginable" (in Benedict Anderson's sense), then Adechina and his colleagues imagined into being a set of ritual practices that replaced any sense of descent-based allegiance with forms of ritual kinship, thus generating what soon was to become a "religion"— and one of virtually universal scope at that: open to anyone whom divination would reveal to be a divinely elected "son of the orichas" (*hijo de santo*). If, in the former case, the task of the historical anthropologist is that of reconstructing what John Peel (1989) called "the cultural work of Yoruba ethnogenesis," in the latter our goal is to delineate what one might provisionally describe as the cultural work of "Yoruba ecclesiogenesis."[14]

* * *

Here a digression is in order concerning the nature and historical significance of the type of institution Ño Remigio-Adechina and his fellow petitioners would have called a *"cabildo de nación."* Modeled after late Medieval Iberian estate-based lay brotherhoods, and more specifically the councils (*cabildos*) of resident foreigners (*gente de nación*) in Castilian cities, the institution of the *cabildos de nación* apparently originated in the efforts of the municipal authorities of Seville to organize (and thereby control) the increasingly large numbers of mendicant Africans and Afro-Europeans swarming the city since the late fifteenth century. But the model of officially accredited volun-

---

within contemporary southwestern Nigeria and/or the Republic of Benin, was based on linguistic and/or cultural commonalities among the slaves so designated, and held any meaning on the African continent itself.

14. This term has been suggested by Erwan Dianteill (2002:132), but whereas he uses it in reference to the processes of formal institutionalization that eventually led to the U.S. Supreme Court's recognition of Ernesto Pichardo's *Church of the Lukumí Babalu Ayé* as an American denomination in 1993 (cf. Palmié 1996), it strikes me that its applicability much antedates the period with which Dianteill is concerned.

tary associations based on self-expressed perceptions of common origin (the original, pre-nation state significance of the Spanish word *nación*) on the part of "foreigners to the realm" quickly diffused to New World urban environments where, as in Havana in the early seventeenth century, the large numbers of free blacks and highly mobile slaves had become a similar administrative problem.[15] It is not clear whether (and to what extent) the Sevillan model of the *cabildo de nación* was offered to Cuba's urban African population as a form of officially sanctioned consociation, or whether it was simply superimposed, *post hoc*, on groupings that had come into existence independently. Yet it is obvious that that the *cabildos de nación* as internally stratified, largely self-governing corporations capable of controlling recruitment of their membership did exert a powerful influence upon the patterns of sociality that developed among enslaved as well as free Africans in urban Cuba. By the second half of the eighteenth century—at the very latest—this institution had come to underwrite the formation of highly differentiated patterns of collective identification. Though records on the participation of *cabildos de nación* in Havana's Corpus Christi processions go back to 1571, (Ortiz 1921) we get a first glimpse of this process in 1755 when the newly appointed Bishop of Havana, Pedro Agustín Morell de Santa Cruz, noting that, for lack of pastoral care, blacks in the city were "living and dying like animals," decided to make a round of the meeting houses of the city's *cabildos de nación* whose members he found engaging in scandalous forms of idolatry. Bishop Morell's suggestion to bring the *cabildos* under the care of parish churches whose priests he encouraged to learn the African languages spoken by their respective parishioners fell on deaf ears. Yet the systematic inventory of the twenty-one propertied *cabildos de nación* existing in the city that Morell compiled (Marrero 1971–78, VIII: 158ff.) gives a good impression of the range of possibilities for collective identification existing for free and enslaved Africans in Havana at the time.[16] In 1821 the British visitor Francis Robert Jameson (1821:21) observed that,

---

15. The literature on the "cabildos de nación" has grown considerably in recent years. The groundbreaking studies of their origin and diffusion are Aimes (1905), Ortiz (1921), Acosta Saignes (1955), Rojas (1956), Sancho de Sopranis (1958), Pike (1967) and Deschamps Chapeaux (1968). More recent treatments include Palmié (1993), López Valdés (1994), Howard (1998), Moreno (1999), Rushing (2002), Brown (2003), and Childs (2003).

16. Five of these were owned by groups calling themselves *carabalí*, three by people who chose *mina* as their common designation, two each by *lucumíes*, *congos*, *mondongos*, and *gangaes*, and one each by *mandingos*, *luangoes*, and *popoes*. In all likelihood, each of these would have been modified by a "sub-ethnic" designation that Morell's list, unfortunately, omits.

The different nations to which the negroes belonged in Africa are marked out in the colonies both by the master and the slave; the former considering them variously characterized in the desired qualities, the latter joining with a true national spirit [sic] in such unions as their lords allow.

No doubt: we can safely assume that the *cabildos* in which members of such nations congregated were in a crucial sense intentional communities rather than entities created by administrative fiat. The "national spirit" Jameson attributed to them, however, was of a rather different sort than he may have imagined:[17] for in sharp contradistinction to the ideologies and political practices that were rapidly transforming the ancient concept of the *natio* in the European mind at the time,[18] the terminology used for—and by—involuntary African migrants to the New Word did not, and arguably could not, reflect the essentially novel (even within its western context) idea that nations were naturally occurring political (or proto-political) entities: internally homogeneous, clearly bounded, held together by common descent, shared language, customs and sentiment, existing as *tantum sui similibus gentes* since time immemorial, and sharply set off from other such entities to which their respective constituents did not (or, at any rate, should not) extend any loyalties.[19]

The case of the Cuban *lucumí* in the late eighteenth and nineteenth centuries certainly discourages any attempt at short-circuiting the onomastics of what, for lack of a better word, I will call *proto-Yoruba* corporate identities in

---

17. In recent years, Jameson has been joined in this by an increasingly large number of contemporary Africanist historians favoring what Paul Lovejoy (1997, 2000), somewhat disingenuously, has called an "Africa-centric" or even "Afrocentric" approach that assumes direct continuities between African and New World forms of identification (e.g. Thornton 1992, Hall 1992, Gomez 1998, Chambers 2000, Lovejoy 2000, or Yai 2001). For trenchant critiques of this so-called "New Revisionism" see Morgan (1997), Caron (1997), and Northup (2000).

18. E.g. Kedourie (1985:13–15)

19. As Ernest Gellner (1983:55) wisely put it: "The great, but valid paradox is this: nations can be defined only in terms of the age of nationalism, rather than, as you might expect, the other way around". The same, one might argue holds for the concept of the "tribe" – which arguably only attained salience in and through its colonial reifications, as well as its successor, "ethnicity" which might well be not just the product of anthropological embarrassment with the former term (in a theoretical as well as political sense), but of largely unchecked intertraffic between scholarly discourses and those pertaining to what has been called a "politics of recognition" gaining prominence in the second half of the twentieth century.

the Bight of Benin with New World data on what might best be understood as Neo-African social formations. To be sure, we *are* dealing with African wine in Castilian bottles. But cépage and vintage are a rather different story. To begin with, the nomenclature produced by the commercially driven proto-ethnology of the slave trade is simply dumbfounding. In a study of the ono-mastic qualifiers attached to slaves whose "primary national identity" was given as "*lucumí*" in the documentary record, López Valdés (1998) counted no less than 137 "variations on a theme," ranging from such likely candidates for *post hoc* interpretation as *lucumí egbá, lucumí egguadó, lucumí iechá, lucumí ifá*, or *lucumí eyó*, to such ethnologically puzzling entities as *lucumí baribá, lu-cumí chanté, lucumí jausá*, and *lucumí kangá*, to completely mysterious des-ignations such as *lucumí yogo de otá, lucumí camisa*, or *lucumí zéza*. But even when they used these terms themselves, the *lucumí* apparently could not be trusted to come up with patterns of naming that latter-day analysts bent on counting them as (proto-)Yoruba ought to feel comfortable with. A case first reported by Deschamps Chapeaux, (1971:42) and recently elaborated on by Childs, (2003:125f.) may serve as a by-no-means-atypical example: here we get a property dispute between members of a *lucumí cabildo* in 1778–80. One faction consisted of Cuban-born members who claimed *lucumí descent* and were led by one Manuel Blanco who was trying to prevent the sale of the *ca-bildo* house his parents once helped to purchase. They were opposed by a fac-tion of *lucumí* newly arrived from Africa who had become members of the *ca-bildo* and now favored the sale. Yet even though all parties to the dispute apparently engaged in forms of sociality for which the term *lucumí* had come to serve as a rubric, as it turned out in court, the *cabildo* had originally been founded ("many years ago") by "the Lucumí nations, specifically the Nangas and Barbaes," and had recently admitted people who testified to being *chabas* and *bambaras*! Who were these people? And what could the term *lucumí* pos-sibly have meant to *any* of them? In all likelihood, we will never know.

Nor could we. For the question itself may well bespeak a fundamental mis-judgment of the realities of social relations on both sides of the Atlantic: one that arises out of a long-standing and pervasive discursive inter-traffic between dated anthropological conceptions of social and / or cultural "units,"[20] popu-lar conceptions of the "tribal" nature of African patterns of sociality reaching back well into the eighteenth century, and the claims of interested contem-

---

20. Most vividly illustrated by the seemingly interminable shelf-life of Murdock (1959) – arguably the epitome, in the Africanist field, of what Amselle (1993) calls "ethnological fetishism".

porary parties, be they "New Revisionist" historians,[21] art historians intent on salvaging essentially romantic concepts of ethnic purity long likened to notions of aesthetic authenticity,[22] or latter-day religious entrepreneurs.[23] For to put the matter baldly: given what we know about the complexity and fluidity of pre-colonial African forms of consociation, why would we want to burden our attempts to operationalize the onomastic emblem *lucumí* with preconceived and patently anachronistic notions of *who* should have been able to legitimately claim membership in a "*natio lucuminorum*" that *we* have defined, *a priori*, in accordance to criteria of "Yoruba-ness" that had only begun to gain currency through the efforts of the CMS, and Christianized Saro such as Samuel Johnson? Would it not be more fruitful—less nominalistic, more historical—to view the *lucumí cabildos*, documented as they are in Cuba since the mid-eighteenth century (i.e. well before the first massive waves of slave imports from the Bight of Benin even reached the island), *not* as the incipient "Yoruba-enclaves" in their New-World role in the generation of cultural forms patently similar to some (but by no means much) of contemporary Yoruba culture appears to suggest, but to treat the very term *lucumí* as an onomastic blanket that covered, at one time this, at other times that "African ethnic" or "cultural" content?[24] That some such contents happened to be "fixed"—not just in the writing of twentieth-century ethnographers and historians, but by the people themselves—would then be less the result of past processes we stand little chance of reconstructing beyond the point where our contact-based sources fall silent, (Amselle 1993) than that of self-conscious endeavors on the part of latter-day intellectuals on both sides of the Atlantic

---

21. See note 17 above. The most extreme case is surely Yai (2001) who comes close to arguing that the concept of the nation was hijacked by Europeans from its African originators (among whom – who would have guessed? – the Yoruba figure prominently), and later superimposed upon them in a distorted and falsified form.

22. Here the work of Robert Faris Thompson (especially Thompson 1983) clearly must be seen as crucial for the case of the Yoruba and their New World "outposts": it is probably no exaggeration to say that Thompson has been the single most influential international advocate of the notion of a creative genius specific to the "Yoruba" – a kind of "Volksgeist" following them (and their descendants or spiritual heirs) westward to the farthest corners of the world (a nice revenge upon Hegel, that). Not since Frobenius' *Und Africa Sprach* (1913) was first translated into French, has any other author exerted more influence in championing Yoruba exceptionalism (and essentialism) than Thompson. On the vicissitudes on the transatlantic art market of the very concept of "ethnic authenticity" Thompson operates with see Steiner (1994).

23. Such as, to name only two examples outstanding for their methodological fastidity, Pichardo and Nieto (1984) and Mason (1992).

24. Here I am following the epistemological argument presented in Peel (1990).

to "recover," unify, and theologically and/or politically *rationalize* precisely those elements of earlier patterns of identification, cultural practice, and esoteric knowledge that *they* thought most amenable to their respective projects and the local conditions under which they aimed to realize them.[25]

* * *

What then of those practices and projects New World actors like Adechina seem to have been involved in, and why do their results nowadays look so stunningly "Yoruba" to us? Were they (and whether they knew it or not) the "carriers" of a "Yoruba" culture, whose outward symptomatology cannot escape our diagnostic gaze—and, besides that, is proudly displayed under that very label by their "spiritual heirs" practicing what is, today, uncontroversial

---

25. This, at any rate, seems to be the position taken by what, currently, are the two most sophisticated interpreters of the New World "Yoruba" experience, J. Lorand Matory (1999. 2001) and David Brown (2003). To be sure, one could imagine a transatlantic continuum of Yoruba-ethnogenetic dynamics: unfolding rapidly, as in the case of Sierra Leone, where it seems that (*pace* Koelle) a relatively cohesive "Aku"-identity had jelled within decades of the colony's foundation among the flood of "recaptives" enslaved in the wars unleashed by the decline of Oyo's imperial hegemony, freed in ever-increasing numbers upon the intensification of the British Atlantic patrols after 1807, and re-aggregated under the authority of emerging leaders such as the early "Aku kings" Thomas Will and John Macaulay (Fyfe 1962: 233f., 292f.); slower in places like northeastern Brazil, where the records on the so-called Mâlé-rebellion of 1835 leave considerable doubt about whether Ilorin- or Sokoto-style Islam (truly jihadist in the second case, merely "panethnic" in the former), some kind of incipient Ibadan-style strong-man politics (Falola 1984), or a locally idiosyncratic combination of historically irrecoverable motives on the part of a – clearly – ethnically heterogeneous insurgent population were predominately operative (Reis and Moraes Farias 1989). The process might have slower yet in western Cuba, where the first half of nineteenth century saw a proliferation of onomastically differentiated Lucumí-identities that only began to consolidate into patterns of "unqualified" Lucumí-ness towards the end of the (by then illegal) slave trade, and – as Romulo Lachatañeré (1992) pointed out as early as 1939 – never reached a truly "ethnic" stage in the eastern part of the island. Not at all paradoxically, such processes of hyper-ethnic (or, shall we say, national?) consolidation might have been slowest still in what we now know as "Yorubaland": unfolding faster in the sprawling, heterogeneous "multi-Yoruba" cities like Lagos, Abeokuta, or Ibadan, than in places where "pre-Yoruba" local political identities were still relatively firmly in place, and where Islam or Christianity had only belatedly made significant inroads. Once we concede so much, however, and whether we like it or not, we are thrown back on the agency of the Ño Remigio/Adechinas and Samuel Johnsons: neither the Yoruba-nation, nor New World forms of òrìs.à religion welled up from the unfathomable depth of the *Volksgeist*: they were actively conjured up.

to call "Yoruba-derived" religions? Or did their agency set into motion a train of cultural developments we might be better off studying in their proper local and historical contexts—rather than referring it to ready-made solutions suggested by the ethnological trait-lists of a time-less "Yoruba culture" sprung from the latter-day anthropological (and native) imagination? Here it is instructive to once more turn to the list of functionaries on the *reglamento* of the *Sociedad de Socorros Mutuos bajo la Advocación de Santa Bárbara Perteneciente a la Nación Lucumí, sus Hijos y Descendientes*. For as David Brown (2003:69ff.) has cogently argued, the majority of officeholders were not just "children and descendants" of *lucumí* in a "biological" sense, but people for whom the term *lucumí* had already come to circumscribe a "vocational" identity. Having been "hailed" by the *oricha*, and interpellated (to misuse an Althusserian vocabulary) into *religious* subject positions created through rituals of consecration, and defined by inclusion into incipient lines (*ramas*) of initiatory descent, they already were the products—and in turn producers— of what, to use Fredrik Barth's hydraulic metaphorics, (1984) we might call an incipient "stream of tradition" carrying the cultural forms of an emerging Afro-Cuban *religion* onward in time, and across the sociological terrain of twentieth century New World history.

Viewed from this angle, the *reglamento*'s roster of dignitaries suddenly reads rather differently. For although the petition in 1900 had been exclusively signed by ageing *lucumí* (none of them under sixty years of age), the *reglamento* reveals not only that, excepting *Adechina*, all of the other six major *babalawos* on the list had *not* been born in Africa (i.e. were island-born Creoles), but that one of them, Luis Pacheco had been initiated by the *criollo* Pedro Pablo Pérez (a "son in Ifá" of the first generation African Estéban Quiñones), and so already represented a *babalawo* at a second generational remove from Africa. Perhaps even more strikingly, another one of the officers of the *Sociedad*, Bonifacio Valdés (Obe Weñe) was a socially white *criollo* of Spanish descent. As Brown (2003:77f.) has shown, Valdés had been initiated into Ifá – and hence "made" into an important twentieth century "vector" of Afro-Cuban divinatory knowledge—by Ño Carlos Adé Bí (Ojuani Boká) who is remembered today as having helped the young Adechina to reconsecrate the African *ikin* (palm nuts used in Ifá-divination) he had "swallowed" before embarking on the middle passage, and then defecated upon arrival in Cuba. According to Brown's superb ethno-historical work (Brown 2003: chapter 2) on the "origins" of the cult of Ifá in Cuba, *all babalawos* active in Cuba (and thus, by implication, the better part of the priesthood of Ifá active in the New World today) trace their initiatory descent back to five "*fundamentos*"—founders— whose crucial ritual activity roughly spans the period between 1880 and

1905.[26] What this means, of course, is that for people like Bonifacio Valdés – and quite possible his initiator Ño Carlos Adé Bí – the term *lucumí* had taken on an entirely novel significance. Even if the category *lucumí* had long been a semantically flexible signifier floating over populations of varying ethnic origins and disposition, both the mode of recruitment into a *lucumí*-identity, and the rationalization of collectivities identifying with the term had radically changed. As George Brandon (1984: 89) pithily phrased it quite some time ago, the difference was that now one "became lucumí not by birth, but by initiation." What once designated the historically fluctuating boundaries of the products of ongoing processes of New World "African ethnogenesis," (Fardon 1987) had now come to congeal into a set of precisely marked lines of initiatory descent ("*ramas*") which, to this day, are recited (though not necessarily in chronological order) in the invocations (*moyuba*) of the names of cultic (rather than "biological") ascendants that precede (and validate) most ritual activities in *regla de ocha* as well as among Cuban priests of Ifá (*babalawos*).

If the fact that a white man like Valdés would occupy a near-apical position in some such genealogies is apt to surprise us, this surely has more to do with our contemporary preconceptions of, and pre-occupations with, notions of race and "African authenticity" than with the concerns of people like Ño Carlos Adé Bí and his African-born contemporaries. For the initiation ritual they devised not only combined the symbolism of rebirth into a sacred commission with an emerging structure of ritual kinship modeled in part on Catholic godparenthood,[27] but in so doing obliterated the notion that sublunar forms of social identification could affect the establishment of a relationship between a human being and a divine entity (whether an *oricha* or Ifá) which originated in the latter's initiative (as revealed by divinatory procedures). We do not know the motives of Ño Carlos Adé Bí and the other African or black Creole *babalawos* involved in Bonifacio Valdés' initiation into the priesthood of Ifá, and

----

26. These were Carlos Adé Bí (Ojuani Boká), Remigio Herrera/Adechina (Obara Melli), Oluguere Kó Kó, Francisco Villalonga (Ifá Bí), and Joaquín Cádiz (Ifá Omí). The latter is of particular interest here, for according to Ortiz (1921) Cádiz was the one who, in 1891, submitted a request to the Spanish colonial authorities to reorganize the "lucumí cabildo" that, in 1893 would become the *Sociedad de Socorros Mutuos bajo la Advocación de Santa Bárbara Perteneciente a la Nación Lucumí, sus Hijos y Descendientes.* The disappearance of his name from the later documents most likely indicates that he died between 1891 and 1893.

27. Drawn up (for the case of Regla de Ocha) in classically "structural" abstraction by Dianteill (2000:86). For a historically nuanced account of the emergence of the "ramas" (lines of initiatory descent) as "chronotopes" of belonging see Brown (2003:98–112)

one could speculate that they hoped to benefit from his social standing as a successful white merchant. But Remigio Herrera-Adechina had already counted white businessmen among the sponsors of his Catholic marriage, and at any rate, Bonifacio Valdés' initiators could not but have rationalized their actions in accordance with a mandate from Ifá himself. Nor could Valdés himself have done otherwise. Whatever acquiring a *lucumí* identity (in the religious sense) may have personally meant to him: in the larger scheme of things to which he submitted in becoming a *babalawo*, his volition was as irrelevant as his skin color. (cf. Palmié 2002b)

But Valdés' case stands only at the beginning of a long ironic history the more recent outcomes of which I will briefly review after a discussion of how the "religion" (for I think we can now safely use this term to designate the practices and forms of identification associated with the term *lucumí* in the early twentieth century) Valdés and his fellow Creole *babalawos* were practicing *finally* became a "*Yoruba*-religion."

* * *

Only a few months after Ño Remigio's death, in the summer of 1905, the young Cuban lawyer Fernando Ortiz (1881–1969) delivered a manuscript to a Spanish publisher which would eventually—and irrevocably—change the name, nature, and ethnological status of the oracular practice on which we can presume Ño Remigio had come to rely financially during the waning year of his life. In what eventually became the founding text of Cuban anthropology, *Los negro brujos* (1906), Ortiz followed the lead of his Brazilian predecessor Raymundo Nina Rodrigues (1862–1906) whose key informant Martiniano Eliseu do Bomfim (1859–1943) had pointed him towards the emergent literature on the southwestern part of the then-still-called Slave-Coast of West Africa in order to aid Nina's attempts to pinpoint the local "African origins" of what earlier Brazilian observers had written up as undifferentiated manifestations of "African fetishism" lingering in the Americas. Armed with Nina's *L'Animisme Fetichiste des Nègres de Bahia* (1900), Samuel Crowther's *Vocabulary of the Yoruba Language* (1848), the American Baptist missionary T.J. Bowen's *Grammar and Dictionary of the Yoruba Language* (1858), Père Bouche's *Etude sur le langue Nago* (1880), and A.B. Ellis' *The Yoruba-Speaking Peoples of the Slave Coast of West Africa* (1894),[28] and largely reasoning from similarity in names of deities and other philological correspondences, Ortiz

---

28. The editions cited conform to the ones Ortiz used.

(1973: 28) categorically pronounced what would become the credo of all future ethnographers of Afro-Cuban religion:

> In the natural war of African religions, the religion of the Yoruba blacks or Nago triumphed both in Cuba and Brazil, though left in a debilitated state by the common enemy of all of them, Catholicism. These blacks are those who entered Cuba as lucumís.

It was as simple as that—and has remained so until today. The litany of both scholarly and practitioners' pronouncements based on the *topos* of a Yoruba / *lucumí* / Nagô / Quêto correspondence is, by now, worthy of a serious bibliographer's effort. More importantly, however, it enabled the growth of a textual formation characterized by rapid rhetorical moves back and forth between ethnographic data pertaining to both sides of the Atlantic—to a degree where it is oftentimes all but clear whether the author is talking about ethnographic facts in the Bight of Benin or the Bay of Havana, a timeless Yoruba religion, or historically specific manifestations of local cultural practices. Whether intended or not, the result tends to be a transatlantic blur of inappropriately aggregated data which, taken at face value, suggest the relative insignificance of space and time when it comes to detecting a distinct Yoruba ethos in Africa or abroad.

I do not intend here to demean the serious comparative efforts which have been based, in good faith and oftentimes to good effect, on such fundamentally ahistorical procedures of short-circuiting Old and New World units of analysis. My own field of research—the anthropology of the African Diaspora—clearly would not exist without them. (Apter 1991, Yelvington 2001) But I think that (the "New Revisionism" notwithstanding) we can engage historically more fruitful positions than to reiterate what Matory (1999:97) calls "the model of agentless collective memory" on which efforts at establishing "African origins" for New World cultural forms have long been based. For, rather than tracing the endlessly repeated *lucumí*=Yoruba equation through the scholarly literature on Cuba, we might do well to consider the questions of: a.) How it was established as a scholarly *topos* in the first place; and b.) How it eventually "sunk in" among practitioners of Afro-Cuban religion to a degree where, as at the 8th World Orisha Congress in Havana, 2003, Cuban *babalawos* could sit down with their Nigerian counterparts, Brazilian *mães* and *pais do santo*, Trinidadian Shango-worshippers, and North American Yoruba-Reversionists and agree that they are practicing essentially the *same* "religion."

The first of these questions is intimately bound up with the role of Martiniano do Bomfim in literally steering two generations of Brazilian, North

American, and French ethnographers of Northeastern Brazil towards the conclusion that what they saw in the *candomblé terreiros*, he, Seu Martiniano, was connected with, were Yoruba cultural forms, and purely preserved ones at that. For what Fernando Ortiz had done in 1906 was little more than transfer Nina Rodrigues' idea that certain Afro-Brazilian cultural expressions could be interpreted in light of an emerging Africanist literature on people for whom the name "Yoruba" was just barely attaining currency.[29] As Braga (1995) first suggested, and as Matory (1999, 2001) has shown in some detail, that idea, in turn, had been Seu Martiniano's: born to freed slave parents in Sao Salvador de Bahia in 1859, Martiniano was taken to Lagos by his father in 1875 where he attended the Faji Presbyterian School where he learned both English and Yoruba, and stayed intermittently until 1884.[30] A Brazilian Creole arriving in Lagos, perhaps a decade and a half after the Ijesha babalawo Philip Jose Meffre,[31] Martiniano do Bomfim's career seems to have inverted that of Meffre: While the African-born ex-slave Meffre returned from Brazil as a practicing *babalawo* and became an evangelical Protestant in Yorubaland, Martiniano do Bomfim arrived in Lagos as a baptized Catholic, and became a *babalawo* there. What is more, while Meffre eventually turned into one of the CMS's most ardent convert-missionaries, and the Reverend James Johnson's primary native source for his 1899 monograph *Yoruba Heathenism*,[32] soon after his return to Bahia Seu Martiniano became one of the most persistent, prolific, and, ultimately, most *effective* "informants" in the history of the discipline of anthropology. We do not know how or exactly when he met the young medical examiner Raymundo Nina Rodrigues, but it is clear that despite Nina's racism and evolutionary speculations, both of his monographs on Afro-Brazilian culture (Nina Rodrigues 1935, 1977) bear the stamp of Seu Martiniano's thought. Late in his life, Martiniano do Bomfim, who like to refer to himself as an English professor and translator, fondly recalled his relationship with Nina, (e.g. Landes 1994[1947]:28) and as he told the reporter from *O Estado do Bahia* in 1936, he and Nina

---

29. As Ortiz himself later admitted (1939), he had written *Los negros brujos* in Spain, and without the benefit of first-hand ethnographic experience (cf. Palmié 1998, 2002)

30. Martiniano do Bomfim's biographical data reappear with good consistency in at least four interviews he gave to Donald Pierson (1942) in 1935–37, Ruth Landes (1947) in 1938–39, E. Franklin Frazier (1942) in 1940, and Lorenzo D. Turner (1942) at about the same time. A discussion of these – as well as another interview he gave to the newspaper *O Estado do Bahia in 1936* – appears in Braga 1995 chapter 2).

31. Whose painful and protracted conversion to CMS-style Christianity Peel (1990) has reconstructed in admirable detail.

32. On which see Peel (1993).

had even planned a trip to Lagos and [Nina] had already [put up] five hundred *contos* when he unfortunately died. Many things would have been revealed, for from Nigeria (the Slave Coast) came the largest number of captives (cited in Braga 1995:45).

Although another Brazilian returnee, the Lagos-based merchant Lourenço Cardoso seems to have introduced Nina to A.B. Ellis' work, Martiniano do Bomfim translated A.L. Hethersett's Yoruba school primer *Iwe Kika Ekerin Li Ede Yoruba* for Nina, (Matory 1999: 93) thus even more firmly linking New World Yoruba research to the emerging CMS literature,[33] and the literary productions of the so-called Lagosian renaissance in particular. Continuing his career as professional informant[34] after Nina's untimely death in 1906, Martiniano do Bomfim went on to leave his intellectual stamp on the work of Brazilian ethnographers Manuel Querino, Artur Ramos, Edison Carneiro. He also served as a handily Anglophone interlocutor to the North Americans Donald Pierson, Ruth Landes, E. Franklin Frazier, Lorenzo Turner, and Melville Herskovits, posthumously impressed the French sociologist Roger Bastide with his "use of his considerable authority to prevent the degeneration of the African cults" (Bastide 1978:165) in instituting what, in fact, were fairly radical innovations, and likely inspired Pierre Fatumbí Verger's studies of the continuing linkages between Bahia and the Bight of Benin. But he also steered the Bahian *candomblé* community itself towards an understanding that their beliefs and practices were (or, at any rate, should be) in conformity with an idea of Yorubaness that had begun to emerge in the Bight of Benin—not the least through the agency of both Christianized Saro and Brazilian travelers like himself. A case in point is his well-documented collaboration with the wealthy trader Eugenia Ana dos Santos (1869–1938), better known as Mãe Aninha, the founder and powerful leader of the *Centro Cruz Santa do Axé do Opô Afonjá* terreiro (*candomblé* house) which the two of them, strategically built up as the standard-bearer of "Yoruba-purity" in Bahia. But, of course, as is evident in the much discussed case of Martiniano's creation in the 1930s

---

33. Hethersett was an African who held the position of Chief Clerk and Interpreter at the Governor's Office in Lagos from the 1880s. Since died in 1896, fifteen years before his primer went into print in 1911, Martiniano must have possessed one of the manuscript versions which had begun to circulate in Lagos at the end of the nineteenth century (Law 1984).

34. Martiniano do Bomfim – quite correctly – preferred to call himself their collaborator. For that he was: there are good grounds for calling him the Brazilian equivalent of George Hunt, Franz Boas' encyclopedic Kwakiutl informant who, like Martiniano do Bomfim, well understood the political potential of the ethnographic genre.

of the ritual office of the *Twelve Obas of Xango*, the concept of "purity of African tradition" he helped to establish and attach to Mãe Aninha's house by proclaiming, at the Second Afro-Brazilian Congress in Bahia (1937), that he had merely revived an ancient Yoruba-institution now lost in Brazil, was a strategic fiction:[35] no such institution ever existed (as Martiniano claimed) at the court of the Alafin of Oyo, and it is tempting to infer that he single-hand-edly invented it for the occasion of the 1937 Congress. But if indeed that was the case, he did not do so from scratch. Whether his inspirations derived from the impressions of Oyo's past splendor he had gleaned during his stay in Lagos, whether he had accessed the Anglophone missionary literature produced dur-ing the Lagos Renaissance, or the more recent ethnographic publications that were beginning to circulate in ever wider circles among the priesthood of the Brazilian *candomblé* in the 1930s (a literature he, himself had helped to shape): Seu Martiniano's creation, the Twelve Obas of Xango, seemed so much in tune with what scholars like Edison Carneiro, Artur Ramos, Ruth Landes, Donald Pierson etc, already *knew* were essential features of a, by now, *book-borne* idea of "Yoruba-ness" that they gladly ratified what, in 1962, *candomblé*-priest *cum* ethnographer Deoscoredes Maximiliano dos Santos, (cited in Butler 2001:146) himself an initiate of *Opô Afonjá* called the "re-establishment of the ancient tradition of the Obas de Xango" which, in his words, "gave still more prestige to Opô Afonjá and demonstrated the competence and knowledge of Iyalorixa Aninha Obá Biyi."[36]

Though less well documented, the Cuban case presents a comparable pic-ture. For there, too, the emergence of a Yoruba tradition was eminently bound

---

35. See the treatment of this episode in Lima (1966), Dantas (1988), Braga (1995), Ma-tory (1999, 2001), and Butler (2001). Just as interesting, in the present context, is the fact that Aninha herself was a descendant of ex-slaves who claimed a *grunci* identity – an eth-nonym that might be taken as pointing towards a region of origin in what today is north-ern Ghana. Aninha herself never denied this: for her, too, the "religiously" defined *Nagô*-identity she acquired when she was initiated into the cult of the orixas at the famous candomblé terreiro Engenho Velho (established around 1830) overrode all previous social attachments and affinities (Butler 2001).

36. In this sense, I think that Matory 's (1999) quarrel with Brazilian scholars such as Dantas (1988) who have argued that northeastern Brazilian anthropologists championed *those* candomblé terreiros which conformed most closely to *their* ideas of "Yoruba purity" (established from the Africanist literature) is unnecessary: in all likelihood, priestly "Africanizers" such as Martiniano and Aninha and anthropologists bent on defending the "cultural superiority" of northeastern Brazilian blacks by assimilating their cultural prac-tices to a (however fictitious) "Yoruba-standard" were engaged in a happy coalition of in-terests.

up with the collaboration between holders of priestly titles, and the single towering figure of native Cuban ethnography in the twentieth century, Fernando Ortiz: a man who has been hailed as the "third discoverer of Cuba" (after Columbus and von Humboldt, that is), but who also was instrumental not only in transferring to Cuba the discursive "Yoruba-connection" Nina Rodrigues and Martiniano do Bomfim had pioneered in Brazil, but in offering it to practitioners of Afro-Cuban religion as a strategy of legitimation. They in turn, as we now know, grabbed it and ran with it.

As far as we know, there was no true equivalent to Martiniano do Bomfim in Cuba.[37] But the priests of Regla de Ocha, Fernando Guerra, and Silvestre Erice, as well as the formidable *olú añá* (consecrated batá drummers) Pablo Roche, Trinidad Torregrosa, and Raúl Díaz might be good candidates. Guerra had met Ortiz at a very early stage in the latter's career (probably around 1909), only a few years after the instantaneous success of *Los negros brujos* (1906) established the young Ortiz as *the* public diagnostician of the new nation's "African problem," and influential advocate of rather gruesome measures to eradicate forms of "black wizardry" threatening to retard the progress of Cuba's civilization. (Palmié 2002a) Under the impact of massive waves of police repression that Ortiz himself had helped to unleash in the aftermath of a case of alleged child-sacrifice in 1904, (Cháves Álvarez 1991, Helg 1995, Palmié 2002a, Bronfman 2004) by the end of the first decade of the twentieth century, Guerra (then probably in his sixties) and his son-in-law, the septuagenarian *lucumí* "Papá" Silvestre Erice, seem to have decided to confront their persecutors. To counter the public constructions of their practices as secretive "African savagery," they strategically opened the doors of the *Sociedad Lucumí Santa Rita de Casia y San Lazaro* Erice had founded in 1902[38] to journalists, scholars, foreign visitors, and even the then chief detective of Havana's civil special police corps, Rafael Roche Monteagudo—several of whom, such as

---

37. Excepting Sarracino (1988) the question of returnees to Cuba, and especially the issue of any back and forth movements between Cuba and West Africa has remained unstudied. Cabrera (1980:179) makes references to the notebooks of one Sixto Samá who, around 1880, had returned from Sierra Leone where he had been educated in a British mission school, but we know nothing about any "English Professors" (in Matory's sense) being active in Cuba.

38. Since Silvestre Erice's name also appears on the list of officers of the *reglamento* of the *Sociedad de Socorros Mutuos bajo la Advocación de Santa Bárbara Perteneciente a la Nación Lucumí, sus Hijos y Descendientes*, it is reasonable to assume that significant ritual as well as social ties, perhaps even overlap in membership, existed between the two *sociedades* right from the start. As will become clear in the following, by 1911, Fernando Guerra clearly was involved in both Sociedades.

the American resident and prolific amateur historian Irene Wright, (1910:149–50) the criminologist Israel Castellanos, (1916) and Roche Monteagudo (1925:79–83) published vivid (though largely antagonistic) accounts.[39] Fernando Ortiz never published a similar account. Yet although he continued to advocate the scientific eradication of "African wizardry" throughout at least the second edition of *Los negros brujos* (1916), it is clear that by 1911 (at the very latest), he had established close relations with Fernando Guerra and the members of both the *Sociedad Lucumí Santa Rita de Casia y San Lazaro* and the *Sociedad de Socorros Mutuos bajo la Advocación de Santa Bárbara*. For his personal papers contain a handwritten letter dating from that year in which Guerra, as secretary of the latter, invites Ortiz, as a "man of the science of good government" to become their honorary president—ostensibly the same office Remigio Herrera-Adechina had held only ten years before![40] We do not know if Ortiz accepted the honor, but it is clear that he reciprocated. For in the summer of 1912, shortly before the outbreak of massive racist violence in the course of the suppression of the Partido Independiente de Color, Ortiz gave legal advice to Guerra and his associates on how to regain official permission to use *batá* drums in their rituals.[41] Finally, in a broadside published in 1914 rebuking journalistic allegations of having surprised Erice and Guerra in morally questionable ritual activities, Guerra emphasized the openness of their practices, assuring the reading public that if the journalists really had been at their meeting house in the barrio of El Cerro on the day in question, their presence would have been noted by two witnesses beyond reproach: Fernando Ortiz, and a colleague from Ireland, whom Ortiz had brought along to observe the ceremonies the *Sociedad* was holding that day. (Palmié 2002a:251f.) As I have argued before, (Palmié 2002a) it is clear that Guerra (who never tired of quoting the articles of the new Cuban constitution guaranteeing freedom of religion) and his priestly colleagues were shrewdly maneuvering to co-opt Ortiz's considerable public authority, and inscribe their *Sociedades'* beliefs and ritual practices into a larger project of self-consciously modern Cuban nation-building. But for our present purposes, it is interesting to note that all of Guerra's writings preserved in Ortiz's personal

---

39. Documenting both altar displays and ceremonial events (Wright evidently attended a ritual featuring divine possession), these publications – as David Brown (2003:59f., 66f., 224–226, 238, 247) has shown – now represent our prime sources for a crucial period in the emergence and consolidation of a specifically Afro-Cuban ritual aesthetic.

40. Instituto de Literatura y Lingüística, Fondo Ortiz, Carpeta 35. For the full text of the letter see Palmié (2002a: 250f.).

41. See Palmié (2002a: 253f.)

archive (or published, as in Castellanos 1916:99) refer to such beliefs and practices as a "Christian lucumí morality." This may relate to the fact that the crucial parts of the 1901 Cuban constitution (a remarkably hybrid document)
were modeled after the Spanish constitution of 1876 (adopted in Cuba in
1881) which retained Catholicism as the official state religion, but allowed the
private practice of other faiths, "as long as they respect Christian morals and
public order." (Bronfman 2004:23) I do not wish to touch upon the never-end-
ing, and utterly confused debate about Catholic syncretism here.[42] But it is
obvious that although the *discursive object* Guerra had launched into circulation in the Cuban public sphere had become "a religion" in the legal sense stipulated by the Cuban constitution, it was not—or not yet—a Yoruba one.

This was to change rather dramatically in the 1930s, and again, Fernando
Ortiz played a significant role in the process. To this day, we are sorely lacking a true intellectual biography of Ortiz, but it is clear that he completely revised his initial assessments of African-derived elements in Cuban national
culture: some time between 1916 and the early 1930s (most likely while in
exile in the USA during the Machado dictatorship, 1930–33) Ortiz turned
himself from a scientific witch-hunter, inspired by Lombrosian criminal anthropology, into the single most effective public advocate for an incorporation of African (and specifically Yoruba-derived) cultural traditions into the
project of building an autonomous and authentic Cuban national culture.
(Palmié 1998) And, once more, his increasingly close contacts to practitioners of Afro-Cuban religion—this time the *cabildo* of Remigio Herrera-
Adechina's daughter Francisca (Pepa) Herrera-Echu Bí (1864–1946) in
Regla—were crucial to this transformation. For when, in May 1937, Ortiz as-
cended the stage at the prestigious Institución Hispanocubana de Cultura, for
a lecture (Ortiz 1938) preceding the first concert-presentation ever, in a "high
cultural" setting (the splendid Teatro Campoamor), of those very drums the
police had been confiscating for decades, and which Remigio Herrera-
Adechina and Fernando Guerra had fought hard to be able to use in private
rituals,[43] Ortiz had become a student, rather than mere patron of the formidable *olú añá* (consecrated master drummer) Pablo Roche (Okilápka). It was
with the help of Roche and his younger colleagues Trinidad Torregrosa's and

---

42. David Brown (2003) has recently revisited it in such a detailed and incisive manner that we might well think of abandoning the term as an analytical instrument – at least
in the case at hand.

43. Ortiz later (1952–55, VI: 322) called the event a "liberation". But it also marked the
beginning of a process that would culminate in the state-organized "folklorization" of Afro-
Cuban religious "art" forms under the socialist regime (cf. Hagedorn 2002).

Raúl Díaz' (all three associated with Pepa Herrera's cult group) that Ortiz eventually compiled his truly stunning monographic chapter on the history, organography, ritual significance, and sociology of the *batá* drum in Cuba, (Ortiz 1952–55, VI: 204–342) and by then, Ortiz was ready to fully acknowledge their contributions. But what was just as remarkable about the 1937 event were the words with which Ortiz opened them:

> Esteemed audience: Aggó Ile! Aggó Ya! Aggó Olofí! Olórum mbae! These words and these ritual gestures are a simple invocation of the Yoruba [sic] gods, so that the spirits, when their sacred chants are reproduced here will not take offense and stop treating us with faithful benevolence. (Ortiz 1938:89)

Reminding the audience that, in the last such event, the Institución Hispanocubana had presented the most advanced modernist compositions by Gilberto Valdés (based on Afro-Cuban themes), Ortiz now promised the listeners not just the "most primitive religious liturgies of the Yoruba negroes and their Cuban descendants as they are preserved here in their ancestral purity," but simultaneously emphasized that the

> lucumí or yoruba [sic] negroes, together with the Dahomeans, are the most civilized in West Africa; [have the] most advanced religion, and whose myths and arts have given rise to ideas about their intimate relations with the ancient peoples of the Mediterranean: with Egypt, Crete, Tartesis, Carthage..." (ibid.:91)

Ortiz, by then had thoroughly digested Frobenius, and it seems that he knew of the debates about Yoruba-origins in the literature that had been emerging from Nigeria since the 1890s.[44] He was also well aware of the impact expositions of African art, and North American "Negro music" had had on the European avant-garde, and had himself played a major role in sparking the primitivist artistic movement known as "Afrocubanismo." (Kutzinski 1993, Moore 1997) But chances are good that his references also were not lost on the three drummers, four *akpuón*[45] and twenty members of the chorus imitating the antiphonal chant pattern of a ritual event: for as Brown (2003:147) makes highly plausible, by the 1930s several *babalawos* (including Eulogio Rodriguez-Tata Gaitán and Guillermo Castro) not only were serving as informants for

---

44. On the various – and conflicting – ways in which Christianized "Yoruba" traced these in accordance to Hebrew, Greek, Christian, Muslim, or (somewhat later) Egyptian models see Law (1976, 1984), Doortmunt (1993) and Peel (2000, especially 295–304).

45. Liturgical experts who lead the chants.

Ortiz, but seem to have gone to "drink water at [his] fountain" (i.e. the impressive library of Africanist literature Ortiz had compiled by then).[46] When Adechina's daughter Pepa died in 1946, in all likelihood, the political significance and legitimatory potential of designating their beliefs and practices as a Cuban continuation of Yoruba traditions had become clear to her, and particularly to the younger members of her cult group.

By the mid-1950s, and in one of the first book-length print publications authored by a practitioner of an Afro-Cuban religion — Nicolás Valentín Angarica's *Manual del Orihaté* — we finally get an explicit claim not just to the Yoruba origins of Regla de Ocha and Ifá, but to their *essential* Yoruba-ness which, so Angarica, was in need of restoration. In the foreword, a Dr. José Roque de la Nuez (Efún Yomí)[47] explicitly chides ethnographer Lydia Cabrera (Ortiz's sister-in-law, whose book *El Monte* had just appeared the year before) for having uncritically compiled data from ill-qualified sources, and, in addition, having generated the mistaken impression of a unified "African language," whereas, so Roque claimed, "it is certain that Africa was the cradle of a FEUDAL civilization, in which tribes of the feudal type existed, and where every tribe had a typical language of its own, different from the language of the other tribes...customs of its own, and a religion in accordance with the religious deity they worshipped...."(Angarica 1955:3). In contrast to profane scholars like Cabrera, Roque (ibid.:4) continues, Angarica had taken the utmost care to rectify such errors, "for a dictionary and a Bible translated into the Yoruba language have [lately] come into his hands." Angarica himself, in turn, emphasized that despite his Creole birth, his "intimate ties to the sentiments of the *lucumíes* and *arará*, and in addition his membership in their Religious Creed, allow [him] to bring to the light of civilization, without distortions, the truth of the Lucumí Religion of Yorubaland" (ibid.: 9). Containing a sophisticated, and theologically highly rationalized account of a "lucumí pantheon" [48] self-consciously modeled after "classical" sources, Angarica's efforts uncannily resemble those of mid-twentieth century Yoruba-theologians such as Lucas (1948) or Idowu (1962). And in this respect, the *Manual del Orihaté* clearly represents a shrewd move to counter both the vil-

---

46. Brown's data derive from a series of letters the *babalawo* José Miguel Gómez Barberas wrote to his colleague Radamés Corona in the late 1970s. In these letters Gómez claimed to have introduced Gaitán and Castro to Ortiz.

47. So far, no one has identified Dr. Roque/Efún Yomí.

48. Which, according to Brown (2003:113–162) early twentieth century "reformers" such as Ña Rosalia/Efuché and Lorenzo Samar Rodríguez/Obadimelli (Angarica's mentor) had only begun to effectively inscribe into ritual practice less than three decades ago.

ifications of an earlier phase of representations of Afro-Cuban religion as African savagery, *and* the primitivism of the Afro-Cubanismo movement that had emerged among intellectuals and artists in the 1930s. (Kutzinski 1993, Moore 1997) In doing so, Angarica strategically positioned himself as the heir to what was now becoming thinkable as a trans-Atlantically extended Yoruba Tradition validated though a rapidly growing scholarly as well as popular literature. But he himself also stands at the beginning of an essentially novel tradition: one out of which, by the 1970s, at the latest, a global movement unified around the worship of deities by now unanimously regarded as of Yoruba origin *and* essence was to emerge.

In the Cuban case, we get the first glimpses of this emergent tradition, when (probably in the late 1950s) the practitioner-author Pedro Arango interpolated some forty pages of Pierre Verger's *Dieux d'Afrique* (1954) into his otherwise unremarkable *Manual de Santería* (reprinted in full in Menendez 1998).[49] Particularly since Verger himself counts among the pioneers of creating the impression of trans-Atlantic Yoruba-continuity by presenting his impressive Bahian data side by side with his equally outstanding data from Southwestern Nigeria and Benin, the effect is stunning. After more than 160 pages of explications of ritual procedures, divination signs and their associated myths, bilingual prayers (Spanish and *lucumí*), or magical recipes, the reader is suddenly plunged into a narrative juxtaposing detailed ethnographic data pertaining to Brazil and different locations in the Bight of Benin, ordered in a fashion that renders their divergences mere local variations on a trans-Atlantic theme: the *òrìṣà*, their attributes, and the forms of worship they receive. Though Arango's textual strategies are still rather clumsy, the impressions they create point the way to the future: that the beliefs and practices associated with the term *lucumí* can, and ought to, be assimilated into this trans-Atlantic spectrum of *òrìṣà*-related—and therefore, ultimately, and essentially Yoruba— cultural forms is now little else but a foregone conclusion.[50]

---

49. Arrango's source was first identified by Dianteill (2000). For the genre of the "manuales" see Palmié (1995), Dianteill (2000), and Dianteill and Swearingen (2003). For the earlier genre of the "libretas" (out of which the "manuales" probably emerged) see Leon (1971) and Hesse (1977).

50. This, of course, was exactly Verger's point: writing about the yearly processions of the "cabildos" of Pepa Herrera and Susana Cantero in Regla which he had witnessed upon the invitation of Lydia Cabrera in the late 1940s, he notes that the chants he heard were "the same as can be heard in the Ibara quarter of Abeokuta on the day of the *Yemanja* festival and there is scarcely any difference between the spectacle of these Cabildos and that of the followers of *Yemanja* bearing the *ere* to the sacred source of *Yemanja* and through the streets of the Ibara quarter" (Verger 1963:215).

Almost predictably, and as in Brazil, the ethnographic interface begins to register these developments at virtually the same time. When Herskovits' student William Bascom[51] went to Cuba in the summers of 1948 and 1950, he had no trouble performing such trans-Atlantic ethnological assimilations. Perhaps unsurprisingly, he "saw many ceremonies in which animals were sacrificed to Yoruba Orishas, Yoruba music was played on African drums, songs with Yoruba words and music were sung, and dancers were 'possessed' by the Orishas."(Bascom 1951:14) Although his claim that two hundred *babalawos* were active in Havana at the time is not unreasonable, the fact that he counts his informant "Akilapa" (i.e. the formidable *olú añá* Pablo Roche-Okilapka) among them, both reveals his misunderstanding of Roche's religious commission, and throws into light the connection Ortiz had obviously engineered between them. Although Bascom claims to have been "able to prove that the Yoruba language is actually spoken, and not just recited" (ibid.:17) in Cuba, in a later essay (Bascom 1953:164) he concedes that "[h]aving to depend on an interpreter in Spanish, I found that with my own limited command of Yoruba, I could at least make some of the elemental enquiries in the African language." While this makes it doubtful whether he actually was able to tell that "[m]any informants, in fact, had a better command of Yoruba than I myself had," Bascom (ibid.:164) clarifies some of the mechanisms by which such linguistic competence was acquired. For

> As part of their training in the Afro-Cuban cults, even the newcomers acquire a vocabulary in an African language which can be identified by comparison with the published dictionaries from Africa. These vocabularies are systematically learned through instruction by those more advanced in the cults, and are copied by hand into note books or copy books of 'santería, *as the Yoruba cults are called.* Handwritten santería copy book are sold, while *the more complete books* may be purchased in typewritten form from stores which specialize in selling paraphernalia used on the altars in the cult houses. (Bascom 1953:163f. emphasis mine)

Chances are that Angarica's mimeographed precursor to *Manual del Orihaté*, *El Lucumí al alcance de todos* (probably late 1940s), a "manual de santería"

---

51. Bascom had done fieldwork in Ifé and Igana in 1937–38 and may have been steered to Cuba by Herskovits who had been in correspondence with Ortiz since the 1920s, and probably wanted Bascom to test the "strength" of Cuban "Yorubanisms". In addition, Bascom's Cuban wife Berta Moreno, took courses with Ortiz at the Universidad de la Habana.

rather than a language primer[52] may have figured among those "more complete books" which were now obviously entering into a complex pattern of intertextuality with ethnographic accounts of performances partly informed by them. What is more, while ethnographers like Bascom were now inscribing Afro-Cuban forms of knowledge that had become partly book-borne and drew on essentialized constructions of Yoruba religion deriving from Christian Nigerian sources or Yoruba-ethnographies, as Dianteill and Swearingen (2003) have argued, practitioners themselves began to plough Cuban ethnographies back into "hierographic" texts designed to guide ritual praxis—and have continued to do so to this very day.[53] The result, it would seem, is a dialectic between heterogeneous texts and practices which, for at least the last half century, has been spiraling steadily towards the *telos* of a transatlantic religious "Yoruba-dom"—however one wishes to understand that term.

* * *

Space will not permit me to trace the complicated—and highly ironic—history which began to unfold with the exodus of hundreds, perhaps thousands of practitioners of what *now* had become thinkable as a New World Yoruba-religion from Revolutionary Cuba after 1959, and the near simultaneous initiation into *Regla de Ocha* of the US African-American cultural entrepreneur Walter Serge King-Obá Efuntola Adelabu Adefunmi I in Matanzas, Cuba in 1958. I have dealt with both issues before, (Palmié 1991, 1995, 1996) and they are, by now, well documented. (e.g. Brandon 1993, Clarke 1997, Brown 2003, Dianteill 2002, Argyriadis and Capone 2004, and Frigerio 2004) But I would like to close by briefly touching an aspect of this history that has not yet—or not to my knowledge, at any rate—received suf-

---

52. The title translates as "Lucumí in Everyone's Reach", and probably was modeled after popular "teach yourself" language primers.

53. Most practitioners of Regla de Ocha and Ifá I have worked with in both Miami and Havana are voracious readers, always on the lookout for new forms of knowledge that help to "recover" forgotten aspects of what they call "la tradición" (cf. Palmié 1995). Such knowledge is often generated from perusal of the most eclectic and unlikely sources (such as the Tibetan and Egyptian Books of the Dead, Kabbalistic or numerological manuals, New Age literature of Mexican or North American origin, and so forth), and are sometimes built into highly original and complex syntheses. However, the crucial point to emphasize here is that none of this takes place in the form of a mere "passive absorption". Apart from sometimes rather idiosyncratic forms of "theological criticism", the Diloggún and Ifá oracles are the ultimately source for confirmations of the "truth" of knowledge produced in this fashion. This, I would strongly argue, also holds for their use of ethnographic texts.

ficient attention: the contributions of late-twentieth century Nigerians to the "cultural work" that has gone into the ecclesiogenetic processes out of which emerged an aspiring world religion centered on the worship of the *òrìṣà/orisha/orixa/oricha*.

The best known, but by no means singular protagonist of this story, is the Nigerian literary scholar, former professor and vice-chancellor of the University of Ile Ife, politician, *babalawo*, and cultural entrepreneur Wande Abimbola (b. 1932)—a man whom Matory (2001: 187) has called a "new Martiniano," and Peel (1990:341) has called an "*araba*[54] *en partes fidelibus*." Most likely, Abimbola's career as the paragon of a new type of transcontinental "Yoruba-dom" began in 1968.[55] That year, he arranged (with the sponsorship of the Nigerian Federal Government!), the bestowing of the old Oyo title of *bálè* (town chief) of Bahia on *candomblé*-priest *cum* ethnographer Deoscoredes Maximiliano dos Santos (*mestre* Didi), an initiate of Mãe Aninha's *Opô Afonjá terreiro*, thus closing the circle between an Oyo of Martiniano do Bomfim's imagination, and a Bahia which now had become a township within an Empire that, to use Matory's (1994) phrase, "was no more." Himself a recent graduate of Northwestern University's African Studies Program, and newly appointed lecturer in Yoruba Studies at Lagos University, Abimbola completed his Ph.D. in Literature, and became a practicing *babalawo* in 1971. In late 1975, we find him on his way to Bahia for a month long trip, sponsored by the University of Ife's Diaspora Research Project. Abimbola's trip had been jointly arranged on location by the linguist Olabiyi Babalola Yai (another emissary from the University of Ife), *mestre* Didi, and the indefatigable French wanderer between African and New World religious worlds, Pierre Verger who had long since established himself in Bahia, but would soon take up a visiting professorship in Ife, undergo initiation into the cult of Ifá in Benin, and become the first African-initiated French *babalawo* active in a New World setting.

In his report presented at the 42. Congrès International des Américanistes in Paris 1976, Abimbola concludes that his observations in Bahia provide clear evidence for "the strong attachment and respect which the people of Brazil still have for the Yoruba divinities." (Abimbola 1979:634) Nonetheless, faced with a loss of linguistic competence in Yoruba, Bahian devotees "do not fully understand the linguistic meaning" of liturgical texts, a situation that is "a painful one to many of the *òrìṣà* devotees who would pay any price to acquire

---

54. Senior *babalawo*.

55. Unless noted otherwise, the following section draws on Abimbola (1979 and 1997).

the linguistic ability necessary for an understanding of their own [religious] repertoire." (ibid.: 634) "Fortunately," Abimbola continues,

> Since the early sixties, the Brazilian government itself has taken at least a token interest in this problem. The first Nigerian was therefore sent to Bahia in the 1960 to teach the Yoruba language. He is the late E.L. Laṣebikan who was already a well-known scholar of the Yoruba language before he left Nigeria. But Laṣebikan was grossly ignorant of the way of the òrìṣà, since in Nigeria he regarded himself as a Christian. Therefore when he first reached Brazil, he could not understand the people whom he had been sent to educate. But he soon adjusted himself and learned more about the òrìṣà as he himself taught the Yoruba language to his students who were mostly made up of babalórìṣà and ìyálórìṣà. During my visit to Brazil, the Bahians fondly remembered Laṣebikan and chanted some of the songs which he taught them. (Abimbola 1979:634f.).

One wonders if Laṣebikan's former students sang CMS hymns to Abimbola! Yet while one might presume that Abimbola would have recognized them, it is clear that the spirits of Bishop Samuel Crowther, James Johnson, and perhaps even Philip Meffre might have hovered over E.L. Laṣebikan's classroom in Bahia. For the question of what constitutes "proper Yoruba" is, of course, intimately bound with the mid-nineteenth century missionary debates about the translation of the Bible into what, in fact, was to turn out a synthetic idiom (largely composed of Egba vocabulary, structured by an Oyo grammar, shot through with Islamicisms, and so forth) which only gradually and unevenly spread through southwestern Nigeria, following the disseminating path of CMS bibles, hymnals, and school primers. (Peel 2000:283–88 et passim) Indeed, whatever his linguistic expertise, Laṣebikan, too, seems to have passed through the trans-Atlantic ordeal that transformed Philip Meffre from an African born Brazilian babalawo into a Yoruba-Christian—if only in reverse. But thanks to his efforts, the criteria that Bishop Charles Philips, in 1890, used to define "Yorubaness"—namely "(1) having a common language, (2) holding the tradition of common origin, regarding Ile-Ife as the cradle of the race" (cited after Peel 2000:286)—were now vigorously being inserted into New World discourses by successors to Laṣebikan unencumbered by the Christian intellectual ballast that had made his travails in Bahia so arduous, but that ironically had been part and parcel of the initial formation of the idea of a "Yoruba nation" in the nineteenth century Bight of Benin.

The next linguistic ambassador of a transcontinental "Yoruba-nation" seems to have been Yai, who—this time financed by the University of Ife—appears to have ingratiated himself with his Bahian hosts so much that "a request was

Figure 3.1 - Bishop Samuel Ajayi Crowther.

sent through the Nigerian Embassy in Brasilia that Yai should be allowed to stay longer." (Abimbola 1979:635) By the winter of 1975, however, Abimbola himself was taking the matter to a higher level of rationalization. Consider his take on the irksome issue of religious syncretism:

> An African devotee of the òrìṣà is at first startled at the syncretism of the Yoruba divinities with the Catholic saints. As a true African interested in the promotion of authentic African traditions, one sometimes wonders whether syncretism is indeed to be encouraged. (Abimbola 1979:636)

Still, so Abimbola in a passage that uncannily echoes the pastoral strategies the Second Vatican Council commended in respect to "syncretistic" Latin American forms of "popular piety" (though, of course, from a *very* different vantage point!), such "syncretism does not obscure the true message of the *òrì.à* to the Brazilian people," for given "the general Catholic atmosphere in which everybody has got to operate" in Brazil, it is "more of an outward than an inward tendency." (ibid.) Besides, "African traditionalists [sic] respect the faith of others as equally authentic, and as an experience they themselves can partake in." (ibid.)

At the time of his pronouncements at the Congrès International des Américanistes, Abimbola, of course, may not have been fully aware of the emergence, in the course of the 1960s of what became known as the "Yoruba-Reversionist" movement in the US. Advocating not only a radically "anti-syncretistic" agenda, (Shaw and Stewart 1994, Palmié 1995) but espousing an ideology reflective of distinctively North American conceptions of the *necessary* coincidence of "Africanity" and "blackness" (as locally conceived), the forms of "Yoruba identity" propagated by Obá Ofuntola's Oyotunji theocratic community Oyotunji in South Carolina, or the Yoruba Theological Archministry in Brooklyn, do not readily admit to the situation Abimbola was facing in Brazil. As he reflected some twenty years later, and from a position at Boston University,

> Some people feel that they don't want to see any white man in this religion. But we keep reminding them that, to start with, white men are there already via Cuba and Brazil, from where the religion came here [i.e. to the US] in the first instance! (Abimbola 1997: 29)

For as he had already pointed out in 1976,

> the important point to note is that the *òrìṣà* in Brazil have ceased to be a property of the black people alone. Both whites and mulatto participate in *òrìṣà* worship, and there are in fact a few people among the elite classes whose sincerity in supporting the *òrìṣà* cannot be called into question. The divinities of the Yoruba known as *òrìṣà* have thanks to the slave trade become a *world religion* offering a new way of life to many black and white people in the two Americas as well as in the Caribbean. (Abimbola 1979:636 emphasis mine)

And so it came to pass. In a highly original inversion of the providentialist interpretations of slavery common to both black Christians in North America since the eighteenth century (from Phyllis Wheatley to Alexander Crummell) and nineteenth century Christian Saro (like Crowther and Johnson),[56] slavery now became the historical medium *not* for the emergence of a Diasporic black Christian *ecclesia* whose members would eventually bring the light of the

---

56. Cf. Peel (1995).

gospel to their "benighted African brethren," but for the transcontinental dissemination of an "African Traditional Religion" whose standard-bearers had
to be propelled abroad in order to eventually carry its message of peace and
racial conciliation across the globe. "We learn from Ifa," Abimbola (1997:29)
would tell the American scholar Ivor Miller some twenty years later,

> That the city of Ilé Ifẹ̀ is the home of Man. It is believed to be the
> place where all humans, both white and black, were created and from
> where they dispersed to other parts of the world. When a person
> comes to Ilé Ifẹ̀, whatever may be his color or nationality, we say
> "Welcome back, welcome home."

Following Abimbola's interpretation, we might say that when, in 1981, he,
mestre Didi and the Puerto Rican *santera* Marta Vega met in New York, and
first hatched the idea of a series of an "International Congress of Òrìṣà Tradition and Culture" under the patronship of the Ọni of Ifẹ̀, they were merely
writing forward a providential narrative, in the making since the beginning
of the world—or, more objectively, since at least beginnings of the CMS efforts in the Bight of Benin around the middle of the nineteenth century.

   In the course of time since 1981 much has changed. And it casts a profoundly different light on the events that may have transpired in the back
rooms of a Havana bodega owned by the well-to-do Spanish-Creole merchant
Bonifacio Valdés, where Ño Carlos Adé Bí and his unknown African-born or
Creole fellow *babalawos* consecrated the first socially white "son of Ifá" and
"father of the secret" (for that is what the term *babalawo* means in contemporary standard Yoruba). As things stand now—after eight International Con-
gresses of Òrìṣà Tradition and Culture since 1981—Ño Carlos Adé Bí's decision is fully vindicated. Whether he knew it or not, Ifá himself had guided
him on a course that, with proper retrospective realignment, today appears as
the first faltering steps towards the globalization of an entity we can nowadays
talk about as a "Yoruba religion" that has transcended both the limits of
"Africanity" and those of "race." Or has it? Surely, the matter is more complicated than the way in which Cuba's Minister of Culture, Abel Prieto presented
it at the eighth such Congress in the summer of 2003—namely that it would
behoove all "*tercermundistas*" to rally around the call of the *òrìṣà*, providing,
as it did, a healthy antidote to the cultural poison emanating from Holly-
wood.[57] But since even the Cuban socialist state has fallen into line with Ifá's

---

57. David Brown's (2003:79–97) account of the vicissitudes of the legitimatory strategies characteristic of what Frigerio (2004) calls "secondary diasporas" provide an apt example of the power politics involved beneath such glib pronouncements.

prognostications, facilitating the acquisition of a prime piece of state-owned Centro Havana real estate by a conglomerate of internet-savvy and globally well-connected, *babalawos* aptly designating themselves as the Asociación Culturál Yorubá de Cuba, who am I to say? The final question, then, may be this: was Samuel Johnson a Yoruba in the same sense that Wande Abimbola, the Youba Theological Archministry or the Asociación Culturál Yorubá de Cuba are projecting these days? I cannot answer it. But I guess it ought to be *both* yes and no.

References

Abimbola, Wande. 1979. "Yoruba Religion in Brazil: Problems and Prospects" *Actes du 42. Congrès International des Américanistes* (Paris 1976). Paris: s.d.A, pp. 619–639

———. 1997. *Ifá Will Mend Our Broken World*. Roxbury: AIM books.

Acosta Saignes, Miguel. 1955. "Las cofradías colonials y el folklore" *Cultura Universitaria* 27:79–102.

Aimes, Hubert. 1905. "African Institutions in the Americas" *Journal of American Folklore* 18:15–32.

Ajayi, Jacob F. Ade. 1994. "Samuel Johnson: Historian of the Yoruba" in: Toyin Falola (ed.) *Pioneer, Patriot and Patriarch: Samuel Johnson and the Yoruba People*. Madison: African Studies Program, University of Wisconsin-Madison, pp. 27–32.

Amselle, Jean-Loup. 1993. "Anthropology and Historicity" *History and Theory Beiheft* 32:12–31.

Angarica, Nicolás Valentín. 1955. *Manual del Orihaté*. La Habana: no publisher.

———. "El Lucumí al alcance de todos". Reprinted in Lázara Ménendes (ed.). 1998. *Estudios Afrocubanos (IV: 4–128)*. La Habana: Universidad de la Habana.

Apter, Andrew H. 1991. "Herskovits' Heritage: Rethinking Syncretism in the African Diaspora" *Diaspora* 1:235–60.

Arango, Pedro. No date. "Manuál de santería". Reprinted in Lázara Ménendes (ed.). 1998. *Estudios Afrocubanos (IV: 130–344)*. La Habana: Universidad de la Habana.

Argyriadis, Kali and Stefania Capone. 2004. "Cubanía et santería: les enjeux politiques de la transnationalisation religieuse" *Civilisations* 51:81–137.

Barth, Fredrik. 1984. "Problems in Conceptualizing Cultural Pluralism, With Illustrations from Somar Oman" in: David Maybury-Lewis (ed.) *The Prospects for Plural Societies*. Washington, D.C.: American Ethnological Society, pp. 77–87.

Bascom, William R. 1951 "The Yoruba in Cuba" *Nigeria Magazine* 37:14–20

———. 1953. "Yoruba Acculturation in Cuba" *Mémoirs de l'Institut Français d'Afrique Noir* 27:163–167.

Bastide, Roger. 1978. *The African Religions of Brazil*. Baltimore: The Johns Hopkins University Press.

Braga, Julio. 1995. *Na Gamela do Feitiço*. Editora da Universidade Ferderal da Bahia.

Brandon, George. 1983. "'The Dead Sell Memories': An Anthropological Study of Santería in New York City" (Ph.D. dissertation, Rutgers University)

Bronfman, Alejandra. 2004. *Measures of Equality: Social Science, Citizenship and Race in Cuba, 1902–1940*. Chapel Hill: University of North Carolina Press.

Brown, David H. 2003. *Santería Enthroned*. Chicago: University of Chicago Press.

Butler, Kim. 2001. "Africa in the Reinvention of Nineteenth Century Afro-Bahian Identity" in: Kristin Mann and Edna Bay (eds.) *Rethinking the African Diaspora*. London: Frank Cass, pp. 135–154.

Cabrera, Lydia. 1980. *Yemayá y Ochún*. Miami: Colección del Chicherekú en el Exilio.

Caron, Peter. 1997. "'Of a nation which the others do not Understand': Bambara Slaves and African Ethnicity in Colonial Louisiana, 1718–60" *Slavery and Abolition* 18: 98–121.

Castellanos, Israel. 1916. *La brujería y el ñáñiguismo en Cuba desde el punto de vista medico-legal*. La Habana: Lloredo y Companía.

Chambers, Douglas. 2000. "Tracing Igbo into the African Diaspora" in: Paul E. Lovejoy (ed.) *Identity in the Shadow of Slavery*. London: Continuum, pp. 55–71.

Chávez Álvarez, Ernesto. 1991. *El crímen de la niña Cecilia*. La Habana: Editorial Ciencias Sociales.

Childs, Matt D. "Pathways to African Ethnicity in the Americas: African National Associations in Cuba During Slavery" in: Toyin Falola and Christian Jennings (eds.) *Sources and Methods in African History*. Rochester: University of Rochester Press, pp. 118–144.

Clarke, Maxine Kamari. 1997. "Genealogies of Reclaimed Nobility: The Geotemporality of Yoruba Belonging" (Ph.D. dissertation, University of California, Santa Cruz)

Dantas Gois, Beatriz. 1988. *Vovó Nagô e Papai Branco*. Rio de Janeiro: Graal.

Danto, Arthur. 1965. *Analytical Philosophy of History*. Cambridge: Cambridge University Press.

Deschamps Chapeaux, Pedro. 1968. "Cabildos: Solo para esclavos" *Cuba: Revista Mensual*, January, pp. 50–51.

————. 1971. *El negro en la economía habanera del siglo XIX*. La Habana: UNEAC.

———— and Juan Pérez de la Riva. 1974. *Contribución a la historia de la gente sin historia*. La Habana: Editorial Ciencias Sociales.

Dianteill, Erwan. 2000. *Des Dieux et des Signes*. Paris: Éditions de l'École des Hautes Études en Sciences Sociales.

————. 2002. "Deterritorialization and Reterritorialization of the Orisha Religion in Africa and the New World (Nigeria, Cuba and the United States)" *International Journal of Urban and Regional Research* 26:121–137.

———— and Martha Swearingen. 2003. "From Hierography to Ethnography and Back: Lydia Cabrera's Texts and the Written Tradition in Afro-Cuban Religions" *Journal of American Folklore* 116:273–292.

Doortmunt, Michel R. 1993. "The Roots of Yoruba Historiography: Classicism, Traditionalism and Pragmatism" in: Toyin Falola (ed.) *African Historiography*. BurntMill: Longman, pp. 52–63.

Falola, Toyin. 1984. *The Political Economy of a Pre-Colonial African State Ibadan, 1830–1900*. Ile Ife: University of Ife Press.

Fardon, Richard. 1987. "'African Ethnogenesis': Limits to the Comparability of Ethnic Phenomena" in: Holy, Ladislav (ed.) *Comparative Anthropology*. Oxford: Basil Blackwell, pp. 168–188.

Frazier, E. Franklin. 1942. "The Negro Family in Bahia, Brazil" *American Sociological Review* 7:465–78.

Frigerio, Alejandro. 2004. "Re-Africanization in Secondary Religious Diasporas: Constructing a World Religion" *Civilisations* 51:39–60.

Frobenius, Leo. 1913. *The Voice of Africa*. London: Hutchinson.

Fyfe, Christopher. 1962. *A History of Sierra Leone*. Oxford: Oxford University Press.

Gellner, Ernest. 1983. *Nations and Nationalism*. Oxford: Blackwell.

Gómez, Michael. 1998. *Exchanging Our Country Marks*. Chapel Hill: University of North Carolina Press.

Hagedorn, Katherine. 2001. *Divine Utterances: The Performance of Afro0Cuban Santería*. Washington, D.C.: Smithsonian Institution Press.

Hall, Gwendolyn Midlo. 1992. *Africans in Colonial Louisiana: The Development of Afro-Creole Culture in the Eighteenth Century*. Baton Rouge: Louisiana State University Press.

Harding, Rachel. 2000. *A Refuge in Thunder: Candomblé and Alternative Spaces of Blackness*. Bloomington: Indiana University Press.

Helg, Aline. 1995. *Our Rightful Share: The Afro-Cuban Struggle for Equality, 1886–1912*. Chapel Hill: University of North Carolina Press.

Herzfeld, Michael. 1982. *Ours Once More: Folklore, Ideology, and the Making of Modern Greece*. Austin: University of Texas Press

Hesse, Axel. 1977. "Eine LIBRETA DE SANTERÍA – Beispiel für den Beginn schriftlicher Tradierung auf Kuba" in: Burchart Brentjes (ed.) *Der Beitrag der Völker Afrikas zur Weltkultur*. Halle: Martin Luther Universität Halle-Wittenberg, pp. 134–62

Howard, Philip. 1998. *Changing History: Afro-Cuban Cabildos and the Societies of Color in the Nineteenth Century*. Baton Rouge: Louisiana State University Press.

Idowu, E. Bolaji. 1962. *Olodumare: God in Yoruba Belief*. London: Longmans.

Jameson, Robert. 1821. *Letters from The Havana During the Year 1820*. London: John Miller.

Johnson, Samuel. 1921. *The History of the Yorubas*. London: Routledge and Kegan Paul.

Kedourie, Elie. 1960. *Nationalism*. London: Hutchinson.

Koelle, Sigismund. 1854. *Polyglotta Africana*. London: Church Missionary House.

Kutzinski, Vera M. 1993. *Sugar's Secrets: Race and the Erotics of Cuban Nationalism*. Charlottesville: University of Virginia Press.

Lachatañeré, Romulo. 1992. *El sistema religioso de los afrocubanos*. La Habana: Editorial Ciencias Sociales.

Landes, Ruth. 1947. *The City of Women*. New York: Macmillan.

Law, Robin. 1976. "Early Yoruba Historiography" *History in Africa* 3:69–89.

———. 1984. "How Truly Traditional is Our Traditional History? The Case of Samuel Johnson and the Recording of Yoruba Oral Tradition" *History in Africa* 11:195–221.

———. 1997. "Ethnicity and the Slave Trade: 'Lucumi' and 'Nago' as Ethnonyms in West Africa" *History in Africa* 24:205–219.

León, Argeliers. 1971. "Un caso de tradición oral escrita" *Islas* 39–40:141–51.

Lima, Vivaldo da Costa. 1966. "Os Obás de Xangô" *Afro-Ásia* 2–3:5–36.

López Valdés, Rafael L. 1998. "Notas para el studio etnohistórico de los esclavos lucumí en Cuba" in: Menendez, Lázara (ed.) *Estudios Afrocubanos (vol.II)*. La Habana: Universidad de la Habana, pp. 311–347

Lovejoy, Paul E. 1997. "The African Diaspora: Revisionist Interpretations of Ethnicity, Culture, and Religion Under Slavery" *Studies in the World History of Slavery, Abolition, and Emancipation* 2: 1–24.

———. 2000. "Identifying Enslaved Africans in the African Diaspora" in: Paul E. Lovejoy (ed.) *Identity in the Shadow of Slavery*. London: Continuum, pp. 1–29.

Lucas, J. Olumide. 1948. *The Religion of the Yorubas*. Lagos: CMS Bookshops.

Marrero, Levi. 1971–78. *Cuba, economía y sociedad*. Madrid: Playor.

Mason, John. 1992. *Orin Òrìsà: Songs for Selected Heads*. Brooklyn: Yoruba Theological Archministry.

Matory, J. Lorand. 1994. *Sex and the Empire That Is No More*. Minneapolis: University of Minnesota Press.

———. 1999. "The English Professors of Brazil: On the Diasporic Roots of the Yorùbá Nation" *Comparative Studies in Society and History* 41:72–103

———. 2001. "The 'Cult of Nations' and the Ritualization of Their Purity" *South Atlantic Quarterly* 100:171–214.

Menendez, Lázara. 1998. *Estudios afrocubanos: Selección de lecturas*. La Habana: Universidad de la Habana.

Moore, Robin. 1997. *Nationalizing Blackness: Afrocubanismo and Artistic Revolution in Havana, 1920–1940*. Pittsburgh: University of Pittsburgh Press.

Moreno, Isidoro. 1999. "Festive Rituals, Religious Associations, and Ethnic Reaffirmation of Black Andalusians: Antecedents of the Black Confraternities and Cabildos in the Americas" in: Jean Muteba Rahier (ed.) *Representations of Blackness and the Performance of Identities*. Westport: Bergin and Garvey, pp. 3–17

Morgan, Philip D. 1997. "The Cultural Implications of the Atlantic Slave Trade: African Regional Origins, American Destinations and New World Developments" *Slavery and Abolition* 18:122–145.

Murdock, George Peter. 1959. *Africa: Its People and Their Culture History*. New York: MacGraw-Hill.

Nina Rodrigues, Raymundo. 1935. *O Animismo Fetichista dos Negros Bahianos*. Rio de Janeiro: Civilização Brasileira.

———. 1977. Os Africanos no Brazil. São Paulo: Nacional.

Northup, David. 2000. "Igbo and Myth Igbo: Culture and Ethnicity in the Atlantic World, 1600–1850" *Slavery and Abolition* 21:1–20.

Ortiz, Fernando. 1973 [1906]. *Los negros brujos*. Miami: Ediciones Universal.

———. 1921. "Los cabildos Afro-cubanos" *Revista Bimestre Cubana* 16:5–39.

———. 1938. "La música sagrada de los negros yoruba en Cuba" *Estudios Afrocubanos* 2:89–104

———. 1939. "Brujos o santeros" *Estudios Afrocubanos* 3:85–90.

———. 1952–55. *Los instrumentos de la música afrocubana* (5 vols.). La Habana: Cárdenas y Cia.

Palmié, Stephan. 1991. *Das Exil der Götter*. Frankfurt: Peter Lang.

———. 1993. "Ethnogenetic Processes and Cultural Transfer in Caribbean Slave Population" in: Wolfgang Binder (ed.) *Slavery in the Americas*. Würzburg: Königshausen und Neumann, pp. 337–63

———. 1995. "Against Sycretism: Africanizing and Cubanizing Discourses in North American òrìsà-Worship" in: Richard Fardon (ed.) *Counterworks: Managing the Diversity of Culture.* London: Routledge, pp. 73–104.

———. 1996. "Which Center, Whose Margin? Notes Towards and Archaeology of U.S. Supreme Court Case 91–948, 1993" in: Olivia Harris (ed.) *Inside and Outside the Law.* London: Routledge, pp. 184–209.

———. 1998. "Fernando Ortiz and the Cooking of History" *Iberoamerikanisches Archiv* 24:1–21.

———. 2002a. *Wizards and Scientists.* Durham: Duke University Press.

———. 2002b. "The Color of the Gods: Notes on a Question Better Left Unasked" in: Berndt Ostendorf (ed.) *Transnational America.* Heidelberg: C. Winter, pp. 163–175.

Peel, J.D.Y. 1989. "The Cultural Work of Yoruba Ethnogenesis" in: Elizabeth Tonkin, Maryon McDonald and Malcolm Chapman (eds.) *History and Ethnicity.* London: Routledge, pp. 189–215.

———. 1990. "The Pastor and the Babalawo: The Interaction of Religions in Nineteenth-Century Yorubaland" *Africa* 60:338–369.

———. 1993. "Between Crowther and Ajayi: The Religious Origins of the Modern Yoruba Intelligentia" in: Toyin Falola (ed.) *African Historiography.* Burnt Mill: Longman, pp. 64–79.

———. 1995. "For Who Hath Despised the Day of Small Things: Missionry Narratives and Historical Anthropology" *Comparative Studies in Society and History* 37:581–607.

———. 2000. *Religious Encounter and the Making of the Yoruba.* Bloomington: Indiana University Press.

Pichardo, Ernesto and Lourdes Nieto 1984. *Odudúwa Obatalá.* Miami: Church of the Lukumí Babalu Ayé.

Pierson, Donald. 1942. *Negroes in Brazil.* Chicago: University of Chicago Press.

Pike, Ruth. 1967. "Sevillan Society in the Sixteenth Century: Slaves and Freedmen" Hispanic American Historical Review 47:344–59.

Reis, João José and Paulo F. de Morães Farias. 1989. "Islam and Slave Resistance in Bahia, Brazil" *Islam et Sociétés au Sud du Sahara* 3:41–66.

Roche Monteagudo, Rafael. 1925. *La policía y sus mistérios.* La Habana: La Moderna Poesía.

Rojas, María Teresa de. 1956. "Algunos datos sobre los negros esclavos y horros n la Habana del siglo XVI" in: *Miscelanea de estudios dedicados a Fernando Ortiz* (vol. II). La Habana: Impresores Úcar García, pp. 1276–127.

Rushing, Fannie Theresa. 2002. "Afro-Cuban Social Organization and Identity in a Colonial Slave Society, 1800–1888" *Colonial Latin American Historical Review* 11:177–201.

Sarracino, Rodolfo. 1988. *Los que volvieron a África*. La Habana: Editorial Ciencias Sociales.

Shaw, Rosalind and Charles Stewart. 1994. "Introduction: Problematizing Syncretism" in harles Stewart and Rosalind Shaw (eds.) *Syncretism/Antisyncretism*. London: Routledge, pp. 1–26

Smith, Robert S. 1994. Samuel Johnson and Yoruba Warfare" in: Toyin Falola (ed.) *Pioneer, Patriot and Patriarch: Samuel Johnson and the Yoruba People*. Madison: African Studies Program, University of Wisconsin-Madison, pp. 139–149.

Steiner, Christopher B. 1994. *African Art in Transit*. Cambridge: Cambridge University Press.

Thompson, Robert Farris. 1983. *Flash of the Spirit*. New York: Random House.

Thornton, John K. 1992. *Africa and Africans in the Making of the Atlantic World, 1400–1680*. Cambridge: Cambridge University Press

Turner, Lorenzo D. 1942. "Some Contacts of Brazilian Ex-Slaves With Nigeria, West Africa" *Journal of Negro History* 27:55–67.

Verger, Pierre. 1954. *Dieux d'Afrique*. Paris: Harmattan

———. 1963. "Afro-Catholic Syncretism in South America" *Nigeria Magazine* 78:211–216.

Wright, Irene. 1910. *Cuba*. New York: Macmillan.

Yai, Olaibi B. 2001. "African Diasporan Concepts and Practice of the Nation and Their Implications in the Modern World" in: Sheila S. Walker (ed.) *African Roots/American Cultures*. Lanham: Rowman and Littlefield, pp. 244–255.

Yelvington, Kevin. 2001. "The Anthropology of Afro-Latin America and the Caribbean: Diasporic Dimensions". *Annual Review of Anthropology* 30:227–60.

CHAPTER 4

CONFUSION AND EMPIRICISM: SEVERAL CONNECTED THOUGHTS

Jane I. Guyer

Introduction

Over twenty years separates two pieces of John Peel's work that have lodged themselves in my mind, and connected themselves to each other, creating a provocative issue to return to. For several years I have been circling around the question of what might constitute empirical anthropological approaches to situations that appear distinctly incoherent. There are many conditions in the world that now seem confused in multiple registers (moral, cognitive, material), indistinct with respect to the level at which "coherence" might be looked for, and deeply puzzling or thrillingly risky (when not terrifyingly unpredictable) to participants as well as analysts. The occasion of a collection in honor of Peel's work offers me the opportunity to speculate about some facets of an approach, using as a springboard his own rigorously crafted arguments, and the Christianity and classical textual scholarship that are central to both the substance and the method of his work.

In 1978 Peel published an extended review of the then-insurgent neo-Marxist movement in intellectual life under the inspired title of "Two Cheers for Empiricism." He argued then that the classic Marxist theoretical categories had to be so expanded if one were to do grounded empirical scholarship (especially on Africa) that ultimately "(t)he only important matters are whether an adequate account of the phenomena...has been given; and how far this account...is consistent with other, more general theories" (1978: 356). The concepts and subject matters he advocated were "concepts applicable in a constant form to all societies or the whole range of a particular kind of phenomena" (1978: 356). The positivist-leaning epistemology that he advocated here has been deeply critiqued since the 1970s. But the practice of identifying and providing evidence for specific dynamics, within contexts taken to be ultimately indicative of some kind of coherence, remains a viable means toward redefining what the salient "wholes" might be in the present profoundly interconnected but seemingly disorderly world.

Fast forward twenty two years to the present, to witness the emergence of "confusion" as a potentially recurrent social "form," or process in Africa, open to empirical study and comparative analysis, and directly implicating our apprehension of interconnections into larger encompassing dynamics. *The Religious Encounter and the Making of the Yoruba* (2000) includes a chapter entitled "Living in an Age of Confusion," depicting a phase of nineteenth century history in Western Nigeria. Although this "age" fits a chronological narrative exposition—between the two orders of "country fashion" communities and a Christian notion of nationhood—Peel does not imply that it can be understood only as a structural "transition." Rather he treats it empirically, as its own configuration, and thereby implicitly as an exemplar of "a whole range" of that kind of phenomenon.

These two pieces seem to me to belong together, as a challenge. Many scholars have found the late twentieth and early twenty-first centuries in Africa fraught with confusions and contradictions, as well as trauma, as the continent's future seems to "go in several directions at once" (Mbembe 2001). In spite of a sense of unique disorientation to the African present, Mbembe has also argued that our current era has something in common with the Africa of the late nineteenth century. He defines it as "*l'Afrique des comptoirs*": an Africa subjected to the destructively competitive demands of extractive commerce and industry in a rapidly expanding world market, and left to its own devices to accommodate its own imaginaries and invent its own social forms. However accurate one finds the parallel from one century's end to the next, it is certainly heuristically suggestive because it opens up the comparative enterprise Peel advocated in 1978. In the new century, states of confusion have become precisely what Peel termed in that early essay a "perennial problem" in the social sciences: a recurrent challenge from "out there" to the adequacy of concepts, methods, and theoretical orientations in the disciplines. He argued there that disciplinary knowledge advances "through extension to new instances of the same kind of structure" (1978: 356). His own relentlessly comprehensive scholarship about social orders, about the multiple and changing social forms through which spirituality and sociality are reproduced, is the tangible manifestation of the qualified empiricism he endorsed in his "Two

Cheers" review. It takes in a great sweep of phenomena, and subjects their relationships to consistent exploration from the evidence. This wide-angle lens
can apply equally to states of confusion as to structure, as Peel implies. One
can ask how confusions are denoted, and whether there are different kinds,
sources, accounts and experiences that fall under this provocative concept.

Such an endeavor must rest first on the signal case. So I take Peel's "empiricism" a step further by triangulating the Yoruba "confusion" of the nineteenth
century through all its possible referents in the cultural repertoires in play at
the time: the Hebrew Bible, the Christian Bible, and Yoruba religion.[1] Both the
noun and the verb—"confusion" and "to confound"—carry weight and are
used at key junctures in all these contexts. To do full justice to the nuances demands more linguistic and critical erudition than I can muster at present, but
tensions in the English translations are suggestive of directions for a social scientist to explore. The Latin etymology implies "mixing together," whereas "confusion" refers throughout the Bible almost uniquely to *dispersing* what had once
been *unitary*.[2] For example, the first biblical confounding was done by God,
when humans worked together to build a great tower. Seeing no limit to what
humans might do with a common language God went down to "confound their
language, that they may not understand one another's speech. So the Lord scattered them abroad from thence upon the face of all the earth; and they left off
to build the city" (Genesis 11:8). The converse of confusion is not order or law
but peace (see I Corinthians 33). Dispersing, however, is not the same thing as
"dividing" within a biblical frame of reference. Dividing is the sacred act of separating the components of a coherent world, naming them and fixing their relationships to one another. Maintenance of the divine distinctions is a religious
injunction; mixing things together, as in the mixtures prohibited in Leviticus,
creates not confusions but "abominations." The precise distinctions made by
the biblical terms reminds us that such words refer to an entire cosmology, and
that shifts can occur in translation as one term is transposed into the resonance
of meanings of another language, culture, historical experience, and system of
spiritual expertise.

---

1. I cannot address the influence of Islamic thought on states of confusion here, but
they would certainly be relevant, as Peel notes of the "conceptual bridgehead" (2000: 194)
that Islam offered to the Yoruba for a later-coming Christianity.

2. A full exploration would require study of the text in Hebrew, through Jewish commentary. From the new Robert Alter translation of *The Five Books of Moses*, and from the
Hebrew original, it appears that not all the instances of "confusion" in English are glosses
for the same term in Hebrew. A more scholarly approach to these concepts would demand
attention to the terms and glosses in all the relevant texts.

Confusion in *The Religious Encounter*

Peel does not precisely define confusion in *The Religious Encounter*. It is his style of exposition that conveys comprehensive and systemic properties. He documents and juxtaposes moral travesties, cognitive illogicalities, ineffective actions and emotional distress. He alludes above all to the disruption of *communities* by civil war (2000: 50); a condition where "principles of action might just as easily undermine as support one another" (2000: 51); the experience of the world as "like a worn-out and cast-off garment"…"spoiled and upside-down" (2000: 50); and the competition between Christian, Islamic and traditional religious practices and politics to build a more orderly idea of a future (paraphrased from the book jacket). The rising centrality of "great men" with their personal clients, rather than elders and experts with their moral communities defined by kinship and occupation, created its own dynamics of arbitrary power. In brief, "social and moral reflection" (2000: 48) on arbitrariness was pervasive: the unpredictable leader, the cruel act, the trickery in diplomacy, the disappearance of a grid of commonly respected reference points, the eruption of war. For the designation of this concatenation comprehensively as an "age of confusion," the reader is referred to Church Missionary Society missionary David Hinderer. He writes that Yoruba see war as "the time of confusion," and cites *orisa* priests saying that, "a god of confusion reigned" (2000: 50). In this juxtaposition, Hinderer is clearly conflating a biblical concept from the Book of Revelation and the Yoruba deity Esu under a common English term.

Before turning to that conceptual elision in the following section, and to what can be lost in the translation of "confusion" from Hebrew and Greek to English and from English to Yoruba, let me note important questions to which I will return again later. What process magnifies and generalizes a designation such as confusion to make it pervasive, or characteristic of an entire era? To what social or political level of inclusion does it index? What "imagined community" is at stake, morally and spiritually? The historical evidence for pervasive disturbance is not convincing enough to make the argument by itself. First of all, Ibadan is the epicenter of Peel's argument, as it was for Samuel Johnson (1921), writing in the midst of the late nineteenth-century confusion, and most recently for Ruth Watson (2003), bringing the history into the colonial period. Centering Ibadan brings its own slant to a Yoruba-wide story. Ibadan has always been seen as particularly and chronically contentious, from its foundation and colonial history (Watson 2003; Falola 1984) to its place in modern state politics up to the present (Agbaje 2002). By contrast, Southern Baptist missionary William H. Clarke wrote of prosperity and order in western Yorubaland in the 1850s, through periods of warfare. Huge markets were attended from a wide radius in spite of the Fulani hostilities, and "beautiful farms were...the elements of success and the foundation of whatever is permanent and durable" (1972: 262). Fulani settlements were tolerated, so that the longstanding relations of pastoral and agricultural economies continued. So the picture of political confusion and decline is remarkably patchwork, geographically, as Peel himself notes in various places: that is, at least, if the Yoruba people are taken as the "whole" under analysis.

Secondly, Peel's account of confusion highlights at least some incidents that almost certainly lay within the routine orders of everyday life. However distressing the descriptions of such events as human sacrifice might be, his accounts are almost exactly the same in content and emotional tone to descriptions of routine religious practice in Yoruba scholarship. Peel quotes Anna Hinderer to describe, "the dignity of the young male victim, the solemn atmosphere in the town before the act, and the relief and rejoicing afterward." (Peel 2000: 70). Awolalu writes of general Yoruba practice, using oral sources: "After immolation, a tense moment has passed. Blood has flowed, and this is a signal that a message had gone from men to the supernatural. The whole atmosphere is then changed. People relax and there is often jubilation" (1979: 177). Not all that was deeply distressing and possibly confusing to some participants departed from the concept of order for others.

Thirdly, Peel's evidence also implies—but he does not yet explore in detail—what seems to be a quite varied recourse to established community-level modes of supplication to explain and resolve disturbances and crises. In principle a Yoruba community's cult complex, like most others, "could answer to the problems recurrent in key areas of life—farming, hunting, trade, disease, and so on—so that there emerged a degree of functional specialization in relation to these niches among the deities of a locality" (Peel 2000: 111). Peel's examples mention several failures in this regard in the late nineteenth century: examples of divination where the supplicants had to go from one deity to another in search of solutions. The Ota chiefs supplicated on behalf of the community after a fire killed thirty-nine people and destroyed most of the town in the wake of a series of other problems (2000: 99). Repeat efforts at prayers and sacrifice failed. The chiefs were desperate, "faced with a pressing problem and a plethora of possible but dubious solutions thrown at them by interested parties on all sides" (2000: 99). The Ondos similarly went through a series of different interventions aimed at containing a run of smallpox epidemics. How is a high rate of failure explainable? There are several possibilities. One that Peel suggests is that failures increase as it becomes more difficult to reconcile "ancient sacred precedent and the messy actuality of the Age of Confusion"

Figure 4.1 - European missionaries at a Yoruba village, 19th century.

(2000: 115). Another explanation might be that the wars had siphoned off a disproportionate number of intellectuals into the overseas slave trade, particularly to Brazil, leaving insufficient expertise to manage a stepped up demand for devotional mediations, and, perhaps, especially at the community level. A further eventuality to consider, and one that is represented by the standard oral history in Idere (where I have worked), holds that flight and exile from war, and return and reinstallation after the peace, were in fact quite effectively mediated by the collective ritual repertoire of Yoruba religion, long before Christianity became a factor in social thought and practice. Their entire religious polity was reinstated in the same location, and on the same spatial and social grid, after years of exile in Iseyin. So there may have been a long cycle within the indigenous religious tradition for which community flight—even scattering—is not best depicted as a confusion.

There may be an important variability here—from event to event and from town to town—for which the history is rather hidden. I am not sure why divination for the collective good is so low-profile in the impressive anthropological and philosophical corpus on divination. Taiwo (2004: 304) is one of few scholars to mention explicitly divination for associations (*ifa egbe*) and for town communities (*ifa ilu*). Did divination for the common good actually go into relative demise under colonialism? This would clearly affect community coherence, regardless of the other pressures of the times. Or did the scholarly

interest in personal trajectories, healing, and micro-sociologies take precedence to the extent that the collective has been relatively ignored? In any event,
the many accounts of divination based on twentieth-century field research
barely discuss cases of collective and political supplication, so we are rather
hard-pressed to understand its apparent failures in some cases in the nineteenth century.

I am experimenting here with narrowing down what might have been considered "confusing" in the nineteenth century, and suggesting a set of disparate
incidents, with varied dynamics, rather than a single systemic resonance.
There is a case to be made for going even further and arguing that even the
"patches" may have had an explanation in Yoruba moral and political philosophy, in the form of the *orisa* Esu. Peel notes a recurrent invocation of Esu,
the trickster god, as the cause of disorder let loose on the world. "The *orisa*
held responsible above all for spoiling and confusing things was Esu; and a
babalawo in Ibadan expressly attributed the troubles of the times to God's release into the world of Esu (confusion) and Ogun (war)...." (2000: 50). Peel
suggests that the cosmic order itself became confused: "This was an uncertain
and competitive world for gods as well as for human beings, in which the *orisa*
had at least as many failures as successes." (2000: 106). This is quite intriguing because Esu is not necessarily construed in this way (as I discuss below),
and Peel does mention, elsewhere in his account, the polyvocality of traditional religion: always "a terrain of constant questioning, contestation, and
exploration" (2000: 121). Different practitioners of the cult made their own
different interpretations. In this case, disorders of inadequate and inept ritual
practice (through loss of expertise, or decline in training) should perhaps be
distinguished from disorders thought by recognized adepts to emanate from
the cosmos itself. Whatever the variant with respect to Esu's implication in the
troubles of the nineteenth century, this *orisa* is certainly an intellectual resource for narrowing down the nature of confusion as seen by those suffering
its effects.

In sum here, there is enough empirical evidence in *The Religious Encounter*
to suggest that confusions and orders can be seen as plural, partial, differen-
tially accounted for, and coexistent, and that their generalization to whole
times and peoples is a projection that needs its own explanation. In Yorubaland, geographical and historical variation in political experience, shifts in
moral response to mundane practices, patchwork failures to mobilize the req-
uisite expertise for entrenching order, and innovations in the attributes of key
metaphysical propositions (such as Esu) create something more like whirlpools
and quick sands than maelstroms and earthquakes. The advantage of breaking down confusion in this way is not, I hope, to be pedantic but rather to

open up the kind of comparative question Peel advocated in "Two Cheers." By locating specific sites and domains, the question of agency can be opened up: in what domains, under what conditions, do people themselves create confusions? How do they see each smaller eddy growing by contagion or replication into something more pervasive? How is significance recognized and diagnosed? Eventually, I argue, we need confusion to take on the active voice: "to confound."

Since Peel is writing about, and also drawing on, the story of Yoruba Christian conversion, one does well to take a voyage through the theology at play. The contrast between two concepts of systemic confusion, at different levels, and a random profusion of limited confusions follows closely the contrast between the singular cosmic apocalypse in the Christian Bible, the recurrent social and spiritual dispersals of the Israelites, and the multiple remediable disturbances that are the work of Esu. I look at the Bible first, making my way next to Esu, and conclude by a short discussion of indeterminacy and human "causal capacity" (Dupre 1993: 214).

Biblical Confusion

Apart from the story of the Tower of Babel, there are rather few references to confusion in the Pentateuch.[3] It is the prophets who develop the idea, often in relation to the hubbub of cities, with their profound spiritual dangers. In terms of a generalized condition, the visions of Daniel constitute the main apocalyptic statement in the Hebrew Bible.[4] In exile in Babylon and in service to its kings, the Israelites were given a complex and precise timeline for their deliverance on condition that they recognize and correct their own faults of waywardness with respect to the Covenant and the Law. "Oh Lord, to us belongeth confusion of face, to our kings, to our princes, and to our fathers, because we have sinned against thee" (Daniel 9:8. King James Version). The prophecy of a sequence of complex political conflicts, each attributed a dura-

---

3. And those there are not, in the King James Bible, the same word in the Hebrew as the confusion of the Tower of Babel (*balal,* in Hebrew). For example, the two allusions to confusion in Leviticus concern the sexual transgressions of bestiality (18:23) and father-daughter incest (20:12), both of which are referred to in the Alter (2004) translation from the Hebrew as "perversions" (*tevel,* in Hebrew). There is a nuanced lexicon for defilement, to which this concept belongs.

4. However, The Book of Daniel has a low (perhaps non-existent?) place in Judaism's annual reading of the entire Pentateuch, where each section has a linked portion from the history and the prophets.

tion in days, culminates in "the end of days": a period of "trouble" during which the people are delivered, under the leadership of Michael, "the great prince." The moral narrative and the political narrative reflect one another; autonomy is reinstated on condition of moral reform, following a period of intense political disorder. In spite of its particularly apocalyptic terminology, the prophecy of Daniel closely resembles recurrent denunciations of the Israelites by their spiritual leaders: predictions, divine threats and chastisements, political restitutions, and subsequent failings. The last verses of the last book of the Hebrew Bible are another roaring indictment and a last chance for a turn of heart before the return of Elijah and the day of judgement.[5] The wicked will be burned up, left with "neither root nor branch," turned into "ashes under the soles of your feet" (Malachi 4). Read in sequence, each Hebrew prophet seems to be turning up the volume about the enduringly strict conditions of autonomy as a people—the "great and dreadful day of the Lord"…"lest I come and smite the earth with a curse" (Malachi 4:5–6)—rather than joining in a chorus about a single "end of days." Their words are part of the on-going history of a specific political-spiritual community's moral vicissitudes.

The Revelation of St. John the Divine in the Christian Bible goes much further. Confusion becomes a single, unique epoch: a phase in a cosmic transformation in which humans figure largely as witnesses, survivors and—if sinful—victims. Through a series of dazzling confrontations between beasts and angels, angelic judgments of the "whoredom" of Babylon, the release of Satan from imprisonment to do his worst on the nations (for a while), and the invocation of fire and brimstone for the wicked, the way is prepared for the Second Coming and the New Jerusalem. The battle is total, and the victory total. The Kingdom admits of no abominations whatsoever. "And there shall be no more curse" (Revelation 22:3). All of being, every person, and not a specific community, is implicated in the whirlwind propulsion into a new world: "the waters which thou sawest, where the whore sitteth, are peoples, and multitudes, and nations, and tongues." (Revelation 17:15). And the "faithful" survive through endurance, as "servants" of God, rather than by the laborious process of collective reform. The age of confusion is an ordeal of triage, identifying and testing the true believers in preparation for the Messianic Second Coming. As a specific "age" of confusion, it is unclear in causation, beyond ritual and moral disciplines for humans to control, and indeterminate in the

---

5. According to Jewish custom, however, a reading in synagogue never ends with words of threat and doom, so another, more encouraging verse from elsewhere in the reading is repeated when the text is performed.

time or nature of its resolution. There is no precise chronology to this "end of days," unlike the numeration in the Book of Daniel. And it may come at any time. Indeed, St. John suggests twice in his last admonitions that it may "come quickly." Thus the *age* of confusion is a magnification and elaboration, encompassing all of creation, of a long tradition of thought about confusion that was originally focused on the vicissitudes of a particular "stiffnecked" people who had been saddled with a unique covenant and an unrelenting law.[6]

Much is at stake then, for moral agency and practical traction on the road toward a future, in identifying the social level of inclusiveness at which the narrative of confusion is pitched. What is the operative social referent for the ruptured connection between action and outcome? Is the experience personal, or collective, or cosmic? Whose intervention creates both the rupture and the resolution? Where does culpability and redemptive action lie, and who is encompassed in it? These two traditions of thought from the Bible differ from each other: the first is national, moral, recurrent, relentless, with no ultimate "escape" to a new state of being. Confusion is associated with dispersal, dispersal with delinquency, and restitution with observance. The other is global, faith-based, once for all time, with total transformation. But both of them index confusion to the social fabric quite differently from the Yoruba thought and practice that one must imagine were most intimately available to people in nineteenth century Western Nigeria.

Yoruba Confusions

In Peel's account, Esu was prominently mentioned by *babalawo* as the cause of the disorganization of a world that had been cast off by the gods. In the era of Christian proselytizing, Esu was amongst the most widely recognized of gods throughout the Yoruba-speaking world (Peel 2000: 108). Generally referred to as the trickster, the messenger of the gods, the guardian of crossroads and thresholds, the god of confusion, Esu is an ever-present source of "indeterminacy and the inexplicable" (Hallen 2000: 73). Insofar as Esu is the source of confusion, it is a confusion of the everyday, the intrinsic, the recurrent. The face of Esu confronts the Ifa diviner on the opposite side of his divining tray (as depicted on the paper cover of *Religious Encounter*) every time he casts for a client.

---

6. I am assured that there is a wide variety of canonical Christian views on Revelation as reality or as metaphor. Catholicism sees it as metaphor, certain sections of Protestantism as real prophecy.

All sources imply (or explicitly argue) that the moral quality of Esu's confusion is deeply ambiguous, or perhaps beyond morality altogether. In the context of other writing on Esu, Peel's particular *babalawo* seems to have had a remarkably biblical interpretation of his role: "God's release into the world... in order to punish men for their disobedience" (2000: 50). Far from representing a moral and judgmental principle, Esu is described elsewhere as causing *gratuitous* trouble. Hallen offers his own addition to the discussion of Esu and evil by noting a moral threshold between *awon araye* (people of the world), to whom anything bad can be attributed, and Esu who rather accounts for that small range of residual conditions for which no moral-social explanation pertains. "The spirit of Esu" (Hallen 2000: 73) is the *final resort* as a moral explanation, when all other motivations for human action fail. Esu is the *orisa* "associated with indeterminacy and the inexplicable" (Hallen 2000: 74), not evil nor indeed a moral commentator of any sort.

In recent years, the literature on "tricksters" in Africa, including Esu, actually suggests creativity rather than negativity. Tricksters open up indeterminate spaces that become sources of invention, creativity and possibility in social life. The sense that Esu may have operated in the past on a potentially dire horizon of moral and material danger has been mitigated, according to the recent ethnography. Esu symbolizes "man weaving a fabric of meaning through the transforming power of his imagination...[disclosing] the radically human character of the whole cosmos" (Pelton 1980: 255–6). Indeed one commentary goes a step further, to claim that Esu actually tames an intrinsic cosmic competitive disorder amongst the gods through his function as their messenger and provider of sacrifices from their acolytes. "Esu seems to provoke trouble deliberately and to take delight in disorder, but he only brings things to a crisis that can be resolved by means of sacrifice. Without Esu the cosmos would be a battlefield of blind aggression". Esu's demand that humans deal actively rather than passively with what is random and inexplicable, is the force "bringing about balanced order through sacrifice" (Witte 1984: 14). Sacrifice was central (Awolalu 1979). It was humans who acted to close the logical vacuum and reinstate causative connections.

How can we judge these accounts in relation to the "reign of Esu" in the nineteenth century? The theology and cosmology are difficult to historicize. Has Esu been tamed by colonial and Christian history into a more playful and innovative, less dangerous, *orisa*? Was he more powerful in the past, and more gratuitously and uncontrollably disorderly? Is a continuing or recurrent sense of confusion due to a failure of divination, or perhaps a failure of sacrifice, at a particular historical juncture? Failures are not yet a source of historical and philosophical study (though see Taiwo 2004). Much of the anthropological literature implies either the power of a closed system to defend itself against skepticism, or else an overwhelming frequency of actual success. Pemberton writes, "rituals of divination are largely understood as a quest, a search for an answer to human suffering in one of its many aspects and a concern to set things right...to create a new context of meaning" (2000: 3–4). John Mack suggests that this gives it a retrospective cast "about telling rather than fore-telling" (2000: 370), and yet in so-doing (according to Fernandez), divination also puts forth a metaphor that "asserts a different possible world from the literal." (2000: 219). The *sense* of order is restored in these accounts, even if order itself is not. In this interpretation, all confusions should be rendered tractable, or at least supportable, if only in one's understanding and in the poetic narrative of Ifa. While it seems very unlikely that patience was limitless, it does seem plausible that the ever presence of Esu can make unpredictability a familiar state of being within Yoruba social and religious practice, across perhaps a variety of historical conditions.

The sense that, even beyond Esu, the Yoruba life-world is *intrinsically* cross-cut by unpredictable forces is conveyed in a wide variety of scholarship. Yoruba philosophy is often presented as being uniquely cognizant of indeterminacy: in the individuality of social careers, the regularity of divination to suggest the way forward and the multiplicity of spiritual forces in the world. The world, *aye*, itself is not predictable. As abstract concept and as *orisa*, *aye* is associated with markets (see Belasco 1980), and even with bad people (*ara alaye*: people of the world). *Aye* has almost the sense of "worldly." In this cosmology, then, humans and the gods create, and recreate, orders and confusions through chains of causation that can start anywhere and circulate through multiple trajectories. And this process is perpetual.

Confusion and Responsibility

This brief comparative extension of the religious ideas that Peel's account puts at play in nineteenth-century Yorubaland may suggest some issues to pursue. First they differ most profoundly at the social level, the frequency and the tractability of the state of confusion. And perhaps a related point: there is variety in the place afforded to human agency and responsibility. Do humans create confusions, and are they responsible for doing anything about them? Or perhaps, conversely, is "confusion" itself—redolent as it is in all these repertoires with some kind of diminution of human agency—a term that slides into a vocabulary of passivity under conditions of powerlessness? Existing concepts of confusion are propelled circumstantially into new social arenas and new discursive frames, transforming as they move. A short detour through textual sources suggests some of the significant thresholds they may cross as they circulate in new ways.

Many works have looked at violence and failures in Africa in the past ten years as infused with religious and cognitive convulsive forces. Ellis and Ter Haar's important recent synthesis argues that: "The contemporary African spirit world is chaotic.... What seems to be required for a greater sense of stability and order...is a higher degree of consensus than exists in the present on the nature of the spirit world and on legitimate ways of access to it." (2004: 190–1). Nigerian political scientist Claude Ake writes of the "disarticulation" (1981: 43) of postcolonial economies, where the parts related incoherently to one another, and of "institutionalizing a Hobbesian regime that turns society into a war of all against all" (lecture, 1996).

Moving against structuralism, recent anthropological work has increasingly used terms such a contingency, indeterminacy, uncertainty and "emergent forms of life" (Fischer 2004) to express a general and profound sense that orders are tenuous and perhaps fleeting constructions, with no clear propensity to develop in the future along lines that can be understood logically from the past. Much of this work demonstrates the quality of indeterminacy itself: the continuing performative construction of orderly ideas and actions out of relatively inchoate cultural and material forms. And much of this literature is brilliantly convincing about micro-processes and states of mind.

Persuasive as it is, however, there are difficulties with this view. It does not always discriminate between an eternal—even if changing—interface between consciousness and forces that escape it, and the dissonances and disorganizations produced by consciousness itself, deliberately or as a predictable entailment of chosen practices. Dupré writes of science that a concept of the disorder of things "leaves an open empirical question how far the world is from true randomness" (1993: 193). He goes on to argue that humans are actually more orderly than the world, constituting "extraordinarily dense concentrations of causal capacity in a world in which such order is in short supply" (Dupré 1993: 216). But if "science aims both to detect order and to create order" (1993: 259), then surely the human imagination can also mobilize "causal capacity" to disrupt and disorganize. So in what terms is agency not only enacted but attributed? An approach through existing narratives of confusion, from different sources, can bring some illumination.

The focus is shifting from orders through contingency and indeterminacy to disorders. The theoretical issues here are complex and contended, as we avoid simply inverting orders and thereby reverting to structural methods of study. The politics and ethics of interpretation are deeply disturbing. So it is important to have accounts of past confusion, such as those by Achille Mbembe, Mike Davis (2000, on *Late Victorian Holocausts*), and John Peel, in the "Age of Confusion," that pay close attention to their specific attributes, rather than treating them as simply a transitional phase in an intrinsically restitutive process. In the intensity of the moment, there is no clear trajectory forward, by definition, and "transition" is a term only applied by those with the luxury of an external standpoint. For the present, I follow Peel in suggesting here that there can be an empirical project alongside the theoretical one: that of identifying theological concepts, cosmic narratives, moralities of agency and horizons of sociality through which people diagnose "confusion," and its attendant social forms and practices that are particular to time and place. Such specificity can then draw attention to the optative, agential processes through which certain narratives may now extend—if they do—from crucibles into comprehensive perceptions, and as propagated into a few grand global apocalyptic versions that override other formulations—like Esu—of enormous sophistication.

References

Agbaje, Adigun. 2002. Personal Rule and Regional Politics: Ibadan Under Military Regimes, 1986–1996. In J.I. Guyer, L. Denzer and A. Agbaje (eds.) *Money Struggles and City Life. Devaluation in Ibadan and Other Urban Centers in Southern Nigeria, 1986–1996.* Portsmouth NH: Heinemann, 3–26.

Ake, Claude. 1981. *A Political Economy of Africa.* London: Longman.

Alter, Robert. 2004. *The Five Books of Moses. A Translation with Commentary.* New York: W.W. Norton.

Awolalu, J.O. 1979. Yoruba *Beliefs and Sacrificial Rites.* London: Longman.

Belasco, Bernard. 1980. *The Entrepreneur as Culture Hero. Preadaptations to Nigerian economic development.* New York: J.F. Bergin.

Clarke, William H. 1972 *Travels and Explorations in Yorubaland, 1854–1858.* Edited with an introduction by J.A. Atanda. Ibadan: Ibadan University Press.

Davis, Mike. 2000. *Late Victorian Holocausts.* Berkeley: University of California Press.

Ellis, Stephen and Gerrie Ter Haar. 2004. *Worlds of Power. Religious Thought and Political Practice in Africa.* London: Hurst and Company

Dupré, John 1993. *The Disorder of Things. The Metaphysical Foundations of the Disunity of Science.* Harvard University Press.

Falola, Toyin. 1984. *The Political Economy of a Pre-colonial African State: Ibadan, 1830–1900.* Ile Ife: University of Ife Press.

Fernandez, James. 1991. Afterword. In P. Peek (ed.) *African Divination Systems. Ways of Knowing*. Bloomington IN: Indiana University Press, 193–221.

Fischer, M.J. 2004. *Emergent Forms of Life and the Anthropological Voice*. New York: Goldfield, Eugene Curtis.

Hallen, Barry. 2000. *The Good, the Bad and the Beautiful. Discourse about Values in Yoruba Culture*. Bloomington IN: Indiana University Press.

Johnson, Samuel. 1921. *The History of the Yorubas*. London: Lowe and Brydone.

Mack, John. 2000. Telling and Foretelling. African Divination and Art in Wider Perspective. In J. Pemberton (ed.) *Insight and Artistry in African Divination*, Washington D.C., 34–44.

Mbembe, Achille. 2001. *On the Postcolony*. Berkeley: University of California Press.

Peel, J.D.Y. 1978. Two Cheers for Empiricism; or, what is the relevance of the history of sociology to its current practice? *British Journal of Sociology*, 347–59.

———. 2000. *Religious Encounter and the Making of the Yoruba*. Bloomington: Indiana University Press.

Pelton, R.D. 1980. *The Trickster in West Africa. A Study of Mythic Irony and Sacred Delight*. Berkeley: University of California Press.

Pemberton III, John. 2000. Introduction. In his (ed.) *Insight and Artistry in African Divination*. Washington D.C.: Smithsonian Institution Press, 1–9.

Taiwo, Olufemi. 2004. Ifa: an account of a divination system and some concluding epistemological questions. In K. Wiredu (ed.) *A Companion to African Philosophy*. Oxford: Blackwell.

Watson, Ruth. 2003. *'Civil Disorder is the Disease of Ibadan'. Chieftaincy and Civil Culture in a Yoruba City*. Oxford: James Curry.

Witte, Hans. 1984. *Ifa and Esu. Iconography of Order and Disorder. Soest-Holand:* Kunsthandel Luttik.

CHAPTER 5

BETWEEN THE YORUBA AND THE DEEP BLUE SEA: THE GRADUAL INTEGRATION OF EWE FISHERMEN ON THE LAGOS-BADAGRY SEABEACH

Axel Klein

The coastlands of Western Nigeria are a characterized by low lying swamps with dense vegetation that have proven a formidable impediment to settlement and cultivation. Rivers running from north to south drain the forests of the hinterland and intersect with salty creeks running from east to west. Saline levels vary according to rainfall patterns and the tidal regime. Most of the year, but particularly after the rains, or when the tide is high, the creeks are navigable to shallow craft. For centuries a lively trade has carried goods and people along the creeks and rivers connecting the large lagoons of Lagos and Porto Novo. To the south of what in Nigeria is known as Badagry creek lies a sand spit, between a few meters and a mile in width and stretching from the western end of Lagos lagoon to Ghana. It is in fact a narrow barrier between the coastal swamplands and the pounding surf of the Atlantic.

Up to the mid nineteenth century this elongated stretch of land played host to temporary trading marts that were locking the communities of the southwest Nigerian forest belt into the Atlantic trading system. It was also a site of religious shrines, a hunting ground, and refuge for exiles and runaways from the expanding trading ports of Lagos and Badagry. After the demise of the slave trade and the development of port facilities at Lagos in the latter part of

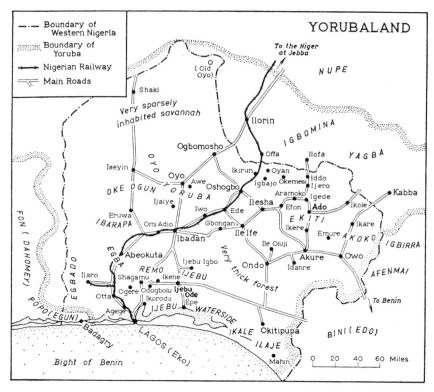

Figure 5.1 - Map of Yorubaland.

the nineteenth century, the economic significance of this strip of coastline was to diminish altogether.

To the north of this strip of land lie coastal swamps that in the mid–nineteenth century provided a safe haven for refugees from the Yoruba wars. With the coming of peace, people moved onto the higher ground on the northern edge of Badagry Creek. Village chiefs of these creek-side communities also claimed suzerainty over beach and forest on the sand spit across the creek, though they had little practical use for it. The small groups of Awori farmers moving into the area from the southeast met and mingled with the westward migration of Egun, traveling along the creeks. Subsistence farmers and in-shore fishermen, they were too removed to benefit from the development of Lagos in any capacity other than running contraband to and from the French colony of Dahomey. Though Rule Britannia established peace, there was very little development. In the words of the District Officer for the Colony District:

A broken slaughter slab and three dry wells serve as monuments of more than seventy years of direct rule. There are no medical or sanitary facilities, and till 1937 there were only two schools, of which one served foreign fishermen's children.[1]

Colony District has now been absorbed into Lagos State and includes the villages of Ilashe, Ikare, Ibeshi, Irewe, Dadi, Ajido, Topo and the town of Badagry. Some of these villages are located on islands, separated from the mainland by the tidal waters of Badagry creek. In these lacustrine communities government services and infrastructure are poorly developed and the traditional authorities continue to play an important role in the distribution of benefits, particularly those accruing from land. Authority over the disposal of land is vested in the village *baale*, and the council of senior chiefs.

Fiercely protective of the farmlands to the north of the creek and the oyster beds, and fishing rights within it, the village *baales* were in the past less concerned about the exact demarcations of their plots along the beach. Each of the three villages owned a stretch more or less opposite to its lacustrine holdings. But given the economic insignificance of this wasteland, villagers were not liable to quarrel over rights of ownership and access.

When, early in the twentieth century, groups of Ewe fishermen from the Keta lagoon in Ghana landed on the shore to set up fishing camps, the elders welcomed them and asked for only token tributes as acknowledgement of their continuing suzerainty. The Awori wanted to cement the bond with their newly found tenants by contracting marital relationships. The newcomers proved reluctant to take up that offer. It seems that they considered themselves as temporary visitors and planned to return to Keta at the end of the fishing season. This failure to enter into marriage alliances with the "sons of the soil" would have far reaching consequences for their descendants, the current occupants of the Seabeach villages.

As so often happens in the history of migration, transitory camps set up by seasonal workers acquired permanence. Crops were planted, the huts turned into houses, and the original leaders of fishing expeditions turned into founding fathers of village communities. Yet today, more than half a century after their arrival, the Ewe fishermen are more marginal and their claim over the land that they have been occupying for several generations more tenuous than ever.

As I will argue below their skills at sea fishing, which made them such welcome tenants in the first place, also provided a formidable obstacle to their

---

1. CSO 30030/S1/ A Report on the Reorganisation of the Badagri District, R.J. Curven (D.O.) 1937. Nigerian National Archives, Ibadan.

integration. The very quantity of the landed catch, and the prevailing organizational arrangements among the Ewe left fishermen dependent on the processing skills of women from their area of origin. Several generations down the line, this history of in-marriage would result in political exclusion, as the Seabeach Ewe continue to be defined as Ghanaian and their rights to the land and other resources fiercely disputed by the Awori chiefs on the northern side of the river. Occupancy of marginal land even after several generations does not produce rights of ownership without intermarriage.

Migrant Fishermen in the Gulf of Guinea

For the Anlo Ewe migration was the logical response to over fishing in the waters of the Keta lagoon, land shortage, and the possibilities of high cash earnings. Migrant fishermen have set up fish camps all along the West African littoral from Ivory Coast to Gabon (Berron 1977; Hill 1986; Lawson 1957; Nukuna 1989; Wyllie 1969). The settlements along the Nigerian coastline follow the classical pattern, but provide a rare incident where a transitory fish camp has turned into a permanent settlement.

According to oral tradition Yovoyan, the first Ewe fishermen, left Keta a lagoon in Ghana—then Togo—in 1914 during the reign of Akran Aholu Kopon (Avoseh 1991). Travelling in his banana boat in the open sea along the shore, he landed first at Cotonou, then at Badagry. Coming ashore he was taken to see the Seriki and the Iman and told them that he had "come to feed the people." The next day he cast his net, and sent the biggest fish to the two dignitaries and the other title holders in the town. Afterwards Yovoyan received permission to cast his net and, in addition, to plant coconut trees on the Seabeach up to the water side, that is the shore of the creek. Yovoyan, however, replied that he was not interested in coconut but only fish. After three years he returned to Ghana with ten kerosine cases full of money.[2]

The Ewe were not the first maritime migrants to arrive from the west. Throughout the eighteenth and nineteenth centuries European merchant ships would recruit specialized boatmen such as the Kru and the Fante in Liberia and Ghana. In the absence of well equipped ports these boatmen were employed to carry cargo from the ships anchoring offshore onto the beach. This hazardous undertaking in the dangerous surf along the coast was well remunerated and a stepping stone for other positions (Brooks 1970; Law 1989; Man-

---

2. CSO Office Lagos, 29979, Intelligence Report on the Central Awori Group in Ikeja and Badagry District of the Colony, Nigerian National Archives, Ibadan.

ning 1985; Smith 1970). Improvements in the port facilities at Lagos and Cou-
tonu made their services redundant in the early twentieth century, and they
turned to other occupations. Some became fishermen, others became clerks
(Tijani 1992), but significantly they soon lost their distinctive collective identity and became absorbed into the main population through intermarriage.

The Ewe, however, had a very different relationship with fishing and the
sea. In Anlo traditional seafaring skills were first acquired by the culture hero
Amaga Le, possibly in the seventeenth century (Greene 1988). They also
learned to use seine-net fishing, possibly from European fishermen working
out of Fort Prindsteen at Keta in the mid nineteenth century onwards. Seine-
net fishing, in contrast to other forms of fishing, is extremely labor intensive
but also very productive. Their seafaring skills and fishing technology were
prerequisites for long distance marine migration. The Ewe required three further conditions: 1. the social organisation for labor recruitment; 2. capital investment in the operation; and 3. the presence of markets.

With the coming of colonial rule, urban development provided ready markets for cheap sources of protein. The fulfilment of the other two was interwoven with Ewe gender relations. The basic unit of the fishing is the net company, with twelve to twenty-five members with different roles. A large team is
needed to paddle the boat across the surf and pay out the net. This is skilled
and risky business as the boat can capsize and injure or even kill the boatmen.
Then the net has to be hauled in, sometimes over many hours depending on
size of net, catch and distance. The full company participates in this task, as
do family members, villagers and even passers by. While hauling in a heavy
net is the quintessential communal exercise, the seine operation depends on
the commitment of the company members. Without minimum numbers the
net cannot be cast and everything comes to a standstill. One way of locking
the team into the operation is by migrating: Moving away from home to temporary fish camps allows the net owner to take advantage of both the migration of fish and the full concentration of the company.

The first Ewe teams to appear on the Nigerian coast founded such fish
camps. Most members would have been men, but they were entirely dependent on the support of the women. Fishing is a full time task after the completion of which the men have little time or energy for other occupations. The
preparation and marketing of the catch is left to the women. Each net company nominates a number of buyers who get the first pick of the catch and
will come to the beach every time the net is cast. These fishwives have to be
well prepared, for once the catch is landed they need to move fast before it
spoils. Some of the wet fish is brought to market right away. The remainder
is preserved by smoking or drying. As a good catch can yield hundreds of kilo

of fish this is challenging work. Smoking shacks have to be prepared, firewood has to be stored, labor and transport arranged. Next the fish, fresh or smoked, is head-loaded to the creek and taken to market by boat. Once at market, many fishwives will buy staples and other goods to take back to the beach on the return journey.

Women then control the sale of fish out and the supply of goods into the community. By processing, sorting and marketing the fish they add value to the product. As purchasers, women provide men with their cash income, and as sellers of food, staples, and luxury goods collect much of it in return. Women are therefore in control of the flow of both goods and money. Moreover, they control the accumulation of surplus and the formation of capital. These funds are invested in various enterprises, including seine nets and banana boats. By financing net companies, female entrepreneurs do not only achieve a return on their investment but also secure a supply of fish for their smoking and retailing operation. The importance of women as sources of finance for artisan fishing ventures has been discussed in different African contexts (Christensen 1977; Hill 1986; Lawson and Kwei 1974; Overa 1995). But what has rarely been discussed is how the interdependence of men and women in the fishing economy of seine netters have impacted settlement and marriage patterns.

Settlement and Marriage Patterns on the Seabeach

The first Ewe fishermen landing at Badagry beach returned to Ghana after a few years' fishing in Nigerian waters. Others, however, decided to stay. In 1920 Nzogola Normeshi obtained permission from the *baale* of Irewe to establish a fishcamp on the Seabeach, then walked for nine days along the beach to Anlo to fetch his wife and followers. Twenty years later Dzogola Koji had become a regular village, with coconut trees stretching to the waters of the creek. According to his grandson, "he had found comfort here." Some agricultural activities were providing an alternative income for fishermen and, with the improvement of transport links to Lagos, alternative opportunities opened up.

Over the next twenty years settlements sprung up all along the Seabeach, from Avijo by the border to Benin Republic in the west, to Sorkpor village close to Tarkwa Bay on the eastern end of Lagos lagoon. The pattern of settlement can be deduced from contemporary arrangements. The villages are mostly named after the founder, who invariably was the *rotor*, or owner of a net company. He would also combine this position with the function of village headman. The accompanying responsibilities are represented in the occupation of the largest compound, which also serves as a place for public gathering. The houses of the net company members are clustered around the central compound. Some of these, particularly the more senior positions such as the treasurer, are settled while others are temporary. There is much coming and going between the Seabeach and the Keta lagoon, but the majority of fishermen are born and settled in Nigeria.

A village may contain a number of compounds in addition to those of the fishermen. A few settlers are working in specialized trades, such as weaving and distilling, or commute to Lagos. In the latter case they only visit the village on weekends and holidays. Most people along the Seabeach are fishermen, and the key unit remains the net company. Village size is therefore limited by the labor demands and constraints of the seine net. A company may have up to twenty-five members, but rarely exceeds this. Villages are at least two kilometres apart, in order to provide each company with a minimum stretch of shoreline needed. Some of the older villages have served as platforms for settlement further east, part of a chain migration towards Lagos. Therefore, families have bases along the entire littoral between the Keta lagoon and Lagos. The high rate of mobility provides most people born on the Seabeach with a web of relatives across the region and back to Ghana, and a very particular sense of identity.

Each village could only be founded with permission from the *baale* in the Awori community across the creek. This followed a pattern in that the *baale* would set a price for the rent and lay down conditions. In Ilashe the ruling *baale* warned the settlers against interfering with married women, but encouraged them to "take a young lady." The fishermen took the land, planted the coconut trees, paid the rent, and provided several catches of fish. But they would return to Keta to marry a woman from their own community using the money earned on the fishing expedition for bride-wealth and setting up a home. In many cases the married couple then moved to Nigeria to make their home and raise their children along the Seabeach.

This pattern continues, and young men along the Seabeach dismiss the idea of marrying one of their Awori neighbours. The reasons vary, including concerns over the financial implications of such an alliance. One informant said that he did not want to pay for the funerals of his wife's relatives. The key determinants, however, were the technical requirements of the fishing. Informants were sceptical of the ability of Awori women to become fully involved in the fishing.

Ilashe Seabeach for example contains 123 adult male residents of whom ninety-seven worked in fishing, and sixty-six were working in one of the three net companies. These members would receive a share of the catch that they then sold to their wives. Company members also have a say in the nomination of fish buyers given privileged access to the catch, and ensure that their wives and female relatives stand to benefit. Most fishermen would also fish in the inshore waters on their own account, or in smaller groups on days when weather conditions or damages to the equipment ruled out working with the seine net.

As diligent fishermen can provide up to 150 kgs of fish a day at the height of the season, women had to mobilize labor through kinship network, and organize marketing networks. There was no doubt that Awori women had the fish processing know-how, and many were experienced market traders. But they rarely worked with the quantities of fish generated by marine fishing. Born into a diversified local economy they had other commitments, such as farming and mat-weaving for which the region was renowned. Moreover, Awori women would experience difficulties in recruiting labor to come to the beach to help with the fish smoking oven, since their families lived on the northern side of the creek and would have had to cross Badagry Creek at short notice.

A marriage to a woman from the neighboring community was therefore not considered a career enhancing prospect. Fishermen depended on their spouses to buy their catch from them. And they were looking toward their wives to accumulate the capital they needed for nets and boats to develop their own operations. As a result of these technical and labor requirements, the Ewe along the Seabeach have become locked into a pattern of endogamy which prevents them from becoming assimilated with their landlords. There was a clear trade-off between establishing a fisheries-based economic model of production, and assimilation into the local politics. The Ewe had mastered the challenges of seine-net fishing by devising a complex division of labor based on gender relations, managerial arrangements and the concept of property. But the needs of the system meant that individual progress depended on the cooperation of a spouse. The fishing economy ruled out intermarriage, and thereby prevented the assimilation of the settlers into the local community. Therefore Seabeach Ewe, even into the third generation, remained "strangers" with no claim over the local resource base and could not emancipate themselves in local arenas of power.

The Rising Value of the Seabeach

Mastery of the sea afforded the Ewe communities with mild prosperity. They were able to build houses, expand their farms, and provide their communities with better facilities than those enjoyed by their Awori neighbors. By collecting rent and trading farm produce, the landlords were also net beneficiaries. Moreover, the Seabeach had previously served no economic purpose and was of religious significance only. This was to change in a most unexpected manner.

In the 1950s Tarkwa village, set on the eastern side of Lagos lagoon and technically at the eastern extreme of the Seabeach, attracted a trickle of visitors. Bars and restaurants opened around the bay to cater to them, while different government departments built rest houses in the village. With the introduction of outboard engines vacationers from Lagos could venture further into the creek. In 1964 a councillor representing the Seabeach on Badagry District Council invited a property developer to Ilashe who found the site compelling. Within months they began building holiday chalets for weekend visitors. These were low-cost constructions from local materials, easily repaired. The main attractions were the palm trees and the white sanded beach.

Ilashe benefited from being in the relative vicinity, but over the next ten years similar chalets sprung up all along the Seabeach. Ewe communities were deeply affected. Tourists provided money for fish and coconuts, drumming up performances and crafts. They hired helpers, cleaners, guards and builders. In some cases personal relationships developed, and visitors evolved into patrons who could even sponsor a net company.

But these benefits came at a cost. Businessmen from Lagos, just like the villager founders of a previous generation, had to negotiate their rights with the owners of the land. In the 1940s the Awori *baales* had been content with payments of high-symbolic and low-material value. Any benefit to be gained from the sand-spit was seen as a bonus. Twenty years later this attitude had changed. To the Awori communities the Seabeach had become a resource. The *baales* succeeded in extracting multiple benefits—jobs and patronage like the Ewe, but most importantly, they could earn rents.

This could be significant. In the mid 1990s, the bigger chalets at Ilashe were leased out to international companies, including airlines, soft drink manufacturers and construction firms, for hundreds of dollars. The smaller ones had individual owners who would pay smaller fees, and would frequently find someone else in what they thought of as their beachside property. But there were even more ambitious projects to develop holiday resorts at various parts of the Seabeach. These generated annual incomes to the Awori chiefs of thousands of dollars. With the coming of wealthy outsiders the real estate value of the erstwhile wasteland had begun to exceed that of the main community. It soon became subject to intense competition between Awori communities and within them. It also set the landlords against their Ewe tenants who began to feel the full disadvantage of their subordinate status.

Land Disputes on the Seabeach

In the late 1960s a team of Lagos based developers became interested in some Seabeach land opposite the Awori village of Ibeshi, and approached the village chiefs. These, headed by Saliu Jinadu, the Ofori of the town, realized the potential of this development and opened negotiations. There was a slight hitch, in that part of the designated area fell under the authority of the neighboring town of Ikare and contained a sacred grove of which they were the ritual guardians. Though it lay closer to Ibeshi than to Ikare, this had never been an issue; but early in 1969 a party of Ikares on the way to the shrine were ambushed and beaten up. Ibeshi was by then a much larger community and enjoyed the support of an outside backer.

The Ikares took their case to court where both sides presented diverse accounts of village origin. At the hearing in 1971 the Ikares claimed that Ibeshi had been founded by a man called Abeshe, expelled from Ikare for adultery with one of the chief's wives. This established Ikare not only as the senior community, but the Ibeshis also owed them rent. The Ibeshis countered with an alternative version of village origin tracing the origin of the founder, one Tesi Ofori right back to Ile Ife. Neither side could substantiate their claims and the court found each version as good as the other.

Next a couple of witnesses were called, referred to in the court records as "some Keta or Ghanaian fishermen," who testified that they had traditionally been paying rent to the Ikares. In the eyes of the court the reliability of the witnesses was questionable because of their migrant status and their working illegally in a domestic occupation. Following several depositions the judge dismissed the evidence with: "This man can obviously not be taken seriously especially when to cap it all he said he is a cleaner for the Europeans who have the chalets on the Green Area" (the Seabeach).[3]

The judge asked for a written contract and receipts when customary tenancy agreements were verbal and indefinite. As in other parts of Nigeria they were marked by "ceremonies which in the absence of recording facilities served as a mark by which the proceedings would be remembered" (Obenson 1977:98). The court therefore ruled that the plaintiffs had not proved their case. The appeals court upheld the ruling.

---

3. Judgement for suit no IK/226/71, Ikea High Court.

Construction began slowly, interrupted by disputes over the sharing of the rental income among the elders in Ibeshi, the issue of the Land Use Decree in 1978 vesting all land ownership in the state, the military coup of 1984, and most importantly the death of the village Baale, Saliu Jenadu, in the same year. When a successor was agreed upon four years later, negotiations had to begin all over again, by which time the optimism of the oil-boom fuelled 1970s had dissipated. The project was never resumed, and the structures were abandoned.

By practically conferring land ownership to Ibeshi the court ruling threw into relief the vulnerability of the Ewe tenants. They had no established claim over their land and had no protection under the law of contract. In the eyes of the court they were foreign migrants working illegally. This was by no means exceptional or even excessive. When up against local big men, the Seabeach Ewe could even fall below the law, as the case of one of the oldest families in the Ibeshi section of the Seabeach shows. The Fiazorli family owned a farm with over 500 coconut trees stretching from close to the high water mark down to the creek. In 1987 this farm was sold to an expatriate by the *baale* of Ibeshi town, with no consultation with the occupant. The family's entitlement to receiving three months notice and compensation of 100 Naira per tree were bluntly disregarded, and the family took the matter to court. A few months after lodging a complaint at the high court in Ikeja, the head of the family disappeared, presumed killed. The family decided to avoid further bloodshed and let the matter rest.

Cases of violent expropriation and the destruction of property are not uncommon. In 1993 a several compounds were burnt down in the village of Akbara in the Ilashe section of the Seabeach, when Ewe villagers had found themselves on the wrong side of an Awori chieftaincy dispute. Again the landlords could unleash the violence against their tenants with no fear of repercussions.

Defining the Status of Native or Stranger

In the court records the fishermen are referred to as "Keta," after their place of origin, or Ghanaian. In the Aworu towns the term of Agoin derived from "Ghanaian" is used to describe the people on the Seabeach. Referring to the fishermen by country of origin rather than ethnic group reinforces their status as strangers, and all that is particularly implied with regard to the land. When asked if the Seabeach Ewe could purchase land to develop their own business, the *baale* of both Ilashe and Ibeshi replied that this was not possible because they were "strangers." The passage of the Native Land Acquisition Law in 1958, which established that a non-Nigerian cannot acquire land without the approval of the government, excluded the Ewe from potential land ownership at the very point when tourism invested the Seabeach with commercial value. Ironically, the law passed to protect rural communities from exploitation by unscrupulous urban businessmen. Awori control over the Seabeach community, meanwhile, extends to all aspects of commercial development. In Ilashe, Ewe have to consult with the *baale* if they want to set up a business such as a chicken farm or an electric mill for grinding cassava. No stone houses can be constructed without the *baale's* permission, which is also needed before the Ewe can fish in the inland waters. Each of the Ewe families with coconut trees on the Seabeach, meanwhile, continue paying rent either in cash or by casting nets and making the catch over.

Describing the people of the Seabeach as "strangers" whose presence is tolerated as long as they abide by the law, can also be used to advantage by outside developers. Particularly where business development affects land farmed or even occupied by the residential dwellings of the Ewe. The physical appearance of the villages, where most of the buildings are constructed from bamboo, palm fronds, and raffia belies the fact that they are the permanent homes to families stretching back for three generations. For traditional authorities and external businessmen there are mutual interests in colluding to exclude a targeted group from a set of rights and privileges. The communities on the Seabeach respond to this discrepancy in status and associated rights by avoiding confrontation. There are vivid memories of the events in February 1983, when some two million people, a majority of them Ghanaians, were forcibly removed by the Nigerian army. Many Ghanaians evicted from their Lagos homes sought refuge on the Seabeach. As in the mid nineteenth century, the rivers and creeks provided a barrier to pursuing soldiers.

The passages of the Aliens Expulsion Order announced by the Minister for Internal Affairs, Ajhaji Ali Baba in January 1983, prompted many of the Seabeach Ewe to become naturalized. Timothy Akojenu, representative for Badagry, argued in the Lagos State House of Assembly that the Seabeach fishermen were "part and parcel of this place," and should be recognized as Nigerian citizens. Lateef Jakande, the Lagos State Governor, visited the Seabeach and promising his support. A committee was formed in the House of Assembly, which collected birth certificates and a list of names of individuals and families eligible for naturalization, verified by the Awori elders. Not only did this entitle them to reside in Nigeria, but also with full civil rights to vote in the elections. Though Nigeria descended into an extended period of military government later that year, the initiative resulted in the inclusion of the Seabeach Ewe in the electoral roll.

Interestingly then, the Seabeach Ewe have been recognized as Nigerian citizens, and allowed to participate in the electoral processes to choose their government. Yet, when it comes to land, they are defined as foreigners and not allowed to hold title of ownership. Much of this is explained by the mechanics of local politics in Lagos State.

When the Lagos State was first carved out of the Western Region in 1967, the Egun-Awori Development Association lobbied hard for the inclusion of the hinterland in the proposed state (Lawal 1993). The Egun Awori District Council was merged with Badagry District Council, only to be split again in 1989, when Ojo and Badagry became Local Government Areas. Ojo, with fifty-seven villages, including Ilashe and Ibeshi, and some 1,011,808 inhabitants,[4] became the most populated LGA. At local government level the traditional authorities are intermeshed with the modern bureaucracy. This is most apparent in the recruitment policy where a clear tendency toward discrimination against non-Yoruba, observed elsewhere in Lagos State, has been apparent (Olugbemi 1987; Peil 1975). Though Ojo has a very mixed population, including large numbers of Igbo and Hausa traders, the Local Government Staff is almost exclusively Yoruba, and mainly Awori. Though the Seabeach-Ewe have found employment in Nigerian parastatals and federal ministries, they have not managed to obtain a single post in the Ojo LGA. The reason provided by staff at the LGA offices, as well as the nearby palace of the Olojo, is that they cannot employ Ghanaians.

Traditional authorities were given an enhanced role in the second republic, with the establishment of a Lagos House of Chiefs, and the payment of stipends. Under the military they became even more important as they provided some form of legitimacy and a forum where popular demands can be presented and channeled to the authorities. The Ojo Regional Chieftaincy Council meets monthly at Ojo Local Government Offices. It contains two tiers, with an inner circle made up of the Olojo of Ojo, the Okiki of Imore, the Ofori of Ibeshi, the Oniba of Iba, the Abiologun of Ikare, the Oba of Ijaneke, and the Oba or Irede. The outer circle comprises six lower ranking chiefs, the Baale of Ilashe, the Baale of Tolu, the Balogun of Ajaromi, the Balogun of Ayetoro, and the Eletu of Ikare. Eight of these traditional rulers draw rental income from Seabeach properties leased to fishermen and developers. It is unlikely that they will support a redefinition of the status of the Ewe allowing them to buy and take ownership of the land they are living and working on.

An interesting process set in therefore with the entrenchment of military government. First it led to a revival of the fortunes of traditional rulers who could provide some form of legitimacy. But more importantly still, the councils organized under the Ministry of Chieftaincy Affairs provided a feedback

---

4. 1991 census.

loop and forum for the presentation of popular demands, an increasingly important function for the ruling soldiers working with neither a network of party activists nor a free press to keep them abreast of developments on the ground. As the economic decline in the 1990s further eroded the government's capacity to deliver services, the chiefs and elders also served to provide a system of administration.

The traditional authorities involved have found ways of using their role to their advantage. These powers, first of all, allowed traditional rulers to influence the definition of what is authentic and legitimate at local circuits of power. Hence while fully naturalized Seabeach Ewe might take up residence, find employment and own property in Lagos, any such privilege could be denied in the Ojo government area where elders habitually refer to them "strangers" and "Ghanaians." With over half the traditional rulers on the regional chieftaincy council drawing an income from Seabeach leases, there is a built-in opposition to reform.

Seabeach tenants, while ineligible for local government employment or to gain the title to a piece of land, could provide one additional benefit: votes. The Babangida government initiated the much discussed, long-drawn-out and eventually thwarted handover to civilian government with a series of elections to different levels of government culminating in the presidential contest. In the Ojo LGA, the Awori rural communities with their Ewe tenants, who were expected to vote with their landlords as is customary in Nigerian politics (Barnes 1996; Peil 1975), were cast in the important role. They were to provide an electoral counterweight to the expanded urban areas around Ojo market, containing large numbers of migrants from Eastern Nigeria. The division of wards already had a distinct rural bias. The 218,000 registered voters of Ajegunle were divided into four wards, while the islands and the Seabeach, with a total of 12,000 registered voters, had three wards between them. The ten wards in total elected the chairman of the council, who in turn appointed his staff. In most of the Seabeach communities voters did as expected, in return for small amounts of money and palm wine. As one elder from Ilashe Seabeach said, "we live with the Ilashes so we must vote with them." In the event, the elections results were annulled and the years of preparation and party political organization were rendered meaningless.

Declaring Identity

Participation in the electoral process had little effect on the sense of identity of the Seabeach Ewe. A survey as to the sense of belonging among the sixty-six active net-company fishermen yielded the following result.

66 Fishermen	Ghana	Nigeria	Benin/Togo
Claiming identity with	45	16	5
Born in Ilashe (39)	27	12	
Born in Ghana (14)	9	5	
Born in Nigeria (13)	9	4	
Born in Benin/Togo			5

Only sixteen out of sixty-six men "claimed" Nigeria, even though forty-four had been born there. The Seabeach retained a particular sense of identity, with Ewe as the predominant language, where maize based *kenke* was staple, as opposed to the cassava based *gari* eaten by the Awori, and with shrines dedicated to such Ewe deities such as Atingale and Vrekete. The easy relationship with the sea, and the regular spectacle of seine-net fishing were further points of contrasts with the inland communities of the Awori. When leaving the enclave for Lagos or other parts of Nigeria, the Seabeach Ewe could employ a repertoire of identities, depending on situation and context. Many of the fishermen have left the Seabeach for work in Nigeria's merchant navy and fleet of fishing trawlers. Here the Ghanaian connection and Ewe language are strong advantages, as Ghana remains the leading marine nation in West Africa. When looking for work in the offices of national corporations and parastatals they will emphasise their Nigerian identity, good English skills, and educational accomplishments. In the informal sectors they will operate as Lagosians and use their Yoruba.

Conclusion

The curious status of the Seabeach Ewe, where they are enfranchised to vote in presidential elections but excluded from local employment or the right to buy land, throws an interesting light on some of the outcomes hoped for from urbanization and democratic rule after independence. There were expectations that resource distribution would be detribalized as, "today it is less essential that a man belongs to a descent group; strangers have full political rights through the ballot box though they are denied participation in the traditional system"(Lloyd 1962:88).

On the Seabeach, democratic mechanisms have been absorbed into the existing methods of political control. Access to the means of production, be this land or jobs, depends on membership of social units which are subject to the rules and practices of distribution (Berry 1985). The system necessarily protects natives and discriminates against strangers, but there are ways of establishing membership—principally through marriage. Yet this most congenial way of obtaining economic and political privileges was precluded by the requirements of fishing: labor, technology, and capital. Without ties of affinity the Ewe have relied on the patron-client paradigm to gain access to resources and political backing.

This was a suitable arrangement in the first period of Seabeach settlement, when there was little interest in the area, and landlords were happy with getting any material benefits at all. With the coming of weekend visitors and property developers the situation changed dramatically. The former wasteland turned into a contested resource at the very time when returning to Keta lagoon was no longer a viable option for fishermen. Seabeach Ewe have, therefore, been faced with the choice of remaining on the Seabeach and in the fishing, but on condition of client status with little formal security, or by asserting their individual rights as Nigerian citizens and moving on. As a community they face a dilemma encountered all over Nigeria, where the formal rights and privileges of citizenship are curtailed by the practical status differences between sons of the soil and strangers. Their origin and the attachment to Ghana obscures the fact that there is an underlying dilemma in the Nigerian polity of balancing the traditional rights between local communities and the general rights of citizens, between custom and civil law. Given the accelerating movement of people both within and across the borders of the Nigerian state, there is an urgent need for clarifying the rights and duties of citizens and aliens.

Bibliography:

Avoseh, T.O. 1938. *A Short History of Badagry*. Lagos: Ifeolu Press.

Barnes, S. 1996. *Decentering Lagos*. Paper presented at Africa's Urban Past, Centre of African Studies, London.

Berron, H. 1977. "Ghanaian Fishermen in Ivory Coast," *Maritime Policy Management*, 4, pp. 209–214.

Berry, S. 1985. *Fathers work for their sons: accumulation, mobility and class formation in an extended Yoruba community*. Berkeley: University of California Press.

Brooks, G. 1970. *Yankee Traders, Old Coasters, and African Middlemen. A History of American Trade with West Africa*. Boston: Boston University Press.

Christensen, J.B. 1977. "Motor Power and Women Power: Technological and Economic Change among the Fanti Fishermen of Ghana," in M.E. Smith (ed.) *Those who live form the Sea. A study in Maritime Anthropology*. New York: West Publishing.

Greene, S. 1988. "Social Change in 18th Century Anlo – The Role of Technology, Markets and Military Conflict," *Africa*, 58, pp. 70–86.

Hill, P. 1986. *Talking with Ewe Fishermen and Shallot Farmers.* Cambridge African Monographs: Cambridge: CUP.

Law, R. 1989. "Between the Sea and the Lagoons: the interaction of maritime and inland navigation on the pre-colonial Slave Coast." *Cahiers d'Etudes Africaine*, 29, pp. 207–237.

Lawal, K. (ed.), 1993. *Urban Transition in Africa: Aspect of Urbanization and Change in Lagos.* Lagos: Pumark Nigeria Ltd.

Lawson, R 1957. "Structure. Migration and Resettlement of Ewe Fishing Units." African Studies 17.

Lawson, R. and Eric Kwei. 1974. *African Entrepreneurship and Economic Growth: a Case Study of the Fishing Industry in Ghana.* Accra: Ghana University Press.

Lloyd, P.C. 1962. *Yoruba Land Law.* Oxford: OUP.

Manning, P. 1985. "Merchants, Porters and Canoemen in the Bight of Benin: Links in the West African Trade Network." In Catherine Coquery-Vidrovitsch and Paul Lovejoy (eds.) *The Workers of the African Trade.* London: Sage.

Nukunya, G.K. 1989. "The Anlo Ewe and Full-time Maritime Fishing," Maritime Anthropological Studies, 2, pp. 154–174.

Obenson, G. 1977. *Land Registration in Nigeria.* (Lagos: self published).

Olugbemi, S.O. 1987. "The Administration of Lagos State 1967–1979" in Ade Adefuye et.al. *History of the Peoples of Lagos.* Lagos: Lantern Press.

Overa, R. 1995. *Entrepreneurial Women in Ghanaian Canoe Fisheries: the case of the Fante fishing town of Moree.* Bergen: Bergen University Centre for Development Studies.

Peil, M. 1975. "Interethnic Contacts in Nigerian Cities," *Africa*, 45, pp. 107–21.

Smith, R. 1970. "The Canoe in West African History," *Journal of African History*, 11, pp. 515–33.

Tijani, I. 1992. *Badagry – Past and Present.* Lagos: Ibro Communications Ltd.

Wyllie, R.W. 1969. "Migrant Anlo Ewe Fishing Companies and Socio-Political Change: A Comparative Study," Africa, 39, pp. 396–410.

CHAPTER 6

"In the Olden Days": Histories of Misbehaving Women in Ado-Odo, Southwestern Nigeria

Andrea Cornwall[1]

Of all the topics that would be guaranteed to animate a fiery discussion in the small Yoruba town of Ado-Odo, that of women's bad behavior was one of the most compelling. Stories would be told, to gasps and cries of disapproval, of women "running here and there after men", refusing to let their husbands "sex" them and being beaten for the cheek of it, and spurning the meagre amounts of money offered to them for housekeeping and sending husbands to the market to see for themselves what their money could buy. Apocryphal tales, indeed, and ones to which there would always be another side of the story. Invariably, these tales would be accompanied by a narrative that I was to initially recognize as the assertion of moral superiority by the "older generation": that *n'igba atijo* (in the olden days), things were not like this.

Older women regularly invoked *igba atijo* to speak about a youth in which obedient, virginal brides-to-be were not even allowed to talk to their prospec-

1. I'd like to express my gratitude to Diana Jeater, for her extremely helpful comments on an earlier draft of this paper, and to David Pratten for reading it at short notice and giving me the encouragement I needed to finish it. I am as ever grateful to J.D.Y. Peel for being such an inspiring and deeply caring supervisor. My thanks to the people I spent time with in Ado are so many, that I can't name them all individually here. I would, however, like to extend especial thanks to Mary and Tokunbo Akinsowon, and my research assistants Dorcas Odu and the late Baba Yemisi Akinsowon, for all they taught me and for all their care.

tive husbands and where husbands were authoritative, responsible providers. Contemporary sexual partnerships between men and women were held up against the yardstick of tales of *igba atijo*, which told of a time in which women conformed to expectations of obedient subservience and did not exercise their agency, nor displayed an active sexuality. These "olden days" were regularly put in service of the telling of cautionary tales that stressed the compliance with authority shown by women and men of that time, their assiduous attention to duty and the seriousness with which they had taken careers as mothers, wives, husbands, fathers and workers. So pervasive was the narrative of the "good old days", that I heard teenagers parroting its moralizing injunctions in complaints about their peers. And the very younger women whose own choices and conduct were so much a focus for critique framed their own commentaries on change with recourse to its insistent refrain.

The explicit focus on discontinuity between that past and this present worked to mask the possibility that things may well not have been quite *so* different. Court cases from nearby Badagry and Otta, stretching from a time beyond the remembered times of the oldest people in Ado into that of their own youth, reveal numbers of women who appeared to be to all intents and purposes no less wilful, wayward and recalcitrant than today's women are accused of being. Contemporary discourses on morality and appropriate wifely behavior may make reference to a golden age in which there was harmony and women knew their place. But they are textured with preoccupations redolent with ideals of womanhood that seem far from consonant with that which historians and anthropologists have come to observe about "the Yoruba" (cf. Sudarkasa 1973; Denzer, 1994; Matory, 1995; Oyewumi, 1998). These narratives are peppered with talk of "harlotry" and "fornication", talk that speaks of another age and another place: that of the prurient Victorian missionaries whose worlds Peel (2000) so eloquently captures, and *their* readings of Yoruba social and sexual life. They are also animated by the religiosity of the present, by the discourses on sexual morality that resound in mosques and churches around the town, and *their* narratives on the wayward ways of today's women.

In this chapter, I return to a topic that was the subject of intense debate with J.D.Y. Peel as I wrote my Ph.D. under his guidance, and to fragments from my thesis in which dissonance between versions of the past came to be quietly buried. At issue were two very different versions of the past that emerged from archival material, principally customary court records, and from oral histories. John and I argued over the nature of evidence and of representation, about the possibility of multiple stories being simultaneously "true" and about what exactly these invocations of "the past in the present"

(Peel, 1984) were all about. The past with which I was concerned was a particular past, that which featured in tales of "the olden days". I sought to make sense of its discursive deployment in moralizing narratives on women's behavior and of the investments different narrators had in promoting a version of "how things used to be" that erased the very possibility of certain forms of female agency. In this chapter, I draw on oral histories, interviews, the accounts of colonial officials, travellers and missionaries and customary court records, to explore the dissonance between versions of the past and what this might have to offer the analysis of gender, religion and social change in south western Nigeria.

Pasts in the Present: Representing "The Olden Days"

Wedged between the two major expressways of the south-western corner of Nigeria, reliant on an economy comprising agriculture, local services and inter-urban and local trade, Ado has roughly equal numbers of Christians and Muslims of all persuasions, and retains a small number of orișa shrines and devotees. Awori indigenes are now outnumbered by the descendants of the Egbado, Egba and Ijesha *alejo* (strangers) who came to the town seeking shelter or opportunities for commerce, and never returned. Amongst the town's principally Yoruba population are "strangers" from further afield, Igbo from the east and Hausa from the north, and immigrants from Togo and Benin, as well as nearby Egun people, who still mainly live outside the town. Proximity to Lagos and its significance in the days before the coastal expressway notwithstanding, Ado has a relaxed feel to it and a history of being, in Peel's (2000) words, "a rather conservative little town".

Sought out as a site for missionary activity in the late years of the nineteenth century, and settled by missionaries in the early years of the twentieth, Ado was also the site for a variety of religious "encounters" (Peel, 2000) that were to shape contemporary gender relations. Missionary accounts make regular mention of the "immoral" ways of the unconverted, as Peel (2000) observes, directing their attention to producing complaint wives out of women given to unseemly ways. Peel's discussion of missionary preoccupation with "fornication" (2000:268), sex and marriage illuminates beautifully some of the moralizing concerns that were so much part of contemporary discourses in Ado. Whilst this chapter merely touches on the surface of some of the issues at stake, my focus here is as much on the significance of continuities in narratives of women's misbehavior, as the ideological uses of a past that conforms less with any essential or "traditional" *Yoruba* notion of appropriate female compliance, but with one that bears the unmistakable traces of Christian and Islamic discourses on women and on morality.[2]

The everyday commentaries that I would so frequently hear when I lived in Ado-Odo in the early 1990s were often framed with reference to another time, a contrastive past that served as a foil against which the troubles of the present could both be narrated and understood. Everyday events—a schoolgirl getting pregnant, a junior wife being troublesome—would spark off discussions that culminated in reflections on how things used to be. Women and men who told me their life stories, chewed over promising pieces of gossip or talked about current problems had recourse to this past, which served both to signify and reinforce their own moral position. Sometimes, accounts of the olden days accompanied tales of lived experience in the past. More often, however, the phrase *n'igba atijo* was used to unleash a torrent of complaints about the present. It came to evoke an unwavering image of an age that is no more: one in which those who invoked it might not even have lived themselves, but which they knew from the cautionary tales of their elders.

So often were the olden days spoken about in conversations about contemporary affairs that they acquired rhetorical resonance beyond a description of other times. They appeared to serve less to inform me and other listeners about what things had actually been like than to provide a vivid and potent contrast with the object of the speaker's disapproval. The message that repeatedly emerged from discussions in which the olden days were implicated was that morally and economically, things have never been so bad (Cornwall 2001, 2002). What, then, did people talk about when they spoke of these "olden days"? The following remarks illustrate the uses to which the older generation put the past:

> In the olden days, girls didn't ask for money from boys as they do today. If a girl was not a virgin, she can't walk in town as people will be abusing her wherever she goes. She can't enter the husband's house before marriage. Unlike today when boys will be petting girls so as to sex them in their rooms, girls will be calling boys here and there to give them money and in no time there is a pregnancy. In the olden days, women would work, work, work to get things to take to the husband's house. In those days you kept yourself clean rather than chasing after men (Iya Abiona, female trader, mid-60s).

---

2. Whilst it would undoubtedly yield interesting insights, I do not here analyse differences within and between discourses on women's misbehavior of different Christian and Muslim entities in the town for lack of space to do justice to the complexities involved.

Figure 6.1 - Yoruba Dowry (bridewealth) Container.

In the olden days, girls could not go near boys. Now girls don't fear anyone. They can even go to boys' rooms. Many women now have men
friends, paint their lips and go to men (Iya Bayo, female trader, late 50s).

In the olden days, they always did dowry—ten years ago you had to
pay dowry before the woman would come. These days everything is
free. If a girl is pregnant, the father sends her to the father of that
pregnancy as he is not going to pay for the care of another man's
pregnancy. Girls, they give themselves to boys free of charge, they just
go to the man without him paying anything. In the olden days, girls
feared their parents and needed their approval. These days, they don't
bother at all (Alhaji Buari, male farmer, early 70s).

In these images sex is tied to money in ambiguous ways—being after
money, but also giving themselves to boys "for free" (i.e. without dowries
being paid first)—and money is associated with avarice and greed rather than
independent, hard work. Attention is focused on the kind of woman who
takes the initiative, demands what she wants and disregards her parents in
pursuit of it. The changes these older people highlight include a shift from

parental choice of marriage partner and the formalization of marriage through dowry payments, to young women seeking their own partners and contracting relationships that begin not with dowries but with pregnancies. Virginity and chastity are the hallmarks of the bygone times, contrasted with images of today's women in active pursuit of men, for sex as well as money.

Women's agency is represented normatively in the subtext of these discussions in equally ambiguous ways. On the one hand, women in the *past* were represented as almost entirely passive: women who, fearing their fathers' disapproval, went along with marriages they had not chosen and with the demands of the men they lived with. Those who asserted themselves either within marriages or by seeking their own choices were cast as behaving badly. On the other hand, women in the *present* were portrayed as too weak to resist the propositions of other men or the lure of money. Women who asserted themselves to rebuff men's advances and who instead "faced the children and their work" (i.e. made them their priority) were applauded. This was not presented as passive, but as a choice that "good women" should, and would, make.

"Civilization" and Its Malcontents

It would be tempting to dismiss all this moaning about how things used to be as the kind of thing that is common the world over, as older people reminisce about the good old days and complain about the present. What surprised me, though, was that older people were not the only ones to complain. Young, unmarried, women and men—the targets of their complaints—used strikingly similar images of the past in their commentaries on the present. I surveyed the opinions of 100 secondary school students, and asked how attitudes to sex and marriage have changed since the time of their grandmothers. Their answers echoed those of older people, and talked of young women chasing after men, impatience, "immorality", "harlotry" and disobedience. Several young people focused their comments specifically on sex:

> Ladies of today don't have patience. Instead of going to school straight she will cross to the boyfriend's house. Mothers were not disvirgined before going to the husband's house, now people who are not even 20 know how to sex or abort (female student, 17).

> Underage now get married and give birth before 15 years, girls and boys meet along the street, under the trees and even at home (male student, 19).

Again and again, the theme of "being after money" peppered their responses:

Girls of today have a very strong affinity for money. Once they see a rich man they will try to have contact with them and by doing so she may go to the man's house and that may result in pregnancy. In the time of our grandmothers all this nonsense has not been happening e.g. nowadays a girl can easily pack to a boy's house but in the time of our grandmother all sorts of this was not happening (male student, 15).

Girls of nowadays like money too much and because of this before any boys chase them they could have been giving him a face and immediately they've got money they will useless themselves in front of the boy. Since the boy is not an impotent he too will have fun with them and as they continue they will get pregnant before marriage. In the olden days before a man could marry he would be forty, now they marry even at ten years. This has caused a lot of problem to the country (male student, 18).

Everybody seemed to be telling me the same thing. Young women were even more vociferous in their criticisms than young men. One young woman said: 'it is the fault of girls because they are dogs.' Another commented that 'many young women just run when pregnant' to their lover's house 'because they are disobedient, stubborn and harlot.' The almost unanimous voice of their responses, to a self-completed, supervised, individual questionnaire, indicated that they may have had an investment in the subject positions from which they spoke to criticise others, and by extension, themselves. And the language they used, all that talk of "harlotry" and "fornicating all around", was the language of chastisement that could so often be heard ringing out from the pulpit or resounding in the mosque.

The school students homed in on one major reason for these changes, in an interesting turn on the otherwise positive normative use of the discourse of "civilization" (olaju):[3]

In that time women obeyed the instruction of the husband, now it has changed. Civilization has created a bad attitude (female student, 17).

There has been total change. There was no civilization before and many did not go to school, they preferred farm and they were always busy, no chance of man going about like today. Now the civilization is on and many girls get pregnant and get married at any time they like (male student, 24).

---

3. See Peel (1978) for a more positive reading of the benefits of "civilization" conveyed to him by informants in Ilesha in those days.

In that time parents found husbands for them and there was a lot of food and land where nobody saw each other that much, but these days everybody's eye is open [the literal meaning of *olaju*], everybody wants to be rich so they have to marry a rich man (female student, 20).

"Civilization", for these students, had brought mixed blessings. A handful stressed positive aspects ranging from improved medical technology and contraception to broadened sexual repertoires that had facilitated greater enjoyment. The majority, however, cast "civilization" as not only creating entirely different possibilities for men and women, but as the driving force behind a series of negative changes, particularly a greatly reduced age at first intercourse, a voracious appetite for money on the part of young women and, as one put it, "hot love" displacing cautious choices in marriage partners. "Civilization" and "the olden days" are counterparts in the discursive construction of gender and social change, polarising time and change and positioning then and now as irrevocably different.

Enduring Arrangements: Marriage in the Olden Days

N'igba atijo, or so older people said, co-wives ate from the same pot, the relations of seniority that permeated sociality formed the basis for relations of respect, husbands were chosen for women who remained compliant and wives were found for men who relied on their fathers' help too much to refuse. Times were good. Order prevailed. It is notable that this kind of order is exactly that which the Reverend Samuel Johnson evokes in his reflections on marriage in a golden age far beyond the boundaries of remembered time:

In ancient times the Yorubas were mostly monogamic; not from any enlightened views on the subject however, but rather from necessity; for, although polygamy was not actually forbidden, yet only rich folk could avail themselves of indulgence in that condition of life. Besides, in a community mainly pastoral and agricultural, where all were peaceful and no-one engaged in any occupation perilous to the lives of its male population, where wants were few, and those easily satisfied, the young men married as soon as they were of an age to support a family, and therefore a superfluous female population was hardly ever known. (1921:113)

From everything I had learned about Ado's past, any such stability seemed far from the experience of the peoples who had come to this town seeking refuge from decades of war and in search of new trading possibilities. For Ado's inhabitants in those days, the town was not the backwater it has become today, but the thriving centre of a regional economy, close to Lagos, the port of Badagry, the border roads to Porto Novo and Cotonou, and the site of an important shrine to the goddess Odudua. Active in the slave trade, brought to its knees by a siege in the mid-nineteenth century that left the town depopulated and desolate, Ado opened its arms to "strangers" from other places and came in peacetime to play a more active part in the local economy, until it was eclipsed by colonial road and rail-building projects that drew trade routes further to the east. Changing times created ambiguous opportunities for women as the cash economy opened up in the early part of the century (Cornwall 2001), making tales of static custom and of endurance and compliance all the more curious.

For many of the elderly women I knew and for some elderly men, their (first) marriages were contracted by their parents or senior relatives. They grew up in the 1920s and 1930s, a time when changes were afoot in this part of the country, with the construction of roads that would take motor traffic and the beginnings of the influx of craftspeople and traders from other, more developed, areas of Yorubaland such as Ilesha and Ijebu. Men and women alike spoke of choices that were made for them in which they had little option but to accept (see Cornwall 2001). Some women ran away, I was told, but in doing so incurred the wrath of their fathers and jeopardised essential support networks.

Betrothals could be made at any time in a girl's life, from birth onwards, I was told; driven by what one older man explained as a shortage of women and others put more squarely as concerns amongst the indigene Awori people about their children marrying Egbado "strangers". Pledging, so repugnant to the British, was common practice in the early part of the century. Young men had to rely on their parents to arrange marriages for them; fathers allocated farm land to their sons, who remained dependents until marriage (cf. Peel 1983 for Ilesha; Fadipe 1970). Subsequent marriages might also be arranged, but in those men had more of a choice: either to ask for a daughter, or to accept one that was offered. Both parents might broker betrothal arrangements. Mothers could promise their daughters to their friends' sons and fathers could arrange marriages with friends or patrons who would take their daughters as wives or as wives for their sons. Friends might arrange between themselves to marry their children to each other, to extend their relationship. Breaking these arrangements was not easy, but it did happen.

Over a period of years, older people told me, the husband-to-be would make contributions and give gifts to the parents to cement the relationship, usually through an intermediary (*alarena*). Promises of marriage would begin with *isihun*, a betrothal fee which marked the start of a series of payments, culminating in the ceremonial payment of schnapps, kola, bitter kola and alligator pepper along with an amount of money that was *idana* ("dowry"). The parents of the bride-to-be could make requests of their future son-in-law as soon as the betrothal was formalised. And betrothals might last for many years, as girls were generally kept at home until judged mature enough to go to their husband. Virginity was prized (Renne 1993), and concerns over securing legitimate reproduction—rather than women's sexual morality per se—were rife, indicating by their presence the degree to which women might have been indulging in pre-marital sex, something that appears to be borne out by colonial and missionary records (see Peel 2000). Sexually transmitted disease was judged a serious problem by the colonial authorities, again some indicator of a degree of sexual networking commented on by Caldwell and colleagues for the past as well as the present (Caldwell et al. 1991; Orubuloye et al. 1991).

Women appear in representations of this era as almost entirely passive. Some women told me that they had not seen their husband until the day of marriage. Unmarried girls were, they told me, forbidden to talk with men or even to share the same bench with them. They couldn't be directly approached by prospective suitors, who instead had to send an intermediary. And nor would their families accept straight away: checks were made to make sure that the family was suitable, paying special attention to the condition of the wives of the house. Prospective husbands would then pay visits to the house, leaving gifts of money for their brides-to-be. Some women were allowed to cook for them when they came. But, I was told, they were not allowed to talk to them. Women were supposed to avoid future husbands if they saw them in town: 'if you saw the husband coming towards you, you would just take another road. It was very shameful to be seen together.' Concern with virginity was often offered as a reason for these practices—that young women shouldn't "give themselves for free."

Once married, older women and men reported that wives in those days had little option but to adjust to whatever situation they found themselves in. Only in the case of infertility, madness or extreme maltreatment, I was told, did women have a recognized reason for extricating themselves from marriages: unlike today, or so the popular refrain would go, when women divorce their husbands if they find a man they like better or who has more money. The practice of levirate left widows to be inherited by a relative of their deceased husband if they were still of reproductive age. I was told that even if a woman did not conceive, she would still stay with her husband, helping to care for their co-wives' children as their own.

Older women and men told me that they had seen divorce in their youth, but only in extreme cases. I asked Yele Akinwonmi, a retired Ado customary court judge, about divorce in the olden days:

> Before the advent of the British there was divorce. The head of the place (*bale*, the head of the compound, sometime the *oba* himself) was the judge and the parents of both parties were brought together with the *alarena*. Unless parents on both sides saw a reason why the woman had to go, it would not be easy for her to divorce because it was a contract between families. The intention of the woman was not considered important in those days. Unless the man was impotent or the woman had no issue, it was not easy for a woman to leave. Unless a woman became too troublesome—fighting, nagging—and she couldn't be subdued by the family. In most cases, the man would get another woman before that one was thrown out.

I was told by older women that women who misbehaved would be brought into line by harsh punishment by their husbands, with the approval of their fathers. Those who sought to go home might be sent straight back to their husbands if they failed to come up with a good reason. Only if they were completely out of control would they be sent home for good. And those who were sent back tarnished the family's reputation and put the links the marriage had created in jeopardy.

In accounts of *igba atijo* told in generalising narratives or situated in the lived pasts of older people, defiant women were almost completely absent. And yet they appeared, in numbers, in customary court records from nearby towns from 1874 onwards. In these cases could be glimpsed representations of female agency that are far from the demure, obedient wives that accounts of *igba atijo* purvey.

Women Who Went Astray?

Through a series of legislative measures, instigated by the colonial authorities due to concerns with the implications of child betrothal and polygyny, the colonial administration mediated women's opportunities to extract themselves from marital arrangements (Fadipe [1939]1970, Mann 1985, Renne 1990).[4] A court was set up in 1874 at Badagry, some ten or so miles south of

---

4. Caldwell et al. (1991) and Peel (1983) detail the impact of legislative and economic change on marriages during this period, for Ekiti and Ilesha respectively. Atanda's account of a revolt in Iseyin and Okeiho following divorce reforms gives a vivid impression of the

Ado. It was run at first by a colonial officer who meted out justice with reference to "Yoruba custom", a practice that was to be formalised in later years
with the institution of the native court system, managed by elders (Atanda
1969).[5] A customary court was in operation in nearby Otta by 1905, and by
1915 Ado had its own court.

Records of court proceedings from Badagry (1874–1906) and Otta (1908–
1920s) are replete with instances of claims for refund of betrothal payments
("a consideration that failed") and of women who had gone astray.[6] Cases reveal instances where women's mothers lined up a better deal and where
women wandered off and got into relationships elsewhere. In many of them,
women appear to be able to represent themselves and their own choices very
articulately; the offers that appear in some of them by women of repaying their
own dowry give an indication that these are women who are not only quite
empowered enough to assert their sexual rights, they also had the economic
means with which to determine their own choices. It is worth giving some examples. In an 1888 case, a claim for betrothal expenses over a long period was
made by a plaintiff who was a known thief, which resulted in his wife-to-be
being laughed at. The records state that the woman, who had been betrothed
at a very young age, later decided that she didn't want him after all: 'she made
up her account and said she would pay back what was due from her to him.'
Unconcerned, it appears, at the implications of his daughter's possible "dis-
virgining" as people in Ado would put it, the father simply states: 'I do not
know if they had cohabited or not.'

---

resistance to the implications of enabling women to divorce their husbands. Atanda argues:
'The [traditional] socio-judicial system did not give much freedom for divorce on flimsy
grounds. Thus the menfolk regarded the traditional system as a check on the loss of wives
through divorce. This was one of the securities which the Native Court system inaugurated
by the British in 1914 destroyed' (1969:501).

5. Across the continent, the customary courts created by colonial governments provide
a rich source of documentation on the conditions under which marriages came to be contracted and dissolved. See, for example, Allman (1996) for Ghana, Mbilinyi (1988) for Tanzania, Jeater (1993) for Zimbabwe; see also Chanock (1985) for the creation of "native law
and custom", and its uses by African patriarchs.

6. Unfortunately, records from Ado's customary court from the colonial period appear
to have perished, and the earliest records I was able to access were from 1964. I draw on
cases from the nearby towns of Badagry (NAI Badadiv 1/2/1) and Otta (OAU Archive) with
the following reservations. While Otta is more like Ado in terms of its ethnic composition
and economic base, Badagry is a port town with a population composed of a variety of
ethnic groups, including non-Yoruba Egun peoples and women may well have experienced
more freedom and have had more opportunities in this context.

One of the most intriguing of these cases is one from 1892.[7] The story begins when Onikoye, a Lagos trader, arranges with the young woman Abesi's parents for her to be his wife. He makes a series of payments, and then asks for her to go to Lagos with him and she refuses. He accuses her of being a prostitute, and says, 'I wrote to her people 3 months ago to ask them to repay me what I had given to them, the girl said I was too old and she did not want to be my wife...' Abesi opens her testimony by cross-examining him: 'When I agreed to be your wife did not my father tell you that I had had connection with a man?...Did my father not send me to Lagos and did I not live there for some time as your wife?...When I returned to Badagry and you asked me to go back with you to Lagos, did I not tell you that I did not like your ways, so would not go with you?...Did I not tell you that if you wished to be my husband, I would be your wife at Badagry, not Lagos?'[8] The case was ruled in her favor.

After spending years courting women, expending considerable sums of money—each item of which is faithfully listed and reclaimed in the records— men would find themselves rejected, passed over for another. Some women were clearly less ready than others to relent, arguing that they were not interested in the husband and finding another man for themselves. Some women would just take the cash and go. One case, from 1893, contains a huge list of expenses lavished on a woman who then ran off with another man, taking her former fiancé's money with her. Another, in the same year, reports a woman taking the money, then going to someone else and refusing to marry her fiancé. Despite being captured, she ran back home to set up home with yet another man.[9]

In cases of extreme recalcitrance, young women were compelled (ultimately unsuccessfully) by force to go to or remain with their husbands, who had eventually to resort to suing for the return of their gifts. A 1905 case from Otta describes how a woman had lost her virginity before marrying, had then had a child and four years later went off 'ostensibly on other business and never returned,' only for her husband to hear that she was with another man. Her long-suffering mother explains that 'before this [marriage] she had led a rather dissolute life for two months until I tied her up and took her to the petitioner.'[10] One 1908 case, also from Otta, details an extreme case of the kind of measures needed to make more recalcitrant women stay:

7. NAI Badadiv 1/2/1: 2/8/1892.
8. NAI Badadiv 1/2/1: 2/8/1892.
9. NAI Badadiv 1/2/1: 18/4/1893; 23/6/1893.
10. NAI Badadiv 1/2/1: 21/11/1905.

One day I saw the town Ogboju sent to my father by [the] Bada of Otta, the Bada is now dead. I was sent for to be delivered in marriage to my husband by force. My father took me over to my husband...I took only calabash when going. I was forcibly detained in my husband's place in shackles for 5 days...I stayed...for 21 days. For ill-treatment from my mother-in-law and my husband's friends I ran away...[11]

Although mention of "divorcement" does not enter the civil court records for Otta until the early 1920s, despite an ordinance permitting the granting of divorces in 1907 (Zabel 1969), it is clear from these records that some women were dissolving marriages after as well as before consummation. It seems that it was not infrequent for women to stay for a while and then leave, citing reasons from bad treatment to boredom. In one 1908 case, for example, a man sought damages 'for the defendant refusing to be the plaintiff's wife.' In her defence, the woman merely said: 'I am tired of staying with him. I would like to get another husband.'[12]

To reach the courts in a time where disputes were usually dissolved by compound heads (baale) or by the oba himself, these cases may well represent the extremes that were shrugged off when I mentioned them to older men and women in Ado. What, then, did other documents written during this time have to say about women, morality and marriage? Snippets of information can be found in travellers' tales from the late nineteenth century, from Clarke's (1972) stories from the 1850s of women lining the trading routes eager to sell goods for cash to Bowen's (1968) tales in the same period of the vibrancy of women's participation in markets. Liet.-Col. Augustus Mockler-Ferryman, writing about southern Nigeria in general, describes stringent norms in place to prevent female sexual "immorality" and then goes on to comment on the "low state of morality" to be found in the area:

Modesty and chastity are qualities which have small place in African life, though infidelity on the part of a wife is subject to the most rigid laws. Adultery is punishable almost at the will of the injured husband, who can demand compensation from the paramour, sell him into slavery or even slay him; while the penalties imposed on the guilty wife extend from simple divorce to death. Polygamy is uni-

11. University of Ife archives, Otta Customary Court records, testimony of Orisafunmi in Orisafunmi vs Akide, 21/8/1908.

12. University of Ife archives, Otta Customary Court records, Talabi vs Taiwo of Otta, 10/7/1908.

versal...There is no question of jealousy, as each wife has her separate hut in the compound, and the greater number of wives a man
has the easier their lives, for the position of wife is no better than that
of servant or laborer, each one having her apportioned daily work,
be it in the household, the field or the market. To show what a low
state of morality really exists, even among the semi-civilised tribes,
we may mention that it is considered no disgrace for a man to lend
one of his wives to another man, or for a wife to be so lent; while
trading on the intrigues of a wife is by no means an unpopular
method of enrichment. (1902:233)

Mockler-Ferryman's misreading of domestic gender relations typifies a tendency in the literature on this topic that Oyewumi was so trenchantly to criticise almost a century later.[13]

Samuel Johnson, in contrast, begins his account of marriage in Yorubaland
by distancing Yoruba polygamy from "tradition" in his evocation of a time in
the more distant past when monogamy was practiced. That Yoruba practice
of this time more resembles the Christianity to which he wished to convert his
countrymen is perhaps no accident. This might be interpreted as a strategy to
present some essential time before the present in which Yoruba were more
Christian in their outlook than in the "corrupted" present. He then explains
several kinds of marriage practice, much of which portrays women as complaint, subservient even, and which underlines, perhaps more than anything
else, concerns about virginity and securing legitimate reproduction rather than
sexual morality per se. It is in Johnson's discussion of a kind of spontaneous
marriage—in which a father sees a man he'd like for a son-in-law and sends
his daughter to him that very day—that the discussion takes another turn. He
observes:

> In such cases a girl that is wild and unruly who is likely to bring
> disgrace on the family receives but a few hours' notice, but a dutiful
> and obedient daughter will always have her feelings consulted, and
> her wishes granted as to her choice of the man and also the time of
> the marriage. (1921:117)

"Wild" and "unruly" women existed, then, even in Johnson's account; they
also occasionally appeared in older women's and men's narratives of their

---

13. Indeed, as is evident from the writing of other colonial officials, the degree of
household drudgery was fairly limited—principally on account of the outsourcing of cooking (see, for example, Clarke, 1972, writing of the mid-19th century).

pasts. But in the particular past that appear so frequently in everyday narratives in Ado, such women are all but erased.

The Good Old Days? Perspectives on Change

Questions arise from this patchwork of evidence about, as Whitehead and Vaughan put it, 'how significant the cultural consequences of colonial rule were, less in imposing new ways of life than in creating new "old" ways of life' (1988:3). Those 'new "old" ways of life' have arguably served to further agendas that have less to do with "tradition" than with the normative views of female sexuality and agency associated with the "civilising" efforts of the Christian missions. In the past described in tales of *igba atijo*, the idea of "useless men" was almost unthinkable. But this was arguably less because men were fulfilling their commitments to their families than because the notion of the husband as breadwinner and provider simply was not part of the frame (cf. Lindsay 2003). And the image of women of the olden days as dependent, nurturing and above all faithful wives and mothers who managed and endured, may embrace fewer and fewer of today's women in the eyes of those whose complaints focus on their behavior and choices, but the extent it ever fitted women of the past is an open question.

Colonial Christian notions of marriage and of the roles of "husbands" and "wives" differed significantly from the kinds of relationships that missionaries found amongst their would-be converts (Peel 2000). Companionate, monogamous, "ring" marriage may have become popular amongst Christian elites in the early decades of twentieth century Lagos (Mann 1985). But it continues to be rare in Ado even up to the present day, and is only really found among the Christian educated middle-class. This is not to say that women and men of other faiths and classes did not have close, caring relationships. But the model of marriage that many people I knew were living was one that bore little resemblance to the idea of the responsible breadwinner, the housewife, the joint household account and a strict sexual division of labor in which women were at a disadvantage. For a start, many of the women I knew did not do a lot of the domestic work themselves. That which they did not contract out—like buying cooked food at least once if not twice a day from food sellers, or at least buying pats of *eba* (a stiff cassava paste eaten with sauce) or sending a child to buy a bowl of beans at lunchtime, or paying someone else a few Naira to do their washing—they would delegate to the children of the compound or a junior relative (cf. Sudarkasa 1973). As Oyewumi (1998) rightly points out, notions of the oppressed Yoruba *aya* are rather far-fetched in a context where so little of the stuff of Western feminist designation of the household as a site for oppression obtains.

The discourses drawn upon by proponents of Christianity and Islam have reconfigured the ways in which claims and contests over conjugal obligations may be played out. Recourse to the particular past represented by talk of *igba atijo* frames some of the current uncertainties and conflicts over the allocation of rights and duties within a timeless order, and the restrictions that are preached at the pulpits of Ado's churches and proclaimed in its mosques and conveyed through narratives about "fornication" and women's inherent sinfulness. These narratives have an uncanny, if unsurprising, echo with the kinds of words and injunctions that might have been uttered by the missionaries that Peel (2000) so vividly describes. *Igba atijo* serves in these discourses as more than a moral caution. It is redolent with the concerns of the present and comes to represent a longing not only for other times, but for other ways. The *igba atijo* where co-wives ate from the same pot, a pot that was filled with food the husband provided, and where women knew their place, describes an idealized nuclear family, complete with breadwinner and housewife: an ideal that the educated Christian elite may have sought to achieve, but remains far distant from everyday gender relations for the bulk of the population then or now.

Although women in the later phases of their life-courses are less likely to be represented as pursuing men and money, they too are the "women of today" who come in for critique. Their positions on *igba atijo* are taken up as not only commentators but also as actors: as mothers, protective of their children, anxious for grandchildren, concerned about being provided for in old age; as mothers-in-law, competing for a share of resources of love as well as care; as senior wives whose husbands bring home obstinate new wives, who may use their sexual allure or medicine to encourage the husband to drive their seniors away. And the men who echoed the women's concerns spoke not only as those who might be giving women money or contending with wives whose expectations exceed their means, but also as fathers whose capacity to intervene has been eroded; or as elderly husbands of younger women who worry about satisfying them sexually. Men may make comments such as that of one man in his 40s who argued, 'in the olden days the husband was responsible for everything. But now you're lucky if he gives half. That's why women are running here and there trying to make money so they can educate their children'. From the work of Johnson (1921) to the narratives of the missionaries that are so meticulously analyzed by Peel (2000), it is evident that men had no such all-encompassing responsibilities in the olden days; and it is entirely probably that such representations of former times, like those of compliant wives, speak for the present, rather than about the time before the normative injunctions of Christianity and Islam shaped marital expectations.

For young people, too, responses are mediated by their own subject-positions that locate them in particular ways in the historical space marked by the present. The tales their elders would spin about the olden days resonate with some of the concerns that occupied them at this stage in their life-courses. This may be 'the time of yuppies [who] want to enjoy their life before they go to the husband', as a woman in her 20s put it, but it also a time when the uncertainties of modern life raise complex challenges for young people. For these young people, growing up in an ever more competitive and economically uncertain environment, life is tough. Yes, young people said, girls are "after money". But this might be due to more than simply their moral weakness. For a start, they pointed out, if a young woman is not cared for properly by her parents, she might spend the whole day without eating and will need some money to get some food. If all her friends have fine clothes, she will feel bad if she hasn't got anyone to give her those things. Young men without a *kobo* (a small amount of money) in their pockets see potential girlfriends going for men with money. They may try to seek romance with these young women, but find that they cannot compete with rivals who can offer them the kinds of things that their parents cannot provide. Young women, faced with peer pressure to have fashionable hairdos and expensive clothing, may succumb to other pressures knowing that gifts have their price. Looking neat, smelling nice and wearing good cloth: all of these things attract a better kind of man, one who might sooner or later become a father of a woman's children and carry her away from the hardships of the present. For some, this is less the stuff of romance than tactics for survival.

It is easy to forget that the women who "love money more than their husbands" or who "do rubbish and nonsense all around", the "harlots" who "useless themselves" and for whom "the next thing is pregnancy", are not only the potential recipients of the money and love of some women's husbands, brothers and sons, but also the daughters, sisters, friends and mothers of others. From the perspectives of those who join in the clamor of condemnation, changing contexts not only of marriage but also of having and bringing up children raise more immediate dilemmas. Such women may take lovers not only for love, but also for the means with which to support their children. As mothers and sisters as well as wives, women may be concerned about the *juju* another man puts on the wife with whom her husband, son or brother is sleeping, or that used by their girlfriends, and now about the threat of HIV/AIDS that casts a deadly shadow over SW Nigeria and is poised to take the lives of millions in the years to come.

Time and Change

What are we to make of the dissonance between these different pasts? Nietsche (1949) talks of the necessity of forgetting, and the importance of selective remembering as an impetus for action. Accounts of the olden days relate to a time that appears to be not just selectively remembered but selectively *forgotten*. The past of *igba atijo* intersects with but does not entirely subsume the particular pasts of some of those who drew on it to frame their narratives of change. Recasting experiences of other times within the frame of a collective, contrastive *igba atijo* works to submerge the particularity of people's own pasts, working it into a narrative that sustains the moralizing messages of the present. And this moralizing works by projecting back onto the past a narrative that comes form another time and place, that which becomes shaped in the encounter between Yoruba and the world religions (Peel 2000).

Levi-Strauss provides a useful lens through which to view the partiality—in both senses—of claims about the past:

> History is…never history, but history-for. It is partial in the sense of being biased even when it claims not to be, for it inevitably remains partial—that is incomplete—and this is itself a form of partiality (1966:257).

Those who told me of *igba atijo* and of their own pasts were invested in a highly partial representation of how things used to be, one that served the subject positions they occupied in the present and sustained their own "projects" as people. Peel argues,

> the past (*qua* representations) must be made through an engagement with its traces: the past (*qua* antecedents) is not just the source of the categories which shape action, but exists in a dialectical relationship with categorizing agents, who make their past as they act to realise their future. (1993:175)

The social imaginary that *igba atijo* represented in narratives of the past was a powerful longing for things not to be as they were today. It was powerful enough, it seemed, to erase any traces that failed to fit the frame. Attitudes to the past seemed to be, in some respects, an attempt to resist the implications of social change. "How things used to be" becomes pivotal in these discourses as an expression of a dismay which was not merely *nostalgic* but was fired with the emotive concerns of actors whose concerns lay precisely in dealing with the uncertainties the present heralded for *their* futures. And yet, in invoking an idealized past in which there was a strict and unyielding division of labor and power between the sexes, and in which women were chaste and obedient, they spoke of a set of preoccupations that had more to do with the kind of preaching one might hear in the Church of Christ, where women were consigned to silence on account of being essentially sinful, or the compound of one of the many self-styled prophets, who have seen their fortunes soar as those of ordinary Nigerians have plummeted, as he sought to explain the ills of today's Nigeria.

What, then, would those in Ado who would preserve an "antiquarian" notion of the past have made of the following tale told by A.B. Ellis (1894: 42–3) about the origins of the town, one that tells of precisely the female agency and active sexuality that today's moralists use the past to bemoan?

> Odudua was once walking alone in the forest when she met a hunter, who was so handsome that the ardent temperament of the goddess at once took fire. The advances which she made to him were favourably received, and they forthwith mutually gratified their passion on the spot. After this, the goddess became still more enamoured, and, unable to tear herself away from her lover, she lived with him for some weeks in a hut, which they constructed of branches at the foot of a large silk-cotton tree. At the end of this time her passion had burnt out, and having become weary of the hunter, she left him; but before doing so she promised to protect him and all others who might come and dwell in the favored spot where she had passed so many pleasant hours. In consequence, many people came and settled there, and a town gradually grew up, which was named Ado, to commemorate the circumstances of its origins. A temple was built for the protecting goddess; and there, on her feast days, sacrifices of cattle and sheep are made, and women abandon themselves indiscriminately to the male worshippers in her honour.[14]

References

Allman, J. (1996) 'Rounding up spinsters: gender chaos and unmarried women in colonial Asante', *Journal of African Studies*, Vol. 37 No 2: 195–214.

Atanda, J.A. (1969) 'The Iseyin-Okeiho rising of 1916: an example of socio-political conflict in colonial Nigeria', *Journal of the Historical Society of Nigeria*, 4(4): 497–514.

---

14. For bringing this story to my attention, I am grateful to J.D.Y Peel.

Caldwell, J.C., I.O. Orubuloye and P. Caldwell (1991) 'The destabilization of the traditional Yoruba sexual system', *Population and Development Review*, 17(2): 229–262.

Chanock, M. (1985) *Law, Custom and Social Order: The Colonial Experience in Malawi and* Zambia, Cambridge: Cambridge University Press.

Clarke, William, H., 1972, *Travels and Explorations in Yorubaland 1854–1858*, Ibadan: Ibadan University Press.

Cornwall, A. (1996) *For Money, Children and Peace: Everyday struggles in changing times in Ado-Odo, S.W. Nigeria*, Unpublished Ph.D. Thesis, School of Oriental and African studies, University of London.

Cornwall, A. (2001) 'Wayward women and useless men: Contest and Change in Gender Relations in Ado-Odo, S.W. Nigeria', in D. Hodgson and S. Mc-Curdy, eds., *"Wicked" Women and the Reconfiguration of Gender in Africa*, New Jersey: Heinemann.

Cornwall, A. (2002) 'Spending power: love, money and the reconfiguration of gender relations in Ado-Odo, southwestern Nigeria', *American Ethnologist*, 29(4): 963–980.

Cornwall, A. (2003) '"To be a man is more than a day's work": Shifting ideals of manliness in Ado-Odo, S.W. Nigeria', in Lisa Lindsay and Stephan Miescher (eds), *Men and Masculinities in Modern Africa*, New Jersey: Heinemann.

Ellis, A.B. ([1894]1964) *The Yoruba-Speaking Peoples of the Slave Coast of West Africa*, London: Chapman and Hall.

Fadipe, N.A. ([1939]1970) *The Sociology of the Yoruba*, edited by Francis Olu Okediji and Oladejo O. Okediji, Ibadan: Ibadan University Press.

Jeater, D. (1993) *Marriage, Perversion and Power: The Construction of Moral Discourse in Southern Rhodesia, 1894–1930*, Oxford: Clarendon.

Johnson, S. ([1921]1973) *The History of the Yorubas from the Earliest Times to the Beginning of the British Protectorate*, ed. O. Johnson, Lagos: C.S.S. Bookshops.

Lévi-Strauss, C. (1966) *The Savage Mind*, London: Weidenfeld and Nicholson.

Lindsay, L. (2003) 'Money, Marriage and Masculinity on the Colonial Nigerian Railway', in L. Lindsay and S. Miescher (eds.), *Men and Masculinities in Modern Africa*, Heinemann.

Mann, K. (1985) *Marrying Well: Marriage, Status and Social Change among the Educated Elite in Colonial Lagos*, Cambridge: Cambridge University Press.

Mbilinyi, M., (1988) 'Runaway Wives in Colonial Tanganyika: Forced Labor and Forced Marriage in Rungwe District 1919–1961', *International Journal of the Sociology of Law*, Vol. 16: 1–29.

Mockler-Ferryman, Liet.-Col. Augustus, 1902, *British Nigeria: A Geographical and Historical Description of the British Possessions Adjacent to the Niger River, West Africa*, Cassell and Co, London.

Orubuloye, I.O., J.C. Caldwell, and P. Caldwell (1991) 'Sexual networking in the Ekiti district of Nigeria', *Studies in Family Planning*, 22(2): 61–73.

Oyewumi, O., (1998) *The Invention of Women: Making an African Sense of Western Gender Discourses*, Wisconsin: University of Minnesota Press.

Peel, J.D.Y. (1978) 'Olaju: A Yoruba concept of development', *Journal of Development Studies* 14:135–165.

Peel, J.D.Y. (1983) *Ijesas and Nigerians*, Cambridge: Cambridge University Press.

Peel, J.D.Y. (1984) Making history: the past in the Ijesha present, *Man* (NS) 19, 111–132.

Peel, J.D.Y. (2000) *Religious Encounter and the Making of the Yoruba*, Bloomington: Indiana University Press.

Renne, E.P. (1990) *Wives, Chiefs and Weavers: Gender Relations in Bunu Yoruba society*, unpublished Ph.D. thesis, New York University.

Renne, E.P. (1993) 'Changes in adolescent sexuality and the perception of virginity in a southwestern Nigerian village', *Health Transition Review*, 3 (supplementary issue):121–133.

Sudarkasa, N. (1973) *Where Women Work: Yoruba Women in the Marketplace and in the Home*, Anthropological Papers 53, Ann Arbor: University of Michigan.

Whitehead, A. and M. Vaughan (1988) 'The crisis over marriage: an overview', paper presented to the 'Crisis over Marriage in Colonial Africa' workshop, Nuffield College, Oxford, December 1988.

Zabel, S. (1969) 'The legislative history of the Gold Coast and Nigerian marriage ordinances. Parts I & II', *Journal of African Law* 13(2):64–79 & 13 (3):158–178.

CHAPTER 7

"LET YOUR GARMENTS ALWAYS BE WHITE..."[1] EXPRESSIONS OF PAST AND PRESENT IN YORUBA RELIGIOUS TEXTILES

Elisha P. Renne

The sea was crystal clear and was as white as a piece of cotton-wool in [a] weaver's shed undergoing looming processes, ready to be turned into thread. The Sky and sand at the sea-side remained snow-white alike without any difference...
> —Abiodun Emanuel, *Celestial Vision*

Yes though I walk through the valley of the shadow of death, it was that valley that I felt the hand of God. I dreamt that I was walking through a field of cotton, cotton wool which was just floating up from the pods. But there was no sound, all round me were cotton pods bursting softly, at my feet a carpet of cotton, in the air, in the sky, bursting pods that made no sound. The cotton wool pressed out gently like small pillows with the wool coming out when your head presses it. Everything was white.
> —Wole Soyinka, *The Interpreters*

---

1. Ecclesiastes 9:8.

Figure 7.1 - Altar draped with white cloth, with portrait of Moses Orimolade, Ogu Oluwa New Jerusalem Church, Eternal Sacred Order of the Cherubim and Seraphim, Mount Zion, Maryland, Lagos, 26 March 2003 (photo by E.P. Renne).

Introduction

In southwestern Nigeria, white cloth is used in a range of spiritual settings—in demarcating sacred space, in marking a spiritual presence, in representing specific religious identities, and in indicating particular forms of dedication to God or other deities. In this chapter, I examine white religious textiles, focusing on the untailored white cloth used by "traditional"[2] Yoruba cult devotees as well as on the tailored white gowns worn by members of the Cherubim and Seraphim Church, one of the Aladura "prayer" Churches which were established in the early twentieth century in response to strictures imposed by mainline Christian churches dominated by Europeans (Peel 1968). I then consider the process whereby Cherubim and Seraphim leaders in the 1920s materially distinguished their own beliefs from those of Yoruba traditional religious practitioners through specific types and uses of white cloth,

---

2. The use of the term, "traditional," is not meant to imply unchanging past practice but rather makes reference to the local English usage of the word, "traditionalist."

relating these garments to church doctrine and practices. Furthermore, the ways that Cherubim and Seraphim (C&S) Church members use white garments to convey messages which relate the particular qualities of textiles (including color) to specific moral states are also discussed. For example, C&S members use clean, white garments to represent their virtuous goodness, while cloths which are stained represent the spiritual laxity of those outside the church. These qualities and associations are discussed in some detail, based on excerpts from the visions recorded in notebooks by W.F Sosan,[3] an early C&S Church leader who regularly met with other "visioners" (ariran) in Abeokuta during the 1930s. In addition to Sosan's unpublished journals, this discussion of Yoruba religious practice and white cloth relies on documents published by Cherubim and Seraphim leaders, such as Captain Abiodun Emanuel (1962), one of the co-founders of the C&S Church in 1925;[4] on Nigerian archival material; and on more recent interviews with C&S Church leaders and members as well as with traditional Yoruba religious practitioners in several parts of southwestern Nigeria.

The process of progressive distinction by which religious groups express new beliefs through material objects—such as the tailored white garments associated with the C&S Church—is then compared with the more recent material distinctions made by many contemporary Pentecostal Church leaders who wear "dress for success" business suits (see Schneider 1978). Both C&S and Pentecostal leaders use clothing made of manufactured imported materials in tailored Western styles. But the garments worn by Pentecostal pastors, such as Evangelist Reinhard Bonnke, convey a different message from the white gowns worn by C&S prophets, whose garments—meant to refer to Biblical texts such as Ecclesiastes 9:8 ("let your garments always be white")—have a sacred quality. The apparently unremarkable business suits worn by Pentecostal evangelists nonetheless communicate church members' concerns with prosperity and "modern" global connections. This form of dress, which is distinctly secular and not white, distinguishes these Pentecostal Churches from "white garment churches" such as the C&S and the Celestial Church of Christ[5]

---

3. It is particularly appropriate for this volume as it was J.D.Y. Peel who convinced Sosan's heirs to deposit these notebooks and letters in the Special Collections section of the Kenneth Dike Memorial Library, University of Ibadan.

4. Some argue that Prophet Moses Orimolade was the founder who was later joined by Captain Abiodun Emanuel (Onovirakpo 1998). Others describe them as co-founders.

5. Marshall (1993:13) notes that "Holiness" church leaders view these Aladura churches as connected with "traditional" African belief and ritual and hence as "the things of Satan and his agents."

as well as from Catholics and Anglicans, with their own forms of religious dress (Renne 2000).

The final section of the chapter considers this process of progressive distinction, beginning with traditional Yoruba religious practices relating to white cloth use. For example, devotees of particular *imole* spirits or *orisa* deities may abandon one cult for another if their prayers—for children, health, or wealth—are not answered (Barber 1981). While conversion to Christianity in the nineteenth and early twentieth centuries might also be conceptualized as a shift to a more rewarding religion, it might also provide a way for thinking about the plethora of Pentecostal Churches which have appeared in southwestern Nigeria since the 1980s and their attractions for those dissatisfied with churches where prayers were unanswered (Corten and Fratani-Marshall 2001; Marshall 1993). The continued dynamics of changing religious affiliations, along with preoccupations with witchcraft and health—topics which help explain the popularity of Pentecostal preachers such as Evangelist Bonnke (Gifford 1987, 1993)—have precedents in both traditional and Aladura Church worship, even while Pentecostal ministers disparage these earlier religious groups (Marshall 1993). This dialectic between the appeal of new solutions to contemporary problems proffered by ever-more recent religious groups—each belittling the practices and beliefs of groups preceding them—and enduring ideas about the sources of misfortune and well-being relate to Peel's (1984:113–14) observations about the importance of examining "the mutual conditioning of past and present." Rather than accepting C&S and later Pentecostal Church leaders' claims that their present practices mark a clean break with past Yoruba religious worship, this paper considers both the continuities of religious thought and practice as well as apparent disjunctures. While the process of progressive distinction in religious practice suggests a linear view of history-as-progress,[6] it might be more appropriate to think of this process as an inversion of the Ijesha "tendency to rework the past so as to make it appear that past practice has governed present practice" (Peel 1984:113). Thus, C&S as well as Pentecostal Church leaders have sought to "make it appear that past practice" has in no way "governed present practice," emphasizing the distinctive changes instituted in their dress and churches, untainted by prior religious worship, often referred to as "pagan practices."[7] A focus on white cloth use (or the lack

---

6. A linear perspective on Ijesha history is also discussed by Peel (1984).

7. This tendency to disparage religious practices that "came before" such as traditional orisha worship led to various local conflicts between early Christians and traditionalists, as documented in British colonial records (Miscellaneous 1930–1942).

thereof) by these different religious groups provides a way of considering the complexity of "the mutual conditioning of past and present" in religious worship in southwestern Nigeria, disentangling some of the ways that "present practice is governed by the model of past [religious] practice," as well as the ways that they are distinguished from one another. To begin, some of the ways that white cloth is used by traditional Yoruba religious devotees will be discussed.

White Cloth in Traditional Yoruba Religious Worship

White cloth was and continues to be used in a range of traditional Yoruba religious practices, which may be characterized in three ways. It is used as protection, as medicine, and as a representation of spiritual connections, although these categories may sometimes overlap. In the latter case, white cloth may be used to express connections between the spirit, natural, and social worlds (Renne 1995). These connections are exemplified by the use of untailored white cloth by members of the *ejinuwon* cult—a water spirit cult of practiced by Bunu Yoruba women living in northeastern Yorubaland (Renne 1995).[8] Their white cloths identify the social group as *ejinuwon* members who, through their offerings made at natural sites such as streams or termite mounds, represent their spiritual connections with the underwater or underground *ejinuwon* spirit world. Similarly, members of other Yoruba *imole* or *orisa* (i.e., spirits, deities, or powers) cults make use of white cloth in their shrines and in religious worship (McKenzie 1997; Murphy and Sanford 2001), the whiteness of members' dress and shrines, both socially identifying them as spirit devotees and signifying their connection with particular spirit beings.[9]

This connection between the natural world and the spirit world made through white cloth may also be seen in many parts of Yorubaland, such as Ikole-Ekiti, where white cloth is ritually wrapped around a large trio of *ose* trees next to the Elekole's palace (Renne and Adepegba 2003). These massive trees, which are associated with the original three sections of Ikole, are

---

8. A related spirit cult, known as *ofosi*, which used white cloth, is no longer practiced in the Northeastern Yoruba area (Kennett 1931; Renne 1995).

9. Women in the Orisa Ila cult use some objects which display many colors on their surface but which may use white cloth on their inner or hidden sides, e.g., the *otun* bottles covered with colored beads but lined inside with white cloth which they carry on their heads.

Figure 7.2 - The three trunks of the large *ose* (baobab) tree near the Elekole's palace are regularly wrapped with white cloth, in part to insure the peaceful unity of the town. Ikole-Ekiti, 29 July 2002 (photo by E.P. Renne).

wrapped with white cloth in order to placate the spirit associated with this tree. It is believed that by doing so, peace and health will prevail in the town (Interview: Olomodikole, Ikole-Ekiti, 7 August 2002). This idea of supplication merges with ideas about using white cloth for protection during times of vulnerability. Thus Bunu Yoruba women who are about to marry—who are perceived as having flighty spirits which may not want to cross over into a new social status (i.e., they might die)—must wear white cloth during traditional marriage rituals (Renne 1995). Likewise, new housing sites may display a pole with a piece of white cloth which will ward off any evil spirits, just as a diviner may reveal that sick children should wear white cloths as protection from those wishing to harm them (e.g., witches). White cloth may also literally be used as medicine as when small pieces of hand-woven white cloth are burnt and ingested or are used to wrap traditional medicines for protection.

There is some indication that these contemporary uses of white cloth have historically been practiced in traditional Yoruba worship. Using Church Missionary Society archival materials, McKenzie (1992:128) cites several examples of white cloth being associated with the spirit world, as in a vision of an [after death] experience:

> Samuel Johnson relates in 1875 that the friend of a babalawo fell gravely ill, sent for his relatives but died before they arrived. His body was wrapped in cloths according to custom. But before the internment his corpse was seen to be moving. It was unwrapped and they found the man had come to life again. In the event he lived for many years. When he recovered he explained how he had seen a great high God "enthroned in a spacious place, from top to bottom in white. On his right is the God Orisa-nla and on his left the God Ifa, both his counselors".

This particular vision stressed the appearance of the Yoruba high God [Olodumare], with the two Yoruba deities, Orisa-nla and Ifa on the right and left [hands], suggesting an influence of Christianity (McKenzie 1992:128), while at the same time the image of Olorun or Olodumare as "from top to bottom in white," reflects more traditional imagery of Olodumare (Idowu 1962:28).[10]

The frequent use of white cloth as protection[11] in traditional Yoruba religious worship also suggests something about the nature of misfortune, often attributed to witches (*aje*) and sorcerers (*oso*), beings who are believed to cause illness, accidents, and death. In order to counter these forces, cult members wear *ala orisa Ila*, white cloth, as one *orisa* devotee explained:

> It is difficult for death to just come and kill a person wearing *ala*.... Those women who are surrounding the head of the *olorisa Ila* [the *orisa* is represented by the woman cult head] are all warriors, they fight for her, and help her to face attacks...At war and peace, we usually put on white cloth. White cloth helps us to win our battles (Interview: *Olorisa Ila*, Ado-Ekiti, 20 August 2002).

---

10. Olodumare is described as an "Essentially White Object, White Material without Pattern" (Idowu 1962:154). Some have attributed the idea of a Yoruba Supreme God to missionary theologians who sought to assimilate traditional Yoruba beliefs with Christian thought (see Peel 2000, 2002:141). More recent descriptions of traditional Yoruba worship are also probably influenced—to some extent—by Christian (and Muslim) beliefs. I make this point to acknowledge these possibilities, but not to say that present explanations are of no historical value.

11. Actually, there is some variation in the characteristics attributed to particular cloths by different diviners. For example, Chief Samuel Pius Faluyi, Onifa of Ado-Ekiti, uses black cloth for protection and white cloth for peace (Interview: Ado-Ekiti, 19 August 2002), although this view was not common.

This connection between whiteness and protective spirituality also suggests a certain moral positioning, i.e., that revealed whiteness represents the opposite of hidden witchcraft. This point is supported by a saying, cited by one diviner who associates the use of white cloth with good character, necessary for someone in his position:

> *Oju kii su kan an mo mo alaso funfun, Osin kii pon kan an mo mo alaso funfun.* Both day and night, anybody wearing white cloth is clearly seen [i.e., their character must be good]. He must be a person of light, he must know that people are watching him, he must be upright in judgment, he must not misrepresent…the voice of Ifa. White cloth is seen as the king of all cloths (Interview: Chief Alameku, Itapa-Ekiti, 30 July 2002).

A similar association between moral goodness and the wearing of white cloth was made by Chief Sunday Saka, who is in charge of the Olokori Ewi Ado shrine in Ado-Ekiti:

> We have a belief in white cloth. We expect every one of us to be white in all spheres—as the outward appearance is white, so also we want our hearts—our inner appearance to be white as chalk, no evil thoughts must be harboured in our hearts, we must be one in manner (Interview: Chief S. Saka, Ado-Ekiti, 19 August 2002).

These ideas about the color white and morality appear to have been developed further as part of the process of Christian conversion, particularly in the Aladura Churches, which are described in the following section.

White Garments and the Cherubim & Seraphim Church

Visions and dreams of heavenly beings contributed to the creation of white prayer gowns by early C&S Church members. Captain Abiodun Emanuel, who joined Moses Orimolade as a co-leader of the church after her famous week-long vision of June 1925 (Omoyajowo 1982), makes several references to angels attired "in a white robe and feather" (Emanuel 1962:11). Indeed, one of the tests she described in her visit to Heaven specifically referred to the distinction made between traditional religious practitioners who use untailored "stitchless" wrappers as opposed to Christians who wear tailored garments:

Figure 7.3 - Olori Omode, of the Imole Olua cult, Itapa-Ekiti, wearing an un-sewn, white cloth wrapper, with two *apo yata* bags with *aso adodo* [red cloth] straps, knotted *aso oke* waistband, holding *uru* with beaded handles, coral necklace, and *otun* (on head)—all signs of her *imole* status. Itapa-Ekiti, 13 June 2003 (photo by E.P. Renne).

> My friend [the angel] promptly revealed that I was to be led to a room where there were clothes and he strictly warned me not to wear any of them. A short while afterwards I was taken to the said room in which I was shown a stitchless [untailored] gown to wear. I refused and explained that people on my planet wore frock gowns and never wore stitchless gowns (Emanuel 1962:15).

While she does not indicate the color of the untailored "stitchless gowns," it was the tailored "white frock" prayer gowns which came to be associated with C&S membership.[12] According to Omoyajowo (1982:61), the actual de-

---

12. Soyinka (1988:179) mentions the distinction made between those wearing tailored cloth (*onikaba*) and those who wear wrappers (*aroso*), a distinction which also implies literacy or its absence. The CMS missionary, Rev. C. A. Gollmer (1885:180), also noted that western dress served as a symbol of Europeans, particularly of their special power.

sign of these first white C&S prayer garments was attributed to Major A. B. Lawrence, "the patterns [of which] were 'revealed to him in visions...' " with "the patterns [sewn] according to his direction." White robes "were first worn by all the members of the Society, "at the time of the first anniversary of the Church which was celebrated by a procession through Lagos in 1926. These were white cassocks with special adornments signifying different ranks" (Omoyajowo 1982:15–16; Peel 1968:75). This remarkable sight attracted many onlookers, some of whom eventually joined the C&S.

While the designs for prayer robes were often revealed in visions, the material representations of the C&S associated with the white prayer garments of C&S Church members were ultimately derived from Biblical sources, in particular, the books of Ezekiel 1:4–15, Isaiah 6:1–7, and Revelation 7:8–14 (see Cherubim and Seraphim Church, 2002). The latter verses make explicit reference to white garments:

> Revelation 7:[8] After this I saw four angels standing at the four corners of the earth, holding back the four winds of the earth, that no wind might blow on the earth or sea or against any tree.... [9] After this I looked and behold, a great multitude which no man could number, from every nation, from all tribes and peoples and tongues, standing before the throne and before the Lamb, clothed in white robes, with palm branches in their hands. [13] Then one of the elders addressed me, saying, "Who are these, clothed in white robes, and whence have they come?"[14] I said to him, "Sir, you know." And he said to me, "These are they who have come out of the great tribulation; they have washed their robes and made them white in the blood of the Lamb.

For church members, the whiteness of C&S prayer garments relates those wearing them to those standing before the Christ, whose blood has "washed their robes and made them white."[13] Aside from their whiteness, prayer garments and associated paraphernalia make reference to these Biblical passages in other, more specific, ways. For example, the four-sided caps of prophets (*woli*) recall the four faces of the Cherubim, while the robes' long sleeves which

---

13. This idea was expressed in a vision of an early convert to Christian in Abeokuta in 1867, recorded by Matthew Luke: "She found her feet lifted up as if she were under the cross; she had gone with Jesus to the judgment hall and had been pleading his innocency with wicked men that rose up to condemn him, saying, 'This innocent man who raised the dead...you are going to kill'...But they did not listen to me, and so they killed him. The drops of blood are as if he is just slain, they dropped on my sin-stained garment and I am clean'" (McKenzie 1992: 132–33).

Figure 7.4 - Prophetess Ekunọla Smart, wearing white dress and 4-cornered *woli* cap, Ondo, 24 February 2003 (photo by E.P. Renne).

are unseamed, drape down over the hands, referring to the wings of these angelic beings. Also, some garments are made with shiny materials or are covered with sequins, emphasizing the luminous beauty of heaven revealed to early church leaders such as Captain Abiodun Emanuel in her vision:

> I passed through the fifth gate into the Fifth Astral plain and I landed in a very large garden where I saw a host of Angels arranged in a way comparable with a guard of honour. The angels I saw all held hymn books and were singing.
>
> It was very remarkable and wonderful to have noted the garden was purely white, the floor of which was like a shimmering mirror so highly polished as if it were gold, in fact I saw nothing of its like in this World (Emanuel 1962:13).

The beauty of prophets' garments also refers to their distinctive leadership position within the church. Thus Prophet Jacob Oke Adeola, the founder of the branch of the C&S known as Ona Iwa-Mimo (Adeola n.d.), had special garments sewn for him made with shiny white satin and damask cloths, while the general membership wore garments of *teru*, a plain white cotton muslin or Osnaberg cloth.[14]

Other prayer gowns are made to copy literally the garments worn by celestial beings seen in dreams, visions, or trances. For example, while in a trance, Prophetess Samson, like Captain Abiodun Emanuel before her, saw angels dressed in various types of garments, one of which she had sewn for herself when she "returned" from her "travels":

> By the time I went into trance, I was walking into heaven, through so many hills, I had only one more hill to get to Jerusalem on high or Jerusalem in heaven, where I was looking at the Angels of the Lord wearing white gowns. They were lining up with everyone covering their head with *ibori* [cape-like head-coverings], and part of the ibori extended from their heads to their back, all of them in full white dress.
>
> There was also a type of gown shown to me by the angels (*malaika Olorun*) of the Lord. It was pure white cloth material—I have sewn it in the same way that I saw it in the vision. I was in a trance for 21 days. Thereafter I decided to sew the dress as it was revealed to me. There was a large wrapper that I also sewed to put over the gown, it was exactly the way I was revealed to me. The wrapper was so big, it touched and swept the ground. One thing is important. I used to sew my other dresses by myself, but this gown was sewn by another tailor because I was still inhabited by the spirit, I was still at the mountain of prayer. I only told the tailor the way the cloth had to be sewn as revealed to me (Interview: Prophetess J. Samson, Ilesa, 27 February 2003).

With the subsequent growth of the C&S Church, other distinctions in dress within the church emerged. While general members, the *aladura*, normally wear white dresses, "prayer warriors" may wear special caps with a red band, and white dresses with a red sash, for special services during the Lenten period. These garments refer to St. Michael as well as to the cherubim and flaming swords mentioned in Genesis 3: 24: "He drove out the man; and at the east of the Garden of Eden he placed the cherubim, and a flaming sword which turned every way, to guard the way to the tree of life" as well as to the

---

14. Captain Queen Dr. Maria Ogunyooye's career is reflected in her use of different types of white cloth. Her first prayer garment was made of a salt sack-cloth while later dresses incorporate materials, some of which she purchased on a shopping trip to London (Ona Iwa Mimo C&S Church 2001:6–8).

Figure 7.5 - Prayer warriors with special caps with a red band (some are embroidered, "prayer warrior") and white dresses with a red sash, St. Saviour's United Church of Cherubim and Seraphim Cathedral, Owo, 28 March 2003.

"fire flashing" described by Ezekiel in his vision of heaven and the seraphim. Some garments worn by C&S leaders literally depict these Biblical icons, as when flaming swords were embroidered on some of the robes of Prophet Adeola. Similarly, portions of Biblical passages may be embroidered on robes, such as one worn by Prophet Adeola which included the phrase, "Alfa ati Omega," referring to Revelation 1: 8.

The use of written passages incorporated into robes exemplify one important distinction made by C&S leaders, many of whom were literate, in contrast to followers of traditional Yoruba religions, who were not.[15] This emphasis on literacy is evident in a number of visions included in the Sosan journals, exemplified in one vision on "The Meaning of Dreams for kings," which was narrated by Matthew Okanlawon on 18 September 1935:

> When I was on my knees praying, I saw somebody in white garments standing. He wrote something on paper and it read, "If only

---

15. This is not to say that Yoruba oral texts were inconsequential or that white cloth was not an important trope in the *odu* used in Ifa divination (Abimbola 1997; Bascom 1969) and *oriki* praise poetry (Barber 1991).

Cherubim and Seraphim are whole before me, then kings would be having fearful dreams and submissiveness." The meaning lies within this Egbe [group] (translation by T. Adekore).

Another vision, described E. A. Lawoyin two months later, on November 18, 1935, refers not only to the importance of writing, but also to the holiness of garments worn by C&S Church leaders and the power of church elders to provide both physical and spiritual healing:

> If only you can behold my endowments [wealth] with your eyes, you will not take me for granted. If only I write your requests on my garment, you would have had more hope. All of us went to an elder who saw all of us present had a disease in the heart. He prayed into his right hand and stroked our chests with the hand, one by one. The elder said Leader Adeolu should wear the holy garment at all times, otherwise a kind of rot will be caused to happen to all the clothes in the box where he kept it and only the Holy Garment will be saved, to show how praiseworthy and powerful the garment is (translation by T. Adekore).

The idea of white Holy Garments, saving other cloths from rot, and the spiritual cure of "a disease of the heart" by the hands and prayers of C&S elders is similar to the association of white cloth with white hearts made by traditional Yoruba religious practitioners.[16] This positive moral imagery, expressed through descriptions of white or holy cloth, is contrasted with the immorality of dark or filthy cloth, mentioned in several visions recorded in the Sosan journals. For example, the velvet and dark cloths described by Wale Adetayo in a vision recorded on November 30, 1935, are associated with "the path of Satan":

> After this, we saw a road which was covered with velvety cloth such that a person sees it, he or she will think it is the path of life. But it is not the path of life and a lot of people were taking the path. The elder said I should come along we were moving in the air and our feet were not touching the ground. We saw an angel wearing black cloth. He himself was dark and he was removing the velvety material from the ground and there were many poisonous things left there. I was

---

16. More recent examples of a preoccupation with the heart as the abode of beneficial or destructive spiritual forces are seen in evangelical booklets, such as *The Heart of Man* (Anonymous nd), which has an Ibadan distributor. I also purchased a poster with similar illustrations in Ilesa in 2003.

then told that this is how the path of Satan is (translation by T. Adekore).

In another vision, the "rotted garments" worn by some are expressive of their wearers' dubious morality:

Prayer garments [aso adura] are the one thing we have that is different from that of this world. We will see that some people will wear garments...stained with gbanja [kola nut]; some people's garments will be burnt, up to the chest; some people will have tobacco stains on theirs; some people will have blood on theirs; some people when they want to sing, saliva will be coming out of their mouths onto their chests and will not dry. Some have rotted their garments [with] graveyard soil and some people's garments [barely cover them]. And some people's own will be flowing and the star will be correcting [guiding] their style in all leadership.

Meaning: The stain of gbanja and tobacco is a forbidden thing. Among those who cannot do without eating gbanja or taking tobacco, it will show on their garments on the last day....Those whose garments are burnt up to the chest are examples of those who take cigarettes and tobacco; those whose saliva are dropping on their chests are examples of those people who do not observe fasting; those whose garments barely cover them are examples of those who are wicked and those who are stubborn; those whose garments are full [flowing] are examples of those who do not take things for granted night and day, those who do all the things we do in this society with all their hearts, those who worship God with all their hearts....(Brother Timothy, 6 October 1935; translation by T. Adekore).

These metonymic qualities of cloth—the tobacco or saliva-stained cloths standing for people unable to follow church strictures as contrasted with the "flowing garments" of the righteous—suggest an intimate spiritual connection between people and the garments they inhabit. This connection is underscored by a vision recorded on November 4, 1935, by John Afinatan:

A house is built in which the walls appear like a place to hang clothes. It is not clothes that will be hung there but human beings. People—a day is coming in which you must not enter / wear such [bodies]. How would you know this if not for prayers without [caring] or getting tired? Many people are coming, not to worship but because of "love of body" (translation by T. Adekore).

This vision makes a particular connection between people's bodies and their garments—which may house people's soul although wearing such cloth will not "save" them. Yet some make a positive spiritual connection between cloth and spirit, as seen in beliefs about the sacred power of some C&S prophets' robes mentioned earlier. Similarly, a large red robe of the late Prophet J. O. Adeola was kept by his son for fear that "people would not know the power of it" for healing (Interview: Senior Apostle S. A. Adeola, Igboho, July 14, 2002; see also Renne and Adepegba 2003).

These interpretive differences over the spiritual powers and meanings of material things may also be seen in red cloth used as garments and sashes, which are associated with warfare (as "prayer warriors" mentioned earlier) against evil forces by many C&S Church members. For some more recent C&S prophets these garments have taken on other meanings:

> That Holy Michael Day is seen as a day of prayer for victory—that red cloth was a vision in heaven. There are some people who are wearing different cloths in different colors. They can be *emere* [people with special spirits] or people who are troubled by evil spirits. People who are praying for them may say that an angel revealed them to make a particular design on such cloths. But the name of Jesus towers above any cloth of any color under any design (Interview: Prophetess J. Samson, Ilesa, March 20, 2003).

This statement is noteworthy as an example of the process of progressive distinction within the C&S Church itself, whereby church leaders distinguish and morally privilege their own beliefs over others. Initially, the use of red cloth in the C&S Church was associated with the Biblical St. Michael—which distinguished their use of red cloth from that of traditional cult devotees such as those worshipping the Yoruba deity, Sango. However, some C&S Church leaders, such as Senior Apostle W. A. Akinyemi of Ondo who once used red cloth later abandoned it, in a decision explained by his daughter: "My father was using red cloth for special prayer in the past, but there was a time he saw a vision that red cloth was for idols. Then he stopped using red cloth…." (Interview: E. Smart, Ondo, February 24, 2003). Prophetess Samson's comments also suggest the way that she is disengaging cloth "of any color" from spiritual sources altogether, relying solely on "the name of Jesus." Thus while she continues to make and wear white garments as head of the C&S Church in Ilesa, her remarks suggest how sacred textiles, associated with sacred texts, divine visions, and early church prophets, become secular things, in other words, mere commodities (Appadurai 1986; Schneider and Weiner 1986; Weiner and Schneider1989), which like any other object, must not be worshiped as an idol. This apparent abandonment of belief in the sacred qualities of particular religious textiles is even more pronounced in the Pentecostal Churches which have emerged in the 1980s in southwestern Nigeria.

Pentecostal Practice: Christ for All Nations (CfaN) Crusades

Pentecostal Churches in southwestern Nigeria range from small congregations to mega-churches. While they have distinct characteristics reflecting individual church founders (Marshall 1993; Marshall-Fratani 1998), these churches share some common concerns, including an emphasis on faith gospel, a belief in demonic forces, and a focus on spiritual healing. These characteristics are evident in the large evangelical crusades which have been carried out by Evangelist Reinhard Bonnke throughout Africa in the last fifteen years. In the past four years, Bonnke has held crusades in several southwestern Nigerian cities, including Lagos (2000), Ibadan (2001), and Owo, Akure, Ilesa, and Ado-Ekiti (all in 2003). The following discussion focuses on the Ado-Ekiti Crusade and Fire Conference, which took place in January 15–19, 2003.

Bonnke arrived the evening before the conference began when he was the guest of a dinner hosted by a group of Ekiti chiefs. The next morning, Bonnke, dressed in a tailored business suit, met for the Fire Conference with registered church leaders representing all Christian denominations in Ekiti State (Interview: Reverend K. Salami, 4 June 2004, Ado-Ekiti). The Ado-Ekiti Stadium, where the Fire Conference was held, was decorated with banners and swags reminiscent of generic business conferences held in Lagos, and characterized by one member of the Ado-Ekiti organizing committee as "up to international standard." No particular dress was worn by Fire Conference participants.[17] In the evening, during the general crusade held near the New Ekiti State Secretariat, Bonnke wore a suit, while some members of the audience wore specially designed CfaN tee-shirts. Only the choir wore cloth that had a local association, a tie-dyed cotton fabric known as *kampala*. However on the last day of the Crusade, Bonnke appeared wearing an *aso-oke agbada* top, given to him by a group of Ekiti chiefs on the evening before the Crusade began. The shiny, narrow-strip hand-woven cloth used for this garment has a distinctly ethnic—

---

17. I was told that some C&S Church members attending the Ado-Ekiti conference wore white gowns. There was no restriction on dress worn at the Crusade and Fire Conference.

Figure 7.6 - Almanac printed by the Christ for All Nations organization showing Evangelist Reinhard Bonnke wearing a shirt made from locally woven *aso oke* cloth at the CfaN Gospel Campaign, Ogbomosho.

Yoruba—association, although its purchase from the market suggests that it was of no particular religious significance. Thus this cloth was especially appropriate for the non-denominational Yoruba gathering where it was worn.[18] Unlike the white cloth of traditional Yoruba religion or of C&S religious prac-

---

18. Bonnke often wears a garment made of cloth associated with the major ethnic group in Nigeria where he is evangelizing. Thus at the Ogbomosho and Ado-Ekiti Crusades, he wore narrow-strip *aso oke* cloth associated with the Yoruba (Picton and Mack 1989). At the Makurdi Crusade in February 2003 (Bradshaw 2003), the chorus wore the black and white hand-woven cloth associated with the Tiv (Lamb and Holmes 1980).

tice, the hand-woven cloth used in Bonnke's Crusade had no connection with spiritual forces or holy texts. Similarly, the business suits worn by Bonnke (and many other Pentecostal evangelists in Nigeria) have no spiritual meaning, but rather are symbolic of his international status and material success, suggesting that he has been favored by God for his faith.

Discussion

Despite the fact that Pentecostal preachers emphasize faith alone, disparaging the use of ecclesiastical vestments and related paraphernalia in religious worship,[19] they nonetheless share some of the concerns of C&S and other Aladura Church leaders and, to some extent, traditional Yoruba religious practitioners as well. For example, the idea of spiritual warfare is remarkable in its continued importance. Thus members of the traditional Yoruba *Orisa Ila* cult in Ado-Ekiti describe being in constant battle with malevolent forces—witches, *emere*, and other spirits— which can cause a range of misfortunes. Similarly, C&S members dress in red and white garments as St. Michael's prayer warriors during Lent to do battle against Satan and witches. Reinhard Bonnke also makes frequent reference to inevitable spiritual warfare, since "Christians who are in the forefront are prime targets for Satan" (Bonnke 2001:264). Some Pentecostal practices have historical antecedents, with both earlier European missionaries and Aladura Church leaders (such as J. O. Babalola; Peel 1968:91), who made bonfires of discarded charms and *juju*, a practice which has become of regular feature of Bonnke's crusades:

> In our great African gospel crusades, there are mighty victories over satanic powers and over sorcery. Gigantic piles of witchcraft materials are brought and buried.[20] Their owners have been delivered from Satanic fears and oppressions when they received Jesus as their Lord and Saviour (Bonnke 2001:31).[21]

---

19. This attitude toward religious dress is a recurrent theme in Protestant critiques of Roman Catholicism, evidenced during the Protestant Reformation in religious tracts with titles such as "A brief discourse against the outvvarde apparell and ministring garmentes of the popishe church" (by Robert Crowley, published in 1578). Three centuries later, when the Bishop of Exeter directed Anglican clergy to wear surplices in 1840, mobs in Exeter pelted those wearing surplices with rotten eggs and vegetables, later referred to as the Surplice Riots (Mayo 1984:102).

20. In the Ado-Ekiti Crusade, an oil drum was used to burn charms.

21. It might be said that while ostensibly ridding people of witchcraft fears, these ritual burnings also reinforce beliefs about the power of witches and Satan through this focus on their presence.

The emphasis of victory over Satan is also related to ideas about healing and fertility, prominent themes in CfaN revivals. This concern with health and child-bearing is also a common theme in traditional Yoruba rituals and in C&S Church practice, although the means by which these twin objectives are achieved differ somewhat. In Pentecostal crusades, barrenness and illness may be conquered with faith and prayer alone. Thus, in the *Telegram Revival Report* of Makurdi Gospel Campaign in February 2003, the cure by prayer of one man who had been diagnosed with HIV-AIDs, is described:

> Reinhard Bonnke prayed for HIV positive to turn into HIV negative…The miraculous had once again followed the preaching of the Word of God; from HIV+ to HIV−, all to the Glory of God (CfaN 2003).

Similarly, Aladura Church members also rely on prayer (along with holy water and anointing oil) in the belief that spiritual healing is an important element in a physical cure, as one woman prophet explained:

> If a person wanted to deliver a baby when Baba [her father, Senior Apostle W.A. Akinyemi] was alive, there was no need of undergoing any operation, my father worked for so many years in the General Hospital in Ondo here until the church said he should not be going to the hospital for such work again because he was already old. People were advised to come to him at home for easy delivery. My father would just lay his hand on pregnant women and he would call Jesus's name, Jehovah, and he would say that every Satanic spirit blocking easy delivery for this woman should be removed. Instantly, the name of the Lord would work in the womb and the child would easily be delivered. In cases when women who faced with difficult deliveries came to him, my father would speak to God and to the womb, and immediately the child would be born (Interview: Ekunọla Smart, Ondo, 24 February 2003).

This reliance on prayer differs from the use of sacrifice and various forms of traditional medicines, along with incantations and prayers, by traditional Yoruba religious devotees to address health problems. Yet while Pentecostal, and C&S Church leaders before them, emphasized these differences in these healing techniques, there is considerable similarity in beliefs about the underlying explanations of illness in all three religious groups. For example, they share beliefs about the causes of illness and infertility, attributing them to particular agents—witches, Satan, or spirits—which must be countered in order for good health, success and fertility to prevail.

Pentecostal and C&S Church leaders downplay these commonalities through a particular "presentist" perspective which stresses their new and unique religious vision, and reworks the past in a certain way. For them, it is not so much their concern with an inability to know the past because of inadequate historical accounts which may be tainted by present interests that characterize their "presentist" perspective. Rather, it is their denial that any aspects of past religious practice and belief intersect with their own present forms of worship. Thus, practices which distinguish earlier religions—such as sacrifice to Yoruba deities by "traditionalists," as well as cure by cult leaders (*olorisa*), diviners (*babalawo*), and "traditional" healers (*onisegun*) are highlighted and disparaged, while continuities in beliefs about witchcraft and well-being are ignored.[22] For C&S Church members, many stress the power of prayer based on Biblical texts (which include the use of white prayer garments) and holy water to counter such demonic forces. For Bonnke and other Pentecostal evangelists, only prayer and faith in Jesus Christ can be used to achieve these ends. In this way, Pentecostal Church leaders and C&S Church leaders before them practice a variation of the "stereotypical reproduction of the past" (Peel 1984:114), although rather than representing past practices as a positive good "govern[ing] present practice," they are represented generically as immoral evils, which are ostensibly eliminated from present church practice altogether. Despite the stereotypical reproduction of the past which defines the present—in terms of either an idealized or an immoral past—the continuities as well as disjunctures in religious belief and practice underscore "the mutual conditioning" of past and present in these three forms of religious worship in southwestern Nigeria.

Conclusion

The use of white cloth is very much part of this process of moral imagining of the past as distinct from the present. In its untailored, plain white form,

---

22. Gifford (1993: 194) has described Bonnke's disregard for African religious precedents:

> Since everything before one's commitment to Jesus is evil, African culture has nothing good in it. 'Witchcraft' is the only category with which Bonnke can treat of it. There is no understanding of the varieties of, say, traditional healers. All institutions through which Africans have been humanized over the centuries are despised and rejected. Thus Bonnke described the results of a crusade in the interior of Zaire: 'Satanic structures as old as the hills were smashed'.

Figure 7.7 - Cover from the video, *Funfun L'Oluwa* (Boye Ventures, Lagos, 2003).

cloth continues to be used in traditional Yoruba religious worship. It has also come to serve as a symbol of traditional religious belief and practice in a range of media, including television and in videos.[23] Cherubim & Seraphim Church members also continue to use white prayer gowns, specifically based on Biblical texts and church founders' visions and dreams. While the tailored aspect of these garments distinguish their wearers' from those making earlier use of white cloth in Yoruba traditional religion, ideas about the association with white cloth with spirituality, with "whiteness of heart," and with unhidden, good intentions persist. Thus while distinguishing the use of white cloth in their own religious practice, C&S Church members have nonetheless perpetuated beliefs about white cloth and its moral associations.

The abandonment of white cloth use by Pentecostal Church members represents another aspect of the process of distinguishing the past from the pres-

---

23. For example, many Nigerian videos, such as *Funfun L'Oluwa* (Whiteness is God), portray "traditional" Yoruba themes, in which actors and actresses dress in white cloth.

ent. In Bonnke's "dream of a Blood-washed Africa..." (Bonnke 2001:33), the "white garments and feathers" of Angels seen by early C&S Church leaders such as Captain Abiodun Emanuel are not present. Nor are "those clothed in white robes," who "have washed their robes and made them white in the blood of the Lamb" (Revelation 7:13–14) evident in Bonnke's dreams and visions. Yet the divine inspiration referred to by such dreams and visions are familiar ideas for followers of the C&S Church and traditional Yoruba religions. The continuing debates over the presence or absence of material objects—such as white cloth and the religious values and meaning that such cloths suggest— underscore the contested role which such objects play in religious worship. While the sacred meanings associated with white cloth use in religious worship in southwestern Nigeria may have been rejected or forgotten by some, for others the connections of white cloth with past practices, with spiritual protection and healing, and with the moral goodness wearing them implies, are benefits too powerful and precious to abandon.

References

Abimbola, W. 1997. *Ifa: An Exposition of Ifa Literary Corpus.* New York: Athelia Henrietta Press.

Adeola, J.O. nd. *Itan Igbe Dide.* Igboho.

Anonymous. n.d. *The Heart of Man or the Spiritual Heart Mirror.* Pretoria, SA: All Nations Gospel Publishers.

Appadurai, A., ed. 1986. *The Social Life of Things.* Cambridge: Cambridge University Press.

Barber, K. 1981. How man makes god in West Africa. *Africa* 51:724–45.

———. 1991. *I Could Speak Until Tomorrow: Oriki, Women, and the Past in a Yoruba Town.* Edinburgh: Edinburgh University Press, for the International African Institute.

Bascom, W.R. 1969. *Ifa Divination: Communication Between Gods and Man in West Africa.* Bloomington: Indiana University Press.

Bonnke, R. 2001. *Evangelism by Fire.* Bad Vilbel, Germany: Full Flame.

Bradshaw, A. 2003. Gospel crusade in Makurdi, Nigeria, 19–23 February '03. *Telegraph Revival Report* (April 2003).

Cherubim & Seraphim Church. 2002. *Church Member's Daily Bible Reading Guide,* 20th edition. Agbo-Igbala, Lagos: Cherubim & Seraphim Church.

Corten, Andre, and Ruth Marshall-Fratani. 2001. *Between Babel and Pentecost: Transnational Pentecostalism in Africa and Latin America.* Bloomington: Indiana University Press.

Emanuel, Mrs. C. Abiodun. 1962. *Celestial Vision of Her Most Rev. Mother Prophetess Capt. Mrs. C. Abiodun Emanuel which originated Cherubim & Seraphim in 1925*, fourth edition (English). Yaba: Charity Press.

Gifford, Paul. 1987. "Africa Shall Be Saved": An appraisal of Reinhard Bonnke's Pan-African Crusade. *Journal of Religion in Africa* 17:63–92.

———. 1993. Reinhard Bonnke's mission to Africa, and his 1991 Nairobi Crusade. In: *New Dimensions in African Christianity*, P. Gifford, ed. Ibadan: Sefer, pp. 186–215.

———. 1998. *African Christianity: Its Public Role*. London: Hurst & Co.

Gollmer, C.A. 1885. *On African symbolic messages*. JRAIGI 14:169–82.

Idowu, E. B. 1962. *Olodumare: God in Yoruba Belief*. Ikeja: Longman.

Kennett, B. 1931. The Afoshi dancers of Kabba Division, Northern Nigeria. *JRAIGBI* 61:435–42.

Lamb, V., and J. Holmes. 1980. *Nigerian Weaving*. Hertingfordbury: Roxford Books.

Marshall, Ruth. 1993. Pentecostalism in Southern Nigeria: An Overview. In: *New Dimensions in African Christianity*, P. Gifford, ed. Ibadan: Sefer, pp. 8–39.

Marshall-Fratani, R. 1998. Mediating the global and local in Nigerian Pentecostalism. *Journal of Religion in Africa* 28(3): 278–315.

Mayo, Janet. 1984. *A History of Ecclesiastical Dress*. London: B.T. Batsford.

McKenzie, P.R. 1992. Dreams and visions in nineteenth century Yoruba religion. In: *Dreaming, Religion, and Society in Africa*, M. Jedrej and R. Shaw, eds. Leiden, New York: E.J. Brill, pp. 126–34.

———. 1997. *Hail Orisha! A Phenomenology of a West African Religion in the Mid-Nineteenth Century*. Leiden: Brill.

Miscellaneous. 1930–1942. Correspondence concerning Cherubim and Seraphim Society Activities in Oyo Province. Oyo Prof 1, File No. 661, Nigerian National Archives, Ibadan.

Murphy, J.M., and M.-M. Sanford, eds. 2001. *Osun Across the Waters*. Bloomington: Indiana University Press.

Omoyajowo, J.A. 1982. *Cherubim and Seraphim: The History of an African Independent Church*. New York: Nok Publishers International.

Ona Iwa Mimo Cherubim & Seraphim Church. 2001. *Silver Jubilee, Queen Captain Maria Omoniyi Ogunyooye*. Lagos: Ojogbon'Niyi Print Services.

Onovirakpo, S.M.O. 1998. *The History and Doctrine of the Cherubim and Seraphim Church of Nigeria*, 2nd ed., rev. Ibadan.

Peel, J.D.Y. 1968. *Aladura: A Religious Movement Among the Yoruba*. Oxford: Oxford University Press, for the International African Institute.

———. 1984. Making history: The past in the Ijesha present. *Man* (NS) 19(1):111–32.

———. 2000. *Religious Encounter and the Making of the Yoruba*. Bloomington: Indiana University Press.

———. 2002. Gender in Yoruba religious change. *Journal of Religion in Africa* 32(2):136–66.

Picton, John, and John Mack. 1989. *African Textiles*. London: The British Museum.

Schneider, J. 1978. Penguins to peacocks: The political economy of European cloth and colors. *American Ethnologist* 5:413–48.

Schneider, J., and A. Weiner. 1986. Cloth and the organization of human experience. *Current Anthropology* 27:178–84.

Sosan, W.F. nd. Unpublished journals. Special Collections, Kenneth Dike Memorial Library, University of Ibadan.

Soyinka, W. 1988. *Ake: The Years of Childhood*. Ibadan: Spectrum.

Renne, E. 1995. *Cloth That Does Not Die: The Meaning of Cloth in Bunu Social Life*. Seattle: University of Washington Press.

———. 2000. Cloth and conversion: Yoruba textiles and ecclesiastical dress. In: *Undressing Religion: Commitment and Conversion from a Cross-Cultural Perspective*, L. Arthur, ed. Oxford: Berg, pp. 7–24.

Renne, E., and C.O. Adepegba. 2003. Yoruba religious textiles. *The Nigerian Field* 68:51–60.

Webster, J. B. 1964. *The African Churches Among the Yoruba 1888–1922*. Oxford: Clarendon Press.

Weiner, A. and J. Schneider. 1989. *Cloth and Human Experience*. Washington DC: Smithsonian Institution Press.

Interviews

Senior Apostle S.A. Adeola, Igboho, 14 July 2002.

Chief Alameku, Itapa-Ekiti, 30 July 2002.

Chief Samuel Pius Faluyi, Ado Ekiti, 19 August 2002.

Olua Ila members, Ado-Ekiti, 20 August 2002.

Chief Sunday Saka, Ado-Ekiti, 19 August 2002.

Reverend Dr. Kunle Salami, Ado-Ekiti, 4 June 2004.

Prophetess Ekunola Smart, Ondo, 24 Feb 2003.

Prophetess Julianah Samson, Ilesa, 27 February, 20 March 2003.

Chief Olomodikole, Ikole-Ekiti, 7 August 2002.

CHAPTER 8

SHRINE SANCTUARY AND MISSION SANCTUARY IN WEST AFRICA

Sandra T. Barnes

The missionaries who arrived in West Africa before colonial conquest faced unique challenges, for they needed to function successfully within the societies where they lived, while at the same time rejecting, or wishing to change, the religious principles that lay at the heart of local social practice. Nor did they find it easy to coexist with African holders of sovereign power. Divergent interpretations of sovereignty and of the meaning of religious practice became especially clear in the matter of sanctuary, where the issues at stake concerned control over the people who sought refuge.

The Rev. Samuel Annear was confronted with this challenge a few months after his 1844 arrival in Badagry, a coastal town in what would become Nigeria, when he offered refuge to a young slave he discovered at the back of his garden. The slave's owner, a powerful chief, threatened war and gathered a formidable militia from the town and neighboring client villages. The next day Annear relinquished the slave, writing that in the end his household would not be "sufficiently strong to bring them to submission by force."[1]

Six months later Annear wrote to Methodist Missionary Society headquarters with a sense of satisfaction that he was now housing and entirely caring for 20 children in the Badagry Mission House, whereas "our brethren of the Church Missionary Society have not been able to succeed in getting a single [one]." To his dismay children were almost openly kidnapped in the town and

---

1. S. Annear, Journal, Nov. 1, 1844, Methodist Missionary Society Archives (hereinafter MMS).

sold into slavery, and therefore when "little ones" were stolen from his own mission house Annear went to great lengths to recover them. Annear believed he must provide protection "as though they were my own children." The CMS failed, Annear wrote, because they did not take children "entirely under their care, and engage to protect them on their own premises."[2]

We can understand the principles underlying these cases only if we make a closer examination of how people gave, and sought, sanctuary in West African societies at times and places where Europeans did not yet play a role. Giving sanctuary was an old and respected practice in Western Africa. Sanctuary traditions were still deeply rooted and widespread at the time missionaries arrived. In several towns, including ancient Lagos, a sacred tree with supernatural powers served as a sanctuary for people accused of crimes if they could reach the tree and embrace it.[3] Farther afield in Igboland, the shrines of Ala and Odo gave asylum to criminals and slaves or people about to be sold as slaves respectively, on the condition they serve the shrines' deity thereafter.[4] Sanctuary was an old principle in Europe, too. There had been a long tradition of providing sanctuary within the Christian church. In English customary law the practice was not abolished until 1723 and in France not until the Revolution.[5]

There were many, varied conventions by which sanctuaries functioned in West Africa in mid-nineteenth century. Sometimes whole towns were sanctuaries which meant people from outside sought refuge in them. Sometimes sanctuaries were separate places inside a town—shrine, sacred landmark, or dwelling—which meant people who sought refuge came either from within the community or from outside it.[6] Whatever the context might have been,

---

2. S. Annear, Letter extract, June 1, 1845, MMS.

3. Chief L.Y. Kalefo II, Olumegbon of Lagos, Interview 10/5/86 (V:2); Abore Olokun, Interview 12/7/86 (VIII.1–2).

4. Meek 1937:78, 135.

5. Encyclopaedia Britannica 1972, 19:992–3.

6. There were other kinds of refuge. First, refugees were created through warfare, exile, and famine. There were widespread conventions for absorbing and settling people such as these who moved in large numbers and settled in separate quarters of a town, separate villages under the patronage of a powerful local chief, or unsettled territories. Second, there were informal ways refugees and others sought protection. They escaped to faraway towns, attached themselves as clients to a prominent individual, and never revealed the reason for their appearance. They also escaped to relatives in another community to seek their protection. (See for example Oguntomisin and Falola 1987.) This essay refers to people who sought refuge singly or in very small numbers and were being protected through a formal tradition such as sanctuary.

any understanding of the terms by which sanctuaries existed came through several kinds of knowledge. One was that the ability to offer asylum depended not simply on providing protection, but on understanding and meeting the conditions that made protection possible. How for example could a town harbor the runaway slave of a neighboring town without provoking reprisals? Another was that the capacity to offer asylum was predicated on understanding the position of a sanctuary in the relations of power in the community, state, or region in which it functioned. How could someone who offended a ruler find safety in the dwelling of his subordinate chief?

Annear's own exposure to understanding the practice of asylum was virtually at his doorstep. His fellow missionary, the Rev. Samuel Crowther, observed that in Badagry itself oppressed slaves, if they were able to escape, could seek refuge in a deity house where, in return for a better life, they were obliged to serve that god ever after—not unlike the Odo and Ala shrines. Crowther compared this custom to that among Jews who gained asylum by laying "hold on the horns of the altar."[7] A fuller understanding of the way sanctuaries were entwined within the ritual and political fabric of a community came from the sanctuary town of Iworo just a few miles east of Badagry and from neighboring regions farther afield.

Sanctuaries and Supernatural Power

Iworo was a sanctuary town, dating at least to 1700.[8] It was always open, providing refuge to anyone needing protection, no matter the cause.[9] The town was something of an anomaly. It was the site of a regional market that met at a point where Iworo controlled a narrow stretch of inland waterway that served as a transportation and communication conduit between communities to its east and west.[10] Yet it was a little town, existing in an environment where larger powers constantly preyed on weaker ones in order to enlarge their spheres of influence and particularly to gain access to favorable opportunities provided by the Atlantic trade. From the time of its beginning

---

7. CA2/M1, S. Crowther, Journal, June 25, 1845, Church Missionary Society Archives (hereafter CMS).

8. CSO 26/30030, W.C. Wormal, V.II, 1935:43ff, Nigeria National Archives, Ibadan (hereafter NNA).

9. Abore Olokun, Interivew 21/6/86 (VI 60–1).

10. CO879/15, African, No. 192, Faulkner to Moloney, March 19, 1879:11, Public Record Office, Kew (hereafter PRO).

to the start of colonial rule intermittent wars raged around Iworo, but no power seems to have overtaken or to have dominated this small place.[11] Even if a war was in progress, the roads to Iworo were always open.[12] When a British administrator inquired into its history he found that during the slave trade years, when the inland waterways were unsafe for travel, there was complete freedom of passage for those on their way to make sacrifices at Iworo.[13]

Yet, the appearance of Iworo inspired dread and awe in those who visited it. Richard Lander came upon the entrance to the town by accident in c.1830, only to be overcome by the sight of human sacrifices with body parts scattered in the branches of a sacred tree and skulls surrounding the base of its trunk. It was "the largest tree I had ever seen."

> Although scenes of horror had become habitual and familiar to me, my feelings, nevertheless, were not entirely blunted, and I encountered a more violent shock, whilst staring at the overwhelming scene, than I ever before experienced. I stood as if fascinated to the spot by the influence of a torpedo, and stupidly gazed on the ghastly spectacle before me, without the power of withdrawing my sight to more agreeable objects, or even of moving hand or foot...[T]he awful stillness and solitude of the place, disturbed only by the sighing of the conscious wind through the sombre foliage, or at intervals by the frightful screaming of voracious vultures, as they flapped their sable wings almost in my face–all tended to overpower me; my heart sickened within my bosom, a dimness came over my eyes, an irrepressible quivering agitated my whole frame, my legs refused to support me, and turning my head, I fell senseless into the arms of Jowdie, my faithful slave![14]

The sacrifices that shocked Lander were made to the deity Elegba (Elegbara, Eshu), the messenger who ran errands between humans and the supernatural world and presided over markets. The deity himself was represented by a simple mound of earth covered by a shed.[15] Elegba was known popularly as a trickster and to scholars as "the principle of unpredictability." To missionar-

---

11. FO/84/920:91, H. Townsend, Jan. 11, 1853, PRO; CSO 26/30030, W.G. Wormal, Vol. II, 1935:19ff, NNA; Abore Olokun, Interview 21/6/86 (VI 60–1). But see CA2.086, Isaac Smith, Journal, Jan. 23, 1850, CMS.

12. Wood 1933[1881]:51.

13. CSO 26/30030, W.G. Wormal, Vol. II, 1935:43ff, NNA.

14. Lander 1830, V.I:264–66.

15. CA2/076, S. Pearse, Journal Extracts, Oct. 13, 1873, CMS.

ies, however, he was the devil or Satan because of his ability to punish those who failed to meet their sacrificial obligations.[16] It was an inappropriate designation, one that divided the sacred world into good and evil, and as such was a violation of local metaphysical principles where both positive and negative characteristics were intrinsic qualities of all deities, albeit in indeterminate and unpredictable ways.

In this context Elegba filled people with alarm. Those who knew Iworo and the Elegba deity who resided there, held the place in "awful veneration,"[17] "too frightening" to be encroached upon by outsiders.[18] So afraid were the people who frequented Iworo market that cowries (the local currency) were left in place as offerings to the deity if they accidentally fell to the ground. The cowries were ankle deep.[19] When the new British Governor in 1863 ordered that a recent human sacrifice be removed from the Elegba shrine and buried, people warned that in a short time he would meet his own end.[20]

Iworo was untouched by external threats up to that point. Before the arrival of the British, outside communities cultivated its friendship.[21] The great conquest states of Dahomey and Oyo and small kingdoms such as Porto Novo and Lagos, all of which were nearby, and had at various periods controlled communities surrounding Iworo, laid not a hand on this sanctuary town.[22] Instead, the rulers of neighboring states sent to Iworo their yearly gifts of slaves or of money to purchase slaves. Even the king of Benin, who extracted tribute from Lagos and other trading centers along the coast, instead sent gifts to Iworo.[23]

Slaves given to Iworo were the sacrificial victims used to appease Elegba. One of the town's distinctive features was that it was strictly divided between those who were ordinary residents and those who were sent as gifts and therefore still enslaved. Gift slaves were destined for sacrifice and stayed in a separate compound, living together as husband and wife and having children, but never knowing when, in the casting of lots, one of them would be sacrificed to Elegba. While they were alive, however, they were servants of the deity. The

16. CA2/022, Coker to Fenn 11/9/1876, CMS; Awolalu 1979:28–30; Drewal 1992:xix.

17. CA2/076, S. Pearse, Journal Extracts, Oct. 13, 1873, CMS.

18. Abore Olokun Interview, 21/6/86 (VI.60–1).

19. CA2/076, S. Pearse, Journal Extracts, July 29, 1861 and Oct. 13, 1873, CMS.

20. CA2/076, S. Pearse, Journal Extracts, June 29, 1863, CMS.

21. CSO.26/30030/S.1, R.J.M. Curwen.1937:9ff, NNA.

22. FO/84/920:91, H. Townsend, Jan. 11, 1853, PRO.

23. CO879/15, African, No. 192, Faulkner to Moloney, March 19, 1879:ll, PRO; CA2/076, S. Pearse, Journal Extracts, July 29, 1861, CMS.

Rev. Samuel Pearse, who spent many years at Badagry, observed that these "unhappy people never attempted to escape, but meekly submit to their own fate" for such was the dread and fear they had of the Iworo Elegba. "It is an ill omen to any of the natives of Iworo to meet up first thing in the morning with any of these doomed people. They are not allowed to enter any house nor shake hands with the natives nor intrude among them."[24]

More than a decade after human sacrifice was prohibited at Iworo, a mission teacher by chance recognized one of these slaves as coming from a house next to his own paternal home many miles distant. The slave had been sent to Iworo as a gift and, although she was spared by the British prohibition against human sacrifice, she remained in service to Elegba. When the teacher took the old woman into his house she quickly renounced her loyalty to Elegba so as to "cleave unto Jesus."[25]

Iworo declined after it was incorporated into the Colony of Lagos in 1863 and became subject to British laws. For a missionary who watched the process, it took only a few years to lose its "ancient glory." The foundation on which its power rested, the awe that Elegba inspired, was receding. Little homage was paid and, in fact, the deity was slowly eclipsed. The king remained faithful to his ancient deities, but he also attended the worship services of local missionaries and asked that a Christian teacher be placed in Iworo so his children could be trained in their school.[26]

So, Iworo built its protective edifice on fear. Its independence was derived from the formidable and mystically awesome spectacle surrounding its patron deity and the fear that supernatural reprisals would attend those who displeased Elegba and violated the town's customs. Iworo's legitimacy as a sanctuary was derived from a singular resource. When its ritually-grounded source of sovereignty was opposed, Iworo could not maintain its aura of invulnerability by turning to other sources of power. There is little evidence that Iworo attempted to grow in size by attacking or otherwise expanding its own spheres of control in the surrounding region. The population was only 500 in about 1876.[27] It existed on its own as a small, autonomous polity, and as a market center. It did not develop the kinds of resources, particularly agricultural productivity or effective regional alliances, that served as alternative sources of strength and that would come to its aid when the authority of the Elegba shrine was challenged. When British officials surveyed the area early in the twentieth century, Iworo's

---

24. *Ibid*, Feb. 23, 1875.
25. *Ibid*, Feb. 23,1875.
26. *Ibid*, Oct. 13, 1873; CSO.26/30030/S.1. R.J.M. Curwen 1937:9ff, NNA.
27. CA2/022, Coker to Fenn 11/9/1876, CMS.

market had taken a secondary role and its government was in decay.[28] This was not, however, the outcome in other sanctuary towns.

Sanctuaries and Material Assets

The story of the sanctuary at Krachi (today's Ghana) could not have been more unlike that of Iworo. At the beginning of the colonial period, German authorities twice executed the priests of its powerful Dente shrine, [29] and twice successors were named to replace them. Earlier the Asante Empire dominated Krachi and tried to keep it undeveloped, but it grew in population and economic strength and successfully rebelled under the leadership of the shrine priest to establish its own sovereign state. Even after independence came to Ghana and the waters of the Volta Dam began to cover the Dente shrine, leaders moved it to safety in the dead of night. Krachi and its protective shrine were threatened at every stage, but they did not collapse.

Throughout its known history the Dente shrine had multiple roles. It was known far and wide as a refuge, especially for slaves who escaped from Ashanti oppression. The shrine was not a fearsome sight. It was located in a cave, covered by a white cloth, overlooking a gorge in the Volta River. The awe in which it was held emerged not from its appearance but from the mystical powers emanating from an oracle housed within the cave. The oracle was consulted on a wide range of concerns, from questions about fertility and health to family and community disputes. Failure to abide by an oracular decision could mean expulsion from the community or payment of a fine. Traditions of nearby peoples spoke of the Krachi deity that could protect them against constant tribal warfare and other misfortunes.[30] Thus Dente was seen as a force that could prevent conflict, and he was the deity that the Asante and other states consulted as to whether or not they should go war. Not least was its role as an "international" court of justice, a role to which we will return.

The shrine controlled significant resources. One was income from trade. Krachi sat at a strategic point on the Volta River from which commercial routes to the north could be controlled. Canoes navigated the river as far as Krachi where a set of cataracts forced shippers to transport goods by land

---

28. CSO 26/30030, W.G. Wormal Vol. II, 1935:43ff, NNA.

29. Maier 1983:142–3, 146–72. Germans controlled Krachi territory on the east bank of the Volta river from 1894 to 1914, when the British ousted the Germans and became the colonial authority.

30. *Ibid*, 17, 34–9, 58.

around the obstacles. The location provided an opportunity to place a toll on goods that were transhipped by land around the cataracts. The most lucrative commodity was salt which came from large deposits of sea salt secured from the Ada lagoon at the mouth of the Volta. Salt was scarce in the interior and much in demand. Transporting it by water to upcountry markets as far as the cataracts saved considerable labor and time. The toll on salt at Krachi is believed to have been one bag of salt for every canoe-load of salt that passed the Krachi cataracts. This salt-toll was then traded by Krachi northward for additional profit. Much of this income went to the Dente priest.[31] A second source of income came from death duties. The Dente deity was consulted in matters of life and death and therefore if a person's death was caused by violating the Dente deity in some way, his or her property went to the shrine. A third source of income consisted of large gratuities paid to Dente priests by people wishing to establish branch shrines in remote areas. Like the Elegba at Iworo, the satellite shrines consisted of a mound of earth for which human sacrifices were required, although animals could substitute when people were not available.[32]

The Dente shrine also controlled increasingly large numbers of people. We do not know how many, but among the Ga (near the coast south of Krachi) one sanctuary had 500 slave refugees.[33] Refugees gave service to the Dente shrine's deity; they provided farm labor to privileged elders; they performed communal labor, built villages, and paid taxes. Krachi was a fertile area and the entire community benefited from the increased labor and agricultural productivity the newcomers provided. It profited as well from the additional military strength refugees gave the community for, if nothing else, this expanded community members' ability to protect themselves and others. It was a self-reinforcing process: growth led to increased prosperity and vice versa. The people of Krachi were socially differentiated, but in less extreme ways than Iworo. Slave refugees continued to be slaves, but in Krachi their lives were no longer in danger. Many came to escape oppression and, while they did not become free people, they were able to live better lives and in some cases start their own villages.[34]

Krachi protected its assets through interdependent relationships. Throughout nearly two centuries of domination, the Asante attempted to keep Krachi in a marginal position, but it was in vain. Asante depended on Krachi for goods that reached Kumase via the Volta River trade route. It relied on the

---

31. *Ibid*, 21, 55.
32. *Ibid*, 43–4, 50.
33. Parker 2000:24.
34. Maier 1983:75.

Dente oracle for advice on whether or not to make war against its enemies. For these reasons, and perhaps because Krachi was a border province and seemed unthreatening to Asante's core holdings, it recognized Dente as a sanctuary by not retrieving its slaves who sought refuge there.

As we have seen, Dente developed other forms of strength beyond the prominence of its oracle that could be used to defend and even expand its position in regional power struggles. This was the key to its survival in a region that was otherwise rent by violence. It was also the key to Krachi's ability to rebel against the Asante, and establish its own state, the political center of which was lodged primarily in the hands of the Dente priest. The combined strength of his supernatural and worldly assets was sufficient to make him more powerful than the titular chief of Krachi. A German historian observed in 1894 that:

> The King has little influence and is completely dependent on the fetish priest and his moods. The Krachi people like all heathens are completely under the spell of the fetish priest and have to fulfill his demands without a murmur.[35]

This arrangement survived into the colonial period.

Ultimately Islam, and not Christianity, provided a contrasting view of supernatural efficacy and an alternative political order that attracted support away from the Dente priest. When a large number of Muslims began moving into Krachi in the 1870s to take advantage of its position on the Volta trade route, the old order was threatened but it did not disappear. Strong political rivalries and factions developed of which the Dente-led population was one and the latter-day Islamic community, which began to prevail in filling positions of authority, was the other. Still, the wider community flourished and the population grew steadily so that by the turn of the century there were between 5,000 and 10,000 people living in the main settlement of Krachi.[36]

Most places of refuge, like Iworo, had a tenuous existence once new forms of authority were introduced. However, others of them were the original cores around which important urban centers grew. The Nupe capital of Bida and the ancient clerical town of Timbuktu, are believed to have begun as sanctuary towns and to have withstood the colonial pressures and social changes that overarching state regimes imposed.[37] The supernatural power that provided a

---

35. H. Klose cited in Maier 1983:55.
36. By 1983, the population of Krachi was 60,000 (Maier 1983:1). For other population figures see Maier 1983:32, 124, 135, 171.
37. Connah 1987:16; Fisher 1973:33.

foundation on which the conventions of sanctuary were enforced, provided the conditions on which other forms of authority could accrete and find legitimacy. It was in these latter expressions of authority, and their residual influence, that we find the sanctuary town's longevity.

Krachi's shrine leaders used their greatest asset—the famous and highly respected powers of the Dente oracle—to amass several forms of material and social value, and these gave them the platform on which to retain positions of influence once colonial legal codes were imposed and the population was exposed to the teachings of world religions. Although Dente and other places of refuge lost their customary ability to offer sanctuary, some of them continued as viable communities because of the multiple ways in which they had, over the decades, established and justified their authority. One of the ways of reinforcing that authority, that has not been examined and to which we now turn, was through judicial processes.

Sanctuaries in Judicial Affairs

No endeavor revealed the relations of power and their interdependencies within a community or region better than the judicial role played by sanctuaries. Serving as a court was a logical progression that went from giving people asylum to settling disputes that brought them there. Serving as a court also had a preventive aspect in that helping people reach settlements could prevent them from taking refuge, and by the same token prevent a breakdown in community relations. Within their own communities sanctuary priests acted as a check on the possible excesses of their fellow leaders by giving vulnerable people a way to defend themselves against false accusations, the impetuousness of vengeance, or oppressive circumstances. The sanctuary provided a protective environment where people could find the unfettered time and the space to reach reasoned judgments or to make settlements.

The Dente priest played an active part in judicial matters, and appeared to have acted as a court of last resort. The priest collected fees from those who sought his services. A traveler in the1870s found the reputation of the priest was enhanced because he heard difficult cases that other leaders failed to decide. "[He] is always referred to, to be consulted as oracle of the nation through Odente, and his word is the judgment by which all must abide."[38]

Sanctuaries played the same role in resolving difficult interstate disputes that they did in resolving fractious relations in their own home communities.

---

38. Maier 1983:54–5.

An Ijebu warrior, Adde Sounlou, spent four years as a refugee in a sanctuary town outside his homeland near the end of the eighteenth century after killing a fellow soldier in a fit of anger. He returned to his family after his own father paid the victim's enraged brother a large sum in compensation. Some years later, Adde Sounlou again killed an important person, and again he took refuge outside his homeland where he remained until compensation was paid for the second crime. We know the story of Adde Sounlou because his son was the well-known captive, Osifekunde, who was sold into slavery as a young man and later told his life story to a French ethnographer.[39] Adde Sounlou enjoyed the benefits of being protected beyond the reach of local justice and the security of knowing that his own authorities or his victims' families would not take the risk of challenging the autonomy of another polity in order to recover him and, as Osifekunde believed, kill him in vengeance. Violating the sovereignty of another polity and its deities by retrieving, injuring, or killing an escapee, risked open confrontation. In explaining how lengthy conflict was precipitated between two Igbo communities from 1891 to 1894, two survivors recalled the war that began after a man who was given sanctuary in a neighboring town was killed by agents from his home community. It was an offense of the greatest magnitude.

> [T]he village which harboured the fugitive usually took arms for what they regarded as a violation of their sovereignty, a desecration of their gods and a frontal attack on their integrity as a people. In fact, until such a village had taken some audacious military measures to bring the offending village to book, neighbouring villages continued to view the host village with some disdain and disregard. In short, its integrity in the comity of villages was drastically jeopardised. It was this cultural milieu that made it almost mandatory for the village so treated to go to war against the aggressor.[40]

The conflict reported here was not an isolated event. Harming an individual while he was living in a place of asylum brought about a similar incident in the same Igbo region. In this case a fugitive was wounded by his townsmen while being protected in a neighboring town. His host shot the assailant which precipitated warfare and the death of fourteen people.[41]

Regional safeguards against violent reprisals of this kind were embedded in cooperative needs that developed among states and autonomous villages.

---

39. Curtin 1967:285.
40. Anyanwu 1988:3.
41. Green 1964:62–3.

Again, the Dente shrine served as a court—in this case as an international court—that resolved disputes between states. A missionary who traveled through the area in the 1878 found that there were negative consequences for states that ignored the Dente priest's judgments.

> The priest is a man of consequence in the country because in all hard cases where the kings of these countries fail to decide in judgment, he is always referred to, to be consulted as oracle of the nation through Odente, and his word is the judgment by which all must abide.[42]

The litigants were required to swear by the Dente deity's oath, an oath requiring a fee. Should anyone break that oath, that person would be subject to the condemnation of the deity and pay a heavy fine.[43]

Sanctuaries were effective as a kind of international court of justice because they held regional power relations in check. They provided a place where states could find redress and avoid the kinds of misunderstandings and rigidities that were preludes to more painful forms of conflict. If they failed to perform judicial functions for a region, the absence of such a judicial mechanism could threaten the delicate safeguards that kept one state from encroaching on another's sovereignty. To act as a court, the authority in charge had to be immune from coercive force—a condition of a place of refuge that had already demonstrated its ability to protect others. Regional courts relied on meta-conventions and widespread hegemonic understandings about what was thought to be the common good in order to establish their authority. The very powers that underpinned the legitimacy of the sanctuary in one context, extended outward into the nearby region and provided the leverage that was needed to bring sovereign polities together to benefit their collective interests. As these illustrations reveal, the common good, relied on the kind of legitimating force that was derived from and inextricably tied to supernaturally imbued power–power that was widely seen as inviolable.

Sanctuaries and the Balance of Power

Without the ability to amass and use force, it would seem that a sanctuary encapsulated within a larger political community would be defenseless, unless of course the sanctuary's leader and the community's most powerful authority figure were one and the same. Such was the case with the Dente shrine

---

42. Maier 1983:54–5, 73.
43. *Ibid*, 58.

whose priest throughout most of its pre-colonial history was the most powerful political figure in Krachi. A similar role was played by those who controlled the Elegba shrine in Iworo. It was not the case in places of refuge like the deity houses in Badagry described by Samuel Crowther where town chiefs were more powerful—militarily speaking—than local shrine priests. Sanctuaries such as these existed within an interdependent set of relationships. The exact nature of these relationships differed from place to place. Yet they tell us how sanctuaries were an important ingredient in maintaining balance among centers of power to the extent that rendered them invulnerable.

One of the most pressing questions was how a local sanctuary could remain free of a ruler's control when protecting someone who may have offended him, escaped from him, or violated the rules of the realm. There was no single answer. In the Kingdom of Gonja, which lay to the north of Krachi, the least threatening officials were given the responsibility of providing refuge to those who sought protection from outside or from within the kingdom. Gonja was divided into fifteen divisions, each ruled by a chief who was descended from the same ruling house. The chiefs of large divisions were eligible to compete for the kingship, whereas those of little divisions were not. Yet, the small divisions, with the least powerful chiefs, were sanctuaries for people fleeing the justice of one another and even the king.[44] In this case, the ability to offer protection went to the authority figures who had the least overall power but in the larger scheme of things had the greatest ability to provide refuge without creating resentments that could lead to confrontation or otherwise undermine the stability of the kingdom. However, as the Dente case showed, there was some risk involved in allowing the marginal divisions of a polity to be the places that absorbed large numbers of newcomers, lest they become strong enough to rebel.

By contrast, some sanctuaries were lodged with authority figures who provided, on the surface, the greatest threat to the ruler. In Maradi (a Hausa kingdom), in the mid-nineteenth century, offenders could find sanctuary with the ruler, any of the four nobles who formed his senior council, or his queen mother. The four noblemen could depose the ruler, exercise checks on his power, and remain immune from trial and punishment.[45] This meant, of course, that the loci of power were distributed among the leading officials of the kingdom with no one official or the ruler able to exercise complete authority over another. Full ruling power was not concentrated in a single, centralized office. In the case of Maradi the rights of sanctuary appear to have been

---

44. Goody 1967:188–9.
45. Smith 1967:117.

embedded within a complex set of relationships. As an individual, each no-
bleman was dominant enough within the kingdom to serve as an autonomous
agent and to provide unquestioned protection to those who sought it. But taken
together, each of the primary authority figures acted as a check against the
other, neutralizing a threat that any one of them acting alone might pose.

The use of a powerful woman's residence as a sanctuary brought still another dimension to the way in which relationships among authority figures
were intertwined. Usually these women held the official title of queen mother
or undertook that role in some way. They were the counterparts of rulers and
were entrusted with providing constraints on a king's misuse of power. They
were not necessarily the actual mother of the ruler, but as their designation
implies they acted as mothers and often led the faction that supported and
protected the royal candidate in his struggle to succeed to the kingship. The
office of queen mother acknowledged and rewarded these protective roles and
the ruler's dependence on them for succeeding to office.[46] Among the Bamileke
(Cameroon) and Kanuri (Nigeria) the ability to offer sanctuary was lodged
with queen mothers over whom the king exercised no legal rights, in the former case, or who was granted the right to operate her own separate court, in
the latter case.[47] Queen Mothers in the Ashanti Kingdom were the counterparts of officials at all levels of government and they participated in virtually
all major decision-making councils of the state, exercised priestly functions,
and had the right to administer public admonitions to their male doubles.
They, like queen mothers far to the east in Onitsha (Nigeria),[48] gave refuge to
fugitives from the ruler's court, even in cases where the death penalty was involved.[49]

Queen mothers were, in many respects, an anomaly. They could not succeed to the highest office. They could not replace a king, and they did not
threaten the foundations on which a ruler's powers were lodged. Their authority was derived from the king. They existed because they had protected
the ruler's interests and because they would continue to do so. It was in this
form of protection—protecting a ruler against himself—that the queen
mother demonstrated the qualities that were essential to a polity's stability and
through which she achieved her privileged, autonomous status.

The right to offer sanctuary came in unexpected ways. In the famed Kingdom of Oyo the houses of officials who were designated to die with the Alaafin

---

46. Barnes 1997.
47. Lebeuf 1963:100, 105.
48. Meek 1937:192.
49. Arhin 1983:93.

(king)–to be his attendants in the other world–were sanctuaries. One of them was the *Ona-Olokun-esin* (*Ab'Oka-ku*), master of the horse, who provided refuge to anyone condemned to death if he could escape to his premises. The *Ona-Olokun-esin* was a palace officer and not part of the governing councils that formed the complex system of councils and town chiefs who functioned as checks and balances in the governance of Oyo. Quite the contrary, he was outside them. No official was as unthreatening. No official was as linked to the well-being of the king. The king's interests were his interests. If they king was denounced and found unfit to rule by the councils charged with that determination, ritual suicide by both the king and the *Ona-Olokun-esin* was mandatory. The *Ona-Olokun-esin* lived or died according to the fortunes of the king. As a result he had unrestricted liberty to live as he wished, tempered by the knowledge that, in providing protection to fugitives, he could not go against the interests of any official who could destabilize the status quo.[50]

Sanctuaries were places to which people who were in jeopardy could find some form of respite—something akin to a court of last resort. On one level sanctuaries were part of the judicial apparatus. The people who sought them out were vulnerable, but those who protected them could not be vulnerable, or be seen as vulnerable. The protectors, or protecting bodies, needed some form of autonomy when undertaking their responsibilities—particularly when they acted within the confines of a sovereign state. They maintained their autonomy because they were deeply implicated in the system of checks and balances on which a political community's equilibrium depended. If they were a threat to the ruling authority, they were neutralized by competing interests. If they were not a threat, they protected competing interests from endangering the status quo. As the examples here indicate, sanctuaries that existed within larger political entities were entwined within and contributed to a complex set of interdependent relationships. It was through these relationships that they were able to attain the kind of legitimacy and independence that rendered them independent in absorbing people into the polity or protecting those who were in peril.

Discussion and Conclusion

The practice of giving sanctuary in pre-colonial West Africa was based on the ability of the host to guarantee protection. It involved taking responsibil-

---

50. Johnson 1921:57.

ity for the whole person in return for which refugees dedicated themselves not simply to the well being of the new community but just as importantly to the deity of the host sanctuary. The conditions that made protection possible were grounded in mystical powers—fear of the deity in Iworo, oracular powers in Krachi. Some sanctuaries expanded their abilities to shelter unprotected peoples, and to grow in size and independence, by accumulating additional sources of ritual and material capital—people, agricultural land, and various kinds of revenue. They worked for what was represented as the common good by providing judicial services that helped to defend people and polities against injustice and maintain local and regional peace. Sanctuaries existed and were allowed various degrees of sovereign control because they were integral to the system of political checks and balances that developed in a particular locale.

Missionaries debated whether or not they should provide sanctuary soon after they began arriving in Badagry in 1842 and nearby coastal towns soon thereafter. The Atlantic slave trade was coming to an end. Yet, despite international prohibitions and seaborne blockades some community members remained active in the trade, and missionaries were caught in the dilemma of whether or not to provide refuge to escaped slaves and other vulnerable people.[51] One side argued that missionaries should not turn their premises into sanctuaries and thereby encroach on the sovereignty of local authorities. Another side took the position that missionaries answered to a higher authority than local citizens and were not beholden to local laws particularly the laws of ungodly rulers. It was an academic debate, because the extent to which a mission house was used as a sanctuary varied from place to place and depended on the desire of an individual missionary either to stay within, or in some cases to ignore, local conventions.[52]

As we have seen, the Rev. Annear appeared not to have observed local conventions when, in 1844, he first attempted to make the mission house a place of refuge by finding and harboring a slave. The slave did not run to him to seek refuge. Rather Annear freed the slave after he found him in a canoe in a creek at the corner of his compound. In so doing, Annear challenged the authority of the owner, a chief who had been a friendly neighbor up to that point. It was nothing less than a violation of the chief's sovereignty and integrity—not unlike the Igbo cases that resulted in warfare. It was as though Annear had invaded the chief's own property and thereby impinged on his right to hold a slave. By this action, Annear showed himself to be an outsider

---

51. For example, debtors, accused criminals, indigents, and aged people with no kin.
52. Ajayi, 1965:117–18.

and thus he became the legitimate target of the chief's determination to seek redress.

Six months later, however, Annear acted in accordance with local practice when he accepted and cared for twenty children in his mission house. It was a dangerous time, the children were vulnerable, and they were sent to safety in the mission. Annear showed then that he had the power to address an unjust practice by redeeming a child if he or she were kidnapped, and by taking responsibility for the whole person, as if that person were his own. This gave him a legitimate role in the community. Annear wrote with some pride of this accomplishment, noting that his counterparts from the Church Missionary Society had failed to attract a single child because they did not take children "entirely under their care, and engage to protect them on their own premises."[53]

Thus, Annear had made the mission house an effective sanctuary, operating under local rules. He guarded those who entrusted themselves to the mission house by redeeming—and having the resources to redeem—any one of them, in this case children who were kidnapped. The children were educated by Annear, which meant they were instructed in the ways of the Christian deity who provided the very supernatural foundation on which the mission house existed. In this, the mission kept faith with local practice, for it was obligatory for those who received sanctuary in the places considered here that they serve the host deity.

Annear also followed local conventions by making himself an integral part of the Badagry community. He served as an intermediary between local merchants and the legitimate British trade. Each side depended on Annear's good offices to conduct business. The Badagry chiefs who were favored in this trade were called the "English chiefs," in that they were loyal to ocean-going British merchants. Annear ruefully noted, however, that the chiefs were only English "for the sake of the gain to be obtained by English vessels coming here." For the chiefs, reflecting on Annear in his mediating role, "everything devolves on the Mission."[54]

As colonial rule was established—it was an uneven process—the old balance of power was transformed to favor the new European order, including an interdependent relationship between missions and British authorities. Backed by British force, the mission houses became more powerful, and therefore capable of achieving greater levels of protection. John Peel described this

---

53. S. Annear, S., Letter Extract, June 1, 1845, MMS.
54. *Ibid,* Journal Extract, Nov. 1, 1844.

process through the eyes of early missionaries, serving in and near Badagry, who told us that early Christian adherents came largely from the ranks of slaves, youth, and other low-status individuals. Most of the people who were putting themselves in the hands of the missions, Peel found, were slaves who dedicated themselves to the Christian god through "conversion," and later bought their freedom.[55] As we have seen, the process whereby those who sought refuge and dedicated themselves to the Christian deity was less of a departure from local practice than it might have seemed to missionaries at the time. Further transformations began still later, toward the end of the nineteenth century, when the colonial government outlawed indigenous slavery and introduced new forms of legal redress and protection.

References

Ajayi, J.F. Ade, *Christian Missions in Nigeria 1841–1891: The Making of a New Elite*, London: Longman, 1965.

Anyanwu, Ukachukwu D., "Warfare in Pre-Colonial Igboland: The Case of the Obowo of Imo State, Nigeria," *African Notes*, XII (1 & 2), 1988:1–11.

Arhin, Kwame,"Strangers and Hosts: A Study in "The Political and Military Roles of Akan Women," in *Female and Male in West Africa*, Christine Oppong (ed), London: George Allen & Unwin, 1983, 91–98.

Awolalu, J. Omosade, *Yoruba Beliefs and Sacrificial Rites*, London: Longman, 1979.

Ayandele, E.A., *The Missionary Impact on Modern Nigeria 1842–1914*, New York: Humanities Press, 1966.

Barnes, Sandra T., "Gender and the Politics of Support and Protection in Pre-Colonial West Africa," in *Queens, Queen Mothers, Priestesses and Power: Case Studies in African Gender*, F. Kaplan (ed), New York: *The New York Academy of Sciences*, 1997, 1–18.

Connah, Graham, *African Civilizations*, Cambridge: Cambridge University Press, 1987.

Curtin, Philip D. (ed), *Africa Remembered*, Madison: University of Wisconsin Press, 1967.

Drewal, Margaret T., *Yoruba Ritual: Performers, Play, Agency*, Bloomington: Indiana University Press, 1992.

---

55. Peel 2000:69, 240–43. Ayandele also found very few "non-immigrant freemen" embraced Christianity until late in the 19th century (1966:332–34).

Fisher, Humphrey J., "Conversion Reconsidered: Some Historical Aspects of Religious Conversion in Black Africa," *Africa* 43(1), 1973:27–40.

Goody, Jack, "The Over-Kingdom of Gonja," in *West African Kingdoms in the Nineteenth Century*, D. Forde and P.M. Kaberry (eds), London: Oxford for International African Institute, 1967, pp. 179–205.

Green, M.M., *Ibo Village Affairs*, New York: Praeger, 1964 [1947].

Johnson, Rev. Samuel, *The History of the Yorubas*, Lagos: C.S.S. Bookshops, 1969 [1921].

Lander, Richard L., *Records of Captain Clapperton's Last Expedition to Africa*, Vol. 1, London: Henry Colburn and Richard Bentley, 1830.

Lebeuf, Annie M.D., "The Role of Women in the Political Organization of African Societies," in *Women of Tropical Africa*, D. Paulme (ed), Berkeley: University of California Press, 1963, 93–119.

Maier, D.J.E., *Priests and Power: The Case of the Dente Shrine in Nineteenth-Century Ghana*, Bloomington: Indiana University Press, 1983.

Meek, C.K., *Law and Authority in a Nigerian Tribe*, Atlantic Highlands, N.J.: Humanities Press, 1980 [1937].

Oguntomisin, G.O. and Toyin Falola, "Refugees in Yorubaland in the Nineteenth Century," *Asian and African Studies*, 21, 1987:165–85.

Parker, John, *Making the Town: Ga State and Society in Early Colonial Accra* Portsmouth, NH: Heinemann, 2000.

Peel. J.D.Y., *Religious Encounter and the Making of the Yoruba*, Bloomington: Indiana University Press, 2000.

Smith, M.G., "A Hausa Kingdom: Maradi under Dan Baskore, 1854–75," in *West African Kingdoms in the Nineteenth Century*, D. Forde and P.M. Kaberry (eds), London: Oxford for International African Institute, 1967, 93–122.

Wood, Rev. J. Buckley, *Historical Notices of Lagos, West Africa and on the Inhabitants of Lagos: Their Character, Pursuits, and Languages*, Lagos: CMS Bookshop, 1933 [1881].

PART C
MEDIA, POLITICS, AND NATIONALISM

CHAPTER 9

TRANSLATION, PUBLICS, AND THE VERNACULAR PRESS IN 1920S LAGOS

Karin Barber

There was an explosion of Yoruba-language newspapers in 1920s Lagos. At the beginning of the decade, the only periodical offering reading material in Yoruba was the long-running Christian Missionary Society fortnightly *In Leisure Hours*. By the end of the decade, Lagos readers had seen the arrival of *Eko Akete* (founded in 1922), *Eleti Ofe* (1923), *Iwe Irohin Osose* (1925), *Eko Igbehin* (1926), and *Akede Eko* (1928). Some of these papers were short-lived, but *Akede Eko* became a well- established feature of Lagos urban life, was distributed to other cities, and continued to be published until 1953. Unlike *In Leisure Hours*, these papers were not produced by missionary organizations but by prominent private individuals among the Lagos professional elite.[1]

This efflorescence of Yoruba-language journalism has been explained as a "response to a revival of cultural nationalism" (Omu 1978:58), expressed as a "growing interest in Yoruba language and literature" (ibid:31–2). In this view, it was a renewal of the much better-documented movement which had taken shape in Lagos in the 1880s and 90s among the elite, but which, as John Peel

---

1. Ibadan saw a parallel development with the establishment of *Irohin Yoruba/The Yoruba News* in 1924, with the difference that this paper was published by an association rather than a private individual: the Egbe Agba-'O-Tan, which was founded in 1914 for the express purpose of promoting the study of Yoruba culture and traditions (see Adeboye 1996:150). Among the Lagos editors, Adeoye Deniga, the owner-editor of *Eko Akete* , worked in the Post Office and as a teacher before turning to full-time journalism; I.B. Thomas, owner-editor of *Akede Eko*, was a schoolmaster and later a salesman and cashier for a mercantile house. See Omu 1978 for further details.

has persuasively argued, had both its roots and much of its continuing impetus in the Christian missions' project of inculturation (Peel 2000:288–95; see also Law 1996). The 1920s newspapers were certainly closely associated with the development of a Yoruba tradition of written poetry and fiction—that centerpiece of cultural nationalism—which had been repeatedly called for in the nineteenth-century Lagos press, but which only really began to take shape in the twentieth century. [2] The 1920s newspapers' intimate, sociable pages provided a space in which new literary styles and genres could be tried out, emulated, and developed in response to a constant flow of readers' letters. Out of this environment came what has been described as "the first known attempt in Yoruba creative writing" (Ogunsina 1992:13), the serialized story of an orphan girl in E.A. Akintan's paper *Eleti Ofe*.[3] It was followed by I.B. Thomas's *Itan Emi Segilola*, generally regarded as the first true Yoruba novel, which began life as a series of fictional letters to the editor of *Akede Eko*, Thomas himself. This epistolary confessional narrative, written in the persona of a Lagos prostitute, drew on the urban slang and popular memories of Lagos life.[4] More generally, the Lagos papers contributed to the creation of a literary culture by publishing a stream of articles on social and political events, local history, shipping news, legal cases and market movements which helped to establish and publicise written Yoruba as a medium through which private

---

2. However, an important earlier effort to record and publish indigenous poetry was E.M. Lijadu's 1886 collection of the poems of Aribiloso, an Egba popular oral poet of the early 19th century, the texts of which Lijadu retrieved and wrote down from the oral memories of Egba elders. Lijadu also did research on Ifa, and published two books which presented numerous Ifa verses to support a theological discussion about the similarities and differences between Yoruba religious ideas and Christianity. The most influential early literate poet was another Egba, Sobo Arobiodu (J.S. Sowande), who published ten volumes of poetry between 1902 and 1936, and whose style of writing was imitated by poets publishing in the 1920s Yoruba-English press (see for example the poem published in *Eleti Ofe*, 29 October 1924, announced as being "in the voice of" Sobo Arobiodu).

3. Falola (1988) mentions an earlier work, *Dolapo Asewo Omo Asewo* (Dolapo the prostitute, daughter of a prostitute) published in the 1890s by an anonymous author. He describes it as "an obscene romantic fiction"; his summary of the plot suggests that it might have been a model for I.B. Thomas's *Itan Emi Segilola*. However it passed into oblivion, and does not figure in Ogunsina's history of the Yoruba novel.

4. In Ibadan, the editor of the bilingual *Yoruba News*, D.A. obasa, was not only an assiduous collector of oral poetic genres, but also one of the first modern Yoruba literate poets (Nnodim 2002). It was in the sociable forum provided by the newspaper that he first tried out the supple, colloquial poetic style for which he is famous. He published three volumes of poems between 1927 and 1945, some of which had previously been published in *The Yoruba News*. Not only did he reserve space for the publication of poetry in this paper, he also wrote some of his editorials in poetic form.

and public life in all its aspects could be conducted, recorded and discussed. The fluent, everyday Yoruba of the newspapers and the social realism of the fiction they published helped to channel a third linguistic stream into written Yoruba literature, the first two streams being oral traditions on the one hand, and the Yoruba Bible—the cadences of which can be heard rolling through the novels of D.O. Fagunwa—with associated liturgical, devotional and educational texts, on the other.[5] The colloquial, realistic strand eventually triumphed in the fiction of the 1960s onwards, blending into itself the resources of oral traditions and Biblical allusion; the result has been one of the most extensive and most remarkable of African-language written literary traditions anywhere in the continent.

But what has not been discussed in the existing rather sparse commentary on the 1920s press is their most striking feature. They were not in fact Yoruba newspapers at all. They were bilingual. They contained sections in English, the nature, extent and positioning of which varied over time and from paper to paper. And this was also true of their two main predecessors which served as their models:[6] the pioneering *Iwe Irohin* published by the CMS mission at Abeokuta from 1859 to 1867, and the *Iwe Irohin Eko* published by Andrew Thomas in Lagos from 1888 to 1892.[7] In none of these publications was the relationship between the English and Yoruba sections that of a mirror image. Some things were said in one language, other things in the other. Even when the "same" piece appeared in both Yoruba and English, it was as if two parallel and independent texts had been generated. There were many things in the Yoruba texts which were withheld from, or simply did not cross into, the English version. The newspapers thus drew attention to the way that Yoruba co-existed in an intimate and yet reticent and detached proximity to English among the early educated elite.

This essay is a very preliminary and provisional look at the 1920s Lagos Yoruba-English newspapers in relation to their predecessors. My tentative ar-

---

5. The most important of these were produced by the CMS: *Ilosiwaju Ero Mimo*, which was the Yoruba translation of *The Pilgrim's Progress*, and *Iwe Kika 1–5*, a series of school readers, written by various hands, which was used from the 1870s well into the 1940s and is fondly remembered today. Their importance as a linguistic and poetic substratum of Yoruba written literature can hardly be overestimated: see Nnodim 2002.

6. The 1920s newspaper owners and editors were clearly aware of *Iwe Irohin Eko*. Not only did they use a similar format and layout, but *Akede Eko* reprinted a macaronic poem, "A beggar's Cry at Lagos/Ebun mi nitori ti Olorun Oluwa" (May 7, 1932), that had first appeared in *Iwe Irohin Eko* (February 16, 1889).

7. There was one "purely vernacular bi-weekly organ", *Iwe Eko*, published by the CMS in 1891, but it expired the same year (Omu 1978:256).

gument is the following. "Cultural nationalism," as an explanation of the Yoruba-English papers' production, only goes so far. The idea of a great vernacular literature as the centerpiece of Yoruba national advancement was a paradigm remarkable for its longevity and stability. The 1920s newspapers certainly drew on it, as did their predecessors and successors, for nearly 150 years. But what they were *doing* in appealing to this paradigm underwent dramatic historical changes. The point of using Yoruba, in double harness with English, changed. This can best be understood in terms of the audiences the bilingual papers implicitly addressed. The overlapping audiences addressed by the *Iwe Irohin* of 1859–67 were not the same as those addressed by *Iwe Irohin Eko* of 1888–92; and an even more remarkable shift occurred in the flurry of 1920s papers. In addressing new configurations of implied readers, the papers helped to constitute new publics and consolidate a sense of what they had in common. This approach allows us to focus on the significance of the relationship between the two languages the papers deploy—the question of what is and is not translated, and how and why parallel discourses co-exist. Bilingual papers convened at least two publics simultaneously—and, in fact, I think that all the papers, from the *Iwe Irohin* of 1859–67 to *Akede Eko* of 1928–53, can be shown to have been addressing more than two—partly overlapping, partly nested within each other, and partly independent. These implicit publics were convened for a purpose. Derek Peterson, in a recent study set in colonial Kenya, has shown how translation, record-keeping, and other kinds of everyday writing in Gikuyu were strategies by which innovators recruited people into new kinds of community, "crystallized a vision of the future…and got people acting in new ways." (Peterson 2004: 242) Similarly, by the horizons of readership evoked in each language, the Yoruba-English papers implicitly constituted a new potential community or communities; and by containing texts addressed to different linguistic audiences within the pages of a single publication, they implied that different sections of the population could potentially be brought into new collective relationships.

Cultural nationalism, from this point view, emerges as protean in its adaptability to different contexts. The focus on publics provides clues to how—and why—the nineteenth century elite's vision of a Yoruba national cultural identity was projected and disseminated outward into the hinterland of warring polities, while the 1920s elite's version of it was projected downward into the Lagos popular masses. Finally, attention to the relations between the two languages in these newspapers further suggests that the construction of Yoruba identity was never a one-way process. The educated elite were well aware that their project of reclaiming vernacular resources and turning them into monuments of civilisation depended on their ability to tap into existing popular and oral traditions whose custodians were not themselves but the indigenes, the pagans, the illiterates and the common people.

The Paradigm of
Language-Literature-Culture-Nation

A "Yoruba literature" lies at the centre of an enduring vision of a Yoruba nation. The term "literature" was originally intended in its broadest sense, and most of the important Yoruba-language publications of the late nineteenth and early twentieth century were works of historiography (for details, see Doortmont 1994, Falola 1999). But the frequent calls in the nineteenth-century Lagos press for literary monuments capable of standing alongside Shakespeare, Longfellow and Homer suggest that a place had been prepared in their scheme of things for literature in the sense of creative writing. These calls were repeated throughout the twentieth century.

In this paradigm, language, literature, custom and nation are seen as an indissoluble circle. Language is the repository and expression of a people's entire way of life; literature is the finest crystallization and conservator of good language; and no nation can be regarded as mature unless it has great works of literature to stand alongside those of the advanced nations. Elements of this paradigm were in place as early as 1855, when Samuel Crowther junior wrote "we doubt not that in proportion as literature thrives among the Egbas and Yorubas, men will not be wanting to come forth with their talents and embellish the pages of African history." (quoted in Peel, 2000:289) After the 1882 Education Ordinance in Lagos, which supported English-language education at the expense of Yoruba (Awoniyi 1978, Law 1996), an articulate pro-Yoruba faction emerged in the Lagos press which called for the study of indigenous verbal arts as the basis for a "national" Yoruba literature. A letter to the *Lagos Observer* decried "the habit of disregarding and ignoring, and, in some cases, totally crying down our Native Language. That a country should rise with a literature entirely foreign almost assumes, to me, the form of an impossibility...." And the sought-for Yoruba national literature is to be found in traditions of the hinterland kingdoms—in the "beauty and poetical embellishments" of the legends of Ile Ife, which stand comparison with the legends of Troy; and in the oratory "delivered in the House of Ogboni at Abeokuta" which is the equal of that of Demosthenes and Cicero.[8] Forty-five years later, in 1927,

---

8. Letter from "Veritas" to *The Lagos Observer*, June 1, 1882.

D.A. Obasa, editor of the *Yoruba News*, in the same vein urged the importance of collecting and preserving from oblivion all the many genres of Yoruba oral poetry, arguing that they stand comparison with the poetry studied in school "such as that of 'Homer', 'Longfellow', 'Shakespeare' and so on." (quoted in Nnodim 2002:165) In 1959, on the eve of Nigerian independence, the author of a Yoruba examination guide for secondary schools states that "Yoruba, as a living and growing language of a new nation just rising to fame in the modern world, needs to be properly developed," (Babajamu 1959:19) and that a vernacular literature drawing on indigenous traditions and local life must be created to stand beside the works of Shakespeare, Shaw, Milton, Pope, Dickens, Chaucer and Swift, so that Yoruba can "become one of the classical languages in the world." (ibid.:240; see also Barber 1997)

The vocabulary hardly changes, though the definition of the "nation" does undergo quiet modification. What is being outlined is a project for the simultaneous development of literature, language, culture, and nation through studying and preserving past traditions, and drawing on them to produce great works of written literature. And it is not at all surprising that a modernizing elite should place such emphasis on the creation of a written vernacular literature, for this is a domain in which oral traditions can simultaneously be recuperated and reformed; a domain in which oral genres can be valued as "literary heritage" without necessarily requiring assent to all their social and religious implications; and a domain in which the project of preservation is inseparable from the project of building for the future. (see Barber 1997, 2000)

Changing Publics

Let us look briefly at how the Yoruba-English Lagos press shifted its horizon of address in the nineteenth century.

The first bilingual paper was the CMS monthly *Iwe Irohin fun awon ara Egba ati Yoruba* (Newspaper for the Egba and Yoruba people), published in Abeokuta from 1859 to 1867. It was mainly written in English by the CMS missionary Henry Townsend, and translated by the mission's Saro agents. The Saro—bicultural and usually bilingual descendants of Yoruba re-captives, who from 1839 onwards had enterprisingly made their way back to Yoruba-speaking cities from Sierra Leone—played a crucial role in the establishment of early Yoruba print culture and the growth of modern linguistic-ethnic Yoruba identity. The intellectual and social context in which this process took place has been superbly and comprehensively treated in J.D.Y. Peel's *Religious Encounter and the Making of the Yoruba*, to which all future scholarship in the area will be indebted.

Those among the Saro who were literate and Christian provided the CMS with its first translators and printers in Abeokuta in the 1840s and 50s—and also with its first audience. This was, in due course, expanded by local Egba converts, equipped by the mission with basic vernacular literacy. Beyond them was a larger community, the traditional Egba polity and its chiefs with whom the mission worked. The imagined "nation" for this newspaper was in the first instance the Egba, not the "Yoruba" as a whole, a concept which had barely begun to be formed; the word "Yoruba" still kept its older meaning of the Oyo people, rather than the amalgamation of political, dialectal and regional groupings now identified by the name. Thus a layered Egba collectivity— made up of the Egba Saro, Egba local converts, and by extension the Egba "nation"—was the newspaper's most immediate audience.[9] The Yoruba language section carried international news items, in keeping with Townsend's stated aim to interest Africans in events "outside the narrow circle of their own country" [i.e. the Egba country].[10] It also carried detailed, pro-Egba reports of local political and military developments. It provided spiritual nourishment for its congregation in the form of *eko* (lessons or moral parables) and a serialized translation of *The Pilgrim's Progress*.

In March 1860 an English *Appendix* was added, and in January 1866 the *Appendix* began to be published as a separate edition. The *Appendix* contained many of the same items (not surprisingly, since the text was originally written in English) but also included pieces that did not appear in the Yoruba version. These give a glimpse of a radically different public. One is a poem "to the honour and memory of President Lincoln" by "A Negro" (July 10, 1863), and another is a poem on "Slaveships" (August 22, 1863). There were also frequent references to Lagos and Freetown as natural components of the paper's constituency: for example, an article in October 1863 which reported that "There are two Debating clubs in Sierra Leone and one at Lagos all commenced within the last six months..." News of CMS missionaries' health and movements was reported, and extracts from the journals of Native Teachers were also sometimes included. Here the audience appears to be the coastal

---

9. However, the language in which it was written looks like early "standard Yoruba" rather than pure Egba. "Standard Yoruba" , pioneered by the CMS, was initially based on a combination of Egba and Oyo linguistic varieties, strongly influenced by English (see Fagborun 1994). Thus the potential to address a pan-Yoruba audience was already being laid down, well before most of the readership was ready to identify with any such category. However, more work on *Iwe Irohin* is needed to confirm this point.

10. Townsend to Venn, quoted in Brown (1964:273). A similar statement, from a CMS printed circular, is quoted by Kopytoff (1965:121).

community of Saro re-captives and liberated slaves, with their experience of the Americas and the Caribbean, their base in Freetown (where the West African operations of the CMS had their headquarters), and their orientation towards a wider black diaspora. According to Peel, it was with this coastal and diasporic "Christian bourgeoisie" (Peel 2000:280) that the educated elite of Abeokuta and Lagos identified most strongly – a *racial* category to which the cultural nationalists later added *cultural* content by reaching into "the rich culture and historical experience that could give it substance, their own Yoruba." (Peel 2000:282) The bilingualism of *Iwe Irohin* at Abeokuta may have played a preparatory part in this historical conjuncture—not only by bringing English (the shared language of the coastal and diasporic "bourgeoisie"), into conjunction with Yoruba (a version of the language of the indigenous independent polity), but also by *addressing* these constituencies from within the pages of a single (even though split) organ. And this address may often have reached its distant as well as its local target. *Iwe Irohin* had an eager readership in Lagos (Brown 1964:272–3), and communications between Abeokuta, Lagos, Badagry, and Freetown were so rapid, even in the 1850s, (see Brown 1964:98 for several telling examples) that the paper and oral versions of some of its news may well have circulated widely among the Anglophone Christian coastal population.

At this point, then, and in this missionary publication, the use of the Yoruba language was still mainly a means of evangelization and a means to constitute a Christian, book-reading community around the mission station. The co-presence of the English and Yoruba languages was made possible in the first place by the mission station's core work of translation and the production of local-language religious texts. Simultaneously immersed in local Egba affairs which could only be conducted through command of the local language, and participating in much wider but shallower diasporic and missionary constituencies in which many participants spoke limited or no Yoruba, the writers of the *Iwe Irohin* seem to have been convening a compound public, no layer of which was reducible or subsumable into the others.

The *Iwe Irohin Eko* in 1888 was launched into a very different environment. Lagos in the 1880s and 90s was, as many studies have emphasized, a heterogeneous, stratified, and highly compartmentalized society. The white administrators and merchants; the Saro professionals, merchants and clergy; the Amaro or Aguda artisans and traders (descendants of slaves repatriated from Brazil and, by extension, Cuba); and the indigenous Lagosians, their numbers swollen by large numbers of Yoruba-speaking immigrants from the hinterland, formed four segments separated spatially and socially. There was also a growing mass of immigrants from non-Yoruba-speaking areas. The Saro elite had minimal interaction with the indigenous inhabitants of Lagos, with whom they rarely had kinship links. In commerce, they were competitors. They had no political motive to engage with the discredited and impoverished Lagos chieftaincy. (Cole 1975:23) Popular Lagosian resistance to British rule took the form of obstructing every scheme for urban "improvement" introduced by the government and supported by the Saro.[11] The Lagos indigenes were predominantly pagan and Muslim, and few were literate. The Saro often preferred to speak English or Sierra Leonean "patois" rather than the Yoruba of the indigenes, (Brown 1964:204) and developed an elaborate Anglophone cultural life which advertised their exclusiveness. Several studies have emphasized the distance and mutual contempt obtaining between the Saro and the "natives." (Echeruo 1977, Brown 1964, Cole 1975)

The Saro elite's links were rather with their kin in the inland kingdoms to which they traced their origin—the Oyo, Egba, Ijesa, Ijebu, and others—through whom alone they could establish functioning trading networks. The interior wars, which had entered a new phase of stalemate in the 1880s, were a matter of intense interest and concern to them, as powerful kingdoms took it in turns to block the trade routes or harass each others' trading partners. Some of the Saro went in person to help the rulers of their ancestral polity negotiate peace; others facilitated the supply of arms to their hinterland contacts. In Lagos, the Saro divided into factions according to their hinterland affiliations, and established clubs in which Saro, Amaro and immigrants from the same polity would have at least limited interaction.

This is the context in which the second Yoruba-English newspaper was founded, more than twenty years after the CMS *Iwe Irohin* ceased publication following the expulsion of the missionaries from Abeokuta in 1867. The new paper was not a missionary organ, and had a general Christian rather than specifically denominational orientation. (Its first issue promised to report even-handedly the affairs of Muslims, pagans, and Christians, but in fact only church events received much coverage.) Founded, edited and published by Andrew Thomas, a Saro printer, the paper first appeared on November 3, 1888, and ran fortnightly until 1892. It was in Yoruba with an English section at the back. Its full title was *Iwe Irohin Eko ati ti Gbogbo Ile Yoruba ati Ilu Miran* (The newspaper of Lagos and of all of Yorubaland and other cities/countries).

The public envisaged by the Yoruba sections of the paper was made clear in its opening editorial. The newspaper was intended

---

11. Projects to widen roads, improve sanitation, regulate weights and measures, improve the water supply and introduce alcohol licensing were all aborted because of the local people's resistance (Brown 1964:33, 292, 320–1).

fun gbogbo orilẹ-ede awa enia dudu ti nso ede Yoruba lati fi ko gbogbo ihin ilẹ wa pọ, iba ṣe ti Ẹgba, Ijẹbu, Ijẹṣa, Ọyọ, Ibadan, Idọkọ, Ẹfọn, Iyagba, ati gbogbo oniruru ẹya enia dudu ti o wa ni ilẹ yi ati ni ilu miran. Inu wa yio dun, a o si dupẹ gidigidi, bi ija ẹya, pe emi ni Idọkọ, emi ni Ijẹṣa, emi ni Ọyọ, ati iru ohun ba wọnni ti o ti nba ilẹ wa jẹ ba le parẹ li arin wa. Nigbana ni a le jumọ ṣiṣẹ rere fun anfani ilu ati orilẹ-ede wa.

for the whole country [or, all the countries] of us black people who speak the Yoruba language in order to gather the news of our land together, whether it is that of the Egba, the Ijebu, the Ijesa, the Oyo, the Ibadan, the Idoko, the Efon, the Iyagba, and all the other different African tribes[12] that exist in this land and in other places. We will be happy, and thankful, if tribal wars, [based on the idea] that "I am Idoko, I am Ijesa, I am Oyo" and so on, which are destroying our country, could disappear amongst us. Only then will we be able to work together for the good of our city and nation.

Here was "the cultural work of Yoruba ethnogenesis" (Peel 1989) at its clearest. The project was to unite the peoples of the independent hinterland polities, and to contribute to the advancement of a new entity, the *orile-ede*—literally "the place of origin defined by language," that is, the country or nation of the Yoruba. Note how the writer (almost certainly Andrew Thomas himself) harnesses the linguistic potential of his medium. Yoruba nouns do not have distinct singular and plural forms, and this means that "Gbogbo orile ede awa enia dudu ti nso ede Yoruba" could be taken to mean "the whole nation/country of us black people who speak Yoruba" – proclaiming the new entity as a fait accompli; or it could be taken to mean "all the countries/nations of us black people who speak Yoruba", referring to the Egba, Ijebu, Ijesa and so on, listed in the next sentence. Is Thomas collecting and synthesising news from these different areas because they are already part of a single nation, or in order to constitute them as such? The text does not specify, but the ambiguity suggests that the work of "ethnogenesis" might have been understood as the realisation of a potentiality for unity already built into the warring kingdoms, which were already, ideally, one in their multiplicity (see also Law, 1996).

---

12. *Eya*: a division, section, branch; *enia dudu*: black people. The use in my translation of the word "tribes" is indicated by the English section of the same issue of the paper, which refers to the need to overcome "tribal jealousies and suicidal distinctions now existing amongst us by which we are distinguishing ourselves as Oyos, Jebu, Egbas, Jeshas &c &c". For an illuminating discussion of the history of this term in relation to Yoruba subgroups see Law (1996).

The newspaper was, in the first instance, calling on the Lagos Saro to unite amongst themselves, and thus to promote peace in the interior, for the Saro had "an exaggerated opinion of their own ability to affect the course" of the interior war. (Cole 1975:63) By extension, the implied audience further included Lagosian immigrants from hinterland polities and the rulers and influential men in the interior, some of whom followed the Lagos press closely and used it to promote their interests. (Cole 1975:83)

Here, then, Yoruba was used to construct an umbrella under which the divided and disparate indigenous "nations" could shelter—it was a medium in which they could recognize what they had in common. The mutual intelligibility of their languages was certainly the most effective, and perhaps the only credible, common denominator amongst them. Following the establishment of a Yoruba koiné, these linguistic varieties could be recognized as dialects of a single language, even before the label "Yoruba" had been generally accepted as a name for it. Unlike the customs, laws, or religious ideas also hopefully proposed as common pan-Yoruba patrimony, a common form of the language—not wholly indigenous to any one of the Yoruba "tribes"—was already in circulation. By writing in the standardised form of Yoruba established by the missionary press, Andrew Thomas put on display the most potent insignia of the new "nation". The public addressed in Yoruba was thus envisaged as stretching out horizontally from the capital to the hinterland.

While the news and legal reports appeared in English as well as Yoruba in this paper, there were many items that appeared only in Yoruba. Among them was a series of articles entitled *"Die ninu ise iyanu ile wa"* (A few of the marvels in our country) which covered topics like traditional trading and judicial practices, wood-carving, and "born-to-die" children. There was also a history of the Oba Adenle, spread out over several instalments. Here, then, it seems that the main agenda is carried out by the Yoruba sections. By simultaneously writing in English, Thomas kept a foothold in the established Lagos Anglophone print culture and buttonholed the Anglicized Saro who were his most immediate audience, since they, in their own estimation, were the ones who could solve the problems of the interior and promote the creation of a unified Yoruba nation.

The 1920s Papers and the Lagos Lower Classes

By the 1920s the orientation of the Saro elite had undergone a marked shift. With the piecemeal incorporation and unification of the hinterland and the introduction of the institutions of indirect rule, the traditional chiefs of Lagos became more influential with the colonial government than formerly, partially displacing the Saro. At the same time the indigenes' resistance to colonial policies became more vocal and better organized, and sections of the Saro elite began to collaborate with them (Cole 1975:73–104). A series of public protests in 1908–9 and again in 1915–16 over the proposed water rate involved not only a coalition of traditional and educated elites, but a mass mobilization of ordinary people. There was a march of 10,000 people on Government House in 1908, a women's demonstration involving the closure of all markets in 1909, crowds of up to 18,000 gathering at the court house in 1916 to demand the release of two Muslims arrested for non-payment of the water rate, and rioting when the police attempted to disperse them. (Okonkwo 1995)

Then, in the early 1920s, two things happened simultaneously to precipitate an upsurge of press activity. The first was the Esugbayi Eleko affair. The traditional ruler of Lagos, the Eleko, was already known for his forthright opposition to the colonial government. In 1920 matters came to a head when he became involved in a dispute among two factions of the Lagos Muslim congregation. The governor withdrew recognition from him, without actually deposing him, and the case became the centre of a political storm. In 1925 he was deposed and deported, and two more Eleko reigned before the pro-Esugbayi faction managed to get him reinstated in 1931. The existing radical and conservative factions among the Saro lined up for and against Esugbayi, and launched intense and protracted campaigns through the press. (Cole 1975; Baker 1974)

The second factor was the introduction of a limited franchise in 1922. Although the property qualification was steep, Herbert Macaulay established a dominant electoral position for himself and his party, the NNDP, by wooing the Lagos population, section by section, association by association, until the traditional chiefs, the market women, and the trade guilds all supported him and could be mobilized in popular campaigns. (Cole 1975:138–9) The need to recruit support among the mass of ordinary Lagosians was matched by a pervasive Saro alarm at the new capacity of the population to act as an organized and articulate mob. Rapid expansion of the education system in the 1920s meant that there was a growing class of disgruntled would-be white collar workers unable to find the jobs their education fitted them for. These people, with primary education that made them literate in Yoruba, but usually not in English, provided a potential new public for the Yoruba-English press. In this context, Saro rediscovery of "native custom," through such practices as the adoption of traditional forms of marriage and the staging of traditional dances, provided the educated elite with "a means of identifying with their new followers, the Yoruba masses." (Mann 1985:74) This symbolic statement of common Yorubaness was a means of consolidating the alliance.

The Yoruba-English press came back to life in an atmosphere of feverish lobbying and campaigning. According to Cole, the Esugbayi Eleko affair stimulated "a spectacular explosion of vernacular literature" which included songs, dances and "native plays," as well as the newspapers and pamphlets explaining the complicated legal issues raised by the case. (Cole 1975:156) The first of the new bilingual papers, *Eko Akete*, founded in July 1922, stated that its purpose was not only to "further the improvement of our own literature" (a familiar, enduring cultural nationalist aim, as we have seen), but also "to inform those who do not understand English of what is going on." And what was going on was political mobilization, court cases and petitions. Certainly, *Eko Akete*'s effort was a success. An editorial by Adeoye Deniga noted gleefully, only two months after the paper's inauguration, that the *Nigerian Pioneer*, hitherto an all-English publication, had now started including sections in Yoruba.

ẸHIN NI ỌMỌ ADIẸ NTỌ 'YA RẸ

A ri i pe ọkan ninu iwe-irohin wa Nigerian Pioneer ti o ti ntẹ Iwe-irohin rẹ ni ede Gẹsi lati ọdun kẹsan ti o ti bere si isẹ yi, nsin wa jẹ ni-sisiyi lati ma tẹ apakan iwe-irohin rẹ ni ede wa.

A dupẹ fun irufẹ jijowu-ẹyẹ bayi, irufẹ nkan bayi ni awọn Oyinbo npe ni Ṣiṣe-afi-ara we ẹni jẹ pipọn oluwa rẹ (Imitation is the sincerest form of flattery) a si ni irufẹ owe yi ni ede wa bayi pe Jijọ lo jọ, ọsupa ko le jọ 'san, tabi Omọde yi jọ ọmọ-jokun jijọ lo jọ on kọ!!! (September 9, 1922, p. 2)

THE CHICK FOLLOWS BEHIND ITS MOTHER

We note that one of our newspapers, the Nigerian Pioneer, which has been published in English since it started nine years ago, is now copying us and publishing one section in our own language.

We give thanks for this kind of emulation, it's this kind of thing that the English call "Imitation is the sincerest form of flattery", and we have a similar proverb in our language which says "It resembles it, but the moon cannot be the equal of the daylight" or "This child resembles *omo-jokun*,[13] he resembles it but he is not it!!!"

---

13. I am unable to translate this word. I am grateful to Dr Akin Oyetade for his suggestion that it may have been a misprint for "Omo-lokun", a Yoruba folktale character. Omo-lokun was a spoilt child whose excessive greed ended up killing his doting parents.

Note how Deniga casts the well-established *Nigerian Pioneer* as his own fledg-ling paper's junior, and demonstrates the superiority of the Yoruba language by first quoting an English saying, then translating it, then capping it with two Yoruba ones whose implications go well beyond "Imitation is the sincerest form of flattery," and make the bolder claim that the *Nigerian Pioneer* cannot possibly, in the nature of things, hope to match *Eko Akete*.

The *Nigerian Pioneer* was the creation of Sir Kitoyi Ajasa, the arch-conserva-tive, pro-British Saro lawyer described by one scholar as "probably the most cel-ebrated 'Black Englishman' of his time." (Omu 1978:45) His motives in includ-ing sections in Yoruba were far from being a sudden conversion to Yoruba cultural nationalism. The *Nigerian Pioneer* remained very much the voice of the Anglophile friends of the colonial government; it continued to give pride of place to its "London letter," "Government House news," and "Reuter's Telegrams." For diversion it included Kiplingesque English rhymed poems of exhortation, and, at one period, a historical series of "Love dramas of the peerage" set in England and Ireland. Its editorials remained cool and suspicious towards enthusiasts of Yoruba language and culture, taking the view that young people need a thor-ough grounding in the European classics before exposing themselves to the du-bious influences of Yoruba indigenous traditions. Nonetheless, in 1923 and 1924 it featured long, accurate translations of key statements arising from the power contest between the conservatives (Kitoyi Ajasa, Henry Carr) and the radicals (Herbert Macaulay, J. Egerton Shyngle, E.O. Moore) whose mutual hostility came to a head during the campaigns triggered by the Esugbayi Eleko affair.[14]

It is clear that Ajasa was rattled by the success of the Yoruba-language press in reaching a new, potentially dangerous public. As well as attempting to counter this with its own Yoruba-language version of events, the *Nigerian Pi-oneer* made frequent, lengthy attacks on the bilingual newspapers for what was

---

14. The key text came on January 12, 1923 when the paper triumphantly announced that the "monster petition" demanding the restoration of government recognition to the Eleko had been rejected by Governor Hugh Clifford. Clifford's reply is published on one side of the page, with an accurate Yoruba translation facing it. On January 19, the text of the monster petition itself is given in Yoruba translation, without the English version which presumably had already been published. The February 16 and 23 issues each published a Yoruba-language letter to the editor from "Otito Koro" [Truth is Bitter], criticising the new Yoruba newspaper *Eleti Ofe* for taking Macaulay's side in the Esugbayi Eleko affair. On July 20 a sermon preached to mark the 30th anniversary of Bishop Oluwole's consecration was published in Yoruba. On May 2 1924, a half column presents a translation of an excerpt from the Journal of the European Civil Service Association in which unfavourable com-mentary is made on the Macaulay party's campaign for Africanisation of civil service posts and its attack on Henry Carr.

depicted as their irresponsible rabble-rousing. "The gullible that could not read in foreign language and would not believe if read to them...would believe only if they could read in the tongue they all understood...The unfortunate tendency is to play up to the mass—to the majority, not knowing that...the voice of the majority is sometimes the voice of the devil itself." (June 27, 1924) The best thing for the bilingual papers to do, in Ajasa's opinion, was simply to cease publication. It was exasperation and fear of the power of the Yoruba medium that drove the *Nigerian Pioneer* to acts of translation. It was provoked into this uncharacteristic exercise not by the opposition's uplifting cultural nationalist sentiments but by its capacity to use Yoruba for astute, targeted and focused political mobilization among the common people of Lagos, which had to be countered. After the Esugbayi Eleko crisis and the initial flurry of electioneering had passed, the *Nigerian Pioneer* no longer included Yoruba translations.

The public being addressed in Yoruba was now a Lagosian public of the lower class. *Eko Igbehin* took this to the point of identifying with them in its motto: "*Fun Olorun, Fun Oba, ati awa mekunnu.*" (For God, For the Oba, and us manual workers). These Christian elite papers sought to align the Muslim and pagan majority in a political struggle, by informing them of on-going events, attacking political opponents, praising their own side's leaders and allies, and offering historical background to the current situation. The use of the Yoruba language at this juncture, then, represents the elites' attempt to widen their constituency by going down the social scale.

The concern with the class connotations of Yoruba as a medium of public communication is made explicit in a "Letter to the editor" in *Eko Akete* of January 1925. The letter begins in a familiar enough vein, that of moderate cultural nationalism, observing that many people go to school in order to learn English, which is fine, and useful in business—but it is madness to learn all kinds of foreign languages and remain ignorant of one's own; the youth of Lagos who boast that they only speak English are making a big mistake; they should make the effort to learn Yoruba. But then the writer shifts his argument. Knowing English is no longer a guarantee of a job. Young people should learn both Yoruba and English so that they will be prepared for any type of work. There are a lot of openings in manual labour, for smiths, carvers, tailors, builders, washermen, soap-makers, and so on, especially now that the Europeans are beginning to go home and give us our trades back. It is true that it is good to be a doctor, lawyer, or surveyor, but we won't all get the chance, and in any case the manual trades are more important "for our progress as a country" ["*fun ilosiwaju wa gege bi Orile-ede*"]. We should not despise such manual workers as "common artisans."

Ju gbogbo rẹ lọ, ko yẹ ki ẹnikẹni sa ede ilu iya rẹ ti, ko yẹ ki a ma ri Iwe-irohin Ilu Oyinbo lọwo nyin li ọsọsẹ l'aika "EKO AKETE" ati Iwe-iro-hin Yoruba miran pẹlu, ko yẹ ki e gb'ojule isẹ Akowe nikan, ko yẹ ki ẹ jẹ ọgbẹri ninu ẹkọ ati imọ Oyinbo [sic]; boribori gbogbo rẹ, ko yẹ ki ẹ ma rena awon osisẹ, ko si yẹ ki ẹ kẹgan Isẹ-ọwọ, nitori ninu rẹ pataki ni ig-bala wa wa gẹgẹ bi Orilẹ-ede.

Above all, no one should despise the language of their motherland, it's not right that the newspapers of England should be seen in your hands every week if you don't also read *Eko Akete* and other Yoruba newspapers as well, it is not right to aspire only to white-collar jobs, it is not right that you should be ignorant of European [*sic*: proba-bly means "Yoruba"] teaching and knowledge; and to crown it all, it is wrong to look down on workers, and to belittle manual work, be-cause it is principally in them that our salvation lies as a nation/country.

Here, then, the duality betokened by the bilingual discourse—by the simul-taneous, adjacent and parallel production of Yoruba and English texts—has taken on a class inflection. English is represented as the language of the pro-fessional and clerkly classes, Yoruba as the idiom of the artisan. Rather than simply being lauded as a repository of cultural value shared by all, Yoruba is firmly linked to skilled manual labour. It is this labour, rather than a gener-alized idea of indigenous cultural heritage, which is presented here as the foundation of "national" dignity and future progress. The somewhat exhor-tatory tone suggests that the speaker probably does not include himself in the same category as his addressees, the category of young men misguidedly fix-ated on white-collar work unobtainable to them. The implied readers of this passage are being talked down to. At the same time, the manual trades are being talked up, idealized, by a writer who does not need to practise them himself. By identifying the Yoruba language in class terms, the rhetoric of progress and patriotism is redirected and the burden of collective advance-ment shifted from the elite to the common people.[15] This flattery was no doubt intended to curry favour with a potential group of supporters for Macaulay's party, the NNDP, with which *Eko Akete* was discreetly allied.

---

15. The theme of the value of artisanal trades in itself was not new. It was much can-vassed in the late nineteenth-century Lagos press. See for example the editorials in the Lagos Observer of 1882 about the foundation of the Rebecca Hussey Slave Charity Institution. But linking artisanal trades to a cultural-nationalist affirmation of the value of the Yoruba language does strike a new note.

Falola considers that the main inspiration of the 1920s Yoruba papers was "the need to propagate Christianity," (Falola 1999:22) and it is true that a strongly moralizing thread runs through the editorials, opinion pieces, topical columns and works of fiction and poetry. But a closer look at the greatest success in Yoruba-language literary journalism—I.B. Thomas's *Itan Emi Segilola*, first published as a serial in *Akede Eko*—suggests that the moralizing mode itself tapped into the popular and the lower class. *Itan Emi Segilola* (The Story of Me, Segilola) was the fictional confessions, couched in the form of letters to the editor, of a Lagos prostitute. "Segilola" (which she stresses was an assumed name, to save the blushes of her former clients) narrates her story in a colloquial style with numerous real-life details of the Lagos of her youth. She claims to have come from a respectable background, but after her father's death her own greed and waywardness led her step-by-step into a life of sin. The pious laments and exhortations—for Segilola is now stricken with a hideous disease, impoverished, deserted by her former lovers, and approaching death—are laid on thick, but this cannot dampen the sheer glee and lubricious detail of the story of her youthful exploits. Rather like the *News of the World*, she has it both ways, titillating the readers while passing judgment.

This story was serialized in thirty-one episodes between July 4, 1929 and March 8, 1930. As it progressed, public interest intensified, and a whole peripheral literature grew up around it—letters to the editor corroborating the truth of Segilola's story, opinion pieces that discussed Segilola as an example of the corruption of modern Lagos, even a donation of 10/- from one reader to alleviate Segilola's suffering. Segilola's reminiscences were full of allusions to popular life in Lagos: for example the Gumbe and Pandero dances "played by the late Adelakun, the drummer," or the story of the white man who was down on his luck and tried to make ends meet by selling bread from door to door until his friends joined together to pay his fare home.

This Yoruba-language literature is clearly rather different from the noble counterparts to Shakespeare and Homer that the newspaper editorials so often called for. It is not a great oral tradition preserved in writing and transmuted into a literary "classic." It is a living tradition of salacious gossip, combined with pious moralising, smuggled into novel form under the guise of real correspondence in the press. Nonetheless, it achieved widespread fame, is still remembered with affection by elderly Yoruba literates, and provided a model for a realist style of writing that later competed with Fagunwa's allegorical and folkloric mode. Immediately after the last episode was published, I.B. Thomas announced that, in response to innumerable requests, the paper would now begin serialising the English translation. It seems that the Anglophone elite— probably including some of the growing population of non-Yoruba-speaking immigrants to Lagos (Baker 1974)—were now agog to find out what the popular Yoruba press was saying. When the English version concluded, further requests and inquiries encouraged Thomas to reprint the Yoruba episodes as a book: and thus the "first Yoruba novel" came into existence. Not only was the Yoruba-English press widening its range to address lower class Lagosians; it was also drawing its inspiration from the seamy side of Lagos life, even while deploring it and bathing it in oceans of pious moralizing.

The long-standing, underlying motives of cultural affirmation and Christian evangelism that shaped Yoruba-language print culture were not abandoned, but they were overlaid by a new and more urgent project of political populism. In the process, it seems likely that the elite paradigm of Yorubaness, implicit in the creation and dissemination of a vernacular print literature, was diffused downward to a more popular audience, while popular urban anecdotes passed upward, available for consumption by the Anglophone elite readership.

Translation and the Untranslatable

An examination of the relations between the English and Yoruba panels of the bilingual newspapers suggests that the construction of a Yoruba cultural identity did not lie exclusively in the hands of the Saro elite. Their project of building Yoruba literature up to classical status depended on their ability to understand and interpret oral and popular genres that had been generated and transmitted by the illiterate indigenous population. The elite's knowledge and understanding of those traditions was unevenly distributed, and in most cases had to be acquired through deliberate painstaking research.

Some of the most influential and articulate Saro in the nineteenth and early twentieth centuries revealed an acute sensitivity to the nature of Yoruba oral textuality. An 1889 article on proverbs by D.B. Vincent (later known as Mojola Agbebi) in *Iwe Irohin Eko* shows a profound understanding of the compositional mode of allusion and incompletion, in which the text and its meaning must be reconstituted by a knowledgeable hearer (see Barber 1999, 2003). An obituary for I.H. Willoughby in 1890 in the same paper similarly adopts a traditional compositional mode in which a sequence of enigmatic formulations is presented and each in turn expanded, explained and applied to the subject. Lijadu's treatment of Ifa verses, though undertaken primarily as a theological inquiry, implicitly reveals an understanding of their complex textual composition. Several of the outstanding works of history, including I.B. Akinyele's *Iwe Itan Ibadan* (1911) and A.K. Ajisafe's *Iwe Itan Abeokuta* (n.d.) are constructed much in the manner of traditional *itan*, which take key epithets, sayings or songs as kernels of the narrative and move between them, using them as springboards, stepping stones or targets. In Akinyele, long quotations of the *oriki* of prominent Ibadan figures form the compositional core of the narrative. In Ajisafe, a much more varied array of popular sayings, songs and epithets underpins and animates the narrative. Akinyele produced a later English version, *The Outlines of Ibadan History,* which omits the *oriki* completely. Ajisafe's English-language *History of Abeokuta* (1916) actually preceded the Yoruba version (Doortmont 1994:166), but the same pattern holds: according to my quick count, the Yoruba text quotes three times as many local sayings, songs, and witticisms to sustain the narrative as the English version, which instead imports the texts of British legal and government documents that are not mentioned in the Yoruba version. They are, in fact, different books.

What I am suggesting is that the authors of these texts not only used traditional compositional modes—which I am prevented by lack of space from doing justice to here—but also found it impossible, undesirable, or unnecessary to transpose them into English. It was the very generative seeds of Yoruba-language composition that would not cross over. This can be seen also in the 1920s bilingual press. Although I.B. Thomas's *Itan Emi Segilola* was based on recent popular culture rather than older oral traditions, it relies, in the traditional manner, on a collection of textual kernels—popular songs, sayings, jokes, epithets, anecdotes and coinages. In the English version, some of these are translated, but they lose their generative properties. They no longer become the source of further text. Here is an example. Segilola recounts an episode in her youth in which her promiscuous behaviour and her dissatisfaction with all her suitors was beginning to attract comment. Her age-mates would sing satirical songs containing veiled criticisms, not explicitly directed against her. But,

O jọ li oju mi bi enipe emi Ṣẹgilọla ni awọn ọmọbirin fi nda orin kan ti wọn nkọ lẹnulọlọyi bayi pe:-
    O sunkun, lati gbe arede
    Baba rẹ ko gbe
    Iya rẹ ko gbe
    Wẹrẹ lo nsun kun
    O! dear Lover! Follow me ! ! !
Nwon npa owe kan bayi pe:- "a hu iwa ibajẹ ṣe bi ti on la nwi, aṣe buruku, o ku ara fu"; emi Ṣẹgilọla gan ni owe n mba wi julọ nitoripe nigbakigba ti orin oke yi ba nta si mi li eti ni emi a ma lero pe emi Ṣẹgilọla ni nwọn npa owe orin na mọ lara. (Thomas, 1930:11)

My translation follows:

It seemed to me that it was I, Segilola, that the young girls were tar-
geting with a certain song that they kept singing, as follows:
> She's weeping to have a church marriage
> Her father did not have one
> Her mother did not have one
> Profusely she sheds tears
> O! dear Lover! Follow me ! ! !

There's a proverb to the effect that: "The badly-behaved person imagines we're talking about him: 'evil-doer, greetings for your suspicions';" I myself, Segilola, was the person this proverb applied to
most, because whenever the above song reached my ears I would
think that it was I, Segilola myself, to whom they were applying the
message contained in the song.

This convoluted passage is built around a kernel, a dense formulation which
attracts attention and invites comment. At its centre is the proverb, "The
badly-behaved person imagines we're talking about him…" This proverb is internally productive: the generalized statement about the badly behaved person flips into dramatic dialogue, when an anonymous speaker mockingly hails
the subject of the proverb, "Greetings for your suspicions." Segilola proceeds
to apply this proverb to herself, to make a comment on her own suspicious
response to the girls' song. The song itself participates in the proverbial mode:
it has to be interpreted by knowing hearers in order to apply it to the right target. She thus quotes one proverb in order to characterize her reactions to another newly coined "proverb," commenting in the process on how coded
meanings are unravelled through application to their intended subject. Put on
display here is the allusive, collaborative, inter-referential mode of text-con-
stitution so characteristic of Yoruba and other oral traditions. The narrative
kernels are potent precisely because they involve the audience/reader in a
process of recognition, completion, and connection which depends on shared
cultural knowledge.

In I.B. Thomas's English version, he translates the song itself, but for the
whole passage after it he contents himself with the following:

> "I conclude that I am reaping what I had sown."

This adequately captures the moral point of the passage—Segilola deserves to
suffer her age-mates' coded taunts because she is in fact guilty—and it does
so with a suitable Biblical counterpart to the Yoruba old and new sayings. But
the vitality and generative, attention-attracting density of the Yoruba passage
is gone.

These bilingual authors' selective omissions and non-translations seem to me to have implicitly recognized the originality and irreducibility of Yoruba textuality. The animating core of it could be acknowledged and appreciated, but it could not be assimilated into the Anglophone world of discourse. In this way the elite seemed to acknowledge that authority, unlike initiative, in the cultural work of Yoruba ethnogenesis was not wholly in their hands.

References

Adeboye, Olufunke A. 1996 *The Ibadan elite, 1893–1966*. Ph.D. thesis, University of Ibadan.

Ajisafe, Ajayi Kolawole 1964 [1916] *History of Abeokuta*. Abeokuta: Fola Bookshops.

Ajisafe, Ajayi Kolawole 1972 [n.d.] *Iwe Itan Abeokuta*. Abeokuta: The Hardcore Society.

Awoniyi, T.A. *Yoruba language in education 1846–1974: a historical survey*. Ibadan: Oxford University Press.

Babajamu, Molomo 1959 *Yoruba Literature For West African School Certificate*. Nigerian Publications Service.

Baker, Pauline H. 1974 *Urbanisation and political change: the politics of Lagos 1917–67*. Berkeley CA: University of California Press.

Barber, Karin 1997 "Time, space and writing in three colonial Yoruba novels", *The Yearbook of English Studies*, 27 (108–129).

Barber, Karin 1999 "Quotation in the constitution of Yorùbá oral texts", in *Research in African Literatures*, 30, 3 (17–41).

Barber, Karin 2000 *The generation of plays: Yoruba popular life in theatre*. Bloomington, Indiana: Indiana University Press.

Barber, Karin 2003 "Text and performance in Africa", *Bulletin of SOAS*, 66, 3 (324–333).

Brown, Spencer Hun 1964 *A history of the people of Lagos, 1852–1886*. Ph.D. dissertation, Northwestern University.

Cole, Patrick 1975 *Modern and traditional elites in the politics of Lagos*. Cambridge: Cambridge University Press.

Doortmont, Michel R. 1994 *Recapturing the past: Samuel Johnson and the construction of Yoruba history*. PhD, Erasmus University of Rotterdam.

Echeruo, Michael J.C. 1977 *Victorian Lagos: aspects of nineteenth century Lagos life*. London: Macmillan.

Fagborun, J. Gbenga 1994 *The Yoruba Koiné–its history and linguistic innovations*. Munich, Newcastle: Lincom Europa.

Falola, Toyin 1988 "Earliest Yoruba writers", in *Perspectives on Nigerian Literature, 1700 to the present*, vol.1, ed. Yemi Ogunbiyi. Guardian Books Nigeria (22–32).

Falola, Toyin 1999 *Yoruba gurus: indigenous production of knowledge in Africa.* Trenton, NJ: Africa World Press.

Kopytoff, Jean Herskovits 1965 *A preface to modern Nigeria.* Madison, WI: University of Wisconsin Press.

Law, R. 1996 "Local amateur scholarship in the construction of Yoruba ethnicity, 1880–1914", in *Ethnicity in Africa*, ed. Louise de la Gorgendière, Kenneth King, and Sarah Vaughan. Centre of African Studies, University of Edinburgh.

Mann, Kristin 1985 *Marrying well: marriage, status and social change among the educated elite in colonial Lagos.* Cambridge: Cambridge University Press.

Nnodim, Rita 2002 *Ewi: Yoruba neo-traditional media poetry – the poetics of a genre.* PhD, University of Birmingham.

Ogunsina, Bisi 1992 *The development of the Yoruba novel 1930–1975.* Ibadan: Gospel Faith Mission Press.

Okonkwo, Rina 1995 *Protest movements in Lagos 1908–1930.* Lewiston, Queenston, Lampeter: The Edward Mellen Press.

Omu, Fred I.A. 1978 *Press and politics in Nigeria, 1880–1937.* Atlantic Highlands, New Jersey: Humanities Press.

Peel, J.D.Y. 1989 "The cultural work of Yoruba ethnogenesis", in *History and Ethnicity*, ed. E. Tonkin et al. London and New York: Routledge (198–215).

Peel, J.D.Y. 2000 *Religious encounter and the making of the Yoruba.* Bloomington, Indiana: Indiana University Press.

Peterson, Derek R. 2004 *Creative writing: translation, bookkeeping, and the work of imagination in colonial Kenya.* Portsmouth, NH: Heinemann.

Thomas, I.B. 1930 *Itan igbesi aiye emi "Segilola, eleyinju ege", elegberun oko l'aiye.* Lagos: CMS Bookshops.

CHAPTER 10

CULTURAL POLITICS AND NATIONALIST HISTORY: A BACKGROUND TO WOLE SOYINKA'S *ISARA*

Insa Nolte

In a recent essay on Christianity and the logic of nationalist assertion, John Peel (2002) examined the relationship between Christianity, cultural modernity and nationalism in Wole Soyinka's novel *Isara: A Voyage Around "Essay"* ([1989] 1991).[1] *Isara* follows the debates and endeavors of the youthful educated elite of the rural-urban Yoruba town Isara in the Remo part of Ijebu province during the early 1940s. At the heart of the novel is Akinyode Soditan, the head teacher of St Peter's Primary School in Abeokuta and a portrait of Wole Soyinka's father, S. A. ("Essay") Soyinka. Soyinka calls Soditan and his group of friends the ex-*Ilés*, an Anglo-Yoruba pun that alludes to the fact that their mission-derived education—rather than trade or circumstance—has shaped their experience beyond the rural-urban town of Isara (cf. 130).

The novel's main narrative is based on the ex-*Ilés*' efforts to support the campaign of the Nigerian labor leader and nationalist politician Samuel A. Akinsanya to become Isara's traditional ruler (*oba*), the *Odemo*, in 1941–43. Characters and parts of the narrative are reconstructed from Soyinka's memory as well as the contents of a tin box he inherited from his father. Unlike in his childhood memory *Aké* (Soyinka 1981), in which Akinsanya also appears

---

1. References to pages in *Isara* (Soyinka [1990] 1991) will appear throughout the rest of the paper as page numbers only. All other sources are referenced with author's name and year (and, where applicable, page numbers) or equivalent.

Figure 10.1 - Wole Soyinka.

(cf. Gibbs 1988: 518–22), Soyinka does not use real names throughout. Moreover, Soyinka disregards chronology and even acknowledges that he "deliberately ruptured" it, implying that this would enable him to examine the major events and relationships which structured and characterized the life of his father's generation without the burden of the particular (v–vi).

This chapter examines the novel's representation of the historical and political background to Akinsanya's contest of the throne. Examining the novel not only as a study in the cultural politics of the generation which gave rise to political independence but also as a cultural product itself (cf. Peel 2002: 139), it focuses on the extent to which Soyinka's representation of nationalist and local politics corresponds with the historical record. The chapter suggests that Soyinka concentrates on the nationalists' mediation and exploration of Britain and its colonial institutions vis-à-vis their own Yoruba cultural and political heritage at the expense of an investigation of local conflict, both in nationalist and local traditional politics.[2] As a result of this, Akinsanya, a controversial figure at the time of his contest for the throne, already appears as the widely popular political leader he would later become.

---

2. The contest over the *Odemo*ship is, since the destruction of *Odemo* Akinsanya's library in 1968, probably best documented in Ijeprof. 1/2428 (I–III) and Ijeprof. 1/2746 in the National Archives in Ibadan.

This chapter illustrates its contention that Soyinka glosses over historical cleavages to enhance Akinsanya's image by discussing four aspects of Akinsanya's candidacy. The first section of the chapter examines Soyinka's account of Akinsanya's decision to contest a traditional office in his hometown and suggests that the author avoids an examination of the personal, ethnic, and ideological tensions within the movement. Soyinka's representation of the drawn-out contest for the *Odemo*ship, examined in the second section, as a triumph of grassroots democracy condenses historical truth about the contest. However, the lack of information about local politics in the novel implies that Akinsanya's popular victory appears as an almost abstract heroic triumph of enlightenment over egotism. The third section explains the historical enmity between the pro-Akinsanya and pro-Erinle sides as the result of conflict between two historical factions in Remo politics. Soyinka's hint at other reasons for the enmity between the two factions enables him to present Akinsanya as a widely popular man. Section four argues that Soyinka's representations of local unity anticipate the politics of the 1950s, when Remo's political factions were eventually united. Soyinka thus indicates Akinsanya's greatness by evoking his later success and political influence. Unlike his supporters, whose difficulties in life are explored by Soyinka, Akinsanya appears as a triumphant agent of change.

Nationalist Politics and Obaship

Soyinka's description of the ex-*Ilés* portrays them in the context of a generation the members of which "derived their distinctive identity as 'enlightened' elements…from their engagement with mission Christianity and its agencies" (Peel 2002: 139), and whose nationalist politics were shaped by a simultaneous appropriation of, and confrontation with, its rhetoric of enlightenment. At the same time, the ex-*Ilés*' ambition to make a Lagos-based union leader the *oba* of their small town—in the early 1940s, Isara had 5–6,000 inhabitants—illustrates that the educated young men from the rural-urban Remo towns were inserted into contemporary nationalist politics in a particular way.

They were—as in Soditan's case—very often members of the first generation of trained exiles who kept in touch with their hometowns. During the nineteenth century, the Ijebu kingdom had forbidden missionary activity in its territory, and Ijebu converts tended to reside in Lagos. However, after the military defeat of Ijebu in 1892, conversion to Christianity (and literacy) had been enthusiastic (cf. Peel 1977). As there were few opportunities for educated

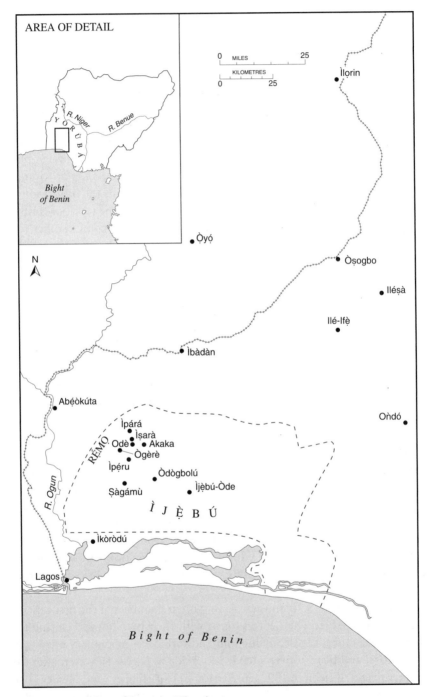

Figure 10.2 - Map of Isara in Nigeria.

workers in the rural-urban towns of Ijebu and Remo, the majority of the newly educated generation moved to the nearby cities of Lagos, Abeokuta and Ibadan, where Christianity had much deeper roots. As a result of this, the Remo migrants entered nationalist politics as provincial newcomers to a well-established and thoroughly cosmopolitan political arena.

Samuel Akinsanya's career reflects these circumstances. His rise within the nationalist movement began in 1923, when he was one of the founders of the Lagos-based Study Circle, which sponsored literary discussions and political debates. Counting prominent Lagosians like H. A. Subair, R. A. Coker, Olatunji Caxton-Martins, and Adetokunbo Ademola among its members, the Study Circle slowly transformed itself into a political group (cf. Coleman 1965: 216). In 1934, Akinsanya became the general secretary of the newly founded Lagos Youth Movement (Nigerian Youth Movement, or NYM, in 1936), whose other founding members included the businessman and aspiring lawyer Obafemi Awolowo, and the editor of the *Nigerian Daily Times* Ernest Ikoli (Crowder [1962] 1978: 218). Reflecting the ascent of a new generation of politicians in Lagos, the NYM grew out of the desire of younger men to differentiate themselves from the already established parties like the Nigerian National Democratic Party (NNDP), which confined itself to Lagos (Coleman 1965: 217–8).

By 1937 branches of the Nigerian Youth Movement were established in several towns outside Lagos. In Ijebu and Remo, the NYM was particularly active politically, and organized popular opposition to *Awujale* Adesanya, the ruler of the capital Ijebu-Ode (cf. below and Ayandele 1992: 166–9). The NYM became the central institution of Nigerian anti-colonial sentiment, organizing demands for a Nigerian university, but also touring the rural-urban towns to educate farmers about agricultural policy and coordinating a strike of the Nigerian Motor Transport Union against higher registration fees for those (mostly African-owned) lorries competing with the railway lines. When palm produce exports were banned from the Western Provinces in 1940, the NYM protested to the governor, Sir Bernard Bourdillon, and achieved a lift of the ban shortly afterwards (cf. Awolowo 1960: 126–139).

In 1941 both Samuel Akinsanya and the then president of the Nigerian Youth Movement (NYM), Ernest Ikoli, wanted to contest a bye-election to the Lagos Legislative Council as NYM representatives.[3] At a general meeting of the Lagos body of the NYM, Akinsanya had the support of the majority with 108 votes against sixty for Ikoli and thirty-seven for another candidate. However,

---

3. In Britain and some British-derived electoral systems, a bye-election is an election outside the regular election timetable. It is usually caused by the need to replace an elected representative who has left office before completing his or her term.

the Central Executive Committee of the NYM, after meeting "to consider these nominations," selected Ikoli. Akinsanya reportedly congratulated Ikoli, but later announced that he would also stand as a candidate (Awolowo 1960: 147). Akinsanya's unwillingness to acquiesce to the NYM decision led to an intensification of political and economic rivalry in the NYM between Dr. Nnamdi Azikiwe and Akinsanya on the one hand, and Obafemi Awolowo and Ikoli on the other.[4] When Akinsanya lost the 1941 bye-election to Ikoli, Azikiwe announced his resignation from the NYM (Coleman 1965: 227).

The lines in the conflict were not determined by ethnic background alone—Ikoli and Azikiwe were Ijaw and Igbo respectively, while both Ikoli's ally Awolowo and Azikiwe's friend Akinsanya were Yoruba from Remo. However, the fact that, along with many Igbo supporters of Azikiwe, a large number of members from Ijebu and Remo left the NYM, points to their problematical position within the nationalist movement. In the early 1940s the nationalist movement in Nigeria still reflected the initial engagement of established elite families, mostly from Lagos, with Christianity and literacy. Therefore, the movement was still predominantly cosmopolitan and Yoruba in origin. However, the growing numbers of the provincial, educated community forced members of the old elite to compete for leadership positions rather than to assume them (Zachernuk 2000: 134).

Often, this led to prejudice and *ressentiments* against the newcomers, which was directed at their place of origin.[5] In many Yoruba communities, origin from a less urbanized area continues to be a source of low prestige, and migrants from such areas are considered to be less civilized, or "farm people," (*ara oko*) by the urban citizens. For the nationalist leaders from the rural-urban towns of Remo, a validation of *oba*ship in their hometowns was not only a pragmatic recognition that *oba*ship still conferred on its holder a considerable degree of power. It also demonstrated that they were "town people" (*ara ilu*), because only towns have *oba*s (Oloko 1984: 23). While many cosmopolitan Nigerian intellectuals and outside observers at the time were of the opinion that, as Nigeria became a modern nation, traditional authority would lose in importance and even disappear (cf. Lloyd 1955; Crowder & Ikime

---

4. After his return from the USA and Ghana in 1937, Azikiwe had founded the newspaper *West African Pilot*, which soon became the newspaper of the nationalist movement. However, in June 1938, Ikoli became editor of the *Lagos Daily Service*, which claimed to be the official organ of the movement. Consequently Azikiwe began to seek political support outside the NYM, especially among Igbo associations and unions.

5. This prejudice was an important factor in the Nigerian debate about the administrative and political status of Lagos (Adebanwi 2004).

1970), it gained a new symbolic importance among provincial nationalist leaders who associated it with claims to urbanity and civilization (cf. Nolte 2003a).

Therefore, Akinsanya's historical decision to contest the vacant throne of the *Odemo* of Isara a few months after he lost the bye-election was a political decision which reflected historical, political, social as well as ethnic tensions within the movement, and may even have inspired Obafemi Awolowo's later formulated vision of a political Yoruba nationalism based on the inclusion of traditional rulers.[6] However, Soyinka plays down the importance of this conflict in the novel. Asked about the movement by Soditan, Akinsanya — still unaware that the ex-*Ilés* are planning to ask him to stand for the *Odemo*ship — points out that after the initial anger, a *rapprochement* is under way:

> What you may not know is that Ernest Ikoli has been to see me. He even wrote letters — I'll show them to you later. For me personally, I have put all the provocation behind me...(197).

As a result of this representation, Akinsanya's decision to contest the throne is, in the novel, the result of a different engagement with national politics than that suggested here: it has very little connection to the movement's internal rifts and pressures, but instead emerges solely as the result of Akinsanya's acceptance of his supporters' assertion that his town needs him (198–9). Akinsanya does promise not to be a "deaf-and-dumb king," implying that his decision will expand the reach of the nationalist movement and take politics to Isara (210). Thus, Soyinka represents what might be seen as Akinsanya's reaching out to a new constituency in the wake of complex struggles over status and leadership within the nationalist movement as his heroic extension of nationalist politics from Lagos to the provinces in response to grassroots needs.

The Contest over the Throne of Isara

Isara is, both in the master narrative and in the smaller tales interwoven with it, intensely interested in different kinds of social practice and their impact on the success of their lives as individuals and as a group. Soditan and his friends reflect on the effect of their Christian-cum-Western education on

---

6. Lloyd (1955: 696) also suggests that in the early to mid-1950s, AG members were much more likely than other party members to be involved in the politics of their (provincial) hometowns.

their lives; they discuss the risks of free enterprise and the lure of money; and they engage with traditional religion and its institutions and practices. But the ex-*Ilés* do not just philosophize about the world; they change it by claiming their hero's place in it. Due to the unrest following the illegal installation of Akinsanya's less popular rival Erinle, a visit by the district officer to Isara for a public hearing is planned. At this event the ex-*Ilés* organize the triumphal appearance of Akinsanya and his numerous local and expatriate supporters, and Akinsanya rides into the town on a white horse. He is marked out as the real *Odemo* already by the weight of responsibility, visible to his supporters, on his shoulders. It is obvious that the ex-*Ilés* will succeed in installing their nationalist *oba*, and they will do so after having prepared the ground for their victory in a democratic manner that is exemplary both for the cultural and the political nation far beyond Isara:

> Where else, for instance, in the entire history of the Yoruba, had a king been chosen by the spectacle of two main contenders seated in an open field, their supporters lined up behind them, visible to all the world? Of course, there had been the earlier murky passages of intrigue, of pressures and treacheries, even of bribery. But that in the end it should come down to what, in effect, was a simple open election? Why, even the legislative council of the nation, now undergoing its fifth decade of experimentation, did not allow such a broad participation of the people (228).

The colonial documents on the case shed more light on the "murky passages of intrigue" Soyinka alludes to. Among the early contestants for the *Odemo*ship after the death of *Odemo* Onabajo Poke (1915–1941) was Joseph Osindeinde, a bookseller, and probably the model for the traditional candidate "Babatola" in the novel (cf. 214). Osindeinde claimed the right to the throne through his membership in the Igan family, whose turn it was to present the next candidate for the throne.[7] Unfortunately for Osindeinde, he was rejected as the *oba* by the *Ifa* oracle. However, not all supporters of Osindeinde were convinced that this rejection had been achieved without manipulation, and he continued to challenge Akinsanya's legitimacy periodically throughout Akinsanya's reign (cf. Ijeprof. 1/2428 (III), 07/03/1943; Ijeprof. 1/2746 (I), 08/03/1948; *Nigerian Tribune*, 22/06/1950). After Akinsanya's death in 1984, Joseph Osindeinde's son, Adeboye

---

7. The noun *ilé* (meaning house) refers both to common residence and shared ancestry. In this meaning it is translated here as 'family'.

Oladele Osindeinde, reigned as the *Odemo* from 1989 until 1994 (*The Daily Sketch*, 02/02/1994, *The Guardian*, 10/02/1994).

As the *Olisa* and regent of the town, I. A. Ifekoya was one of the highest-ranking officers of the civic town association or *Osugbo* of Isara, where the divination was held. He was also, in reality as in Soyinka's novel, Akinsanya's main opponent and had written to Akinsanya in the middle of July in order to convince him not to contest the throne (cf. 253). However, Samuel Akinsanya ignored Ifekoya's letter and quickly proved to be a much more popular candidate than Joseph Osindeinde. Only Osindeinde's timely removal from the contest allowed the *Olisa* to nominate a candidate who might stand a chance against Akinsanya. After Osindeinde's rejection by the oracle, Ifekoya threw his weight behind the well-liked J. S. Erinle (cf. Ijeprof. 1/2428 (II), 13/07/1942).

Unlike Soyinka suggests (197), it was Akinsanya who was first installed as *Odemo* by his supporters on July 31, 1941. His unauthorized enthronement was followed three days later by another unsanctioned installation of J. S. Erinle as *Odemo*. One of the reasons for Akinsanya's swift installation was very likely the attempt to prove that he was eligible to wear the crown. Doubts over his eligibility emerged early on in the dispute over the *Odemo*ship, because the Afonlade family, through which he claimed to be related to the throne, was not widely recognized at the time. Akinsanya's opponent, the powerful chief *Olisa* Ifekoya, was also a historian and writer, and he had authored the first published history of Isara, *Iwe Itan Ilu Isara (Ijebu Remo)*,[8] in 1929. In Ifekoya's book, Igan and Rokodo, the founders of Osindeinde's and Erinle's families, are both listed. However, no mention is made of an Afonlade or Afonlade family.[9]

To claim legitimacy for Akinsanya, his supporters first asserted that Afonlade was the first *Odemo* before Ode-Omo [the hunter-prince usually acknowledged as Isara's founder] moved to Isara (Ijeprof. 1/2428 (II), 21/08/1941). Later, they would argue that Afonlade had descended from Fey-isara, a son of Ode-Omo and the *Odemo* after Ode-Omo's death (Ijeprof. 1/2428 (II), 13/07/1942). In both cases, Akinsanya's right to the throne of Isara was established by challenging established notions of tradition. How-

---

8. Translation: A history book of the town Isara (Ijebu Remo).

9. In another history of Isara, *Itan Ilu Isara* (A history of Isara town), published in 1980 and co-authored by Joseph Osindeinde, Afonlade is mentioned as the "present ruling house (1980: unnumbered page)." However, elsewhere the authors argue that "Awon idile merin ti nje oba ni Isara ni wonyi (1) Igan, (2) Rokodo, (3) Erinsiba, (4) Poke-bi-Owula (sic)" (The four families who(se members) become rulers in Isara are (1) Igan, (2) Rokodo, (3)Erinsiba, (4) Poke-bi-Owula), leaving out Afonlade (Osindeinde et al. 1980: 8).

ever, the lack of a recognized traditional pedigree at the time—more recently produced histories and chieftaincy declarations of Isara have adopted a master narrative which includes Akinsanya's family—did not adversely affect Akinsanya. As Soyinka's novel suggests (210–1), Akinsanya's legitimacy was probably (also) confirmed to his supporters by his previous political achievements.

Reflecting the town's deep divisions, Erinle and Akinsanya were both installed by their own faction of the *Osugbo*, Isara's town association responsible for aiding the *oba* in governing and ensuring the well-being of the town. Soyinka refers to the political and spiritual importance of the *Osugbo* through events in the private lives of Akinyode Soditan's family, as well as in the struggle to install Akinsanya. Thus, the *Osugbo* is implicated in the narrative surrounding Soditan's mother Mariam, her missing moneybox and the burial of his uncle Tenten (81–102). However, the *Osugbo* is also the source of spiritual power that allows Akinsanya's local supporter Jagun to expedite the death of *Olisa* Ifekoya's ally, and virtual prisoner, Agunrin Odubona (212–3, 237). However, Soyinka's description of Odubona's death "for the public good" (237) suggests that, as the main traditional institution of the town, the *Osugbo* remained united behind Akinsanya.

In response to the two installations, and in a manner similar to that described by Soyinka (250–262), District Officer E. R. Ward came to Isara in August 1941, and held a public meeting with all the chiefs and town council members. However, unlike the novel allows the reader to imagine, Ward did not recognize Akinsanya as the *Odemo*. Instead, in a way similar to Soditan's friend Sotikare (214), he expressed his preference for the "uneducated [but] suitable" earlier candidate Osindeinde (Ijeprof. 1/2428 (II), 21/08/ 1941). Yet neither Akinsanya nor Erinle withdrew from the contest, and eventually the two factions came to a final clash over the division of Isara's *Osugbo*.

Since February 1942, each section of the *Osugbo* had held its own funerals. However, in January 1943 Ifekoya was able to persuade the senior sanitary inspector not to sign the death certificates presented by Akinsanya's supporters, thus preventing them from burying their dead (Ijeprof. 1/2428 (II), 18/01/1943). At this stage, the local administration had exhausted itself by insisting on procedure, and both sides had corresponded extensively first with Resident E. V. S. Thomas, and from 1942 with E. N. Dickenson. Eventually, Chief Commissioner Whiteley broke the *Olisa*'s hold over Isara. Stating that overall public opinion in Isara was in favor of Akinsanya, as were the majority of the traditional kingmakers, he was prepared to accept him as the new *Odemo*. Regarding Akinsanya's eligibility for the throne, he stated,

Erinle's eligibility could not seriously be questioned, and whatever doubt there might have been in the case of Akinsanya is resolved I think by...the fact that the majority of the leading Emos [princes and kingmakers in Isara] by supporting his candidature tacitly accept his eligibility (Ijeprof. 1/2428 (II), 27/06/1943).

Thus, unlike the novel suggests, the town and *Osugbo* were not united behind Akinsanya, and the people of Isara did not directly decide the contest over the throne. Instead, administrative indecision and partiality at the local level (see also below) allowed the town to be so thoroughly divided that no peaceful solution could be found. Only Akinsanya's eventual recognition by a senior colonial administrator enabled him to act as the *Odemo*, and to attempt a reunification of the town after two divisive years. Akinsanya's desperate need for administrative support even after his recognition is illustrated by the fact that in his first letter to the Resident as the *Odemo*, he asked for his personal intervention in Isara politics. He also demanded the official suspension of his formidable enemy, *Olisa* Ifekoya (Ijeprof. 1/2746 (I), 23/09/1943).[10]

However, the main reason for Akinsanya's recognition as the *Odemo* was the fact that his support in Isara and beyond remained strong throughout the conflict. His followers believed in Akinsanya and refused to be intimidated by any of his opponents' arguments and political manoeuvres. In this sense, Soyinka's representation of Akinsanya's procession as "a simple open election" which overcame "the earlier murky passages of intrigue" (228) is an image for the triumph of grassroots demands over political machinations. Thus Soyinka's evocation of a popular victory for Akinsanya condenses the historical truth about his widespread support.

Yet the assurances throughout the novel that the town (and its *Osugbo*) are behind Akinsanya reduce the depth of local politics and imply that the change affected by Soditan and his friends—Akinsanya's victory—is really a victory of progress and enlightenment over individual machinations. Nationalist politics and the ex-*Ilés*' enlightenment do not lead to the triumph of democratic demands over authoritarian structures and the racist state so despised by the ex-*Ilés*, but to a public-spirited overcoming of selfish intrigues by their hero. Similarly transforming the demands for political enlightenment into the personal, Soditan's father points out after a discussion about Akinsanya's candi-

---

10. A critique of the town's dependence on the colonial administration is formulated elsewhere in the novel, when Pa Josiah, Soditan's father, laments that he has to "wait on the white intruder to decide who is going to sit on the throne of [his] ancestors (211)."

dature that it is human weakness—jealousy—which men of change must overcome:

> Far too many of our own people don't wish their own kind any good or success. That is why the black man is not making progress in this world (211).

The Candidates and Their Politics

Soyinka strongly suggests that the ex-*Ilés* as well as the majority of Isara's residents support Akinsanya because he is a man of progress in the way the ex-*Ilés* understand and welcome it. As Pa Josiah explains to his son Soditan, the town trusts that in these times of political transformation, the ex-*Ilés* can mediate between the town and the colonial government without being cowed by authority:

> Times are changing. The white man is here and he pokes his nose into everything. So it is a good thing that we have those who understand his way of thinking and can pass on to him our thoughts on matters which concern us (32).

Meanwhile, not all ex-*Ilés* think that leadership in modern nationalist politics is compatible with traditional authority, and Soditan's friend Sotikare even believes that Akinsanya is lowering himself when he competes for the *Odemo*ship (see above). Sotikare's friends disagree with this view and, in the ensuing conversation, legitimize the continuing existence of *oba*ship as well as its present political relevance. Soditan points to the existence of kingship in England, where, presumably, it is a civilized institution, while Ogunba—a schoolteacher—points to the ongoing transformation of Nigerian society:

> Adjustments are being made to a new age, and the obaship is only one of the institutions that are affected....Akinsanya is merely representative of a new breed (215–216).

While the novel does not say much about the background of Erinle and his supporters, it strongly encourages a reading of the contest as that of a pro-Akinsanya faction committed to progress and enlightenment and unafraid to challenge the colonial government versus that of a conservative pro-Erinle faction, the strength of which lies in the local entrenchment of the *Olisa* (cf. Peel 2002: 144–5). Yet based on his educational achievements, Akinsanya's historical rival J. S. Erinle could easily have belonged to the group of friends supporting his candidature for the *Odemo*ship.

Like *Isara*'s Akinyode Soditan, Erinle was a graduate of St. Andrew's College in Oyo, fictionalized in the novel as St Simeon's Seminary at Ilesa. In 1941, when the dispute over the *Odemo*ship arose, Erinle was, again like the novel's central character, a school headmaster involved in politics at home. He had served as the headmaster of St. Saviour's Secondary School in Ijebu-Ode for several years. Moreover, Erinle had been politically active for many years and had held an elected seat on Remo's highest administrative council since 1938 (Ijeprof. 1/2428 (I), 28/07/1941).

Erinle's background and career in education clearly illustrate that "filling the position with an enlightened person," as Soyinka puts it in the novel (215–216), was not simply a question of having education; it was a matter of outlook and politics. Centering on rival visions of Isara's historical identity and relation to its surrounding towns, the Erinle and Akinsanya factions put forward different images of Isara during the fight over the *Odemo*ship. These images were, at least on the surface, not so much concerned with nationalist politics as they were with traditional hierarchies and local administration. Politically, the Erinle and Akinsanya factions had emerged in relation to a long-established political conflict in Remo.

Few written sources about the Ijebu kingdom date from before the nineteenth century, but the Ijebu kingdom, with its capital at Ijebu-Ode, had probably established its *entrepôt* trading position between the lagoon and the hinterland by the fifteenth century. Bordering on Egba territory, the Remo towns constituted the westernmost district of Ijebu (cf. Ogunkoya 1955). After the destruction of old Oyo and the foundation of the new military power of Ibadan in the first half of the nineteenth century, the north-western Remo towns of Ipara, Isara, Ode Remo, Makun, Ogere and Iperu found themselves situated along the trading route from Lagos to Ibadan. Confident of their own economic and political position, and with close traditional ties to the capital and spiritual center Ijebu-Ode, leaders from these towns challenged the power of Ofin, then the local capital and the seat of the *Akarigbo*. However, following the end of Ijebu's alliance with Ibadan, these center-oriented towns were defeated in 1864 (Epega [1919] 1932: 22–4).

After this victory, *Akarigbo* Igimisoje established himself as the leader of a centralized Remo by attracting other towns to settle nearby and thus creating the present capital Sagámù. Through careful diplomacy with Britain, the *Akarigbo* was able not only to establish his paramountcy in Remo but also his independence from Ijebu-Ode; and, after the military defeat of Ijebu by the British in 1892, Remo was administered from Lagos. In 1914 Remo was— against the wishes of most of its traditional and civic leaders—excised from the Colony of Lagos and administered as part of Ijebu Division, which remained a part of Abeokuta Division until 1921. The reintegration of Remo into Ijebu was linked to the introduction of direct taxation to the area in 1918, and the Remo taxpayers in effect subsidized colonial projects in Ijebu-Ode (cf. Ayandele 1992: 140–1). For this reason, many local leaders and traditional rulers supported the agitation of *Akarigbo* Christopher Adedoyin for Remo's administrative (and fiscal) independence under his paramountcy throughout the 1920s and 1930s.

However, a sizeable minority of Remo leaders—mostly based in the old center-oriented towns in the northwest of Remo, including Isara—was indignant about the *Akarigbo*'s claims for paramountcy. Many leaders in these towns believed that the *Akarigbo* had never been more than a *primus inter pares* among the Remo rulers and that, like other rulers, he was subject to the spiritual authority and historical leadership of the *oba* of Ijebu-Ode, the *Awujale*. They argued that sources referring to the *Akarigbo* as a pre-colonial paramount ruler were based solely on exaggerated representations made by past *Akarigbos* to the ignorant British (cf. Epega [1919] 1934). Samuel Akinsanya, who had already in 1933 attempted to convince the powerful Remo politicians G. I. Delo-Dosunmu from Sagamu and M. S. Sowole from (also center-oriented) Ipara to withdraw their support for the *Akarigbo*, was, together with the prominent historian D. O. Epega from Ode Remo, one of the leaders of the pro-Ijebu-Ode side (Ayandele 1992: 143).

Unfortunately, the case of the pro-Ijebu-Ode side was made more difficult by the fact that British intervention had also discredited the political and spiritual leadership provided by the capital. In 1929 the ethnographer and administrator Amaury Talbot had revived the Gbelegbuwa family's eligibility for the throne of the *Awujale* of Ijebu-Ode in disregard of local tradition. When in 1933 a member of Gbelegbuwa family was installed under the name Daniel Adesanya, traditional and elite leaders in Ijebu-Ode and beyond, including Akinsanya and later the NYM (see above), fiercely opposed him. Meanwhile, demonstrating his great political skill, *Akarigbo* Adedoyin was one of Adesanya's supporters (cf. Ayandele 1991: 97–107). When, a few years later, Adedoyin demanded Remo independence from Ijebu-Ode, the fact that *Awujale* Adesanya was considered illegitimate by a large part of the population made matters much easier for the *Akarigbo*.[11]

---

11. Daniel Adesanya found it difficult to concentrate on Remo politics while he sought to establish and maintain his hold on the throne. Meanwhile, his existence created a political dilemma for the centre-oriented towns in Remo: if they rejected the *Akarigbo*'s authority for the *Awujale*'s, they declared their allegiance to an *Awujale* who was widely considered as an impostor.

In 1937 the political pressure from Remo finally led to an official inquiry into the status of Remo under Justice Martindale. The inquiry confirmed the *Akarigbo*'s claims both for independence from Ijebu-Ode and his paramountcy in Remo; and, a year later, Remo received its own native administration. As a result of Remo's administrative independence from Ijebu, *Akarigbo* Christopher Adedoyin was also recognized as Remo's paramount ruler and the head of the Remo Native Administration. I. A. Ifekoya, the published historian and *Olisa* of Isara, as well as schoolmaster J. S. Erinle, were only two of the many members of the local elite who were personally involved in organizing support for Remo independence, and when in 1938 Remo received its own Native Administration, J. S. Erinle was elected into the Remo Native Administration Council (Ijeprof. 1/2428 (I), 28/07/1941).

Thus, both Akinsanya and Erinle had some experience of political mobilization and agitation before they contested the *Odemo*ship, with Erinle having emerged on the side of victory in 1938, when Remo became independent. Akinsanya on the other hand had already made many local enemies. Apart from the *Olisa* of Isara and a section of Isara elites, his opponents included the *Akarigbo* as well as the rulers of Isara's main neighboring towns of Ode Remo, Ipara and Akaka, all of whom had supported *Akarigbo* Adedoyin.[12] Thanks to his earlier agitation against *Awujale* Adesanya in 1933, Akinsanya did not even have a potentially useful ally in the former capital Ijebu-Ode. Consequently, Akinsanya had very little local support in traditional politics before his recognition as *Odemo*.

Akinsanya's and Erinle's historical dispute appears somewhat removed from the "enlightenment" sought by the ex-*Ilés* in their investigations of power and the traditional. While references to the administrative reorganization are made in the novel—Soditan's friend Sipe reflects in a fairly unimpressed manner on the fact that "Isara now belong[s] to Remo (183)"—Soyinka's description of the Akinsanya dispute suggests that the politics of his election are reflected in the ex-*Ilés*' discussions. These center on the practices of the colonial state and the European powers as well as on their attempts to reconcile their understanding of traditional power with their self-perceived modernity. While these concerns were clearly not directly relevant for the conflict in the Akinsanya case, a structural link exists between Akinsanya's argument in the historical dispute and the logic of nationalist assertion in the novel.

Peel astutely observes that many of the ex-*Ilés*' debates follow a dialectical movement in which traditional practice, after comparison with an analogous

---

12. A section of the elites in the former rebel towns of Ode Remo and Ipara, however, had opposed Adedoyin.

example from the institutions associated with cultural modernity, is revalorized (cf. Peel 2002: 141–4). By insisting that the *Akarigbo*'s paramount status in Remo was only derived from the British, Akinsanya both examined and critiqued the colonial customization of local tradition and revalorized its past practice. Akinsanya's version of the Remo past appropriated and simultaneously undermined the claims to modernity of Christian and colonial discourse by pointing out that democratic traditions had existed locally long before the establishment of British rule.

By opposing the *Akarigbo*'s claims to paramount authority over Remo, Akinsanya attempted to shape nationalist politics in Remo as the politics of a traditional political culture based on co-operation and parliamentary discourse. Yet, by concentrating on Akinsanya's opposition to the public authoritarianism of the colonial state, Soyinka bypasses this chance to explore Akinsanya's attempt to reverse the more obscured suppression of local egalitarian traditions by colonial and local interests. However, Akinsanya's political vision of a more democratic Remo was, historically, not successful, and a reference to this struggle might have destabilized Soyinka's description of Akinsanya as a triumphant agent of historical change.

Nationalist Politics and Remo Unity

Ignoring the historical conflict that formed the political background to the contest between Erinle and Akinsanya, Soyinka describes the roles of the paramount rulers of Ijebu and Remo, the *Awujale* and the *Akarigbo*, as supportive of Akinsanya. In fact, in the novel, the *Akarigbo* of Remo appears so solidly in favor of Akinsanya that he warns him about Erinle's planned illegal installation (198). Instead of provincial politics, Soyinka presents Akinsanya's anti-colonial politics as potentially dangerous for him. In a meeting with Akinsanya, Akinyode Soditan points out that while the support of the other traditional rulers for Akinsanya is ensured, his political activities might alienate the British and endanger his ambitions:

> But you know how things are. If you continue to terrify the government with your politics, the Resident will be instructed to get under these people and turn them round: Do you want such a troublemaker as a brother Oba?—that kind of thing (199).

Indeed District Officer Ward, who refused to recognize Akinsanya, was no supporter of the nationalist politician, and neither were many of his local colleagues, one of whom noted in the 1945 Annual Report that,

The Odemo of Ishara (Samuel Akinsanya), formerly leader of the Youth Movement in Lagos, has continued to be the leading critic of Government, and a dangerously plausible and convincing one (CSO 26, IPAR 1945).

However, without *Akarigbo* Christopher Adedoyin's intense dislike of Akinsanya, based on Akinsanya's earlier opposition to his paramount position in Remo (see above), Ward could not have drawn out Akinsanya's case for as long as he eventually did. Although Ward publicly professed a dislike for both Akinsanya and Erinle, his close co-operation with the *Akarigbo* de facto favored Erinle. Thus, after the first public hearing Ward recommended that, if the contestants did not withdraw, they should be referred to the Remo Native Court of Appeal, the president of which was *Akarigbo* Adedoyin (Ijeprof. 1/2428 (II), 21/08/1941). Ward also overlooked the *Akarigbo*'s interventions on behalf of Erinle, which included the despatch of a number of Native Authority Policemen to Isara. In Isara, they guarded *Olisa* Ifekoya's house, where Erinle lived, giving the impression that his installation had been officially recognized (Ijeprof. 1/2428 (I), 30/08/1941). Both men also colluded in keeping Akinsanya in the dark about administrative decisions, and addressed all formal correspondence in the dispute to the regent Ifekoya's house where Erinle had access to it.

When Akinsanya complained about his treatment to Resident E. V. S. Thomas, Acting Chief Commissioner G. G. Shute officially referred the dispute—perhaps naively, perhaps intentionally—to the Remo Native Administration Council. Unlike in the novel (236), the inquiry was a tour de force in political manipulation. Of sixty-nine members of the Remo Native Administration Council, only twenty-nine members were present to hear the testimony given by six witnesses about Isara custom. Of these, only one was a supporter of Adesanya, while the other five—including the *Olisa*, who accused Akinsanya of being of slave origin—were supporters of Erinle. At the end of the meeting, the council voted on the two contestants for the *Odemo*-ship, and the resulting vote was split twenty to nine for Erinle and Akinsanya respectively (Ijeprof. 1/2428 (I), 26/09/1941). One of Akinsanya's supporters, J. T. Ogun from Mákún, a fellow center-oriented quarter of Sagamu with a long history of political rivalry with the *Akarigbo*'s quarter Ofin, complained to the Resident:

> Although the District Officer was present, the meeting to my mind was not all that it ought to be. I cannot hesitate to say that the Akarigbo dominated the meeting rather too much... The Akarigbo encouraged overwhelming cross-examination of Akisanya's [sic] peo-

ple, while he always opposed questions being put to Erinle's people (Ijeprof. 1/2428 (I), 30/09/1941).

The complaints of Akinsanya and his followers to Resident Thomas about the Remo Native Administration Council and District Officer Ward were eventually upheld by Acting Chief Commissioner Shute, and the council's report was considered unsatisfactory. Ward was accused of prejudice, and, after having been asked to augment his report, he was transferred to The Gambia (Ijeprof. 1/2428 (II), 13/07/1942). However, the *Akarigbo* remained Remo's paramount ruler. After Akinsanya's recognition by Chief Commissioner Whiteley in 1943, he and *Olisa* Ifekoya remained Akinsanya's bitter political enemies. Both men were involved in numerous further attempts to discredit and dethrone Akinsanya during the 1940s (cf. Ijeprof. 1/2428 (III)).

In the novel, Soyinka has given his literary Akinsanya the political support the real Akinsanya would only have after Adedoyin's death in 1952. By that time, Akinsanya's former rival Obafemi Awolowo had returned from his studies in the UK and founded the political party Action Group (AG). With Akinsanya's help, Awolowo was able to instrumentalize and unify existing opposition to *Akarigbo* Adedoyin in the center-oriented Remo towns. Adedoyin was affiliated with the NYM's successor organization that was eventually called National Council of Nigerian Citizens (NCNC).[13] Therefore, the AG became the party of the opposition, and the results of the first stage of the Western Regional Elections in 1951 show that the NCNC obtained most votes in the towns which supported the *Akarigbo*, while the AG tended to win in the center-oriented towns. Three months after the AG's inauguration in March 1951, *Odemo* Akinsanya became its chairman for Remo (*Nigerian Tribune*, 05/06/1951).

In 1952 *Akarigbo* Christopher Adedoyin died, and his son Adeleke contested the throne. However, the Remo Divisional Council, which had once been fully under his father's control, refused to recognize his claim. Apart from historical opposition to the *Akarigbo* in the center-oriented towns, many former supporters of Remo independence later came to resent the degree of control exercised by the *Akarigbo*. This resentment was also based on the perception that Adedoyin had continually favored the infrastructural development of his own community Ofin (in Sagamu) to the disadvantage of other towns. The Action

---

13. Christopher Adedoyin's son Adeleke Adedoyin was a Lagos-based lawyer and very prominent NCNC member. Soyinka may refer to Adeleke Adedoyin as the lawyer "Prince Adedoyin" used by the ex-*Ilés* to support their case (198).

Group also actively courted politicians from Ijebu and Remo who felt disadvantaged in other political parties.[14]

The new, AG-dominated council forced Adeleke Adedoyin to leave Sagamu, and gave its full support to Moses Awolesi, a friend of Akinsanya and Awolowo as well as an Action Group member. As the new *Akarigbo*, Awolesi was able to unite Remo behind the AG (cf. Nolte 2003b). Like the literary *Akarigbo* in Soyinka's novel, *Akarigbo* Awolesi supported and promoted *Odemo* Akinsanya's political ambitions, and both men participated in Obafemi Awolowo's AG government of the Western Region.

The temporal dislocation created by Soyinka by situating Akinsanya in a politically receptive and welcoming provincial environment, which includes both the *Awujale* and the *Akarigbo*, has the effect of letting Akinsanya's later success appear as a part of him that has always been present. Reflecting an understanding of the self in which all later achievements are already contained in their essence, the novel's description of Akinsanya clearly anticipates his subsequent leadership role.

Soyinka's setting of the dispute over the *Odemo*ship in the background of the local politics of a later, more unified decade is also extended to smaller details in the novel. For example, Soyinka refers to the Isara Native Administration Court that oversees the open ground on which the contest between Erinle and Akinsanya is carried out (4, 250). However, no such court existed at the time. In 1915, a native court was established in neighboring Ode Remo (short: Ode) in order to serve Ode, the nearby villages, the surrounding towns of Isara, Ipara, Akaka, and, until it received its own court two years later, Ògèrè. From the beginning, the presidency of the court was rotated among the rulers of the towns served by it (Ijeprof. 8/8, 09/12/1915). However, politicking and intra-town rivalry often affected the proceedings of the court, and the court members from Ode—where the court clerk was usually stationed—could sometimes use their proximity to the court and its proceedings to their advantage (cf. Ijeprof. 6/13, J 5/1930A).

When the *Odemo* was recognized by government in 1943, he found he had to work with rulers who had all opposed him politically in 1937–8 (see above). The *oba* of Ode Remo, the *Alaye Ode*, had even played an instrumental role in manipulating the Remo Native Administration Council's vote on Akinsanya and Erinle (Ijeprof. 1/2428 (I), 26/09/1941). In 1945 the *Odemò* began to boycott the Ode Remo Native Administration Court because, he alleged, the clerk and

---

14. In 1953, six of 60 inaugural and executive members of the AG were from Remo Division, and two more came from Ikorodu, which was part of the pre-colonial Remo district (Sklar 1963: 108–110).

the other joint presidents had conspired against him to prevent any cases from being heard during his presidency (Ijeprof. 2/C32 (I), 04/05/1945). While the complaints arising from his boycott would, in the short term, contribute to Akinsanya's continued difficulties in the late 1940s, the *Odemo* eventually succeeded in establishing a court in Isara in the 1950s. Like Remo's political unity, the Native Administration Court appears in Isara a decade early, silencing any notion that the *Odemo* might be subject to interference from neighboring towns.

Yet Soyinka does not gloss over the vagaries of local rivalry entirely. Thus, both Soditan's friend Sipe and Akinsanya himself are concerned about the construction of the new road from Ibadan, which the *Alake* of Abeokuta wants to keep almost entirely within Egba territory, whereas the ex-*Ilés* would like it to run through both Isara and neighboring Ipara (184, 242).[15] There are also some explorations of Isara's closeness and rivalry with neighboring Ode. In the marital dispute between Node and his youngest wife Binutu, her relatives from Ode lay siege on Node's house before Isara diplomacy resolves the matter amicably (96). Also from Ode are Erinle's relatives in Rokodo compound, who mistake the sanitary inspector Goriola for a spy (221–5). In both cases, town rivalry is shown to be the result of personal decisions, with no explicit link to political questions. As Erinle's relatives also demonstrate a surprising lack of sophistication—it is only in the discussion of the magic used by them that traditional religious practice ever appears laughable—one could even suggest that Soyinka describes local rivalry not in terms of political interests, but in terms of individual concerns and cultural practice.

Conclusion

This chapter has illustrated that, by focusing on the engagement of local intellectuals with cultural modernity during the 1940s, *Isara* does not fully reflect contemporary concerns over the direction of nationalist politics and the heritage of authoritarian local government. This allows Soyinka to represent

---

15. The road was eventually built as a 'trunk A road' linking Lagos and Ibadan by the AG government and it did lead through Ipara. However, despite Akinsanya's desire to have it run through Isara, it bypassed the town (albeit by less than a kilometre) and instead went through Ode. Locally, this is attributed to the intervention of AG financier Gbadamosi from Ikorodu, who was related to Ode on the maternal side. In 1968 and 1969, the Isara Progressive Union (IPU), a group led by Isara citizens close to failed *Odemo*ship candidate Osindeinde, fostered popular discontent with Akinsanya by embarking on the building of an access road from the Lagos-Ibadan road to the local health centre (cf. Osindeinde et al 1980: 16–22).

Akinsanya as an undisputed champion of popular politics. In a debate that emerged in response to Soyinka's critical distance to the *Négritude* movement, the author has on occasion been accused of lack of "authenticity" (cf. Feuser 1988). In a similar vein, Owomoyela has argued that Akinsanya's contest for the throne of Isara appears one-dimensional. He suggests that the climax of the book, Akinsanya's procession, simply describes his victory as the development challenge of an "African pathology":

> Akinsanya, destined to become the new Odemo, rides in triumph into the village on the white horse Bahia, while Akinyode [Soditan]... surveys the marks of the deficiency of the old regime evident on the bodies of Isara citizens and in their physical environment: yaws-eaten bodies, heads ringed by ringworm, necks distended by goiter, and the like (258–9). In short, Akinsanya's ascension, the triumph of the "enlightened" (216) over the retrogrades, promises an end of disease and dis-ease in Isara (Owomoyela 1994: 78–9).

However, such a criticism of *Isara* is not only inappropriate for accusing the author of not writing a different book, but it also falsely assumes that Akinsanya's contest for the throne constitutes the focal point of the novel.[16] The author himself suggests that the novel is centered on the personal, intellectual and spiritual life of Akinyode Soditan and his friends (v–vi). *Isara* is framed by an evocation of Soditan's potential, linked in complex ways to the name of Ashtabula, the Ohio hometown of his American pen friend Wade Cudeback. Soditan asks the "Spirit of Layeni," based in Òdogbolu at the border between Ijebu and Remo, whether he will be successful in life, and receives the (then) mysterious reply "Find Asabula." He later receives letters from Cudeback in Ashtabula, and when his pen friend comes to Isara during Akinsanya's procession and implied election as *Odemo*, Akinyode Soditan has, in his hour of triumph, also brought Ashtabula to Isara (3, 38–9, 245–6, 262).

As Peel has pointed out, by exploring the impact of the ex-*Ilés* complex and contradictory forms of knowledge and social practice on Akinsanya's campaign for the throne, the novel is concerned with their relationship to power as a personal, spiritual, and a public force (cf. Peel 2002: 139). This understanding of power as encompassing private success, public politics and the realm of cultural practice is ambiguous, and it allows Soyinka to portray the concerns of the ex-*Ilés* exemplarily, but without reducing them to the subjects of historical forces and movements. Akinsanya, while part of their group, is

---

16. Owomoyela concedes the possibility of this point in a footnote.

at the same time removed from them. While the ex-*Ilés* change history by supporting his candidacy in their different ways, the novel abandons Akinsanya at the moment in which he sets out to attain his office. Yet his future success is foreseen by the novel's description of a present in which he already enjoys the status of a popular hero (260–1).

By describing Isara as the aim of the ex-*Ilés*' efforts, *Isara* also contributes to the continuing debates on Yorubaness. Peel has suggested that the historical imagination of the Yoruba as a modern cultural nation was tied in with the emergence of a Christian educated elite and its consideration of Biblical ideas about the "nation" or "ethnos" (Peel 2000: 281). Yet the localization of the Bible in the "national" language also inspired a re-ordering of the national space, an attempt to constitute centers and reference points for the emerging nation. Shaped by the historical trajectories and political rivalries of the past, this re-ordering of space was competitive. Cultivating the localizing strategies of the mission, many of the emerging nation's intellectuals attempted to capture its essence through the historical perspectives of the polities which constituted it. At the time of writing, rival historical and cultural perspectives continue to coexist within Yoruba nationalism, often refracted and shaped in turn by the insertion of the greater part of the Yoruba into the colonial and postcolonial state of Nigeria.

As a contribution to this political and cultural project, Soyinka's representation of Akinsanya supports a reading of *Isara* in which Akinsanya represents nationalist politics while the town stands for Ijebu and Remo, and, beyond that, the Yoruba and even Nigerian nation. Like a literary peace offering, Soyinka's retrospectively viewed nationalist movement does not include enemies of "enlightenment," nor is his Remo divided into factions. In *Isara*, Soyinka includes almost everyone—with the exception of *Olisa*, Erinle and their nameless followers—on the side of his hero Akinsanya, and he diplomatically shares with them the retrospective glory of the early nationalist movement and the later success of Akinsanya's political career.

The novel's refusal to expose the differences and struggles both within the nationalist movement and in provincial affairs is a political assertion and an attempt to go beyond nationalist politics at the same time. Soyinka's description of Ijebu, often viewed as an awkward political entity within Nigeria, constitutes it as a central location of the making of the Yoruba and Nigerian nation. But rising above the historical politics of internal division, the debates and engagements of Akinyode Soditan and his friends stand not only for the political but also for the intellectual history of Nigeria. This refusal to get entangled in historical rivalries suggests that *Isara* is also an attempt to go beyond nationalist concerns and to present in the debates of the ex-*Ilés* and in the victory of Akinsanya a more general critique of Western claims to the "ownership" of cultural modernity.

References

Books and Articles

Adebanwi, W. 2004. "The City, Hegemony and Ethno-Spatial Politics: The Press and the Struggle for Lagos in Colonial Nigeria" in *Nationalism and Ethnic Politics*, Vol. 9, 25–51.

Awolowo. O. 1960. *Awo: The Autobiography of Chief Obafemi Awolowo*, London: Cambridge University Press.

Ayandele, E. 1992. *The Ijebu of Yorubaland. Politics, Economy and Society*, Ibadan: Heinemann.

Coleman, J. 1965. *Nigeria. Background to Nationalism*, Berkeley: University of California Press.

Crowder, M. & Ikime, O. (eds.), 1970. *West African Chiefs. Their Changing Status under Colonial Rule and Independence*, Ile Ife: University of Ife Press.

Crowder, M. [1962] 1978. *The Story of Nigeria*, London: Faber.

Epega, D. [1919] 1934, *Iwe Itan Ijebu ati Ilu Miran*, Ode Remo: Imole Oluwa Institute.

Feuser, W. 1988. "Wole Soyinka: The Problem of Authenticity" in *Black American Literature Forum*, Vol. 22 (3), 555–575.

Gibbs, J. 1988. "Biography into Autobiography: Wole Soyinka and the Relatives who inhabit 'Ake'" in *The Journal of Modern African Studies*, Vol. 26 (3), 517–548.

Ifekoya, I. 1929. *Iwe Itan Ilu Isara (Ijebu Remo)*, Lagos: Ife-Olu Printing Works.

Lloyd, P. 1955. "The Development of Political Parties in Western Nigeria" in *The American Political Science Review*, Vol. 49 (3), 693–707.

Nolte, I. 2003a. "Negotiating party politics and traditional authority: Obafemi Awolowo in Ijebu-Remo, Nigeria, 1949–1955" in W. van Binsbergen (ed.), *The Dynamics of Power and the Rule of Law*, Münster, Germany: LIT Verlag, 51–67.

Nolte, I. 2003b. "Obas and Party Politics: The Emergence of a Postcolonial Political Identity in Ijebu-Remo, 1948–1966" in O. Vaughan (ed.), *Indigenous Structures & Governance in Nigeria*, Ibadan, Nigeria: Bookcraft Press.

Ogunkoya, B. 1956. "The Early History of Ijebu" in *Journal of the Historical Society of Nigeria*, Vol. I (1), 48–58.

Oloko, B. 1984. "Modernisation and the Legitimacy of Traditional Rulers in Nigeria," paper presented at the National Conference on the Role of Traditional Rulers in the Governance of Nigeria, Institute of African Studies, University of Ibadan, September 11 to 14, 1984.

Osindeinde, J; S. Lesi & J. Talabi 1980. *Itan Ilu Isara*, Lagos: Jafo Commercial Printers.

Owomoyela, O. 1994. "With Friends like these…A critique of pervasive anti-Africanisms in Current African Studies Epistemology and Methodology" in *African Studies Review*, Vol. 37 (3), 77–101.

Peel, J. 1977. "Conversion and Tradition in two African Societies: Ijebu and Buganda" in *Past & Present, a journal of historical* studies, No. 77, 108–141.

Peel, J. 2000. *Religious Encounter and the Making of the Yoruba*, Bloomington: Indiana University Press.

Peel, J. 2002. "Christianity and the logic of nationalist assertion in Wole Soyinka's *Isara*" in D. Maxwell and I. Lawrie (eds.), *Christianity and the African Imagination. Essays in Honour of Adrian Hastings*, Leiden: Brill, pp. 127–155.

Sklar, R. 1963. *Nigerian Political Parties: Power in an Emergent African Nation*, Princeton: Princeton University Press.

Soyinka, W. [1989] 1991. *Isara. A Voyage Around 'Essay'*, London: Methuen.

Soyinka, W. 1981. *Aké. The Years of Childhood*, London: Collings.

Zachernuk, P. 2000. *Colonial Subjects. An African Intelligentsia and Atlantic Ideas*, Charlottesville: University Press of Virginia.

Newspaper Articles

Nigerian Tribune, 22/06/1950, "Igan Family disclaims Oshindeinde".
Nigerian Tribune, 05/06/1951, "General Saki Elected Remo AG Chairman".
Nigerian Tribune, 7 July 1951, "Awolowo and Sowole Will Represent Remo".
The Daily Sketch, 02/02/1994, "Odemo's Death is Natural – Family".
The Guardian, 10/02/1994, "Odemo of Isara Passes On".

Archival Sources (all from the National Archives Ibadan)

CSO 26, Ijebu Province Annual Reports (IPAR).
Ijeprof. 1/2428 (I), "The Odemo of Isara" (1941–2).
Ijeprof. 1/2428 (II), "The Odemo of Isara" (1942–3).
Ijeprof. 1/2428 (III), "The Odemo of Isara" (1944–50).
Ijeprof. 1/2746 (I), "Isara Affairs" (1943–8).
Ijeprof. 2/C32 (I), "Remo Affairs 1" (1935–45).
Ijeprof. 6/13, J 5/1930A, "Ode Remo Native Court Inspection".
Ijeprof. 8/8, "Ijebu-Ode Office Miscellaneous Papers Relating to Ijebu Chieftaincy Matters".

CHAPTER 11

RELIGION, PUBLIC SPACE, AND THE PRESS IN CONTEMPORARY NIGERIA

Matthews A. Ojo

Introduction

The mass media is a dominant institution in contemporary society. Particularly, in urban areas, both electronic and print media affect the daily lives of people in many ways as the media continues to perform the traditional roles of conveying information and providing entertainment. However, in contemporary times, the media has also become the purveyor of ideology and consciousness (Thompson, 1990).

The print media has continued to occupy a central place in the continuous change and crisis in Nigeria's social, political and economic arena. Particularly in the years of military dictatorships, the print media was in the forefront of articulating and maintaining a consistent and continuous opposition to the regimes. The print media has continued to provide not only information about events, but has also molded public opinion in the country. The creation of a civil society in Nigeria in the turbulent era of military regimes was greatly fostered by the press. Unlike the electronic media, which has largely been under government control, the press on the other hand has largely been privately-owned and thus has been able to maintain some independence to safeguard its readership—the major reason for its commercial viability. Even in the democratic regime that began in 1999, the press has largely maintained a critical position on various government policies. Consequently, the print media has adopted various styles in maintaining itself as the conscience of the people and in reflecting the aspirations of the people.

A major research project titled "The Role of Print and Electronic Media in the Constitution of New Religious Publics in Yorubaland," undertaken between 1997 and 1999 under the leadership of Professors Louis Brenner and J. D. Y. Peel of the School of Oriental and African Studies, London, and Professor Karin Barber and Paulo F. Moraes Farias of the Centre of West African Studies, University of Birmingham, has enabled me, among other things, to reflect critically on how the production and the consumption of the print and electronic media influence the constitution of new forms of "new religious publics"; and on the interrelationships that exist between diverse forms of religious consciousness which are opened up by the media. Of particular interest is the role the print media continues to play in the creation of an identity for the civil society, and investing certain forms of power on this society. Religious organizations constitute a significant part of this civil society. In addition, I have investigated the projection of religious message, symbols, and associated activities from the private to the public sphere through the medium of the press. Indeed, since the late 1970s, religion has occupied much attention and space in the press and in public sphere. This transformation has altered the position of religion within the pluralistic background in the country, and has intensified the contest for public space among the three major religions: Christianity, Islam, and Traditional African Religion. It is this continuing interest in the relationship between religion, the public sphere and the press that informs the focus of this chapter.

The Nature of Nigerian Print Media

Studies about the media and religion in Nigeria are rare. The existing literature often discusses the press from the journalistic perspective, and hardly takes religion into account. Increase H. E. Coker (1970), Dayo Duyile (1985), and R. A. Akinfeleye (1985), among others, focus on the historical development of the Nigerian press; while Fred Omu (1978) pays attention to the relationship between politics and the press. It was Andrew Walls (1978) who first provided us with an insight into the relationship of religion and the press in Nigeria. His article focuses on how the press and religion are united and used for war propaganda and for fostering group identity in the Biafran enclave during the Nigerian civil war, 1967–70. Panta Umechukwu (1995) makes a content analysis of the reportage of religious violence by two Nigerian news weeklies between 1986 and 1991. He reveals poor performance by the media in the coverage of such a sensitive issue. Rosalind Hackett (1998) notes how the burgeoning Christian Charismatic and Pentecostal movements are favoring electronic media as suitable sites for the transmission of their teachings and building their empires. Although she pays much attention to the television, audio, and video forms, her revelation could also be extended to the press. While studies from Nigeria have been few, many have been published about the American press and religion. Stewart Hoover (1993) discusses American newspapers' coverage of religion from the perspective of the readers. Mark Silk (1995), on the other hand, provides more comprehensive analysis of religion new in the American press. S. Hoover and K. Lundby (1997) examine the intersection between religion, the media, and culture, but have few discussions specifically devoted to the press.

The history of the Nigerian Press could be traced to two divergent attempts of European missionaries in Nigeria. In 1846 Rev. Hope Waddell, a missionary of the Church of Scotland, based in Calabar, South Eastern Nigeria, set up a printing press that concentrated on printing religious materials. On Dec. 3, 1859, Rev. Henry Townsend, a Christian Missionary Society missionary based in Abeokuta, published the first newspaper which he called *Iwe Irohin Fun Awon Ara Egba ati Yoruba*. While the efforts of Rev. Townsend stimulated the evolution of the Nigerian Press, that of Waddell brought into being the commercial press in Nigeria.[1]

The second newspaper, *The Anglo African*, appeared on June 6,1863. It was pro-colonial government in its reportage, and it was generously supported with government advertisements. It folded on December 30, 1865.[2] Seventeen years after the death of *The Anglo African*, the third newspaper, the *Lagos Times and the Gold Coast Advertiser*, first appeared on November 10, 1880. Between 1880 and 1920 about seven newspapers, altogether, came into existence, and most ceased publication within their first ten years.

By the 1920s, the nationalist agitation was partly reflected in the establishment of more newspapers that sought to further the nationalist agenda. This period also witnessed the birth of provincial and indigenous language newspapers. Most of the newspapers had pungent and critical editorials against British rule. The only surviving paper of that era is the *Daily Times*, which was first published by the same organization on June 1, 1926. The *Daily Times*, because of its well-organized and efficient management, dictated the pace in newspaper management, printing technology, training of journalists, systematic production-planning and circulation designs in the country. Up till early 1980s, *Daily Times* was playing the lead role in the newspaper business. How-

---

1. Dayo Duyile, *Makers of Nigerian Press* (Lagos: Gong Communications (Nig.) Ltd., 1987), pp 1-6 & 14–18.
    2. *Ibid.*, p. 68.

ever, its pro-government reportage resulted in the loss of readership, and in September 2004 it was sold to a private interest. Its new management has suspended publication until late 2004.

Further development in the history of the newspaper industry took place around the late 1950s when vigorous political electioneering campaigns partly resulted in the publishing of various newspapers to promote the interest of political leaders and their parties. For example, the Action Group of Chief Obafemi Awolowo published *The Tribune* in 1949 as a political organ mainly to counter Zik's paper, *The Telegraph*, that was established in 1948.

The 1960s witnessed the commencement of the Nigerian government's involvement in publishing newspapers.[3] Various governments either took over existing newspapers or established new ones. The Federal Government acquired *The Daily Times* at this time, while the Northern Nigerian government established the *New Nigerian* after taking over an existing newspaper, the *Nigerian Citizen.*

Early in the 1970s the scene shifted from government ownership, and the period witnessed the unprecedented proliferation of private national and provincial newspaper in Nigeria. Chief Olu Aboderin opened the scene in 1973 when he established the *Punch* newspaper, while Chief M.K.O. Abiola established the *National Concord* in 1980. In 1975 Sam Amuka Pemu, a renowned journalist, produced the *Vanguard* newspaper. In February 27, 1982, Alex Ibru came up with *Sunday Guardian*, and by July of that year he began daily publication.

The 1980s was the boom era of magazines, especially in Southwestern Nigeria. Initially, news magazines (which dealt with serious issues and were meant for well-informed, educated people) were published, but in the mid-1980s, Mr. Muyiwa Adetiba came up with *Prime People* a magazine that revolutionized the practice of journalism. The magazine projected the sensuous, sensational, and incredulous dimensions into the human-interest publications.[4] *Prime People* was essentially a tabloid, and devoted interest to gossips concerning important people in the society. With the advent of *Prime People*, magazine publication in Nigeria could be said to have assumed three categories, namely: news magazines (e.g., *Newswatch*, *The News*); the general human interest magazines (e.g., *Poise*, *Vintage People*, *Prime People*, *Today's Choice*); and fun and romantic affairs magazines which involved non-sensa-

---

3. Tador, M., 'History of the Nigerian Press' in Tony Momoh and Godwin Omole (eds), *The Press in Nigeria* (Lagos: Nigerian Press Council 1996), pp. 47-49.

4. An Interview with Mr. Jimi Kayode, the director of Nigerian Institute of Journalism, Ogba, Lagos.

tional aspects of the lives of the individuals and things happening in the society (e.g., *Hearts, Better Lovers, Passion, Ikebe Super, Hints, Super Story*).

From such a small beginning, by 2000 Nigeria's print media had become perhaps the most vibrant in Africa, with about fourteen dailies, most of which had national readership and coverage, six news weeklies, three regular weekly tabloids, and about five evening papers all publishing in English. In addition to the national papers, there are a large number of regional newspapers and magazines in the English and indigenous languages. The variety represents a colossal development of the press since its beginning in 1859.

Despite being the largest newspaper industry in Africa, the Nigerian print media has a checkered history under successive military governments in the country. At various times from the early 1970s, some papers have been banned when the government considered them to be too critical. In addition, there have been seizure of copies of the papers, censoring of journalists, occupation of the premises by security agents, unilateral confiscation of properties of newspapers, arrest and detention of journalists, and so on.[5] These anti-press activities coming from the government require us to reflect on the nature of the Nigerian press.

First, the Nigerian press is an institution that derives its active life from the political sphere. Although, it was the activity of a missionary of the Church Missionary Society that brought the press into being, however by the late nineteenth century, the press had been devoting much attention to social and political issues. More important, the press derives its news content predominantly from the political arena. Presently, about 50% of news appearing in the papers come from events and activities generated by the government and its agencies. The papers owned by the government are expected to devote much attention to reporting the activities of government, mostly in admirable terms.

Secondly, the press as an institution derives legitimacy from the political realm. There are a number of laws that regulate the establishment and operation of newspapers in the country. Although the 1979 constitution allows for the establishment of newspapers by any Nigerian, subject to regulation by the National Assembly,[6] in reality any newspapers could be closed down at any time. Some laws are made stiff to curb the freedom of the press. Although the Nigerian Press Council was established by Decree No. 85 of 1992 as a self-reg-

---

5. A human rights has documented some anti-press activities by the government between 1994 and 1997. See Babatunde Olugboji, *Suppression of Press Freedom in Nigeria* (Lagos: Constitutional Rights Project, 1997).

6. Section 36 (2). This has been retained in the new Constitution. See Section 22 and 39 (2) of the Constitution of the Federal Republic of Nigeria, 1999.

ulatory body, yet the government does not take into account whenever it has any complaint against the press. Therefore, government control on the press is strong.

While the political authority provides the legal framework for their existence, the survival of newspapers depends on the generosity of the business arena. Most media houses survive because they obtain regular and fat advertisements and sponsorships from the business sectors. This need became strengthened in the mid-1970s when business entrepreneurs began to establish independent newspapers. *The Punch*, the *National Concord, The Guardian* (Lagos, Nigeria) and the *Vanguard* were established in 1974, 1980, 1982, and 1985 respectively by entrepreneurs who used their business connections to provide more advertisements for their respective papers.

Lastly, the print media as an institution are acceptable to Nigerians because they operate within certain cultural contexts with pre-defined moral values. These moral values are both religious and cultural, and both act together to give respectability to the press from the readership. In addition, for survival, the print media must overtly promote certain viewpoints which its readership share or will subscribe to.

As the fourth estate of the realm, the press has always been looked upon as a strong pillar of democracy because it channels democratic culture through the free flow of information. But the reality is that the press is always subject to manipulation by the political realm. Even when the press becomes a combative public organ, as it has been under recent Nigerian military regimes, it must still fulfill its basic role of gathering, processing, and disseminating information for public good.

From the foregoing, it is clear that the press is essentially political. However, from the 1990s, the Nigerian press has been devoting much attention to reporting religion and giving prominence to the activities and pronouncements of religious leaders. This paper will attempt to account for this shift. It will be argued that the failure of the centralized state to respond to the needs and aspiration of the people has enabled the press to turn increasingly to the religious sphere as the only articulate segment of the civil society. In addition, religion offers stability that contrasts sharply with the instability of the political realm, and the press has continued to receive favorite backing from religious bodies and institutions. More importantly, pronouncements from religious leaders, no matter how distasteful to the political authority, still carry a sanctity that the military rulers cannot question, disturb or regulate.

Although religious news has been featured in the newspapers since the nineteenth century, religion took prominent space and shifted to the front cover during the great debate on the inclusion or otherwise of the Sharia legal system in the national constitution in 1977 (Ofonagoro, 1978). By the early 1980s, the religious riots in Northern Nigeria and the controversy surrounding Nigeria's admission into the membership of the Organization of the Islamic Conference (OIC) all helped to put religion into a dominant position in the press and in the public arena. These religious events polarized the population into Christian versus Muslims, which corresponded to the existing North-South divide. These events had much bearing on the political life of the country.

With the proliferation of newspapers from the 1980s, the ensuing religious divide, and the competition to win readership and maintain large circulation, many newspapers resorted to using various appeals, including the religious. Religion was so used because, in many places, it reinforces ethnic and regional identities. Indeed, by the 1990s, the reportage of religion in the press had assumed a wide proportion, and socio-cultural and religious issues affecting the people at the grassroots have occupied a greater attention.

Religious Reportage in the Secular Media

The Nigerian press represents different orientation to news coverage and reporting, and basically the origin of these newspapers determine their orientation. Moreover, in their reportage, the Nigerian press has greatly reflected the changes in the society. Although economic and political issues have continued to dominate, attention is also given to socio-cultural issues, particularly religion.

For a preliminary assessment of religion reportage in the press, five newspapers were selected for analysis. In terms of the quantity of religious items reported in these newspapers, the *Daily Sketch, Nigerian Tribune, National Concord*, and *The Punch* ranked among the first four.

The coverage of religious organizations and religious activities in the selected papers is very comprehensive in scope and very diverse as well. Three consecutive months, January, February, and March were selected for analysis. In each of these months, there was at least one major religious event of national significance. Activities marking the beginning of the year and the end of the Ramadan fasting occurred in January. In February, Nigerians were first informed of the impending visit of Pope John Paul II to Nigeria, and there was an uprising by Shiites in the North calling for the release of their detained leader, Ibrahim El-Zak Zaky. In March, the Pope visited Nigeria, and Benson Idahosa, the foremost Nigerian Pentecostal minister, died at the age of 59. Because of the quantity of the data available, I have used statistical analysis to summarize them. The *Daily Monitor* is also analyzed because it is the only daily that carries more of Islamic items than Christian ones. Table 01 shows the quantity of religious reportage in the selected dailies.

News constitutes the main focus of the Nigerian dailies. News that borders on religion is mostly political commentaries by church leaders, and of religious disturbances in the country. Generally, events surrounding religious festivals are covered. Newsworthy events like the death of Archbishop Idahosa, and the visit of the Pope in March were covered. Occasionally, the dailies report on unusual activities in the churches or about church leaders. Features or articles are usually more serious, and are lengthy discussions on previous and current news on religion. They contain more facts than news, because they are the output of thorough investigation. They are usually not less than half a page.

Materials considered as advertisements are paid for, and their contents addressed to the public. The two categories included in this section are public notices of registration of churches with the Corporate Affairs Commission of the Ministry of Internal Affairs, and occasional advertisements of forthcoming church activities. The commodification of the religious symbols and its consequent commercialization has given rise to the bureaucratization of church structures. Churches now register their organizations like business companies; they adopt organizational and administrative strategies devised by profit-oriented companies. This is evident in the number of religious announcements and advertisements in both the print and electronic media.

Announcements are unpaid notices of church activities that are put in the bulletin board or in the announcement column. They are in smaller prints as editors try to maximize available space. The announcements columns depend on items submitted by the churches, and the space the editors can make available. *The Punch* and *Nigerian Tribune* have the best and regular columns for announcements.

Photographs are news items that are reported with captions to photographs taken during church activities. Excluded are photographs from the archives and libraries of the dailies. Interviews are limited to those on church leaders or those items whose contents dwell on religion.

Overall, religion is receiving much attention in the Nigerian press. News items dominate accounting for a mean of 29.27% of the total Christian items in all the four selected dailies covered in the three-month period of January to March 1998. Next were announcements of forthcoming church programs, which accounted for a mean of 22.76. Photographs were evenly distributed every month with a mean of 16.03%, and interviews were the least with a mean of 1.51%. Table 02 gives the mean of the various categories of religious reportage in the selected dailies in the three-month period.

Table 01. Frequency of Religious Reportage in Selected Nigerian Dailies According to Months

Title	News No	News %	Features No	Features %	Sermons No	Sermons %	Advertisements No	Advertisements %	Announcements No	Announcements %	Photographs No	Photographs %	Interviews No	Interviews %	Christian Items No	Christian Items %	Islamic Items No	Islamic Items %	Total
January 1998																			
Sketch	89	38.5	19	8.2	11	4.7	13	5.6	42	18.1	55	23.8	2	0.8	231	69.1	103	30.8	334
Punch	52	26.1	43	21.6	14	7	42	21.1	27	13.5	19	9.5	2	1	199	79.9	50	20	249
Tribune	56	30.2	23	12.4	26	14	8	4.3	57	30.8	12	6.4	3	1.6	185	73.7	66	26.2	251
Concord	49	43.7	15	13.3	10	8.9	8	7.1	21	18.7	8	7.1	1	0.8	112	73.2	41	26.7	153
February 1998																			
Sketch	57	30.6	11	5.9	11	5.9	20	10.7	63	33.8	23	12.3	1	0.5	186	76.8	56	23.1	242
Punch	75	38	11	5.5	16	8.1	41	20.8	39	19.7	15	7.6	0	0	197	85.2	34	14.7	231
Tribune	42	25.4	22	13.3	17	10.3	15	9.0	53	32.1	14	8.4	2	1.2	165	90.1	18	9.8	183
Concord	38	29.2	9	6.9	18	13.8	6	4.6	36	27.6	17	13.0	6	4.6	130	88.4	17	11.5	147
March 1998																			
Sketch	67	20.6	26	8.6	16	4.9	17	5.2	59	18.2	131	40	6	1.8	324	89.7	37	10.2	361
Punch	58	22.8	31	12.2	21	8.2	45	17.7	49	19.2	45	17.7	5	1.9	254	90.3	27	9.6	281
Tribune	50	24.5	35	17.1	9	4.4	14	6.8	45	22	48	23.5	3	1.4	204	91.4	19	8.5	223
Concord	49	21.6	42	18.5	18	7.9	15	6.6	44	19.4	52	23	6	2.6	226	91.4	21	8.5	247

Table 02. The Mean of Various Aspects of Religious Reportage in the Nigerian Press January to March 1998 in Four Selected Dailies (All in Percentage of Overall Total of Christian Items)

	News	Features	Sermons	Advertise-ments	Announce-ments	Photo-graphs	Inter-views
Sketch	29.90	7.57	5.17	7.17	23.37	25.37	1.03
Punch	28.97	13.10	7.77	19.87	17.47	11.60	0.97
Nigerian Tribune	26.70	14.27	9.57	6.7	28.3	12.77	1.40
National Concord	31.50	12.90	10.2	6.10	21.90	14.37	2.67
Overall Mean	29.27	11.96	8.18	9.96	22.76	16.03	1.51

Sermonizing to an Irreligious Public

A prominent part of religious items in the secular press is the sermons. These sermons are written on a regular basis by different eminent pastors, and they range from spiritual development to contemporary issues such as politics and economy. The contents of the sermons are often stereotyped, and most of them deal with personal salvation and Christian growth. W. F. Kumuyi, who writes in the *National Concord*, adopts a holiness orientation, while David Oyedepo, who writes in the same paper, represent the liberal prosperity-type of contemporary Christianity. E. A. Adeboye represents a middle course in between. Tunde Bakare who writes in the tabloid, *National Encomium*, often dwells on socio-political issues and empowerment of the Christian church as an institution within the ever-changing Nigerian society. Islamic sermons are only published on Fridays and usually in a paper published only once per week.

It was the *National Concord*, owned by the late M. K. O. Abiola, a Muslim, that first introduced a regular, weekly column for Christian sermons in the *Sunday Concord* from the mid-1980s. However, by the early 1990s, the inclusion of Christian sermons as a regular column either on Sundays or during the week days have become a prominent and permanent features of all the four papers selected. *The Punch* leads with four regular sermon columns, each half a page, spread throughout the week. Next is the *National Concord* with a minimum of three, and at times four regular columns. The *Nigerian Tribune* has only one Christian sermon column on Sunday, and there is a sermon column on New Age Religions. Most of the sermons touch on the experiential aspect of religion. Examples of the captions of these columns are "Voice of Hope in These Tough Times," "Help for the Present Hour," "Family Matters," etc. Though diverse, they are written to meet the needs of many Nigerians in the

Table 03. Frequency of Sermons in Eight Nigerian Dailies (January–May 1998)

Name	Year established	Christian sermons	Islamic sermons	Other religions	Total
Nigerian Tribune	1949	4	1	1	6
The Punch	1974	5	1	0	6
Daily Sketch	1964	4	1	0	5
Vanguard	1985	3	2	0	5
National Concord*	1980	4	1	0	5
The Guardian	1982	2	1	0	3
Daily Monitor*	1997	1	1	0	2
Daily Times	1926	0	1	0	1
TOTAL		23	9	1	33

*Proprietors of these papers are Muslims.

contemporary milieu. The continuing relevance of Christianity in the public sphere was buttressed when the weekly tabloids began to have regular sermon columns from early 1998.

Sermons columns have been very regular in the dailies. These sermons have become means of de-secularizing the papers, and portraying them as agents interested in the christianization and Islamization of the society, and thus confer legitimacy on the activities of the papers. Unarguably, religion has become a smokescreen in the public sphere, and a tool for mediating the harsh economic socio-political reality in the country. It is, therefore, in the interest of the papers to move in the same direction as the aspiration of the people.

The newspapers have also become a religious market place where religious organizations advertise themselves. A prominent feature of this is the statutory notices of registration, and the number of notices of application for registration to the Corporate Affairs Commission of the Federal Ministry of Internal Affairs has been revealed in the qualitative data above. The diversification of the choices in terms of quality, content, style and shape of religious organizations is really astounding.

The Press and Religious Crises

One major issue that has been reported immensely in recent times in the papers is the controversy over the implementation of the Sharia in some states in Northern Nigeria. The Sharia controversy began in the second week of Oc-

Table 04

Title	Total No. of Issues	News Items	Essays/ Features	Letters to Editors	Editorial	Inter- views	Cartoons
The Guardian*	31	44	11	6	1	2	NIL
The Punch**	17	47	7	6	NIL	3	3

*All daily issues consulted. **Collection based on Saturdays and Sundays only.

tober 1999, when the Governor of Zamfara State, Alhaji Ahmed Sani, signed two bills for the establishment of Sharia courts, and subsequently proclaimed the state an Islamic state.

The press coverage on the Sharia controversy is really complex, and opinions expressed on the issues reflect a variety of perceptions. The coverage by *The Guardian* is the best organized and articulate. *The Punch* has more news content but less in-depth examination of the issues involved in the controversy. Initially the press coverage of *The Guardian* appeared under News mostly on pp. 1 to 5. Thereafter, a separate column captioned "The *Sharia* Debate" was created from time to time for fuller news reports. Thirdly, the column "Policy and Politics" occasionally was devoted to essays or in-depth analysis of the issue. The table below reflects a breakdown of religious news pertaining to the Sharia controversy that appeared in *The Guardian* and *The Punch* between October 14 and December 23, 1999.

Media coverage of the Sharia controversy was disproportionately higher in the news content. Most of these news items were about further developments in the implementation of the Sharia in Zamfara and other Northern States. Public comments, press releases and press conferences in support or against the Sharia were all covered as news. Unlike the Sharia debate of 1977-78, there were fewer published opinions from the ordinary Nigerians, thus reflecting a great shift of interest in the whole matter. Instead of the generality speaking through the press, the press this time articulated what it considered the interest of the political elite. Governor Sani and other leading protagonists and antagonists of the Sharia were interviewed, while the cartoons reflect the less serious side of the controversy.

A good analysis of the press coverage of the Sharia controversy is to examine what *topoi* the reportage represents. Mark Silk, the journalist and historian, has argued that news stories are usually stereotypical. Topoi, according to Silk (1995: 50–51), provides focus and general conceptions of journalistic narratives. Silk has concluded that:

> All in all, the topoi used by the news media are like reflections on a
> pond, sometimes clear and distinct, sometimes distorted.... The topoi

will mirror public attitudes, if only because it is in the nature of the media to be comprehensible to the undifferentiated audience it seeks...(1995: 53).

In the Nigerian press coverage of the *Sharia*, it is clear that a set of public perceptions guided the media treatment of the crisis. This public perception usually operates at a level of appropriateness, i.e. generally acceptable "broad public discourses about policy, sentiment, taste, and value" (Hoover, 1998:3). Like other subjects in the media, religion has its familiar story types or topoi, and the topoi applied to religious news are derived from religious sources. Silk therefore identified seven topoi under which religion in the news can be sub-sumed—good works, tolerance, hypocrisy, false prophecy, inclusion, super-natural belief, and declension.

Two relevant topoi, which were clearly reflected in the press coverage of the *Sharia* controversy, are "tolerance" and "false prophecy." The topos of toler-ance assumes a peaceful co-existence of adherents of different religions in a religious pluralistic society. Tolerance has an added advantage of guarantee-ing the secularity of the Nigerian state and curbing the excesses of any reli-gion. Most of the news reports on the Sharia controversy were quick to point out that the implementation of the Sharia meant that Zamfara had become an Islamic state. Questions were then raised about what becomes of the in-terests of non-Moslems in an Islamic state.[7] Hence, the press coverage was quick to highlight the effect of the Zamfara experiment on religious tolerance in the country. In his analysis of the issue, the *Guardian* Political Correspon-dent, Chukwudi Abiandu, quoted a Lagos Moslem who asked if the Zamfara people and governor are conscious of their responsibilities to non-Moslems who have co-existed with their Moslem brothers for ages.[8] To buttress the fact that the Sharia issue would breed intolerance, many papers reported the con-tinuous exodus of non-Moslems and non-indigenes from the state.[9] In addi-tion, the restiveness and fear gripping the Christian community in the North featured in the content of the news coverage.

Another issue bordering on tolerance/intolerance featured in news cover-age is the allegation of the gradual Islamization of Nigeria either through forceful conversion or installing a Moslem as the President of the country. The secretary of the Pentecostal Fellowship of Nigeria in the North, Rev. Raphael

---

7. See 'The North Splits over Sharia,' *Sunday Punch*, October 17, 1999, p. 3.

8. 'The *Sharia* Debacle and Governance in Nigeria', *The Guardian*, October 25, 1999, p. 8.

9. *The Punch*, October 16, 1999, p. 35.

Opawoye, made such an allegation in a press release.[10] Although Section 10 of the 1999 constitution prohibits the federal or state government from adopting any religion as a state religion, and further protects Nigerians against discrimination on account of religion, ethnic affiliation, the press reported the concern of Nigerians about the possible breach of these constitutional provisions. The press further noted that the balance of religious pluralism that had existed in the country was being threatened by the Zamfara adventure. Therefore, in the reportage of the Sharia, the press considered itself as the protector of the religious rights of Nigerians against the intolerant onslaught of the Sharia. Whenever religious news is treated in the perspective of false religion, the reaction of the media is usually to join crusades against such eccentricities in religion. It seems that a life-consuming religion, as the Sharia in Nigeria is, is socially regressive and thus hostile to mankind's deepest aspirations. Media coverage of the Sharia is not about marginal religious groups but about a mainline religion, which is consciously keen in destroying the social order and the national fabric of unity. Looking at the Sharia issue as a classic example of false prophesy was further strengthened by tales of atrocities about the consequences of the implementation of Sharia in Muslims countries such as Algeria and Sudan. Therefore, Ahmed Sani's concept of the Sharia has become a dangerous representation of religion, which the society has to fight against.

Governor Ahmed Sani was regarded as a self-style prophet and a deviant within a society that was adjusting to positive change. To the press, here was a constitutional leader attempting to manipulate the country's constitution and religious sentiments and thus establish himself as a religious leader. For example, Ahmed Sani was reported as saying that the proclamation of Sharia law in Zamfara was a divine revelation, and any Muslim opposing it is not a true Muslim.[11] It is therefore interesting that most newspapers gave prominence to the attack of Ibrahim El-Zak Zaky, the leader of the Islamiyah Brotherhood Movement, a strict Islamic sect, on the Zamfara governor. El-Zak Zaky said that the Sharia is an Islamic legal system and can only be applied by an Islamic government, and not by a political leader such as Sani. He added that wherever Sharia operates, it is supreme, but such cannot operate in the present dispensation in Nigeria. He then called on Governor Sani to endeavor to enforce Islamic moral principles in the state before contemplating the Sharia.[12]

---

10. *Sunday Punch,* October 31, 1999, pp. 1 and 2.
11. *Sunday Punch,* October 17, 1999, p. 14.
12. *The Guardian,* October 14, 1999, p. 4.

Sani Ahmed was a false prophet, no doubt—that was the judgment of the Nigerian press. For example, a big photograph of the man on *The Guardian* edition of March 5, 2000, had a bold caption, "THE MAN WHO ALMOST BROUGHT NIGERIA TO ITS KNEES."[13]

In addition, the media portrayed Ahmed as hypocritical in his quest to implement the Sharia. Some press reports commented that the Sharia would descend heavily on petty thieves while, what Nigerians call "pen robbers," i.e., government functionaries in high positions who embezzle millions of public funds go free. This hypocrisy became manifest on March 22, 2000, when a cow thief, Bello Jangedi, had his right hand amputated in Zamfara State. This latest development attracted condemnation in the press. It is therefore not surprising that the Sharia issue was treated as a false prophecy by the press.

Other issues covered by the press on the Sharia debate included the constitutionality and legality of the implementation of the Sharia, the international and diplomatic implications of the implementation of the Sharia in Nigeria in the light of the global promotion of human rights, and the political implication of the action of Governor Ahmed Sani, particularly the suggestion that the Zamfara experiment would destabilize the country and eventually lead to the disintegration of the country.

The Sharia debate is far more than just a religious or political issue; hence the wide diversity in the press coverage of the controversy. It calls into question the role of religion in governance, the need to redefine the secularity of the state, and the need to guarantee religious pluralism and peaceful co-existence in the country. The dilemma of the press in reporting this issue informs its wide perspective.

From the foregoing analysis, it is evident that the media has always been torn among three main perspectives of religious news—treating news purely as religious matters or treating it as political issues. A third perspective is to treat religious news as a hybrid of the above two. First, when religious news is generated by religious institutions themselves, e.g. sermons, advertisements, festivals, they are treated as religion per se because they represent a kind of community faith. Within this perspective, the supernatural aspect of religion, its community spirit, and its benefits to individuals are emphasized. However, when the media generate the news through investigation and reportage, religion is more likely to be treated as a political issue. Within this perspective, the role of religion in contributing to the interplay of power within the soci-

---

13. *The Guardian*, March 5, 2000, p. 1

ety, its manipulation by politicians, and its transformative potentials are highlighted.

The Sharia contest could be seen as a contest for both religious and political space by an obscure segment of the political elite. Certainly, the press acted not only as an adjudicator but as a participant in the context. In the final analysis, according to Hoover (1998:11), media coverage of religion is deeply embedded in the perception of the role of religion in democratic public life.

Conclusion

As clearly shown, religion is no longer marginal to the press. Since religious life is a major part of culture, it follows that it should be portrayed in the press. The media has continued to give prominent coverage to religion partly because it is the most articulate section of the civil society that withstood the onslaught of military dictatorship between 1993 and May 1999. With the decline of the state, the religious realm continues to meet the needs and aspirations of Nigerians, and thus generate news for the media.

The Nigerian press represents itself as the mediator between the public and the individual. The scope of its power is largely determined by the unfolding socio-political events in the country. In the 1960s and 1970s, newspapers were very cheap and their circulation was rather large. Economic decline from the late 1980s has been costly, but they still enjoy popular readership. To cope with declines in circulation, the newspapers and magazines have resorted to publishing advertisements from businesses and government agencies, and announcements from religious organizations.

As already noted, the newspapers often serve as the mediator between the public sphere and the private sphere. The coverage and reporting of such religious news of national dimension is purely journalistic. However, the style of reportage indicates the sectional interest of the newspapers concerned. For example, during the controversy about Nigeria's membership of the OIC, the style of reportage by the *National Concord* was clearly in support of Islam, in fact it published various articles defending Muslims.

The secular media are really not secular in their content and style because of the attention they devote to reporting religion. Religion in the Nigerian press, I surely believe, serves a secular purpose of sanctioning a public space that is not religious. In fact, the Nigerian press approach religion and report religion with values and presuppositions that the public widely shares. Therefore, while not strictly forming opinion for the people, they are at least expressing the opinion of the people.

References

Ayandele, E. A. "The Missionary Factor in Northern Nigeria" in O. U. Kalu, ed., *The History of Christianity in West Africa*, (London, Longman, 1980),

Coker, Increase H. E. *Landmarks of the Nigerian Press* (Lagos, 1970).

Duyile, D. *Makers of Nigerian Press*, (Lagos, 1987).

Federal Ministry of Information, *Report of the Constitution Drafting Committee*, (Lagos: 1976).

Hackett R. I. J. "Charismatic/Pentecostal Appropriation of Media Technologies in Nigeria and Ghana," *Journal of Religion in Africa* Vol. XXXVIII, 3 (1998), pp. 258-277.

Hoover, Stewart M. "Privatism, authority and autonomy in American newspaper coverage of religion: the readers speak" in Chris Arthur, ed., *Religion and the Media, An Introductory Reader* (Cardiff, 1993), pp. 261-274.

Hoover, Stewart M. & Lundby, K., eds. *Rethinking Media, Religion and Culture* (London, 1997).

Hoover, Stewart M. *Religion in the News* (London, 1998).

Kukah, Matthew H. "The Politicisation of Fundamentalism in Nigeria" in Paul Gifford, ed., *New Dimensions in African Christianity* (Nairobi: All African Council of Churches, 1993).

Lovin, R. "Religion and politics" in M. Hawkesworth and M. Kogan, eds., *Encyclopedia of Government and Politics*, vol. 1 (London: Routledge, 1992).

Marshall-Fratani, R. "Mediating The Global and Local in Nigerian Pentecostalism", *Journal of Religion in Africa* xxviii, 3 (1998).

Marshall, R. "Pentecostalism in Southern Nigeria: An Overview" in Paul Grifford, ed., *New Dimensions in African Christianity* (Ibadan: Sefer Books Ltd., 1993).

Nabofa, M. I. *Religious Communication: A Study in African Traditional Religion* (Ibadan: Daystar Press, 1994).

Nwabueze, B. O. *Nigeria 1993: The Political Crisis and Solutions* (Ibadan: Spectrum Books, 1994).

Ofonagoro, W. I. et al., *The Great Debate* (Lagos, 1977).

Ojo, M. A. & Akinrinade, O. "Religion and Politics in Contemporary Nigeria: A Study of the 1986 OIC Crisis," *Journal of Asian and African Affairs*, vol. IV, No 1, Fall 1992, pp. 44-59.

Ojo, Matthews A. "On the beat: In Lagos, Religion's Above the Fold" *Religion in the News*, Vol. 2, No. 2, Summer 1999, pp. 7-8, & 22.

Olugboji, Babatunde, *Suppression of Press Freedom in Nigeria* (Lagos, 1997).

Olupona, Jacob K. "Religious Pluralism and Civil Religion in Africa," *Dialogue & Alliance*, vol. 2, No. 4, Winter 1988-89.

Omu, Fred, *Press and Politics in Nigeria 1880-1937* (Ibadan, 1978).

Silk Mark, *Unsecular Media: Making News of Religion in America* (Urbana & Chicago, 1995).

Tador, M. "History of the Nigerian Press" in Tony Momoh & Godwin Omole (eds), *The Press in Nigeria* (Lagos, 1996).

The Constitution of the Federal Republic of Nigeria, 1999.

Thompson, J. B. *Ideology and Modern Culture* (Cambridge: Polity Press 1990).

Ukah, F-K. A. S. "Religion and Mass Media: A Sociological Perspective" M.A. Dissertation, Department of Religious Studies, University of Ibadan, Ibadan, Nigeria (1997).

Umechukwu, Panta, O. J. *The Press Coverage of Religious Violence in Nigeria* (Enugu, Ugovin Publishers, 1995).

Walls, Andrew, "Religion and the Press in "The Enclave" in the Nigerian Civil War" in Edward Fashole-Luke et al., eds. *Christianity in Independent Africa* (London, Rex Collins, 1978), pp. 207-215.

PART D
ALADURA AND
PENTECOSTALISM

CHAPTER 12

"Those Who Trade with God Never Lose": The Economics of Pentecostal Activism in Nigeria

Asonzeh F-K. Ukah[1]

Introduction

For many observers and scholars of the religious scene in Nigeria, the last three decades of the twentieth century presented an important era of religious effervescence in the country. There were two significant transformations during that period which heavily impacted on the religious culture of the people. The first was political: the country was under a profligate military dictatorship for almost twenty-five years. The second was economic: the period of military dictatorship occasioned economic deterioration and the imposition of World Bank and International Monetary Fund (IMF) supervised deregulation of the economy. IMF conditionality translated to a wide range of requirements imposed on the country as a condition for receiving assistance which brought about unprecedented hardship on the masses. These two facets of transformation touched every aspect of social life. The disorder, tension,

1. The author would like to specially thank Patti Esohe Asonzeh-Ukah and Dr. Emelda Ngufor-Samba for comments on an early draft of this paper. Also, particular thanks to Aniete Udoh for assistance during the author's fieldwork on the RCCG in Nigeria.

Figure 12.1 - Banner for a Pentecostal preacher in Lagos.

and apathy that resulted from these processes of change brought about an increased level and diversity of religious demand by the masses.

About this time, a new strand of Christianity emerged, first within university campuses in the south of the country, and later, in urban centers of the south. This brand of Christianity is generally called Pentecostalism, but it is more appropriately called neo-Pentecostalism, a new version of an old religious practice and teaching. Pentecostalism is not new in Nigeria. It was part of the country's religious scene since the first decades of the twentieth century (Turner 1979; Kalu 2000; cf. Peel 1968a; b; 2000). In the midst of legitimacy crises, social decay, state failure, massive corruption, endemic graduate-unemployment, environmental degradation, unprecedented abuse of human rights, and crippling poverty of many amidst the scandalous wealth of a few, new churches and ministries proliferated. One of the significant things about the new Pentecostalism is its leadership which is mainly made of young, university-educated men and women who demonstrate great zeal for all that is modern, particularly mass media, organization, and advertising / marketing strategies. These leaders are not only religious leaders; they are also economic visionaries who creatively respond to the demands of their immediate environment. The ways they achieve this mix is both new and innovative. Numerous Pentecostal groups emerged about this period. Many other existing churches such as the Redeemed Christian Church of God (RCCG) transformed their social identity to conform to the cultural milieu. Of both categories, the RCCG stands out as a market leader of the pack that changed its social and theological character from a church in the holiness movement to a neo-Pentecostal, prosperity-preaching church.

The RCCG: A Brief History

According to the present leader of the RCCG[2], Pastor Enoch Adeboye, the RCCG is, according to divine revelation, "the church of distinctions."[3] A close examination of the history and practices of this church shows that indeed this is an accurate description of the church. As we shall show in this discussion, one significant area that distinguishes this church from others is its theology and sociology of God, particularly in matters that relate to wealth and material wellbeing. In the fifty-three years of its existence, the RCCG has undergone a series of transformations from a small prayer band within a fringe *Aladura* Christian group to a distinctively structured religious organization. It has moved from a tribal or ethnic religious movement made up of mainly Yoruba to an international phenomenon, spreading from Nigeria to the entire West African sub-region, and then to the whole continent (except Muslim North Africa). Within its fold are Africans and non-Africans, diverse groups of people from diverse cultural backgrounds.

The founder of this group is the Rev. Josiah Akindayomi, an estranged prophet and Apostle in the Eternal Sacred Order of Cherubim & Seraphim

---

2. Fieldwork on the RCCG was carried out in Nigeria between April and July 2001 and again between July and November 2003. Data from this fieldwork formed the core of my PhD. Dissertation (Ukah 2003b). The research was part of a larger study carried out under a collaborative research project on 'Local Action in the Context of Global Influences in Africa' based at the University of Bayreuth, Germany. I acknowledge the support of Professor Dr. Ulrich Berner, my supervisor at Bayreuth, and also that of *Sonderforschungsbereich/Forschungskolleg 560* during the period of research and writing up my dissertation. I also thank Professor Dr. Ute Luig of the Institute for Ethnology, Free University of Berlin/Germany, for her engaging interesting my research. As well, I thank Professor J.D.Y. Peel of the School of Oriental and African Studies (SOAS), University of London for his comments on my initial manuscript.

3. E. A. Adeboye, *Redemption Light*, vol. 8, no. 3, p. 21. *Redemption Light* is the official newsmagazine of the RCCG published monthly by the national headquarters of the church in Lagos.

Figure 12.2 - Billboards advertising Pentecostal preachers.

(C&S) church. Born in 1909, Josiah became a traditional healer before converting to the Anglican Church Missionary Society (CMS) in 1927. After only
four years in the Anglican Church, he joined the just established C&S movement in 1931. Josiah was literate in Yoruba, but not in English. In 1940, he
migrated under divine instructions, from the town of Ondo, his place of birth
and conversion, to Lagos, through Ile-Ife, the ancient city of the Yoruba regarded as the cradle of civilization and the center of the world. It was at Ile-
Ife that Josiah was formally commissioned as a peripatetic preacher and
prophet of the C&S. A year later, he took a wife. Restless in Ile-Ife, Josiah migrated further from home to Lagos, where he settled in the suburb of Ebute-
Metta. He rose to the rank of prophet and Apostle in the C&S, and formed a
small band of followers around him which he called *Egbe Ogo Oluwa*, the
"Glory of God Fellowship." In 1952 he had some problems with the leadership
of the C&S movement and was consequently excommunicated for insubordi-
nation to authority. He transformed his small band into a church and changed
the name to The Redeemed Christian Church of God, claiming it was a name
divinely revealed to him. For four years (1956–60) this church was affiliated

with the Apostolic Faith Mission of South Africa (AFM), a relationship that was terminated after Nigeria gained political independence in 1960 and severed diplomatic relationship with Apartheid South Africa. The church grew slowly, and when Josiah died in November 1980, there were thirty-nine parishes located in Lagos and its environs with a membership of less than a thousand.

Before his death, the founder of the church nominated a university teacher, Dr. Enoch Adeboye, with a doctoral degree in mathematics, as successor. Adeboye had spent only seven years as a member of this church, and was himself only thirty-nine years old when he took over the reins of power in January 1981. At the end of that year, the church had forty-two parishes. For the first ten years of his leadership, Adeboye gradually repositioned the church socially and doctrinally. He inserted it into the glittering world of global media technologies. The transformation of the church was itself a response to the wider processes of social change in the Nigerian society.

In May 1988 the new leader created what came to be known as the "Model Parishes," as against the "Classical Parishes" that existed prior to that time. The latter were almost like a pietistic movement; women were not allowed to wear trousers, earrings or face make-ups and they had to cover their hair during fellowship. Electronic instruments and bands were banned. All services were conducted in Yoruba. Virtually all the members of the Classical Parishes were Yoruba. The Model Parishes, on the other hand, permitted all the things that were outlawed in the Classical Parishes, in addition to being located at such strategic but "profane" places as hotels, night clubs, cinema halls, high-brow city centers and other places where "worldly people" are found. Services were mainly in English and not translated into Yoruba. The vision behind the Model Parishes "was to reach the younger folk, graduates, upwardly-mobile executives, which the older folk (meaning the Classical Parishes) could not have done due to a lot of limitations."[4]

While Classical Parishes emphasized holiness, Model Parishes emphasize modernity and prosperity, and flaunt images of wealth as an index of grace and salvation. This new strand of parishes, then as now, symbolize what is best in the material world; they bring home to people such icons of high modernity as new media, global consumption appetites, and worldly grace. They introduced trans-cultural elements from outside the Yoruba cultural mi-

---

4. Pastor Pitan Adeboye, "No Contest between Classical and Model Parishes", *Lifeway*, vol. 1, no. 3, August – September 2001, p. 23. (Pastor Pitan Adeboye who is from Kwara state is no relation of Pastor Enoch Adeboye, who hails from Osun state.)

lieu into the church. The "success" of the Model Parishes resulted from a low-ering of the strict standards that governed the conduct of personal life in Classical Parishes.[5] The people who trooped into the church were taught to increase their expenditure, time, conviction, and commitment in the cause of the church. Members of the Model Parishes are in the main *networkers*, mobile middle class men and women who criss-cross Nigerian society and try to extend their connections all over Africa and the world. The rapid increase and expansion of the Model Parishes soon became the driving force in the early 1990s for the local multiplication of parishes as well as the founding of parishes in Europe and North America.

In the middle of the 1990s, tension arose between the different members of the two strands of parishes. The Model Parishes claimed and boasted of being responsible for turning the fortunes of the church around, of being progressive and outward looking; in other words of being modern and global in both content and outlook. They called the Classical Parishes local and parochial. The members of the Classical Parishes were enraged about this and, in turn, claimed of keeping the original vision of the founder, remaining faithful to the founding inspiration, biblically grounded and warding off worldly temptations from creeping into the church. As a result of this squabble, the leader of the church initiated a third strand of parishes, the Unity Parishes, in January 1997, which consciously combined the characteristics of the first two strands of parishes, creating what many in the church believed would in the long run be a harmony in the midst of diversity (Ukah 2004: 128–134).

By redefining the "cost" of belonging to the church through the creation of Model Parishes, Adeboye stimulated religious demand, making the church attractive to many educated and upwardly mobile urban dwellers. Thus, he permanently changed the social, economic and demographic structures of the church. From thirty-nine parishes in 1981, the RCCG has, as at August 2002, 6,265 parishes worldwide, more than seventy percent of which are of the Model Parish variety. This is a marked case of expansion and vitality.

Economic Reorientations of the RCCG

The new leader of the RCCG transformed the church he inherited from a poor church to arguably the richest Pentecostal church in Nigeria. The first step

---

5. In economic terms, the removal of restrictions over membership can be likened to a discount on a purchase; it stimulates and sustains demand.

in achieving this feat was the inauguration of a new series of teachings principally on the person of God and his relationship with wealth as well as his intentions for those who believe in him. The introduction of specific ideas of God
(to be discussed presently) was made a component of social action and organization which profoundly altered the fortunes of the church after some time.
While the founder of the RCCG taught his followers that wealth was a distraction, and so forbade the taking of offerings during religious services,[6] his successor disseminated the idea that "poverty is a curse" from the devil or some
evil persons.[7] According to Adeboye, "it is the devil that has taught us that if
we are rich we will not be able to serve God properly. What God says is that
the love of money is the root of all evil and not that money is the root of all
evil."[8] He further argues that poverty is evil because it is antithetical to what
God intends for his people which is wealth and material abundance. What God
desires for his followers flows from the divine nature which is pure goodness
and perfection.

As we can see, the new leader anchors his *new* teaching[9] on the nature of
God, who, for him, loves wealthy people. In an often-neglected book, *How to
Turn your Austerity to Prosperity* (1989), Adeboye first articulated his doctrine
of God and wealth. Significantly, the publication of this book coincided with
the onset of social and economic hardship in Nigeria. This was precipitated
by the fall in oil prices in 1981 and the subsequent introduction of the IMF-
imposed Structural Adjustment Programme (SAP), or what was known in the
local parlance as "Austerity Measures" (Marshall 1992; Osaghae 1995; 1998).
The theology of God which Adeboye expounded in his book has a direct relevance for economic behavior, for according to him, following his prescriptions is "the surest and shortest way" to complete, "supernatural" prosperity.[10]

The conceptualisation of prosperity by Adeboye is three-dimensional: (i)
material comfort and wellbeing; (ii) health and healthy living; and (iii) salvation of the soul. This tripartite conception is based on 3 John 1:2 which states
inter alia, "Beloved, I wish above all things that thou mayest prosper and be

---

6. Adeola Akinremi, "Some Old Landmarks", *Redemption Light*, vol. 7, no. 7, August
2002, p. 33. (*Redemption Light* is the official newsmagazine of the RCCG).

7. E. A. Adeboye, "Reversing the Irreversible", *Redemption Testimonies*, no. 89, July
2002, pp. 2–3.

8. E. A. Adeboye, *The Tree by the Riverside*, Lagos: CRM Books, 1995, p. 21.

9. The old teaching is that of the founder of the church who, according to his son, Pastor Ifeoluwa Akindayomi, preached *against* wealth as a distractive and corrupting influence
on believers (personal interview with Ifeoluwa Akindayomi, RCCG National HQ, Ebute-
Metta, Lagos, 06.06.01).

10. Adeboye, *How to Turn your Austerity...*, p. 26.

in health, even as thy soul prospereth."[11] Material comfort and wellbeing is described in line with Deuteronomy 28:11 to mean:

> cars, houses, clothes, land, anything money can buy—material things!.... [Y]ou will have children, as many as you want, and you will have lots of money to take care of them. If you have any domestic animal—goat, sheep, poultry and cattle—God says they will keep on prospering. If you plant anything, it will come out very well.[12]

This teaching is further based on a prior reasoning that "God is not poor at all by any standard." Furthermore, Adeboye reasons that "the closest friends of God [in the Bible] were wealthy people [...] God is the God of the rich, and his closest friends are very wealthy [...]. The rich are friends of the rich, and the poor are friends of the poor. Therefore God decided to befriend the rich."[13] To be poor, according to this strand of thought, completely excludes one from the friendship of God since "[b]irds of the same [sic, of a] feather flock together" and poverty is an evil as well as a curse which brings hatred and destruction in its wake.[14]

Adeboye further teaches that a true born-again Christian ought to be prosperous by virtue of claiming the riches of Christ:

> [t]here is no reason for every [sic, any] true follower of Jesus Christ to die in poverty [since] Jesus Christ became poor that we might become rich. He had no house so that you can build a house and not die [as] a tenant. He had no wardrobe so that you can have a big one. He did not have a horse so that you can have a big car. Refuse to die in poverty.[15]

Such reasoning is simple, straightforward and attractive. It advocates that Jesus had already accomplished all that is needed to achieve the good things of this world. Through his sacrificial poverty and suffering, He has, so to speak, created "a credit account," that human beings (for whom he made the sacrifice) are now free to draw upon.[16] Being poor, therefore, is attributed to either unbelief or a curse. In an intriguing passage, Adeboye asserts unambiguously "poverty is a curse and...prosperity is not evil."[17]

---

11. All bible reference from the Authorized King James Version of *The Holy Bible* (which Adeboye uses in his texts).

12. *How to Turn your Prosperity*, pp. 8–9.

13. *Ibid.*, pp. 2–3.

14. *Ibid.*, pp. 3 & 6.

15. E. A. Adeboye, *The Siege is Over*, Lagos: CRM, 1997, p. 49.

16. Thanks to Professor JDY Peel for the "credit account" metaphor, (Email communication 20 June 2002).

17. E. A. Adeboye, *I Know Who I am*, Lagos, CRM, 1994, p. 22.

Curses that bring about poverty come from three possible sources, namely: i) God; ii) Satan; and, iii) man. God sometimes uses the afflictions of witches and wizards to "cane" an individual who is defaulting on such divine precepts of paying tithes. Curses from either Satan (and witches and wizards) or man are easily broken through the sincere invocation of the name of Jesus Christ who has power and authority to set humans free from their effects. Curses from God, however, demand more actions. They are removed through: i) repentance; and, ii) the payment of tithes to the church. The payment of tithes brings to an end the curses which God places on the finances of certain individuals.[18]

In addition to the above teaching on the causes of poverty and ways of getting out of it, Adeboye stipulates four spiritual laws that he believes to operate with economic consequences. The first and simplest of these laws is *the law of harvest*. This law states that a person reaps what she / he sows. In other words, what a believer gives as tithes and offerings or donations to the house of God, or the man of God, is what she / he should expect to get in return. The second is *the law of unlimited returns*. If a believer goes beyond the requirement of the law and makes generous cash offerings to the house of God and men of God, then, "all the devourers that have been eating up your money, all abortive efforts that you have been making, He [God] will silence them."[19] The combination of the first two laws brings about "tremendous prosperity" to believers who operate by their dictates. The third is *the law of total returns*. According to Adeboye, this law states that "If you give your all to God, God will give you His all."[20] In other words, when a believer gives all she / he has to the house of God through men of God, then God will reward the person with three-dimensional prosperity: wealth, health and salvation. The last of the laws is *the law of diligence*, which states that if a believer is diligent in obeying all of the above laws, then God will reward the person with tremendous wealth such that she / he will lend to nations. Obeying these spiritual laws will mean that an individual will: i) sow; ii) sow all; iii) sow into the right soil; and, iv) sow at the right time.[21]

The underlining principle for this range of laws is in the nature of an economic transaction between believers and God. This point is not disguised in the "economic theology" of the RCCG. The church teaches that extraordinary wealth demands supernatural intervention. And in order to secure that intervention, a believer needs to perform extraordinary actions. Supernatural prosperity is such that only God gives a person through "double" (or concentrated

18. Adeboye, *How to turn Austerity*…pp. 18–21.
19. *Ibid.*, 24.
20. *Idem.*
21. *Ibid.*, pp. 23–25.

/ compound) blessings which is secured "by doing something special that will move God and cause him to bless you more than he intended."[22] This special thing which the believer is admonished to do is giving money to the church. "Those who will get blessing from God will have to go beyond ordinary giving of offering or paying of tithes. Daily they look for an opportunity to do something special to God that will compel Him to do more than what He wanted to do for them. Those who trade with God never lose."[23]

For the wealthy, this teaching is a source of comfort; for the poor it is a source of encouragement to improve their situation. However, the teaching is more significant for the former group than for the latter. This was the message the rich had long wanted to hear rather than the "old" theology that demonized wealth and antagonized wealthy people. Wealthy business people, who now see themselves as special friends of God, soon became points of distribution of "God's wealth" in the religious marketplace. The new doctrine galvanized and mobilized them to participate in the promotion of Pentecostal enterprises in the country. Efforts were made by the church to redirect the thinking and actions of the rich by mobilizing their resources and influence to support church programs and activities. The RCCG made special efforts to target and recruit this group of people through proselytizing (An-Na'im 199: 5). For example, in 1990 the leader of the church set up a special-purpose group called Christ the Redeemer's Friendship Universal (CRFU). According to the church, the CRFU "targets those people in positions of authority who invariably are rich and affluent" (Bankole 1999: 62). To be a member of this group requires a college education. Or, as a waiver, a prospective candidate would have distinguished him/herself as a successful business person. There is a registration fee and an annual due that each member pays which goes into the treasury of the church. Adopting the principle of "like attracts like," the responsibility of this group is to recruit the rich, wealthy and powerful members of the society to the cause of the church. Consequently, successful business executives, captains of industries and political figures have now become the financiers of RCCG expansion. Today, about forty per cent of RCCG members are in the professional, administrative and managerial occupations; more than eighty percent of its clergy are drawn from this pool of graduates of tertiary institutions. The RCCG, much like many other Pentecostal groups in the country, deliberately and systematically skims "more of the cream of society than the dregs" (Stark and Bainbridge 1985: 395). The CRFU has

---

22. *Ibid.*, p. 29.
23. *Idem.*

branches in all the states of the federation. Members make regular contributions to the church in addition to unspecified sums of moneys that individuals are encouraged to donate to the church.

Because the membership of the CRFU is dominated by business people who understand the language of economic transaction, the economic theology developed by the leadership of the RCCG becomes very appealing. Underlying all the laws enumerated above is what the leader of the church calls "the law of exchange": what a believer gives to God is part of an elaborate transaction, an investment, in which there will be a return or a profit. The reiteration of this teaching was the beginning of a new paradigm in human and resource management in the church.

From Theology to Economics: Trading with God

The essence of theological reorientation of the RCCG is to alter conduct and practice of its members. For the new leadership, influencing behavior towards a desired end is topmost in its repositioning of the church within the main stream of religious practice in the country. Religious behavior, for the new cadre of leadership, is not confined to church rituals but significantly, involves economic practice. Such reorientation set a new order of priority for the group's economy which greatly enhanced its capacity for competition and survival. One of the first important steps taken by the church was to redefine the purpose of tithes. It is compulsory for every member of the church to pay ten per cent of his/her income to the church. During the era of the founder, tithing was "used to cater for the needy like the widows, orphans, the unemployed" (Tijani 1985: 29). In the new dispensation, tithing is reserved for the welfare of the pastors of the church.[24] The leadership of the RCCG provides a variety of ways in which individuals (whether or not they are members of the church), corporate organizations, and the political class can engage in reasonable exchange relationship with God.

Individual Exchange

For individuals, there exist different forms of giving to God through the church, such as: i) the tithe, which is the obligatory giving of 10% of one's in-

---

24. *RCCG: Our Fundamental Beliefs in the Bible*, (Lagos: RCCG National HQ, 1999), art. 24.

come, or profit on business transactions, and gifts to the church; ii) thanks-giving offerings; iii) love offerings; iv) Sunday and voluntary offerings. (It is not unusual for there to be six offerings during a Sunday service.) In addition to the above, different types of cash offerings are taken during such weekday programs as bible study, choir practice, healing service and prayer meetings. The basis of the different offerings is exchange: if you give to God, he will give to you in return.

In the RCCG, individuals are taught to engage in exchange relationship through "giving": Adeboye teaches that "[w]hen you begin to give extraordinar-ily, you will begin to receive extraordinarily…It is a key that opens the door of abundance.…When you are giving you are loading your cloud and when the cloud is full then it is going to fall down as rain [of abundance]."[25] For Adeboye, this key constitutes a natural law. The law of harvest works better "when it is coupled with other laws. The best explanation to this is, if you plant in a good soil, it will germinate and produce fruits but if you add fertilizer, then the result will be better still."[26] Giving should be to ministers and representatives of God.

Some forms of giving are called "sowing"; it is related to the law of har-vest. Sowing is defined as something (money) given by a Christian to a pas-tor for a particular purpose. "You sow specifically in order to reap specifi-cally." This law, for Adeboye, makes it possible for a person to practically control his / her future. "We can become the controller of the wealth of this nation if we just…sow aggressively…sow consistently…[and] sow as if some-thing is wrong with us."[27] The harvest is proportional to the seed cultivated.

> If you want a double portion of wealth, you have to do something greater than what Solomon did. You have to give an offering the kind that you had never given before. God is a God of principles: Do what nobody had done before; He will respond by giving you something that nobody had ever got before.[28]

---

25. Pastor E. A. Adeboye, "Keys to Prosperity", text of sermon delivered at the monthly Holy Ghost Service at the Redemption Camp, Ogun State, Nigeria, 6 July 2001, (http://www.rccg.org/Holy_Ghost_Service/Monthly_Holy_Ghosat%20Service/jul2001.htm (accessed 14.09.01), pp. 6–7.

26. Adeboye, *How to turn your Austerity to Prosperity, op. cit.*, p. 18.

27. Adeboye, "What Happens when…?" sermon preached at the Holy Ghost Service, Redemption Camp, 1 February 2002, http://www.rccg.org/Holy_Ghost_Service/Monthly_Holy_Ghost%20Service/feb2002.htm (accessed 06.04.02).

28. Adeboye, "God of Double Portion", sermon preached at the HGS, Redemption Camp, 1 March 2002, http://www.rccg.org/Holy_Ghost_Service/Monthly_Holy_Ghost%20Service/mar2002.htm (accessed 21.05.02).

Giving is a strong theological pillar in the RCCG, as we have seen. Adeboye aptly calls this "the principle of nothing goes for nothing,"[29] which regulates the laws which we have itemized above. Adeboye recently demonstrated aspects of these teachings when he announced that God instructed him to set up four groups of people who would carry out four different tasks for the RCCG in return for divine favours.[30]

i)   Group One: A thousand (1000) people who will be willing to fast for sixty (60) days a year for the next ten (10) years; half of this fasting period must be continuous. Reward: Any gift of the Holy Spirit they should desire, such as the gift of healing, or of working miracles or of prophecy, they will get.

ii)   Group Two: A thousand (1000) people who will volunteer to do manual work for sixty days in a year for the next ten (10) years at the church's Redemption Camp free of charge. Reward: God will enable them to enjoy divine health for the next ten years.

iii) Group Three: A thousand (1000) people who are willing and able to give God one million naira a year for the next ten (10) years. Reward: God will begin to show them the true meaning of prosperity.

iv)   Group Four: A hundred (100) people who are willing and able to give ten million naira each year to the church for the next ten (10) years. Reward: God will quietly transfer the wealth of nations to them. For the different groups, no matter how hard their enemies may try, they will be alive for the next ten (10) years.[31]

Underpinning these diverse teachings is the neatly formulated maxim: "He who cannot be generous with money, surely will not be generous with anointing."[32] Adeboye articulates three kinds of blessings which human beings re-

---

29. RCCG pastors, in the main, re-echo the teachings they hear from Adeboye in line with the doctrine of "Follow Your Leader." A senior pastor of the church recently reaffirmed the doctrine of *quid pro quo* when he said, "I agree and believe that nothing goes for nothing", (Pastor James Fadele, *Redemption Light*, vol. 7, no. 5, June 2002, p. 22).

30. This principle of "Nothing goes for nothing" is very popular among Nigerians who use it to describe the general decadence and pervasive corruption among civil servants who demand bribes and personal gratification before carrying out their legitimate duties (cf. Osaghae 1998 *passim*).

31. Adeboye, "God of Double Portion", *op. cit.* At each anniversary of the delivery of this sermon, the groups were expanded, first to five, and again to seven in 2004 with some minor modifications. See, http://www.rccg.org/Pastor_E_A_Adeboye/covenant_partnership_group_with_.htm, (accessed 24.10.2004).

32. Adeboye, *The Holy Spirit in the Life of Peter*, (Part 1), Lagos: CRM, 1999, p. 47.

ceive in return for what they give to God: i) "double blessings;" ii) "compound blessing"; and, iii) "concentrated blessing." "There is only one way by which you can get this greater blessing. It is by doing something special that will move God and cause him to bless you more than he intended."[33] The RCCG's teaching is clear that the degree of anointing one gets is correlated with the amount of money one gives. Giving is regulated by the law of exchange.

According to Adeboye, there is a form of giving which is the *principle of the first fruits*. This is giving to God the first fruits of one's increase:

> If you get a job, the first salary is called the first fruit. If you are a con-
> tractor, you register a company and that company gets a contract, the
> profit on that contract is a first fruit. Or at the beginning of the year,
> there is an increment on your salary—the increment on the first
> month is first fruit.[34]

Corporate Exchange

Having reformulated its doctrines of God and wealth, the RCCG was able, from the late 1980s to attract upwardly mobile, university educated and am-bitious young men and women. These young people with unmet dreams and bright ideas were encouraged to become pastors and church elders, manning parishes and other para-church organisations within the church. In the mid-1990s, a novel practice became noticeable in the church. The aggressive pol-icy of proselytizing the upper middle class of the society paid off with man-agers and corporate heads of many organizations, particularly in the southwest of the country, joining the church or one of its numerous interdenominational groups. These organizations were encouraged, or cajoled, to go into partner-ship with the church by sponsoring the church's activities. Such corporate sponsorship comes in different forms: i) Some of the companies make finan-cial commitments to the church in forms of "donations"; ii) some companies also provide equipment such as electricity generating plants, communications gadgets, trucks and vans or even constructing buildings for the church; iii) some companies, in addition to one or two of the above, provide personnel, logistics and expertise for hosting large congregations.

There is an almost endless list of companies that have become involved in RCCG events. The first that made the headlines in national dailies was the Nigerian Brewery Limited (NBL), the largest producer of a range of alcoholic

---

33. Adeboye, *How to turn your Austerity to Prosperity*, *op. cit.*, p. 24.
34. Adeboye, "Keys to Prosperity", p. 10.

beverages such as beer and malt drinks in the country. In 1997 the NBL gave the church the sum of twenty million naira as a "donation" towards the hosting of the church's annual program at Lekki beach in Lagos. In exchange for this donation, the NBL was given the sole right to market its soft drink products. By prohibiting the sale of any other brand of soft drink during the event, the church made it possible for NBL to recoup its "investment" in the sponsorship deal. In a similar way, other corporate bodies manufacturing household products have joined the sponsors' club in order to have their wares displayed and marketed during the church's numerous events. Such companies include Procter & Gamble, (manufacturers of Ariel detergent, pampers and sanitary pads); Unilever Nigeria Plc (manufacturers of OMO detergent and other household items); Nestle Foods (makers of Nescafé and Milo beverages and ice cream); Coca-Cola and 7UP companies; banks; insurance companies and mobile phone providers. These companies also embark on aggressive advertizing of the church's programs and leaders. They put out advertorials in national media (Newspapers, radio and television), erect countless impressive and expensive billboards, print posters, car bumper stickers and banners announcing the church's programs and inviting the public to come and participate.

Exchange with the Political Class

The RCCG is also strongly connected to the political ruling elite in the country. Because of its non-adversarial posture towards politicians, and also as result of its ability to gather a huge crowd during some of its programs, politicians have found it expedient to fraternize with the group in the hope of getting political support particularly during elections. The country's present leader, Olusegun Obasanjo, is a personal friend of Adeboye, the church's General Overseer.[35] Obasanjo sometimes attends the church's services or sends an official representative. Sometimes also Obasanjo invites Adeboye to the State House in Abuja to conduct special prayers and delivery services. Top political officers of the state, who may not necessarily be Christians, often visit the church's Redemption Camp. These politicians make huge "donations" to the church. It is on record that the leader of the church openly told his followers to vote for a particular political party (Erinoso 1999: 47). This type of political behavior is also seen as a form of trading with God; paying one's dues to God through the church secures for the person positions of power and privi-

---

35. *Redemption Light*, vol. 7, no, June 2002, p. 27. See also "Comments of his Excellency the President of the Federal Republic of Nigeria" in Ojo (2001: 1–2); Obasanjo (n.d).

lege in society. In turn, the church admonishes that "All Christians are to obey the law of the country, obey the government and authority," for "All authority that exists is established by God" (Romans 13: 1b).[36]

Towards an Interpretation

Pentecostalism in Nigeria, as elsewhere, is a protean phenomenon encompassing so much variety and complexity. One variety that stresses worldly goods as much as other-worldly rewards is represented by the RCCG. As the most popular brand of religious ideology, involvement in Pentecostal Churches in Nigeria provides the youth with the leverage to deal with strains in contemporary Nigerian society. Such strains include social meaninglessness, unemployment, cultural practices that are considered retrogressive, and poverty. The attractiveness of the RCCG today is partly accounted for by the fact that upwardly-mobile people switch from low status to high status religious groups where they hope to, and do, meet like-minded people, establish social and economic connections as well as meet people of similar moral or religious conviction. The search for these objectives brings along certain degree of religious distinctiveness, one that is heavily advertised and marketed by a church such as the RCCG.

Central to the transformation of the RCCG is changes in doctrines. The behavior of the church in the post-founder era has been modeled against its new doctrines on God, wealth and well-being. We deduce from the doctrines and practices of the RCCG that the relationship between God and humans is not simply one of social exchange, but involves also economic exchange. Two significant factors that characterise this exchange transaction are: i) competition; and, ii) self-interest or the profit motive. Part of the popularity of Nigerian Pentecostalism is its employment of market imageries as well as its appeal to self-interest, self-love or the profit motive. These same reasons also account for corporate sponsorship of Pentecostal programs in the country.

The social, economic and political contexts in which a religious organization such as the RCCG flourishes are significant in properly understanding religious change as a form of cultural change, and the influence of economic practices on religious behavior and vice versa. In a society in which the state has repudiated its essential duties of regulating social and economic

---

36. *The RCCG: Our Fundamental Beliefs in the Bible*, (1999) art. 13. On some of the social and theological consequences of the rapprochement between the RCCG and the Nigerian political class, see Ukah 2004.

practices, civil society may evolve some forms of practices to fill the vacuum. The RCCG is operating in the context of near-economic melt-down of the Nigerian state, where companies are increasingly folding as a result of dwindling business. In this context of alienation and (social, political and economic) dislocations, the leader of the RCCG, who is a charismatic-prophetic figure, emerged to reinterpret and reformulate religious doctrines in a way that is deemed relevant to his followers and to groups and organizations eager to bring about change. The convergence between the context and the emergence of charismatic personalities has produced changes that transcend the religious sphere, changes that directly impinge on the economic and political spheres of social organization. Religious organizations not only provide religion, they are increasingly providing material, economic and social services (wealth and security) and alternatives to dominant political framework.

The church provides sales outlets in exchange for financial support and sponsorship by corporations. Corporations suffering from legitimacy problems recruit prominent religious leaders to become their spokespersons, appealing to the members of their congregations to patronize the companies' goods and services. Adeboye advises his audience in 2001 to "buy and use the products" of Procter and Gamble.[37] Such transactions are increasingly altering the economic behavior of corporate groups which now are openly exhibiting what I have elsewhere called "corporate religiosity" (Ukah 2003b): the appropriation of a distinct public religious identity. This identity goes beyond taking on explicitly religious names such as "Haggai Community Bank" and "Redeemed Motors Limited." Some businesses now begin each working day with prayers; they conduct midday prayer meetings for staff on company premises. Company executives double as pastors, and employ company resources and facilities for religious ends. While it is the case that some firms are increasingly adopting a religious image and posture, some Pentecostal Churches such as the RCCG and its main rival, the Winners Chapel, are increasingly adopting distinctive business strategies such as corporate advertizing, strategic marketing, diversification of products and services, business organizational structures, and systems of recruitment, promotion, and remuneration.[38] In the trading engagement with God, the RCCG has posi-

---

37. http://www.rccg.org/Eyewitness_Report/Conve.../summary_of_49th_annual_convetio.html (accessed 16.08.01).

38. RCCG's remuneration of its clergy is pegged to the Federal Government's salary scale (Personal interview with Pastor S. T. Adetoye, RCCG National HQ, Ebute-Metta, Lagos, 12.06.01).

tioned itself as "the sacred trading agent," or "religious middleman," articulating and conducting this transaction on behalf of God. The leader of the church defines the parameters of this engagement, and functions as the oracle of God, the pre-eminent channel of grace and wealth. As Adam Smith (1937 [1776]) rightly pointed out long ago, in a true exchange relationship, both parties to the transaction must benefit: while there is strong and open rivalry among Pentecostal Churches for members and to attract corporate patronage and sponsorship, the churches have become the locus of an aggressive rivalry among global and local business organizations competing for a share of the Pentecostal market for their services and products.

While not completely ruling out or ignoring the claim of divine intervention by RCCG leaders, the success of the group is intimately linked to strategic adaptations of both doctrines and practices to social, economic, political, and cultural changes in early twenty-first-century Nigeria. Significantly, changes in methods of recruitment which specifically target professional, administrative, and managerial groups for proselytization, as well as organizational restructuring which privileges donors with ecclesiastical positions, have contributed to improving the fortunes of the church. Also, one aspect of the church's strategic adaptation has seen the group model its products to suit the taste of consumer demands (of both individuals and corporate organizations) (Ukah 2003). This is perhaps where the church's greatest social and economic significance lies. Considering the popular and corporate appeal of the RCCG, this new strategic repositioning does not appear to undermine its "plausibility structure," as Peter Berger (1967:157) suggests, because of its doctrinal emphases on the power of God to make all things new through the church. The church has managed to accommodate dominant consumer culture and capitalist market practices while not losing its other-worldly foci (Ukah 2003b).

Conclusion

A characteristic feature of the Nigerian religious economy is the proliferation of divisions within Pentecostalism. This feature is increasingly transforming Pentecostal groups into competing religious firms who aggressively utilize marketing and business strategies in securing a clientele for their goods and services. Further, the pressure to be successful in terms of positive public image and mobilization of resources such as social power, wealth, and prestige, compels some of these churches to go into alliances with secure economic firms and businesses in what is purely an exchange relationship. Scholars are increasingly recognizing economic features of religious practice (Gill 1998; Noll 2002; Chestnut 2003).

As our discussion has shown, a significant factor in the transformation of the RCCG into an economic empire is the reformulation of the church's idea of God, or the social nature of God. This change from a God who loves "the wretched of the earth" (in the famous phrase of Fanon) to a God who loves and befriends the rich and powerful of society is almost revolutionary in its impact. This change coincides with the transformation of the church from a powerless, storefront, and marginal group to a powerful political and economic force in Nigeria. This change is fundamental in justifying the new wealth and socio-political power of the church in the midst of state collapse and near economic collapse.

This change also illustrates the power of religious ideas to bring about social, economic, and political change. In order to understand religious change in Africa, it is important to note what Rodney Stark aptly calls the "sociology of Gods" (Stark 2000; 2001; 2003): "the most fundamental aspect of any religion is its conception of the supernatural" (Stark and Finke 2000: 34). While we have shown in this discussion how religious beliefs have influenced economic and corporate behavior, it is equally the case that economic self-interest (of both individuals and corporate business) has considerable influence on Pentecostal beliefs and practices. In this respect, Peter Berger (1981: 86) is right when he observed that "[v]ested interests clearly do affect [religious] beliefs, but the way in which people understand their own interests is in turn influenced *by* their beliefs" (emphasis in original).

The ongoing cultural change in Nigeria has given rise to a "new religious class" which is made up of captains of corporate organizations, intellectuals (university professors both serving and retired), military, and para-military officers, top politicians (in and out of government), and government bureaucrats who also double as religious leaders (pastors, deacons, and elders) of Pentecostal organisations. An important feature of these new-paradigm leaders is their high level of educational attainment and socio-economic status prior to their Pentecostal commitment. For this group of religious professionals, there is a strong intermingling of vested economic interests and religious beliefs and conduct. The new wave pastors and the corporate businesses and institutions they represent are the primary financiers of Pentecostal mobilisation in Nigeria (Ukah 2002). The new generation of pastors espouses discernible values, life style, tastes, and preferences which it brings into the practices and belief system(s) of Nigerian Pentecostalism. It is proper to suppose that the group influences the vested interested of other religious actors and their economic behavior. Further, it is to be expected that the new religious class will display specific forms of political preferences. Consequently, this category of religious actors requires an in-depth sociological investigate into its influence on the general Pentecostal culture in the country, an investigation that goes beyond the scope of our present discussion.

Nigerian Pentecostalism is both a religious institution and big business. While I do not totally subscribe to Karl Maier's (2000: 263) reductionism that "religion is a thriving business in Nigeria", there is an evident interpenetration of religion and economics in Nigeria. There is a monetary turn in much of Nigerian Pentecostalism.[39] There are, however, some formidable hurdles facing a study of the economics of Nigerian Pentecostalism. The most important of these are: i) the almost sacred secrecy surrounding the accounts of churches; ii) the lack of records of most financial dealings in these churches; and, iii) suspicion of outsiders, which is partly a result of competition and rivalry among church leaders / founders. Where churches are run as business empires with the leader-founder acting as the executive director, and his wife (who usually is the second-in-command) acting as treasurer/ financial secretary, transparency and public accessibility are difficult to obtain by non-members.

Nigeria is currently experiencing a complex period of fundamental transformations. Perhaps no area best captures the rapidity and intensity of cultural change as the ongoing *religious turmoil*. The sphere of religious change brings together all the other facets of change such as socio-cultural, political, ideological, ecological, and economic. It is difficult to predict the outcome of these changes. However, it is generally believed that what is happening will provide a lasting impetus for the dynamic growth of the Nigerian society.

References

An-Na'im, Abdullahi Ahmed. Ed. 1999. *Proselytization and Communal Self-Determination in Africa*, Maryknoll, New York: Orbis Books.

Bankole, Olusegun. 1999. *Trees Clap their Hands: A Photobook on the Redeemed Christian Church of God*, Lagos: El-Shalom Publishers.

Berger, Peter L. 1967. *The Sacred Canopy: Elements of a Sociological Theory of Religion*. New York: Doubleday Books.

Berger, Peter L. 1981. "New Attack on the Legitimacy of business", *Harvard Business Review*, 16 October: 82.89.

Chestnut, Andrew R. 2003. *Competitive Spirits: Latin America's New Religious Economy*, Oxford: Oxford University Press.

---

39. See Ukah, "Pastors and Profit: A Comparative Study of the Mobilization and Organization of Money in West African Pentecostalism", Proposal submitted to Institut française de Recherche en Afrique (French Institute for Research in Africa) IFRA-Ibadan, for the Research Program *Transnational Networks and New Religious Actors in West Africa* (Phase II), 2004/2005.

Erinoso, Kolawole Joseph. 1999. *The Life and Ministry of Pastor Adeboye, the General Overseer of the Redeemed Christian Church of God*, BA Long Essay, Lagos State University

Gill, Anthony. 1998. *Rendering unto Caesar: The Catholic Church and the State in Latin America*, Chicago: The University of Chicago Press.

Kalu, Ogbu U. 2000. *Power, Poverty and Prayer: The Challenges of Poverty and Pluralism in African Christianity, 1960–1996*. Frankfurt am Main: Peter Lang.

Maier, Karl. 2000. *This House has Fallen: Nigeria in Crisis*. London: Penguin Books.

Marshall, Ruth. 1992. "Pentecostalism in Southern Nigeria: An Overview". In Paul Gifford, ed. *New Dimensions in African Christianity*. Ibadan: Sefer Publications: 7–32.

Noll, Mark A. Ed. 2002.*God and Mammon: Protestants, Money, and the Market, 1790–1860*, Oxford: Oxford University Press.

Obasanjo, Olusegun. n. d. *This Animal Called Man*, Abeokuta, Nigeria: ALF Publications.

Ojo, Tony, 2001. *Let Somebody Shout Hallelujah: The Life and Ministry of Pastor Enoch Adejare Adeboye*, Lagos: Honeycomb Cards and Prints.

Osaghae, Eghosa E. 1995. *Structural Adjustment and Ethnicity in Nigeria*. Uppsala: Nordiska Afrikainstitutet.

Osaghae, Eghosa E. 1998. *Crippled Giant: Nigeria since Independence*. London: Hurt & Company.

Peel, J. D. Y. 1968a. "Syncretism and Religious Change", *Comparative Studies in Society and History*, vol. X: 121–141.

Peel, J. D. Y. 1968b. *Aladura: A Religious Movement among the Yoruba*, Oxford: Oxford University Press.

Peel, J.D.Y. 2000. *Religious Encounter and the Making of the Yoruba*. Bloomington, Indiana: Indiana University Press.

Smith, Adam. 1937 [1776]. *The Wealth of Nations*, New York: Modern Library.

Stark, Rodney and Roger Finke. 2000. *Acts of Faith: Explaining the Human side of Religion*, Berkeley: University of California Press.

Stark, Rodney. 2000. "Religious Effects: In Praise of 'Idealistic Hamburg'". *Review of Religious Research*, vol. 41, no. 3: 289–310.

Stark, Rodney. 2001. *One True God: Historical Consequences of Monotheism*, Princeton: Princeton University Press.

Stark, Rodney. 2003. *For the Glory of God*, Princeton: Princeton University Press.

Stark, Rodney and William Sims Bainbridge. 1985. *The Future of Religion: Secularization, Revival, and Cult Formation*. Berkeley: University of California Press.

Tijani, Adebisi R. 1985. The Establishment of the Redeemed Christian Church of God in Ilesa. Long Essay, Department of Religious Studies, Oyo State College of Education, Ilasa.

Turner, Harold W. 1979. *Religious Innovations in Africa: Collected Essays on New Religious Movements.* Boston, MA: G.K. Hall & Co.

Ukah, Asonzeh F-K. 2002. "Reklame für Gott: Religiöse Werbung in Nigeria. In: Tobias Wendl (Hg), *Afrikanishe Reklamekunst,* Wuppertal: Peter Hammer Verlag GmbH: 148–153.

Ukah, Asonzeh F.-K. 2003a. "Advertising God: Nigerian Christian Video-Films and the Power of Consumer Culture", *Journal of Religion in Africa,* XXX/2: 203–231.

Ukah, Asonzeh F.-K. 2003b. *The Redeemed Christian Church of God (RCCG), Nigeria. Local Identities and Global Processes in African Pentecostalism.* (http://opus.ub.uni-bayreuth.de/volltexte/2004/73/pdf/Ukah.pdf).

Ukah, Asonzeh F.-K. 2004. "(Re)Branding God: The Transformation of the Redeemed Christian Church of God (RCCG), Nigeria", Paper presented at the West Africa Seminar, Department of Anthropology, University College London, (UCL), England, 26 November.

Weber, Max. 1996[1920]. *The Protestant Ethic and the Spirit of Capitalism.* Trans. Talcott Parsons, California: Roxbury Publishing Company.

CHAPTER 13

Mediating Tradition: Pentecostal Pastors, African Priests, and Chiefs in Ghanaian Popular Films

Birgit Meyer

Introduction[1]

In the context of debates about the "invention" or "imagination of tradition" (Hobsbawm and Ranger 1983, Ranger 1993), Africanists realized that the long-taken-for-granted dualism of tradition and modernity is inadequate as an analytic device and in need of deconstruction. The fact that this dualism appears to be continuously called upon in contemporary debates does not prove its theoretical usefulness, but does testify to its persistence as a discur-

1. The material on which this article is based has been assembled during fieldwork in Ghana between 1996 and 2002. The research takes place in the context of the research program Modern Mass Media, Religion and the Imagination of Communities and is sponsored by the Netherlands Foundation for Scientific Research (NWO) through a PIONIER-grant. Earlier versions of this paper, or parts thereof, have been presented at the Conference Chieftaincy and Democracy in Africa, Accra, 6–10 January 2003, the Mass media-Religion Seminar at the University of Amsterdam, the Ghana Studies Group at the African Studies Centre Leiden, and the Department of Anthropology at the University of Toronto. These discussions were important for me to build my argument. I am particularly grateful to Francio Guadeloupe, Stephen Hughes, Lotte Hoek, Michael Lambek, Martijn Oosterbaan, Mattijs van de Port, Marleen de Witte, Rijk van Dijk and Jojada Verrips for their stimulating comments and Toyin Falola for copy editing and correcting mistakes.

sive frame. In his magisterial *Religious Encounter and the Making of the Yoruba*, John Peel (2003), to whom this essay is dedicated,[2] has shown in detail how the emergence of this discursive frame is situated in nineteenth-century en-counters between Yoruba and Church Missionary Society missionaries. While Yoruba Christianity and Yoruba Culture were mutually constitutive of each other, and hence impossible to be disentangled in temporal terms (in the sense of the latter being "prior" to the former), Christian discourse itself produced a temporalizing dualism of "traditional religion" and Christianity, which in-formed, and still informs, calls for the Africanization of Christianity as much as it advocates discarding African elements in favor of a more global, Pente-costal-charismatic perspective. Indeed, the dualism of Christianity and tradi-tional religion[3] appears to be remarkably resilient as a discursive frame through which arguments for and against African religious and cultural tra-ditions are being made—as a set of practices and values to "return" to or "to be left behind" (Engelke 2004, Gyekye 1997, Meyer 1998, Steegstra 2004). Throughout Africa, debates take place along these fault lines, with Pentecostal-charismatic churches making a fervent case against traditional culture and re-ligion. In so doing, these churches link up with older, nineteenth-century mis-sionary attitudes towards African cultural and religious traditions as expressions of "heathendom." While these derogatory attitudes have a long record of being contested—by African converts, theologians, intellectuals, and state cultural policies, they still play a key role in contemporary debates about African culture. The contesting imaginations of tradition mobilized in these debates are increasingly channeled through the recently liberalized and com-mercialized mass media.

In Ghana the appropriate imagination of local cultural and religious tradi-tions is a continuous bone of contention involving state politics of identity and at times traditional councils, on the one hand, and Christian, especially

---

2. I met John Peel for the first time in 1994, in the context of a Satterthwaite Sympo-sium organized by Dick Werbner. I was taken by John's serious engagement with my work, which still was to yield a dissertation, and his generous, thought-provoking comments. His publications on the dynamics of Christianity and Yoruba religion and culture have been a tremendous source of inspiration and provided a sense of direction for my own work.

3. I realize that the use of the term 'traditional religion' is problematic because it is part and parcel of the discursive frame introduced by Christianity. The fact that there seems to be no alternative at hand – even the designation ATR (African Traditional Religion), used by those seeking to revive African religious traditions, seems to be locked up in the dis-course it seeks to critique – pinpoints that, rather than searching for an adequate, neutral designation, it is necessary to unpack the discursive formation in which traditional reli-gion is addressed. This actually is one of the key concerns of this article.

Pentecostal, understandings of tradition on the other. To put it somewhat crudely: the state politics of identity, which thrived especially under the Rawlings regime (1981–1992), emphasized—in an Nkrumahist tradition—the importance of "our cultural heritage" for the enlightenment of the nation and the deployment of "African personality." Tradition, here, is located in the past and needs to be (re)turned to in order to develop national identity and pride. From this perspective, Christianity is looked upon as a foreign religion, which colonized Africans' consciousness, whereas tradition is constructed as a repository of authenticity. Pentecostals, on the other hand, tend to represent local religious traditions as dangerous and diabolic, and propagate "a complete break with the past" (Meyer 1998). As in many other postcolonial countries (cf. Ginsburg, Abu-Lughod, Larkin 2002), in Ghana, too, mass media were gradually liberalized and commercialized in the wake of the country's return to democracy in 1992, and this transformed the role of the state in the politics of representing national culture. With the liberalization and commercialization of hitherto-state-controlled media as film, TV, radio, and the press, the public sphere was transformed significantly (Meyer 2004). In particular Pentecostal-charismatic groups, which have become increasingly popular since the mid 1980s (Gifford 1998, 2004), have adopted audiovisual media with much success and started to openly counter state politics of tradition and identity. Whereas the views put forward are not new as such, it is important to recognize that they are articulated in a new setting—the public sphere—and make extensive use of newly accessible media technologies, in particular (digital) video.

Next to Pentecostal-charismatic churches propagating their message through new media channels, developing new formats and styles in the process, individual cultural entrepreneurs also started to engage in conveying Christian views in the sphere of music, popular painting, and theatre, and video-films. Thriving on the discursive frame "Christianity versus traditional religion," these products more or less openly emphasize the superiority of Christianity by defining it against the alleged primitiveness of traditional religion. A particular case in point is the video-film industry, which emerged in the last fifteen years, and which owes a great deal of its popularity to visualizing Pentecostal-influenced imaginations of traditional religion. Featured as a visual extension of Pentecostal discourse into the sphere of entertainment, video-films tend to vest the Christian God with the power to see and grant vision, whereas its opponents, usually located in the sphere of traditional religion, are presented as operating "in the dark," and have much to conceal. While those depicted as mean—if not bloodthirsty and barbaric—Africans, who owe their power to a bond with uncanny spirits, lament that they are misrepresented,[4] they have little means to venture alternative imaginations. Likewise social groups in defense of traditional religion as an identity resource, such as the neo-traditional movement Afrikania which seeks to articulate a decent and respectable version of "African traditional religion," find it difficult to crack the dominant Pentecostal imagination.

In this essay, I will focus on contemporary imaginations of traditional religion in the medium of video and the reactions they ensue. Particular emphasis will be placed on the way in which video relates to practices of religious mediation in the context of both Pentecostalism and traditional religion. As the possibility for any religion to articulate its message and access the invisible or supernatural depends on mediation, it requires certain techniques or even technologies and practices of using them. Indeed, as the Dutch philosopher Hent de Vries puts it, "mediatization and the technology it entails form the condition of possibility for all revelation—for its revealability, so to speak" (2002: 28). In this sense, the media called upon in practices of religious mediation play a constitutive role in conceptualizing the supernatural and establishing links between the supernatural and human beings in general, and leaders and followers in particular. As media do not merely operate as neutral vehicles for pre-existing contents, the availability of a new medium such as video raises complicated questions with regard to existing practices of mediation. Whether, to mention two extreme positions, video may be perceived as attractive and easy to incorporate, or as inappropriate and threatening, depends on how this medium is perceived to relate to existing practices of mediation. From this perspective, it is possible to grasp the apparent ease by which visual technology such as video seems to be incorporated by Pentecostals, as well as the reservations traditional representatives have vis-à-vis this technology. And, more importantly in this essay, this perspective is useful to understand how a great deal of popular video-films not only depict Pentecostals' power to reveal what priests and chiefs allegedly seek to conceal, but echo, or even mimic, Pentecostal mediation practices. It should be noted that, although video is an *audio*-visual medium, in the Ghanaian context the sound dimension of video plays a subordinate role. Both video-filmmakers and au-

---

4. For instance, during a consultation on religion and media in May 2002, traditional representatives complained bitterly about the fact that most independent video-filmmakers misrepresented traditional religion, and drew an image of priests as mean and false. One of the filmmakers present, William Akuffo, retorted that video-films would not seek to offer adequate representations of traditional religion, but to depict traditional religion as most viewers imagined it to be. This shows that video-films are inscribed in a longstanding Christian tradition of imagining African religious traditions.

diences emphasize the visual aspects of video-films to a much larger extent. This may be due to the fact that the sound quality of video-films is so bad that dialogues are difficult to follow. Aware of the limitations of sound, which is partly due to poor equipment, video-filmmakers strive to make films which can be grasped by looking at the images alone.[5]

My point here is not simply that these imaginations visualize tradition from a Pentecostal angle—they certainly do, and this can be easily traced back to nineteenth-century Protestant missionary discourses in which the claim of bringing "light into the dark" was a key trope (Meyer 1999a). More importantly, I wish to argue that in the context of a great deal of video-films, imaginations of tradition tend to thrive on a dualism of revelation and concealment, which asserts the ultimate power of vision associated with Pentecostal Christianity. The first section situates the video-film industry in relation to Pentecostal religion and its marked presence in the public sphere. Secondly, focusing on representations of pastors in films, it will be shown that, as vision and revelation are central in Pentecostalism, it lends itself easily to adopting visual media such as video, and conversely visual media can easily accommodate Pentecostalism. By contrast, and this is the theme of the third and most extensive section, matters are much more complicated with regard to priests and chiefs. Depicted as having something to hide, they are pursued by the light of Christianity. Although they dislike being represented in this way, they tend to promote secrecy and claim that visual technology is unable to capture their practice—a point realized all too well by video-filmmakers, who thus can't help but imagine tradition in their own way. Lastly, I will briefly present a recent video-film genre, the epic film. This genre, which is driven by aesthetic concerns, seeks to eschew the Christian hegemony by creating beautiful, "new" traditions. On the whole, I hope to show that contemporary imaginations of tradition in Ghana are inscribed into a long history of Christian representations of "heathendom," yet are also shaped by the possibilities and limitations of new visual media.

---

5. This has a long tradition in Ghana. Audiences were fond of Indian films, which would be shown without subtitles and without being dubbed. Also English-spoken celluloid films were often in such a bad state that the sound was impossible to hear.

The Video-Film Industry and Pentecostal Christianity

Until 1992, following Nkrumahist ideas, the state regarded film and television as privileged means to create national unity and pride. Filmmakers were employed as civil servants in the Ghana Film Industry Corporation (GFIC) which was devoted to state politics of representation. Although there was a shortage of funds, as celluloid is an expensive technology, the urge to make profitable films appealing to popular taste was not emphasized until the GFIC broke down financially and eventually was sold to a Malaysian TV company in 1996.[6] The video-film industry, which emerged in the course of the last fifteen years, was instigated by independent, self-trained cultural entrepreneurs at a time when the state-sponsored film industry was breaking down (Aveh 2000; Meyer 1999b; Sutherland-Addy 2000). In the new mediascape emerging in the wake of democratization, video-filmmakers need to produce profitable films. Although independent self-trained video-filmmakers are heavily criticized by their trained colleagues (who often worked for the GFIC) for misrepresenting Ghanaian culture and religion, they are unable to accommodate these criticisms which are voiced over and over again.[7]

For instance, during the Ghana Film Awards celebrations (held in Accra on October 11, 2002), the chairman of the jury lamented the present state of the film industry and requested that "juju [a term used for "magic," BM] and special effects should be kept to an absolute minimum"—a stance which had guided the jury in their nomination of (video-) films[8] and implied that movies along these lines would not receive any award. In the same vein, the representative of the National Commission on Culture and the Minister of Communication asked (video-)filmmakers to come up with better stories more in

---

6. Due to a lack of funds, the GFIC started to experiment with video from the early 1990s onward, in response to the popularity of video-films made by independent filmmakers, such as William Akuffo, Alfred Hackman, Socrate Safo and Hammond Mensah. Their films, in contrast to GFIC productions, took as a point of departure popular stories about snake-men, ghosts and witches.

7. Though independent video-filmmakers would love to be recognized by the establishment at home and in international arenas such as the prestigious African film festival Fespaco in Burkina Faso, they state that they cannot afford to make films that flop. They have to satisfy the expectations of popular audiences, who are perceived as misguided, superstitious and non pc by the establishment.

8. Celluloid technology completely broke down in Ghana; all movies made are shot with (digital) video-cameras.

line with local cultural traditions and strive to present a more positive image of Ghana. Yet, as many producers and viewers kept assuring me, it is precisely the visualization and subsequent defeat of occult forces by the Christian God which makes these films popular among the urban masses. Hence, video-film-makers are positioned in a social field in which they encounter popular, Pentecostal imaginations of tradition, on the one hand, and statist imaginations on the other. Whatever their personal views—and many video-filmmakers are not in favor of Pentecostalism, or even regard it as "crap" (Meyer 2004)—they tend to adopt Pentecostal styles so as to ensure audience appeal. A notable exception is the new genre of epic films which seeks to eschew the Pentecostal hegemony (see section 4).

Indeed, video-filmmakers are severely constrained by expectations of their local audiences on whose approval they depend, while, at the same time, they have to live up to the requirements of the Film Censorship Board and compete with Nigerian films (Haynes 2000) which have gained ever more popularity in Ghana, especially through their strong emphasis on the fight between the Christian God and the "powers of darkness" or juju.[9] Many (targeted) viewers are more or less tightly committed to the new Pentecostal-charismatic churches that started to thrive in the mid 1980s. These churches pose a major challenge to mainline churches, which also seek to accommodate this expressive form of Christianity so as to avoid the loss of ever more members (Meyer 1999a). The new Pentecostal-charismatic churches stress their global outlook and promise born-again believers to link them not only with the Holy Spirit but also insert them into global Pentecostal infrastructures. As intimated above, in contrast to state-driven modes of representing cultural and religious traditions in terms of "heritage," Pentecostalism demonizes these traditions and talks much about ancestral curses and the like which impede progress in life for the individual and the nation.

Pentecostal-charismatic churches use effectively new ICT to produce recorded tapes of sermons and lessons, and get programs on TV, thereby rearticulating their message in line with the specific modes of communication in the information age. Not only do they display a remarkable public presence through their elaborate use of audio-visual media, Christian practice itself is being recast in line with the availability of new visual technologies (De Witte 2003). In this way, Pentecostalism has become a major public presence which

---

9. Ghanaian video-films have increasingly come under pressure of Nigerian films. As the Nigerian market is much bigger, producers have a larger budget at their disposal, and this has an impact and the quality of the film. Moreover, Nigerian films bring in more special effects and violence than is the case in Ghanaian films.

cannot be overlooked. It also is echoed in the works by artists in the fields of popular painting, music, and video-films. As in Pentecostal sermons, in video-films much emphasis is placed on the "powers of darkness," making use of spectacular computer-derived special effects. Although the visualization of evil is the main attraction of these films, occult subject matter is always couched in a dualistic frame, which asserts the ultimate power of God. Put differently, calling upon the alleged superiority of Christianity as a frame makes it possible to depict all those matters from which good Christians are expected to abstain.

Pastors in Video-Films: the Power of Vision[10]

Pentecostal-charismatic Christianity revolves around the figures of pastors who founded their own church. Charismatic pastors are viewed as new icons of power and success (cf. Marshall-Fratani 2001), and in line with the Prosperity Gospel by which their conspicuously-displayed expensive garments and posh cars are taken to be signs of divine blessing. As intimated above, in Pentecostal-charismatic churches, both vision and the Bible hold a central place. Pastors claim to get visions by the grace of God, or even to have the Spirit of Discernment through the Holy Spirit. Referring to biblical passages in a highly eclectic manner, they turn these visions into divine revelations, thereby vesting them with authority. The marked emphasis on vision and the ability to see is a key feature of Pentecostal religious practice, in which, similar to American popular Protestantism, "the act of looking itself contributes to religious formation and, indeed, constitutes a powerful practice of belief" (Morgan 1998: 3). Popular Protestant aesthetic, to use Morgan's terms, "pivots on seeing as real what one has imagined" (ibid.: 26).[11] While visuality and, more particularly, claims of making visible what remains in the dark, have been key tropes in nineteenth-century missionary discourse, video technology has only recently started to play a key role in Christian preaching practices (De Witte

---

10. This section summarizes and relies on Meyer (in press), a paper in which I explore the elective affinity between Pentecostal vision and video-films in some detail.

11. It would be interesting to explore the genealogy of Protestant looking practices from nineteenth century missions to current Pentecostal churches. As I showed elsewhere, the lithograph of The Broad and the Narrow Path offered a kind of didactic device, which taught that true vision could only be achieved by viewing images through the prism of biblical texts (Meyer 1999a). While Pentecostal pastors quote the bible extensively to authorize their visions, they seek to penetrate the invisible to a much larger extent than was the case in missionary Protestantism.

2003). If in the old missionary projects visual tropes were mobilized in oral and written texts, for instance by talking through allegory (Meyer 1999a: 31ff; Peel 2003: 162ff), now video is easily accessible. Inspired by the format and style of American televangelism, many Pentecostal preachers find audiovisual media highly suitable to address their followers, and to advocate their church to a broad audience. While Pentecostals, in line with Protestant understandings of the Second Commandment, refrain from making images of the divine, they use audiovisual technology to aggrandize the pastor as a true man of God—a man with true vision, whose charisma is created, or at least affirmed, by projecting his endlessly reproduced image onto the television screens.[12] The question of whether this endless reproduction does not merely popularize pastors' image, but actually causes its inflation and eventually banalizes the message, is a matter of debate in Pentecostal circles. Yet even though the adoption of audiovisual media into Pentecostal practices of mediation is perceived as problematic, it seems to be irreversible. Pentecostals excel not only in making visible images of charismatic pastors all over the place, but also in asserting their ability to have visions, and thus be closer to God than churches which lay less emphasis on visions. In short, Pentecostals' self-representation revolves around the performance of visibility, thereby creating the, of course questionable, impression of utmost transparency.[13]

In video-films, born-again Christians, and certainly the pastor, are not just objects of the viewers' gaze, but above all celebrated as the harbingers of the vision offered by the camera itself. Pastors' visual capacities are technologically extended by the camera, in the sense that the camera mimics the pastors' ability to reveal what otherwise remains concealed to the naked eye. Many video-films are framed as confessions or testimonies, and make ample refer-

---

12. Not only do Pentecostal churches strive to buy airtime and broadcast a program around the church leader, many also use video technology in the context of services, so that close up images of the pastor and other speakers are projected into every corner and outside of the church building. A very interesting comparative case is that of the Brazilian Charismatic Catholic Priest Marcello Rossi, who is a singer and film star, and who is heavily involved with mediating his image through new visual technology. For a perceptive analysis of the possibilities and constraints entailed by the adoption of these new media see D'Abreu (2002).

13. In the context of this essay it would lead too far to go into the ways in which the claim of transparency is countered by rumors which state that Pentecostal pastors' powers actually derive from hidden sources, for instance Mami Water and other occult forces. These rumors, as will become clear below, tie into dominant imaginations of African spirits as prone to conceal. In this way these rumored criticisms leave intact the performance of visibility in the context of Pentecostal Christianity.

ence to biblical texts, either in the beginning or at the end, or state something like "To God be the Glory." They are often presented as *revelations*, thereby inscribing films into Pentecostal notions of vision and practices of discernment. Video-films address viewers as Christians in dire need of vision, and seek to please them by offering them the privileged perspective of the omniscient eye of God, through a camera-mediated mimesis, which gives insight into the realm of the "powers of darkness."

These points can be illustrated by briefly introducing the video-film *Stolen Bible I & II* (Idikoko Ventures 2001/02), a movie in two parts about a jobless man (Ken), who joins a secret society, Jaguda Buja, whose members got their riches by sacrificing the people they love most in life—an ongoing theme in Ghanaian and Nigerian films and in popular culture—and who congregate around a coffin in a secret room situated in a posh office complex. While they enter the building dressed in the fashion of office people, they have to change clothes (wearing black pants to a bare chest) before entering the secret room. They worship a spirit who emerges from a calabash and who is marked as African by being adorned with feathers and attributed with other paraphernalia characteristic of traditional powers in the popular imagination. Instead of his loving wife Nora, Ken tries to sacrifice another woman, who got into prostitution out of poverty. His plan, however fails, because the prostitute calls the name of Jesus in time—in the Pentecostal language of video-films the sure device to protect oneself against occult forces. He starts to get rich after having sacrificed his wife in a scene involving special effects such as a snake coming out of her mouth. Ken's spiritual murder goes unnoticed and he can keep up appearances. He even gets a high position in his church because the pastor is pleased by his lavish gifts—clearly a church that is motivated more by the urge for money than truly serving God. [14] Yet, when the pastor is about to honor him in public, Nora's spirit arrives and turns Ken mad—"you cannot go to heaven with a stolen bible"[15]—and makes him lose

---

14. While in many video-films born again pastors feature as heroes, there are also movies which are critical about them and unmask them as fakes, thus eventually leaving intact the ideal image of the genuine man of God. See for instance *Candidates for Hell* (Extra 'O'Film Producers, 1995), which revolves around a satanic pastor who uses his church as a business device and owes his powers to Mami Water. This theme features over and over again, most recently in the Nigerian film Church Bu$ine$$, which was also popular in Ghana.

15. This statement means that Ken, rather than being a true born-again believer, has achieved his status through feeding the pastor with money. However, as ultimately money cannot buy God's blessings, Ken does not deserve calling himself a Christian. Through this title, the film echoes criticisms that many Pentecostal churches are just money-generating

Figure 13.1 - Scene from *Stolen Bible*.

all his riches. Roaming about in the streets as a mad man, one day he bumps into the former prostitute, who had become a staunch born-again Christian in the meantime. She takes him to a spectacular deliverance session, where a truly powerful and genuine Pentecostal pastor delivers him from the "powers of darkness." The film ends with a number of spectacular scenes (see Figure 13.1). When this pastor lays his hands on Ken and vests him with his divine power, Ken not only falls down and is exorcised, his secret society is also drawn into the born-again sphere of influence. The movie flips from inside the church to Jaguda Buja's secret room, and a power contest ensues. The members of the secret society make use of a calabash filled with water, the surface of which mirrors what happens to Ken in the church. The occultists try to strike back by miraculously sending a member into the church. When the pastor and the congregation pray as hard as they can over the intruder, he

---

businesses (see previous note). At the same time, by introducing the genuine pastor at the end (see below) the true charismatic pastor is praised.

transforms into a snake and vanishes. The fire of the Holy Spirit touches the secret shrine, and its members perish. The power of the Christian God to make visible the "powers of darkness" and defeat them has once again been affirmed. Importantly, the power of Christian vision is not confined to appearance alone, but is shown to have a material impact, by demonstrating a person's true nature as a snake (an animal coded as occult force), or by compressing time and space and burning the far-away secret room.

Interestingly, I had the chance to interview Rev. Edmund Ossei Akoto of the *Fifth Community Baptist Chapel* (Madina, a suburb of Accra), who was much in favor of Ghanaian films and had played the role of the genuine pastor in *Stolen Bible*. He explained to me that, as Pentecostals seek to reach further than the mere confines of the church service and to turn their members into full-time Christians, there is need to venture into the sphere of popular entertainment and contribute to a Christian mass culture. In his view many Ghanaian and Nigerian video-films "reveal the operation of the powers of darkness. They give ideas about how demonic forces operate, how to counteract evil forces with the blood of Christ, how to apply faith to counteract." Yet, the forces should not only be portrayed, but there should be no doubt that God overcomes these forces. Thus, he said, "to me, the ending [of a film] is the message. From here I make my own assessment and judgment." When I enquired how he could be sure that the depictions of the "powers of darkness" in films, and the special effects used in these representations, would actually reveal what happens in the invisible realm, he asserted with confidence that in his view, "about 80% of these visualizations were correct." He claimed to know this from his own experiences with deliverance, through which he witnessed how evil forces manifest themselves through people, and also heard people confess.

Thus, when his old school mate, the producer, director and actor Augustine Abbey (alias Idikoko) asked him to play the role of a pastor in *Stolen Bible*, he happily agreed. Akoto remembered the deliverance scene as intense, powerful and highly realistic, and he was "at his best." He let himself go, as he usually does when he is in church. Knowing that many people would watch the film, he wanted to "really preach a message." Yet this time it went even better than otherwise, because normally when he does deliverance he is tense, fearful, and very cautious. In this situation, however, there was no fear and thus he could perform very well. For him it was "great fun to cast out devils!"

Hence, the power of this type of film seems to derive from the extent to which it is able to appear as real, as a documentation of the spiritual realm, rather than just fiction. It has to make viewers forget that they merely watch a film (indeed, if people express their dislike of a film they say that it is "too artificial"). In other words, a successful film depends on effacing all traces of contrivance so as to convincingly feature as revelation, thereby bridging what happens in the visible and invisible realm with the help of the camera. It has to make people believe.

Akoto's statement captures nicely the predicament of video-film production. While films are organized as revelations of the struggle between divine and demonic forces, they obviously cannot simply record what goes on in the invisible realm. Rather, as his statement shows, they have to set up, and in a sense mimic the presence and power of the Holy Spirit in order to make it seem as real as possible. Yet, this kind of power seems to lend itself easily to being visualized by visual media. There seems to be an elective affinity between Pentecostal vision practices and the way in which the camera is put to work in Ghanaian video-films, between Pentecostal dramatizations of the struggle between God and the devil in the context of deliverance and the visual "spectacularization of the spectral"(Comaroff and Comaroff 1999: 21), which is the climax of this kind of movie. Both Pentecostal practices and films converge in the urge to reveal what remains hidden to the naked eye, yet is shown to have such a strong, eventually destructive influence on the visible world. In this sense both engage in the performance of visibility, making it seem as if pastors don't have anything to hide. Video-films appear to affirm Pentecostal pastors' self-image as great revealers, whereas, as will become clear in the next section, traditional representatives are depicted as prone to conceal.

Objects of Revelation: Priests and Chiefs

Priests and Chiefs on Screen

The summary of *Stolen Bible* illustrates how the relationship between pastors and occult forces typically is represented in video-films. If the camera acts as an extension of Pentecostal vision and contributes to the performance of visibility, those associated with traditional religion—traditional priests, modern occultists, and chiefs—ultimately become objects of this vision and are scrutinized through the Power of the Holy Spirit. The already mentioned scenes in *Stolen Bible* which visualize the spiritual struggle between the power of God and the devil, fought by the pastor and the secret society, illuminate what is at stake. The members of the secret society, the movie pinpoints, also attempt to see what is going on in the church (see Figure 13.2). At first, their visual device, the calabash filled with water whose surface works as a screen, is quite successful, and they even are able to send a member over to the church through spiritual means. In the long run, however, it is the pastor

Figure 13.2 - Scene from *Stolen Bible*.

who is able to make visible or, in religious language, reveal the true nature of the devil worshippers, and this enhances his power, whereas his opponents perish.

This depiction of priests as powerful and having the capacity to see, yet inferior to the vision granted by the Holy Spirit, is a key feature of many films. Far from simply turning traditional powers into "harmless folklore," as Peel (1994: 163) aptly characterized deliberate attempts on the part of mission churches to Africanize Christianity by incorporating traditional elements, video-films, in the same way as Pentecostal sermons take these powers seriously and demonize them. For instance, in *Time*, the first Ghanaian-Nigerian co-production (Miracle Films, D'Joh Mediacraft and Igo Films, 2000), the priest is sinister and strong, he can read a person's mind, disappear and reappear at a different place, and exchange human life for riches. *Time* pictures the priest in the way he is typically imagined as located in the wilderness. Marked as African, again in line with the popular imagination, he represents "African power," which even inspires awe from its most fervent opponents (see Figure 13.3). Indeed, Pentecostals deem African power to be strong and ef-

Figure 13.3 - Scene from *Time*.

fective, and hence fear it with all their heart. Like *Stolen Bible*, *Time* also pictures the story of a man who has turned poor (in this case because of mischief in his wife's family), and comes under the control of a powerful priest. This priest has his shrine in the bush, near the village where the man has taken refuge because life in the city has become unaffordable for him. He eventually accepts to receive a black pot with feathers and blood from the priest, which makes him rich whilst his dear wife gets sicker and sicker, until she dies. He keeps her body in a cupboard in his bedroom, where she vomits banknotes. In the end, however, the Holy Spirit is victorious and all the evildoers die. In the last scene we see the shrine being burned through the fire of the Holy Spirit, because a young Pentecostal woman who was to be sacrificed loudly called the name of Jesus just in time.

Thus, in video-films the dualism between God and the devil is played out by focusing on struggles between Christianity and African powers, in which the former eventually triumph over the latter. Video-films, in the same way as Pentecostal discourse, assert the superiority of vision and visibility, and claim to shed light on the realm of traditional religion—or in Pentecostal discourse:

the "powers of darkness"—so as to destroy it. If pastors, and in extension the camera itself and this type of films as a whole, are featured as great revealers, priests are represented as prone to conceal, yet are ultimately overcome by the power of Christian vision.

Although the neo-traditional movement Afrikania, which was founded by a former Catholic Priest in the 1980s and initially received much government support (Bogaard 1993),[16] seeks to make traditional priesthood respectable by a careful, though not very successful management and formatting of traditional imagery, it is clear that priests only rarely appear in public and do not have the means to counter the images which their opponents draw of them. This is somewhat different in the case of chiefs. Chiefs are important public personalities who pose as representatives of traditional society, yet at the same time quite successfully resist being trapped in the dichotomy of modernity and tradition which underlies the very legitimization of chieftaincy as an institution. In recent years, in the context of global programs seeking to instigate "good governance," chiefs seek to generate publicity and present themselves as custodians not only of tradition, but also of the well-being of the people. As chiefs are important public personalities who attend public functions to a much larger extent than priests, even Pentecostals would be reluctant to condemn chieftaincy straightforwardly. While Ghanaian video-films' negative stance towards local religious traditions also shows in the representation of chiefs, their representation is less equivocal, as will become clear below.

While some films featuring chiefs link up with a rather crude, stereotypical perspective in which chiefs are impediments of development, others deal with chief's occult powers or the ways in which they get, as film maker Seth Ashong-Katai put it, "power through powers," and bring them close to priests. Still other and more recent films to be discussed in the final section of this essay offer more positive, and increasingly virtual images of chiefs and traditional culture in general. In *Nkrabea—My Destiny* (Amahilbee Productions 1992) and *Mataa: Our Missing Children* (Galaxy Productions 1992), for instance, chieftaincy is associated with evil powers and "blood money." *Nkrabea*, a film based on a "true story," deals with Nana Addae from Sefwi-Bekwai, who makes money through worshipping the bloodthirsty spirit Degadu. Degadu, who occupies a *secret* room, offers money and power in exchange for human

---

16. After 1992, when Christianity started to become so markedly present in public space, matters became much more difficult for Afrikania. As the government was less prone to emphasize the importance of the African heritage, Afrikania became increasingly marginalized. Lacking funds and know how, Afrikania is unable to bring across its concerns in the media, and mainly features as an object of representation.

heads. The film evolves around the sad case of the boy Kofi, who is killed and beheaded by his own uncle in order to be sacrificed (for a detailed analysis see Meyer 1998). In *Mataa* a rich and mean cocaine dealer (Jonas) who terrorizes his (fishing) village and even wants to become chief, has made a pact with *Mami Water*, a beautiful lady presiding over her empire of commodities at the bottom of the ocean. In return for the money and protection she provides for him, she requires the sacrifice of little children, and eventually she wants the ultimate sacrifice: the heart of his dear niece. Both films explicitly address the question of receiving "power through powers" and refer to pre-colonial chief-taincy practices, in which chiefs derived their power from the "black stool" sanctified with human blood (usually that of slaves) (cf. Gilbert 1995).

In the last couple of years there have been also numerous Nigerian films which present as problematical the phenomenon of "big men" or "chiefs" as new, immoral figures of power and success. The attraction of these films certainly lies in the fact that they take the mysteriousness of power as a point of departure, and set out to make visible the void around which chiefs' power seems to evolve. In order to grasp this nexus of "power through powers," it is useful to recall Em-manuel Akyeampong's view that the "culture of power" in contemporary Ghana is characterized by different and shifting centers and epicenters of power "which are rooted in the fusion of the secular and sacred worlds" (1996: 167). This not only prevents attempts at fully monopolizing and centralizing power, for in-stance by the state, but also means that access to spiritual forces—from old vil-lage gods to the forces of the wilderness, from new spirits at the bottom of the ocean to the Holy Spirit—is a prerequisite for generating power, and accounts for its dynamics. In a sense, these films' claim to lay bare the mysteriousness of chiefs' power, without however demystifying it. In the same way as with regard to priests, the powers on which chiefly power ultimately depends is affirmed as existing, yet couched in secrecy in hence in dire need of revelation.

Talking Back: Secrecy Versus Visual Representability

What do priests and chiefs think of such visual representations? Whilst conducting my research on the video-film industry in Accra, I did not come across any priest, nor did I encounter public statements from, for instance, Afrikania, about representations of priests in Ghanaian and Nigerian video-films. The priests I interviewed during my fieldwork in Peki, in the early 1990s, lamented how much they felt misrepresented by Christian discourse. For their part, they did not see themselves as devil-worshippers, yet as they were marginalized they were unable to counter this negative image. They are certainly not in favor of the ways in which priests are represented in video-

films. In December 1996 I had the chance to talk to Nii Kojo Armah II, Ga
divisional chief of Jamestown and a professional photographer. He had been
a member of the Film Censorship Board for more than twenty-five years,[17]
and had been made a chief in the early 1980s. In our conversation, he expressed how critical he was regarding the representation of spiritual forces
or juju:

> I like action films, thrillers, melodrama. Films carry a lot of educa-
> tional aspects for the younger generation. But when it comes to
> these juju things, video-filmmakers are doing certain things they
> don't understand. When they start playing with juju I don't like to
> watch it, because I find it childish. The real thing itself is there, but
> they are using their imagination to create something that they don't
> know. I will sleep. We can't fight it, because when you are in this
> status you go through the real thing. I can't talk about it here, but
> you experience the real thing itself to a point were I didn't know
> where I was....

What struck me most in our talk was that he disagreed with the fact that
video-film makers just imagined how juju would work, thus creating "something they don't know," yet at the same time asserted that the "real thing,"
which he had experienced for instance when he was installed as a chief and
kept in a dark room for a week, was unrepresentable. Hence he could not
just demand more adequate representations, unbiased by a Christian perspective. The following conversation between us reveals the intricacies concerning not only the representation of invisible and secret powers on which
the power of chiefs and priests ultimately depends, but also its very representability.

> NKA:....and there are certain places, where you go with a camera and
> the camera cannot function. It has happened to me. I was holding a
> camera and the camera just got locked. I took another camera and I
> started trembling. Instead of loading the camera the flash would not
> work. I thought "Am I nervous?" I put everything in order and went
> back. It was worse.
> BM: What did you want to photograph?

---

17. Any film to be shown in public or sold as a home video are to be taken to the Censorship Board to get approved. In my experience, this examination is not subject to a systematic procedure. Whether a film is approved depends very much on which Board members, who have been appointed so as to represent major groups in society, are present.

NKA: A shrine. It got to a point where I couldn't do anything. Indeed, there were many secrets and nobody talked about them.
BM: But why is there no film that deals with it in an adequate way?
NKA: Who is going to give you the secrets? When I go to a ritual I won't tell you.
…The things that happen to you, when you come, you can't even talk to them. When I see people creating these things in a movie, they are fooling themselves. They don't know what they are playing with. Somebody may tell them this is the way it is, the way they do it, but the real thing itself, they do not understand. The first time I had to go in a palanquin [a hammock-like device in which a chief is carried around at ceremonial occasions, BM], there was nothing wrong with me, but when the elderly men came, I was held and they took me and the old man poured libation and after the second one, I felt as if my legs were not there. And then the third one, I was not there. All of a sudden all I could remember [was that] I was off.

In these reflections Armah speaks from his experience as a photographer *and* a chief. He contrasts secrecy, which underpins the power of chiefs and thus chieftaincy as an institution, and visual representability. Both appear incompatible: how it really is, he claims, cannot be shown in a film. Thus, the problem, according to Armah, is not simply that video-filmmakers offer wrong visualizations of what otherwise remains secret and inaccessible to the public, the problem lies in the fact that certain things seem to "refuse to be photographed" (cf. Spyer 2001) or represented to the outside world and featured in films. Clearly a line is drawn here between a set of secluded and exclusive rituals which make a person a chief and are at the base of his power, and his public image. The power(s) on which chieftaincy and, by implication, priesthood rely are claimed to be shrouded in secrecy and thus inaccessible and unrepresentable, only the public aspects of these offices seem to lend themselves to be depicted truthfully. This, at any rate is what contemporary documentaries about chiefs (e.g. the videos of the funeral of the old and the installation of the new Asantehene) usually engage in, thereby confining chieftaincy to its public dimension and keeping more or less silent about the issue of "power through powers" which appears to inform feature films such as those discussed above.

The alleged impossibility or at least undesirability of representing through visual mediation, so succinctly indicated by Armah, also pertains to the representation of local religious practices and juju at large. Here, too, the most important aspects are barred from view. This alleged invisibility seems to collide with the medium of video, which thrives on the easy accessibility of visual technology and is devoted, or even compelled, to visualize. Exactly for this reason, as I tried to point out in the previous section, video is so easily made to work as an extension of Pentecostal viewing practices. Video is a machine programmed to create a potentially endless series of digital doubles of everything. It does not only mimic the eye, but also posits what is to be seen and how, creating the world as an image (as Heidegger put it). As a technology it is part and parcel of a new regime of visibility, in which visuality is a proof of true existence. In the context of Ghanaian and Nigerian video-films, the technological potential of video is further enhanced by embedding films in Christian practices of seeing. Parasitically thriving on the popularity of Pentecostalism, as I tried to argue above, these films derive part of their appeal from the claim to offer revelations.

Pentecostalism's affinity with visual media contrasts strikingly with Armah's dismissal of visual media. This suggests major differences in practices of religious mediation which make for traditional religion's different attitude towards a new medium such as video. Yet, it is important to realize that Armah, far from being confined to a traditional past, speaks from a position that realizes the importance of visuality and the power of visual images in contemporary Ghana. On the basis of his personal and professional experience he explicitly refers to photography and video to state his case, thereby suggesting that these visual media are unsuited to be incorporated into traditional mediation practices in a prosthetic manner, as is the case with Pentecostalism. At the same time, the deliberate emphasis on certain traditional practices as undepictable through technologies of audio-visual reproduction serves to underline the uniqueness of the indigenous powers backing chieftaincy and priesthood. Modern technology, as it were, is called upon so as to assert and explain the distinct otherness of traditional power. By dismissing the use of visual media, Armah asserts that the power of chiefs and priests resists this kind of mediation. This power is there, and overwhelms even a man with Western education and training as a photographer as is Armah.

In this sense, the deliberate reference to visual technology is part and parcel of discourses on indigenous African powers, rather than merely being opposed to them (cf. Spyer ibid). Referring to the impossibility to represent secret (and sacred) power sources, Armah ties into the "performance of secrecy" which is the main way through which priests and chiefs tend to assert their power in public. Yet, this should not mislead us to draw the much too facile conclusion that whereas Pentecostals are associated with visibility and hence easily adopt visual technology, priests and chiefs are custodians of secrecy and hence once and for all at loggerheads with these technologies. While both seem to focus on one pole of the opposition revelation and concealment, it is important to realize that this focusing—and the performance of visibility or secrecy ensued by it—reflects a long history of the relationship between Christianity and traditional religion. Employing an allegorical opposition of light and darkness, Christianity has always been hegemonic in imagining traditional religion as its other. It remains to be seen to what extent traditional representatives will deal with new visual technologies in the future, and how these technologies may impinge on mediation practices.[18] While certain practices of religious mediation may be more prone to incorporate certain media than others, as is the case with visual technology for Pentecostals, one should also be wary of claims of an essential impossibility to adopt new media into certain religious practices (cf. Morris 2000, Sanchez 2001).[19]

Video-Filmmakers and Imaged Tradition

Armah's point that the power of chiefs and priests does not at all lend itself to visualization, as it thrives on secrecy and concealment, is recognized by video-filmmakers. During my research I understood that it is indeed difficult for them to depict traditional powers convincingly. For one thing, they realize that in the register of tradition of which chieftaincy and priesthood are part, not everything is convertible into images: "there may be just one small and scanty pot in a shrine, but tremendous power dwells in it," my friend and video-filmmaker Ashiagbor Akwetey-Kanyi told me. However, "for film you need to exaggerate, one cannot do with the image of a simple pot in order to depict a shrine." Thus the compulsion to tell a story through spectacular images requires that video-filmmakers recur to the imagination. And indeed, I heard many of them assert that instead of seeking to represent how traditional religion really works, they create it in line with Christian imaginations

---

18. In this context I would like to draw attention to the work of Mattijs van de Port (in press) on Candomblé in Salvador, Brazil. Although priests emphasize the impossibly to represent the secret sources of power through visual technologies, followers start to introduce video so as to record aspects of their initiation into Candomblé. In this way Candomblé does not remain outside the new visual regime that increasingly characterizes the life worlds of the followers.

19. Thus, it would be interesting to conduct detailed research on how priests and chiefs incorporate media as photography and video in their religious practice. The claim that traditional powers themselves may not be photographed, or resist to appear on images is familiar to any tourist or anthropologist encountering ritual performances. On the other hand, as Behrend has shown (2003) these reproductive technologies may be called upon in certain healing practices, for instance in order to protect or harm an absent person who is substituted by his or her photograph.

Figure 13.4 - Video depiction of tradition.

thereof—and thus they use all sorts of objects which in reality will never be found in a shrine, for example, colorful masks produced for tourists, weird pieces of cloth, non-descriptive bones, and ornaments. Hence shrines pictured in video-films are much more visual than real ones. Video-film makers not only imagine, but "image" tradition (see Figure 13.4).

At the same time, I understood (also by being present on location) that even the visualization of "how Christians imagine traditional religion" is not without risks. For there seems to be no clear-cut boundary between fake shrines, their entourage and related paraphernalia set up in front of the camera on the one hand, and "the real thing," on the other; between the representation and its referent. I learned that, all too easily, spirits, which always roam about in search of new dwelling places, may enter such a fake abode. They can make it real even if it bears no resemblance with a real shrine out there, which, as stated above, does not necessarily consist of images and thus does not fit in with the regime of visibility on which video thrives. This is also reason for some video-film makers to make sure to replace some of the required ingredients by fake-things (e.g. alcohol by water, blood by red liquid) and only make nonsensical incantations in no really existing language. The set designer Nina Nwabueze told me that she always prays when she makes a fetish-shrine, for fear that the forces depicted may materialize and turn against her. Likewise, actors who play a role involving occult forces tend to consult their pastors and pray with them so as to be protected. The point here is that there is no clear-cut boundary between reality and fiction, and that what starts as fiction can create a reality of its own, more image-prone than the reality it initially set out to depict, and thus all the more dangerous.

While certainly the camera mimics the Pentecostal performance of visibility, it would be mistaken to state that making visible that which remains concealed from the naked eye deconstructs and undoes it as a mere figment of the imagination. In the complicated interplay of concealment and revelation at stake here, simulation always entails the risk of mimesis, and in the murky zone in between there emerge new, auratic forms (cf. Samuel Weber 1996). What is at work here, interestingly, is the logic of the secret, which by its very existence appears to magnify reality, as Simmel put it, when he wrote "the secret offers, so to speak, the possibility of a second world next to the obvious one, and the latter is influenced by the former in the strongest way" (1922:272, translation BM).[20] Thus here too, as Michael Taussig argues in *Defacement*, "attempts to unmask appearances may actually compound the mystery thereof" (1999: 56). Exactly this happens in the case of the video-films, which, by claiming to reveal what is otherwise unrepresentable, offer new mystifications of what they claim to represent. Video technology and Pentecostal practices of vision are implied in the "mystery-making impact of unmasking" (ibid.). Hence, it would be much too simple to adopt a straightforward reading of Walter Benjamin's *The Work of Art in the Age of Technological Reproducibility* (1978) and thus associate the refusal to be photographed with the presence of the aura, and video technology with its loss (cf. Dasgupta in press; Spyer 2001). Clearly, compelled as they are to visualize, video-filmmakers eagerly fill up the void resulting from the alleged impossibility to depict the secret.[21] Indeed, initial invisibility and thus unrepresentability does not put an

---

20. "Das Geheimnis bietet sozusagen die Möglichkeit einer zweiten Welt neben der offenbaren, und diese wird von jener auf das stärkste beeinflusst."

21. Of course, all sorts of knowledge about what happens in the confines of secrecy circulate in society (cf. Michael Taussig's notion of the "public secret"). The point, it seems, above all is not to blur the boundary between public and secret dimensions in representations of chiefs and priests. Only what is official is to be represented, and by the same token what is represented features as official. In other words, the secret is assigned a certain role and place in the politics of representation.

end to visualization, but calls for a new space for the imagination and the creation of new auratic forms.

"Tradition and Colour at Its Best"

So far, it may seem as if video-films, as they parasitically feed upon and extend Pentecostal viewing practices, are irredeemably trapped in an interplay with traditional religion, in which films, as extensions of pastors' vision reveal what chiefs and priests seek to conceal, without ever doing away with the tradition thus constructed. Diabolizing traditional priests and chiefs affirms their power and binds Christianity in a symbiotic relation with the powers it despises so articulately. Pentecostalism seems to need this image of the other so as to demonstrate its superior power, but is also haunted by it. Yet, the recent phenomenon of the epic film seems to escape this trap, as it seems to open up tradition to the imagination without diabolizing it.

The genre of epic films emerged first in Nigeria, and was introduced to Ghana by Samuel Nyamekye, owner of Miracle Films and producer of the already mentioned movie *Time*, and dubbed as Mr. Quality in his self-advertisement.[22] In 2001 he brought out *Asɛm* (director Kenny McCauley) and in 2002 *Dabi Dabi I & II* (director Kenny McCauley).[23] These films are situated in an imaginary village long before the intrusion of colonialism and Christian missions. In the trailer at the beginning, *Asɛm* promises viewers "tradition and colour at its best" and situates the narrative by the following introduction, given in Akan, but printed in English:

> In a time long ago, the deeds of men held the traditional community through taboos and laws. But when the deeds, words, taboos and laws outlive their time, will there be the needed change? In the quiet

---

22. This genre, of course, exists in the sphere of African art films for a long time already. What is new is that video-filmmakers, who depend on popular appeal, started to adopt this genre. This genre was quite popular in 2001 and 2002. I understood through conversations with Ghanaian friends, that more recently, video-filmmakers started to make movies featuring missionaries. These films seem to be immediate reflections of colonial missionary discourse. Until now I did not have the chance to see such films.

23. Interestingly, MacCauley has been trained at the National Film and Television Institute, which opposes independent filmmakers' demonizing representations of tradition and culture. McCauley agreed to work on these films because they did not take as a point of departure the usual opposition of Christianity and heathendom, which characterized many earlier Miracle Film productions.

Figure 13.5 - Video representation of a chief.

serene village of Sekyerekrom taboos and laws are upheld. But the peace is about to be shattered in this quiet village. Will the old stand or will the old pass?

The characters in *Asεm* wear white cotton loincloth, supplemented, in the case of women, with a bra from the same material; all walk barefooted. Both men and women wear necklaces from beads around neck, feet and arms. The women have their hair plated and also wear beads around their waists. They live in a small village, situated in the bush, in houses made from mud and sticks, roofed with grass. They live by farming and hunting. The priest plays an important role in restoring the moral order, as, once he is possessed, he can see into people's minds. Regularly the chief, usually dressed in antelope skin and also adorned with beads, his elders and the queen-mother meet under a tree, all seated on Akan-stools (see Figure 13.5). While the elders speak Twi (subtitled in English), the chief himself speaks English. At this time, the rules are strict: if a taboo is broken the perpetrator is banned from the village or even killed.

Interestingly, by showing "tradition and colour at its best" the film aestheticizes tradition, but at the same time criticizes the irrationality of traditional law. This is already conveyed by the blurb on the tape which has to advertise the film to potential buyers, thereby framing their expectations:

> In the kingdom of Sekyekrom tradition is supreme and reasoning is nothing. Opanin Kufour is accused of murdering the king's daughter. He is found guilty and sentenced to death by the traditional laws. He is innocent. Will the traditional law listen to his plea?

Clearly the chief, as the ultimate embodiment of "traditional law," does not listen and thus makes a terrible mistake.

It is important to emphasize that the genre of epic film departs in a marked way from all videos I saw before, i.e. by concentrating on and even cherishing village tradition. Yet epics are always located in a space and at a time before the introduction of Christianity, thus avoiding successfully having to take sides for one religion at the expense of the other. Audiences, in any case, are much more sympathetic to tradition when it is depicted as an all-encompassing life world, than when it is an option to choose at the expense of Christianity.[24] I watched a number of epic films in small video-cinemas in 2002 in Accra, and noticed that especially young urbanites appreciated them, stating that through these films they got an impression of the past and village culture.

I have to confess that my first reaction to this type of film was quite negative. Knowing a bit about Ghanaian history, to my taste these films were all too much made up. As, in my view, things were not like this in the past, I saw these films as great examples of "invention of tradition," and false.[25] In the case of the genre of epic film, I somehow assumed that the producers, directors, and actors involved, as well as the audiences, took these films as real representations of the past. So it seemed to me that they took for "real" what I, with the hindsight of the historical anthropologist, could qualify as "invented" and, in line with Ranger (1983: 247) as totally misunderstanding the realities of pre-colonial Africa, which had been much more flexible than these invented traditions claimed.

---

24. Video- films which are explicitly critical of Christianity and positive towards tradition usually flop, as many of my video-filmmaker friends already painfully experienced.

25. In principle, as explained above video-films echoing a Pentecostal perspective also engage in inventing tradition. Yet they evoked a less strong reaction on my part, as I could immediately situate them as visualizing Christian imaginations of tradition – a theme I have been interested in for a long time. That these were part of an ideological project was beyond doubt for me. In the case of the genre of epic film, however, I somewhat naively expected a genuine search for history, not deliberate imaginations thereof with little attention for facts. I thus wrongly assumed that, while anthropologists view traditions as constructed, the people on the ground would be convinced of their authenticity (we deconstruct, they believe).

Yet I soon realized that this was much too simple. An interview with Samuel Nymekye immediately made me realize that he had adopted epic films because he sensed that people were eager to see some village scenes. This was convenient for him, as he found it increasingly difficult to make films able to compete with the lavish and conspicuous display of expensive costumes in Nigerian films. It became clear to me that he saw the genre of the epic not so much as a true representation of the past, but more as an imagination feeding as much on fact as on creativity. My understanding was much furthered in an interview with Emeka Nwabueze, a Nigerian living in Ghana who owned *First Image Creations*, a company devoted to creating props for films, and who worked with Miracle Films. His great passion was the creation of props for films about chiefs. When I expressed my surprise about how tradition, [as a matter of or at least from the past], could be created in the here and now, he said: "we create an unexisting culture or an unexisting tradition, something absolutely new." This he repeated many times in his attempt to explain to me that artistic creativity is needed to create images of tradition. The challenge for Emeka was to make different images for every film, not to use the same costumes, to always show traditions in a new way. Of course, he said, he knew that "in the past every hut was red," but his aim was to bring in a change, to give it other colors: "Set design is everything."

When I asked him how his notion of "creating unexisting traditions" or even "new traditions" was limited by the use of certain materials, I learned that he would only use materials of which he knew that they were common in and belonged to Africa: beads, feathers in different colors, skins, certain signs printed on white cloth, raffia, snails. He also once created a bra from a cobra skin, although in the olden days people would not wear a bra. He gets his inspiration from photo-books on African arts and culture, and mixes all the parts he sees and thus creates "imaginary cultures" which have no resemblance with true ones. For Emeka, the chief was the spill around which he created his "unexisting traditions." Indeed, in a movie like *Asɛm* no attempt is made to make the chief, nor his entourage, resemble any real setting. Rather the whole scene is made up of different elements, which combine into a distinct style. Deliberately stressing that the aim is not to truthfully depict a traditional culture that existed once upon a time, for the set designer the characters depicted in *Asɛm* feature as artificial images in an artificial environment. Producers, actors and audiences did not seem to be worried by the artificiality of the chief and his entourage. Rather, the chief and other characters feature as icons which make it possible to imagine tradition in the here and now.

Of course, the questions posed in the beginning of *Asɛm* are rhetorical, as they have already been answered by the course of time. Today, at least in an urban context, traditional laws and taboos are easily breached, and do not determine the course of everyday life. Indeed it appears that "the old has passed." If the question "will the old stand or will the old pass?" is posed in the here and now, the point is to offer a frame to more or less freely imagine tradition as a matter of the past in the here and now. In this endeavor, the imaginary chief with his insistence of maintaining the old ways of the ancestors is not an option to follow, but only an image condensing a nostalgia of a tradition long lost. In contrast to Pentecostal-oriented imaginations of tradition, epic films such as *Asɛm* lock tradition up in the past and merely celebrate its aesthetic beauty. It does not inspire awe or command fear. The point here, it seems to me, is not a break with the past understood as an abode of occult forces, nor a return to the values and norms of the past. The epic film, by contrast, deliberately adopts aesthetic devices to signify tradition. Tradition, in this sense, is not an option to follow or reject, but rather a style able to convey a longing for matters of the past, which are truly made up yet carry the label of authenticity. In this sense, epic films offer an alternative to the discursive frame Christianity versus traditional religion, which forces people to take sides and identify themselves with one option. It remains to be seen how far the imagination of tradition put forward by epic films will impinge on debates about tradition in Ghana, which still to a large extent seem to be trapped in the opposition of Christianity and traditional religion.

Conclusion

Truly, "when the old ways are alive, traditions need neither be revived nor invented," as Hobsbawm (1983: 1) put it. While the thrust of *The Invention of Tradition* was to pinpoint to historians and anthropologists the need not to take for granted what was made to appear as old, and to engage in deconstruction, this essay sought to draw attention to the fact that imaginations of tradition continue to play an important role in debates about culture and identity in Ghana, and that the introduction of video and the retreat of the state from film production has even brought imaginations of tradition on TV and cinema screens. Video-films, I tried to show, offer deliberate imaginations of tradition, either as satanic and negative, or by proudly asserting the newness and spectacular nature of what has to pose as old so as to satisfy a nostalgic longing for something authentic. The imagination, as Jean-François Bayart (1996) has pointed out, is not unreal as opposed to the empirical reality of everyday life, but forms a space in which ideas about what reality is, about cause, effect and the production of knowledge, about morals and identity, are being worked out. Thus imaginations are not just constructions waiting to be de-constructed, but play a key role in creating people's life-world by appearing as taken-for-granted and convincing (cf. Anderson 1999).

I showed that contemporary imaginations of tradition are to a large extent trapped in the discursive frame of "Christianity versus traditional religion," which has its roots in nineteenth-century encounters between missionaries and Africans. Even though what is circumscribed—inadequately—as traditional religion cannot be thought outside of the discursive frame that made African gods inferior to Christianity, the resilience of the traditional, or African, in the imagination of even those who despise it is truly remarkable. In this frame, tradition is either cherished as a realm to return to, or, according to Christian—or at least Pentecostal-charismatic—parlance, to be rejected. Tradition, though not alive in its own terms, still is a powerful resource for the imagination, and bears upon questions of personal and even national identity. Video-films, in order to be successful, tend to mimic Pentecostal attitudes toward traditional religion as populated with old and new occult forces. Though these forces are viewed as extremely dangerous, they are ultimately (to be) overcome by divine power that thrives on the possibility to reveal. In this sense, video-films feed upon and enhance the predominance of Pentecostal imaginations of traditional religion, yet add a visual dimension to these imaginations.

My main concern is not simply to point at the continuity of Christian imaginations of tradition. Importantly, in this essay I sought to draw attention to the new arena in which imaginations of tradition are displayed and the media used in this process. Thus instead of merely seeking to deconstruct imaginations of tradition or asserting continuities in the politics of representation, I have argued that we have to ask how traditions are mediated, by whom, through which media, and for what purpose. In Pentecostal imaginations of tradition, priests and chiefs are turned into objects of vision, made visible by the power of the Holy Spirit who allegedly throws light even upon the darkest secret. Vision here is a weapon in the struggle to reveal what priests seek to conceal and traditional religion is to be discarded in favor of Christianity. In epic films, traditional life is excessively aestheticized, and deliberately turned into beautiful images, a hotchpotch of folkloristic, purposely neutral signs which no single ethnic group could claim as its own. Both imaginations approach tradition through a visual lens, and make it subject to spectators' gaze. Whereas it induces fear in the case of Pentecostal-inclined video-films, epic films present tradition as a site of aesthetic pleasure.

Although this essay has approached Christianity and traditional religion through the prism of video-films, I think that the question of mediation is of broader importance for the ways in which religions feature in the public arena. While it seems that Pentecostal Christianity has eagerly and efficiently accommodated audiovisual media, thus taking advantage of the easy availability of new audiovisual technology, in Ghana's contemporary mediascape traditional religion is, above all, an object of representation. It remains to be seen if and to what extent traditional representatives themselves take up this challenge and adopt audiovisual media. In any case, access to audiovisual technology and the willingness and ability to embrace visuality as a dominant mode of representation appears to be crucial for achieving power in Ghana's contemporary mass mediated public sphere.

References

Akyeampong, Emmanuel, *Drink, Power and Cultural Change. A Social History of Alcohol in Ghana, c. 1800 to Recent Times.* Oxford: James Currey, 1996.

Anderson, Benedict, *Imagined Communities. Reflections on the Origins and Spread of Nationalism.*9th Impression. London: Verso, 1999.

Aveh, Africanus, Ghanaian Video Films of the 1990s: An Annotated Select Filmography. In: Kofi Anyidoho & James Gibbs (eds.), FonTomFon. Contemporary Ghanaian Literature, Theatre and Film, *Matatu* 21–22, 2000 : 283–300.

Bayart, Jean François, *L'illusion identitaire.* Paris: Fayard, 1996.

Behrend, Heike, Photo Magic: Photographs in Practices of Healing and Harming in East Africa. *Journal of Religion in Africa* 33 (2): 129–145, 2002.

Benjamin, Walter, The Work of Art in the Age of Mechanical Reproduction, in *Illuminations.* New York: Schocken Books. 1978.

Boogard, Paulien, Afrikania of: Hervormde traditionele religie. Een politiek-religieuze beweging in Ghana. University of Amsterdam: MA-Thesis, 1993.

Comaroff, Jean and John Comaroff , Alien-Nation: Zombies, Immigrants, and Millenial Capitalism. *Codesria Bulletin* 3 &4, 1999: 21.

D'Abreu, Ze, On Charisma, Mediation & Broken Screens. *Etnofoor* 15 (1/2), 2002: 240–259.

Dasgupta, Sudeep, Gods in the Marketplace: Refin(d)ing the Public under the Aura of the Religious. In: B. Meyer & A. Moors (eds.), Religion, Media and the Public Sphere. Bloomington: Indiana University Press, forthcoming.

Engelke, Mathew, Discontinuity and the Discourse of Conversion. *Journal of Religion in Africa* 34(1–2): 82–109.

Gyekye, Kwame, *Tradition and Modernity. Philosophical Reflections on the African Experience.* Oxford: Oxford University Press, 1997.

Gifford, Paul, *African Christianity. Its Public Role.* Bloomington and Indianapolis: Indiana University Press, 1998.

Gifford, Paul, *Ghana's New Christianity: Pentecostalism in a Globalising African Economy.* London: Hurst, 2004.

Gilbert, Michelle, The Christian Executioner: Christianity and Chieftaincy as Rivals. *Journal of Religion in Africa* 25 (4), 1995: 347–386.

Ginsburg, Faye D., Abu-Lughod, Lila and Brian Larkin (eds.), *Media Worlds. Anthropology on New Terrain.* Berkeley and Los Angeles: University of California Press, 2002.

Haynes, Jonathan (ed.). *Nigerian Video Films.* Athens, Ohio: Ohio University Center for International Studies, 2000.

Hobsbawm, Eric, Introduction: Inventing Traditions. In: E. Hobsbawm & T. Ranger (eds.), *The Invention of Tradition.* Cambridge: Cambridge University Press, 1983. Pp. 1–14.

Marshall-Fratani, Ruth, Prospérité miraculeuse: les pasteurs pentecôtistes et lárgent de dieu au Nigeria. *Politique Africaine* 82, 2001: 24–44.

Meyer, Birgit, 1998a "Make a complete break with the past." Memory and Post-colonial Modernity in Ghanaian Pentecostalist discourse. *Journal of Religion in Africa* XXVII (3): 316–349.

——— 1998b The Power of Money: Politics, Occult Forces, and Pentecostalism in Ghana. *African Studies Review* 41 (3): 15–37.

——— 1999a *Translating the Devil. Religion and Modernity Among the Ewe in Ghana.* Edinburgh: Edinburgh University Press.

——— 1999b Popular Ghanaian Cinema and "African Heritage". *Africa Today* 46 (2): 93–114.

——— 2001 Prières, fusils et meurtre rituel. Le cinéma populaire et ses nouvelles figures du pouvoir et du success au Ghana. *Politique Africaine* No. 82: 45–62.

——— 2004 "Praise the Lord." Popular Cinema and Pentecostalite Style in Ghana's New Public Sphere. *American Ethnologist* 31 (1): 92–110.

——— forthcoming. Impossible Representations. In: B.Meyer & A. Moors (eds), *Religion, Media and the Public Sphere.* Bloomington: Indiana University Press.

Morgan. David, *Visual Piety. A History and Theory of Popular Religious Images.* Berkeley and Los Angeles: University of California Press, 1998.

Morris, Rosalind, *In the Place of Origins. Modernity and Its Mediums in Northern Thailand.* Durham and London: Duke University Press, 2000.

Peel, J.D.Y., Historicity and Pluralism in Some Recent Studies of Yoruba Religion. Review Article. *Africa* 64(1), 1994: 150–66.

———— *Religious Encounter and the Making of the Yoruba.* Bloomington: Indiana University, 2003.

Pels, Peter, Introduction. In: B. Meyer & P. Pels (eds.), *Magic and Modernity. Interfaces of Revelation and Concealment.* Stanford: Stanford University Press, 2003.

Port, Mattijs van de, Visualizing the Sacred and the Secret. Televisual Realities and the Religious Imagination in Bahian Candomblé. Under review at American Ethnologist, nd.

Ranger, Terence, The Invention of Tradition in Colonial Africa. In: E. Hobsbawm & T. Ranger (eds.), *The Invention of Tradition.* Cambridge: Cambridge University Press, 1983. Pp. 211–262.

Ranger, Terence, The Invention of Tradition Revisited: The Case of Colonial Africa. In T. Ranger & O. Vaughan (eds.), *Legitimacy and the State in Twentieth-Century Africa. Essays in Honour of A.H.M. Kirk-Greene.* Pp. 62–111. Houndmills: Macmillan, 1993.

Sanchez, Rafael, Channel-Surfing: Media, Mediumship, and State Authority in the María Lionza Possession Cult (Venezuela). In: Hent de Vries and Samuel Weber (eds.), *Religion and Media.* Stanford: Stanford University Press, 2001. Pp. 388–434.

Simmel, Georg, *Soziologie. Untersuchungen über die Formen der Vergesellschaftung.* München & Leipzig: Verlang von Duncker & Humblot, 1922.

Spyer, Patricia, The Cassowary Will Not Be Photographed. In: Hent de Vries and Samuel Weber (eds.), *Religion and Media.* Stanford: Stanford University Press, 2001. Pp. 304–320.

Steegstra, Marijke, *Resilient Rituals. Krobo Initiation and the Politics of Culture in Ghana.* Münster: Lit Verlag, 2004.

Sutherland-Addy, Esi, The Ghanaian Feature Video Phenomenon. Thematic Concerns and Aesthetic Resources. In: Kofi Anyidoho & James Gibbs (eds.), FonTomFon. Contemporary Ghanaian Literature, Theatre and Film. *Matatu* 21–22, 2000: 265–277.

Taussig, Michael, *Defacement. Public Secrecy and the Labor of the Negative.* Stanford: Stanford University Press, 1999.

Weber, Samuel, *Mass Mediauras. Form Technics Media.* Stanford: Stanford University Press, 1996.

Witte, Marleen de, Altar Media's *Living Word*: Televised Charismatic Christianity in Ghana. *Journal of Religion in Africa* 33 (2), 2003: 172–202.

CHAPTER 14

CONTINUITY OR CHANGE? ALADURA AND BORN-AGAIN YORUBA CHRISTIANITY IN LONDON

Hermione Harris

The scholarship of John Peel on the Yoruba of Southwestern Nigeria has spanned nearly four decades. Although covering local history, law, politics, and social and intellectual developments, much of his work has concentrated on religious change.[1] Combining first-hand research with the exploration of Church Missionary Society archives, he has charted the progress of Yoruba religiosity over the last two centuries.

His conclusions therefore arise from detailed historical analysis. "Conversion in Africa," he argues, is "a process of impassioned communication, whose outcome, while conditioned by the assumptions, interests and resources of the participants, is in the fullest sense the product of their interaction," whether between "individuals or cultures" (1990:339). This was written in the context of the conversation between the pastor (the bearer of mission Christianity) and the *babalawo* (the indigenous diviner-priest in mid-nineteenth century Yorubaland), but all religious change is a question of encounter. The precise nature of this exchange is historically and geographically specific, but it is seldom simply a one-way transition from one praxis to another, or a mix of elements from old and new in some syncretic "mechanical assignation of cultural traits" (Peel 1968:140).[2] What Peel rigorously examines in the origi-

---

1. Eg.: 1967, 1968, 1990, 1994, 2000.
2. See Stewart and Shaw 1994 for a discussion on the concept of syncretism.

nal attraction of Christianity to the Yoruba, and then in the formation of an
independent prophetic movement in the twentieth century, is "the mutual assimilation of two religious cultures" (2000:249)—the indigenous and the
Christian—in two historical periods.

While alert to innovation, this approach assumes that "the explanation of
change has to be grounded in an appreciation of the continuities through
change" (Peel 2000:255). But recently, the natural bent of the anthropologist
towards tracing convergences rather than recognizing rupture has been questioned. Kiernan (1992) has challenged Sundkler's classic characterization of
South African Zionism as "New Wine in Old Wineskins" (1961:238); Engelke
(2004) urges closer attention to Zimbabwean conversion narratives that stress
the move into independency as a radical break. This emphasis has also
emerged in the context of the new forms of Pentecostalism sweeping Africa,
Asia, and Latin America, which are predicated on rejection of previous religiosities and "re-birth" into a new life. [3] Joel Robbins (2003) writes of "the perils of continuity thinking", which emphasizes the similarities between indigenous and Pentecostal practice, rather than looking at the meanings ascribed
by worshippers to what they do and say. These avowals of breaking with the
past are consistent with the rejection of previous patterns of ritual behavior;
claims of rupture should inform sociological analysis.

Yet the discourse of Yoruba religiosity is comprised of more than participants' explanations and the form of their ritual practice. There are also underlying epistemological assumptions, and these remain constant. Although
presented in contemporary packaging by successive generations of worshippers, the search for spiritual empowerment is the enduring leitmotiv of Yoruba
ritual.

Peel's own explorations of conversion and Yoruba religious change, both in
the nineteenth and twentieth centuries, are located in Nigeria. Now there is
another theatre in which to explore themes in the nature and extent of religious innovation. This is the burgeoning Yoruba diaspora. Although now
spread throughout Africa, Europe and the United States, Yoruba seeking work
and education have traveled particularly to Britain as the ex-colonial metrop-
olis. There they have established their own churches which cater to their particular needs according to their own understanding of their experience. Chief
amongst these are the Aladura, or "praying" churches, convinced of the effi-

---

3. The 'new' Pentecostal movement refers to the contemporary rise of charismatic
Christianity in the developing world. Although 'traditional' Pentecostalism, such as described by Hollenweger (1972) influenced the movement in Nigeria, the two differ in certain aspects of theology and ritual practice, as well as their social base.

cacy of prayer, and the later arrivals on the Nigerian religious scene, the Pentecostal "Born-Agains".

The Cherubim and Seraphim

The Cherubim and Seraphim Church (C&S) in Britain started in 1965 when a group of Yoruba met to pray for their forthcoming exams. They were all already members of the C&S, founded in Nigeria in 1925, as part of the popular Aladura movement (Peel 1968).[4] By 1971 they had purchased their own church, where 2–300 white-robed members clapped, sang, danced, and drummed to Yoruba rhythms. Throughout the service several men and women would start to shake, their faces contorted with the power of the Spirit in their bodies, hissing, shouting or speaking in tongues. But these manifestations of the Spirit would be controlled by elders if not accompanied by coherent "visions," interpretations of images seen whilst in trance which convey messages from God. The subjects of these revelations echoed those raised in the spontaneous prayers: exams, family, fertility, travel, employment, finance, immigration, "sudden death," hidden dangers and the triumphs and tribulations of daily life. C&S Prophets were also available for private consultation about plans and problems. With trance-access to the realm of invisible powers which affect the course of events, clients were advised on ritual and mundane action to reinforce their projects.

Thirty years on, the sizes of congregations have dwindled dramatically. This is partly because of the fragmentation of the C&S, as elders and prophets gathered their clients together and established their own churches. The original leader, Special Apostle Abidoye, heads a C&S coordinating council, but even he does not know how many branches now exist. Estimates vary from 50 to 100, ranging from gatherings in private houses to churches with substantial properties. There are branches of the C&S in Birmingham and other provincial cities, and Abidoye travels to visit churches inaugurated in Europe and the USA. Although it is impossible to estimate the number of adherents, the C&S, as the Aladura movement as a whole, is still a significant part of Yoruba religious practice in London.[5]

---

4. Apart from Peel 1968, the most significant studies of the C&S in Nigeria include Omoyajowo 1982, 1984, Probst 1989 and Ray 1993.

5. Findings from Africa indicate that although they are losing ground to the Pentecostals, the African independent/initiated churches (AICs) still have significant followings (Gifford 1998:62–3; Meyer 1998:341 endnote 4; 2004:452). In London, apart from the Cherubim and Seraphim there are several other Yoruba Aladura churches. The Church of

The leaders of the major branches are drawn from the body of the original "worker-students" who arrived in the 1960s. From modest backgrounds, they often financed their education through menial jobs in London, contending with inadequate living conditions, financial hardship, family problems, academic difficulties, and ill-health, besides encountering hardening institutional and personal racism. But the C&S helped them retain their dreams of the elite position that they would occupy in post-independence Nigeria, as accountants, engineers and other professionals. Some never achieved their goals, and stayed in England. The majority succeeded. Although they may have taken up to ten years to gain their qualifications, they eventually returned home. The Yoruba population in London is therefore no longer mainly composed of elderly ex-students; it is their adult children's generation who take advantage of their British passports to escape the worsening political and economic situation in Nigeria.[6] Some do attend the C&S, but many more head for the "Born-Agains."

Kingsway International Christian Church and the "Born-Agains"

Every Sunday 2–3,000 worshippers stream into a converted warehouse on an East London industrial estate. Inside, the carpeted foyer looks more like a corporate headquarters, but the sound of singing and clapping from the auditorium conveys the religious nature of the business. The focal point in the huge hall is the stage, where the neatly dressed female vocalists are backed by keyboard, percussion and electric guitar. They lead the singing, a mixture of gospel, pop and rock. The high point of the service is the appearance of the Yoruba Pastor Mathew Ashimolowo, who founded the church in London in the 1980s. His preaching, reiterating the promise of wealth and success, is a professional, highly charged performance.

The majority of those packing the hall are West African—pastors estimate that 60% to 80% of the membership are from Nigeria, mostly of Yoruba origin—but they are joined by other African, African-Caribbean, Asian and Black British worshippers. The proceedings are in English, but the cosmo-

---

the Lord is a longstanding example; the Celestial Church of Christ, much given to elaborate ritual, is going strong. The Brotherhood of the Cross and Star is predominantly patronised by Ibo. Surprisingly, apart from Kerridge 1995, there is little research on AICs in England.

6. Maier (2000) gives a vivid account of the disarray of Nigerian public life; Jumare (1997) documents the disaffection and exodus of the academic community.

politan ambitions of the church are indicated by the forty national flags hanging around the walls. A few women wear indigenous blouses and wrappers, but a large proportion of the congregation are young men and women dressed in smart street styles. There appears to be no clash between being cool and giving your life to Jesus. Spontaneous prayer is offered as though conducting an emphatic argument, voices raised, fingers wagging, eyes clenched. Some break into glossolalia. Their intensity is reflected back into the hall by the cameras that swoop over the congregation, sending their images to large monitors positioned around the walls. Every half hour the lights are dimmed, and the screens are filled with advertisements for church events, products, and the locations of other KICC branches.

The topics of prayer, preaching, and "testimony" include those heard in C&S, reflecting the common preoccupations of a migrant community. But there is less emphasis on education, and far more on material success. Many have already gained their qualifications at colleges and universities not only in Nigeria but also throughout Europe and the United States. Although some have poorly paid work in the service sector, or with mini-cab and parking firms, others work with local authorities, are successful professionals, or run their own businesses. As members of a black diaspora, they inevitably encounter a range of problems. But by and large they are better educated, more widely traveled and more prosperous than their parents' generation.

Although KICC is one of the largest Born-Again churches in London, it is by no means the only one. Several, such as the Glory House ("Where Miracles Happen"), or the Redeemed Christian Church of God (RCCG)[7] owe their origins to Yoruba Pastors. Others, such as the Kensington Temple, or the Universal Church of the Kingdom of God (UCKG)[8] were founded by Pastors from other ethnic diasporas, but have a large Nigerian membership. Organizations differ in their orientation, but none identify themselves as "African". They see themselves as part of a contemporary international movement, the charismatic Christianity exploding across the developing world.[9] They not only reject the older African independent / initiated churches (AICs) such as the C&S, but

---

7. For the RCCG, see Hunt and Lightly 2001, one of the only studies of 'new' Nigerian churches to date.

8. For UCKG see Freston 2001.

9. 'In 2000 there were 83 million Independents and 126 Pentecostal-charismatics in Africa' (Meyer 2004:451). There has been a corresponding growth of literature. Recent sources include Maxwell 1998 on Zimbabwe, Meyer 1999 and Gifford 2004 on Ghana, Marshall 1993, 1995 on Nigeria. Overviews include Martin 1990, 2002; Cox 1996; Gifford 1998; Coleman 2000 and Corten and Marshall-Fratani 2001.

represent their religion as a complete rupture with the past. Significantly, it was on Nigerian campuses that this new Pentecostal movement took root in the 1980s,[10] and it is amongst this well-educated generation that Nigerian Pentecostalism has spread, both at home and in the diaspora. Yoruba Pentecostals see themselves as "born again" into modernity.

Pentecostalism, "Modernity" and Globalization

Yet if we look at what it means to be "modern" in Nigeria over the last century, we can discern a line of continuity. As Peel demonstrates (1968), many of the original members of the C&S in Yorubaland, as with other Aladura churches, were the first in their families to receive education, and to migrate to towns in the first half of the twentieth century to seek employment. Christian, literate, working for colonial commerce and administration, they represented an emerging pan-Yoruba petty bourgeoisie, the modernity of their day. After independence in 1960 some amongst their children's generation migrated further to make the transition into an expanding post-independence Nigerian middle class through qualifications gained in England. Their membership of the C&S supported them in their endeavors. Now it is their sons' and daughters' generation, including the Yoruba elite, who come here to work and study, and who seek out churches where they feel at home—most often the Born-Agains.

Each successive generation has therefore represented an advancement in education, occupation, pan-ethnicity and geographical mobility according to what is seen as the modernity of the age. "The modern" is not a static, homogenizing category (Comaroff and Comaroff 1993:xi–xv; Moore and Sanders 2001:12–13; Bastian 2001). It also has many meanings; in this context it refers to a cluster of attributes to which individuals aspire, rather than an objective socio-economic state. The way in which Yoruba modernity has been imagined has changed over time. Early models were based on European colonialism—literacy, Christianity, bureaucracy and the trappings of a western life-style. With independence and the growth of international markets, Nigerian modernity gradually adapted to the emergence of trans-national institutions and movements. It is particularly the influence of North American capitalism which suffuses the global age.

It is the cultural style of this contemporary modernity that advertises the "newness" of the Born-Agains. A salient feature of globalization is the devel-

---

10. For the Nigerian Born-Again movement, see Hackett 1995, 1998; Ojo 1987, 1988, 1995; Marshall 1993, 1995; Marshall-Fratani 1998.

opment of technology. Appadurai (1996), among others, has argued that the interrelation of mass migration with the transformation of methods of communication have revolutionized both the speed and geographical range of interconnections. The Born-Agains project an image that is congruent with this mobility, that they have left the local and are part of a global movement—the Kingsway *International* Christian Church. Ashimolowo has founded branches back in Nigeria, besides Europe and the USA; Pentecostal pastors jet around the world working the Born-Again circuit—and are often introduced as having "just flown in" from some distant location. The size of their imagined stage is indicated by Ashimolowo's promise in his preaching that members' success will make "world news".[11] C&S leaders travel too, but not on the scale of the large international Born-Again organizations.

Born-Again mastery of the media conveys the same message. With their considerable financial resources, the KICC put out a wealth of publications: regular mail-shots with fliers for meetings and services, books, tapes, videos and CDs. To compare the irregular typeface and unpredictable font of the C&S hymnal to the glossy professionalism of these "products" is to set a local Nigerian printing press against a US-style publishing house. So with other technological apparatus. The C&S has a website, but not their own cable TV channel as does KICC. Some C&S churches have ticker-tape screens relaying biblical texts, but not the elaborate CCTV monitors of Kingsway. Aladura prayer-houses have long had musical instruments and amplifiers, for music is an essential and vibrant accompaniment to prayer. But they have nothing to compare with the equipment and sound-systems of the large Born-Again halls. Whereas C&S worship includes Yoruba rhythms and language, the model for KICC is North America. When Yoruba pastors are preaching, American inflections and pronunciation slip into their speech.

But religious practice consists of more than cultural style. Although presented in a different package, many Born Again aims and understandings have much in common with epistemologies they claim to have left behind.

The Search for Empowerment

As Peel has amply demonstrated, the thrust of Yoruba indigenous religion has always been eminently practical, addressing the needs of everyday existence rather than worrying about the life to come. Aladura followed in this

---

11. KICC all-night vigil 1.10.04.

tradition, their prayer and prophecy directed towards members' daily concerns. The C&S presents itself as a problem-solving church; "Without problems there would be no C&S", Elders say. The Born-Agains also deal with overcoming personal difficulties—but there is a difference in emphasis. Both Aladura and Pentecostals aim towards what Yoruba call "the good things in life", a state of well-being that embraces health, wealth, children and longevity. But whereas worker-students' attention was focused on returning safely with qualifications and family to Nigeria, the vistas offered to the contemporary diaspora stretch way beyond Britain to global horizons. Born-Again sermons abound with promises of property, employment in upper echelons, and untold wealth. Money, consumer goods, successful employment, and high social status are not only desirable, but indicate a right relationship with God. In what has come to be known as the prosperity gospel, a major movement within new Pentecostalism, material success has been elevated to an article of faith.[12] Among his many publications, Ashimolowo's four books on *101 Answers to Money Problems* (2000a) urge "experience of God's Prosperity", explaining "investment, saving smartly and the purpose of real estate". His preaching on the surmounting of "failure", and the equation of miracles with unashamed materialism, is repeated across London in a variety of Born-Again venues. The KICC pastor's promise that "God will change your story", diverting the narrative of individual lives towards success, is a principal theme in the rhetoric of Born-Agains.

These differences reflect the respective dreams of successive phases in the Yoruba diaspora. But what both generations seek is empowerment, fortification of their capacity to confront obstacles and achieve their goals. The key concept behind this search for efficacy is that of spiritual power, the unseen energy that articulates the universe, and provides a reservoir of strength and protection. Notions of spiritual power provide the basis for both the aim and the technology of ritual action in much indigenous religious practice. Peel (1993) has reminded us of Bryan Wilson's comprehensive study *Magic and the Millennium* (1973) which documents the search for thaumaturgy, that is "the belief in, and the demand for, supernatural communications and manifestations of power that have immediate personal significance" (ibid: 70). Wilson was charting indigenous movements up to the mid-twentieth century. But recent studies have shown that far from the "disenchantment" of the universe in

---

12. An earlier version of Nigerian Pentecostalism was the millenarian 'Holiness' movement which condemns consumerism and immorality. This has been largely eclipsed by 'Faith' teaching which embraces Prosperity (Gifford 2001). While Prosperity is the main tendency in Britain, some preachers incorporate Holiness tenets in their preaching.

succeeding decades, notions of "occult forces" and unseen power are moulding themselves to African modernity (Comaroff and Comaroff 1993; Geschiere 1997; Moore and Sanders 2001; van Dijk 2001).

Yet in spite of this persistence, power *per se,* as distinct from its uses and abuses, is rarely examined. Curiously, in the light of its significance, it seems to be as much taken for granted by ethnographers as it is for those that assume its presence in their daily lives.[13] Wilson, as many others, has stressed the significance of this quest for Aladura[14] and similar African independent churches.[15] But with the possible exception of Hackett (1993), few have examined the concept of spiritual empowerment itself. In order to assess the extent of disjuncture between Aladura and the Born-Agains, it is essential to compare the epistemological foundations of their practice. This is not only to trace the continuities between the two. The recasting of the Spirit also sheds light on the developments in Yoruba religiosity in London, and the Pentecostal claim that the past has been left behind.

Power and the Spirit

It is often difficult to tell whether anthropological neglect of spiritual power reflects the lack of indigenous exegesis, or whether the subject has not been researched. Ashforth, in his discussion of witchcraft in a South African township, argues that "it is necessary to countenance something akin to the phenomenon known in religious experience as the Mystery in relation to…unseen powers, that is an engagement with something..beyond human apprehension.….(T)he putative action of witchcraft, along with the very real fears relating to them, spring from, relate to, and are located in, realms of being which are both ineffable and open to transcendence—that are not subject to forms of knowledge adequately represented by clear and distinct ideas" (2001:219).

Even if this accurately represents the situation in Soweto, this is not a conclusion that can be universally applied to indigenous understandings of un-

---

13. Fogelson and Adam (1977) and Arens and Karp (1989) provide some ethnographic material, but the problem of comparative terminology is not sufficiently addressed. Indigenous semantics often make it hard to determine whether there is a concept of unseen force distinct from the entities so animated (Moore and Sanders 2001:3–6; Geshiere 1997:13–14.) Any broad study of spiritual power would have to tackle this question.

14. See Turner 1967, Peel 1968, Hackett 1983, Ray 1993.

15. Eg. Mbon (1992) on the Nigerian Brotherhood of the Cross and Star; Beckman (1975) on Ghanaian independency and Kiernan (1990) and Comaroff (1985) on South African Zionists.

seen energy. It echoes New Age uncertainty rather than ethnography. The 2002 *Mind Body Spirit* Festival in London advertised one of its workshops as "The Field: The Quest for the Secret Force of the Universe, the key to life itself may lie in the vibrations that connect everything"—"vibrations" remains undefined. For the modern magicians studied by Luhrmann (1992), the quest for power lies at the heart of their practice, yet in the context of a secular mainstream, the value of the concept lies in its ambiguity (ibid. 215). "Magical forces exist, they say, but no-one can properly describe them, because no-one really understands how the magic works" (ibid. 205).

The Cherubim and Seraphim, however, do have a clear idea as to the principles behind the operation of spiritual power—as to how power "works". As Mudimbe argues, African thought-systems must be "made explicit within the framework of their own rationality",[16] so, although no member would spontaneously provide a neat model of these regularities, a profile of the Spirit may be drawn from conscious exposition by Elders, as well as deduced from an analysis of ritual text and action. For power is a constant topic in C&S discourse. Members pray for power; they sing about it, dance for it, and embody power in possession. Power is the subject of dream and vision, and ritual techniques seek to control spiritual energies and deploy them for practical ends. Choruses celebrate the C&S access to the Spirit:

> Send down the Power, send down the Power,
> Send down the Power, O Lord

"This church is based on spiritual power. Without spiritual power there would be no church," said an Elder. *Agbara Emi Mimo*, the power of the Holy Spirit, is the key concept in Aladura epistemology—and therefore of the religious praxis of the C&S.

In elucidating the concept, Elders often employ indigenous examples, for the same discourse animates both practices. The original Yoruba word for unseen energy was *ase*. Pierre Verger, one of the first to pay attention to this Yoruba preoccupation defines it thus:

> Nor are the Gods the only beings animated by it: it is the principle of all that lives or acts or moves. All life is *ase*. So is everything which

---

16. *The Invention of Africa: Gnosis, Philosophy, and the Order of Knowledge.* London: James Curry 1988:x quoted in Nyamnjoh 2001: 28–9.

exhibits power, whether in action…or in passive resistance like that of the boulders lying by the wayside" (1966:36–7).[17]

Subsequent scholars have gone even further:

The fundamental concept of life-force—that exists in many forms and varying amounts—is at the foundation of Yoruba philosophy and social organisation (H and M Drewal 1990:6).[18]

When speaking in Yoruba about "power" the C&S do not use the word *ase*, but *agbara*, as in the Yoruba Bible. It is likely that the Yoruba Bishop Crowther, translating the Bible in the 1880s, wanted to signal a radical break with indigenous ritual by using by a term which referred to physical rather than spiritual strength; *ase* carried too much symbolic weight. But Aladura carried former meanings into their readings of the scriptures, which confirmed a world full of unseen forces and divine powers.

For the C&S—as for the worshippers of indigenous deities, the *orisa*—the source of all power is *Olodumare*, the Almighty God, *Olorun*, God in Heaven. For the C&S he is *Jah Jehovah*, the God of Power, and *Olorun Iye ati Agbara* the God of Life and Power. C&S prayer is also addressed to the Father and to the Son, but it is the Holy Spirit, *Emi Mimo*, which is privileged in the triumvirate of the Trinity. *Mimo* means holy. *Emi*, spirit, holds the multiple meanings of unseen being, the locus of an entity's power and this power itself. In the C&S translation of *Emi (mimo)* the terms "(Holy) Spirit" and "(spiritual) power" are used interchangeably. *Mi* means "breath," so the concept of spirit incorporates interrelated associations with vitality. An elder explained, "Power comes from life, life from breath, and from your spirit comes the power."

In indigenous religious practice, the power of the Creator was solicited from *orisa*, borrowed from spirits, accessed through incantation (*ofo*), or derived from the manipulation of medicinal ingredients (*oogun*) popularly referred to as "juju". Aladura hope to tap *Agbara Emi Mimo* not through supplication to lesser deities, but directly from the supreme source. In 1928 the Anglican synod in Nigeria, focusing on individual ritual acts rather than appreciating the logic of spiritual power lying behind them, dismissed C&S practice as "replacing superstition with superstition" (Turner 1979:124). But the C&S had no problem

---

17. It is likely that Verger was alerted to the significance of *ase* by the work of Fr. Palcide Tempels, whose exploration of 'la force vitale' in *La Philosophie Bantoue* was first published in 1945.

18. Other accounts of *ase* include Drewal 1992; Apter 1992; Hallen and Sodipo 1986.

in advertising their church as replacing "heathenish practices" with something better. Unlike the Born-Agains, they spontaneously indicated equivalences: prayer and fasting has replaced sacrifice; *oogun* is abandoned in favor of consecrated candles, blessed water and olive oil, prayer gowns and ritual texts all of which contained reservoirs of performative power. The old Ifa oracle was supplanted by prophetic visions. A 1970s chorus exhorted:

> Herbalists, leave your juju alone
> Come and take Holy Water

The Principles of Power

It was because they shared an understanding of unseen power that Aladura could supplant indigenous practice. For the C&S, the master-metaphor for power is electricity, a parallel that had already surfaced in the world of *orisa* and *oogun* (Peel 2000:217–18). Like electricity it is conceived as a dynamic current, not a static quality; it possesses particular characteristics, and operates according to certain principles. It is these that underpin Aladura ritual and provide a logic for the effectiveness of prayer.

Primarily, "power" is a principle of general efficacy, necessary to progress in any area of life, mundane or spiritual. This theme runs through the whole of Yoruba cultural discourse. Advertising is a case in point: "Aspro for power". Guinness promises "power and goodness"; politicians and persons of wealth or influence are assumed to have great reservoirs of spiritual power. Although eliding here with socio-political authority, the one cannot be reduced to the other. Any manifestation of well-being is seen as a refraction of this vitality. So with the C&S:

> Jah Jehovah! The Holy Spirit in Heaven, come and descend it upon us! The power that we will never go ashamed, that our prayer will never go unanswered, that the pregnant women will bear easily, that you will provide for those looking for children; people looking for job will get good jobs, that the fold [i.e. members of the church] will be multiplying. The power by which we shall be prophesying, and that all our prayer will be accepted by thee. O God of the Holy Spirit!…the power for joy, for rest of mind, that we will never have trouble in our homes; the power to fight impediments in our ways, that we will never be ashamed. We beg thee to come and endow us with thy power.…(Prayer 9.1.71)[19]

---

19. Translated from the Yoruba by a C&S Elder.

A weak spirit, a lack of power, therefore denotes enfeeblement. A vision in a Sunday service warned a Brother:

> The Lord says that you must pray fervently against anything that may make you lose your spiritual power....I do not want your life to be like a dead fish, like an old shoe....(20.4.69)

By tapping the power of Olodumare, through indigenous or Christian ritual, an individual hopes to become a potent personality. This provides the capacity to "over-power" others, to co-opt their power, control their actions or fend off their malice. For *agbara*, as was *ase*, is a comparative, hierarchical concept. As a C&S elder explained:

> A lot of spiritual things are a matter of one spirit being stronger than another. So with *oogun*, the spirits you call up may be stronger than the spirit of the person you want to influence, and so you will dominate him. A lesser power must always submit to a higher one, unless it is being used by a greater spirit.

Superior power is necessary not only to realize ambition, but to provide protection against unseen attack. For power is not only a positive force; it is morally neutral. Orthodox Christian dualism of good and evil distorts the understanding of *agbara*. In C&S assumptions, as with indigenous epistemology, spiritual power in itself it is neither good nor bad, but may be used for either. As an elder explained: "Power is like electricity; it gives you light, it also instantly kills you". Both prayer and medicine can mobilize destructive forces as well as erect defences against invisible assault. At the same time, even the power of witchcraft, described below as the ultimate malignity, could, in indigenous thinking, bring benefit as well as wreak harm.[20]

Power and Protection

These assaults can come from many quarters. As did the Ifa oracle, dream and vision reveal the activities of "evil hands" and "the powers of darkness" which loom large in the Yoruba imagination. Yoruba in London, as their parents before them, are quick to attribute failure and misfortune to the jealousy and spite of others. Problems are personalized. As a C&S sister complained:

---

20. See M Drewal 1992; H & M Drewal 1990; Bastian 2001 amongst others. This moral ambiguity is also emphasised in studies of contemporary witchcraft elsewhere, e.g. Geschiere 1997:12–15.

> Sometimes you have studied from morning to night. You have done everything you can, but you still don't pass [your exam]. So then you know that it may be because someone is jealous of you and is putting impediment in your way.

Revelation constantly reinforces this aetiology of misfortune:

> Watch and pray. The enemies are digging holes in your way so that you may fall in, and these enemies are appearing as friends.... (Vision: 5.9.70)

The collective term for a range of adversaries is that of "enemies" (*ota*) (Oyetade 1996). The C&S and other Aladura churches accepted the reality of the Yoruba panoply of destructive forces, rebranding them as "branches of the Devil". Satanic power appears in a variety of guises: it can be mobilized though a curse (*epe*), or embodied in the charms and incantations of juju and *oogun buruku*, harmful medicine whose ingredients are available in London as well as Lagos. The dramatis personae of the cast of evildoers also include a range of evil spirits (*emi buruku*) associated with disease and disaster, but the ultimate assault is thought to be that of witchcraft (*aje*). Yoruba witches conform to the African stereotype—women whose destructive activities invert normal social behavior and feminine roles. Emerging at night, their *emi* flies through the darkness to sap the spirit of their victims, sabotaging reproduction and attacking children. C&S visions constantly confirm their presence:

> I was made to see some little children in a small room.... These are the ones the Holy Spirit has been guarding from witchcraft and the powers of evildoers.... (Vision: 7.12.69)

Aladura find ample Biblical justification for these malign forces. The pages of both the Old and the New Testaments are shot through with references to witchcraft and evil spirits; of the 150 psalms (which are favorite C&S texts), fifty-six mention "enemies" explicitly, whilst others refer to a variety of ill-wishers and their malice. But missions in the late nineteenth and early twentieth centuries could not tolerate this "superstition". Their failure to acknowledge this integral part of Yoruba cosmology left converts feeling defenceless. If protective ritual and juju were ridiculed, or prohibited as paganism, what would provide fortification against attack? As a contemporary C&S member commented, "GP can't deal with witchcraft". But in Aladura thinking, the Devil is ultimately an entity of God's own creation. His defeat by the Archangel Michael (Rev. 12:7–12) proves that satanic power is inferior to that of the Holy Spirit. Through prayer and ritual, therefore, the C&S can enlist the protective power of God to withstand attack. Armed with insight into the activities of unseen forces through revelation, appropriate action can be taken to influence these powers, avert misfortune and realize ambitions.

While incorporating Yoruba epistemology into their practice, the C&S condemn indigenous techniques of tapping spiritual power. The original Constitution stated that:

> The Order…believes in the curative effects of prayer for all afflictions, spiritual and temporal, but condemns and abhors the use of charms or fetish, witchcraft or sorcery of any kind and all heathenish sacrifices and practices.
>
> (Eternal Sacred Order of the C&S. 1930. *The Cherubim and Seraphim Memorandum and Articles of Association*. para 10)

Visions convey the same message of breaking with the past:

> As my word was over the enemies of old, so is my word today. If you want to worship the true God, we should realise that these *orisa,* they have ears but they cannot hear, eyes and they cannot see, they have mouths, but they cannot talk.…(Vision. C&S Service 1970)[21]

But now C&S leaders are aware that for a younger generation, their ritual practice appears not so much as a rejection of tradition, as they intend, but a perpetuation of it. Today, when contemporary Yoruba culture has moved further away from the world of the *orisa,* they see that the youth find the prayer-gown, the spiritual armor of the C&S, "old-fashioned". Younger Yoruba are not so attracted to the use of candles, incense, water and other ritual items imbued with power. They cannot relate to the pollution taboos preventing the debilitation of spiritual power though the removal of shoes and covering of women's hair during prayer. The exclusion of menstruating women from services or from contact with "powerful" objects sits uneasily with the image of modern womanhood embraced by the Born-Agains. At a Council of C&S Churches meeting (20.1.01), bemoaning the lack of younger members, a Brother, painfully aware of current criticism, exclaimed: "Look at us! We are too syncretist, too Sango-like! That is what is driving them away!"—Sango being the God of Thunder who possessed his priests.

Attitudes toward tradition lie at the heart of Born-Again antagonism to Aladura. Towards the end of 2000, the C&S approached Premier Christian Radio, an Evangelical Pentecostal station, requesting them to run an adver-

---

21. Cf. Psalm 115:4–7; 135: 15–17.

tisement for their bible class, the "Theological School". This was refused, on the grounds that complaints had been received about the church:

> One Lady who complained suggested that 'they [the C&S] invoke curses on any of their members who stop going to their churches' and that 'they see all sorts of evil visions.....they mix pagan and Bible worship together'. She said that she knew former members who have had 'very nasty experiences'.

The letter went on to claim that the C&S did not qualify for membership of the African and Caribbean Evangelical Alliance, who have

> raised concerns about the use of visions and revelations. In addition, many African Churches would not consider the Cherubim and Seraphim churches to be orthodox in the Christian faith and would not consider them a church.
>
> (Letter to C&S Council of Churches 21.10.00).

The key to Born-Again virulence against the C&S, as with the Anglican Synod decades ago, is what they see as "paganism" in Aladura practice. By being reborn, dedicating their lives to God, the new Nigerian Pentecostals reject not only their own personal history, but that of indigenous Yoruba religious culture as a whole.

Pentecostalism and Powers

Yet despite this derision, there are features of Born-Again discourse that have a familiar ring. Although presented in a contemporary package, many of the themes of Aladura concern reappear in Pentecostal settings. For, despite appearances, the C&S and KICC share the basic premise of their practice: the ubiquitous Yoruba search for spiritual empowerment. Marshall affirms that that "Nigerians tend to respect or fear displays of spiritual power, which they generally recognise born-agains as possessing" (1993:232). Meyer (1998) indicates that Ghanaians are turning to Pentecostalism as a new "modern" source of power. Although indigenous terminology has been abandoned in favor of the English term "power", the Yoruba concept persists both in its salience and characteristics. Hackett has vividly demonstrated the significance of the discourse of empowerment to contemporary Nigerian preachers and their adherents (1993:397–402). So in the diaspora. The crowds at a KICC night-vigil had been summoned in the publicity to "Experience the Power" (1.10.04). This energy does not remain an external force. Worshippers seek the fortification of their own spirit through infusion of the divine: "Fill us with your power; live inside of me," they sing. Charged with this vitality, they will overcome all obstacles to the success which lies just around the corner: "By thy great power…nothing, absolutely nothing…is too difficult for thee."

These "obstacles" are presented not in terms of objective socio-economic disadvantage of minority communities, or the effects of institutionalized racism, but in typical Yoruba fashion are personalized: "*someone* trying to destroy your career…". "Enemies" lurk everywhere: they could be human beings spreading malicious rumors; they could be family or false friends using medicine or witchcraft; they could be evil spirits. A "Success and Prayer Night" (5.3.2004) was advertised as "Breaking the Curse". These agents of the Devil operate either through mundane methods of obstruction, or undermine their victim through unseen power. Either way, the means to resist lies in personal empowerment. By recruiting the superior force of the Holy Spirit, weaker destructive energies are overcome. The common theme in C&S revelation of "protection over the little children" is echoed in Born Again assurances; Ashimolowo "saw a wall of fire" around the children, and promised that "there would be no loss" (1.10.04). In both Aladura and Pentecostal discourse, fire is a potent metaphor for the Spirit, speaking to Moses from the burning bush (Exod.3:2) and appearing as tongues of fire at Pentecost (Acts 2:3). Fire also speaks of the intrinsic ambiguity of power: as a destructive force (Deut. 4:24) it protects through the incineration of evil. At another all-night service, worshippers were invited to burn slips of paper inscribed with their problems: "Bring in documentation of your challenges, add them to the bonfire and watch God answer by fire" (5.11.2004).

Although Ashimolowo did not mention witchcraft specifically, this potential threat to children was clearly implied. For *aje* is still part of the Pentecostal scene. Nigerian Born-Again literature, as the secular media, is explicit about evil entities (Marshall 1993, 1995; Marshall-Fratani 1998; Peel 2000:315). Diaspora Born-Again practice cannot be read off from Nigerian experience, for Pentecostalism is also shaped by local context (Martin 1990, 2002). But writings of Yoruba Born-Again pastors, such as Bishop David Oyedepo, founder of the popular "Winners' Chapel", reach British audiences and alert them to a range of invisible threats. One of KICC's recorded phone messages warns of "the spirit of witchcraft" (11.1.01). When inviting various categories of the afflicted to come forward for prayer during services, Ashimolowo rebukes infirmities of mind and body as "spirits"; "the spirit that pollutes the womb", "the spirit of failure". His exhortation to "take authority" over them is significant: "authority" translates as *ase*. When he promises that "the power of darkness is broken", the operational logic of "over-powering" evil forces remains much the same as before.

The Spirit and the Self

If there is indeed an acceptance of the indigenous hermeneutic of spiritual powers, what, then, distinguishes Born-Again epistemology from Aladura? Are there differences in the way the Spirit is conceived, and which enable Pentecostals to perceive a rupture with the past rather than recognize continuity?

A significant development is the individualization of the Spirit. The C&S Holy Spirit was never completely impersonal, and was credited with some character. But his human aspect assumed much less significance than his spiritual. In Born-Again epistemology, this is reversed. "The Spirit is not an 'it'," said Ashimolowo, "he's a personality" (Sermon 24.9.00). The cover of one of his books, *1001 Truths About Your Best Friend the HOLY SPIRIT* (1997) goes further: "Friendship with the Holy Spirit means communion, direction, intimacy and depth in the things of God…Ask your friend to walk with you, talk to you and take you into the depth of the Father's will.…Truly, he is your greatest and best friend." In traditional Pentecostalism and evangelical religion, this companionate role is reserved for Jesus; for Born-Agains the personal relationship is also with God and his spiritual manifestation. Congregations are told that "this is a time of intimacy and growth in your relationship with God". This "intimacy" goes beyond mere "friendship" and assumes more emotional dimensions. Popular choruses drive home the message: "I'm in love, sweet Holy Spirit, I'm in love"; "I just want to…say I love you. You are everything to me…"; "One night with the King changes everything…I'll never be the same". Oyedepo, visiting the Glory House in London, told the congregation that "God is waiting for a passionate love affair with you" (29.10.00).

These sentiments bear much affinity with contemporary secular cultural emphasis on "relationships". But there are two sides to a love affair; Born-Again discourse pays much attention to the personhood of the worshipper, and constructing the individual subject. This is signalled by the structure of space: the replacement of altar, cross, and candles on the platform with choir, musicians, and preacher. It is reinforced by the virtual representation of participants and pastor continuously relayed back to the congregation. It is the whole person — physical, psychological, emotional, as well as spiritual — which is celebrated in the new Yoruba Pentecostal practice. This includes an appeal to the sensory dimension of individuality which is not discernable to the same extent in Aladura. Music is an essential part of C&S worship, but aural stimulation is never absent in KICC services; keyboard meanderings accompany both prayer and preaching. Tactile sensation is stirred by preachers' directions to touch your neighbors, addressing them with exhortatory phrases.

Sermons in all Born-Again churches abound with mentions of "seeing", "voicing", "hearing", "walking"—metaphors for the connection with the Spirit and the rewards this brings. "If you can see it, you can have it" said Albert Odulele (Glory House 29.10.00).

This "seeing" does not refer to visioning or dreams, but to personal imagination and aspiration. Ashimolowo's book, *Breaking Barriers* (2000b) is subtitled: *Changing Your Speech, Sight, Hearing and Thought from Negative to Positive*. One of the great attractions of Aladura is the encouragement prophetic promises provide, and the personal optimism promoted by prayer. But in Born-Again practice, psychological parlance is overt. "Your negatives are taken by God...", but you must also think yourself into becoming a "stranger to failure". Ashimolowo explains why a "newly called" man may evolve an ambitious "vision" for his life: "This is because God is using what is called incentive motivation; that is using the positive to challenge a person" (2000:77). The "vision" has nothing to do with Aladura revelation, but the enhanced personal hopes of the convert. Conceptions of personal spirit are also only partially held in common between the two independent Yoruba religiosities: in both C&S and KICC epistemology, individuals have their own power, but whereas Aladura conceive of this energy as a refraction of the power of God, Born-Again discourse posits reserves of potential to be released by a mixture of prayer and positive thought. In his book *The Release of Power*, Oyedepo explains that:

> The gift of power will not come until you stir it up. There's a power deposit inside you, but it takes prayer to cause it to be released (1996:59).

In KICC there is much talk of "breakthrough". One meaning of this epiphany is to "bring out what is in you". All this sounds remarkably similar to North American secular self-help literature. Take, for example, an excerpt from a best-seller of this genre, Anthony Robbins' *Unlimited Power*:

> We can all unleash the magic within us. We must simply learn how to turn on and use our minds and bodies in the most powerful and advantageous ways (1988:29).

For the KICC, the most "advantageous way" is becoming Born-Again in the Spirit. This is a phrase common to all Pentecostals, but there is a significant distinction between the orthodox tradition and Born-Again praxis which bears on the individualism of Nigerian Pentecostals. True conversion is commonly marked in Pentecostalism by the eponymous moment of the Holy Spirit's descent on the Apostles (Acts 2:1–4). Speaking in tongues, falling into trance, indicates baptism by the Holy Spirit, and selection by God for spiritual re-birth. But contemporary Nigerian Pentecostals do not wait for heaven-sent signs; to be born again is to "open your heart to the Spirit", to decide to dedicate your life to God. Sometimes it is hard to distinguish enthusiastic Born-Again prayer from trance. Both are manifested in the body, with bending back, swinging arms, and contorted facial expressions. But unlike Aladura, where the Spirit takes the possessed far from their surroundings, in Born-Again practice worshippers do not appear to be out of conscious control. Glossolalia is commended as experienced prayer, but does not necessarily involve dissociation. Although some may personally experience oblivion, possession is not privileged in Born-Again practice, either as a mark of divine approval, or as a means of receiving messages from God.

This emphasis on individual will is accompanied by developments in ritual democracy. Aladura broke with indigenous ritual and orthodox Christian practice in rendering direct communication with the divine a possibility for all. Yet not every Aladura has the "gift of the Spirit"; only a minority have the capacity to vision, and influence others through their revelations. Yoruba Pentecostalism now takes this egalitarianism a step further, removing a potential mark of inequality by decentering possession. A privileged association with the Spirit depends only on a rational personal decision.

Revelation, however, is still there, but is the preserve of the leading Pastor. Although not betraying signs of trance, when Ashimolowo declared that he "saw" the children surrounded by fire, he is exercising his prophetic gift. Given the authority invested in Pentecostal leaders, it seems paradoxical to argue that this monopoly of revelation indicates a new spiritual democracy in the church at large, but devolution of prophecy to the Pastors leaves a congregation composed of equal individuals. With Born-Agains there are no "grades", no spiritual hierarchy as in Aladura. Access to God is unmediated by symbol or involuntary spiritual privilege.

This Born-Again emphasis on the *person* rather than on the organization of which they are a part, is appropriate for a global age. Part of the transformation that Nigeria has undergone in the space of a few generations is accommodation with cultural individualism (La Fontaine 1985; Abrahams 1986:56). Not that indigenous Yoruba society was wholly collective; it has been, as now, a competitive culture with individual choice and aspiration inserted into traditional hierarchical structures.[22] Yet, as Lawuyi (1991) argues,

---

22. H. and M. Drewal (1990:105) and M. Drewal (1992) argue that ritual and cultural life were energised by innovation and individual preference.

in pre-independence Yorubaland, self-actualization was constrained by strong social pressures to conform. In what Nyamnjoh (2001:31) has called "domesticated agency", individual interests were realized within the context of the collectivity.

During the last century, these restrictions began to give way. The penetration of market relations and the rights and duties of national citizenship began to remove areas of Yoruba life from the norms of social reciprocity. Private ownership, legal autonomy, political enfranchisement, and monetized exchange diluted old moral allegiances. What Matory (1994:47) calls "this new capitalist negotiation of self" challenged previous principles of seniority and gender. The Aladura movement was itself a response to this process and to the loosening of links between personal identity and group membership, whether of kinship, ritual, locality or occupation.

For the succeeding generation, that which now constitutes the Nigerian diaspora, the constraints of geography, gender, family and age are also giving way. The political and social significance of birthplace and kin has more to do with personal ties of "clientism" than collective interest. Culturally, the pressures towards individualism have gathered momentum, and the contemporary climate of self-preoccupation now surrounds the Yoruba migrant to Europe or the USA. Its socio-economic underpinnings of advanced industrial capital and attendant consumerism foster the construction of identity around individual acquisition, whether of material goods or techniques of self-improvement. C&S prayer and prophecy assisted those negotiating the transition for ascribed to achieved status, and a changing sense of self. Born-Again discourse goes a step further towards legitimizing individual ambition, and translating self-actuation into Christian practice. The configuration of epistemological assumptions, the shape of spiritual power, has shifted accordingly.

Conclusion

These developments do not constitute a linear progression. Neither Aladura nor the new Pentecostalism is an homogenous movement.[23] Leaders imprint different emphases on their churches, with some C&S branches now leaning towards a Pentecostal style, and some Born-Again practice reminiscent of Aladura. Individuals may also move between the C&S and the Born-Agains in

---

23. Gifford makes the same point in relation to Ghanaian Pentecostalism, stressing ' the tendency for each succeeding wave [of charismatic Christianity] to affect all existing churches, making 'pure' or 'non-hybrid' types hard to find' (2004:27).

their search for spiritual support. It has been recognized that "traditional" religion, mainline churches and AICs "are in ongoing exchange, conflict and dialogue with each other" (Meyer 2004:450). Peel's "encounter." Pentecostal practice now needs to be added to the mix. Despite Born-Again repudiation of other religiosities, elements of their ritual practice reappear. For example, although rejecting most Aladura ritual symbols, Oyedepo promotes anointing with oil to augment personal spirit;[24] "When you have the anointing," Ashimolowo writes, "you have the strength no force can overcome" (1999:13). KICC credits the communion bread and wine with the performative power to "defeat enemies," and "change a nobody to somebody" (1.10.04). The status of prophecy is now also indeterminate in both movements. The diminution of displays of Spirit in C&S services over the years, the reduction of time given to visions whether in public or private, demonstrates a self-conscious move away from dependence on revelation towards reliance on individual prayer. On the other hand, it will be interesting to see whether the increasing demand for prophecy in Ghanaian Pentecostalism (Gifford 2004:89–90), which receives its impetus from Nigeria, will be reflected in Yoruba practice in London.

How far, then, does Born-Again practice represent a rupture, as Pentecostals claim? It depends on whose perspective predominates. There has always been a tension in anthropology between the researcher's interpretations, and the explanations of the people they study—"the observer's and the actor's model" it was called in functionalist days, the emic versus the etic. Peel (1994) alludes to these approaches in his review of three studies of African religion published in the early 1990s. Appreciating Drewal's rich 1992 study of Yoruba ritual, Peel (1994:151) notes her "sensitivity to the self-understanding that Yoruba performers have of it" with material drawn from "clearly individuated ritual agents" (ibid.:152). This is in contrast to Apter's analysis of Yoruba ritual (1992) in which he searches for the "'deep' interpretations and hidden meanings" behind *orisa* worship. "[W]e have heard of 'multivocality' in ritual discourse" Peel writes, "but we have not yet heard many actual voices...." (1994:154).

The voices of Yoruba converts, whether to Christianity, Aladura, or the new Pentecostalism, proclaim their break with the past. In search of modernity, each turned away from a previous religious practice: Christians abandoning indigenous ritual, the C&S seeking alternatives both to missions and "medicine," Born-Agains rejecting Aladura and mainstream churches. In asserting their innovation, the Born-Agains speak the loudest of all.

---

24. 'We know from Scripture that power comes from anointing'. (Oyedepo, quoted in Gifford 2004:60)

The argument for "rupture" in the analysis of Nigerian Pentecostalism respects the claims participants make of their own experience. As such it is valid. However, to trace cosmological connections with the past behind apparent difference is not to erase Born-Again interpretations. To chart continuity is not to argue that Yoruba "can only understand the world in terms of their received categories" (Robbins 2003:230), that they are trapped in some Popperian "closed" world-view, but to recognize that in the appeal of the new, in the personal contemplation of change, there must be something that resonates with the familiar, even if not consciously identified. If, as Peel would encourage us to do, we see religious change as a *process*, then connections, and the conversation between old and new, emerge. As Robbins himself argues, Pentecostalism introduces its own ontology, but situates the traditional world-view within it (2003:223). The key concept in both, the thread that weaves through Yoruba religious change over the last century, whether in Nigeria or in the diaspora, is the search for spiritual empowerment. By taking unseen vitality as a distinct concept, rather than as an unexamined backdrop to religious practice, both continuity and change become apparent. Although adapted to circumstance, the operating principles of spiritual power remain, providing the logic for both C&S prayer and Born-Again "miracles".

To pit "continuity" versus "rupture" in understanding the relationship between Aladura and the Born-Agains is therefore to pose a false dichotomy. We can trace continuities behind epistemological change, but acknowledge that Pentecostals revolutionize their relationship with God, and feel born afresh into the Spirit.

References

Abrahams, Roger D. 1986. Ordinary and extraordinary experience, in *The Anthropology of Experience*, ed. Victor Turner and Edward Bruner, 45–72. Chicago: University of Illinois Press.

Appadurai, Arjun. 1996. *Modernity at Large: Cultural Dimensions of Globalization*. Minneapolis: University of Minnesota Press.

Apter, Andrew. 1992. *Black Critics and Kings: the Hermeneutics of Power in Yoruba Society*. Chicago: University of Chicago Press.

Arens, William and Ivan Karp (eds.) 1989. *Creativity of Power: Cosmology and Action in African Societies*. Washington DC: Smithsonian Institution Press.

Ashforth, Adam. 2001. On Living in a World with Witches. Everyday Epistemology and Spiritual Insecurity in a Modern African City, in *Magical Interpretations, Material Realities; modernity, witchcraft and the occult in post-*

colonial Africa, eds. Henrietta Moore and Todd Sanders. 206–225. London: Routledge.

Ashimolowo, Mathew. 1997. *101 Truths about your Best Friend the Holy Spirit.* London: Mattyson Media.

———— 1999. *Anointing 101.* London: Mattyson Media.

———— 2000a. *101 Answers to Money Problems.* London: Mattyson Media.

———— 2000b. *Breaking Barriers: Tearing down Invisible Barriers: changing your Speech, Sight, Hearing and Thought from Negative to Positive.* London: Mattyson Media.

Bastian, Misty. 2001. Vulture Men, Campus Cultists and teenaged witches: modern magic in Nigerian popular media, in *Magical Interpretations, Material Realities; modernity, witchcraft and the occult in postcolonial Africa.* eds. Henrietta Moore and Todd Sanders, 71–96. London: Routledge.

Beckman, David M. 1975. *Eden Revival: Spiritual Churches in Ghana.* St Louis: Concordia Publishing House.

Coleman, Simon. 2000. *The Globalisation of Charismatic Christianity: spreading the Gospel of Prosperity.* Cambridge: Cambridge University Press.

Comaroff, Jean. 1985. *Body of Power: Spirit of Resistance.* Chicago: University of Chicago Press.

———— and John Comaroff. 1993. *Modernity and its Malcontents; ritual and power in post-colonial Africa.* Chicago: University of Chicago Press.

Corten, André and Ruth Marshall-Fratani. 2001. *Between Babel and Pentecost: Transnational Pentecostalism in Africa and Latin America.* London: C. Hurst & Co.

Cox, Harvey. 1996. *Fire from Heaven.* London: Cassell.

Drewal, Henry John and Margaret Thompson Drewal. [1983] 1990. *Gelede: Art and Female Power among the Yoruba.* Bloomington: Indiana University Press.

Drewal, Margaret Thompson. 1992. *Yoruba Ritual: Performers, Play, Agency.* Bloomington: Indiana University Press.

Engelke, Mathew. 2004. Discontinuity and the Discourse of Conversion. *Journal of Religion in Africa* 34:1–2. 82–109.

Freston, Paul. 2001. The transnationalisation of Brazilian Pentecostalism: the Universal Church of the Kingdom of God, in *Between Babel and Pentecost: Transnational Pentecostalism in Africa and Latin America,* ed. André Corten and Ruth Marshall Fratani 196–215. London: C.Hurst & Co.

Fogelson, Raymond D., and Richard N. Adams, eds. 1977. *The Anthropology of Power.* London: The Academic Press.

Geschiere, Peter. 1997. *The Modernity of Witchcraft; politics and the occult in post-colonial Africa.* Charlottesville: University of Virginia Press.

Gifford, Paul. 1998. *African Christianity and its Public Role*. London: Hurst & Co.

———— 2004. *Ghana's New Christianity, Pentecostalism in a globalising African economy*. London: Hurst & Co.

Hackett, Rosalind. 1983. Power and authority in Nigerian independent churches. *West African Religion* 20:1,2; 37–54.

———— 1995. The gospel of prosperity in West Africa, in *Religion and the Transformation of Capitalism*, ed. R. Roberts, 199–214. London: Routledge.

———— 1998. Charismatic/Pentecostal appropriation of media technologies in Nigeria and Ghana. *Journal of Religion in Africa* 18:3, 258–77.

Hallen, Barry, and J.O. Sopido. 1986. *Knowledge, Belief and Witchcraft: Analytic Experiments in African Philosophy*. London: Ethnographica.

Harris, Hermione. 2002. *The Cherubim and Seraphim: the Concept and Practice of Spiritual Empowerment in an African Church in London*. Unpublished PhD thesis, SOAS, University of London.

Hollenweger, W.J. 1972. *The Pentecostals*. London: SCM Press.

Hunt, Stephen and Nicola Lightly. 2001. The British black Pentecostal 'revival': identity and belief in the 'new' Nigerian churches. *Ethnic and Racial Studies* 24:1, 104–24.

Jumare, Ibrahim. 1997. The displacement of the Nigerian academic community. *Journal of Asian and African Studies* 32:1–2, 110–19.

Kerridge, Roy. 1995. *The Storm is Passing Over: A Look at Black Churches in Britain*. London: Thames and Hudson.

Kiernan, J.P. 1990. *The Production and Management of Therapeutic Power in Zionist Churches within a Zulu City*. Lewiston: The Edwin Mellen Press.

———— 1992. The Herder and the Rustler: deciphering the affinity between Zulu Diviner and Zionist Prophet. *African Studies* 51:2, 230–242.

La Fontaine, Jean S. 1985. Person and individual: some anthropological reflections, in *The Category of the Person*, eds. Michael Carrithers, Steven Collings, and Steven Lukes, 123–40. Cambridge: Cambridge University Press.

Lawuyi, Olatunde 1991. Self-potential as a Yoruba ultimate, in *Ultimate Reality and Meaning* 14:1, 21–29.

Luhrmann, T.M. 1992. *Persuasions of the Witch's Craft: Ritual Magic in Contemporary England*. Oxford: Blackwell.

Maier, Karl. 2000. *This House has Fallen: Nigeria in Crisis*. Harmondsworth: Allen Lane.

Marshall, Ruth. 1993. Power in the name of Jesus: social transformation and Pentecostalism in Western Nigeria 'revisited', in *Legitimacy and the State in*

Twentieth Century Africa, ed. Terence Ranger and Olufemi Vaughan, 213–46. Oxford: Macmillan.

——— 1995. 'God is not a democrat': Pentecostalism and democratisation in Nigeria, in *The Christian Churches and the Democratisation of Africa*, ed. Paul Gifford, 239–60. Leiden: Brill.

Marshall-Fratani, Ruth. 1998. Mediating the global and local in Nigerian Pentecostalism. *Journal of Religion in Africa* 28:3, 278–315.

Martin, David. 1990. *Tongues of Fire: The Explosion of Protestantism in Latin America*. Oxford: Blackwell.

——— 2002: *Pentecostalism: The World their Parish*. Oxford: Blackwell.

Matory, J. Lorand. 1994. *Sex and the Empire that is no more: Gender and the Politics of Metaphor in Oyo Yoruba Religion*. Minneapolis: University of Minnesota Press.

Maxwell, David. 1998. 'Delivered from the Spirit of Poverty? Pentecostalism, Prosperity and Modernity in Zimbabwe. *Journal of Religion in Africa* 28:3, 350–373.

Mbon, Friday M. 1992. *Brotherhood of the Cross and Star: a New Religious Movement in Nigeria*. Frankfurt-am-Main: Lang.

Meyer, Birgit. 1998. 'Make a Complete Break with the Past.' Memory and postcolonial modernity on Ghanaian Pentecostal discourse. *Journal of Religion in Africa*. 28: 3. 316–349.

——— 2004. Christianity in Africa: from African Independent to Pentecostal-Charismatic Churches. *Annual Review of Anthropology* 33: 447–74.

Moore, Henrietta and Todd Sanders. Eds. 2001. *Magical Interpretations, Material Realities; modernity, witchcraft and the occult in postcolonial Africa*. London: Routledge.

Nyamnjoh, Francis. 2001. Delusions of Development and the Enrichment of Witchcraft discourses in Cameroon, in *Magical Interpretations, Material Realities; modernity, witchcraft and the occult in postcolonial Africa*. eds. Henrietta Moore and Todd Sanders. 28–49. London: Routledge.

Ojo, Matthews A. 1987. *The Growth of Campus Christianity and Charismatic Movements in Western Nigeria*. Unpublished PhD thesis, Kings College, University of London.

——— 1988. The contextual significance of the charismatic movements in Independent Nigeria. *Africa* 58:2, 175–92.

——— 1995. The charismatic movement in Nigeria today. *International Bulletin of Missionary Research* 19:3, 114–18.

Omoyajowo, J. Akinyele. 1982. *Cherubim and Seraphim: The History of an African Independent Church*. New York: Nok Publishers International Ltd.

———— 1984. *Diversity in Unity: the Development and Expansion of the Cherubim and Seraphim Church of Nigeria.* Lanham: University Press of America Inc.

Oyedepo, David O 1996. *The Release of Power.* Lagos: Dominion Publishing House.

Oyetade, B. Akintunde. c.1996. *Ota: Enemy in Yoruba Belief.* Unpublished article.

Peel, J.D.Y. 1967. Religious Change among the Yoruba. *Africa* 37: 292–306.

———— 1968. *Aladura: A Religious Movement among the Yoruba.* Oxford: Oxford University Press.

———— 1990. The Pastor and the *Babalawo*: the encounter of religions in nineteenth-century Yorubaland. *Africa* 60:3, 338–69.

———— 1993. An Africanist revisits magic and the millennium, in *Secularization, Rationalism, and Sectarianism: Essays in Honour of Bryan R. Wilson*, ed. Eileen Barker, James Beckford, and Karel Dobbelaere, 81–100. Oxford: Clarendon Press.

———— 1994. Historicity and pluralism in some recent studies of Yoruba religion. *Africa* 64:1, 150–66.

———— 2000. *Religious Encounter and the Making of the Yoruba.* Bloomington: Indiana University Press.

Probst, Peter. 1989. The letter and the spirit: literacy and religious authority in the history of the Aladura Movement in Western Nigeria. *Africa* 59:4, 478–95.

Ray, Benjamin. 1993. Aladura Christianity: a Yoruba religion. *Journal of Religion in Africa*, 23:3, 266–91.

Robbins, Anthony. 1988. *Unlimited Power: The New Science of Personal Achievement.* London: Simon and Schuster.

Robbins, Joel. 2003. On the Paradoxes of Global Pentecostalism and the Perils of Continuity Thinking. *Religion* 33. 221–231.

Stewart, Charles, and Rosalind Shaw. 1994. *Syncretism/Anti-Syncretism: the Politics of Religious Synthesis.* London: Routledge.

Sundkler, Bengt. [1948] 1961. *Bantu Prophets in South Africa.* London: Oxford University Press.

Turner, Harold. W. 1967. *African Independent Church* (2 vols.). Oxford: Clarendon Press.

———— 1979. *Religious Innovation in Africa: Collected Essays on New Religious Movements.* Boston: G.K. Hall & Co.

Van Dijk, Rijk. 2001. Witchcraft and Scepticism by Proxy; Pentecostalism and laughter in urban Malawi. In *Magical Interpretations, Material Realities; modernity, witchcraft and the occult in postcolonial Africa*, eds. Henrietta Moore and Todd Sanders. 97–117. London: Routledge.

Verger, Pierre. 1966. The Yoruba High God–a review of the sources. *Odu* 2:2, 19–40.

Wilson, Bryan. 1973. *Magic and the Millennium: a Sociological Study of Religious Movements of Protest among Tribal and Third-World Peoples.* London: Heinemann.

CHAPTER 15

"Ndi Afe Ocha": The Early Aladura of Igboland, 1925–1975

Ogbu U. Kalu

Introduction

The Igbo people of southeastern Nigeria identify the African Indigenous Church people by describing their white garments or *soutane* rather than by their prayer habits as the Yoruba do, who call them the "people of prayer," or Aladura. The Igbo refer to them as *"Ndi afe ocha,"* people with white garments. When this religious phenomenon exploded into the religious landscape in the twilight of the colonial period, offering an alternative path to heaven that was buttressed with charismatic resources such as visions, healing, prophecy, orality, and raucous liturgy that borrowed much from the prohibited indigenous musical tradition, people responded in various ways including the negative epithet that suggested that only the priests of the mission-founded churches could wear white cassocks. Therefore, the Aladura must be fake. Indeed, a proverb entered into the language that "no one goes to the white garment people with clear eyes." Some problems must have distorted the person's vision, disorganized the mind, and invited a desperate solution. This Igbo proverb merely modified what used to be said about a visit to the *"dibia afa,"* the diviner: People do not pay social calls on the diviner just to find out about the ritual agent's well-being. The early Aladura internalized the hostile environment and hid their garments in their bags when going for worship. Some groups sacralized the subterfuge. For instance, one of the rules among the Christ Apostle Church, Onu Uzo Ndu (The Gate of Life) decreed that,

Any anointed person for whom the vision recommends the sewing of a red, yellow or green uniform, should have it blessed and kept in the church to be worn only on important occasions and not outside. May God help us to do this. Amen.[1]

Many stored their white, green, red, and yellow garments in the church premises.

Certain themes dominate the reconstruction of the profile of the early Aladura of Igboland. First, are the roots and provenance, or trajectories, amidst the competition that dogged their heels in hostile environments fraught with guardians of groves and mission-founded churches. Second, is an explanation for their survival and growth. How did the Igbo respond when this form encountered the cultural soil of communities? These are relevant questions because in spite of the competing theories about the Aladura, little scholarship has focused on the Igbo simply because it has been portrayed as a Yoruba religion. Scholarship on this phenomenon in Nigeria benefited from detailed, pioneering efforts, in the 1960–1970 period, by H. W Turner, J. D. Y. Peel, and R. C. Mitchell who were based in the University College, Ibadan. In the following decade, the Ibadan tradition inspired indigenous scholars such as J. Akin Omoyajowo and A. O. Iwuagwu. In the 1980s, a larger corps of researchers worked in this field including Rosalind Hackett, Chris Oshun, Friday Mbon, S. C. Amadi, A. A. Agbaje, and Deidre Crumbley. In the 1990s, David Olayiwola, C. O. Oladipo, Akin Omoyajowo, Jr., and Afe Adogame made major contributions. Thus, there are full-length studies on the Aladura generally, and specifically on the Cherubim and Seraphim, Church of the Lord, Christ Apostolic Church, Celestial Church in Yorubaland, and Brotherhood of Cross, and Star in the Cross River basin. Many journal articles and undergraduate degree projects contribute to the large quantities of data.[2] Only iwuagwu studied the phenomenon in Igboland as a part of eastern Nigeria.[3]

The subtitle betrays the motive or focus of each study. Thus, Turner's interest was the Christian authenticity of the movement. He examined the life and faith of the Church of the Lord, gave them a clean bill of health, and promoted their membership in the World Council of Churches. Turner influenced Ndiokwere's comparison of the understanding and performance of prophecy

---

1. Apostle Echefu, *Order of Service and Church Method*. Pamphlet for Doctrine and Practice. (Aba. nd. ca 1960) no. 9.

2. These fifteen works and more are listed in the bibliography section of Afe U. Adogame, *Celestial Church of Christ* (Frankfurt: Peter Lang, 1998): 230–251.

3. A.O. iwuagwu, "The Spiritual Churches in the Eastern States of Nigeria: a selected study", University of Ibadan PhD dissertation, Dept. of Religious Studies, 1971.

in the Bible and among the Independent Churches. The same applies to Oladipo's delineation of the development of the doctrine of the Holy Spirit among the Aladura. Concern for syncretism, religious change, nationalism, and protest against colonialism informed the researches by Mitchell, Peel, and Oshun. Peel and Mitchell did their researches in those halcyon years of *uhuru,,* before the citizens realized that *uhuru* might be worse than the yaws of colonialism. So, the regnant discourse was sect/church typology. Being sociologists, they strained to deploy Weberian models. But their comprehensive interpretations showed sensitivity to African Christian initiative and how this charismatic religiosity reshaped the religious landscape by contesting the grounds dominated by traditionalists, Christians, and Muslims. This fitted into the nationalist mood. But, contrary to the conflict model in Oshun's study, Mitchell saw little of political concern in Nigerian Aladura movement though prominent Aladura members participated in government and politics. Peel used the case of Ibadan city to demonstrate that their members participated in ethnic organizations just as any other member of established churches. As he argued,

> it might be said that the Aladuras support, more emphatically than most, the common standards of social morality as they are interpreted by Yoruba Christians.[4]

From Horton's intervention, it became clearer that Peel was concerned with how a community converts from the covenants with the gods of their fathers to a more charismatic form of Christianity; how the indigenous Christianity performed the same tasks of explanation, prediction, and control of space-time events. Using the Ijebu as a case study, he would further explore the ambience in tradition and conversion to new religious movements. The terminology, "New Religious Movement," became more fashionable with Hackett's work on Calabar. Thus, her colleague, Mbon , deployed a phenomenological method of studying New Religious Movements in *Brother of Star and Cross*. This scientific, sanitized study differed greatly from Helen Akpabio's revealing account entitled, *Seat of Satan Exposed!* It was billed as the account from an insider who had deserted the inner sanctum of the BSC.[5]

The major contribution of the Aladura religiosity has been its "fit" in the indigenous worldview. Thus, Adogame focused on the politics of cultural identity by examining the fit of Celestial Church's construction and efficacy

---

4. Peel, *Aladura,*1968: 237.
5. Helen E. Ukpabio, *The Seat of Satan Exposed* (Calabar: Splendour Printers, 1992)

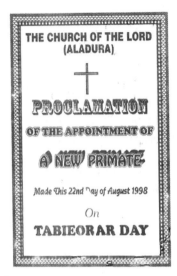

Figure 15.1 - Aladura document.

of rituals in the Yoruba cultural matrix. Two approaches to the matter could be identified: Olayiwola traced the deployment of some indigenous Yoruba cultural ideas and symbols (for instance, *ase*) in Aladura liturgy. This sounded like acculturation. Benjamin Ray riposted that there was more than met the eye; that the Aladura carved a deeply Yoruba religious stamp in shaping a new version of Christianity, that was a unique synthesis of Biblical belief, Christian liturgical forms, and Yoruba religious and ritual concepts. He used a number of indices to underscore the creativity. These consisted of belief in invisible spiritual forces, especially malevolent spiritual powers, belief in the efficacy of ritual action and construction of ritual space as the foundation for contact between this world and God in the heavenly realm, function of revelation (dreams, visions, prophecies), and meaning of ritual symbols and traditions about the founders. Prayer replaces divination and sacrifice for controlling malevolent spiritual forces.[6] Put simply, the Aladura mined the interior of indigenous Yoruba worldview to build a new understanding of Christianity and succeeded in an environment where people eschewed dogma and minimized doctrinal differences.

This raises the question about the appropriation of Aladura religiosity among non-Yoruba peoples of Nigeria. It is interesting to observe how researches pioneered from Ibadan, Ife, and Calabar set the tone and interest in

---

6. Benjamin Ray, *"Aladura* Christianity", *Jnl. of Religion in Africa*, 23, 3 (1993): 266–291.

the study of the Aladura phenomenon. Though Turner worked briefly with Sam Epelle as his assistant, from the University of Nigeria, Nsukka, the research in the area did not consolidate. Even Turner's papers that Andrew Walls stored at Nsukka were lost during the Nigerian Civil War. The papers recovered from groundnut sellers in the 1970s consisted of data collected by Epelle from Ibibio and *riverine* communities. This is quite understandable because the demographic pattern of Aladura movement is that it predominates among the Yoruba of southwestern Nigeria, followed by the Ibibio and the Ijaw of southeastern Nigeria. The low provenance among the Igbo deserves an explanation. Igbo scholars owe a debt to A.O. Iwuagwu's reconstruction of early Aladura in Igboland. He is an Anglican priest who rose to the rank of a bishop. Employing the church/sect dichotomy, he treated the new movement as if it was an aberrant form, and paid scant attention to typology.

Anatomy of "Ndi Afe Ocha"

Among the Igbo, the movement emerged after missionary Christianity had consolidated, and remained a predominantly urban phenomenon during the fifty years under consideration.[7] The early groups formed in either towns or in the village of the founder. A rural location hindered growth and such movements sought relocation in towns. Thus, groups that formed in the two commercial towns of Aba and Onitsha prospered greatly and spread to other towns. Geography mattered: Aba grew as a trading center on the river that connected Igboland with the Niger Delta communities. The *onumiri* (water front) section of the town was the commercial center for the Kalabari traders from the Niger Delta. A number of religious groups emerged: some Liberians brought the Sabbatharian Seven Day Adventism; the Garrick Braide agents proselytized prominently especially after 1918. Moreover, the construction of the southern railway line between Enugu and Port Harcourt, 1913–1916, enhanced Aba's importance and brought many non-Igbo people who came as railway workers. The religious horizon enlarged. Similarly, Onitsha's location on the banks of the famous River Niger made it important for commercial and Christian groups. Individual biographies are also important because each founder was an intrepid entrepreneur under the colonial canopy. Their life patterns explained the provenance of the movement.

Period-focused study is at the core of the writing of church history. Though stories about Aladura type groups increased in the 1940s, there is a story that

---

7. see, C.O .Nwanunobi, "Sect as an urban phenomenon in contemporary eastern Nigeria", *Anthropos*, 75, (1980): 117–128.

the Sacred Order of Cherubim and Seraphim was brought to Igboland through a man from Ihube in Okigwe District. He was suddenly afflicted with strange ailments and hard fortune. Finally, he left his civil service employment in the Post and Telegraph in northern Nigeria, and was led by the spirit to return home. He had a revelation that a cave with clear water existed in the top layer of the nearby hills. According to oral tradition, the man was soon visited by a delegation from Lagos to declare that spring as one of their holy grounds. That was in 1925, the foundation year of the movement. There is no indication that a vibrant branch of the Cherubim and Seraphim was opened at Ihube, but they registered a presence. The period between 1925–1955 was the teething period as various denominations tried to establish in a hostile terrain. The rate and pattern of the "collapse of pagandom in Igboland" meant that the mission churches scrambled and competed with one another rather intensely in Igboland leaving little room for any home grown variety. After the First World War, the use of education as an instrument of evangelization ensured that Igbo communities competed among themselves to invite missionary groups. By the 1940s Igbo entrepreneurs were already founding secondary schools. The collusion between missions and the colonial officers ensured a monopoly that essayed to snuff out indigenous religious adventurers. But matters changed in the period between 1956 and 1965. First, nationalism contested missionary ideology and encouraged indigenous expressions. Some revivalist religious forms such as Godianism and God's Kingdom Society tried to nurture political Christianity. Godianism was an invented nationalist argument that Africans had the concept of God before missionaries came, and that Africans had a religion, that could be dubbed Godianism, provable from a web of myths. They built churches replicating Western architectural forms, polity and liturgy, without the use of the Christian canon. Chief K.O. Onyioha, the high priest (from Nkporo in Bende District), was an eloquent nationalist and religious entrepreneur. Godianism thrived on the founder's rhetoric; as the man grew old, the movement declined with him. Daniel Ilega has shown how the protagonists of God's Kingdom Society recruited Christian idioms and Old Testament liturgy for constructing a nationalist rhetoric. [8]

In the midst of political independence, 1960–1967, Aladura Christianity benefited from the softened grounds to enjoy its heyday in Igboland. Though clienteles still dominated its membership structure, the class content changed.

---

8. U.R.Onunwa, "Godianism: the quest for world peace", *Areopagus* (Hongkong), 3.2 (Epiphany, 1990): 16-21; D.I. Ilega, "Religion and Godless Nationalism in Colonial Nigeria", *Jn. Of Religion in Africa*, 18, 2 (1988).

The Civil War,1967–1970, proved a boon because it was a religion meant for unsettled times when people sought both quick and miraculous resources for coping. The range of its typology broadened: the Apostolic and Zionist types had predominated; now, new types surged such as the vitalistic type that emphasized the quest for power even with occult and kabbalistic means, and nativistic types, or prayer houses, that indulged in traditional rituals and symbols mixed with a veneer of Christian symbolism. Many types of Aladura proliferated into the hinterlands at the heels of fleeing patrons. Messianic types in which the leader claims to be one or the other of the Trinity, moved from across the Ibibio and Cross River borders into Igboland during the Civil War. Two examples are the The Spiritual King's Church or The Spiritual Kingdom Church popularly known as Edidem Bassey or Jesus of Ikot Ekpene (after the name of the founder, John Akpan Bassey) and The Brotherhood of Cross and Star, known simply as "OOO" (the initials of the founder, Obu Obu Olumba). That war scrambled the religious landscape of Igboland more than many historians have acknowledged. Indeed, between 1966–1976, Igboland witnessed a major religious revival that constituted the bedrock of the new Charismatic-Pentecostal phenomenon that has shaped the contemporary face of Christianity among the Igbo. The complex relationship between the Aladura and the new charismatism is a key aspect of the story of the last period. Thus, the vertical expansion of the movement could be profiled in four time frames: 1925–1955, 1956–1965, 1966–1970, and 1971–1975.

Paul Gifford used the statistics from two surveys of Christian forms in Ghana to argue that the salience of Charismatic-Pentecostalism has robbed the Aladura of both numbers and significance. [9] The situation in Igboland is more complex. A religious revival started during the Civil War and gathered intensity with each passing decade. All religious forms benefited whether indigenous, Aladura, charismatic, Pentecostal, or mainline denominations. Since the Aladura were the most charismatic until after the civil war, their dominance of left-wing Christianity was duly challenged; they became the butt of the attacks from various Christian strands, and they must have lost numbers and reputation in the decades between 1970–1990.There is no denying that nationalist historiography built up the movement, variously profiling it as Africa's contribution to world Christianity, its religious creative genius, whose achievement on the gospel-culture interface has spurred the emergence of African spirituality. Others demur, pointing to Turner's warning about

---

9. Paul Gifford, *African Christianity: Its Public Role*(Bloomington, IN: Indiana University Press,1998)

some "pagan features," and to the tendency to romanticize the movement by sociologists. Some argue that a Christian yardstick should be applied to evaluate a Christian movement. But anti-Western ideology has turned syncretism into a dirty epithet that westerners applied to African creativity, and church-sect has become a non-viable conceptual scheme. Few scholars have pursued Turner's concern for typology and his revision of Sundkler's typology.[10] Obviously, the enlargement of scale yielded a number of new forms that knew little about their Biblical roots. Furthermore, encapsulation strategies by mainline churches soon absorbed much of the liturgical innovations of "Ndi afe ocha" who gained respectability and grew exponentially. By the end of our period, they came out of the closet and wore their white garments in carol services and other public parades. What happened?

Strange Bells of Strange Healers, 1925–1955

Beyond the story of the Ihube man who discovered the cave used by the Zionist Cherubim and Seraphim for their annual holy retreat, the movement was patronized preeminently by the "stranger elements" from Yorubaland in the commercial city of Aba in the 1930s. This explains the epithet, *Ndi Chochi Oluwa* since they addressed God as *Oluwa*. These were employees of the Nigerian Railway Company, United African Company, Bank of British West Africa, or middlemen traders in industrial goods. A few of them evangelized the community. There is a popular anecdote about a woman leader who would walk round the town, every morning, ringing her bell, and imploring people to repent and pray. This morning cry became an object of ridicule as if designed to comment on what people did at night. Between 1930–1955, a few branches of the Cherubim and Seraphim were started by the various splinter groups that had emerged within the movement. It acquired little significance in the religious landscape. Small groups of C.S. could be traced in the towns that served as colonial administrative centers such as Enugu, Port Harcourt and Owerri. In this early period, the new spirituality was established by Yoruba indigenes and could hardly transcend the gap between indigenes and immigrants. The strange language, rituals, and the virulent opposition of the mainline churches competed against the allure of the joyful liturgy and miracles of healing.

---

10. H.W. Turner, "A typology for African Religious Movements", *Jnl. of Religion in Africa*,1,1 (1967):1–34; "Pagan Features in African Independent Churches", *Practical Anthropology*, 12, 4 (1965): 145–156; "Problems in the Study of African Independent Churches", *Numen*, 13, 1 (1966): 27–42.

More significant was the foundation and provenance of the Apostolic church type that thrived from 1940s. They were not transplanted by Yoruba indigenes. The explanation for their salience might also lie in the resonance with mainline evangelical Protestantism. They resembled the Faith Tabernacle that had emerged in the mid–1920s and survived in the eastern region when the votaries in western Nigeria abandoned it for the Apostolic Church and later founded the Christ Apostolic Church.[11] Moreover, the Apostolic types shared much with the Garrick Braide church that exploded into Igboland from 1918 and remained very strong through 1939.[12] The decline started in the 1940s because education became a major instrument for evangelization, and the Braidists lacked the structure and funds for sustainable operation. Soon the Catholics, Seventh Day Adventists, Niger Delta Pastorate, and the Qua Iboe Church shared many of the mission fields and schools of the Braidists in southern Igboland. The Apostolic type operated for the most part in southern Igboland, as did the Braidists. The question, therefore, is how the Apostolic type survived where the Braidists had failed. The story of three enterprises could illustrate the enigma.

The first Apostolic type was the Abosso Apostolic Faith Church. Its origin is the Apostolic Faith, Light of Hope, with headquarters in Portland, Oregon, USA. It is an offshoot of the Azusa Street Revival because Florence Louise Crawford was a holiness worker who assisted William Seymour in editing the magazine, *Apostolic Faith*. She left and founded her own organization in 1906. She was an ardent restorationist who believed in divine healing, faith living and millenialism. The organization opened its mission field in Liberia where the patrons distinguished themselves from the American church by adding the honorific title, Abosso, meaning, *mother*. It spoke to the vision of a nurturing household of faith. Ordinarily, this would not have qualified for an Aladura type except that the African variety modified some ingredients of the American home base. As is the case with religious entrepreneurship, biographies are essential, especially the conversion and call of the founders. They are usually embellished with vivid divine interventions in the lives of the founders. These stories are preserved orally and some in written form as a part of the heritage and legitimacy of the group. In this case, a certain Daniel Ejiofor had been reared as a Primitive Methodist from Amaba village near Ovim that was an important railroad junction and a Methodist mission station. In 1927 the

---

11. O.U. Kalu, "Doing Mission Through the Post Office: The Naked Faith People of Igboland, 1920–1960"*Neue Zeitschrift fur Missionwissenschaft*, 56, 4 (2000): 263–280.

12. See, O.U. Kalu, *Embattled Gods: Christianization of Igboland, 1841–1991* (Trenton, NJ: Africa World Press, 2003): 144–146.

Primitive Methodists built a major school for girls at Ovim and moved their operational post at Ihube to the new location. Amaba village is also near Okigwe, the administrative seat of the District Officer. Daniel traveled to the United States to study Engineering. There he encountered the Apostolic Church, Light of Hope in New York, and experienced the salvation stages leading to spirit baptism. But disaster struck: he became increasingly restless, inattentive to his studies, and finally failed to cope with the demanding but secular course of study. Prophecy is a hallmark of the church's mode of communication. Bishop W.E Gray prophesied to him that he should return to witness to his people but at a risk that they may kill him. After some hesitation, he obeyed but rejoined the Methodist Church at Amaba village. His revivalist and charismatic evangelical work created much excitement. But his relationship with the village pastor soured, and he was forced to obey the original prophecy by founding the Abosso Apostolic Church in 1941. October 24 is celebrated annually as the founder's day.

Ejiofor linked himself closely to the New York base and branches in Liberia and Ghana. Occasionally, these sent delegations to encourage the work. But he achieved local prominence through charismatic gifts and evangelistic tours. For instance, it was alleged that he prophesied to a woman that she would give birth on a certain date and it happened. There were magical dimensions such as commanding a little baby to walk, or a child to lift a heavy suitcase, or when he walked into a river in his *soutane* and emerged dry. Rumors drove hordes to his village; so did his healing powers. This paid for his evangelical tours and funded the foundations of many stations. Abosso stations grew out of the bishop's tours and from the evangelical ardor of those who benefited from his ministrations. For instance, those he healed in Port Harcourt opened stations in the contiguous Delta communities as Buguma and Degema. Others opened in northern Nigerian towns among southern immigrants. In 1970 the Amaba Headquarters made the obviously exaggerated claim that they had about 500 stations and over 40,000 members. Once a year, all the leaders would gather at Amaba for motivational talks spiced with the presence of visitors from New York and other parts of West Africa. The self-representation as belonging to an international body inspire local agency.

This group subscribed to all the core tenets of Apostolic Churches such as adult baptism by immersion, faith healing, foot washing, sacred mourning and weeping, a robust eschatology, and a polity that ranged hierarchically from apostles, prophets, and bishops, to deacons, evangelists, and Levites. When the founder died in 1955, the successor, Pastor J.C. Ndukwe, could not claim his title of bishop because, though the authoritative text for belief, polity, and practices is the Bible, the mode of accession to any position is solely by prophecy and revelation. Revelation could come through dreams and visions, but they privileged glossolalia (followed by the exercise of the gift of interpretation) so as to avoid manipulation or intervention by an evil spirit. Though Trinitarian, the theology is akin to the position held by Oneness Pentecostals that subsumes the trinity under Christ. Its Constitution says that "when one person of the Trinity is patent, the others are latent." But, they declared, God's dispensational name in our times is Our Lord Jesus Christ. The gender ideology is patriarchal. As common among the Apostolic type, polygamy is permitted while divorce is rejected.[13]

Healing is a central doctrine, and the process of indigenization is embedded in the healing practices. Diagnosis is by revelation, as well as the therapeutic strategy. The inventory includes: placing a cross on the afflicted; ritual bath in water, river,or pool, according to a prescribed number; and herbalism. The Abosso healer sometimes performs as the indigenous *dibia ogwu*, medicine man. He employs instruments such as the palm oil, coconut water, spittle, sand, olive oil, and the bark from revealed trees. The non-canonical dimension is the number and shapes and types of crosses deployed through revelation for healing. These are placed on the center of the head, the forehead, and the chest of the afflicted. Revelations about the secret names and meanings of the shapes of crosses soon capture the distinctive character of the pastoral theology and practice of the Abosso. This dimension creates some measure of ambiguity in their attitude toward indigenous culture, and opened the door to esoteric spirituality. Yet they condemn indigenous religion and practices, cultures and organizations. Members cannot participate in village festivals, rituals and clubs. In the colonial society, members should pay taxes but should not swear oaths, or join secular clubs or trade unions. Purity is the essence of a Christian life; sanctification is a process on the heavenly journey. Both the Methodist and Apostolic roots have restrained the charismatic purviews of the group, and the rural setting has limited both its numbers and the patronage of richer segment of the population.

Another variety of the Apostolic Church came to Nigeria from Britain under the auspices of Idris Vaughan and George Perfect, and spread through Efik and the Ibibio communities into Aba,(Igboland) by the late 1930s.[14] In

---

13. *The Abosso Apostolic Faith Church. Constitution and Doctrines.* New York, 1964. Reprinted Mile 2, Diobu, Port Harcourt, 1965:1–13.

14. I.J. Vaughan, *Nigerian: The Origins of Apostolic Church Pentecostalism in Nigeria, 1931–1952* (Essex: The Ipswich Book Company, 1991). After his retirement, Idris Vaughan spent time to tell his story in *Missionary with a limp,* and the story of the Apostolic church's venture in Nigeria.

1940 a major schism occurred. Various accounts exist: Some claim that devotees from the Ngwa sub-tribe were angered that they lacked access to leadership positions in a church located in their communities; others claim that the European leadership favored Efiks and Ibibio indigenes, were authoritarian, and practiced certain liberal ethics, perhaps around faith healing. This may be connected with a similar rumpus in Lagos that led to the formation of the Christ Apostolic Church. But it may have reflected the religious mood of the times when indigenous people felt emboldened to exercise *agency*, give *voice* against the hegemonic control of Christianity by the whites, and dared to *exit*. As long as the religious forms were connected with white roots, their experimentations did not appear exotic. Religious agency at this time manifested in other non-Christian ways as in the quest for occult materials from India, patronage of Masonic Lodges and Rosicrucianism. The Apostolic Church in Igboland splintered into various branches. Apostle J.A. Anyahuru formed his own, The Apostolic True Church Mission. Apostle J.W. Nwanke called his own group, Christ Apostolic Church Gospel Mission. In 1950 the two united under the rubric, The Apostolic Christian Church of Nigeria, with the older man, Anyahuru, as president and Nwanke as his vice president. Given the background, the Apostolic Christian Church's Constitution enshrined an effort to avoid further splintering by insisting that every body

> should contribute towards the support of the cause of the church as taught in the word of God. He should keep the counsels of the church within the church and keep the unity of the spirit in the bond of peace.[15]

According to the *Memoirs and Records of Chief Apostle B.N. Adiele*, by the end of our period, the body claimed a membership of about 10,000 in twenty-five branches, a third of which is located in Aba Town.[16] Some branches existed in the northwestern region of Nigeria, across the River Niger.

A farmer and trader, Adiele had joined the Apostolic Church in the 1930s, was ordained a pastor in 1938, and trained in the Bible School without full ordination until the schism. He was a good example of the frustrated cadre of trained indigenous people in the church. He succeeded the two founders in 1962, and built up the organization for a number of years. However, there was little of innovation in their ministry beyond what they inherited. The political protest within religious bounds appears to have been the driving motif.

---

15. Printed in Aba, 1952:9.

16. Printed in Aba, 1966. This story has been reconstructed from the pamphlets and interviews done at two points in time, 1975 and 1977–80.

Their engagement in school apostolate was equally minimal given their size and limited resources. Yet they constructed a high sense of community through charitable programs that aided disadvantaged people in the town.

The largest Apostolic type was the Christ Apostolic Church, Holy Prophetess Odozi Obodo, founded by an illiterate woman, Madam Agnes Okoye, in 1947 at Fegge ward, Onitsha town. Agnes was married to a Ghanaian with whom she had a son, Okoh. But she developed an incurable stomach problem that afflicted her through sixteen years at a great cost. Then she heard that a Christ Apostolic Church prophetess was coming to minister at Broderick Hall, Enugu. She was healed and baptized there in 1945; she responded to a prophecy about a divine unction, and immediately started her own healing ministry. At this point, she moved to Onitsha, and through a divine revelation acquired a large piece of property owned by a man who had benefited from her charismatic ministry. This remains the sprawling headquarters of the organization, sporting a housing project, a training school, administrative facilities, a healing Pool of Bethesda, and conference center. A little further out is an asylum for mentally challenged people. She nurtured a contact with the Christ Apostolic Church headquarters in Ibadan. In 1950, a delegation visited, approved, and integrated her ministry into the functions of the *Constitution, Practices and Guiding Principles of Christ Apostolic Church, 1953.*

But also, creatively, they honored her uniqueness in order to encourage a Yoruba religious form that would move into a non-Yoruba territory. First, the gender ideology within the Christ Apostolic Church was contested in her significant role. Her forte included a gift of "word of knowledge," prophecy, healing and a disciplined prayerful, fasting life. She would deliver her prophecy in a somber mood in the Igbo language to those kneeling before her, as the prescribed posture. It is alleged that she saw about 400 people daily. The *CAC Calendar, 1965* puts the size at 300 churches, four located in Onitsha.[17] By 1970 the group grew to 400 churches according to the Onitsha headquarters. As many flocked from the entire eastern region of Nigeria, she acquired the accolade as a Holy Prophetess whose ministry was a Reformer of the Land, Odozi Obodo. She used this appellation to distinguish the church that she founded, and it was permitted. Second, the Ibadan headquarters allowed her domination of the Igbo mission field to the extent that some male leaders later protested. Some would later claim that they are directly under the National Headquarters, Ibadan, and rejected the subtitle that advertised her. But many

---

17. Printed in Ibadan, 1965; see, iwuagwu, "The Spiritual Churches in the Eastern States Nigeria," chapter 9.

looked up to her. For instance, power was concentrated under the General Superintendent, Right Reverend Okoh, guided by his mother's visions. Onitsha acted on behalf of the General Council of the Christ Apostolic Church in posting ministers and running the church. She organized a monthly meeting of all pastors, evangelists and catechists. Each station sent three delegates including a woman, an elder and whoever was in charge of the station. She allowed each station to be self-supporting, pay for the minister, keep all their tithes and income, and give only voluntary gifts to the headquarters. She assisted weak parishes and paid for the education of ministers, and encouraged them to celebrate the origin of her ministry as the founder's day. These policies made her very popular and blocked dissent. She licensed a number of Praying Men to tour stations enlivening the healing and charismatic lives of the people. Tarrying was mandatory and provided occasion for "helping seekers." This was a strategy for enabling people to access the charismatic gifts, appropriate the spirituality, and learn the language of the ministry.

Third, she indigenized the liturgy into Igbo. Worship would begin with Abu Otuto, songs of praise, and intensify in three stages: first, an indigenous rumba or kokoma music tradition will get everybody dancing and clapping; then, the dance beat will become faster with indigenous varieties as the Nganga or Nwajaga and Edere. Third, as the mood warms, the music will turn to the hot Nwakpe or Nwadubere. By this time, the worship would resemble an Igbo festival event. Undoubtedly, this impressed people and catalyzed growth. They sacralized the Igbo rites of passage and yet stayed close to the constitution of the CAC. To avoid the hostility of the other churches, her ministers dressed as Anglican Church priests while she herself wore frocks. The group expanded into the rural areas at the heels of the healed.

She was such a great force in the religious landscape that she influenced little groups as the Uno Uzo Ndu (The Gate of Life) Christ Apostolic Church. This started with a woman, Madam Ukaegbu, a tobacco trader in Aba, who had a similar experience as Agnes Okoye. It was a stomach ailment that resisted treatment. A doctor told her in 1950 that she was pregnant when she was not. She was healed in a rump of Garrick Braide's Christ Army Church in 1952. The following year she started her own healing ministry. Indeed, the name of the church was revealed to a thirteen year old boy, Henry Onyeji. The church became more organized after 1960 when Apostle S. N. Echefu joined as the full-time administrator. His 1970 memoir is a good source about this group, in which he designated himself as the "elect of God and co-founder." He was barely literate, but a simple, sincere man who joined the church when he was about forty years old. His career wove together three strands of the Aladura movement: The Garrick Braide, Church of the Lord, and Christ

Apostolic Church. His story is a human angle tale of a man who resisted the call until the prophecies including an escape from a motor accident convinced him. Prophet J.O. Oshitelu, founder of The Church of the Lord, visited Aba in 1956, picked him out of a large crowd, and prophesied a divine call on his life. As a trader, he traveled often from Aba to Onitsha where he came under the influence of the Holy Prophetess Odozi Obodo, and later teamed up with Madam Ukaegbu.

The Gate of Life is primarily a healing ministry that has borrowed beliefs and practices from Garrick Braide and the Christ Apostolic Church. Echefu authored the binding principles of conduct in two documents, the *Guiding Principles of the Church* and *Order of Service and Church Method*. A third important document is a collection of four of his sermons, *Tracts and Pamphlets*.[18] A careful reading of these documents would show Echefu's understanding of the Old Testament roots of the contemporary church, and the lessons that he learnt from the Christ Apostolic Church and Christ Army Church: Levitical laws that buttress rigorous fasting, prohibitions, polity, and gender ideology. As he concluded, "the members of Onu Uzo Ndu are chosen by God and the Apostle is the Shepherd elected by God for his Israel." There is no indication that Madam Ukaegbu fought to regain prominence as Echefu legitimized his ascendancy. The provenance of this organization is within the Delta basin (Port Harcourt, Azumini, Opobo) and in central and north eastern Igbo areas such as Orlu and Abakiliki. The center is in Aba. By the end of our period, Echefu's memoir claimed a membership of one thousand. The liturgy is mainly from the Christ Army, using the Igbo Hymn Book, some choruses such as "*Ime mma ya, ime mma ya, di uku*" ("his goodness, his goodness, is great"!), and the Christ Army Creed. The highlight in the worship is the performance by prophets and visionaries as they recount visitations by angels and significant dreams. Unlike the Christ Apostolic Church, they adopt Cherubim and Seraphim practices such the use of candles, and colored vestments decorated with crosses to indicate differentiations in status and charismatic power. They have sacred spaces such as wilderness, watersides, and hills.

In summary, the Apostolic type of Aladura Christianity dominated the early incursion into Igboland. Some Zionist forms existed, and the messianic *Edidem* group at Ikot Ekpene claimed that Igbo people gave the leader the fourth of the determinant visions in the construction of his lofty religious stature. His forte was not healing but the ability to give power to people. This resonated with indigenous religious tradition when spiritual forces give power to

---

18. Printed in Aba, 1966, 1968, 1970.

people to control space-time events. Ikot Ekpene is near the commercial town of Aba; so, it would be a short trip to acquire power for prospering in the competitive urban environment. But there is little evidence of proliferation of this form in Igboland in the pre 1960 period. The Apostolic type came into Igboland from three sources: America, Britain, and Yorubaland; yet missionaries did not come from these places specifically to evangelize Igboland. Igbo appropriation of the Apostolic type of Aladura Christianity benefited from schisms, vision-driven evangelism, and a creativity that became increasingly eclectic as entrepreneurs wove many traditions together based on their understanding of the Bible. As it engaged the indigenous worldview, the struggle to retain the Bible as the authoritative text grew apparent. The pneumatic dimension to Christianity attracted as healing and miraculous power remained central. The indigenized liturgy in Igbo language and culture drew members to bold experimentation. Under the colonial canopy, the quest for religious autonomy was matched by deliberate linkage to a protective umbrella. The founders must have exploited the unsettled geopolitics and world war dislocation to contest the monopoly by mainline churches. It could be surmised that the Apostolic type survived because they retained the features of evangelicalism to the degree that it was not strange in an environment dominated by mission churches. However, faced with the intense competition in the religious market, many remained small in number and provenance.

The temper of the late colonial period was characterized by a religious entrepreneurial mood that enlarged the religious space. The leaders had contact with mission-founded churches, but they did not secede; they simply transgressed institutional boundaries, adopted other Christian forms, exercised individual autonomy of freedom of choice to experiment with new rituals and new interpretations of the Bible. They ingeniously crafted their own doctrinal formulae. For some, the vista for adventure widened with time. For instance, Joseph Ikechukwu Anyanwu was born in Ogbuebulu village in Umuahia in 1916. Though the father was a votary of indigenous religion, he attended a Methodist primary school, and was baptized a Methodist in 1935, before becoming a laborer at the Agricultural Center, Umudike. When he was posted to Nkwerre, an angel convicted him about tithes; he joined the Faith Tabernacle. The angel visited again and persuaded him to resign from the job just when he was to be promoted to the rank of overseer. Against all persuasions, he obeyed and returned to his village where he joined the Apostolic Church and was re-baptized in 1937. The angel came again and urged him through visions, signs, and wonders (strange fire, strange fish and strange rain) to found his own, St Joseph's Chosen Church of God in 1947. Based mostly in Benin and its environs, his healing powers created traffic jams as people would line up to receive his blessings. He dropped his surname and re-tained Ikechukwu that means, "God's power." He opened branches in Igbo towns such as Onitsha, Aba, Oboro-Umuahia, Ohafia, and Obizi near Ow-erri. His *Immutable Rules and Conduct* and *Memoirs and Records* (1966) tell the story of this ministry and indicate the eclectic extent that he borrowed from his past spiritual journey.[19] But soon another visit from a friendly angel suggested that he should marry seven wives contrary to the marriage rules in-herited from Apostolic Church and enshrined in the "immutable rules." The fact was that he had no son, although serial monogamy with seven women had given him many daughters. His successful ministry, which claimed about 100,000 adherents in thirty-three locations, collapsed with a whimper when his subalterns met in a conference, and suspended their founder in 1970! Newspapers guffawed with ribald jokes.

As the emphasis on visions deepened, differences emerged among the early Aladura of Igboland over the use of instruments in healing. For instance, three young men, Ogede, Onwuasoanya, and Eliaku, members of Christ Apostolic Church, Onitsha, believed that they had a vision to found a new church, in 1958. They called it, Christ Chosen Church. Soon, a quarrel ensued: Onwua-soanya returned to the Christ Apostolic Church ; Eliaku formed his own, The Christ Disciple Church in 1959; while Ogede inherited the mantle of the Christ Chosen Church. To carve an image, they devised new rituals. The en-largement of scale created the gradual shift from the Biblical roots in a period that witnessed an increasingly, bold religious entrepreneurship.[20] Yet, the motif of purity that runs as a creeping plant through Aladura spirituality must have served as a self-integrative force in the midst of the insecurity unleashed by new cultural forces. The resonance between the core structure of Yoruba in-digenous worldview and the Igbo ensured that the Igbo response to Aladura spirituality did not differ significantly.

Sabbatharian Aladura of Igboland, 1918–1975

The literature has not adequately distinguished between Sunday worship-pers and Sabbatharians among the Aladura. Admittedly, this variety became

---

19. Printed in Benin, 1966.

20. See Joseph Eliaku, *Memoirs of Eliaku* (Onitsha, 1966); S.A. Orisakwe, editor, *Christ Disciple Church: Song of Praises* (Onitsha, 1965). This contains practices, order of service and choruses for worship. From these one could assess the emphases in their theology and practices.

most prominent in Igboland after our period. It was a form of home-grown, Igbo Aladura. For instance, the vertical pattern of growth is as follows:[21]

Decade	No. of groups founded
1916–1925	1
1926–1935	–
1936–1945	–
1946–1955	2
1956–1965	4
1966–1975	19
1976–1985	68
1986–1990	62 (in five years)

Thus, 138 of the 156 groups emerged in the two decades 1970–1990. Indeed, it was a post-civil war phenomenon in Igboland as sixteen new groups sprouted between 1971–1975. Its growth could be explained as an instrument of Igbo survival strategy after the civil war. It grew just at the same time that youthful charismatics found fillip in Bible Christianity. A revival of many competing types reshaped the religious landscape. The pattern of the geographical spread (1916–1990) is as follows:

Culture Area	No. of groups
Southern Igboland	28
Northwest	76
Central	32
Northern	9
Eastern	4
Northeastern	7

Most are located in the axis from Onitsha to the boundaries of Udi. However, indigenous Sabbatharianism started with Dede Ekeke Lolo of Akwete in southern Igboland around 1918. This priest of *Iyieke* shrine had a vision that some Christians would come to attack the reign of his gods. He excitedly called for a canoe and paddled out into the river in a prophetic dramatization of the flight of the gods. In 1918 the Garrick Braide agents arrived with holy

---

21. See Kalu, *Embattled Gods,* 302. The only full study of sabbatharianism in Igboland is by my student J.O. Anyaegbu, "Sabbatharianism in Igboland, 1916–1990" PhD dissertation, Dept. of Religion, University of Nigeria, Nsukka, 1993.

water to attack shrines.[22] Dede was deeply impressed by the ministry of the disciples, but wove an alternative Sabbatharian ministry from the encounter. He trained four disciples including Mark Onuabuchi, Jeremiah Osolu (of Amichi), and Ikpeogu (of Ogbunike). Mark, the most enterprising, founded Christ's Healing Mission, and trained Michael Amakeze of Nnobi, who founded Holy Sabbath Christ the King, and Samuel Nnabueze Okpala of Nnobi, who founded Christ Holy Sabbath. These, especially Amakeze, who is nicknamed "Musa," trained a corps of devotees who initiated the proliferation of Sabbath movements in the northwestern culture theatre. Onitsha and Nnewi, which are big commercial towns, host twenty-five of the seventy-six in that culture zone, just as Aba town alone hosts twenty out of the twenty-eight in southern Igboland. The Owerri-Nkwerre axis dominates in the central culture area. The numbers in the north, east and north-eastern culture areas remained insignificant. For instance, the only significant Sabbatharian presence in the old Bende District (eastern culture theatre) was founded by Hyde Onuaguluchi who has an engineering firm that digs boreholes for the government. He opened a branch wherever his company worked.

Sabbath movement shares an identical typology as the Sunday worshipping Aladura. For instance, Musa's group is just like the Cherubim and Seraphim who affirm the centrality of Christ but indulge in certain use of indigenous instruments in cleansing rituals and healing that orthodox Christians would reject. Thus, there are Zionists with internal differences. For instance, Musa trained Hyde Onuaguluchi whose Holy Sabbath Christ Mission adopts an Israelitist posture. He is an educated, urbane man who rejected some of the practices of his mentor, Musa. Some are vitalistic such as Tim S. Okoye's God's Holy Sabbath Synagogue in Onitsha. He is completely Hebraist, denies Christ, and mixes Jewish traditions with occult. Enoch Ugwuegbu founded Holy Sabbath Church at 30 New Cemetery Road, Onitsha, in 1976. He is nativistic in his articulation of ancestor worship, reincarnation, sacrifices at cross roads, use of such things as palm fronds and coconut oil. In a ceremony called "waking," they call the spirits of the dead after forty days to inform the living about the cause of death. This is necromancy. Smaller nativistic forms operate in rural areas as prayer houses. The gender ideology is same as among the rest of the Aladura even when there are female prophetesses and founders.

---

22. O.U. Kalu, "Waves from the Rivers: The Spread of Garrick Braide Movement in Igboland, 1914–1939", *Jnl. of the Historical Society of Nigeria*, 8, 4 (1977): 95-110. On Dede Ekeke Lolo, see S.C. Chuta, "Africans in the Christianisation of Igboland", PhD dissertation, Dept. of Religion, University of Nigeria, 1985.

Sabbath observers operate in an association named ASDON (Association of Sabbath Day Observers in Nigeria). This association has tried to streamline beliefs and practices so as to define the boundaries between Christian and non-Christian forms, and to link with the United Council of Sabbatharians International. Their register is a good source of information on this denomination.

Why has this movement grown? First is the enlarged space for charismatic religiosity; second is a streak of interest in the Old Testament that was central in the apologetics of the early Aladura and has seeped into even Pentecostalism. The Riches of Christ, a Pentecostal group founded by Edozie Mba, became Sabbatharian in due course. Third is the example of the Seventh Day Adventists that expanded in southern Igboland, and built schools that competed with other missionary churches. The white example validated what started with a priest of a local shrine. Fourth, the majority of Sabbatharians are vitalistic. In the politics of recovery from the civil war, many found their rituals attractive.

The Calabash of Blood and Revival, 1960–1975

It could be argued that nationalism created an atmosphere in which the monopoly of the religious space by the missionaries could be challenged. Increased urbanization, literacy / education, modernization, the impact of the world wars, a rise in the level of social expectation, change in consumption habits, intensified religious pluralism in the period,1960–1966. The stress in the new and exploding urban centers induced a heightened level of religious quest. The Civil War, 1967–1970, scrambled the landscape and created a wealth of new cultural forces that had impact on the religious sphere. Two discourses have prevailed. The instrumentalist discourse focuses on the deprivation / compensation theory and effects of the war. It points to disillusionment with the secular order, craving for an alternative means of surviving the war and "civil peace," and the effect of social dislocation that decentralized the missionary church structures and opened a field for new players who regaled in personal autonomy. The religious agenda of the past lost significance; denominational identities became less important as people fled for refuge. In the polarized, competitive religious market, a religious war ensued for the control of the moral landscape. The nominalism and bureaucracy of the ageing mainline churches hindered them. The civil war reconfigured religious commitment and distribution pattern. A second discourse privileges a religious explanation , especially the contours of multiple spiritual revivals. It does not deny that stress, vulnerability and insecurity produced contrary forces such as revitalization of indigenous religion, intense charismaticalism, and secularism as people disdained the gods that failed to save them during the crisis. But it argues that God used the social suffering to create a new religious environment. Suffering is the way to spiritual renewal. The limited purview of this discourse must be noted because it leaves the impression that all that happened was a Christian revival. In fact, it was a broad-based religious revival whose impact has remained. The renaissance of indigenous religion during this period, revitalized cultism that caused the urbanization of the modern public space as the elite arm themselves with medicine to empower their competition for the scarce resources in the public space.

The two charismatic forces were the Aladura and the sprouting of a Christian revival among young people. Both served as a commentary on the power failure in missionary spirituality. The mainline churches continued to be significant during the war but their operations were disorganized by the war conditions. They provided relief materials but their devotees wanted charismatic, powerful, divine intervention. Groups that had flexible infrastructure, and spoke to the need for quick solutions, stood the chance to gain. Healing in the midst of inadequate health care delivery, prayer houses in refugee camps, prophecies, and visions for poorly armed soldiers promoted the resources of the Aladura as the death toll in the war spiraled. Thus, the Aladura gained during the crisis. As Andrew Walls observed,

> the effectiveness of Christian faith or of any particular manifestation of it, is accordingly open to the test whether it gives access to power or prosperity or protection against natural or spiritual enemies, purposes to which much traditional practice was directed....[23]

Cyril Okorocha's study of religious conversion among the Igbo concurred that a cherished value among the Igbo is *nka na nzere* (long life with dignity); therefore, the core religious quest is *ezi ndu*, a good life that embraces physical health, material prosperity, fertility, individual success, communal satisfaction and practical guidance. It is like the *shalom* of the Jews. However, as John Peel admonished, there could be an equally important process of transvaluation, "that the most important human objectives lay beyond earthly existence, not within it."[24]

---

23. Christopher Fyfe and Andrew F. Walls, eds, *Christianity in Africa in the 1990s*(Edinburgh: Center for African Studies, University of Edinburgh,1996), 5.

24. C.C. Okorocha, *The Meaning of Religious Conversion in Africa: The Case of the Igbo of Nigeria* (Aldershot: Avebury, 1987): 206, 278; J. Peel, *Religious Encounter and the Making of the Yoruba* (Bloomington: Indiana University Press, 2000):165.

Accounts that appeared after the war commented profusely on the growth and importance of Aladura spirituality in the period, 1966–1970. Vertical expansion into the hinterland was buttressed by horizontal growth into the cultural soil of communities. Alex Madiebo was a chief protagonist in the war. His book, *The Nigerian Revolution and Biafran War* commented on the rise of spiritualism and its destructive impact on the morale of the Biafran army. He observed that,

> The insurmountable hardship facing the army were being exploited for personal benefits by certain unscrupulous individuals through spiritualism. Many officers men realizing that we lacked the material force to prosecute the war successfully resorted to spiritualism and prayers as the only alternative way of surviving the war.[25]

A certain quack known simply as "Mr Wise" was a beneficiary of false adulation; his visions controlled the soldiers. Ben Gbulie, another war leader, used this facet as an explanation scheme in his book, *The Fall of Biafra.*

Stephen Ellis, in his study of the civil war in Liberia, confirmed a similar trend reported in Igboland: that as the war intensified, forcing people back to their villages, a renaissance of indigenous religiosity started.[26] People deployed magic, divination, ancient modes of coping, and other sources of power that aided life in pre-colonial periods, for survival amidst social suffering. Yet overcrowding, economic stress, and the quest for a safe haven from war forced people to break ancient prohibitions by entering and farming in sacred groves, fishing forbidden types of fishes, and reassessing the power of some indigenous gods. Those that could not perform watched as their groves overgrew with grass.

Just as the war was starting, the Scripture Union that operated among secondary schools became prominent in mobilizing the youth into prayer and Bible study camps.[27] Gradually, a spiritual revival broke out among them. Scholars differ about the exact timing. Richard Burgess would place it before 1970 because the Bible study regimen catalyzed a revival. Many young people

---

25. Alex Madiebo, *The Nigerian Revolution and Biafran War* (Enugu: Fourth Dimension Publishers, 1980), 15; Ben Gbulie, *The Fall of Biafra* (Enugu: Fourth Dimension Publishers, 1989). See Chinua Achebe, *Girls at War and Other Stories* (London, Heinemann, 1972).

26. Stephen Ellis, *Mask of Anarchy* (London: Hurst & Co., 1999).

27. Bill Roberts, *Life and Death Among the Ibos* (London, 1970); Frances Lawjua Bolton, *And We Beheld His Glory: A Personal Account of the Revival in Eastern Nigeria in 1970/71* (Harlow: Christ the King Publishing, 1992).

rediscovered the Bible as a source of comfort, guide, conversion, problem solver, and ethical renewal. Bill Roberts, the leader, did not encourage glossolalia. Others recognize it as a balm in Gilead that aided the survival in the post-civil war period.[28] Though the spirituality of the SU became more charismatic, it was still restrained. In fact, many of the young Bible preachers were members of Aladura churches and prayer houses during the civil war. Two intriguing aspects of Igbo church history are that some of the early Aladura in Igboland emerged from the evangelical churches; and many of the contemporary Pentecostal groups emerged from among the Aladura. The post-civil war period witnessed a three-way struggle for the religious space among Christian groups that intensified with the years: the Aladura competed against both the youthful charismatics and the mainline churches. Meanwhile, the mainline churches essayed to recover the years that the locust ate, and battled against both the Aladura and the new fangled charismatics with much venom.

It has been shown that northwestern Igboland was the most successful mission field of the Aladura, both Sunday and Sabbath worshippers. It was also the origin of the missionary enterprises of the Anglicans who came in 1857 and the Roman Catholics who came in 1885. So, it could serve as a good example of the battlefield in the religious war of the period: the Roman Catholic Church under the indomitable Archbishop Francis Arinze commissioned a study on the Aladura, encouraged Father Ikeobi to start a charismatic prayer meeting every Tuesday in Onitsha, and permitted Fr. McNutt's charismatic team from the United States to tour his archdiocese in 1971. He ordered his diocesan priests to attend, and brought his mother to receive a healing ministration from the McNutt team. Later, Fr. Edeh was permitted to start a Holy Ghost Ministry at Elele.[29] These encapsulating strategies were designed to shut out both genres of charismatic groups and block the patronage by the "faithful." He seemed to have succeeded because a survey of seventy-nine leaders of the youthful charismatics indicates that only about 10% came from the Roman Catholic Church, while 43% came from the Anglican Church.[30]

---

28. Richard Burgess, "The Civil War Revival and Its Pentecostal Progeny: A Religious Movement among the Igbo People of Eastern Nigeria, 1967–2002," PhD dissertation, Dept. of Theology, University of Birmingham, June, 2004), chapter 3. See Kalu, *Embattled Gods*, (2003), Chapter 10: Balm in Gilead.

29. See Hilary Achunike, "Catholic Charismatic Movement in Igboland, 1970–1990," PhD dissertation, Dept. of Religion, University of Nigeria, Nsukka, 2001.

30. Burgess, "The Civil War", 169.

The growth pattern of charismatic Christians who founded Pentecostal groups in that culture area is as follows:[31]

Period	No. of Pentecostal Ministries Founded
1970–1974	6
1975–1979	8
1980–1984	11
1985–1989	25
total	51

The statistics do not tell the story of an energetic, vibrant evangelism, group bonding, activism and diversity of ministerial emphases that comprised of deliverance, healing, evangelism, intercessory, specialized focus on prisons and children. Opposition came from mission churches especially Roman Catholics in Onitsha and Presbyterians in Enugu. To illustrate only one from Raphael Okafor's testimony: he was one of the leaders, and kept a daily diary of their activities. He noted in his diary entry:

> 28th March 1971: Enu Onitsha campaign continues. Emmanuel Church authorities refused their church compound again. We moved to the Anglican Girls' School, Inland town, Onitsha and began around 5.00 pm. People still attended despite the disruptions.[32]

Emmanuel Church belonged to the Roman Catholics and the Girls' School to the accommodating Anglicans.

The focus here is the impact of the charismatic youths on the Aladura. First, a number of the youth who had patronized the Aladura deserted to the charismatic groups. One illustration is a young man who was a firebrand in the new charismatic movement. Stephen Okafor (a friend, not a relation of Raphael) was one of the three founders of Our Hour of Redemption. He was a trader from the village of Ojoto, near Onitsha, was brought up as a Roman Catholic but converted to Aladura in 1963. He rose to a position of trust in Ufuma Practical Prayer Band, a powerful prayer house founded by Madam Nwokolo at Ufuma. Okafor went to collect relief materials from the Scripture Union camp in 1969 when he heard a sermon that changed him. He then recruited

---

31. Kalu, *Embattled Gods*, 278.

32. Cit. O.U. Kalu, "Passive Revolution and Its Saboteurs: African Christian Initiative in the Era of Decolonization, 1955–1975", in Brian Stanley, ed. *Mission, Nationalism and the End of Empire* (Grand Rapids, Eerdmans, 2003), 274.

his two friends, Raphael Okafor and Arthur Oruizu. But the prophetess perceived a new spirit at work and drove the three young men away from her compound. They formed an evangelistic preaching band that flowered in years. His career is a composite image of the new religious environment. Second, a lively debate ensued among the new charismatics that demonized the Aladura. Desertion became mandatory; former members repented of their dalliance, and underwent deliverance rituals as they queried the use of instruments in healing and liturgy. Many young people found the SU environment to be safe: it provided the spiritual power they sought, challenged the gender barriers in the mainline churches, served as an instrument of moral and self integration, and a coping mechanism in the new times. They combined a devotion to the Bible with a passion for saving souls. Yet it was a daring act to be a "Bible carrier" when others were struggling to recover the material loss from the civil war. The society taunted them. In their zeal, some formed new Pentecostal ministries. Third, the breakup of some Aladura groups took different forms: Some, as Victory Christian Mission led by Onuigbo, turned the formerly Aladura churches into Pentecostal churches. In others, the internal debate splintered the group. For instance, Christ Ascension Mission resolved that each branch should decide what to do. The Port Harcourt branch retained its Aladura form; Aba split into two: Mike Okonkwo took one part and created the very large Pentecostal church, True Redeemed Evangelical Mission. He relocated in Lagos, and is the current President of the Pentecostal Association of Nigeria. The Enugu branch, under the original founder, discontinued the use of some of their symbolism and instruments, and has maintained a strong relationship with Pentecostal groups.

Testimonies of those who had been in nativistic and vitalistic Aladura movements, the reports from deliverance contexts, and accounts of those who had been deeply connected to messianic Aladura forms, generated immense data for tarring and feathering the movement in spite of the large connections in their origins. As Rosebud Okorocha wrote to Bill Roberts in May 1971,

> those who have bound by satanic Prayer Bands have received the Lord
> through this group and many who do not go to church now share
> Christian fellowship with us.[33]

In spite of the attacks, the Messianic and Sabbatharian forms grew faster than other forms of Aladura. Perhaps, they provided more miraculous answers. For instance, The Brotherhood of Cross and Star swept into Igboland in the post-

---

33. Cit. Burgess, "Civil War", 174.

civil war period, offering that if devotees knocked their foreheads three times on the ground, the leader would appear to them and answer their requests positively.

Aladuras and charismatics were like estranged bedfellows. The major points of contention were over the centrality of the Bible, its use and hermeneutics, and attitude to indigenous culture. They demonized the Aladura for incorporating elements of indigenous religion, occultism in belief system and rituals, low-level evangelism, magical use of the Bible such as use of psalms and candles for acquiring power, or beating a victim with the Bible as a means of cleansing.[34] Pentecostal Biblicism nurtured a certain hermeneutics of trust that discountenanced the elements of popular religiosity among the Aladura. Both provided a large space for the Holy Spirit, but the Pentecostals showed a greater sensitivity to the prospective intrusion of unholy spirits. Equally important is the attitude of Igbo converts to indigenous culture. The young people lacked the accommodating or dialogical attitude found among the Yoruba. Though certain parts of Igboland retain culture as mark of identity, it would appear that the Igbo convert is more willing to desert the covenant with the gods of the fathers and to abandon the culture including even the language. This war against indigenous culture has militated against the process of enculturation of the gospel in Igboland. By the end our period, the increasing salience of youthful charismatic influence went full circle with the charismatisation of the mainline churches. A Pentecostal wind blew outside Pentecostalism. The battle of the early 1970s against the youth petered off in the 1980s. The pace of growth of the Charismatic-Pentecostal genre soon outpaced the Aladura in a harsh terrain where their halcyon days were few.

---

34. O.U. Kalu, "Estranged Bedfellows?: The Demonization of the Aladura in African Pentecostal Rhetoric", Missionalia, 28, 2/3 (Aug./Nov. 2000): 121–142.

CHAPTER 16

Afro-Brazilian Religion, Progressive Catholicism, and Pentecostalism in Northeast Brazil: Notes on Confluence

Miriam Cristina M. Rabelo[1]

Introduction

In the best tradition of Weberian social sciences, John Peel's approach to Yoruba religion is essentially historical. As we all know Weber's sociology is historical in the strong sense: not only does it show the advantages of complementing the study of society and culture with the study of history but affirms the vital link that exists between these disciplines. John Peel's work proves how fruitful it is for anthropology to place culture and history in ongoing dialogue.

This dialogue requires that anthropology move away from defining culture as a fixed structure of meanings underlying historical development. To define culture in such terms means not only overlooking the historical processes through which certain configurations of meanings crystallize but also ignoring the essential openness of such configurations. This of course is a very Weberian theme. In Weber's own view culture illuminates a segment of reality with meaning: it is a horizon of understanding which shapes action. But cul-

---

1. I would like to thank Mark Cravalho for revising the text and making valuable comments.

tural horizons are far from fixed, moving as action itself unfolds, as new questions or problems are posed by the actions of the others (individuals and groups) toward which it is oriented, as a certain history proceeds.

The turning to history, however, can hardly lead away from the anthropologist's concern with contextual analysis—after all, the past is never immune to the interests of the present. Moreover conceptions of time encoded in a society's major narratives have an important impact on historical practice. As Peel notes, making history on the plane of social action directed at releasing a future is closely involved with making history in the sense of giving accounts of the past. The contexts of meanings and interests that define a certain present cannot be overlooked in analysis of the past.

The articulation of cultural and historical analysis seems to require a reflection on temporality or rather on the relations between past, present and future. Peel's own reflection takes the form of a powerful critique of presentism. In claiming that the past as we know it can only be a fabrication of the present, presentism not only questions the value of historical analysis but completely severs our vital links with the past. Peel's critical position is brilliantly summoned in a discussion of Yoruba ethnicity: "Against this 'presentism,' I argue for a properly cultural and historical explanation of ethnicity. But 'culture' must not be seen as a mere precipitate or bequest of the past. Rather, it is an active reflexion on the past, a cultural work. And because work supposes a real object, in this case historical experience, an adequate explanation must be a fully historical one."

To substitute the omnipotence of the present for the determination of the past is still to remain within a one-sided or linear model of temporality: in both cases one misses the complex dialectic or mutual conditioning of present and past (and future) at work in every cultural context. In a recent lecture Peel has noted that understanding the specificities of context requires attention to the history of what was brought to context. All contexts are, after all, confluences. The idea of confluence brings out the complex temporal dimensions of context. In approaching contexts of religious encounter as confluences, analysis is able to move from the situation itself of the encounter to the histories through which different traditions came together.

Of course at issue here is the conception of tradition or culture that informs our approach to the religious encounter. In Weber's own view culture illuminates a segment of reality with meaning: it is a horizon of understanding which shapes action. But cultural horizons are far from fixed, moving as action itself unfolds, as new questions or problems are posed by the actions of the others toward which it is oriented, as a certain dialogue proceeds. By linking culture to history, Weber's sociology of religion is able to focus both on the uniqueness of different religious traditions and on their essential openness, on the areas of interpenetration and conflict through which they dialogue with other cultural understandings.

Peel argues that situated comparison—where the religions compared are present in a single context—is the most productive strategy for understanding the distinct import of the different world religions to local settings and thus for highlighting their specificities, *qua* traditions. Apart from obvious methodological reasons, he observes that situated comparison enables the anthropologist to "address one of the key ways in which religious traditions have been always shaped: through the practical comparisons made between religions by their adherents or potential adherents" (2003). This observation suggests that, to understand confluence as a historically constituted encounter of religious traditions, we must also approach it as a space of action, or rather social relation, to use two of Weber's sociological concepts. Social action is in fact a pivotal concept in Weberian sociology. Not only does it provide Weber with a means for articulating culture and history, but it also offers a renewed approach to both culture and history.

Articulating culture and history through action Peel (2000) moves beyond both the explanation of religious change from the viewpoint of the internal content of religious traditions and a reduction of religious processes to the logic of socio-economic transformations. In fact, despite their differences, both approaches neglect the intricate mediations of social action—and end up conflating what are often more diversified interests and projects. Attention to the complex dynamics of interests and ideas in the study of the history of Christianity in Yorubaland allows for a more nuanced picture of the ways by which the efforts of missionaries were tied up with the British colonial enterprise. It also leads to a finer perception of the different agents and constellations of interests that played a decisive role in the expansion of the mission and in the transformation of its initial features: from the mediating role of the *babalawos*, intellectuals of Yoruba culture, to the disseminating role of native mission agents whose work contributed both to the spread of Christianity and its adjustment to local culture.

Peel's work, I think, highlights not only the value of analysis aimed at locating the complex relations of actors and interests in a given context, but also the need that an understanding of the temporality of action guide analysis of far-reaching processes of change. To construct the past as a mere fabrication of the present is to forget that it is sedimented in experience as habit, as a set of crystallized investments in the world which are always also possibilities of acting. And if following Peel we can claim that the effectiveness of the future lies in its links with the past, this is precisely because the past is not exterior to existence but inherited possibilities that, in being taken over, open up a field of action. This means of course that the past provides guidelines for action but not as a causal force determining present and future in any linear way. As Gadamer (1994) points out, recovery of the past is never mere repetition: even if it is not explicitly articulated as such, reacquisition is also a rediscovery and renewed exploration of the past in the present. Recovery of tradition is always already an application of tradition.

Now, just as the past is never immune to the present, but possibilities that are only available through recovery, the interests and goals that guide this work of appropriation are not formulated in a time-free space from which they stand completely untouched by the action which itself unfolds in time. On close attention we find that clear-cut ends are often the product of a retrospective look, one placed at the conclusion of the action, explicitly engaged in explaining or justifying it. To the actors the future is always somewhat indeterminate; as Peel (2000) shows in his recent book, to the Yoruba dealing with the European missionaries in the Age of Confusion it was even more so. Through action a more or less vague sketch of the future is progressively filled. But action is rarely the mere fulfillment of a ready-made project: the actors' intentions and projects are clarified and altered in the unfolding of action. This obviously means that context greatly affects action, but it also means that what counts as context itself changes as the action unfolds. In neglecting the temporal mediations of social action, historical analysis runs the risk of reifying meanings that are often more fluid, and that to the social actors were not always so distinct and clear.

But historical analysis must still deal with the temporality of far-reaching processes of change. The main challenge for a study of history built around the concept of action is to avoid reducing history to a mere collection of scattered facts and reducing the facts and actions of individuals to the power of some sort of overarching historical reason. Particularly concerned with understanding the emergence of certain structures in history, Weber's sociology provides a good example. As Merleau-Ponty (1973) notes, Weber deals with the challenge not by positing an overarching line of historical development, which reduces facts to the raw material of historical logic, but through an understanding of the essential indeterminacy of events—the different possibilities which they enclose and which always depend on human initiative for their full development. The past holds the key to the future but only the future places us in the position to fully discern the truth of the past: by joining scattered events, taking up and further developing the initiatives of others, action both projects the past in the direction of a certain coming to be and grounds the future in the past.

Rather than positing an unvarying historical essence behind the concrete manifestations of world religions, an action-oriented approach enables us to locate continuity in the renewed efforts of religious agents and followers to re-cover the meaning of tradition and apply it to present, in the historically con-tingent ways by which these efforts are taken over and further developed by others, crystallized in certain institutions and styles of interpretation. Contra religious agents, we can always argue that this process is never pure repetition but always creation of meaning. Contra anthropological accounts, however, it can always be argued that if all interpretation is oriented by the concrete in-terests of the present, recovery of the past is rarely pure fabrication, itself working through tradition in search of its truth in the present. Confluence is dialogue—as long as we acknowledge that mystification and intolerance, rather than greater understanding, can also come as a result—proceeding through a dynamics of question and answer, clarification and application of meaning. The contexts that provide the anthropologist with an opportunity for situated comparison are also, by the very fact that they promote dialogue and confrontation, those that provide the religious agents with greater op-portunity to make explicit their own religious traditions.

Clearly the temporality of action does not give us access to the temporal-ity of the far-reaching processes of change promoted by the expansion of world religions. There is always a certain difficulty in maintaining a produc-tive balance between them. Overcoming this difficulty depends in part on se-lecting the right strategy of presentation or narration, a strategy that can move from one to the other and back in a circle of growing contextualization and progressive particularization. Peel's recent work on the history of Christian-ity in Yorubaland is certainly a good example. His text is filled with quotes and summaries from the journals of missionaries, describing the mission's rou-tine, commenting on everyday encounters and conflicts, and reflecting on the choices that they faced throughout daily work. These are obviously contextu-alized by reference to wider socio-economic processes, and are taken as fur-ther examples of long-term dynamics of religious change. But they also shed light on the uncertainties that afflicted the missionaries, on the open-ended character of their endeavors, the unfulfilled hopes, and the distortions to which they often felt their work was subjected. The result of the coexistence of these two narratives within the text—the grand narrative of Christianity in Yorubaland, which the historian reconstitutes, and the short, everyday nar-ratives of the agents also seeking to make sense of their practice—is double. On the one hand it shows the daily efforts of missionaries connected to other actions and events, stretching beyond their immediate consequences, already forming a pattern, which the actors themselves could not discern as well as the historian, but in whose identification they were nonetheless engaged as narrators. On the other hand it shows how the structures, which the historian highlights were precipitated by certain choices, developing tendencies, which, although already implicit in these choices, required action to be matured or fully realized, and required the future to recognize itself as a tendency already present in the past.

* * *

In this chapter I examine a particular instance of religious encounter or confluence of different religious traditions. Present at the encounter were two very different modalities of Christianity, Pentecostalism and the Progressive Catholicism of the Ecclesial Base Communities (CEBs), and a syncretic Afro-Brazilian religion, known as jarê. The setting was an area of family-based agri-culture, Nova Redenção, a municipality in the center portion of the state of Bahia, Northeast Brazil. Around the village of Nova Redenção were seven rural neighborhoods of peasant families. This is where in 1987 I carried out field-work for my doctoral dissertation (Rabelo, 1990) under the supervision of John Peel. As in most of the rural Northeast, the Catholic Church held a main position in the local religious field: its building stood in the centre of the vil-lage, surrounded by the houses of the local elite. But during the early eight-ies under the initiative of a progressive clergy, lay groups of Catholics multi-plied in the rural neighborhoods, among peasant families. These were the Ecclesial Base Communities. Before CEBs were formed under the initiative of a progressive clergy rural neighborhoods were already home to the jarê and its *caboclos*, spirits of the bush known to possess great healing powers.

Nova Redenção was a zone of confluence from its very beginning: a meet-ing place of migrants and of traditions. The jarê is a syncretic cult in which West African deities or *orixás* have been largely assimilated to a generic class of native spirits, the *caboclos*—possibly a good example of what Bastide (1960) described as the degeneration of African religion in rural Brazil[2]. Pop-ular Catholicism is very much present in the world of the jarê, and more gen-erally in the religious imagination of the Northeast. If tradition is used to refer

---

2. Bastide (1960) was especially concerned with identifying the conditions which en-abled the preservation of African religion in Brazil. He defended the idea that the Brazil-ian rural milieu made particularly difficult the survival of African religion – the spatial dis-persion of Africans in vast areas of the rural Northeast hindered the reorganization of *orixá* cult and promoted a more intense syncretism with Amerindian religious practices. This view has contributed to a certain lack of interest among anthropologists in researching rural based Afro-Brazilian religions and, more significantly, also to the dissemination of a neg-ative view of these cults, generally taken as deviations from a pure or authentic religious form.

to origin, to the original as opposed to innovation, then the jarê does not qualify exactly as tradition. Nevertheless it is worth noting that the emergence of both CEB Catholicism and Pentecostalism significantly altered the balance traditionally prevailing in the local religious field between different modes of religious practice, between laity and clergy, popular and erudite, hegemonic and subordinate religious productions. In a way they both presented a modernizing approach to relations within this field.

During the time I resided in Redenção reconfigurations within the religious field could be readily observed. The late 1980s were a period of demobilization of the local CEBs (as of the CEB movement in the rest of Brazil). The jarê remained a central reference in the area. Though largely invisible to the local elite of town, it delimited an important field of exchanges with the supernatural, of healing and entertainment. Pentecostalism then held a very insignificant position: only one temple of the Assembly of God in town. Ten years later the situation had drastically changed: Pentecostal churches multiplied and the jarê lost some of its pervasive power as healing cult. There were still CEBs in the rural neighborhoods but from inclusive communities of the poor they had been redefined as exclusive groups of church people.

In describing this very particular instance of religious encounter I will attempt to further explore the notion of confluence as a matter not only of time—or temporality—but also of spaciality. More particularly I will consider the ways by which the articulations of time and space promoted by these religious traditions, and embodied in the actions of their carriers, shaped the dynamics of the encounter. Given the complexity of the question examined here, and my own limitations as a researcher, I have opted for considering confluence from the vantage point of the jarê, that is, by examining CEBs and Pentecostalism in relation to central features of Afro-Brazilian cult. I should note from the start that I am analysing a very particular and relatively small territorial context—not Brazil but a locality (district) in the state of Bahia—it is the context in which I carried out fieldwork. To explain this context, however, I will resort to a discussion of wider socio-historical processes that affected the religious formation of the country, and of Northeast Brazil in particular. Also worth clarifying, I am not going to engage in long term historical analysis. Such endeavor, although certainly necessary for a more comprehensive understanding of religious encounters, not only falls out of the scope of the present chapter, but equally out of my own competence as a researcher.

Nova Redenção is located in the Chapada Diamantina region of central Bahia, and cut by the Paraguaçu River. Roughly speaking, the region can be divided into two historically and geographically distinct areas: the west, a mountainous and humid area which was traditionally a settlement of miners and diamond prospectors, and the east, mostly low and dry land, largely occupied by a migrant population of peasant cultivators. This latter region, where Redenção is located, originally supplied foodstuff to the mining population of the west. By the 1950s, however, it specialized in commercial crops (castor oil), and this shift to castor oil production was largely responsible for the horizontal expansion of the peasantry in the area. During the period of military rule the region was marked by an acute process of land concentration, and many peasant families were expelled from their plots. The living conditions of the district's overwhelming peasant population have seriously deteriorated since then.

The jarê can be defined as a "candomblé de caboclo," an Afro-Brazilian cult in which Yoruba deities or *orixás*, worshipped in the more traditional Candomblé houses of the Bahian Recôncavo,[3] have been assimilated to a generic class of native spirits, the *caboclos*, held to be Indians or descendents of the Brazilian Indians. The cult is based on the Chapada Diamantina and its origins, closely related to the development of diamond mining in the region, date back to the mid-nineteenth century. During the period of great prosperity generated by mining (roughly between 1817 and 1840) there was considerable influx of Afro-descendents to the Chapada (as slave labor), but the presence of Africans actually goes back to the eighteenth century, when *quilombo* formations (communities of runaway slaves) were reported in the region. From the mining centres of the Chapada the jarê spread into the surrounding areas of peasant agriculture, acquiring both new adepts and features. Basically in these latter zones syncretism is far more pronounced—the influence of popular Catholicism is greater, and links to African tradition much weaker (Senna, 1984).

Outsiders to Redenção are not immediately confronted with the world of the jarê. Not only were most jarê houses located in the rural neighborhoods, but people were somewhat reluctant to admit participation to educated members of the elite. Practically all of the district's jarê houses or *terreiros* are headed by peasant cultivators. Jarê leaders retain central functions as healers and are thus generally referred to as *curadores*. There is no formal instruction available to healers; initiation as a special period reserved for the transmission

---

3. The Bahian Recôncavo is the region around the Bay of All Saints, where Salvador, Brazil's first capital city, is located. Due to the main political and economic role played by this region during colonial period it received a massive influx of African slave labour. The urban centres of the Recôncavo were, according to Bastide, a main area of preservation of African tradition and development of the candomblé.

of sacred knowledge hardly exists in the local jarê and only in a very loose sense it might be said that healers control a specialized body of knowledge. Though treatment in the house of a *curador* for afflictions caused by the *caboclos* is a necessary step in the making of healers, healing power is thought of less as an acquisition made through learning than as an unexpected gift gradually revealed in its exercise and, as *curadores* themselves like to point out, only accepted after a painful trajectory of suffering in the hands of their spirit-guides.

Jarê houses do not form rigidly organized groups, and membership in a *terreiro* does not create exclusive social relations; bonds between members tend to overlap and strengthen existing relations of neighborhood, kinship, and co-parenthood (*compadrio*). A healer's circle of adepts is markedly female: the vast majority of jarê goers are women, and most men who attend rituals stand in a position of occasional visitors or observers. Both women and men, however, occasionally consult *curadores* and undergo treatment in the jarê for a wide range of problems.

The *curadores* of Redenção are not the keepers of African memory usually sought by researchers. Most were not raised in areas of strong African presence and did not start their religious careers within the jarê. The spirits who possess them are no longer identified exclusively as African *orixás*, but generally referred to as *caboclos, encantados* (enchanted beings), or *guias* (guides). Before becoming jarê masters, many worked in *sessão*, healing cults centred on the incorporation of spirit-guides, closely related to the Catimbó of Amerindian origin. Sessão and jarê are in fact regarded as two different lines of healing, and *curadores* claim that the choice between them depends ultimately on the preference of clients and nature of the case. Their religious experience, moreover, has strong links with Catholicism:

> I know that everything you need in the world is already there. The world is a pantry, everything you search for inside it you'll find, for God provided for everything....Everything that came to my mind was ordered by Jesus Christ. I never learned a prayer from a book nor did anyone teach me. All I have was a gift from God. I always pray for Jesus and when I have something to do, I go to bed today and tomorrow I know how to do it. I come to the altar, light a candle and beg Jesus and all the living saints in heaven and the words I have to say come to my memory.

Agenor, author of the quote above, was a relatively well known jarê master. He was also directly involved in some of the Catholic traditions that, imported from Iberia, developed in the region largely free for the direct interference of the clergy. Every year in celebration of the Maji he led a group of revellers that re-enacted the journey of the three kings during a six day walk throughout the neighboring countryside. At the jarês held in his house the dance of *caboclos* was preceded by a long session of Catholic prayers, sung in Latin.

In the local religious imagination Catholicism delimits a world where even *caboclos* have a place, a rich pantry of characters and powers, provided by God himself. Agenor's image of the pantry captures nicely the territorial character of Catholicism, a church religion whose own limits are made to coincide with the limits of the known world, in all possible gradations of vice and virtue. Both the virtuous devout and the unremitting sinner find room in the vast plan of God; they manifest different relations or degrees of proximity to the sacred. Brazilian anthropologist R. Fernandes (1982) provides very interesting insights into the spatial dimensions of Catholic worldview. Represented spatially, he argues, the world image of Catholicism articulates diversity and unity in terms of two intersecting planes: the horizontal plane of this worldly existence and the vertical plane of other worldly salvation. In this scheme the diversity that coexists in the first plane is conciliated by reference to the second: as one moves upward within the vertical plane lines converge to a common point. Midway between human kind and the Holy Trinity, diversity and higher level unity are the saints—still diverse in their histories and areas of performance as sacred mediators, but all of them committed to heavenly enterprise. As Fernandes points out this spatial design also describes the typical Catholic strategy of dealing with difference: dissolving diversity into higher level unity and unifying particular claims by reference to universal ones.

The Catholicism that laid roots in Brazilian soil was marked by this ambiguous articulation of diversity and unity. It proved flexible enough to assimilate elements from the traditions it sought to subjugate, plastic enough to accommodate difference within its overarching umbrella of faith. The festive side of Portuguese Christianity with its emphasis on medieval mysteries and revelries was a powerful instrument in the assimilation of Indians and Africans to the dominant colonial order. Clearly such plasticity had limits and favored syncretic practices that often escaped completely the control of the church hierarchy. In fact the Church was never entirely successful in maintaining control over Catholic practice throughout the country. The social conditions prevailing in the interior determined from the outset the development of a popular Catholicism that was relatively free from Church interference, centered on lay devotional practices. Distant from the main poles of economic development and scattered throughout vast and isolated areas, rural communities offered limited access to a clergy that was both numerically and organizationally weak.

This brief historical overview suggests that the syncretic religious imagination of the rural Northeast must be explained in terms both historical and spatial. The articulation of time and space in the analysis of syncretism is especially relevant for understanding the jarê. The religious production of local healers is set against a historical background of intensive spatial mobility, entailing different relations to the land and often a complete lack of it. The past experienced by *curadores* as squatters, tenants, sharecroppers, and day laborers is a clear example of the fluidity of local peasant histories. Most have struggled with the difficulty, almost impossibility, of maintaining stable ties to the land: clearing bush and cultivating plots in vast and unoccupied properties, they were soon placed under the authority of overseers, material embodiments of distant and unknown landowners; settling as sharecroppers, they were often back on the move as small conflicts were enough to break what were then only personal agreements, revealing the extreme fragility of their condition. In the past land was available, one had only choose a site for cultivation, clear the bush and settle with the family. With the expansion of cattle grazing farms later in the seventies, cultivated plots (*roças*) gave way to pasture as peasants were expelled from what became farmer's land. Migration to the rich urban centers of southern Brazil was greatly intensified. São Paulo appeared as an alternative to the bad days in Bahia; some who returned managed to purchase small plots in the district, after an extended period of drought had once again made land available to newcomers. In São Paulo curadores from Redenção found a receptive clientele for their religious and healing services. Establishing themselves as healers in the big city brought them close to Umbanda, a modern syncretic version of African religion, adapted to the needs of a racially and culturally mixed population in search of integration to modern society and protection in face of its many risks. Those who returned to Redenção brought Umbanda practices to the jarê, in a movement which curiously reversed the process itself of Umbanda formation, from the African based Northeast to the prosperous and more Europeanized South.

To the peasants that occupied the district during the '40s and '50s, the passage of time was thus marked by movement: the past emerged as geographical distance and space bore the clear attribute of history. Movement was also integral to the process by which some became *curadores*, not only preserving along with jarê practice, activities as *sessão* masters and leaders of popular Catholicism, but also bringing to the jarê elements from both these traditions (and later also from Umbanda). As activity of powers in space, movement equally helps explain the success of the jarê in the area, as compared to the sessão. Healers' gradual shift to the jarê reflects the growing importance of the cult for a population of migrants who were not themselves originally familiar with it and who came to see the jarê as more powerful and effective than the *sessão*.

One of the main differences between jarê and *sessão* lies precisely in the nature of the action that unfolds during rituals. The *sessão* lacks the drumming and dancing of African ritual, which are considered defining elements of the jarê, also known as *couro* (leather), because of the leather topped drums used in rituals. Sacred space in the *sessão* emerges through the singing and speaking of otherwise motionless bodies. In jarê rituals, by contrast, it is a direct function of motion. Not only does the jarê reframe the ritual's central action—possession by *caboclos*—in terms of movement, but, more significantly, it democratizes action: whereas only the healer is possessed by his spirit-guides during a *sessão*, any of the attendants at a jarê can be caught by *caboclos*. To healers this means that the jarê is far more demanding and risky than the *sessão*: no longer centred exclusively on his well known spirit-guides the jarê makes room for an entire village of *caboclos* and forces the healer to publicly deal with them. The good will of these spirits, moreover, cannot be taken for granted; though *caboclos* can and do heal, their main goal during rituals is to play or more precisely to fool around (*vadiar*), as songs point out. To attendants this means that jarê rituals create an arena of power that is clearly more appealing to the senses—more entertaining and beautiful to watch—and more compelling, more likely to place them at the centre of the main action performed: the play of *caboclos*. In the jarê play can turn into serious business (and vice versa), aesthetic experience can become possession by the object of admiration, and in the relation between humans and *caboclos* the question of agency cannot be settled in any straightforward manner:

> This [*caboclo*] Indian I don't know why he caught me. I went to a festival in the hills. There were two drums there, at my sister's house. We had given the Caruru de Cosme e Damião[4] and I said: "I'm gonna have a jarê here". "But do you know how to?" "No, I said, but let's do it!" So we started beating the drums and I was singing whatever came to my mind. Then all of a sudden this guy started dancing with a *caboclo* called Bugue (from bugre, Indian). And the man turned brute and wild, he danced real pretty and I thought it was pretty. I thought it was beautiful! Then after he danced the *caboclo* Bugue, he danced the Indian. Such a beauty, the Indian! "*Madinha* (godmother), there in the hills, what a beautiful thing, the *caboclo* Indian". But why did I have to want the Indian? I don't know, I thought it was beautiful, really beautiful. Then one day at Agenor's they sang for the Indian, when I realized I was already

---

4. A traditional feast in honour of the twin saints of Catholicism, who are also playful child *caboclos* of the jarê, centred around a caruru meal, of African origin.

yelling and dancing (possessed). I think he [the *caboclo*] saw me there (in the hills) he liked me too, so he leaned on me.

The play of *caboclos* in the jarê weaved several important threads of local peasant history. The *caboclos* were wild, brute, unpredictable Indians from the bush, African slaves and fearful African witches, hunters and cowboys from the backlands. Their songs addressed the formation of a racially mixed and migrant peasantry, and dramatically subverted the negative stereotypes ordinarily associated with its Indian and African origins. The open structure of rituals made them capable of incorporating and involving participants in the creation of vivid extracts of social drama, which further elaborated their historical experience. To exemplify this last point I now turn to a particular ritual which I attended during fieldwork. The ritual was centered on the visit of Mineiro (miner), one of the rural *caboclos* of the jarê, during the closing of Vavá's *terreiro*, at the beginning of Lent. Vavá was then greatly dissatisfied with his reduced and uncooperative circle of clients and planned to achieve greater influence as a *sessão* healer in the neighboring town of Ibiquera, where he claimed to have important connections. At a certain point of the ritual, he was caught by Mineiro:

> "I thank you all. I send you my blessing, in the name of the father and the Holy Ghost, amen. (…) I, *caboclo* Mineiro, I am leaving now forever, amen. To this *aldeia* (Indian village) I shall not return. Farewell my children. The day has come for *caboclo* Mineiro to leave. If you want to see me you will now have to go to the town of Ibiquera. There you can still find me. No my children, it's not that I'm abandoning you, that I will no longer like you. My days here are over. Jesus, Mary, Joseph is among us all. Amen, Jesus.
>
> "Amen", reply the participants, still confused as to the meaning of Mineiro's words.
>
> "Now we shall work in Ibiquera, when we finish there, we shall return to our center in Minas and Goiás[5].
>
> People are now silent. The *caboclo* sings then continues the speech:
>
> "Thank you, my children for trusting me. May Jesus light your path.…Those whom I cherished the most were the ones who most despised me. This is a land of deceit but I bless you all, I spread holy miracles upon you all."
>
> Some of those present are truly moved. Mineiro proceeds with his revelations:

---

5. States whose development was closely linked to mining activities.

"There are many people here in this *aldeia* tonight. I can pick out by finger those of you who are faithful to my house, the rest are full of deceit."

People turn to one another and comment on the words of Mineiro. A woman cries.

"Look my child...stop crying, you're blessed...Wherever I am I shall look after you....You have to accept it, calm down. I shall look after you".

Once more the *caboclo* raises his hand to bless the group and adds: "Here you'll never find me again". Then he moves to the small altar compartment adjoining the *barracāo*. People line up to consult with Mineiro for the last time. One by one they approach the *caboclo*, who is now seated on a stool, and kneel by his feet.

Mineiro's last visit articulates central themes of the jarê. It is certainly a good example of the cult's plasticity, the creativity of healers and the personal relations that develop between jarê goers and *caboclos* (particularly the healer's *caboclos*). It also shows the importance of Catholic imagery within the jarê and the ways by which it connects to the history of local *curadores* and their followers: Mineiro's experience of displacement, religious work, and eventual betrayal by his followers, links the trials of Christ to the difficult histories of healers and peasants. Mythical past, and lived past, re-describe each other in very important ways. Discovered to lie behind the events that make up a personal history, mythical past gains concreteness; re-described in terms of mythical plot, personal past is infused with greater reach. Finally it is worth noting that the last episode of Mineiro's visit points to the significance of healing in the framing of relations between humans and spirits.

From the perspective of the jarê the person is continually interacting with things, spirits and people she cannot control and of whom she knows only too little. The world is fragmented into shifting relations which invariably produce ill feeling; it is full of threats and surprises. Healing is above all an attempt to regulate these relations, by reverting a previous state of vulnerability in which the body is said to be open (*corpo aberto*). It involves two main operations: the *revista* or divination session and the *trabalho*. The *revista* is a private consultation between the *curador*, or rather his *caboclo*, and the patient, which seeks to unveil the wider relational context underlying affliction. The *trabalho* comprises a series of measures performed on the patient's body during public rituals. It represents a public, dramatized and embodied resolution to a story that was largely shaped in the private context of the *revista*.

The motive of expulsion of sickness causing agents is present at various moments during the performance, creating an arena of struggle around the sick body. *Curadores*, however, do not heal simply by objectifying and finally expelling illness agents. They also seek to close or seal the patient's body, protecting it from the powers that surround it and continually threaten its integrity. The *trabalho* is pervaded by a rich imagery of restoration of weakened bodily extremities, and gradual enclosure of the body within a circle of protection. But it is not regarded as a final solution to the problem: the maintenance of health requires that the patient follow a series of behavioral and dietary rules known as *resguardo* (from the verb *guardar*, to keep). It is their effect of opening the body that makes certain actions and foods subject to restrictions. The *resguardo* encapsulates the memory of the events that defined a past episode of illness and healing, and stresses their determining influence upon the present. As long as this memory lives on—in terms of obedience to the *resguardo*—the person is able to prolong the state of security and protection which the healer has inscribed on her body. It is forgetfulness, by contrast, that eventually destroys the thin advantage granted by healing.

The jarê was a major reference in the district when, under the initiative of a progressive Italian priest, the first base communities (CEBs) were created: lay Catholic groups of peasant families that met to read the Bible, discuss their problems, devise collective strategies to assist one another and improve their situation. The CEBs were formed in the territory of the jarê: not in town (where the main church building stood as marker of the power of Catholic religion) but in the rural neighborhoods. Like the jarê they were loosely structured groups of neighbors and kin in which women participated actively. And yet despite this proximity to the jarê there was no tension between CEBs and *terreiros*, no competition for adepts, but a rather peaceful coexistence. From the perspective of followers, their participation in both groups posed no problem. Local peasants were used to being involved in religious activities of distinct backgrounds. Their religious experience was plural in that it covered different sets of relationship with what were often very distinct spirits and powers, saints and *caboclos*. Though *curadores* themselves kept a distance from the base communities, many of their followers were closely involved in CEB practice. Moreover neither CEBs nor the jarê made exclusive demands upon followers and members; neither laid stress on values of separateness and purity or practiced any form of proselytism. When it came to dealing with outsiders the jarê was surrounded by a silence which only interest and renewed efforts could break. Although many CEB members had some sort of connection with Afro-Brazilian cult—either as mere attendants to rituals, occasional clients of *curadores,* or children of *caboclos*—they saw no reason to publicize it. Thus the jarê remained largely invisible to the foreign pastoral agents (besides the Italian priest, an Austrian couple) who promoted CEB organization in the district. The progressive clergy was not particularly concerned with identifying jarê-goers and had only a vague idea of the nature of the jarê as a particular mode of religious practice. Recovering the Catholic theme of the community of the poor and working through this theme to promote popular organization was the main focus of their activities.

The rise and rapid development of the CEBs in Brazil were part of wider transformations taking place among sectors of the Catholic Church during the sixties and seventies. To state it briefly, progressive church intellectuals adopted a strong position in defense of human rights, a position which they redefined as central to the Church's mission of constructing the kingdom of God on earth. This project actually entailed a radical redefinition of the role of the Catholic Church in society. In the context of violent repression against most forms of popular organization (unions, parties, social movements) which followed the military's rise to power in Brazil, the CEBs became one of the few available channels of popular expression and mobilization (Krischke and Mainwaring, 1986).

It was only in the mid-seventies with the arrival of a progressive Italian priest to the area that the first attempts were made to organize CEBs in the district of Redenção. By the early eighties the base communities had already emerged as a new force in the local political scenario, redefining traditional patterns of political and religious practice. From a close association with the elite of merchants and landowners, the local Catholic Church moved to the side of the poor and became increasingly involved in the defense of their rights. From a previous ritualistic emphasis on sacraments it came to encourage the appropriation of biblical texts by the laity. In the particular style of biblical interpretation favored by the CEBs, biblical texts, and the community's everyday life and problems, each provide a key to understanding the other. In these texts CEB members are encouraged to find not only a reflection on the community's collective situation of oppression but the possibility of overcoming oppression through the unity of the weak and poor.

CEB discourse actually places great emphasis on the category of poverty. This category links directly to the notion of weakness (*fraqueza*) through which peasants and impoverished town dwellers describe their own unfavorable condition and generally refer to themselves as weak (*fracos*). As a descriptive category, poverty is inclusive enough to unify the multiple fragments that compose local peasant history—now owners of small tracks of land, local peasants have lived through different relations of land and labor, and still find themselves moving between the categories of wage laborers and small producers. In the CEBs they are joined, and their differences played down, by reference to the generic attribute of poverty, the definition of which is at once socio-economic and religious, for the poor are not only those who live in scarcity but the followers of God's message of brotherly love. And here we come to yet another dimension of poverty within base communities: more than a descriptive term it is also an action category, pointing directly to the role of the poor in constructing God's kingdom on earth. In the CEBs the poor become a collective agent of change, or liberation (a central term in the discourse of the progressive clergy): the strength of the poor derives from their unity.

CEBs everywhere recovered and extended traditional communitarian practices: community members labored together to assist one another in construction and agricultural work, visited the sick and collectively celebrated important dates of the Catholic calendar. Despite their novelty within the religious field, CEBs still represented a certain line of continuity with popular Catholicism. Like the messianic movements of late Nineteenth Century, however, this continuity was based on the elimination of ambiguities, that is, on the radicalization of the communitarian elements of Catholic religion. The ethics of brotherhood favored within the CEBs not only unified peasant families around ideals of solidarity and selfless love but also provided an interpretive key for assessing wider contexts of inequality and exploitation. Through a metaphoric strategy that confers to collectivities and socio-economic arrangements the qualities of individuals and of person-to-person relations, the CEBs contrasted the solidarity of the poor to the inherent selfishness and individualism of the rich, their refusal to share. The opposition between brotherly love and individual interest was reproduced and expanded in a series of others: religion vs. politics; charity vs. greed; community vs. capitalism; good vs. evil. There was a general tendency within the base communities to interpret both past and future according to the essentially moral logic of these oppositions.

Revitalizing communitarian action CEBs brought some material improvement to rural neighborhoods. Pastoral agents also sought to recover and systematize popular knowledge of healing plants, and organized groups of women who were trained to provide assistance for the most common problems afflicting rural dwellers. One of Redenção's pastoral agents was a trained nurse from Austria who brought with her several boxes of donated medication which she prescribed and distributed free of charge. In a context where basic medical assistance was lacking and drugs sold at abusive prices in the town's only pharmacy, the initiative of Church leaders was greatly welcome by the population and for some time very successful.

The rapid growth of the CEBs during the early eighties and the achievements of community action had also an important impact in the political field: soon local politicians were forced to negotiate directly with CEB representatives, some of whom engaged in party politics joining the then emerging Partido dos Trabalhadores (PT) and organizing an opposition to the conservative rural workers trade-union. By the late eighties, however, changes in the local balance of power came to question the base community's legitimacy to speak for the poor. A major drawback in the process of CEB mobilization was the implementation of a new state rural development program in the region, the Projeto Nordeste, centered on a methodology of participation which bore some resemblance to the CEB's own style of practice. The plan was designed to give associations of small producers direct access to World Bank funds for the development of their own community projects. Neighborhood based organizations of peasants had only to legally register as associations to qualify for inclusion in the program. As a consequence, most CEBs were transformed into associations and, even in areas where there had been no previous base community experience, associations were rapidly created. In some of the rural neighborhoods CEBs were kept alive but drastically reduced to very small groups. The shift from CEB to association was not merely nominal; it entailed changes in the dynamics of meetings and patterns of political participation. Groups became increasingly involved in long debates about the allocation of funds and the administration of community resources acquired through the project. Pastoral agents were highly critical of the Projeto Nordeste which they interpreted as a political strategy for the demobilization of peasants. They claimed that, in the CEBs, the material benefits conquered by members stood as a sign of their power to jointly confront a given system of domination; they represented an initial step toward more radical and wide reaching political struggles. In the associations, by contrast, improvements were made to appear rather as a result of negotiation and compromise; a wider perspective of change was lost and peasant action sadly reduced to a dynamics of bargaining with the state for what were ultimately only minor material benefits. One CEB leader explained his view in a slightly different color:

> **Zé Ligeiro:** We are all in the association. I, for example, belong to the association but only as a means to serve us to get those things we didn't have and not to make us forget the community....I think we can't leave the community because it's the path of liberation. Now, if the person only cares for living the moment, for getting immediate results, then that's the project (Projeto Nordeste). But we also need to build a path for the next life.
> **Miriam:** And what's the path of liberation, Zé?
> **Zé:** From our readings of the Bible I understand that the path of liberation...that to be liberated, we shouldn't look at things to criticize, we shouldn't care about hunger, sickness....That is, we should care for all these things here on earth, but we can't forget the path that we

want for our soul, right? Because that's the last path for us, the end of our lives. While we're here on earth we may eat or starve or study, that's all fine, but we can't forget that day of the end of our life, 'cause that's gonna be forever. It's really a death not to have a right to come back to the world. So I think the community is for these things, with my little understanding that's what I think. 'Cause at first nobody ever saw…who was it that saw a poor fellow in his mate's house reading the Bible? I'll tell you the truth the first time I saw people reading the Bible was here, in this region here. There where I come from I never saw it. I saw the Bible but in the hands of the *crentes* (Protestants), but we never really took part in their things. I don't know if it's the *crente* that's right, or if it's I who am right, or if it's the priest, but I think that each should follow his own path, free of projects, because I don't think projects are a path of liberation. The project is a path of deceit, of deceiving the poor.

Zé Ligeiro was an active CEB leader who remained faithful to the community as it was facing a serious threat of dissolution. His general assessment of the association was not much different from that of the priest: it was an impediment for the free organization of the poor, a clear deviation from the true path of liberation. But though aware of the negative effects of the development program, he was also acutely aware of the impossibility of refusing its short term benefits. In the everyday lives of local peasants being poor was also being in no position to refuse any kind of financial aid. This was a main source of disagreement between the pastoral agents and peasants; in fact the deepening of the divergences in respect to the association forced a certain redefinition of the CEBs: from inclusive communities of the poor they came to be perceived as exclusive groups of Church people.

In his defense of the CEBs, Zé Ligeiro reveals yet another difference between the progressive clergy and its lay followers. Like the clergy, Zé speaks of liberation but in his own version it is less the political construction of God's Kingdom on earth than religious attention to the path of the soul. Not Liberation Theology but Popular Catholicism is the central reference in Zé's discourse. Religion concerns itself with the soul; it stresses the finite and thus relative character of our earthly existence, and prepares us for the life that truly matters. Insofar as it places undue emphasis on the material demands of this worldly life and leads away from liberation, the association is nothing but deceit. Insofar as they turn to the soul, all religions are inherently good and man is in no position to judge between them. Catholicism (lay and clerical) and Protestantism are but variations within the path that leads to salvation. CEB

Catholics in particular share with the *crentes* the quotidian practice of reading the Bible. Before the CEBs, Zé notes, the Bible was associated exclusively with the few *crentes* that were then found in the region.

There are actually important elements that draw the CEBs close to Protestant tradition. Like historical Protestantism, CEBs were directly committed to the rationalization of religious practice, turning away from ritualism and emphasizing the study and interpretation of the Bible by the laity. CEBs were also critical of the model of negotiation that presided relations between laity and clergy within the Catholic Church and which, on yet another plane, organized exchanges between humans and saints. Though the initial radicalism of the progressive clergy with regard to the conservative elements of Catholicism was later replaced by a more tolerant view based on an attitude of respect for popular religion, CEB intellectuals sought to substitute a militant approach to faith—centered on the theme of constructing God's Kingdom on earth—for the traditional logic of the vow. This meant minimizing the role of intermediaries and moving from a circuit of discontinuous relations with representatives of the sacred toward the establishment of enduring bonds with God. In this respect, however, the solution worked out by the CEBs was substantially different from that of historical Protestantism: not individual religious qualification but an ethics of brotherhood defined the space of God's people. In the logic of the CEBs the poor were the natural carriers of this ethics, and in its development lay their power to subvert a situation based on the selfishness and greed of a few.

The *crentes* who established themselves in the district of Redenção were not historical Protestants but Pentecostals. In the late 1980s there was only a small congregation of the Assembly of God. Its temple was located in town and it drew its reduced membership from an incipient middle sector of merchants, shop owners, teachers. There were practically no Pentecostals in the rural neighborhoods. During the 1990s nine other congregations were established in town and there was a marked increase in the number of followers. Among the groups with a larger number of adepts were the Congregação Cristã do Brasil (Christian Congregation of Brazil) and the Igreja Deus é Amor (God is Love Church).[6] Despite an initial attempt the neo-Pentecostal Igreja Universal had not succeeded

---

6. The Congregação Cristã do Brasil was the country's first Pentecostal church founded in 1910. According to Freston (1994) it represented, along with the Assembly of God, a more traditional Pentecostalism, which, along with an emphasis on a personal experience of the Holy Spirit, also established rigid patterns of moral conduct among adepts. Freston sees the Igreja Pentecostal Deus é Amor, founded in 1962, as part of a second wave of Pentecostal growth in the country. It launched an open warfare against Afro-Brazilian religions and greatly emphasized healing. Differently from the neo-Pentecostalism of the 1970s and

in establishing a congregation in the district. The Pentecostal boom coincided with important socio-economic and political changes taking place in the district. Nova Redenção had been promoted a municipal center, politically emancipated from the city of Andaraí. This contributed not only to an intensification of local political activities, but also to the implementation of services that were formerly lacking in town and the consolidation of a small urban middle class sector. On the other hand the decline of castor oil production and the growing pauperization of peasant families forced an increasing number of men to engage in temporary labor in the region's agro-industrial complexes. This often meant traveling great distances and spending several months away from home. Many peasant families moved to town where at least water was available, swelling the numbers of the urban poor. This relatively new impoverished urban sector was especially attracted to the Pentecostal message.

In contrast with both the jarê and the CEBs, Pentecostal churches were predominantly urban. The visibility afforded by a location in the city both enhanced the glory of God and the power of the church to represent His work. From this space of visibility Pentecostals launched an open attack against the jarê, associating it to a past of ignorance and deceit, and announcing a future of clarity (and prosperity) reserved for those who sided with the Lord. Whereas jarê-goers had always preferred to keep to themselves their involvement with caboclos, Pentecostals openly expressed their religious affiliation.

Pentecostalism rejected the collective project of the CEBs, and re-established the logic of negotiation so common to popular Catholicism and to the jarê. Differently from Catholicism, however, crentes appeal not to intermediaries but to God himself. In doing so they seek to completely abolish the ambiguity that pervades relations with the tricky and playful caboclos. Permanently engaged in exchanges with God their victory is affirmed to be certain. This view is explicitly articulated in healing, which is a central element in Pentecostal practice.

Pentecostalism frames healing as the re-enactment of a struggle between good and evil, a struggle that has already been fought and won in the otherworld. In every new instance, victory over affliction is dependent on the sufferer's efforts to secure an alliance with God. In the church these efforts are weaved into practices that, while aimed to reinforce and renew the person's own choice for God, are also designed to promote visibility: to uncover, show and expose both evil and grace. Three sets of practices are particularly relevant for the understanding of healing: exorcisms, revelations, and the bap-

---

1980s, however, it adhered to a very strict moral code, placing high demands among followers. It is worth noting that in most present day Pentecostal churches one finds not rigid differences but rather distinct combinations between these styles of practice.

tism of fire. In the first *caboclos* are publicly expelled from the bodies of the faithful during healing sessions, called upon by pastors and compelled to reveal the name under which they conceal their devilish nature. In the second it is the personal problems and secret faults of adepts that are unveiled, publicly exposed to the congregation in the form of divinely inspired revelations. Usually voiced by church members with recognized authority in the group, revelations are presented through enunciations of the type "there's someone here that…" followed by some specification of the problem and a request that the person to whom it is directed step forward and show herself to receive God's blessing. Healing emerges from the conjunction of public confession and acceptance of grace. Finally the third set of practices is geared toward producing the experience of the Holy Spirit in the bodies of adepts through intense prayer. In church services this experience occurs during long prayer sessions in which individual prayers are pronounced out loud by adepts and gradually dissolved into indistinct sound. As prayers intensify some speak in tongues, others cry, visibly moved. There are those among them that sway their bodies to and fro, bounce, jump, and shake all over, in movements and gestures that are reminiscent of possession by the *caboclos*. They have been filled by the Holy Spirit, transformed into a dwelling of sacred power. Healing is thought to result directly from this experience of empowerment. In fact as adepts liberate their bodies from vice and dedicate more and more to prayer, it may come to them as a gift that does not require the mediation of a third party and that is no longer exclusively bound to church ritual.

So if the CEBs approached healing as a collective issue, related to a broader context of poverty whose solution demanded joint action, Pentecostal churches treated it as a question of producing and maintaining personal transformation. This certainly brought them close to their Afro-Brazilian opponents. However, despite similarities with the jarê, Pentecostalism also introduced important changes in the practice of healing, all of which relate to its underlying strategy of announcing and making visible the transformation effected on the bodies and lives of adepts. I would like to single out two of these changes. The first relates to the maintenance of the state of security and protection brought about by healing. In both jarê and Pentecostalism this goal required some measure of body discipline. But whereas the discipline followed by jarê goers (as dictated in the *resguardo*) centers almost exclusively on the avoidance of certain foods, that is, on practices that remain largely unnoticed by outsiders; the discipline of *crentes* is explicitly directed toward making noticeable their singular state: from dress, to posture, to behavior everything about the *crente* must stand as a sign of transformation.

The second change introduced by the churches has to do with the internal structure of healing. As we noted above, the jarê constructs healing through the articulation of *revista* and *trabalho,* in such a way that the public resolution of affliction in ritual follows the private exploration of causes in the encounter between healer and patient. Local Pentecostal churches, by contrast, condense these distinct moments in such ritual sequences as exorcism, revelation and the baptism of fire. No longer developed in the context of a private encounter, the explanations which are offered to affliction become less personal, more generic. There is a loss of specificity and detail in favor of public visibility; emphasis on the dramatic resolution of affliction takes the place of the jarê's minute search for origins in particular events and relationships of the past.

In a way the Pentecostals churches that established themselves in the district proved better equipped than CEBs and jarê to adjust to a context of urban growth, increasing disarticulation of local peasant agriculture—indeed, of the local peasantry—and growing pauperization. Keeping an official distance from politics—that is, rejecting the CEBs' clear-cut political stand—Pentecostal churches did not position themselves against negotiation with local political power, and placed no great restriction on possibilities of obtaining short-term advantages in what had become a much more diversified political field. Like the jarê, they addressed individual distress and promoted healing, but associated those elements with the idea that victory was certain for those who allied themselves with God, and made healing directly available to devotees. Many of these features of Pentecostalism have been noted in other comparative analyses of religious alternatives in Brazil (Prandi, 1991; Burdick, 1998). In pointing them out here I am not suggesting that Pentecostalism was the only viable religious response to local modernity or that it has succeeded in neutralizing the force of other existing religious alternatives. It is worth noting that several elements of CEB practice—indeed of CEB Catholicism—were incorporated into the Movimento dos Sem Terra (Movement of the Landless) which, during the '90s, emerged as an important political force in the region, having already promoted two successful land occupations in the municipality of Redenção. And although the number of jarê houses has declined, the jarê and its *caboclos* remain a reference around which the district's peasant population can weave a common identity on the basis of shared historical experience. I believe this reference will still stimulate new articulations in the religious field.

Conclusion

This paper has been an attempt to explore the notion of confluence in the understanding of contexts of religious encounter, first by working out some of the theoretical issues it raises within John Peel's work, and second by presenting a particular instance of confluence, the meeting of religious traditions in the Bahian district of Nova Redenção: the jarê, the Catholicism of CEBs, and Pentecostalism. From the standpoint of the case described here, I would now like to turn once more to the idea of confluence and explore some of its theoretical implications.

The jarê resulted from a complex history of religious encounter. A more recent part of this history involved the spread of the Afro-Brazilian cult outside the traditional mining centers of the Chapada, and its success among a population of migrants recently settled in the region. Establishing themselves close to important historical centers of jarê, peasant healers gradually exchanged the *sessão* for the *couro* (drums). Generating an arena of play through the use of multiple media and democratizing access to the main ritual action, the jarê soon proved more attractive than the *sessão*. Comparing the two attendants and clients emphasized the visibility and beauty of the powers stirred by the drums—in the jarê people see things happen (and become directly involved in action), whereas *curadores* noted that having to control these powers placed greater demands on them as religious leaders—a discourse which affirmed their own power. *Curadores'* strategical move to the jarê also resulted in a creative addition of elements to the cult—images, characters, objects and stories—most of which were taken from the vast pantry of Catholicism. As I tried to show these additions were part of a dynamics of dialogue, neither an indication of loss of tradition (as some sort of compensation for this loss) nor simply a motivated reinvention of tradition. Indeed as ability for dialogue, and more particularly as the development of a certain style of dialogue, creativity is certainly a constitutive dimension of every religious encounter, one that can be easily overlooked or misinterpreted when tradition is viewed as some fixed historical content, and which the adoption of an action frame of reference greatly helps clarifying.

But there is still another aspect of confluence that stands out in the study of the jarê. The biography of local healers shows that their gradual shift from *sessão* to jarê as well as the transformations which they brought to Afro-Brazilian cult must be understood against a background of intensive spatial mobility, and as the result of a series of concrete investments in place. Confluence is as much a matter of space as it is of time—or, to put it differently, not only time but also space must be held a problem in the analysis of religious encounters. By this I want to suggest that to fully develop the notion of confluence, as proposed by Peel, one must undertake the project of a spatial history.

At a very general level this idea rests on the understanding that time and space are always intimately connected in our experience of place: the passage of time is lived also as change in / of place and places not only "mark" time but are themselves discovered and explored through movement (which is at once spatial and temporal). Places, writes Casey, have an "eventmental" character (1996: 38), they co-locate time and space. This idea has important implications for the study of religion and more particularly for the study of religious encounters.

Embedded in every religion's major narratives is a particular mode of framing relations between past, present and future. In his study of the history of Christianity in Yorubaland, for instance, Peel (2000) notes that whereas the narratives presented by missionaries were essentially stories of redemption, that stressed the liberating power of an otherworldly future, the religious narratives of the Yoruba focused on a power whose source lay in the past, and whose appropriation, for this-worldly success, was a recovery of origins. Whereas the first were theological, the second were archaeological. When we move from worldviews to religious organization and practice we find that these temporal frameworks are always closely knit to patterns of relating to place. In fact more than simply observing that place serves as an important marker of time, we learn that the spatial project of a religion, the particular spatial arrangements it promotes are also ways by which it makes room for certain modes of presentation and disclosure of past, present and future. Let me exemplify this by reference to the ethnographic material I presented here.

The peripheral location of the jarê affirms both the cult's grounding on the power of wild and untamed spirits and its identification with the local peasantry whose own history of migration and search for available land established enduring links with the bush. The play of *caboclos* in the jarê recreates peasant history as a history of Indians and Africans set in the fringes of rural society. Like the past which they evoke, *caboclos* are essentially ambiguous spirits, at once foreign and native, distant and near. Their presence in ritual opens up a field of experimentation in the present, a field in which jarê goers can themselves "play" with different possibilities of being in place. The power that stems from this play of people and spirits can always be channeled towards healing. But it remains largely unavailable to outsiders, like peasant themselves, hidden from dominant society.

The ecclesial base communities that were formed in the district promoted a radical re-centering of peripherality—like *terreiros*, CEBs were all located in the rural neighborhoods. Differently from the jarê, however, the spatial strategy of the CEBs was part of an explicit project of redefining wider society from the periphery. This relates directly to the way salvation was interpreted within the community. CEB members still understood salvation through the general logic of Catholicism, as dependent on the renunciation of immediate this-worldly benefits in favor of an otherworldly goal—participation in the kingdom of God. But in the CEBs the kingdom of God was thought to be anticipated in place—the periphery, where an ethics of brotherhood was already being put to practice by the poor—and to require, for its advent, concrete investments in place—the transformation of society according to this ethics. If place was a source of healing in the jarê, in the base communities it was a focus for redemption. Whereas in the jarê the healing power of place related to peasants' culturally plural and historically specific experience, in the CEBs the redemptory power of place referred to their generic experience of poverty. Agency in the CEBs was thus essentially collective agency, a "we" that had to be both recovered from place and discovered as potency for the transformation of place.

To Pentecostals the kingdom of God has no location in the present—its effects can be experimented concretely in the lives and bodies of the faithful (and must be publicly shown) but belonging to a remote otherworldly future it cannot be recreated in place. From the perspective of *crentes* every person is faced with a choice between two conflicting and irreconcilable paths; the true Christian has chosen the path of light. This choice requires moving away from the past that is held to be firmly rooted in place. To be in the world but not of the world—as the *crentes* frequently describe their existential condition—is an attempt to break away from surrounding place and radically engage with the sacred. In rejecting the past however, Pentecostals seek less to reconstruct their polluted entourage according to a set of moral principles than to multiply the signs of God's power; this "spatial strategy" is to exhibit power rather than impose order, make visible rather than actively transform. Thus the significance of a temple in town—the periphery cannot provide the visibility necessary to affirm God's favor. Faced with the unremitting presence of suffering and sin *crentes* exhibit not only the temple as a marker of distance (and difference), but their bodies. Always somewhat displaced or in tension with the places where worldly past is established, the body in Pentecostalism becomes itself a focus for place. It is visible as a product of the disciplined efforts of Christians to break away from the past. It is noticeable also as a body-subject that savors the benefits of an alliance with God, a place where these benefits accumulate and through which they can be made accessible to others. Finally it is experienced as vase or dwelling for the Holy Spirit, periodically loosened and liberated from worldly constraints, prepared to be reconstructed according to divine rule.

Pushed aside as a matter of secondary concern in the CEBs, the individual body thus reappears in local Pentecostal churches as an object of continuous investment. This certainly brings Pentecostalism close to the jarê. With the body come also the *caboclos*. They are granted an important place in some of the local churches, object of explicit attention in exorcisms. But they also resurge in a less overt form and, as a set of historically constituted embodied dispositions toward sacred, pervade also the experience of the Holy Spirit. It is worth noting, in passing, that the embodied experiences promoted within religious contexts are certainly a field where dialogue and interpenetration between religious forms is made possible and takes place, one that deserves more attention in studies of confluence. In looking at members' experiences of the Holy Spirit we find that, despite its explicit denial of the past, Pentecostal practice is itself founded on reacquisition: the encompassing power of the Spirit seems to originate precisely in the recovery and reframing of sensuous experiences derived from other domains of practice, among which figure undoubtedly relations with *caboclos*.

So, to conclude, I would like to point to yet another meaning of confluence which Pentecostal experience highlights: confluence is also a *place* where past, present and future meet. While new to many local contexts, and very much "modern" in its underlying ethos, Pentecostalism also connects deeply with many traditional modes of religiosity in its emphasis on immanence, this-worldly concerns and empowerment (cf. Peel, 2003). In dealing with the growth and success of Pentecostal churches, analysis can always move between two opposing alternatives. It may emphasize the explanatory force of the past and conclude that, in the end, it is tradition that determines the new modes of religion that will succeed in local contexts or, alternatively, it may argue that it is rather the demands of the future—embodied in the growing effects of globalization in local contexts—that determine whether and how tradition will be recovered. But, taken as elements in a causal chain, neither the past nor the future fully explain behavior: the past provides the framework for the future, but expectations regarding the future also provide the guidelines for an indefinite search and renewed exploration of the past. As Merleau-Ponty (1970) notes, there is a continuous movement by us toward the past and of the reanimated past toward us. Peel's work suggests that, in order to capture this movement, anthropology might well return to Weber's concern with articulating history and culture through the mediation of social action. This means also exploring the ways by which the practice of religious agents and their followers works through possibilities available from the past, lending it sense or directionality, while at the same time infusing the future with some sense of familiarity and return. Anthropology certainly has much to contribute to understanding how past and future, the local and the global, tradition and modernity "fold" upon each other in the social experience of so many groups and societies, provided that it in its own narrative, it keeps a productive balance—or tension—between the distinct temporal and spatial frames at play in confluence.

References

Bastide, Roger (1960). *As Religiões Africanas no Brasil*. São Paulo: Livraria Pioneira Editora.

Burdick, John (1998). *Procurando Deus no Brasil*. Rio de Janeiro: Mauad.

Casey, Edward (1996). How to Get from Space to Place in a Fairly Short Stretch of Time. In Steven Feld and Keith Basso (eds.), *Senses of Place*. Santa Fe: School of America Research Press.

Fernandes, Rubem C. (1982). *Os cavaleiros de Bom Jesus: uma introdução às religiões populares*. São Paulo: Brasiliense, 1982..

Freston, Paul (1994). Breve histórico do pentecostalismo brasileiro. In: *Nem Anjos nem demônios: interpretações sociológicas do pentecostalismo*. Rio de Janeiro: Vozes.

Gadamer, Hans G. (1989) *Truth and Method*. New York: Continuum.

Krischke, Paul and Mainwaring, Scott (eds). (1986). *A Igreja das Bases em Tempo de Transição (1974–1985)*. Porto Alegre: L&PM.

Merleau-Ponty, Maurice (1973). *Adventures of the Dialectic*. Evanston: Northwestern University Press.

Merleau-Ponty, Maurice (1970). Institution in Personal and Public History. In *Themes from the Lectures at the College de France, 1952–1960*. Evanston: Northwestern University Press.

Peel, John D.Y. (2003). Transitions, Transvaluation, Traditions: Some Weberian Themes for the Anthropology of Religion. The Roy A. Rappaport Distinguished Lecture in the Anthropology of Religion. Meeting of the Society for the Anthropology of Religion, Providence, Rhode Island.

——— (2000). *Religious Encounter and the Making of the Yoruba*. Bloomington: Indiana University Press.

——— (1987). The Cultural Work of Yoruba Ethnogenesis. In Tonkin, E., M. McDonald and M. Chapman, (eds.), History and Ethnicity (London, 1987), 198–215.

Prandi, Reginaldo (1991). *Os Candomblés de São Paulo*. São Paulo, Hucitec.

Rabelo, Miriam C.M. (1990). Play and struggle: dimensions of the religious experience of peasants in Nova Redenção, Bahia. Ph.D. dissertation, University of Liverpool, UK.

Senna, Ronaldo (1984). Manifestações religiosas na Chapada Diamantina. Doctoral Dissertation, Universidade de São Paulo, Brazil.

Part E
Christianity and Knowledge Without Borders

CHAPTER 17

Managing Christian-Muslim Relations in Africa

Matthew Hassan Kukah

When the cold war ended in 1989, the United States was convinced that it had achieved a moral and an ideological victory over the Soviet Union. It considered that its moral obligation was to husband the rest of the world along the path of western, liberal democracy nudged on by the invisible hand of the market. World expectation and attention really focused along those lines. The United States took it upon itself to gather together the debris of the dreams of the peoples of the former Soviet Union ("the Evil Empire") after it imploded. Along with other European powers, the United States played a very significant role in helping the newly independent countries to democratize and open up their markets, believing that the world was now going to march to the same drumbeat.

However, as it turned out, most of the prognostications have been awfully wrong. Our hopes that we were standing at the portals of the "brave new world" of liberal democracy where all would live in freedom and pursue market economic dreams soon came crashing as ethnic wars broke out in the Balkans. The process of putting life back to these countries consumed the energies of the United States and its European allies right into the end of the millennium. The world had barely welcomed in the new millennium when it was awakened by what was by far the worst single event in recent times: September 11, 2001. The world woke up to the news that the main perpetrator of this evil was one Osama bin Laden. The said Osama bin Laden, it would later be revealed, had enjoyed a cosy relationship with the US Central Intelligence Agency (CIA) in the days of the war against the Soviet Union in Afghanistan. We were further told that bin Laden was the leader of a terrorist network known as al-Qaeda and that they were determined to take the war to the United States of America on their own soil. The world would not be the same again.

Earlier, on the African continent, a stunned world had watched in disbelief as Mr. Nelson Mandela, hitherto, the world's most prominent prisoner, walked out of the gates of prison to freedom on February 11, 1990. These images were Africa's own treasured mementos, not unlike those from the fallen Berlin Wall. Four years later, the miracle found even greater expression with the freed prisoner becoming the leader of a country which had hitherto run the world's most vilified system of oppression, apartheid. An ecstatic Archbishop Desmond Tutu, the foremost moral opponent of apartheid, declared his people of South Africa the "Rainbow People of God!" Many optimists now believed that Africa at last had found its soul just in time to enable the continent to negotiate the final turn into the new millennium. Then Rwanda came as a rude shock to the continent in particular and the world in general. Overnight, with machetes, knives, bows, arrows, and other local weapons, the Hutu allegedly slaughtered approximately 800,000 of their fellow Tutsi countrymen and women. Despite being a poor reflection of the reality, the world watched this implosion with disbelief, but saw it as the boiling over of the poisoned pot of ethnicity. So, we might ask, why does the world continue to live in such cyclical phases? Why does the bad news appear so quickly to drive out the good news? We are still unable to capture the essence of what is going on because, as Amartya Sen (1998 winner of the Nobel Prize for Economics) has argued: "Modern conflicts that call for analysis in terms of contemporary events and machinations are then interpreted as ancient feuds, real or imagined, that place today's players in pre-ordained roles in an allegedly ancestral play."[1]

Post-September 11 has cast the world in a new shape altogether and everyone is asking, what exactly is happening? Is it a "clash of civilisations" or a clash of cultural expectations and interpretations of civilizations? If either be so, which or whose civilization would we be talking about? Either way, George Bush has since cast the conflict in a moral tone as one between "Hell's Devils" and "Heaven's Angels." Only recently, General Boykin, a senior military officer and right wing Pentecostal Christian extended this Manichean paradigm of the conflict when he stated that he believed "his Jesus" is certain to conquer "Satan, the Muslim god." What is most important is that, either way, Africa

---

1. Amatya Sen, "Civilisational Imprisonments: How to Misunderstand Everybody Else in the World," *The New Republic.* June 10, 2002, p. 28.

now finds itself sucked into a war that it did not really start and has a very limited role to play in. Just as it was before and after colonialism, Africa has found itself caught in the power play of western hegemonies as the struggle for contention and control of resources in and outside its own continent intensifies. These interests have always been wrapped in the dubious fig leaf of religion, culture or higher civilization. And, when the west sneezes in the process, Africa and African citizens find themselves conscripted to fight proxy wars that have very little to do with their realities, wars that they mistakenly associate with religion. The result is that in Africa and Asia today, citizens who subscribe to Islam and Christianity are experiencing severe strains and difficulties in their relationships. They are subsequently called upon to "dialogue" and find ways for peaceful coexistence, to borrow the common clichés. It is the struggle for this dialogue that this essay is concerned with. To do this, I will divide the essay into four sections. In Section 1 I will try to place the issues before us in a historical context, attempting to examine the problems of dialogue from an African perspective. In Section 2 I will take on the issues of the strategies and themes for engaging in this dialogue. In Section 3 I will examine these themes against the backdrop of Globalization in the post-September 11 world. Finally, in Section 4 I will summarize the arguments and identify some of key themes that could be incorporated in state policy by way of recommendations.

History, Evangelization and Empire Building

Even in the best of times, history has always been a very contentious subject. Being largely cast as the footprints of glorious knights in moral shining armour, it is not surprising that this view of history has ignored some realities while preoccupying itself with sanctifying those footprints of the conquerors. In the pages of history lie accounts of Africa as "a dark continent," occupied by soulless creatures and savages in dire need of salvation and civilization. Whether as colonialists who conquered lands, kingdoms, empires and subjugated kings, or as missionaries who vanquished and exorcised the devil from the souls of the Africans explains their real motives, they are part of the texture of our various crises and conflicts as a people and in defining our relations with other civilizations. There are still some nagging questions that have refused to go away. I believe that we need to spend more time asking more questions than seeking simple answers to the African condition today. But, I am aware that this is not the essence of this initiative.

I believe that we do not need to rewrite history, but we need to sincerely confront these carefully crafted or distorted accounts of our histories and cultures, accounts that justified colonial excesses, assaults on our cultures that still serve as determinants for unjust economic, social and political relationships. It is these convoluted and distorted views of ourselves, and our willingness to unquestionably internalize these skewed views, that make conflict along ethnic and religious lines part of our daily national lives across Africa. For example, should we not be interested in finding answers to some questions: How dark was the continent of Africa before the coming of both the missionaries and the colonialists? Assuming that this continent was so dark, how did the gold diggers, fortune seekers and soul seekers from Europe and Arabia find their way into the gold and oil fields of Africa? What were the cultural, social and spiritual histories of Africa that preceded European colonialism? What became of those Empires and kingdoms that created their own civilizations well before European states emerged? What was really at stake in Africa? Were Christian missionaries seeking to rescue Africa for Christ or expand the hegemonic frontiers of their home countries as some have contended? What accounted for the intensity of conflict between, for example, Protestant and Catholic missionaries on the one hand or Irish missionaries and British missionaries and colonialists on the other? Indeed, what were the implications of the so-called scramble for Africa and the subsequent partitioning arising from the Berlin Conference of 1885? What were the implications of Africans being parcelled out as subjects of queens and kings of Europe and what were the implications of Catholics being subjects of Protestant queens or Protestants being subjects of queens or kings who claimed to be Christians and custodians of the Catholic faith? And what about Muslims being the subjects of Christian kings and queens whose faith they did not accept? What were the implications of slavery in this relationship?

Historically, Islam preceded Christianity by hundreds of years in some parts of Africa. Before the advent of colonialism, Islam had been the local colonizer in many parts of Africa, though it encountered other civilizations through trade and lived peacefully side by side with local authorities and cultures in such places as the coastal cities of Eastern Africa and Southwestern Nigeria. Unlike Christianity, Islam sometimes used empire building and conquest to spread the frontiers of its faith and thus consolidate faith and power. This is the story of the Sokoto caliphate in what is now Northern Nigeria. Not so with Christianity in many respects. By the time Christianity came to Africa, its appetite for empire had been curtailed by developments in Europe. Thus, Christian missionaries did not seek direct conquests of lands as a means of establishing Christian kingdoms but rather, western kings and queens, seeking empire and wealth, used Christianity as an entry-point but, beyond the diamond and mineral fields, they never sought to establish a kingdom for Christ in Africa in the way of the Muslim caliphate. The end of "Christendom" in parts of Europe had seen the expulsion of religion from the state. Yet, when colonialism reared its head in Africa, Christianity paid the price in many respects. Thanks to a distorted view of history, missionaries were considered "brothers" and "sisters" of the colonialists and were tarred with the same brush, but in some parts of Africa such as Nigeria, the post-colonial state that emerged ensured that British interests were better protected by connivance with the traditional Muslim ruling classes whose feudal systems approximated British royalty. It is necessary to make these points because, even today, the sources of our crises can only be better appreciated against the backdrop of these histories. Indeed, right from the beginning, this contradiction preoccupied the thinking of the first generation of the African literary and political elites.

The late Jomo Kenyatta, one of the first generation of leading Pan Africanists and first President of Kenya, cast this predicament in words that have been told and retold by African scholars. I find them rather apt. In his book, *Facing Mount Kenya*, Jomo Kenyatta, the anthropologist turned politician, told the following story. Known as "The Gentleman of the Jungle," the story went like this: A man built his house. An elephant came and asked if he could find a place to shelter his trunk from the rain. The man conceded, but the elephant went on to eject the man from the house. Commotion ensued and the lion appeared on the scene to find out what was happening. When the lion heard the case, he suggested that a panel be set up to investigate the matter. The panel, made up of the buffalo, rhinoceros, fox, and hyena were called in to listen to the case and make recommendations. The panel decided to take evidence from the man who had been evicted from his house. Unfortunately, in the process of hearing the man's evidence, the animals in the panel decided that it was better to save time so the case was dismissed on the grounds that the man had not confined himself to the facts of the case and there were inconsistencies in his account. The animals retired to the house of the elephant for a meal and also to write their final report and make recommendations. After the meal, they then delivered their judgement to the man: "In our minds, you tried to make a case, but it lacked merit. However, in sympathy, we give you another space to build yourself a new house." Fearing the animals and some repercussion, the man did not appeal but quietly went ahead to put up another building. He had barely finished building when the rhinoceros moved in. The charade about justice and a panel continued with the same judgement offering him a new piece of land. Convinced of the injustice, the man decided that his new house would have to be the last house he would build. This time, he built a grand house that was better than anything he had ever built. No sooner had he finished than, predictably, all the kings of the jungle, lion, elephant, fox, mainly the various members of who sat on the panels regarding his case, moved into the new house. Each wanted the beautiful house for himself. But they soon got involved in a fight as to who would own the house. While they quarrelled and argued inside the house, the man stepped out and set the house on fire, thus burning down all his tormentors, the so-called kings of the jungle! Surveying his burnt house and his oppressors, the man said: "Peace is costly, but it is worth the expense."[2]

The fact here is that to many, these stories of historical injustices are a distraction because the common expression is: "Forget the past and move forward." We are told often that slavery existed in Africa before, but we cannot continue to dwell on the past about which we can do nothing. Colonialism has long ended and Africans should get on with life and not continue to make excuses. We are told to look at the "Asian Tigers" who underwent colonialism, but now have picked themselves up. If only African leaders would be less corrupt, manage their resources well, embrace democracy and open markets, reduce ethnic and religious wars and focus on development, all would be well. With so much religion on the continent, dialogue should be the new catchword, we are told. But, whatever may be the level of our preoccupation with finding peace or using religion as a force of reconciliation, there is an urgent need for us to come to grips with how some very deep historical memories still shape how people see religion, history and politics in a world that has become gradually concerned with power to the exclusion of human welfare.

It is important to note that underlining the crises in the world and in Africa are the issues of the persistence of injustice in resource management, control, allocation and distribution. Both victims of injustice and the perpetrators of injustice are appealing to the same divine elements as a basis for their claims. There is very little difference in terms of conviction and divine claims between Osama bin Laden and George Bush. Their moral claims to leading a divine cavalry to rout out evil in the world are basically the same as is their rhetoric. Today, the world has become far more dangerous. And despite Africa having nothing directly to do with the quarrels between Bush and the United States on the one hand and oil rich Iraq on the other, Africa has suffered severe col-

---

2. Quoted in Chinua Achebe, *Home and Exile* (Oxford University Press, 2001) pp. 65–7.

lateral damage since the war started. The result is that dialogue between Islam and Christianity has become much more difficult now than it ever was before.

Africa has now become caught up in the war against terrorism spearheaded by the US. But occasionally, by some Freudian slip, we get to know the reasons for this war. From George Bush claiming that "Saddam Hussein tried to kill my father," Halliburton's scandalous mega-dollar contracts on the oil fields of Iraq to the refusal of the US to allow such "moral rebels" like the Russians or the French a piece of the action in the multi-billion dollar reconstruction contracts of Iraq, we now know that the war against terrorism has more than one script. Yet, despite not being in the line of fire, African lives have been lost from Kenya to Nigeria with relations between Christians and Muslims coming under severe strain. The volatility of these relations is better captured in the hundreds of lives that were lost in the Nigerian Muslim city of Kano when an argument over an Osama bin Laden poster led to a fracas. So, while the US continues with its mission of empire building and the pursuit of self-interests, the texture of African life is constantly overstretched. It is within this maze that we are asked to find a way to dialogue between Islam and Christianity in Africa and elsewhere. Against the backdrop of what we have said, and given the moral inconsistencies that becloud America's foreign policies, how might this dialogue be conducted now that we have all been conscripted to fight terrorism? These are some of the difficulties. Yet, we must look carefully for some strands in the wind to make dialogue possible.

Ingredients for Dialogue of Religions

The real issue here is how to answer the how and the why questions of dialogue. Who needs dialogue and why? And, how might this dialogue be conducted? What issues should dialogue be concerned with? It seems to me that, in Africa, dialogue among religions has tended to shy away from the very difficult questions and has preoccupied itself more with attacking the symptoms rather than the cancer of injustice, which is at the heart of the crisis that dialogue has been trying to resolve. In the heat of internal crises, various governments are quick to stampede religious leaders by conjuring up such words and themes as tolerance, peace, harmony, unity, coexistence, and other bland words as magic wands to calm frayed nerves. What is more, dialogue in many African countries has tended to focus on Christian leaders teaming up with Muslim leaders, holding hands and smiling while the cameras click and click around the corridors of the powerful. These pictures are then sent out through the media and they are supposed to send out signals to the effect that if ordinary Christians and Muslims see that their leaders are working together in peace and harmony, they would follow suit. These cycles of dialogue have been going on in Nigeria for many years and yet, as it is clear, the violence has not relented. If anything, in the last few years, religiously induced violence has claimed thousands of lives in the country. Sadly, neither the religious leaders themselves nor those whose policies generate tension and violence seem prepared to face the real issues of why violence persists in African societies. By and large, in almost all circumstances, instances of so called violence between Christians and Muslims have always been in reaction to certain government policies undertaken by government largely for its own self-interest. Thus, when religious leaders are shown to be in a cosy relationship with a government that ordinary citizens do not trust, they are merely compounding the issues. Two examples will serve here.

Immediately after Mr. Frederick Chiluba became president of Zambia, he declared Zambia a "Christian state." This generated curious responses from Nigeria. On the surface, many of my friends and colleagues were surprised when I insisted that this was a very dangerous gamble. A friend of mine, obviously scandalized by my lack of enthusiasm, praised Chiluba, arguing that, after all, Muslims have never had qualms with doing the same thing! Well, I said to him, if we object to Muslim politicians doing this in principle, surely, Christian politicians doing the same thing should not make (what is wrong) right simply because they claim to be Christians. I sensed that Chiluba was merely clutching at a straw and hoping to extend his political mileage. Sadly, three years ago, and after serving two terms as president under very dubious circumstances, Chiluba's political career ended in humiliation unbecoming of a Christian presiding over a Christian state. Chiluba has fought a very bitter and scandalous divorce, and is standing trial for stealing state resources.

Similarly, Nigeria has had its fair share of opportunistic decisions by politicians. The issue of whether or not it is right for a president, governor or any senior government official or politician to have a chapel built in the seat of government has generated controversy. I personally do not believe it is necessary because it has serious implications for the future given that all occupants of the place are birds of passage and the structure needs to be insulated from the vagaries of politics and other social norms. My position is that such a structure should be religion neutral to command loyalty of all citizens across the religious divide. The reactions of Christians in Nigeria have been, "it is our turn." After all, they argue, the Muslims have built mosques in the same premises and the president is a believer. However, with Freemasons and Ifa worshippers now in prominent positions of power in Nigeria and actively in government, we can only await what structures will be erected next in the State

House in future. To my mind, it is these opportunistic and haphazard policies that deepen tensions between believers and finally generate anxieties and tensions between Christians and Muslims. Imagine what will happen when a Muslim president decides he needs a different mosque because his predecessor belongs to a different Muslim faction (*Darika*) or a Protestant president who decides that all the Catholic statutes and images have to be pulled down because Catholics worship Mary. These are some of the possible problems which those blinded by power do not see now.

Politicians were elected to deliver goods and services to their citizens. Despite this bogus spirituality across the land in many African countries, elections are rigged and citizens lose a sense of moral direction, corruption persists and social chaos looms, providing ingredients for violence by hungry citizens (which will then be called a crisis between Christians and Muslims). Over the years, religious violence in Nigeria has been generated not by Christians and Muslims suddenly fighting over the right to build mosques, churches, or worship. On the contrary, these tensions have been generated as a result of jealousies nursed by the feelings that governments are making decisions that favor one religious group against the other. The decision to admit Nigeria into the Organization of the Islamic Conference (OIC) in 1986, threw Nigeria into a crisis that lingered for nearly ten years. The decision to set up a Muslim Pilgrims Board for Muslims began in the former northern region and was contested by non-Muslim bureaucrats when it became a national initiative. So, today, Nigerian Christians have a Christian Pilgrims Board and, all things considered, one aspect of the dialogue has been resolved. Today, Nigeria is perhaps the only country that is wasting millions of dollars in a venture that ordinarily has nothing to do with the government. I do not know of any other country that spends the resources that Nigeria spends on these pilgrimages. But, having tasted the benefits of the patronage that comes from these initiatives, the governments and politicians have held onto the pilgrimages as a means of garnering support for political ends. While all this goes on, the business of governance, delivery of services, ensuring justice and the rule of law, and clarifying the moral options for governance become abandoned as religious leaders find themselves jostling for positions and patronage from the governments it is supposed to guide. In the year 2000, the Federal Government of Nigeria set up what it called the National Reconciliation Committee (NAREC) made up of a gathering of both Christians and Muslim leaders. They have had very little effect in dealing with such issues in Nigeria as the Sharia crisis. Both sides were unable to rise beyond the confines of their religious barricades in the heat of the crisis. The result is that, except for the federal government, very little is known about what that body is doing. But, while all this goes on, suffering and poverty persist in the land.

During these national self-induced crises, religious leaders are often asked to find suitable Biblical or Koranic injunctions that speak about peace, unity, harmony, or tolerance. Sometimes, these leaders preoccupy themselves with explaining the substance of their belief systems to one another in the name of dialogue. The idea here is to create the impression that the violence that societies experience can be averted if only Muslims come to a greater understanding and appreciation of what Christians believe in or vice versa. The result again is that more and more literature is generated with Christians and Muslims believing that they are the ones who are not living according to the dictates of their faiths. But the process of generating this literature is itself problematic. For example, who writes the material for this education? Will Christians be expected to water down what they believe regarding Jesus Christ as son of god, since Muslims are most offended by what they consider to be the heretical claim that God had a son? Or will Muslims be expected to come round to appreciating the fact that Jesus was not just one among a chain of prophets but the subject of prophesy? The reality is that in my personal experience, most people who have tried this line of dialogue find it an exercise in futility because, in the end, it opens up new wounds rather than heal. But more importantly, is it really the case that understanding one another's faith is enough condition for ensuring tolerance among believers? On a secular plane, can we argue that a condition for peaceful business competition within car manufacturing companies for example, will be better guaranteed if Ford learns more about the central beliefs and strategies of Toyota company? Only stringent regulations can regulate their conduct. It is the absence of these regulations that adds to the confusion that we face so constantly.

I have made these points not because I am cynical about dialogue or do not believe in it. However, it does seem to me that in many respects we run the risk of barking up the wrong tree in the name of dialogue. In the developing countries of Africa there is need to first of all understand the circumstances that have led to the crises that dialogue has always tried to resolve. If we do this, we shall then be compelled to address the deeper historical questions outside the realm of mere belief systems held by Christians and Muslims. For example, let us take the two most notorious African countries where tensions between Christians and Muslims have persisted with intensity, namely, Nigeria and the Sudan. Both countries are former British colonies. In both cases, the British consciously created a North-South dichotomy based on religious and educational differences. In both cases, the South ended up with a western educated elite trained by Christian missionaries. But, in both cases, the British consciously schemed and plotted to hand power over to the Northern Muslim elites rather than the so-called Christians in the South. In both cases, the Muslim ruling classes had fought the British, but when defeated, they had tactically aligned with the British to guarantee the survival of their interests and religion. Yet, deep down, they had treated the British with some level of contempt as infidels. In both cases, the British erected walls of separation that sought to protect Islam from incursion by Christian missionaries. Whatever may have been the good intentions, the reality is that post-colonial politics has been shaped by the prejudices that were nurtured on both sides over these walls of separation. Time and politics have not successfully bridged these walls. Instead, the political elites on both sides have found solace and comfort in them in moments of political crisis. The so-called labels of the Muslim-North and the Christian/Animist South, popularized by the British, have become the defining identities of citizens from both sides till today. They define relational perceptions of differences and prejudices. These inherently conflicting cleavages account for the tensions that both Christians and Muslims experience as they continue to see those labels as a basis for justifying the chasm in power and social relations, with each seeing the other in negative terms. Against this background therefore, it is to my mind rather futile for us to continue to speak as if we can conjure up unity when these problems have not been resolved or appreciated. British colonialism lasted for well over sixty years in both countries, and yet today, the British expect ill-equipped African states to resolve tensions, crises and walls of prejudices that they built over these years. I am therefore making the case that indeed there is need for us to rethink what we have always referred to as "religious crises" in former colonies, whether they are Nigeria, Sudan, Uganda or Rwanda. This is because in the main, these crises are largely the crises generated by the structural weakness and inefficiency inherent in the post-colonial state. In some cases, the colonial state exacerbated tensions along religious lines as we have indicated above, in other cases even where there were ethnic homogeneity as in Rwanda, the colonial state manufactured ethnic differences to sustain its divide and rule strategies. These are the stark conditions in which we are being stampeded with demands to engage in dialogue. But, my argument is that although dialogue is an imperative and therefore not impossible, there is need for us to rethink our histories and experiences not as Muslims or Christians, but primarily as citizens who were collectively violated and need to regain our lost heritage as a people. I therefore propose a two-pronged approach.

First of all, I propose a dialogue between the state and its citizens; and here, I speak of the state as an agent for the delivery of services and good governance to its citizens. Historically, both the colonial and the post-colonial states failed to generate popular support among citizens due to the absence of a platform of legitimacy. The lack of infrastructure and institutions to resolve some of the lingering contradictions of the colonial state such as the monopoly of power by tiny elites along ethnic or religious lines, lack of transparency and accountability, lack of popular participation and the constant harassment of citizens all have meant that in the main, the state now as then has still not been able to generate the loyalty and support of its citizens. The colonial state was considered oppressive because of people's experiences with hard labor, unjust taxation and racism. In both Sudan and Nigeria, the prolonged periods of military rule (again largely by Northern Muslim military officers) tended to heighten and deepen tensions and also generate resentment between Christians and Muslims. On the surface, Christians in both countries continuously felt marginalized, resented the state and often charged it with pursuing pro-Islamic agendas such as the sponsorship of pilgrimages or the building of mosques for Muslims with state resources. But, as we have tried to argue, in the final analysis, these politicians are interested in the capture and control of power and not religion whether it be Christianity or Islam. Here, the issues of good governance and the state's seeming lack of capacity to fight corruption are beyond the purview of dialogue since the issues can only be resolved if a state lives by the rule of law. It is therefore futile to think that we can resolve issues of injustice, oppression and corruption by merely encouraging Christians and Muslims leaders to engage in dialogue. Religion cannot be a force of stability in an unstable state. What is more, those ordinary Muslims and Christians who genuinely feel strongly and deeply convinced about their religious values are the first to detect the moral waywardness of leaders who preach one thing and do another. This was the experience of ordinary decent Muslims in Sudan or Nigeria in the heat of the Sharia crises in both states. This is what triggers off the moral revulsion that leads some believers to take to the path of violence as a way of expressing righteous indignation against those of their own faith who merely seek to manipulate the religions!

Thus, the only condition around which dialogue can become a very fruitful exercise is in an environment in which the state takes its sovereignty seriously and begins to address, very coherently, the issues of the welfare of its citizens. It is citizenship anchored on the rule of law and other supporting institutions that offers the only viable platform for meaningful dialogue. It is the absence of these institutions that has put so much pressure on the religious bodies to mediate in conflicts which the state has generated but which the religious bodies have no mechanisms (such as courts or police) to address.

When a state establishes the basis for citizenship, its police and the courts can then mediate in conflict. It is against this background that citizens can be brought to justice not as Christians or Muslims but as Sudanese, Nigerians, South Africans, Liberians, and so on who have infringed upon the law. After all, when anyone commits a crime in Europe or America, they face the consequences of the law as citizens, not as Muslims or Christians. It is this lack of an institutional platform erected by a legitimate state that makes it possible for criminals who should be prosecuted for crimes of murder or arson to challenge the state on the grounds that they are being persecuted because they are Christians or Muslims. In his comments on this, Taker Amir concludes that, "Co-citizenship is the encounter of persons as equal actors in society and polity who, while influenced by culture and religion and ethnicity, cannot be reduced to the roles assigned to them in the name of communal identities, loyalties and perceived interests."[3] In a state of injustice, religion must always continue "asking for trouble" by raising difficult questions for the state to address.

Secondly, there is dialogue that must include a concerted attempt at reexamining the nature of the issues of the moment, namely, how Western interests, right from the period of colonial rule, had nothing to do with the spread of Christianity but the pursuit of secular power, domination and economic opportunities. Indeed, the situation is even worse now that Europe has entered what it calls a post-Christian era as it struggles to ensure its interests and security. Conflicts generated in Africa now are conflicts around minerals and other resources in developing countries. The injustices perpetrated by multinational corporations and their governments on the continent of Africa over the scramble for diamonds, gold, oil, and so on goes beyond what Christians and Muslims can be called upon to resolve. It is important to underscore this point because of the asymmetrical power relations between these weak states and a combination of powerful western interests, which are allied with multinational corporations. Transparency International, the Bonn-based anti corruption organization has now exploded the myth that corruption is a function of weak states in Africa by compiling a Bribe Payers' Index, showing those western countries from where multinational corporations are more prone to give bribes in pursuit of their business in developing countries. The focus of the findings was, "The propensity of companies from 21 leading exporting countries to pay bribes to senior government officials."[4] Resource generation, management and allocation are moral issues and not the function of mere dry laws and human caprice. Unless anchored on the principles that ensure the care and protection of the weak and the common good of all, nations with re-

---

3. Taker Amir, "Issues in Religious Dialogue," www. Islamonline.net.
4. Transparency International Report, 2003: *Explanatory Notes and Comparative Tables.* Spain, Germany, France, USA, Japan were just slightly above the average in the rankings!

sources such as Zaire, Nigeria or Angola will continue to be islands of violence in a sea of massive poverty and squalor.

Religion and Dialogue in a Globalized World

Much attention has been given to the positive dimensions of globalization and it seems that we are all supposed to be celebrating this new dawn of a world that has further shrunk and made any place in the world just a mouse-click away. Those who celebrated globalization created the impression that it was a fallout of the end of the Cold War and that, indeed, its existence, if properly handled, could actually bring us all closer to values of our common humanity. However, if anything, the world is getting increasingly violent and intolerant, while world poverty and inequalities are rising and deepening. There are, therefore, many central questions, which need to engage our minds, such as, What kind of world do we want to live in? What is the future of the United Nations and other international institutions such as the European Union, the World Bank and the International Monetary Fund in relation to this new situation? What are the moral responsibilities of the super powers that continue to define power in naked and material terms without a sense of moral balance? It is clear that contrary to the assumptions that welcomed the end of the Cold War, the new world order of justice and fairness towards all that we much expected has still not yet been born. What is even more threatening are the consequences of the policies of new empire builders and their impact on developing nations. So far, what separates the challenges of today from those of yesterday lies more in the fact that the tunes have changed, but the message is essentially the same.

The project of Western Empire building is couched now in different but perhaps more palatable idioms. In his book, *The Breaking of Nations*, Robert Cooper, a close adviser to British Prime Minister Tony Blair, has come to the conclusion that the world is best understood within the context of premodern, modern, and post-modern societies. But there is very little in the substance of the debate that changes the assumptions of who is on the saddle and who ought to be the horse. The thrust of Mr. Cooper's argument, as I understand him, is that Europe and the US live in post-modern societies and they have a responsibility and duty to, first of all, figure out the threats posed by the pre-modern societies where presumably, life is still in its Hobbsean state being, nasty, brutish and short. With pre-modern states characterized by state failure, chaos and anarchy, Cooper argues that post-modern societies must ensure that pre-modern chaos does not intrude into their space, never mind that this space that is now being well guarded and fortified owes its wealth and continued strength to the extraction of resources from the pre-modern world. After all, as he says, the Roman Empire collapsed not from the threat of superior Empires like the Persian Empire, but from the barbarians.[5] He further argues: "We may not be interested in chaos, but chaos is interested in us. In fact, chaos or at least the crime that lives within it, needs the civilised world and preys upon it. At its worst, in the form of terrorism, chaos can become a serious threat to the whole international order. Terrorism represents the privatisation of war, the premodern with teeth."[6]

Against this background, what should constitute the elements of dialogue at this level? To be sure, there is enough evidence to suggest that, since the role of religion is in severe decline in the West, dialogue within religions with the same Christian traditions are not a viable option in the eyes of this post-modern bug bear. After all, the European Union has at least for now, rejected recognition of any Christian roots in defining its history and identity as was shown over the debates on its Constitution. Christianity is not about to engage in dialogue with paganism, the now dominant religious beliefs that can claim local origins in Europe. There is very little to suggest any urgency in Africa over a quest for dialogue with Oriental religions with their minimal presence. We are left with a new form of Islam which is demonized as fundamentalism, characterized by tolerance and terrorism as the only variants of religion that poses a real threat to world order. Although Africa has suffered collateral damage from America's war with its former collaborators of yesterday, Africa is once again being asked to fight this war in the name of international security.

Clearly, the threat to a new order should be of concern to all citizens of the world. But, do we have a new international community whose principles and policies should be cherished by all and where all are equal? So far, we have the United Nations and the World Court as the only institutions that show our collective commitment to living within some reasonable ground rules. Now that the United States has decided to place its interests and citizens above the principles of the United Nations and the International Criminal Court (ICC), what should other nations do in our collective search for justice and equality? How should Africa and the world deal with the issues of the inequalities and perceived injustices that have spawned the globe and now account for the perpetration of chaos and disorder about which people like Cooper waxes so lyri-

---

5. Robert Cooper, *The Breaking of Nations: Order and Chaos in the 21st Century* (Atlantic Books. London. 2003) p. 70.

6. Cooper, *The Breaking of Nations*, op. cit., p. 77.

cally? So far, Osama bin Laden has sought to rally some troops from some parts of Africa, but it is only in relation to his war with the West and the United States. So, how might Africa fit into this war?

First of all, I believe that there is need to rethink more forcefully, the issues surrounding globalization. There has been more concentration on the economic dimensions of globalization to the exclusion of its impact on our collective humanity. Hence, as they say, although globalization means freedom of movement, this freedom is only free for goods and not for human beings. A clear framework for addressing these issues must include the incorporation of the supremacy of the human person over mere economic ideals. Otherwise, the new world would not be better than the old order of Communism with its command structure which undermined the individual human person in favor of the state. Secondly, there is the attendant problem of immigrants and asylum-seekers in European nations. Many Western nations are reluctant to tackle head-on the challenges posed by the mass movement of human beings across borders. However, there is a need to show the connection between these movements and the international interests that sparked off the internal civil wars leading to these migrations in the first place. From Latin America, Asia, Africa, and the Middle East, the movements of human beings to the United States and Europe are sometimes caused by wars externally driven as part of the fallout of the Cold War, the struggle for domination and control of resources, etc. The reason for the first and second wars against Saddam Hussein's Iraq (1990 and 2003) was oil then and oil now. But, they have set off trends which have spawned the deep crises that lie ahead among religions. Under Saddam Hussein, Christians enjoyed some levels of religious liberty. But a post Saddam Hussein Iraq has now led the same George Bush and his generals who have called themselves "warriors for Christ" to now align themselves with a faction of Islam that is vehemently anti Christian. Who is going to facilitate the dialogue between Christians and Shiites in the new Iraq?

Thirdly, there is the problem of deepening inequalities that have become even more prevalent than they were fifty or so years ago. Of course, one of the advantages of globalization lies in the fact that through the Internet and other sources of instant information despatches such as Cable News Network, CNN give us immediate information. Naturally, citizens from different parts of the world feel they also wish to replicate what they see on these screens in their own countries. Thus, when ambitious citizens see life on the other side, they reason, "If the mountain will not come to the Mohammed, then Mohammed had better go to the Mountain." Thus, the flow of human traffic has to be taken as fallout of globalization. Dialogue should include how best to protect these vulnerable people, many of whom have become victims of human trafficking, the modern day slavery.

Fourthly, there seems to be evidence to suggest that amidst all this, the world feels itself torn between the challenges of "individualism" and the sense of being a "human family." The era of the "war of all against all" may be in retreat, but it depends on how much civil society groups, the human rights community, and the faith-based communities prepare for this fight for human dignity. The contradictions thrown up by trade agreements such as those encapsulated in the World Trade Organisation (WTO) raise many troubling moral questions about justice. The crippling policies of the World Bank and the International Monetary Fund, the Paris Club, and other lending institutions, continue to have negative impact on poor countries. The existence of the World Court is a testimony that the world wishes to create a common ground for the respect of human rights of all citizens of the world. But it does not help that the United States believes that its citizens are above the principles of that court.

Fifthly, there are still more burning issues such as the role of religion in re-defining the place of women in many of our societies in Africa and elsewhere. There is no doubt that in many developing countries in Africa, religion is being used as a tool of legitimating the tyranny under which women live. There is need for religion to redefine and re-echo the teachings of scriptures as regards the equality of God's children and the need for the word of God to trump negative cultural norms.

Sixthly, is the issue of the status of minorities, especially religious minorities. In many countries today, despite being signatories to various statutes and conventions, there are nations where citizens still do not have their rights on grounds that they constitute ethnic, numerical or religious minorities. Again, as in the case of women, there is need for religion to provide a moral basis for a proper appreciation of the fact that the state's primary obligations are to their weakest members of its society. The quest by ordinary Muslims to live under Sharia law has its own good points and in principle should not pose a problem. However, as we have seen in Nigeria, weak states provide a dangerous platform for political demagogues to play with the fires of religion as a means of consolidating their hold on power. The experience of Nigeria with Sharia law has shown that the hypocrisy of so-called Muslim politicians is perhaps far more dangerous a threat to both religious harmony and democracy. The charade that characterised the trials of the two Muslim women, Safiyya and Amina, who were convicted for adultery by lower Sharia Courts sent out mixed signals as to the efficacy and propriety of the application of Sharia Law even within the Muslim community. Unfortunately, during the Sharia crisis, all sides were left more damaged as far as prospects for dialogue were concerned. The unnecessary loss of lives is evidence of what could happen when politicians seek to extend their political mileage through the application of religious idioms.

Summary and Conclusion

In this essay, I have tried to address the issues of dialogue by presenting the problems raised by some of our assumptions about what constitutes Christian-Muslim dialogue and its projected outcomes. I have done this largely in order to move away from the assumptions that dialogue is simply about getting Christian and Muslim leaders to come together so as to ensure that religion becomes a means to achieving peace. This goal may be desirable, but it is an insufficient means for explaining the difficult issues that constantly cause the breakdown of our moral universe by way of open conflict in weak states. I have tried to argue that there is need for us to come to a proper understanding and re-reading of our colonial histories and the negative impact of this legacy on our polities. I argue that the sources of conflict in and among many religions in former colonies go back to deep-seated historical experiences, some of which were contrived by the colonial regime to strengthen its hold and control. Thus, I have tried to show that it is not enough to merely seek to learn about one another's religions as many people have always argued. I have argued that the absence of strong policy frameworks within new states for guaranteeing the efficient domestic delivery of the fruits of good governance make dialogue a futile exercise, since a hungry man remains an angry man. There is no doubt that religious education is very important and can lay a foundation for addressing the problems of statecraft and the place of religion in society. As Professor Kayode Makinde of the Babcock University in Nigeria has noted, "While the visible nation's bankruptcy is such that worries even the a-religious secular minded citizens, there is still a general concern expressed at the idea of renewal and national rebirth mid-wifed by religious education. Religious education should serve as the catalyst of moral regeneration and integration."[7]

A poor reading of history by some Muslim scholars in relation to African history has tended to create the impression that Western colonialism was synonymous with missionary evangelism. Despite the overlapping interests, the issues are far more complex, but these prejudices persist. The result is that even some of the best scholars, such as the renowned Professor Ali Mazrui, continue to mistakenly use the words West and Christianity synonymously. Consequently, these Muslims treat Christians in Africa as if they are reposi-

---

7. J. A. Kayode Makinde, "Trends and Tensions in Religious Indoctrination and Education: Babcock University as a Case Study." Paper presented at a National Workshop on Religious Pluralism and Democratic Governance in Nigeria, Centre for Research and Documentation, July 27–28th, 2001, p. 6.

tories of Western interests, thus beclouding our ability to realize that in the eyes of the same Western nations, we are never treated separately neither do Americans, Germans or the French speak of themselves as French, American or German Christians. Rather, state interests are paramount and various peoples with their religious or cultural traditions are held together by the mesh of citizenship which then becomes the basis for their claiming their rights and privileges from the state. The absence of a sense of citizenship against the backdrop of the failure of institutions in Africa means that ordinary people continue to negotiate with the state as Muslims or Christians, Hutus or Tutsis, thus making conflict, tension, and violence inevitable. Under these circumstances, religion and religious leaders cannot be summoned to mediate in conflicts that are the result of such deep-seated state failure.

It is also important to note that conflict in African societies has been engendered more by the universal claims of Christianity and Islam than the failure of its human agents. These universal claims contrast with the non-conflicting nature of African traditional religions, which did not seek to evangelize across cultures. Professor Chinua Achebe tells a story that best explains this, and can be replicated by many communities across the continent of Africa. As the story goes, the people of Ogidi (where Achebe comes from) claimed that a certain tribe migrated and finally settled among them. These strangers were welcomed and given a place to settle by the people of Ogidi. But, after settling down, the strangers made a request that seemed most strange to their hosts: they expressed the wish to be shown how to worship the local gods of the people of Ogidi apparently as evidence of their loyalty and wish to become fully integrated into their new community. Although the people of Ogidi found this irrational and incomprehensible, they reacted with pity instead. They gave their guests two gods but they insisted that these new gods must never be called *Udo* (the name of the official Ogidi god). These new gods were to be given names that denoted that they were subordinates and only the son and daughter of *Udo*. In reviewing this story, Professor Achebe concluded: "Surely, such a people cannot have any notion of the psychology of religious imperialism. And that innocence would have placed them at a great disadvantage later when they came to deal with European evangelism. Perhaps the audacity of some stranger wandering thousands of miles from his home to tell them they were worshipping false gods may have left them open mouthed in amazement." [8]

Finally, despite the difficulties enumerated above, I believe there are prospects for dialogue among religions in Africa. However, it must never be

---

8. Chinua Achebe: *Home and Exile*, op cit., pp. 12–13.

forgotten that Christians or Muslims, Animists or Atheists are primarily citizens of nation–states. It is the duty and responsibility of the state to create the constitutional basis delineating the role and place of religion. Where countries have weak constitutional basis for corporate existence and ambiguous definition of the role and place of religion, there can be problems. In Africa, post-independence states were caught up with either civil wars or military dictatorships. The post-colonial elite merely inherited the same colonial states and went ahead to re-enact the same contradictions that had guided relations between citizens and state. After independence, these countries dissipated their energies as conscripted soldiers in the barren cold war which had nothing to do with the interests of Africa. In the process, the continent's history was marked by civil wars, military and civilian dictatorships. Now after fifty years of the Cold War, except for its minerals and oil resources, both sides in the Cold War have deserted Africa. Indeed, even the new states of the former Soviet Union who were the enemy yesterday, now all enjoy greater support from the European Union and the United States, their new allies. Western reaction to the Balkan wars and the reaction to Rwanda testify to this. However, as the continent struggles to climb out of the years of military repression, it is required to lay minimum conditions for relevance in this new phase of its history.

It is therefore gratifying to note that more and more African countries are embracing democracy, thus creating the necessary condition for cross cutting cleavages beyond regions, ethnicity and religion as basis for political party affiliations. This development will take the pressure away from the religious groups as politics offers a new platform and basis for representation. The role of religious bodies in a democracy is a completely different one. But we must note that democracy by itself is an insufficient precondition for any form of dialogue among peoples, nor is it a guarantee for a just state. The killings in Rwanda happened under a democracy. Thus, the role of the religious bodies is to serve as watchdogs for the "common good." However, despite its weaknesses, democracy lays a condition for reducing conflicts and ensuring the delivery of services. Conflicts are here to stay with us in the world. The end of the Cold War has only changed the context of conflict. However, as they say, "democracies do not go to war," because democratic societies provide a haven for the pursuit of individual, communal and national growth. It is the absence of these firm roots that make many seemingly ordinary arguments in Africa boil over, leading to violence in the name of religion or ethnicity. When frustration and sentiments gestate over a long period of time in an undemocratic environment of poverty, the slightest spark can cause havoc. For example, the crisis over the application of Islamic Law or the hosting of Miss World in Nigeria claimed many lives and led to massive destruction of properties. These occurred when a faltering democracy was struggling with its faltering steps out of the dungeon of prolonged military rule. At the heart of it all was the crisis of powerlessness felt by a people who, rightly or wrongly, felt threatened by the suffocating fumes of the world that was spinning out of their control. Some times, the issues of dialogue could threaten to divide a society in the short term. But whether we are negotiating our differences or points of agreement over what may seem to be religious, minority, or women rights, it is only a democratic environment, no matter how imperfect, that offers us a *terra firma* on which to get started. We must seek to defend democracy despite its imperfections while struggling to tailor its ideals to suit our peculiar collective norms. Democracy was never meant to be a one size-fits-all dress, nor should its claims be conceived of as being cast in stone. Its ideals remain contested terrains. Navigating around them is what politics is about. Religion offers the lubricant that enables the machine of state to move smoothly.

CHAPTER 18

Conversion, Conquest, and the Qua Iboe Mission

David Pratten[1]

One of the most striking and important comments in John Peel's monograph *Religious Encounter* is a characteristically unambiguous statement that the study of Christianity in Africa is at *least* and irreducibly the analysis of religious change.[1] This statement is important because it signals two significant strands of John's thinking and scholarship. The first is his critique of those studies of Christianity in Africa that overplay the ties between conversion and conquest, between Christianity and colonialism. We are urged, therefore, to explore the internal imperatives as well as the external dynamics of religious change on the continent. The second related point is the way this statement signals his emphasis on the cultural frameworks and historicity in which religious encounters are experienced. The body of John's work on Christianity in Africa, including most importantly *Aladura* and *Religious Encounter,* demonstrates indisputably both that the links between missions and colonial orders require a situational analysis, and that, as he says, "the mission situation is shaped by those whom a mission seeks to convert as well as by the power behind the mission."[2]

This stress on historical contingency and cultural continuity is a consistent theme in John's writings. In an analysis of mission conversion published in 1976, John's attentions shifted eastwards across Nigeria from his familiar Yoruba focus to the mass conversion of Igbo, Ibibio and Ijaw in the palm oil

---

1. I wish to thank, of course, John Peel, for his comments on an earlier draft. My thanks also to John Cardoo of the Qua Iboe Fellowship for facilitating my access to the church's archives held at the Public Record Office of Northern Ireland (PRONI) in Belfast.

1. Peel, 2000, p. 4.

2. Ibid., p. 7.

belt. Here, he and his co-author, Robin Horton, wrote that "the only way to explain religious innovation is to relate it to the experience of its authors in the social context of its emergence."[3] Theirs was a broad ranging critique of the argument that conversion in Owerri and Calabar Provinces was a consequence of incorporation into the new world economy and the imposition of new political roles under the colonial system. [4] In their response Horton and Peel argued that converts in Eastern Nigeria did not see Christianity as promising a new kind of power, white power, as an alternative to success in the modern world but as a means to such success.[5] Proximate, socio-structural factors such as intense competition between the mission denominations, and the rapid socialization of school children into Christianity were evidently important. Yet, to attribute conversion to these socio-structural factors alone would be to argue that hardly anyone *chose* to be Christian. John has revisited and refined this argument in subsequent debates where in each case his most powerful critique has been to locate agency with the converts themselves.[6]

One of the mission churches that figures in the debate about the causes of conversion in southeastern Nigeria was the Qua Iboe Mission, which takes its name from one of the "oil rivers" of the eastern Niger Delta. This chapter is an account of, firstly, the imperatives of conversion, and secondly, the dynamics of conquest in the early years of the Qua Iboe Mission. As John Peel has so expertly shown, mission archives are rich in narratives of conversion that, with scrutiny, care, and ethnographic sensitivity, can illuminate the subjectivity of the convert and the localized meanings of religious change.[7] Following John's sociological lead, the emphasis here is on identifying those who joined the new mission and the "opportunity costs" of their conversion.[8] The pathways to conversion that this analysis suggests highlights the role of brokers of religious power and knowledge, the dispossessed, the old and the young.[9] And as this analysis points to the marginal social status of early converts, so the focus on the Qua Iboe Mission's slow and halting expansion into the Ibibio and Annang-speaking hinterland in the second section offers evidence of the contingent, problematic and opportunistic relationship between Christianity and colonialism.

---

3. Horton and Peel, 1976, p. 497.
4. Ifeka-Moller, 1974, p. 61.
5. Horton and Peel, 1976, p. 484.
6. Peel, 2000, pp. 4–6.
7. Peel, 1995.
8. Peel, 2000, p. 216.
9. Peel, 1968; 1968; 1990; 2000; 2002.

European missionary activity on the Qua Iboe river and its hinterland developed in the immediate aftermath of King Jaja's reign at Opobo. Several European traders tested Jaja's embargo, including Harford, who held scripture meetings his trading post in Ibeno. This experience, along with the Ibeno traders' experience of the Scottish missions along the coast in Calabar, led the chiefs of Ibeno to request a missionary of their own. The message was passed, via merchants and the United Presbyterian Church of Scotland Mission in Calabar, to several British training colleges. Set on a missionary path after the Sankey revival in his native Belfast several years previously, Samuel Bill, then studying at the Harley Missionary College in London, responded to the request. Bill arrived at the mouth of the Qua Iboe river in 1887, and established a non-denominational evangelical Protestant mission in those areas recently released from Jaja's blockade with the intention of expanding northward up the river. Bill preached through a translator because he had learned Efik from his Scottish colleagues in Calabar which, although understood by younger converts, was not comprehended by the elders who spoke the Ibeno dialect. A former Sierra Leonian trader, Williams, helped Bill with translation while Elder Dempster, the steamer company, provided a free service to the fledgling mission outpost.

Pathways to Conversion

A year passed before there were any converts to the Qua Iboe Mission. The first was a young man called Min Ekong, who was from one of the leading fishing families in Ibeno. His father had died when he was twelve. His grandfather was a shrine priest, and Min would have succeeded to minister to several of the principal Ibeno spirits. From his own accounts Min Ekong's initiation into the *nyena* shrine priesthood was well advanced; he had conducted full sacrifices at the shrine on his own, had mastered the means of producing the "voice of the spirit," and was observing various food prohibitions. His grandfather warned him that divulging the shrine's secrets would incur a fine, or worse, from a certain Igbo village, which suggests that the shrine was part of a regional complex.[11] Soon after his initiation into the warrior society (*ékóŋ*), however, Min became the house-boy of the newly arrived Samuel Bill and assumed the Christian name of David. In 1891 he accompanied Bill on

---

11. David Ekong: First Pastor of the Qua Iboe Church, (G. Bill), 1964, PRONI: D/3301/GB/5. David Ekong's grandfather was the chief priest of what Talbot called the great Juju Ainyena (Talbot, 1923 p. 103.).

furlough to Belfast, and on his return he became the mission's first Ibibio preacher.

The chiefs, Egbo Egbo and Ukut Ibuno, who had initially requested the European missionary at Ibeno, proved reluctant converts. Both were traders whose livelihoods depended on the gin trade. After two years Egbo Egbo began to take instruction and was ministered to daily. Once he had renounced the gin trade and had pensioned off eleven of his twelve wives he was baptised.[12] His power in village politics and in the "palaver-house" fell considerably, but Egbo Egbo became one of the first church elders appointed to oversee the expanding congregation in Ibeno. Ukut Ibuno recanted while suffering from rheumatic fever.[13] He had been a renowned "witch killer," and in this he was not alone among the Qua Iboe Mission's first converts. Asukpa Ikaeto, another renowned "killer of wizards" had been accused of wizardry himself and had fled in fear that his life was to be taken on account of it.[14] He was an Ibibio sold to one of the Ibeno chiefs as a child, and had become a diviner and executioner. The palm grove to which he escaped was known as Mimbo Town, near Eket, which became a haven for former slaves and those fleeing accusations of wrongdoing. Influenced by Christian traders from Ibeno who rested at this spot, Asukpa built a small hut of bamboo and mats for evening services and had prepared a band of six enquirers for baptism. In 1899 he invited David Ekong to establish a mission station at Mimbo Town.[15]

Mission accounts exalted the moral and ethical characteristics of these early converts' prior "heathen" lives. That Ukat Ibuno was a fair trader, well-loved by his customers and who always returned money paid to him during his middleman dealings, indicated his common decency. The wise counsel of David Ekong's grandfather, that he should have nothing to do with *egbo* men who dealt unjustly with a poor man, and that he should refrain from using charms to make himself brave, win a girl's love, or make himself rich, were all presented as appropriate standards of conduct in preparation for his life as the church's most important messenger.[16] These accounts must be seen, however, as one among many devices by which the mission constituted their congrega-

---

12. Egbo Egbo: Ibuno Chief and Christian, (R. L. M'Keown), n.d., PRONI: D/3301/GC/4/1.

13. The late Ukat Ibuno, (D. Ekong), n.d., PRONI: D/3301/GA/6.

14. David Ekong to Mr Niblock, 10 June 1897, PRONI: D/3301/AB/1.

15. Asukpa was suspended from the church in 1901 for committing adultery (S.A. Bill to Edward, 12 October 1901, PRONI: D/3301/AG/1.).

16. David Ekong: First Pastor of the Qua Iboe Church, (G. Bill), 1964, PRONI: D/3301/GB/5.

tions as moral communities. Indeed, rather than illustrating prior moral proclivities towards Christianity, the conversions of Min Ekong, Ukat Ibuno and Asukpa suggest that those who were initially drawn to the mission were very powerful individuals who had a prior history of "religious quest."[17]

In the two cases of Ukot Ibuno and Asukpa, illness and persecution were contributory factors in their conversion, but it is intriguing, nevertheless, that "witch killers" should be among the pioneer flock. What the missionaries meant when they referred to Ukat Ibuno as the "elected leader in killing witches" or to Asukpa as the "public executioner" is not clear. Most commonly it was the diviner (*ídìɔŋ*) who detected witches, but another highly secret category of witch seer was known as *ukpötia* or *ùkpòtíô*.[18] Goldie translates this word as headstrong and reckless. This definition is accurate in the sense that *ùkpòtíô's* fearlessness means they consider themselves immune and all-powerful, but in general use it refers to a person of unassailable spiritual power. *Ùkpòtíô's* power extended beyond the ordinary Annang and Ibibio sense of power as someone who has been tested (*òkpɔsɔŋ*), and beyond the prognosticative and spirit-invoking capacities of a diviner (*ídìɔŋ*). Rather, an *ùkpòtíô* person was endowed with powers of a highly ambiguous nature and with very "witch-like" capacities, including the ability to meet with fellow *ùkpòtíô* in distant places, usually at night and often at the top of tall trees.[19] This points to the way in which brokers in knowledge and power, *ùkpòtíô* and *ídìɔŋ*, who, in religious terms were among the most powerfully protected, were among the first to embrace Christianity.[20] They did not fear these new forces but rather were interested in assimilating this new, exotic and foreign source of power.

Among the Qua Iboe converts there were those for whom the adage "the nearer the kirk the farther from God" applied, yet in the main the reverse was true. Samuel Bill, Archie Baillie, John Kirk and later recruits to the mission focused on conversion at close quarters, especially in situations where the mission profited both from the salvation of souls and from their labor. Qua Iboe evangelism was most effective among house staff of the mission quarters, and

---

17. C.f. Peel, 1990; 2000, p. 227.

18. The term *ukpötia* or *ùkpòtíô* remains associated with the Eket region. 'Nka Ukpotio' was the name taken by bands of young men during a witch-hunt in the 1970s (Offiong, 1982), and which re-emerged in Eket in 2002.

19. Jeffreys noted another category of witch-finders in Eket, young children. In 1928 a young boy had accused 8 people of witchcraft who all succumbed to the *esere* bean ordeal. The boy told Jeffreys that he could leave his body at night and join the dances of the witches who themselves had the power of looking like trees (Jeffreys, 1966 p. 97).

20. Peel, 1990, pp. 350–359.

then among apprentices at the saw mill in Ibeno and the coffee plantation opened in Okat station.[21] Other indirect avenues, such as the government smallpox vaccination campaign, which Bill assisted in 1902, were also seen as a means of consolidating the mission, in this case to Eket. In other circumstances the demonstration of these powers of "healing" might have swollen the congregation, but instead men and women were injected at the same time in the same room, and as the exposure of women's buttocks to men was a potentially lethal act of spiritual sanction against men, the vaccinations were mired in controversy. Nevertheless, the provision of basic medical services and staffing the dispensaries that were established at the mission stations, were perceived, along with proficiency in Efik, as key requirements in the recruitment of European missionaries. Bill insisted that his missionaries "work at the medicine" when they returned to Britain on furlough.

The circle of converts at Ibeno was a tight one, and was extended in part by marriage among them. In 1895 the mission celebrated its first marriage when David Ekong married Mary, one of Chief Egbo Egbo's daughters on whom he renounced his bride-price claim. John Ewainan, appointed as a teacher at Impanek, was married to David Ekong's sister, Eka Ito. His cousin, Robert Anderson, also became a mission teacher. One of the eleven wives that Egbo Egbo "put away" upon his conversion, Adiaha, who had been banished from Eket after giving birth to twins and had later became a slave before marrying Egbo Egbo, also went on to marry one of the Qua Iboe Mission's first preachers, Ibok. Marriages such as these consolidated the small congregation. It was this set of core families at Ibeno who trained and fostered the mission's later recruits, and these marriages anticipated later initiatives with the founding of the Girls Institute in 1908, which sought to become a "means of rescuing many from a life of heathenism, and preparing them for a useful career as the wives of some of our Christian teachers."[22]

As Peel has argued so forcefully in the Yoruba context, the dominant orientation of Ibibio and Annang towards all religions was the search for individual and collective power, for personal protection, healing, fertility, and

---

21. 3,000 coffee seedlings were given by the government for the scheme but the low price of coffee made the scheme uneconomic and it was abandoned after only one season.

22. QIM Occasional Paper, August 1901, (32), PRONI, D/3301/EA/2. 'We give them a little secular education to develop the intellect and make them better able to understand the Great Truths we wish them to grasp. We give them domestic training, that they may develop wifely instincts an we insist on their continuing their manual or outdoor work as necessary to the training of an African girl...' (QIM Occasional Paper, November 1908, (61), PRONI, D/3301/EA/2.). See Bastian, 2000 for an analysis of the reconfiguring of gender roles through such schools in an Igbo context.

practical guidance through life's uncertainties.[23] Conversion was a choice, and the costs and benefits, which differed according to age and gender, were weighed up carefully.[24] The social advantages of belonging to the Christian community were especially relevant for those who had little to lose. The poor and marginalized included former slaves, strangers, and categories of social outcast in which twin-mothers predominated. Many had physically lived outside the Annang or Ibibio village in ad hoc settlements established by slaves, or in spaces such as the "twin mother's village" that were isolated by ritual embargoes. Conversion offered these groups haven and re-integration. At Ibeno and beyond, therefore, conversion appealed to the disempowered and those, like young men and women, who were least integrated into the social and religious networks of Ibibio life.

The majority of the small pioneer flock were a motley crew of social misfits. One of the terms under which Samuel Bill accepted land from the Ibeno chiefs was that any person accused of witchcraft, or who was being unlawfully sold as a slave, could take permanent and unmolested refuge on mission ground. By 1892 there were thirty-five church members at Ibeno, and six inquirers.[25] Asukpa's community in Mimbo Town, and those who sought refuge at Ibeno, suggest that a significant proportion of the first converts were former slaves. Small parties of escaped slaves regularly swelled the "refugee" population of the mission station. In March 1899 the missionaries received the largest group of these "refugees," some 130 who were mainly women (there were twenty-one men and a few children). Little was known of their origin— somewhere in the Niger Territories (300 miles to the north). Sold to "Arab" slavers, they had been made to march from one town to another until they found themselves north of Old Calabar on the Cross River from where they made their escape in their owners' canoes. The mission housed them for six weeks during which they were put to work by Bill, and cut firewood and processed oil in order to purchase food. Through the mission they were able to contact a British expeditionary force who sent two large canoes to carry them on the initial stage of a long journey back to the homes they had left probably several years previously.[26]

In 1890, three years after Bill's arrival, the number of the so-called "refugees" and their families living on mission ground was thirty-four. Among them was the church's second convert, Etia, the first woman to enter the Qua

23. Peel, 2000, p. 219.
24. Cf. Peel, 2002, p. 137 on the Yoruba case.
25. M'Keown, 1912, p. 74.
26. S.A. Bill to Mr Hamilton, 20 March 1899, PRONI: D/3301/AG/1.

Iboe Mission. The widow of a chief in the village of Impanek at the mouth of the Qua Iboe River, she escaped the attentions of his family toward her son by fleeing with him to Duke Town, Calabar. She saw the Scottish missionaries there but was afraid of entering the church for fear of being bewitched. On her return she married again, but was accused of causing the death of a child in her new husband's family and of being a witch. Facing summary execution or the *esere* bean ordeal, Etia ate the poisonous bean and survived its effects. She was banished from Impanek, however, and settled near the Qua Iboe mission station. When her second husband died, she refused an offer of protection from the village chief, and requested land in the mission compound from Samuel Bill. Etia burned the wooden stakes representing her ancestors, and the plate in which, at noon each day, she poured water for her bush soul to drink. Skilful in the use of herbs, Etia became famous as a children's doctor, and later when twin infanticide was prohibited she nursed twin children until their mothers lost their fear of them.[27]

The Christian congregation was especially appealing to elderly women like Etia, especially those without children and with no one to support or bury them.[28] Fellowship within the Christian congregation became an important form of social insurance. A woman from Ibeno said, "I seem to gain [a] great deal by being a Christian, friends give me presents every now and again to keep me from want." Without a son or daughter of her own becoming a Christian meant she had gained many friends who would bury her when she died.[29] Hearing that in heaven everything a person possesses will remain with them forever, an old woman who had entered the inquirer's class in Eket stated that:

> I have been a mother of many children fully trusting they will support me when I grow old [and] unable to work, but instead they all died and leave me without any child to care for me....I will become a Christian that I may go to where there is no parting from friends and property.[30]

It seems that there was a great deal of interest in the mission from young women too, but they were less able to confirm this curiosity. The social pres-

---

27. From Darkness to Light: The Story of Etia, (G. Bill), n.d., PRONI: D/3301/GC/9/24. In 1899 mothers of twins in Okat and Mkpok were enabled to go about their daily work while 'egbo' is roaming the town without being flogged. The law was ratified by the swearing of mbiam – 'that is each part, after taking oath, tastes a mysterious concoction out of a still more mysterious little jar (*QIM Occasional Paper*, May 1899, (23), PRONI, D/3301/EA/2.).

28. Peel, 2000, p. 238.

29. David Ekong to Mr Keown, 16 July 1923, PRONI: D/3301/AB/1.

30. David Ekong to Mr Keown, 28 October 1925, PRONI: D/3301/AB/1.

sures upon young girls to enter the pre-marital fattening society (*mbòbó*) were great, and the "patriarchal panic" at the conversion of those responsible for the reproduction of the lineage was violent.[31] Reports that women were flogged by their husbands for going to church or attending inquirers' classes were widespread, and there were many accounts of more serious assaults. When a man in Etinan in 1904 heard that one of his wives had gone to church for the first time he cut her throat with a matchet.[32] Another Etinan man called his household together to make a feast and sacrifice, but one of his wives refused to take part and said she had heard in church that a man cannot serve two masters. Having decided "to serve the true god, rather than the devil," her husband "went to Ju-ju and told the God to kill her." Three days later the woman died. He said "ju-ju" killed her, but John Kirk, who had opened the Etininan station in 1988, claimed that the husband had poisoned her.[33]

Poisoning, in fact, became a common topic of discourse at the turn of the century. Kirk claimed that he knew of several people who had been poisoned at Etinan after his arrival, including the man who gave the ground on which the mission house itself was built. He also claimed that it was common knowledge that people poisoned for money. The man responsible for a series of poisonings in Etinan disclosed his complicity before a large crowd of people in the mission yard. He even named those who had paid him for his work, and said that the price he generally received was 1,100 manillas, or about £5.[34] This discourse on poisoning was part of a significant innovation in the occult imagination of Ibibio and Annang society at the turn of the century. The physical and social mobility of the period was not only associated with Christian conversion, but with religious change more broadly as the western Ibibio-speaking areas witnessed the introduction of a new mode of witchcraft, *ifót*. In everyday discourse *ifót* is a witch who kills by poisoning. This belief was linked to rumors that people in Calabar, its supposed source, did not live to an old age as they were consumed by a cycle of witchcraft flesh-debts.[35] Hence sto-

---

31. Peel, 2002, p. 155.

32. *QIM Occasional Paper*, February 1904, (42), PRONI, D/3301/EA/3. He subsequently burned down his own compound, and shot himself in the throat.

33. *QIM Occasional Paper*, February 1902, (34), PRONI, D/3301/EA/3.

34. The Etinan poisoner ended up in prison for poisoning four children to whom he had apparently given too high a dose which caused them to vomit before it could have effect.

35. In Calabar itself, those accused of *ifót* were subjected to a poison ordeal called *esere* made up of Calabar beans (*Physostigma Venenosum*). The bean was considered *ibét* (ritually forbidden) to *ifót* in the same way as food prohibitions are *ibét* to Annang and Ibibio clans. See Latham, 1972 in which he argues that witchcraft accusations in Calabar were the

ries of witchcraft familiar in Ikom folk tales as recorded by a District Commissioner, Dayrell, began to circulate in Ibibio and Annang. They related tales of "bewitched" foods, of nocturnal transformations into a witch-bird (the owl), of chiefs and head men predominating among the witches, of witches' feasts, and of the consumption of human flesh.[36]

Younger men who had yet to marry and had yet to invest in their initiation into the ancestral masquerade society (*ékpó*) had less to lose than their seniors for whom the costs of conversion involved social severance and sanctions. At the Okat station that Archie Bailie opened in 1895, a man who has been attending services for over a year, and seemed earnest in his conviction, suddenly stopped coming. When Bailie went to inquire the reason for his absence, he said that his fellow *ékpó* members had threatened that, if he returned to either church or class, they would put him out of the society, prevent him cutting his palm fruit, and deprive him of all the other privileges of that organization "which to an Ibibio means so much."[37] These were very real sanctions and could be invoked against the most well-integrated within society, as Ekpo Uro Usoro's story indicates. It is not clear precisely how, but he had "displeased a chief and incurred the wrath" of the *ékpó* society in Ikot Akpata.[38] He fled to a Christian friend in Okat, where he received the news that his wife had been sold, his children appropriated, his farm plundered, and his compound razed. He joined the enquirer's class at the mission station in Okat, but Bailie's negotiation with the chiefs of Ikot Akpata to return the man's family and property proved futile. His suggestion that Ekpo Uro Usoro would be reconciled with the village if he was allowed to visit Okat Mission, not to work on Sundays, take no part in public sacrifices, and not be forced to contribute to any "heathen play" was met by a yell of derision. Ekpo did not go back to Ikot-Akpata; instead he built a house near the mission ground in Okat where he lived "in peace and security."[39]

As the missionaries themselves recognized, those young converts who had yet to enter *ékpó* felt they had little to lose at the time of their conversion.[40] The high proportion of young men among the converts led deputations of

---

result of social and political tensions arising from the conflict between traditional status systems and the new status of wealth based on overseas trade. The physical effects of the *esere* bean ordeal are detailed in Simmons, 1956 pp. 225–226.

36. Dayrell, 1913 p. 34.

37. *QIM Occasional Paper*, August 1901, (32), PRONI, D/3301/EA/2.

38. The *ékpó* society is often referred to in Missionary narratives as Akpan-Oyoho.

39. *QIM Occasional Paper*, February 1903, (38), PRONI, D/3301/EA/3.

40. The Qua Iboe Mission Makes History, (J. W. Westgarth), 1946, PRONI: D/3301/GA/2.

chiefs to visit the mission stations and ask whether the church gospel compelled the young to be Christian. The young men saw being a Christian as their exclusive preserve, a sphere of religious and political opportunity not meant for the chiefs and elders. The widespread demand for schools was a reflection of young men's anxiety to improve themselves, and did not mean, as the mission recognized, that they were thirsting for the Gospel. The Qua Iboe Mission was compelled to open numerous schools around each of the six central stations in response to the companies of young men "whose anxiety for teachers is almost painful."[41] These little schools lacked equipment and in the absence of a certified instructor many of the teachers were "ignorant of any method of teaching."[42]

These young men were influential in the spread of the church. One Sunday in Etinan in the early 1900s there were 1,268 members of the congregation of whom at least 800 were young men and boys, with the remainder all young women.[43] While there was clearly widespread appeal among young men in general, the role of influential individuals and of the ties binding groups of young men together in bands of fellowship cannot be overestimated. At Ikot Akpan, the mission depended on a single young man who ran the school and who had attracted twenty others into the new church. Such positions were pathways to power and promotion, and in this case the young man's ambitions over-reached. He began to sell European gin, and wishing to raise himself up among the chiefs, he married additional wives. When he was removed from the church, only two of the twenty he brought with him remained.[44]

At Etinan, Kirk's account of the conversion of Akpan Udo Ema, who was one of the first young men to be baptized there, indicates that the "bands of young" men came in various guises:

> Before we came he was one of the worst men in this town or for that matter in any of the towns in this neighbourhood, and he had a following of young men like himself for he was the son of a powerful chief and had therefore considerable standing in the place. Some of his past life could not be mentioned—'let darkness cover it'....Shortly after we came here, he and his young men went to a town ten miles

41. M'Keown, 1912, p. 169.

42. Ibid p. 162. One of the problems was that in the expansion of the church and in the need to reach as many places as possible very few young men would give up their lives to teaching, objecting both to the meagre salary and to being tied to a rural backwater. In 1902 Bill decided to ask teachers for a commitment of only 6 months.

43. Ibid., p. 127.

44. Ibid., p. 114.

Figure 18.1 - A lady missionary in late nineteenth century Africa.

> away and seized a lot of cattle and goats and as many yams as they
> were able to carry. These were all brought to his house where a divi-
> sion was made of the captured spoil. But in the mercy of God all this
> was soon to be changed. He and his companions settled down to
> learn to read in our little school, and he also came to the inquirers
> class when there were only five names on the roll. [45]

Once Akpan Udo Ema had converted he made restitution for his robberies,
and with eight of his gang learned to read the New Testament in seven months.
His wife was baptized a few months later. On the morning of her baptism she
became the first woman in the district to wear a dress, and for this reason the
heads of the secret societies were said to have made an order that Akpan and
his wife were to be killed wherever they were caught in any of the towns within
a ten mile radius.

While the attraction of Qua Iboe Christianity for young men was widespread, its path was far from smooth, and during this period young men's allegiances to the Qua Iboe Mission appeared to be highly provisional.[46] Two issues concerned young men most. One was gin trading, the profits from which
were quicker than on any other commodity. The other issue that was being
"seriously discussed among a lot of young men" was "wife palaver." "The young

45. Akpan Udo-Ema, (J. Kirk), n.d., PRONI: D/3301/GA/3.
46. Peel, 2000, p. 229.

men declare they don't want a number of wives, just one at a time. They wish an arrangement made by which when a wife displeases her husband, or turns out badly, or troubles him with too many palavers, he may dismiss her, and put another into her place."[47] It was not polygamy that the young converts wanted, but flexibility regarding labor and divorce. Since these were essentially economic grievances, the two issues, gin and marriage, would flare up as the principal cause of "backsliding" whenever economic fortunes declined.

Conversion interrupted the initiatory cycle by which men's societies reproduced themselves. By the early 1900s those who converted to Christianity and resisted initiation into *ékpó* were therefore also the subject of concerted and violent coercion: "The heathen people made palaver, because Christian young men were growing up without joining Egbo, or rather without paying fees to be made members of that powerful society."[48] In 1905 *ékpó* "made a strong stand for the old customs, and have practically blotted out the work at two of the out-stations, where they killed several enquirers."[49] By 1906 the Christian converts "grew cold," and there was a clamor for polygamy and liberty to trade in gin.[50] During the season of *ékpó* performances in 1907, the mission reported that young Christians had "lately shown a disposition to return to playing."[51] The following year the secret societies had "resorted to their old trick of putting ju-ju signs in front of the Christians" houses with the idea of bringing some calamity on the home."[52] The missions sought vigorously to defend their flocks both because they opposed the secret societies as bastions of idol worship, and for more practical, economic reasons. Both the *ékpó* elders and the mission stations needed money. Written contracts between chiefs and young men, between *ékpó* and Christians, and between the church and residents of their compounds, became a common feature of dispute settlement. In April 1915, for instance, Westgarth drew up an agreement between the chiefs and schoolboys of Ediano. The mission boys agreed not to "spoil" *ékpó* while chiefs agreed not to attack the school.[53]

---

47. *QIM Occasional Paper*, August 1905, (48), PRONI, D/3301/EA/3.

48. M'Keown, 1912, p. 73. At Ibiam, roads were closed to prevent school boys from attending school and church. Their books were taken from them and thrown into the bush....school boys were fined 35s merely for holding 'prayers' in one of their houses while an egbo play was going on elsewhere (B. Welsh to Mr Bedwell, October 1913, NAE: CAL-PROF 13/6/108.).

49. *QIM Occasional Paper*, February 1905, (46), PRONI, D/3301/EA/3.

50. *QIM Quarterly*, May 1906, (51), PRONI, D/3301/EA/4.

51. *QIM Quarterly*, February 1908, (58), PRONI, D/3301/EA/4.

52. *QIM Quarterly*, May 1908, (59), PRONI, D/3301/EA/4.

53. Diary, J.W. Westgarth, 14 April 1915, PRONI: D/3301/CB/1.

Narratives of early converts illustrate something of their motivations for joining the Qua Iboe Mission fellowship, but very few dwell on non-instrumental factors. The foremost element of Annang and Ibibio spirituality was the quest for power. The cultural continuity that underlay the process of Christian conversion here was the exploration for and testing of power. In Ibibio and Annang society, power (*ódùdù*) is transmitted from an omnipotent deity (*àbàssì éñɔ̀ŋ*) who is remote and hidden deep in the sky. *Àbàssì éñɔ̀ŋ* is served in the worldly arena by numerous spirits (*ñdêm*), the most significant of whom is the god of the soil (*àbàssì ìkpá ísɔ̀ŋ*). The power of these distant deities is not conceived in abstract or impersonal terms. Instead force, power, and influence are conceived within personal relationships as personal and collective progress are perceived to be caused by individual competitors, rivals and enemies. Using power in this way is conceived as putting "pressure" (*úfík*) on another and of having "influence" (*ábàyá*—to intimidate and frighten). Unless it is revealed in the specialist investigations of a diviner (*ídíɔ̀ŋ*), the possession and source of a person's power remains secret. The recognition of power is therefore based on the public achievements of a person, a feature captured in the saying "performance makes a person strong" (*"édínám ówó ánám ówó édí òkpɔ̀sɔ̀ŋ"*). Status and wealth must have been achieved as a result of overcoming the tests, trials, and threats of a neighbor or a kinsman. Hence, those who have suppressed a rival's power constitute a category of the strong and powerful (*òkpɔ̀sɔ̀ŋ ówó*—powerful person).

Several aspects of this spiritual cosmology were significant in the conversion process including continuities in the structure of spiritual frameworks, the acquisition of power over rivals, and the importance given to the public testing of religious power. Christianity's conceptions of God and Devil, Heaven and Hell, intersected with a complex duality of powers in Ibibio cosmology. In translations of the Bible and in everyday speak the remote all-controlling beneficial sky god, *àbàssì éñɔ̀ŋ* became *Abassi*, and was translated for God. The ancestral spirits, *ékpó*, as represented in masquerade performances, became the Devil.[54] This duality resonates with a structural distinction in Ibibio belief between the powers of up and down, earth and sky. Where the sky deity is linked to antidotes and protection, the earth's powers are associated with malevolence. The parallels between Ibibio belief in a supreme deity (*àbàssì éñɔ̀ŋ*) and the Christian God emerge in accounts such as that of the conversion of Ofon Omana, an orphan at Okat:

> On our arrival at Okat we found Ofon very jealous for the worship
> of his ancestor's gods.... He informs me that every sickness he had

---

54. C.f. Meyer, 1999; Peel, 2000 pp. 255–265.

from childhood was attributed to the ju-jus. And as soon as the Idiong man pointed out the offended ju-jus he was carried to and laid down before the piece of wood which represented it whilst his parents offered the sacrifice....in common with all Ibibios he believed—that there were two great gods. Abasi Enjong, or the god above, Abasi Isong, or the god below; that the Idiong men (sorcerers) occasionally see Abasi Enjong, but never see Abasi Isong; that all things were made by these two gods; that the souls of the 'Big Men' and the good people go to the good country called Idung Ikpo...that the bad, that is to say, witches, murderers, and a few of the most abandoned must for caused by evil spirits; that these must as far as possible be appeased.[55]

Where there are glimpses of the spiritual quest in accounts of conversion they intersect with underlying notions of spiritual puzzlement directed beyond ancestral and household shrines. Ibibio evangelists for instance pointed to faith in àbàssì as a moral foundation and a form of proto-Christianity. Jimmy Udo Ema, the first preacher in Etinan, for example, recalled that when his mother was "baffled by the evil spirits" after she was banished from her village for giving birth to twins, she would turn to Abasi (God the Creator) and prayed earnestly to Him in her loneliness and separation from her husband and people.[56]

Of Ibibio conceptions of power John Westgarth, who joined the mission in 1906, was quite accurate when he said that, "Rising and falling fortunes are attributed not so much to ability or fortuitous circumstances, as to some secret opponent working their "magic" in the dark."[57] A chief who converted said that the thing that kept him away from the church was "the fear that if he destroyed his 'medicine' his enemies would get power over him."[58] The index of power in Ibibio-speaking societies was gauged by wealth and health. Indeed, as a search for power and protection, the imperatives of health and healing threw the lines of the religious encounter into stark relief. It is from such experiences as that of Robert Atai, the Qua Iboe evangelist at Ibesit, which point to a broad dynamic of religious change which focused on the tensions over the attribution of the causes of illness. Robert Atai's account also reminds

---

55. *QIM Occasional Paper*, August 1900, (28), PRONI, D/3301/EA/2.

56. Jimmy Udo Ema: Evangelist and Pastor, (J. W. Westgarth), n.d., PRONI: D/3301/GC/5/1..

57. Westgarth, 1946 p. 35.

58. *QIM Quarterly*, November 1927, (135), D/3301/EA/12..

us of the very personal motives—of mistrust and discouragement, of being accepted and being loved—that conversion involved:

> My father died when I was a few months old, when my mother and I came under the care of uncles. These uncles worshipped the gods of their fathers. One was called 'Afang Ukpon'. I was brought up to know and worship this god. My eldest uncle was the priest who ministered to this God. He placed a clay dish at the root of a big tree near our compound. This he filled with water and told us that our souls were in the water, under the shelter of the tree. If a boy or girl became sick then this priest said that the water had dried in the plate. This made the children's souls feel hot. Then he would offer a fowl and put more water in the plate, believing this will cause the fever to leave the children. Once a year we went in a company to this god. The priest damped our bodies with water from the plate and blessed us in the form of a kind of prayer, saying the god would keep our bodies cool. He also put round our necks leaves of the palm tree which had been dipped in the plate. These palm leaves were a sign of our peace and freedom from sickness.
>
> When I was seven years old I began to feel discouraged of going to this god any more. When the feast in its honour was held in my uncle's yard I refused to attend. This made the uncle, who had joined the Church, love me more. He took an interest in me and led me to Christ. He also sent me to live with the native pastor in our town to learn from him more about God....Many years passed and some of my uncles had died. Lightning twice struck the tree that sheltered the plate. This incident made my surviving uncles and my mother to shake and fear that we were all going to die. They trusted the tree to protect us and it failed. They thought the thunder had destroyed our souls, but this made them think, and god opened the hearts of my mother and my uncles to see and know that all souls are in God's care. At Christmas 1918 after the epidemic of influenza, my mother saw that God is above all evil powers and is able to save from death. Thus she came to the Church, and five years afterwards she confessed to the world the reception of her Saviour....The old Ju-Ju tree is dead and the land about it is farmed, but we are praising the Saviour. The plate is rotted away and the water dried up, but we are alive and believing that God alone can save both body and soul.[59]

---

59. *QIM Quarterly*, August 1930, (146), PRONI, D/3301/EA/14.

Robert Atai's family's shared trauma in the face of natural calamities contributed to a religious uncertainty in which the power of the Christian churches, like all forms of power in Annang society, was judged on its worldly effects and in terms of its performance against competitors—in this case the power of the *ábáŋ úkpɔŋ* (soul) shrine. The influenza epidemic of 1918–19 to which Atai refers caused an estimated 4,000 deaths in Opobo District, and a further 12,996 in Uyo and Abak.[60] His mother's conversion was one of a range of religious reactions among survivors of the epidemic. The D. O. at Eket reported that it was popularly believed the influenza deaths were caused by the poison of *ifót* witchcraft, and that *esere* bean ordeals had accounted for 110 suspected witches.[61] Both *ídɔ́ŋ* and mission used the epidemic, along with other events of the period, to prove their power through public testing and performance. *Ídɔ́ŋ* diviners broadcast that the influenza epidemic was the result of the *ídɔ́ŋ* spirit's anger at the presence of the Qua Iboe Mission. Several church buildings were attacked and razed to the ground during 1918, though the effects on the church's standing did not last. With a near-total solar eclipse on May 29, 1919, the missionaries let it be known through the teachers that the "heathen" should be "dismayed by the signs of the heaven." The following Sunday the church buildings were crowded.[62]

Conquest and Contingency

As Peel illustrates, while many of its early converts were socially peripheral, so Christianity's initial advance was also slow and halting.[64] In the Ibibio case it is important to stress the historical contingency with which Christianity and colonialism penetrated the palm oil producing hinterland. In 1895 the protectorate, which had been extended over the hinterland in 1893, was renamed the "Oil Rivers and Niger Coast Protectorate." Consuls and vice-consuls visited the Qua Iboe River for several years prior to the turn of the century, though their attempts to open interior roads and suppress "obnoxious practices" had little impact. Sometimes in tandem, sometimes in spite of each

---

60. Flu Epidemic: Calabar Province, 1919, NAE: CALPROF 5/9/69.

61. Jeffreys, 1966 p. 96.

62. *QIM Quarterly*, November 1919, (103), PRONI, D/3301/EA/9. Across the region the influenza epidemic was also thought to have been caused by poisonous gas released by German troops during the First World War. In Ukanafun, bonfires of scented leaves were lit around family compounds to dispel the fumes.

64. Peel, 2000 pp. 242–247.

other, though often because of common fears, however, the forces of conquest and Christianity began to move inland. Two related anxieties developed in the years between Samuel Bill's arrival at Ibeno in 1887 and the opening of the last colonial district office in the southern Annang town of Abak in 1909: the British concern over Aro slave-traders determined the violent pattern of colonial conquest across the hinterland: and the missionaries' fear of the secret societies developed as a discourse on inter-generational conflict and judicial practice.

Samuel Bill's relationship with the British consuls on the coast was indifferent in most matters. In 1898 Etinan chiefs implored him not to interfere with their customs of *ídìɔŋ*, polygamy and twin-infanticide. Bill replied that he was not disposed to constant appeals to the British Consul, but if reports of such practices came to his knowledge he would "attempt to use or call in any force to aid us." [65] On the subject of punitive expeditions staged by the British Government against hinterland communities he was equivocal. Bill allowed the mission's launch to be used to tow government troops between the coastal towns but refused to transport them if they were preparing an expedition. On one issue, however, Bill's antipathy for the *ékpê* ("egbo") society, he freely invoked the threat of the consul.

The Qua Iboe Mission presented contrasting views on the various Ibibio secret societies, especially the leopard society (*ékpê*), the ancestral masquerade (*ékpó*), and the warrior cult (*ékóŋ*). The mission's response was comparable to the Church Missionary Society's attitude towards the Yoruba Ogboni society that Peel has described.[66] On the one hand the "heathen plays" were represented as idolatrous bastions of paganism, and on the other as an integral part of the political and judicial fabric of Ibibio society. In one moment, therefore the Ibibio secret societies would figure as the most serious obstacle to the spread of the Gospel, and as Baillie's reflections indicate, their diabolization was achieved through association with criminal cults reported from across west Africa:

> The gin trade and our work mostly clash among the more ambitious young men who desire to get on and make money, for the profits on this article of commerce are greater and their returns speedier than on other commodities so many of them are not prepared to make the sacrifice that the gospel demands. Whilst the 'wife palaver' and the gin question are tremendous hindrances to Missionary enterprise, the

---

65. S.A. Bill to Mr Niblock, 16 December 1898, PRONI: D/3301/AG/1.
66. C.f. Peel, 2000 p. 270.

secret organisations are avowedly hostile and openly opposed to all Christian work. They are numerous and practically rule the country. Everyone lives in terror of them, and all their laws are readily obeyed. Their power is unlimited, they rob and oppress, they sell men and women into slavery and offer human sacrifices. I could tell of many dark crimes committed by them near my own station, but at present shall just say that from the Porrah, or Human leopard Society of Sierra Leone, who tear and eat human victims, or the Silent Ones of the Lower Niger whose aim is to rid Africa of all white influence, down to the immoral *Ékóŋ* men, of our own tribe, they have all declared against the Gospel and use their great influence in retarding its progress.[67]

In more pragmatic moments, however, it was the influence of the secret societies in civil litigation that exorcised the mission. Indeed, Bill had recommended the establishment of a Native Court at Ibeno for many years precisely because he saw it as the most effective way of breaking up "Egbo law" in which, as he put it, "the plaintiff is really also the judge and the executioner and the defendant has no chance."[68]

The experiences at the Enen out-station of the Qua Iboe Missionary, reported by Gamble in 1918, were representative of this ongoing struggle with the secret societies and of the ways in which the mission invoked colonial sanctions to its cause. At Midim the head of *ékpó* and the village chief claimed that *ékpó* would shoot the schoolboys if they refused to join the society. During Gamble's attempts to negotiate, the *ékpó* leaders raised the stakes; they threatened to knock down the school, and proposed a law that a boy should pay a fine of a cow and £5 if he refused to join *ékpó*:

At this stage there was much shouting outside, and about 40 masked men with bows and arrows surrounded the school. I was not at all sure that I wanted to die at that moment, and I inwardly prayed for grace to be kept calm.... Just then one Egbo man inside gave an awful shout, and rushed towards the door. The boys caught him and I cautioned him that he must not move until our palaver was finished. They all charged me with allowing the scholars to break the Egbo regulations, threatening to kill the boys who would not make drums for

---

67. *Qua Iboe Mission Quarterly*, August 1906, (52), PRONI, D/3301/EA/4.
68. S.A. Bill to Mr Niblock, 20 August 1899, PRONI: D/3301/AG/1.

them. Finally I had to draw a circle, and step inside it, saying that I stood there protected by British law.[69]

The most significant conjunction of colonial and Christian interests surrounded an event in the year following the opening of the mission's third station at Etinan.[70] The first incursion of protectorate forces inland to the western Ibibio-speaking territory was triggered by the mission's direct opposition to Ibibio burial practices. The terms of the various treaties designed to prevent slavery had included provisions to stop certain social practices, the killing of twins, the *esere* bean ordeal, and the sacrifice of human beings at burials.[71] The raid was approved in March 1899, following the efforts of John Kirk to prevent the sacrifice of a young man as part of burial rites in the village of Mkpok. In their efforts to save the victim and capture the chief responsible, Kirk and the District Commissioner Horace Bedwell were injured.[72]

While the village of Mkpok was quickly overrun following these reports, the expedition force of seven officers, 180 troops and over 200 carriers led by Major Leonard met with surprising resistance. Leonard thought that with such a display of power, fighting would be unnecessary, but he was mistaken as the sortie to Eket, which had been intended to last two or three days, became protracted in conflict with the neighboring Afaha section of Ubium and lasted as many weeks.[73] Leonard's expedition penetrated a distance of sixty miles up the banks of the river, and claimed to have razed fourteen towns with 150 others who surrendered signing treaties by which they agreed to open and maintain roads, refrain from seizing people in "palavers," and from all practices that

---

69. *QIM Quarterly*, February 1918, (97), PRONI, D/3301/EA/8.

70. The first preacher in Etinan, Jimmy Udo Ema, was the son of a twin-mother and had been raised in the bush of twin mothers (*íkɔ́t íbáàn ékpó*) in Afaha Iman (Jimmy Udo Ema: Evangelist and Pastor, (J. W. Westgarth), n.d., PRONI: D/3301/GC/5/1.). When he granted land for the church Chief Udo Ema chose a former burial ground in order to test the mission.

71. An agreement was signed with Duke Ephraim and other Chiefs to abolish twin murder in January 1855 for instance though Old Town was destroyed by HMS Antelope on instructions from Vice-Consul Lynslanger because the inhabitants had permitted human sacrifice during the treaty signings. The treaty signed between Consul Hutchinson and the Chiefs of Calabar in January 1856 secured British ships exclusive trading rights. Under the treaty the chiefs aggreed to protect missionaries, to abolish the poison nut ordeal and to hand over orphaned and twin children to the Scottish Mission. Thomas Joseph Hutchinson (Consul) and the Chiefs of Old Calabar Town and Old Calabar, 21 January 1856, NAE: IKOTDIST 15/8/2.

72. Noah, 1984 p. 42.

73. *QIM Occasional Paper*, May 1899, (23), PRONI, D/3301/EA/2.

would lessen the value of human life (including practices such as human sacrifices, twin murders, burial of widows, and killing of supposed witches).[74] It quickly became apparent, however, that despite the advertised destruction of the "Fetish Quae" (Eket), the area remained distinctly hostile and the Ekets regularly attacked soldiers and road-making parties, and rescued prisoners.[75]

Sir Ralph Moor, the Consul-General of the Niger Coast Protectorate, thought that a major force must have supported and stiffened the resistance displayed by the Ibibio villages during the expedition of 1899. It became commonplace to trace every local manifestation of opposition to British rule to the influence of Aro Igbo, and gradually Aro enmity was built into an obsession.[76] In this conception the Aro's regional force was exaggerated, as satellite trading settlements were taken for military garrisons. Moor became increasingly convinced that Ibibio leaders were compromised by their complicity in Aro slave-dealing atrocities, that the Aro had infiltrated their ranks, and that in order to bring the Ibibio under British rule the Aro should be subjugated. Colonial conceptions of Aro influence were spurred on by the Qua Iboe Mission's commentators and the link they drew between the Aro, the slave trade and the secret societies:

> Order has been restored and good government introduced so that the whole country is opened up, and now awaits the herald of the cross to take possession in one King's name. About fifty miles farther up there is one of the most powerful tribes in Africa, called the Aroes....They are the soldiers of the country, to whom the surrounding tribes pay tribute that they may fight for them.... They keep the trade of the interior from coming down to the coast, and have effectually [sic.] resisted every overture of the Government for years, so that theirs is really the closed land of the West Coast. The Aroes are also the great slave traders of the coast, so that slavery cannot be abolished until they are dealt with. They are also the originators of the great secret societies of the country connected with witchcraft...For several years the Government have contemplated sending an expedition against them....At the present time they are preparing for the long-looked-for advance....It will be the largest thing of the kind that has ever been organized on the West Coast.[77]

The Aro Expedition was "the severest single blow" that the British dealt to the Aro oligarchy, though its impact was considerably less decisive than the

---

74. S.A. Bill to Mr Hamilton, 20 March 1899, PRONI: D/3301/AG/1.
75. *QIM Occasional Paper*, November 1899, (25), PRONI, D/3301/EA/2.
76. Anene, 1956 pp. 21, 23.
77. *QIM Occasional Paper*, August 1901, (32), PRONI, D/3301/EA/2.

British had hoped for.[78] The punitive Aro expedition of 1901 was justified on the grounds of stopping slave raiding, abolishing the "fetish hierarchy," and stimulating legitimate trade. Initially the British claimed to have freed the protectorate forever from the evils of slave dealing since they assumed, mistakenly, that slaves were procured by raids and that once law and order had been imposed then slave dealing would cease. They failed to understand the intricacies of the Aro trading system, and reports of revivals of the Long Juju and of ongoing slave deals and markets quickly suggested that their triumph was premature.

The Aro expedition had wider consequences for the region as a whole. After raiding Arochukwu, the four columns of the force led by Lt. Col. Montanaro swept through Ikot Ekpene. They met resistance, notably at Anwa Oko, but the patrols themselves soon divided the region into divisions with native courts and councils established at strategic locations. Political officers urged these councils to further undermine Aro standing by passing bylaws that would impress upon the Aro that their rights to trade and settle were conditional upon permission from local rulers.[79] By the end of 1899, as a result of the government expeditions, the towns and villages around Eket which had been closed to the Qua Iboe Mission had begun to invite the church in. Despite its misgivings about the punitive raids, there was considerable excitement within the mission in 1901 at the news that large tracts of densely populated country at the head of the Qua Iboe River (the Obium and Aro country) were being opened up "to the entrance of the trader and the missionary" by the British military expeditions.[80]

The relationship between the Qua Iboe mission and the institutions of colonialism became more explicit with the creation of these new courts. When it opened in December 1899 Bill became the clerk of the monthly Ibeno Native Court.[81] He also recommended fourteen chiefs from various towns to sit as assessors on the court, of whom seven were Christians. They included Egbo Egbo, whose status was restored by his appointment as the court's first president, a position he used to prohibit human sacrifice, twin infanticide and trial by ordeal in Ibeno.[82] The physical conjunction of church and court worked to the mission's benefit in other ways too. During their itinerating work the Eu-

---

78. Afigbo, 1971 p. 3.

79. Ibid p. 6.

80. *QIM Occasional Paper*, August 1901, (32), PRONI, D/3301/EA/2.

81. S.A. Bill to His Excellency the High Commissioner, Southern Nigeria, 20 October 1904, PRONI: D/3301/AG/1.

82. Egbo Egbo died during the smallpox epidemic of 1901.

Figure 18.2 - Church in Qua Iboe.

ropean missionaries lodged in the court houses. At Etinan the church was located near the new Native Court and litigants would arrive from neighboring communities on the Sunday to be ready for the opening of the court session on Monday morning. In this way the imposing external improvements of the church compound and congregation were widely advertised and those lodging for the night with converts would accompany their hosts to church.

It was commerce, not the expeditionary forces, however, that the Belfast missionaries followed north along the river. The first Christians to penetrate the creeks and tributaries of the Qua Iboe, however, were Opobo and Ibani traders who settled along the creeks and tributaries that criss-crossed the southern Ibibio and Annang region. These became small Christian communities of up to forty converts attending their own mud chapels built on the beaches. The second Qua Iboe Mission station was opened on the site of a shop Harford had run at Okat.[83] Despite the fact that waterside markets were already home to Christian communities, and that the northern reaches had

---

83. For some, like Samuel Akpan Ekang who became a mission evangelist, Harford's presence on the river had prompted his intellectual path to conversion: 'When I was about eight or nine years of age, my father gave me to one of Mr John Harford's clerks to live

been "pacified" by the expeditions, the mission's expansion was piecemeal and faltering. Crucially the church did not have the resources to expand rapidly. It lacked significant finances from its home base, it could not raise funds from trade because of an existing trading monopoly agreed by the Ibenos, and it therefore lacked trained ministers and teachers for many years.[84] Up to 1908 the mission was financed both by the local church and from home funds. Afterwards the council adopted a principle of self-sufficiency. This severely handicapped the church since the majority of converts were young people, which as the European missionaries knew very well, was, "another way of saying that they are poor."[85]

Weekly cash offerings were supplemented by the sales of palm oil which made the mission dependent on the fortunes of the export market. With the permission of the chiefs, young converts harvested oil-palm plots, processed the oil, and donated the proceeds of the sale to the church. Many chiefs, however, refused to grant schoolboys access to communal palm, who therefore resorted to various means in order to raise funds for mission buildings or teachers' wages.[86] Some learned carpentry from the mission and hired themselves out, giving a third, a half, or even the whole of the money received to the church as offerings. At Ibeno, Bill raised funds by selling cut timber from his steam sawmill. Other donations were received from Qua Iboe graduates who had moved on to the government school in Bonny. The students there received a cup of rice and a ship's biscuit for their daily food ration. The biscuits could be sold at five-a-penny, and twenty-four Eket boys studying at the school raised £1 2s 8d to be spent on a new church in their village of Atabong by saving and selling part of their daily allowance.[87] By these means the church's annual donations from local Christians in Qua Iboe had risen slowly from less than £100 per year to £300 in 1908, £550 in 1909, and £1,000 in 1910.[88]

---

with him and learn English' (*QIM Occasional Paper*, February 1905, (46), PRONI, D/3301/EA/3.).

84. In 1888 a small society called the 'Qua Iboe Missionary Association' was formed in Belfast and had raised just £70 in its first year. These original sponsors cut their funding in 1891 and advised Bill to move on to the Congo. Instead he returned home to Belfast that year and following a series of talks in Mission Halls formed an interdenominational council which became the first auxiliary of the mission.

85. M'Keown, 1912 p. 96.

86. In some localities whole groves of oil palms were reserved by the secret societies, and 'a Ju-ju mark', presumably an *èyèì*, was put on each tree to prohibit anyone from touching the fruit (Ibid).

87. Ibid pp. 96–97.

88. Ibid p. 90.

Throughout this period the southern Annang region to the west of the Qua Iboe River earned a reputation for fierce resistance and lawlessness. Across the region the government's grip was shaky and seasonal. During the rainy season, when government troops could not travel inland, communities took the opportunity to settle scores. Kirk records a "little war" between Afa-Ofiong and Etinan in the autumn of 1904. Both were heavily armed with Snider rifles, with the Afa Ofiong having "sold a number of boys and girls lately, and bought war material with the proceeds."[89] After the expedition to Abak in 1904 the district quietened down, but the country on the other side of the river remained "unsettled, and men wanted by the Police for their misdeeds found refuge there. Court messengers sent by the District Officer were badly treated and law and order was impossible."[90]

As a result of a series of inter-denominational delimitation conferences held from 1904 onwards, the Annang and Ibibio areas of Calabar Province were apportioned to the Qua Iboe Mission which therefore became the dominant mission in the region.[91] To the north, in Ikot Ekpene Division, were the Primitive Methodists, to the east the Calabar and Cross River areas were occupied by the United Free Church of Scotland, and to the west the lower Niger river was covered by the Niger Delta Pastorate of the Church Missionary Society. The Catholic Church refused to participate, and their attempts to gain a foothold in Annang and Ibibio territory exercised the Qua Iboe missionaries throughout this period. The first mission station in Abak Division was established at Ikot Idung near Abak in 1904, the same year that Samuel Bill declined an offer of an appointment as the Political Officer of "Kwa Ibo District."

The Qua Iboe Mission was able to secure support and enhance its authority in the Annang hinterland stations, such as Ikot Idung, by vouching for villages and saving them from attack as the expedition forces passed through. Evidence from fifteen years of patrols in Annang territory, from Roger Casement's journeys to the founding of Abak station, indicates that the Annang proved a constant irritant to British military forces. [92] While the Ikot Ekpene, Itu, and Uyo stations were opened in 1903, it was not until 1909, when the Ikot Ekpene patrol marched south, that the district station was established at Abak. On their route, at Ikwek (north of Abak), the column was attacked by the Obongs, Midims, Ikot Imos, and Afaha Obongs

---

89. *QIM Occasional Paper*, August 1904, (44), PRONI, D/3301/EA/3.
90. The Qua Iboe Mission Makes History, (J. W. Westgarth), 1946, PRONI: D/3301/GA/2.
91. Udo, 1972.
92. Northrup, 1979.

with cap guns and matchets.[93] This conflict led to widespread displacement, and many lineages in southwestern Annang villages who call themselves ńtɔ̃ Abak (the children of Abak) trace their settlement to this incident. After making tortuous progress with the construction of the new Qua Iboe stations at Ikot Idung, Smith vouched for the village when troops approached to launch the government expedition against the troublesome Annang district in 1909. He guaranteed that carriers would not be molested after the regular force had passed, and that the village would sell provisions to the troops. Smith himself treated the wounded casualties of the punitive raid from the villages further north.[94] Spared the ravages of the punitive raid, the population of Ikot Idung and neighboring Annang villages were not slow to notice the mission's growing influence.

References

Afigbo, A.E. 'The Eclipse of the Aro Slaving Oligarchy of South-Eastern Nigeria, 1901–27', *Journal of the Historical Society of Nigeria* 6(1), 1971, pp. 3–24.

Anene, J.C. 'The Protectorate Government of Southern Nigeria and the Aros 1900–1902', *Journal of the Historical Society of Nigeria* 1, 1956, pp. 20–26.

Bastian, M.L. 'Young Converts: Christian Missions, Gender and Youth in Onitsha, Nigeria 1880–1929', *Anthropological Quarterly* 73(3), 2000, pp. 145–158.

Dayrell, E. *Ikom Folk Stories from Southern Nigeria*, London: Royal Anthropological Institute, 1913.

Horton, R. & J.D.Y. Peel 'Conversion and Confusion: A rejoinder on Christianity in Eastern Nigeria', *Canadian Journal of African Studies* 10(3), 1976, pp. 481–498.

Ifeka-Moller, C. 'White Power: Social-structural Factors in Conversion to Christianity, Eastern Nigeria, 1921–1966', *Canadian Journal of African Studies* 9(1), 1974, pp. 55–72.

Jeffreys, M.D.W. 'Witchcraft in Calabar Province', *African Studies* 25(2), 1966, pp. 95–100.

Latham, A.J.H. 'Witchcraft Accusations and Economic Tension in Pre-Colonial Calabar', *Journal of African History* 13(2), 1972, pp. 249–260.

Meyer, B. *Translating the Devil: religion and modernity among the Ewe in Ghana*, Edinburgh: Edinburgh University Press, 1999.

---

93. Johnson, 1932. 'Afaha Obong, Annang Sub-Tribe, Abak District', NAE: CSE 1/85/4782A.
94. M'Keown, 1912 pp. 144–146.

M'Keown, R.L. *Twenty-five Years in Qua Iboe: the Story of Missionary Effort in Nigeria*, London: Morgan and Scott, 1912.

Noah, M.E. 'The Establishment of British Rule among the Ibibio, 1835–1910. Part One: The Military Approach', *Nigeria Magazine* (148), 1984, pp. 38–51.

Northrup, D. 'Roger Casement and the Aro', *Ikenga* 4(1), 1979, pp. 46–50.

Offiong, D.A. 'The 1978–79 Akpan Ekwong Anti-Witchcraft Crusade in Nigeria', *Anthropologica* XXIV, 1982, pp. 27–42.

Peel, J.D.Y. *Aladura: A Religious Movement Among the Yoruba*, London: Oxford University Press, 1968.

———— 'Syncretism and Religious Change', *Comparative Studies in Society and History* 10(2), 1968, pp. 121–141.

———— 'The Pastor and the Babalawo - the Interaction of Religions in 19th-Century Yorubaland', *Africa* 60(3), 1990, pp. 338–369.

———— 'For Who Hath Despised the Day of Small Things? Missionary Narratives and Historical Anthropology', *Comparative Studies in Society and History* 37(3), 1995, pp. 581–607.

———— *Religious Encounter and the Making of the Yoruba*, Bloomington: Indiana University Press, 2000.

———— 'Gender in Yoruba Religious Change', *Journal of religion in Africa*, 2002, pp. 136–166.

Simmons, D.C. 'Efik divination, ordeals and omens', *Southwestern Journal of Anthropology* 12(2), 1956, pp. 223–228.

Talbot, P. A. *Life in Southern Nigeria. The Magic, Beliefs and Customs of the Ibibio Tribe*, London: Frank Cass, 1923.

Udo, E. A. 'The missionary scramble for spheres of Influence in Eastern Nigeria, 1900–1952', *Ikenga* 1(2), 1972, pp. 22–36.

Westgarth, J.W. *The Holy Spirit and the Primitive Mind: A remarkable account of a spiritual awakening in darkest Africa*, London: Victory Press, 1946.

CHAPTER 19

CHRISTIANITY, COLONIAL RULE, AND ETHNICITY: THE MISSION OF THE WHITE FATHERS AMONG THE DAGARA (GHANA/BURKINA FASO)[1]

Carola Lentz

In 1985 the Bishop of Wa, the Archbishop of Tamale and more than fifty priests celebrated an especially festive mass in the large brick church of Jirapa in North-Western Ghana. For the first time, a young Dagara, Alphonsus Bakyil, a Ghanaian, was entering the order of the White Fathers, which since 1929 had converted thousands of men and women from the North-West and the neighboring French colony to Catholicism. At the same time, Father Remigius McCoy from Canada, at that time Father-Superior in Jirapa, was celebrating the jubilee of his ordination. In his commemoratory sermon, Bishop Kpiebaya, a Dagao[2] from Kaleo, reflected on the history of the mission in North-West Ghana:

---

1. This is a shortened and revised version of a chapter of my forthcoming book *Ethnicity and the Making of History in Northern Ghana*, Edinburgh: Edinburgh University Press. The paper is based on extended fieldwork as well as archival studies which I have carried out on Lawra District and the neighbouring areas in Burkina Faso since 1987. For more details on the history of the area and a list of all interviews and archival sources perused, see Lentz 1998.

2. Dagara ethnic names are a matter of controversy. British colonial administrators introduced the terms 'Dagarti' and 'Lobi', which many Ghanaians continue to use. French administrators used 'Dagari', in reference to the plural forms of the Mooré language. Most

What we are really celebrating here today is God's love for the Da-gaabas. We are among those fortunate people of the world whom He has chosen to bless again and again. Christianity came to us nearly fifty-six years ago, but little more than twenty of those had passed be-fore the first Dagati priest in Ghana was ordained [in 1951]. And less than nine years later...the first diocese in the Northwest was estab-lished with a Dagati bishop at its head. Great things were happening in our small corner of the Lord's vineyard....The first place in the Northwest to receive the Word of God now sends forth the first mis-sionary priest of the Northwest to carry that Word beyond the fron-tiers of Ghana. This day the Church in Jirapa and the Church of Wa diocese have truly come of age! (quoted in McCoy 1988: 238–9)

Bishop Kpiebaya's words bespoke gratitude that God had chosen the Dagaba (Dagara) as his people, satisfaction with the successful Africanization of the Catholic Church, and ethnic pride. Today, Dagara bishops officiate in three of the four dioceses in Northern Ghana, Wa, Damongo, and the Arch-Dio-cese of Tamale, and most members of the Tamale theological seminary's fac-ulty come from the North-West, a fact that irritates many non-Dagara. For Bishop Kpiebaya and many others, being Dagara and being Catholic are inti-mately linked, although in the region around Wa, and Kaleo especially, there were and are numerous Muslim Dagara as well as many families that were for-merly Christians, but have since returned to their traditional practices. Catholic Dagara, however, have in the course of several decades developed an ethnic sense of community which has also influenced the self-understanding of the non-Catholic Dagara, and which transcends the small-scale colonial ethnic categories and the local patriotism of the "native states," the colonially introduced chiefdoms.

Inspired by J. D. Y. Peel's magisterial work (2000) on the role of Christianity in the making of the Yoruba, this article discusses the intimate connections

---

of those so labelled (Dagarti, Dagari) reject these names as pejorative, but there has been much discussion over what to use instead. Some believe that the people living around Wa, Nadawli and Jirapa form a distinct group, namely the Dagaba (sg. Dagao; the British 'Da-garti'), who speak 'Dagaare', and that the term Dagara (or 'Lobr') should be reserved for the population of Lawra, Nandom and parts of South-West Burkina Faso (the British 'Lobi'). Others hold that 'Dagara' is the only correct term for both the language and the ethnic group. For details relevant to the controversy, see Lentz 1997: 42–54; see also Hawkins (2002: 39–45, 93–5) who continues to use Jack Goody's invented name 'LoDa-gaa'. Because my work focusses on the northern dialect group, I generally use the term 'Da-gara', unless referring specifically to the population of Jirapa and further south.

between evangelization and ethnicity in a case of a much smaller scale, involving a population of several hundred thousand which, although regionally dominant, constitutes a "minority" in the national setting of modern-day Ghana. Yet there are many parallels with the Yoruba case: the linguistic work of the mission played a crucial role in forging a new sense of ethnic community, and the mission-educated elite, prime movers of ethnic unity, came to play an important role in administration and politics, both at local and regional as well as national levels. Furthermore, as among the Yoruba, European missionaries, Dagara converts, and non-proselytized elders and chiefs engaged in heated debates about local religious practices and beliefs, and about the compatibility of "traditional culture" with the new creed or the necessity of reforms. A crucial difference, however, is that the White Fathers' activities in North-Western Ghana (and South-Western Burkina Faso) began only some thirty years after the establishment of colonial rule. British (and French) "pacification," the introduction of chiefs in formerly "stateless" societies, as well as massive labor migration produced a new socio-political landscape, and eventually lent colonially-created ethnic categories tangible reality. From the start, therefore, the new religious community had to position itself vis-à-vis these new self-understandings and practices which the British, however, tended to defend as "traditional" against Catholic reformist enthusiasm. As Peel has convincingly argued, relations between colonialism and the missionary project are contingent, the mission among the Dagara being a case in point. This article explores the ways in which the missionaries and their converts used, but also subverted and challenged colonial ethnic categories, contested chiefly authority, and debated cultural norms. I shall deal first with the beginnings of the mission and its development into a mass movement, which, in the early 1930s, became enmeshed in conflicts with the colonial government and the chiefs. I shall then discuss the ethnic categories used by missionaries, and sketch out the new infrastructure and social networks that the mission came to create in the course of time. I will also show how the codification of native law by the chiefs occurred against the backdrop of the challenge presented by Catholic converts, and how colonial administrators, chiefs, missionaries and converts engaged in intense discussions about the meaning of earth-shrine rituals, funerals, and marriage practices. Finally I shall examine the establishment of Catholic schools, from which emerged a Dagara elite quite different from the chiefs' sons.

Mass Conversion and Conflicts with the Colonial Regime

Until 1929 the British would not permit any Christian mission to establish a presence in the North-West. When in 1905 the White Fathers first expressed an interest in opening a mission station in the Northern Territories, the chief commissioner had political reservations vis-à-vis the White Fathers, who were based in the neighboring French colony. He was also concerned that religious competition with Islam, dominant in the urban polity of Wa, might make the pacification of the "Lobi" and "Dagarti" even more difficult than it already was.[3] The White Fathers had to follow the chief commissioner's suggestion and opened their first mission station in the North-East of the Northern Territories, at Navrongo, where, however, they were only able to win relatively few converts.[4] Nonetheless, the presence of the missionaries changed the British view of the White Fathers. Despite some tensions between converts and chiefs, missionary work struck them as politically relatively harmless, and Catholic education as useful.[5] The White Fathers' renewed attempts to extend their radius of activity to the North-West in order to forestall the expansion of the American Protestant Missionary Society were supported by Lawra District Commissioner Eyre-Smith. Himself an Irish Catholic, he was generally well-disposed to the White Fathers, and recommended the Dagaba to them as a hard-working, honest, peaceable, and gracious tribe, open to innovation, who one day might make good Catholics. However, the chief commissioner and the governor continued to have political reservations regarding the "French" White Fathers. Only via the intervention of the apostolic delegate, who turned to the governor in Accra for help, was permission attained to open a mission station in Jirapa in 1929.[6]

---

3. Detail of tour of inspection in March and April 1906, National Archives of Ghana, Accra (NAG), ADM 56/1/43: 9; letter of Oscar Morin to Mgr Bazin, Navrongo, 4 June 1906, Vicariat apostolique du Soudan Français, Chronique trimestrielle 1904–09, Archives Générales des Missionaires d'Afrique, Rom (A.G.M.Afr), AO2: 226. On this, see also Der 1983: 94–5. On the (pre)history of the White Fathers in the neighbouring French colony, see Somé 1996.

4. After fifteen years of proselytising, the White Fathers only counted 422 baptised individuals and about 500 catechists; see Northern Territories, Annual Report 1922–23 (Colonial Reports).

5. On this, see Thomas 1975: 432–6; see also Der 1983: 40–7; Naameh 1986: 166–8.

6. On this, see History of Navrongo etc., A.G.M.Afr., Dos 291/6; John McNulty, *The fiftieth anniversary of the evangelization of North-West Ghana*, Jirapa 1979, A.G.M.Afr., N

The White Fathers thus began their work in the North-West at a time when the colonial geography of administrative districts and native states had long since become fact. The chiefs, at least, had by now become familiar with the new political order, having even adopted the colonial ethnic categories and neo-traditional rituals.[7] The founding of the mission in Jirapa came at a time of intense debate over political reform. Eyre-Smith's critical reports on abuses of the chiefly office had sensitized the district commissioner and his superiors to the potential for conflict that was brewing in some areas due to the arbitrariness of the chiefs. And so it was that colonial officials observed the work of the White Fathers with even greater mistrust, and soon saw confirmed their fears that the mission might very well destabilize the political order they had so carefully built.

In the first year after the mission station was opened, the three White Fathers who had been delegated to Jirapa from Navrongo, with Father McCoy as their superior, learned the local language in accordance with the evangelization method of their order. At the bidding of the district commissioner, the paramount chief of Jirapa, Jirapa Naa Ganaa, allotted the new settlers a plot of land and provided labor to build the station. Otherwise Ganaa and most of the other inhabitants of Jirapa kept their distance. With the support of the British medical officer stationed in Lawra, the missionaries soon set up a medical post. Since their modern medicine cured many illnesses like yaws, dysentery, and sleeping sickness—something traditional diviners and medicines failed to do—trust in the White Fathers gradually increased. According to the mission's statistics, more than 16,000 patients sought treatment at the station in 1931–32.[8] The reputation of the White Fathers as powerful healers, as Father McCoy recalled (1988: 55–61), was furthered particularly by the "miracle" healing of a headman whose relatives had long given up hope for recovery. Medical treatment was always accompanied by prayer and religious instruction. However, the missionaries also used modern, worldly methods of winning devotees, such as records, films and football, which soon became

---

189/3; also Lesourd 1938; Paternot 1949: 27–8; Der 1974; McCoy 1988: 33–4; Naameh 1986: 169; Der 1983: 118–24.

7. On the colonial introduction of chieftaincy and its local appropriation, see Lentz 2000a, 2003, on the history of ethnicity in the North-West, Lentz 2000b.

8. Préfecture Apostolique de Navrongo, Rapport Annuel, A.G.M. Afr., AO 15. For Sean Hawkins (1997; 2002, ch. 6), the successful provision of medical care is the first and foremost reason for the success of the White Fathers' mission. He sees the second reason in the population's dissatisfaction with the colonial political system, especially the chiefs (see below).

a favorite sport among village youths.[9] Already by the end of 1931 the White Fathers counted sixty-eight baptised Christians and 432 catechumens, while the number of those who sojourned to Jirapa Sunday after Sunday, or who stayed there several weeks on end for catechism instruction, finally obtaining a Mary medal, went into the thousands.[10]

Among the primary factors contributing to the exponential spread of the new belief were the return labor migrants, who, driven by curiosity, stopped over in Jirapa and then spread word of the new powerful cult in their home villages. The new faith was especially attractive to those young migrants who may already have been introduced to the Christian religion in Ashanti and the colony. On the one hand, it allowed them to overcome the stigma of "primitiveness," and of being "uncivilized," with which they were confronted when away from home. On the other hand, with its emphasis on the individual and its criticism of unquestioned subordination to one's elders, it offered potential backing in family conflicts over decisions to migrate, the distribution of income from migration, and marriage preferences.[11] Conversely, their experience of having survived apart from the extended family and their ancestral cult back home, "without frequently consulting the family fetish," contributed to their receptiveness for the new religion.[12]

Isolated conflicts between converts and chiefs already seem to have arisen at the start of 1932, as some headmen later reported to Lawra District Commissioner Guinness. Many converts met in their villages to pray daily, and re-

---

9. See Der 1983: 56–7; McCoy 1988: 50–1.

10. See Préfecture Apostolique de Navrongo, Rapport Annuel, A.G.M. Afr., AO 15; Der 1983: 48. The DC estimated the number of catechists at 12,000 to 13,000; Lawra-Tumu District, Annual Report 1931–32, Northern Regional Archives, Tamale (RAT), NRG 8/3/27. The catechumenate consisted of three stages and took four years altogether. After participating for three to six months in the Sunday instruction for the catechism and undertaking two days work for the mission, the converts received a medal with a picture of the Virgin Mary. After a total of two years instruction and passing marks on an examination they received a rosary, and finally, after a further two years instruction and change to a Christian way of life, they were baptised. On this, see Rapport du sup. Rég. P. Blin, November 1933–January 1934, A.G.M. Afr. Dos. 198/7; McCoy 1988: 315; Lesourd 1938; Paternot 1949: 136–9.

11. For the relationship between the mission and individualisation, see also Birgit Meyer's study (1999) on the Protestant mission among the Peki-Ewe.

12. DC Lawra-Tumu Eyre-Smith, in Northern Territories, Annual Report 1923–24 (Colonial Reports). Here I draw on material collected in biographical interviews with early converts, who were all labour migrants before becoming Christians. However, obviously not all labour migrants converted. A systematic study of the relationship between Christianisation and labour migration in the North-West has yet to be undertaken.

fused to take part in sacrifices at the earth shrine or to work for their chief on Sundays. The only "Whites" whom they would still recognize, according to Guinness, were the "White Fathers":

> [C]ertain men…have been going about making wild statements such as that 'there were no more Chiefs now and no white men any longer but the White Fathers' and 'they should not obey their Headmen any more'.…The headman of Bazin further states that 'a certain gang' has walked about the country carrying a red cloth on a stick, and giving out that the authority of the Chiefs was at an end.[13]

When asked, the headman of Bazin admitted that he did not know the significance of the red flag. However, he and other chiefs saw another Christian symbol as a direct attack on the dignity of the chiefs, namely the Mary medals that converts wore proudly around their necks, which bore a certain similarity to the chiefs' medals.[14] In general, chiefs tended to see the Christians, and particularly the catechists, to be potential rivals.[15]

In summer 1932, the flow of converts to Jirapa and the conflicts with the chiefs reached a peak in connection with an occurrence that Catholic chroniclers later came to call the "rain event," raising it to the status of the single most important event that paved the way for the realization of a Christian mass movement. As Chief Commissioner Duncan-Johnstone noted in his diary, 1932 was a year of "food shortages." In Tamale, there was less rainfall than there had been in any of the previous twenty-three years.[16] Despite all the offerings at the earth shrines and rainmakers' supplications, no rain fell in Lawra District either. Only in Jirapa, noted Guinness, did any rain fall, and "[t]he White Fathers are making a lot of converts in consequence."[17] As Father McCoy writes in his memoirs, one village headman is supposed to have gone to the White Fathers with his elders and promised to take up the new faith, even destroying all "fetishes," if only rain could be summoned. And in fact, on that very day, it is said to have rained heavily in that village, a sign sent by

---

13. DC Lawra-Tumu to CCNT, 8 Sep. 1932, NAG, ADM 56/1/301.

14. It is also striking that the converts only destroyed the ancestral shrines in their homes after acquiring their medals. Naameh (1986: 196–7, 204–5) therefore assumes that the Christian medals were seen as powerful 'fetishes'.

15. Interview with Archbishop Peter Dery, Tamale, 7 Jan. 1995; on the conflicts of Dery's father Porekuu with the Nandom Naa, see also McCoy 1988: 75–83.

16. CCNT, Diary, 25.7 and 4 Aug. 1932, Rhodes House Library (RHL), Mss. Afr.s. 593.

17. Lawra-Tumu District, Informal Diary, 16 and 21 July 1932, RAT, NRG 8/4/62.

God, as Father McCoy believed, which was to aid Christianity achieve a breakthrough.[18] In any case, an increasing number of delegations came to Jirapa to pray for rain. As Guinness reported, the missionaries emphatically preached to them, that "they could not expect rain if they prayed to God and to their old Fetishes as well. Those of them who were doing so therefore went home and destroyed their own Fetishes."[19]

Guinness accused the White Fathers of inciting their converts to religious fanaticism, but Father Paquet assured Guinness "that he has never instructed his people to force their neighbours' consciences," and Father McCoy delivered "a strong moral lecture" to the "iconoclasts" before the district commissioner sentenced them to prison.[20]

Whether this measure was in line with his own convictions, or a tactical attempt to avoid the escalation of conflicts with the colonial government, remains uncertain. In the eyes of the missionaries and, later, Catholic historians, neither the mass conversions nor the conflicts with the chiefs were politically motivated. The converts were merely opposing restrictions on the exercise of their new belief, which inevitably ended in conflicts with many chiefs and lineage elders.[21] By contrast, colonial officials tended to read these events politically, though in two contrasting manners. Eyre-Smith regarded the mass conversion to be a true "revolution" that expressed the people's aversion to the "tyranny" of the chiefs imposed upon them.[22] For Guinness and most of the other British administrators, on the other hand, the popularity of the White Fathers was "merely the result of a fortunate and apparently miraculous answer to a prayer for rain,"[23] after which the missionaries had begun to incite those in their flock to resist the chiefs. Chief Commissioner Duncan-Johnstone saw parallels with the Watchtower Movement, which in the 1920s had challenged the colonial hierarchy in Northern Rhodesia. He doubted

---

18. There are different versions of the exact timing and the identity of the affected village (or villages): McCoy's recollections (1988: 109–24, 247–9, 285–6) mention Daffiama and then numerous other villages; Paternot (1949: 123–31), Der (1983: 49–50) and Naameh (1986: 179–84) write about Jirapa itself.

19. DC Lawra-Tumu to CCNT, 8 Sep. 1932, NAG, ADM 56/1/301. See also Duncan-Johnstone, Diary, 10.8 and 14, 15 and 19 Sep. 1932, RHL, Mss. Afr.s. 593.

20. Lawra-Tumu District, Informal Diary, 26 and 30 July 1932, RAT, NRG 8/4/62.

21. See, for example, Der 1983: 48–57; Naameh 1986: 206–24; Bekye 1991: 269–309.

22. Eyre-Smith to Secretary for Native Affairs, 2 March 1933, NAG, ADM 11/1/824, §40–43. This interpretation of conversion as the expression of anti-colonial protests is also shared by Hawkins (1997: 55–65).

23. CCNT to Secretary for Native Affairs, 1 April 1933, NAG, ADM 11/1/824.

whether a "fanatic" like McCoy was the right man for an area like Lawra District, "among such a high spirited and excited people."[24]

The district commissioners on the spot reacted to the conflicts of 1932 and 1933 with a combination of tough intervention in support of the chiefs and a readiness to compromise. Guinness, for example, sentenced the "iconoclasts" and other active Christians to several months' imprisonment with hard labor. However, he also ordered that a weekday be designated on which converts might go to attend mass in Jirapa, undisturbed by their chiefs.[25] Some time later District Commissioner Armstrong called a meeting of missionaries and chiefs in Lawra, at which the latter were once again obliged to cease exacting Sunday work, while the former promised to enjoin their followers to fulfil their other obligations to their chiefs.[26] The introduction of taxation in 1936, which did away with obligatory roadwork, further de-escalated the conflicts between chiefs and converts.

"The history of the relations between the native authorities and the Mission have passed from outright antagonism to compromise and then more compromise": in these words District Commissioner Ellison ultimately summed up matters in 1939.[27] One contributing factor was certainly that the White Fathers themselves had no interest whatsoever in being at odds with the colonial government. They had their own ideas concerning the characteristics of "real chiefs who thoroughly understand the meaning of authority and who have always in their mind the good of their subjects,"[28] but in principle shared the colonial aim of disciplining the Africans. They were themselves surprised by the success of their mission and were genuinely concerned about how the new Christian movement was to be controlled. Following the "rain event" the number of converts rapidly increased, and by December 1932 mission reports already recorded over 20,000 believers in the North-West.[29]

---

24. CCNT, Diary, 30 Sep. 1932, NAG, ADM 56/1/301; see also CCNT to Colonial Secretary, Gold Coast Confidential, 14 Dec. 1934, enclosures 1 and 3, Public Record Office, London (PRO), CO 96/720/31002. On the perspective of the missionaries, see McCoy 1988: 133–8.

25. Guinness to CCNT, 8 Sep. 1932, NAG, ADM 56/1/301. The local calendar was based on a six-day week structured in accordance with regularly occurring markets. As a result, the missionaries, in their work outside Jirapa, initially declared that day on which they visited a particular area to be Sunday. Only in the course of 1932 did a uniform Sunday gradually become part of the local calendar; on this, see McCoy 1988: 99–102.

26. Lawra-Tumu District, Informal Diary, 6 May 1935, RAT, NRG 8/4/76.

27. Lawra-Tumu District, Annual Report 1938–39, RAT, NRG 8/3/78: 34.

28. F. Barsalou to CCNT, 4 Sep. 1934, enclosure 6 in Gold Coast Confidential of 14 Dec. 1934, PRO, CO 96/720/31002.

29. See Préfecture Apostolique de Navrongo, Rapport Annuel, 1932–33, A.G.M. Afr., AO 15, also Northern Territories, Annual Report, 1932–33, RAT, NRG 8/3/46. However,

However, within a few short years, the systematic training of catechists made it possible to discipline believers and transform what had once been a radical "sect" into a well-organized church. Since the catechists, initially trained for three and then for four years in Jirapa, were sent back to the villages to serve the new congregations there, and since more mission stations were set up—at Kaleo in 1932 and Nandom in 1933, as well as at Dissin and Dano on French territory—the weekly stream of pilgrims to Jirapa also gradually abated.[30] In the three mission stations of Jirapa, Kaleo, and Nandom the numbers of baptised Christians increased from a good 500 in 1933–34 to just under 10,000 in 1937–38.[31] District Commissioner Ellison estimated that by now a quarter of the population of the Lawra Confederacy "followed" the White Fathers,[32] and in some areas, such as the chiefdom of Nandom, the congregation eventually counted over 15,000 baptised Catholics, more than two-thirds of the population.[33]

Although the anti-authoritarian impulse had been harnessed and gradual accommodation between converts and chiefs had been achieved, the new religious community in many respects continued to present a challenge to the power of the elders supported by the ancestors, and to the colonial political order. It offered an entirely different framework of collective identification than the native states, produced a different infrastructure, drew ethnic boundaries differently from the colonial government, and contended with the chiefs over the definition of customary law.

Pays Dagari: a Catholic Trans-Border Community

The mission principle of the White Fathers was "one post, one language" (Lesourd 1938). Linguistic criteria already played a role in the decision to work in the North-West. The White Fathers hoped that they could profit from their familiarity with the Mooré by proselytizing the linguistically related "Dagari."

---

following his visit to the new mission stations, the Regional Superior of Navrongo, P. Blin, warned against exaggerating the figures; Rapport sur la Préfecture de Navrongo, November 1933–January 1934, A.G.M.Afr.Dos. 198/7.

30. On the training of the catechists, see McCoy 1988: 94–103; Naameh 1986: 257–61.

31. See Préfecture Apostolique de Navrongo, Rapport Annuel, 1932–33, A.G.M. Afr., AO 15; also Der 1983: 62–4.

32. Lawra-Tumu District, Annual Report 1938–39, RAT, NRG 8/3/78: 34–7.

33. Préfecture Apostolique de Navrongo, Rapport Annuel, 1950–51, A.G.M. Afr., AO 15. This figure obviously includes the children of the first converts.

Differences in dialect or culture and political boundaries were not terribly important in evangelization, so long as the people could only understand the missionaries' message. As a result, the *pays Dagari*, as the White Fathers, who spoke French among themselves, called their new mission area, transcended all colonial boundaries and existing ethnographic conventions. Lesourd (1938) and Paternot (1949: 23) even have the *territoire dagari* stretching from 10° to 12° latitude, from Wa to Boromo. The area shown in Paternot's cartographic sketch (see map on next page) still forms the basis for many Dagara intellectuals' idea of "Dagaraland."

Despite more widely drawn ethnic boundaries, the White Fathers' notions of the "Dagari" (in the French-speaking context) or the "Dagaaba" (in the English-speaking context) by no means gainsaid colonial ethnography. The missionaries not only shared colonial officials' essentialist understanding of ethnicity, they also adopted the current colonial ethnic stereotypes and, if only partly, the colonial nomenclature. The "tribe of the Dagaris" was seen as a horticultural, hard-working, modest and hospitable tribe, "with rather docile customs and quite open to European penetration" (Lesourd 1938), unlike the still "untamed" Lobi. Like French officials, Paternot stressed the close relationship of the "Dagari" with the "Ouilé." He even obtained his initial information on the Dagari from the *commandant du cercle* in Diébougou (1949: 23–4, 149–50).[34] Father McCoy, working in British territory, spoke of the Dagaaba, Wala, LoWilli and Lobi, though he probably only later adopted the term "LoWilli" from Goody (1956), meaning by "Lobi" not the Lobi-Dagarti of the colonial officials, but the recently in-migrated Birifor south of Wa.[35]

Alongside language, religious aspects also influenced how Christians defined ethnic boundaries, much as colonial officials had created ethnic categories from the administrative point of view. The White Fathers' missionary success among the Dagara was unparalleled in Africa. This therefore presented missionaries, and later the local priesthood, with the pressing question as to what distinguished the Dagara from other groups. In the first instance, as in the sermon of Bishop Kpiebaya quoted earlier, they referred to God's ineffable will. However, they also sought and continue to seek a psychology, traditional religion and social organization peculiar to the Dagara that were supposed to have favored conversion. "Their naturally religious background and incorporeal concept of God," argued McCoy (1988: 229), together with a rather high moral code and a value system similar to that of Christianity, made

---

34. Paternot's listing of the 'main characteristics of our Dagari' (1949: 33) did not differ from colonial ethnographies (see Tauxier 1912, Delafosse 1912, Labouret 1931).

35. McCoy 1988: 230, 311 fn. 2 to Ch. 2.

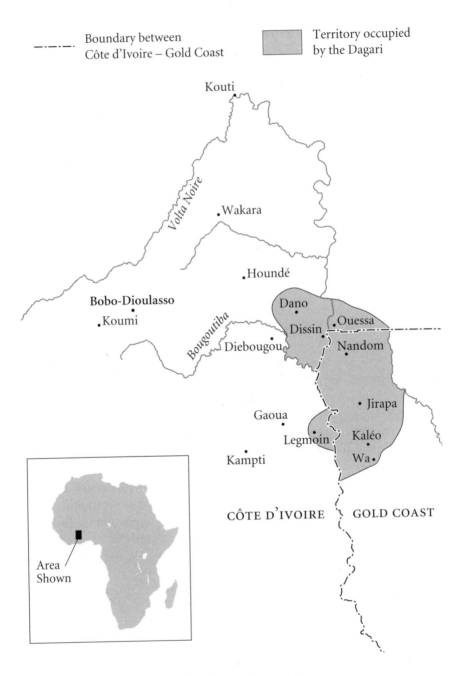

Figure 19.1 - Territoire Dagari, after Paternot 1949.

it relatively easy for them to accept the Ngwinsore ['God's way', i.e. the Christian faith]. Other Catholic authors regard not only the intellectual affinity of "animistic monotheism" (Girault 1959) to the Christian doctrine, but also of Christian symbols and rituals to local religious practices as factors that facilitated the mass shift to Christianity.[36]

In any event, being "Dagari" or "Dagaaba" came in the eyes of missionaries and converts to be regarded as synonymous with a receptiveness to Catholicism. If, however, a group would not allow itself be proselytized, or only hesitantly, then it had to be a different tribe, regardless of any linguistic or cultural similarities to the Dagara. Thus Father McCoy, for example, referred to the "Birofo" (by which he meant the Dagara inhabitants of Birifu), who resisted proselytization, as a distinct ethnic group and "a very special people," despite their close ties with their "Dagati cousins" (1988: 217–18).[37] Among the Wala too, who are closely related to the Dagaba linguistically, the missionaries stressed difference, not similarity. Ardron, District Commissioner of Wa, even complained about the increase in ethnic tensions caused by the construction of the mission station in Kaleo: "Mission influence over the Dagarti has tended to put a strain on traditional loyalty and friendship between the ruling Wala and the subject Dagarti."[38] However, considering the conflicts between the Wa Na and the Dagaba toward the end of the nineteenth century, one cannot but question Ardron's harmonious view of the Wala-Dagaba relationship of the past.[39] In fact, the Dagaba most likely used the new Catholic congregation as a means of defence against the Wala's continuing assertion of power, as Ardron also wrote. The conversion of many Dagaba to Christianity thus strengthened the mainly religious (and politically) defined boundary between the Wala and

---

36. On this, see Naameh 1986: 198–224; Mukassa 1987: 124–38; Der 1983: 53–8; Dabire 1983: 226–55; Bekye 1991: 274–309. On the problematic construction of a uniform 'traditional religion' by Dagara priests, see Goody 1975, Somé 1991, and Hawkins 1996, 1998.

37. Strong criticism of this distinction and of McCoy's comments on Birifu can be found in Gandah (1967/1993: 64–8). Gandah, himself the son of the Birifu Naa, whom McCoy accused of religious intolerance, joined the Ahmadiyya movement in 1941 while a schoolboy in Tamale, this although many of his brothers are Catholics.

38. DC Wa to CCNT, 5 Feb. 1937, RAT, NRG 8/19/7. See also McCoy 1988: 136–8, on the quarrel with DC Ardron.

39. See Wilks 1989, Chs. 5, 6 and 7, also the present work, Ch. 1. In addition, when the mission station opened in Kaleo, Wa was preoccupied with internal conflicts. The success of the Ahmadiyya mission amongst one of the competing Wala factions exacerbated the local power struggle to the point at which violence finally broke out.

the Dagaba that also existed in the pre-colonial period. Just as, for many Wala Muslims, a Wala who becomes a Christian is no longer "a proper Wala," so too, in the eyes of Dagara Catholics, a Dagara who turns to Islam is no longer "a proper Dagara."

The association of Dagara-ness with Catholicism has also reinforced the ethnic distinction from the Sisala, especially in Lambussie where Christian Dagara farmers live on Sisala land. The dominance of the Dagara language in evangelization has led to almost all catechists, and later the local priesthood too, being Dagara, as they still are. In a sense, the Sisala would have been required to undergo a double conversion, to Christianity and to Dagara speech. Few were prepared to do this, particularly since the material advantages of belonging to the new religion, schools, medical posts, and other development projects had scarcely reached Sisala villages. Only Peter Dery, who refers to himself as "of mixed Sisala–Dagaba origin," and who became Bishop of the new Diocese of Wa in 1960, ensured that all catechists and priests who were active in Sisala areas, whether Dagara or not, learned and used Sisala.[40]

While ethnic boundaries "to the outside," to the Sisala and Wala, were stressed, the small-scale ethnic differences between the Dagarti, Lobi and Lobi-Dagarti, which had been emphasized by the British, lost their significance. In the eyes of the White Fathers, they were dealing with one large people living on both sides of the international border.[41] This unity also began to take shape in practice through the masses of Dagara who sojourned to Jirapa from all over, including villages in French territory, in order to take part in the catechism.[42] In the summer of 1932 more than ten thousand followers and onlookers frequently gathered together in Jirapa, and the flood of Dagara from Upper Volta took on such proportions that French colonial authorities became concerned that some of the many pilgrims might become emigrants, resulting in a drain of taxpayers and labor power. In 1933, therefore, the responsible French *commandant de cercle* called a meeting with representatives of the White Fathers from Ouagadougou, Bobo Dioulasso, Navrongo, and Jirapa. After the proposal to close the border was rejected, the commandant finally suggested that the missionaries open stations on French territory too, thus making the pilgrims' journey to Jirapa unnecessary. The choice fell on Dano and Dissin, places that had the most converts up to that point. In turn, the

---

40. Interview, Tamale, 7 Jan. 1995. On this, see also Tengan (1991: 25–30, 208–15), one of the first Dagara priests to be raised in the Sisala area, and a fluent Sisala speaker.

41. See Lesourd 1938; Paternot 1949: 23–33; McCoy 1988: 35–8.

42. On this, see Lesourd 1938; Paternot 1949: 141–53.

White Fathers had to promise to send all Upper Volta converts in Jirapa back to the new stations on French territory.[43]

The brief period of a large, trans-border religious community thus gave way to a separate development of Catholicism. Thus, from teaching the catechists to training the local clergy, to the production of written material, the "British" and "French" vicariates reproduced certain colonial idiosyncrasies. However, in neither local community did the awareness of belonging to a trans-border, pan-Dagara community ever disappear.

A New Infrastructure

Although the mission had to recognize the international border, the territorial organization of the Catholic Church within the North-West stood, and continues to stand, in a tense relationship to the colonial political geography of the native states. Jirapa was recommended to the White Fathers as "the most central of the Dagati [sic] villages" (McCoy 1988: 34, 48), and evangelical work benefited from the colonial infrastructure, including roads and paths. However, in the course of time they altered it in a way that was to have secular political consequences. Colonial officials probably also recommended Jirapa, because it kept the mission at a distance from the district station. When, in 1932–33, additional mission stations were to be built, and the White Fathers considered Lawra as a potential site, Lawra Naa Lobi Binni, together with District Commissioner Armstrong apparently rejected any such idea.[44] Nandom Naa Konkuu thought otherwise. True, he had imprisoned some of the "iconoclasts," and also jailed Porekuu, a particularly active catechist who had built a chapel in Zimuopere that attracted a thousand converts, for incitement against the chiefs. Yet at the same time, he offered to let the White Fathers build a church in Nandom, hoping this move would pull the rug from under Zimuopere's unwanted rivalry, as Father McCoy reckoned in hindsight (1988: 78–82, 250–1). This coincided with the tactical considerations of the White Fathers who did not want to further heighten anxieties amongst the divisional chiefs that their power was threatened. Moreover, Konkuu is said to have acted exactly as the Jirapa Naa had done

---

43. On the so-called 'Ouessa conference', see Diaire de Ouagadougou, 17 and 14 Jan. 1933, A.G.M.Afr.; Lesourd 1938; McCoy 1988: 125–8; Naameh 1986: 185–7; Somé 1993: 104–12. On the further development of the mission stations at Dissin and Dano, see Somé 1993: 307–17.

44. On this, see Der 1983: 52, 61. Lawra only became a parish of its own in 1966.

some years earlier, in that he allotted the missionaries a barren piece of land allegedly haunted by spirits, and waited to see whether they would drive out the White Fathers or the White Fathers be driven out by them.[45] Later, colonial officials heaped praise on the Nandom Naa for having successfully managed "to steer his course between the diametrically opposed creeds of his people, keep on good terms with the mission, and with a purely pagan belief adjudicate impartially."[46]

New stations were situated to facilitate effective evangelization, that is, in easily accessible areas preferably with a large number of converts, although local power relations also had to be taken into account. Nevertheless the parish boundaries cross-cut those of the divisions, a situation that time and again gave rise to conflicts. District Commissioner Ellison, for example, reported the Lawra Naa complained that the converts of Lissa were not prepared to recognize his authority in settling a dispute over the creation of a Christian cemetery, but instead turned to Nandom. Ellison suspected that affiliation with the Nandom parish might actually lead to political secession, as the Lawra Naa feared, and advised the mission "to confine their activities and conform to Administrative areas."[47] However, the missionaries were not able to follow this advice, nor did they want to. Until 1960 the spiritual needs of Dagara converts living on Sisala land in Tumu and Lambussie were served by the Nandom mission. This happened also to correspond perfectly to their social ties, given that many of them had only recently migrated into the Sisala area from villages in Nandom Division. Although after 1960 parts of the former Nandom parish had become parishes in their own right, the idea of a "greater Nandom," that emerged from the early days of Catholicism, is in the minds of many still alive today and engendered the potential for political conflict when, for instance, new administrative districts were to be created.[48]

The material infrastructure created by the White Fathers also tended to compete with that of the native authorities, or at least had different geographical foci. The settlement of the mission in Jirapa, for example, involved building a church and a catechism school, followed by the opening of a girls' school, a hospital, and a credit union, which boosted the local economy and increased the population of Jirapa so that it came to outnumber that of Lawra. Since the

45. Interview with Archbishop Peter Dery, Tamale, 7 Jan. 1995.

46. Lawra-Tumu District, Annual Report 1938–39, RAT, NRG 8/3/78: 6. See also Northern Territories, Annual Report 1936–37, PRO, CO 96/738, No. 31196: 73.

47. Lawra-Tumu District, Informal Diary, 28 March 1935, RAT, NRG 8/4/76; see also 20, 26 March 1935, ibid.

48. On this, see Lentz 2002.

1970s, therefore, the Jirapa Naa and the Jirapa Youth Association have been petitioning for a district of their own, which was finally granted in the late 1980s, though jointly with Lambussie.[49] Like Jirapa, Nandom also grew in importance, which it might not have done had it not been for the White Fathers. Initially opposed by the Nandom Naa, but later coming under his protection, a lively Sunday market developed here; and after 1940, a daily market in the street leading to the mission followed.[50] In 1937 the region's first Catholic primary school for boys opened, followed in 1950 by a middle school, then in 1958 a primary school, and a middle school for girls, and finally, in 1968, a secondary school, as well as a hospital, two technical craft schools, and various agricultural development projects. Yet apart from a brief period in the 1960s, Nandom never succeeded in achieving the rank of district headquarters.

The Church also created new social networks which corresponded neither to the longstanding collective identities of patriclan and earth shrine, nor to the "local patriotism" of the colonial native states. The masses held in Jirapa, particularly those held in the early years, which attracted thousands of believers, clearly illustrated the existence of a large community of Dagara speakers. No political occasion could bring together in Lawra District so many people who could communicate in a single language.[51] The central catechism school and the mobility of its graduates, who were normally not assigned to their own villages, the need to transcend the boundaries of culture and dialect in search of a Christian spouse, the Christian schools, whose pupils and teachers were recruited almost exclusively from among the Dagaba, the rise of a local clergy, new associations, courses and festivals, which mobilized Dagaba believers from across the North-West: all of this helped make a living reality a language area and a new, broadly inclusive definition of a great Dagaba/Dagara community, at least for Catholics.

However, the fact that, in British territory, the expansion of this language area progressed from Jirapa had consequences that were later to give rise to conflicts. The first Dagaare catechism was printed in 1931, soon followed by a two-volume comprehensive version for catechism training, numerous prayers, school primers and a dictionary, all texts translated by the White Fathers, in

---

49. See Lentz 1995.

50. The Nandom Naa complained that the Sunday market was not paying market fees to the native authority and was competing with the six-day market; see Lawra-Tumu District, Informal Diary, 12 and 17 Sep. 1934, RAT, NRG 8/4/62. For the later accommodation, see Informal Diary, 19 and 21. 1.1940, also 2 April 1942, NAG, ADM 61/5/16.

51. On this, see also the report of a service held in Nandom by DC Amory, Northern Territories, Annual Report 1936–37, Appendix A: 13, PRO, CO 96/738 No. 31196; see also the photographs of masses held in Dissin and Dano in Lesourd 1938.

consultation with their catechists, into the dialect most familiar to the latter, namely that used in Jirapa and its environs.[52] Because it was the first to be put into writing, the Jirapa dialect was predominant in the training of catechists and priests, as well as in religious services and schools. Even if other dialects could be used in sermons and oral explications, the Dagaare of Jirapa continued to predominate by virtue of the fact that it had a written form and so became a sort of standard speech even adopted by native authority schools.[53] Speakers of other dialects were thus at a distinct disadvantage—at least, this is the current view of many educated Dagara from Nandom, where the dialect spoken is the one that predominates among the Dagara congregations of Upper Volta, having there been given a written form by the White Fathers.[54]

As with the chiefs of the various divisions in the native administration, the educated of the various dialect groups compete with one another over scarce resources and influence. Nevertheless, Christians share the conviction that Dagara or Dagaare constitutes a large trans-border language area. At the same time, however, the Catholic basis for this community also implied certain ideas concerning the content of a Dagara/Dagaba identity. In the following section, I shall deal with the tension between these ideas and native customs as codified by the chiefs.

Christian Law versus Native Custom

In central aspects of life, the Catholic Church prescribed and still prescribes norms that collided with local values and practices. Conflicts, between converts on the one hand and chiefs, earth priests and non-Christian elders on the other, flared up particularly when converts refused to continue making sacrifices to the ancestors or the earth deity, or to take part in any other "pagan" rituals. Furthermore, there were disputes over particular burial ceremonies and the regulation of marriage and divorce, questions touching on relationships between young and old, and between men and women. However, despite their deep-seated differences of opinion, the adversaries negotiated compromises so that they could, more or less, live together in peace.

One example of a practical compromise involved the sacrifices that the earth priest made prior to the construction of a new house, a practice Christians rejected. The Lawra District Commissioner laid down that "[c]onverts

---

52. On this, see McCoy 1988: 98–9; Der 1983: 272–3, 294–8.
53. On this, see Lawra-Tumu District, Annual Report 1941–42, RAT, NRG 8/3/108: 5; Informal Diary, 25 Jan. 1944, NAG, ADM 61/5/16.
54. On this, see Bemile 2000: 211–22.

wishing to build new compounds will in future give the Tengdana a 'dash' and a paper from the Fathers."[55] The former ritual of sacrifice was therefore divided into a voluntary, religious part and a secular, political component, obligatory for everyone, including Christians, a move that protected one of the earth priests' sources of income. Similar compromises were reached for funeral customs. When Father McCoy complained that "pagan" relatives were refusing to bury deceased Christians without the usual rituals of sacrifice, District Commissioner Ellison suggested that chiefs and tendanas permit the establishment of Christian cemeteries. A failure to do so would likely result in a state of permanent conflict "where converts are desecrating land which is consecrated by native custom."[56] At a gathering held in Lawra in May 1935, to which District Commissioner Armstrong invited the White Fathers and all the divisional chiefs and sub-chiefs, these and other regulations, such as those regarding Sunday work, were publicly affirmed.

Yet these compromises were just a sort of framework agreement; the details continued to be a matter of dispute. Disagreements ensued not only over the actual allotment of Christian cemeteries,[57] but also over the question of whether Christians still had to provide material contributions to sacrifices at the earth shrine. The missionaries advocated the abolition of the native custom "by which stray sheep, goats or anything else found on the land had to be taken to the Tindana who then makes the owner make a small sacrifice to the land god," but District Commissioner Armstrong saw no reason why this "age-old custom" should be changed.[58] Because of the district commissioners' refusal to budge on this and other matters, Bishop Morin finally demanded that the colonial government endeavor to clarify the fundamental principles according to which conflicts between "native custom" and "Christian law" could be reconciled. "Native legislation," he demanded in a memorandum, must provide for comprehensive liberty of conscience and belief.[59]

---

55. Lawra-Tumu District, Informal Diary, 28 Dec. 1934, RAT, NRG 8/4/62; see also 13 Dec. 1934, ibid.; 6 Jan. 1935, RAT, NRG 8/4/76.

56. Lawra-Tumu District Informal Diary, 13 Dec. 1934, RAT, NRG 8/4/62; see also Informal Diary, 6 Jan. 1935, RAT, NRG 8/4/76. For the Christian view of 'pagan' funerals, see Lesourd 1938, Appendix.

57. See, for example, Lawra-Tumu District Informal Diary, 20 and 28 March 1935 (at Lissa), RAT, NRG 8/4/76; DC Lawra-Tumu to CCNT, 18 April 1935, NAG, ADM 56/1/301 (at Karni).

58. Lawra-Tumu District, Informal Diary, 12 June 1935, RAT, NRG 8/4/76.

59. Bishop Morin, Memorandum, 14 Dec. 1936, RAT, NRG 8/19/7. Six of the ten conflicts listed by Morin concerned questions of marriage and divorce, which had not yet been brought up at all in the local negotiations.

Morin persuaded the Catholic Bishops of the Gold Coast to hand over his memorandum as a joint petition to the governor, which Chief Commissioner Jones took greatly amiss. Nevertheless, all political officers were now instructed to report on the state of relations between Christians and non-Christians in their districts. All of them, even Ellison in Lawra, and Ardron in Wa, disputed Morin's accusation that Christians were being hindered in the practice of their faith. Ardron asserted quite the contrary, that the converts caused the divisiveness in the village communities with their "attitude of superiority over their own kith and kin," and further complained they were provoking "tribal friction."[60] Ellison was concerned that freedom of conscience might turn into a pretext for the preferential treatment of Christians, "thereby disrupting the authority of the family or family groups."[61] The governor ultimately rejected Morin's demand for a new arrangement of the relationship between the mission and the native authorities and referred the "rare cases of conflict" back to the district commissioners.[62]

In 1937, therefore, the Lawra-Tumu District Commissioner summoned another public meeting, at which the chiefs and the White Fathers agreed on a mode of compromise regarding earth-shrine rituals, funerals and Christian marriages.[63] In practice, however, conflicts continued to break out, which then had to be brought before the native courts or the district commissioners, launching renewed debate over contradictions between customary law and Christian ethics, the authority of the elders and chiefs, the rights of women, and the leeway granted for the exercise of individual liberty.[64] To Bishop Morin, conversion to Christianity represented a transition to the new order of "Christian law," which he regarded to be more binding than "pagan beliefs and customs."[65] Chief Commissioner Jones, on the other hand, only granted the status of legal code to "native law" (and naturally also British civil law), while he regarded "Christian law," to which Morin referred, to be nothing more than a "Christian code of ethics."[66] Jones was sympathetic to the chiefs, who regarded Christian activities "as a break in the administrative control of the Chiefs and in the magical authority of family heads and Tindana which

---

60. DC Wa to CCNT, 5 Feb. 1937, RAT, NRG 8/19/7.

61. DC Lawra-Tumu to CCNT, 6 Feb. 1937, ibid.

62. Colonial Secretary to Bishop Porter, Cape Coast, 25 Oct. 1937, ibid.

63. See Annual Report Northern Territories 1937–38, PRO, CO 98/72: 34, 88–90. On this, see also Hawkins 2002: 249–51.

64. See Lawra-Tumu District, Annual Report 1938–39, RAT, NRG 8/3/78: 34–6; Informal Diary, 13 and 17 Jan. 1940, 1 and 2 Feb. 1940, 23.4, 4.11 and 29 Dec. 1942, and 16 and 18 May 1944, NAG, ADM 61/5/16. See also Hawkins 1989: 130–2.

65. Morin Memorandum, 14 Dec. 1936, RAT, NRG 8/19/7.

66. CCNT to Colonial Secretary, 9 March 1937, RAT, NRG 8/19/7: 1, 4.

they [the chiefs] believe to be essential for the maintenance of peace and good order in the community."[67]

At the heart of the debate stood the authority of family heads and the rights of husbands. The missionaries demanded freedom of conscience for their often young converts, and also that the district commissioners aid in the assertion of the right to freedom of religion, if necessary, even against the wishes of lineage elders. Colonial officials, by contrast, defended the authority of the old men, which should under no circumstances be challenged if the social order should be kept from breaking down.[68]

The debate reveals that the new religious mass movement represented a challenge for the colonial authorities. Despite all the civilizing rhetoric, the colonial state's project was a minimalist one, at least until the Second World War. So long as the public order was not dramatically threatened, the aim was to interfere as little as possible in domestic matters. It was only the petitions submitted by missionaries that forced the colonial authorities to intervene in the social dynamics, which they would have preferred to leave to their own devices and to the neo-traditional control of the chiefs. Thus, for example, the persecution and even killing of "witches" was tacitly tolerated, becoming a target for administrative action only when the White Fathers began hiding women who were being persecuted as witches.[69] And it was only when the White Fathers began protecting Christian girls who were to be married against their will from the attacks of their fathers and husbands that an intense debate was set off regarding the "marriage custom."[70]

Here Lawra District Commissioner Ellison and his colleagues defended the soundness and humaneness of local marriage customs against the Christian norm of indissoluble church marriages. Ellison even found the relevant practices of the Lobi and Dagarti "far in advance of European custom less than a century ago."[71] "It is totally untrue," he explained, "to imagine that any woman by native custom is bound in marriage any further than the dictates of her own heart."[72] The White Fathers never directly responded to the assertion by

---

67. CCNT to Colonial Secretary, 9 March 1937, RAT, NRG 8/19/7: 11; see also DC Lawra-Tumu to CCNT, 18 April 1935, NAG, ADM 56/1/301.

68. DC Lawra-Tumu to CCNT, 6 Feb. 1937, RAT, NRG 8/19/7.

69. See Lesourd 1938; Paternot 1949: 67–75; McCoy 1988: 64–9. However, DC Eyre-Smith is known to have severely punished witch hunts; see Lawra-Tumu District, Informal Diary, 20 July 1932, RAT, NRG 8/4/62.

70. On this, see the examples in McCoy 1988: 149–65.

71. Lawra-Tumu District, Annual Report 1938–39, RAT, NRG 8/3/78.

72. DC Lawra-Tumu to CCNT, 6 Feb. 1937, RAT, NRG 8/19/7.

colonial authorities that Catholic norms dictating the indissolubility of marriage robbed women of one of the most important means of exerting pressure on their husbands. They did, however, insist that the traditional "marriage customs," namely bridewealth, polygamy, and "forced marriage" were aimed at the unrestricted control of women by men, making them the property of their husbands and the latter's clans, "just as purchased cattle" (McCoy 1988: 154). In their eyes, Christian marriage decidedly raised a woman's status.[73]

The chiefs used the conflicts between the colonial authorities and the missionaries to strengthen their own position wherever they could. Hardly any chiefs converted, mainly because they would then have to give up polygamy, one of the pillars of chiefly power. For many chiefs, converts and catechists provided welcome scapegoats who could be blamed for all problems relating to the enforcement of roadwork and other colonial decrees. However, whether a chief chose confrontation or cooperation with the Christians depended ultimately on local power relations.

The rest of the population too, apart from a core group of devoted Christians, soon adopted a rather pragmatic attitude to the opportunities presented by the new faith, as the missionaries themselves fully admitted.[74] The healing of many hitherto incurable illnesses, rain, and a degree of protection against attacks by chiefs were some of the definite advantages of associating with the White Fathers.[75] Later came further benefits, such as participation in development projects and credit unions, access to formal education, and with it new opportunities for social advancement. In negotiating everyday conflicts, one could play off against each other customary law, Christian norms and, under certain circumstances, even British civil law in order to further one's interests. Among young labor migrants from Nandom, for example, it became customary to get married in church before going off to the mines, "so that the Roman Catholic rules of divorce shall keep the girl on ice for him," a strategy that District Commissioner Amherst found extraordinarily unfair to the young

---

73. See McCoy 1988: 149–53, 161. On the ambivalent significance of the mission for the status of Dagara women and the development of Christian education for girls in Lawra District, see Behrends 2002.

74. See Barsalou to CCNT, 4 Sep. 1934, enclosure 6 in Gold Coast Confidential, 14 Dec. 1934, PRO, CO 96/720/31002; see also Lesourd 1938; Naameh 1986: 240–2; also Goody 1975 on the initial role of Christianity as simply an additional cult, not a wholly new one.

75. The missionaries explained very precisely to converts the restrictions on the rights of the chiefs and unofficially backed them up before the native courts too. See, for example, Northern Territories, Annual Report 1935–36, RAT, NRG 8/3/53: 49.

women, who were then frequently accused of marital infidelity.[76] Conversely, many men suspected that women only became Catholics in order to escape their unwanted unchristian husbands, or because they could no longer be repudiated by their Christian spouses, even if the former failed to be faithful.

In spite of the prevailing pragmatism, the new religion forced all the affected parties to elucidate local norms in a manner that had not been necessary earlier. The colonial codification of customary law took place in this context. It may, therefore, have tacitly incorporated a number of Christian norms and declared them to be integral to local tradition. Conversely, the missionaries were continually forced to integrate local practices into Christian rules of behavior and ritual.[77]

The Emergence of a Christian Educated Elite

For British colonial authorities the stabilization of the chieftaincy was accorded a higher priority than modernization or "development" of the protectorate, including formal education. The first petition from the White Fathers to open a school in Nandom was therefore rejected. First, there was ostensibly not enough qualified teaching staff available;[78] secondly, the colonial government asserted that it needed educated native clerks, not catechists or priests; and thirdly, Chief Commissioner Jones feared, educated Christians might undermine the authority of the native chiefs. He regarded "semi-literate catechists," who believed themselves to be superior leaders to the chiefs, as the main culprits in conflicts between the latter and converts.[79] Power, the director of education, did not support the opening of Catholic schools either, not until native authority schools were firmly established for the education of the chiefs' sons. He argued that "the chiefs and ruling classes, conservative in view and often polygamous in habit, will be usually the last to send their children to a Christian mission school." Mission schools therefore entailed "a danger of setting up an educated class among the lower orders before the ruling

---

76. Lawra-Tumu District, Informal Diary, 4 Nov. 1942, NAG, ADM 61/5/16.

77. After the late 1950s, and especially in the wake of the Second Vatican Council, the local clergy explicitly discussed a re-evaluation of local cultural practices that the White Fathers had forbidden as 'heathen'; see Naameh 1986, Chs. 7, 8; Bemile 1987, Mukassa 1987, Bekye 1991, Kpiebaya 1991.

78. CCNT to Colonial Secretary, 18 Oct. 1934, enclosure 3, in Gold Coast Confidential, 14 Dec. 1934, PRO, CO 96/720/31002.

79. CCNT to Revd. Father Barsalou, 13 Aug. 1934, enclosure 5, ibid.

classes become literate, and of weakening, in this way, the authority of the Native Administration which in the early stages it is essential to support."[80] Nevertheless, a second petition to set up a mission school in Nandom was accepted and approved. In the meantime, mission school graduates from Navrongo and Bolgatanga had proved their worth as native clerks, and it had also become increasingly clear that the native authority schools could not produce enough graduates on their own to cover the demand for administrative personnel. In 1937 St Paul's Primary School opened its doors in Nandom, first as an infants' school, and from 1939 as a fully accredited primary boarding school.

Apart from the Catholic primary school for girls opened in Jirapa in 1940, St Paul's Primary School for boys was until the early 1950s the only mission school in the entire North-West. Unlike the Lawra Confederacy Native Authority School, therefore, it recruited its pupils not only in parishes belonging to Lawra-Tumu District, but also in Kaleo, and adjacent areas. In the school, the Sisala constituted a negligible minority. Most of the boys were Dagara and Dagaba, and, as one of the first pupils recalled, they were initially astonished at the differences in the dialects they spoke.[81] On the other hand, they became aware of the size of their own ethnic and linguistic community and made friends with boys from all over the North-West. However, this new sense of community appears to have come about "incidentally." Unlike in the native authority schools, the White Fathers did not teach the basics of local culture and history, nor did they wish their pupils to become socialized into any sort of "local patriotism." According to one former pupil, at the newly founded St Andrew's Middle School in Nandom, it was only in the 1950s that "tribal dances" began to be performed occasionally alongside English folk dances—in which case everybody then had to learn the dances of fellow pupils from other regions—while in "dramatization," scenes with local themes and stories told in Dagara were sometimes staged alongside English plays.[82] The missionaries firmly sought to avoid the formation of groups along the lines of shared origin and dialect, and the boys had to speak English as much as possible. The community toward which pupils were to

---

80. Power to Colonial Secretary, 18 Sep. 1934, enclosure 2, ibid. On the conflicts over the school in Nandom, see also Thomas 1975a: 640–4; Der 1983: 181–90; McCoy 1988: 145–7.

81. Father Irenaeus Songliedong, in McCoy 1988: 290.

82. Interview with Father Gervase Sentuu, Hamile, 24 Dec. 1993. As in the native authority schools, the boarding regime followed the model of the English boarding school, but it did not borrow from the chieftaincy.

develop their sense of responsibility and of which they were to become productive members was not the tribe or the chiefdom, but the Catholic Church.

In a sense, Power's expectation that the mission school would produce an "educated class" that did not stem from the chieftaincy proved well-founded. Only Catholic children were accepted into St Paul's, chiefs' sons being among them only in the rarest of cases. Whoever had not yet converted by the late 1930s had more or less explicitly decided against Christianity. Such men therefore usually did not permit their children to go to the mission school. Conversely, Catholic parents did not wish to send their children to the native authority school, and even after World War II, when native authority day schools were opened in many villages, most Catholics hesitated to expose their offspring to the moral and spiritual dangers of a lay school. Consequently, school attendance split the population into two camps: Catholics on the one hand and the non-Catholic chiefs' sons and relatives on the other, each side mostly keeping to themselves.

Whether educated Catholics really belonged to the "lower orders" of local society, as Power expected, is, however, questionable. Until 1946 no school fees were levied,[83] and thereafter fees only amounted to five shillings, half the sum charged by the native authority school. However, the privilege of formal education was mostly a matter for the sons of catechists who received a fixed salary from the mission and often worked relatively large farms, aided energetically by some of their congregation. Catechists, who had learnt reading, writing, and arithmetic, wanted their own children to have access to higher education so that these might enter higher social positions as priests or teachers, and because they usually lived separated from their families in other villages, their children's school attendance met with less resistance from relatives, who regarded school children as "lost" to the family. Finally, because of their close relationship with the missionaries, catechists had better opportunities than other parents to secure for their children a spot at school when the capacity of the educational system to take on pupils was limited.

Before the White Fathers opened a middle school in Nandom in 1950, Catholic pupils could only obtain further education in Navrongo or Bolgatanga.[84] The first graduates of these senior schools mostly became priests or teachers. Future priests were sent to the theological seminary that was first opened in Wiagha in 1946, and subsequently moved to Tamale in 1953. Future teachers mainly worked for the first two or three years as "pupil teachers,"

---

83. On this, see Der 1983: 205.
84. On this, see McCoy 1988: 145–6, 282–3, 288.

and then taught in the Catholic schools at Nandom and Jirapa.[85] Yet by no means did all mission pupils remain loyal to the White Fathers. Some were frightened off by the missionaries' authoritarian and paternalistic teaching style and their treatment of employees, or they were simply attracted by the promise of better pay in other types of employment.[86] The boundary between mission school pupils and native authority school graduates therefore cannot be drawn too rigidly: especially in later years there were always pupils who changed between the two educational systems, as well as mission pupils who subsequently worked in occupational fields not affiliated with the church. Nonetheless, the mission schools and the native authority schools did exist separately, being mostly self-reproducing institutions each with their own educational goals in which pupils had different experiences, created different friendship networks, and normally also pursued different careers.

The central point in all this is that the mission of the White Fathers not only drew the boundaries of the "Dagaaba" community and defined its culture differently from the colonial authorities or chiefs, it also promoted the formation of a separate educated elite, which was later to participate actively in the debates concerning ethnic politics and cultural practice. Locally, mission schools also provided social groups with access to education who would otherwise not have been educated at all, or at least not at such an early stage, by the native authority schools, due to their remoteness from the chiefs. In the regional context, the great success of the mission and the educational efforts of the White Fathers in the North-West not only led to the Dagaba dominating the ranks of Catholic priesthood and other Catholic institutions in Northern Ghana today, but also to their disproportional predominance in many higher-level positions in the North's regional administration—a situation that has by no means won them only friends.

References

Bekye, Paul K. (1991): *Divine Revelation and Traditional Religions with Particular Reference to the Dagaaba of West Africa*. Rom: Leberit Press.

Bemile, Paul (ed.) (1987): *From Assistant Fetish Priest to Archbishop: Studies in Honour of Archbishop Dery*. New York: Vantage Press.

---

85. On the priests' seminary, see McCoy 1988: 14–15, 200–1; Der 1983: 412–28; on teacher-training, see Bening 1990: 111–18.

86. On this, see Bening 1990: 112–13; also my interview with Severio Termaghre, Nandom, 12 Dec. 1989.

Bemile, Sebastian (2000): 'Promotion of Ghanaian languages and its impact on national unity: the Dagara language case', in: Carola Lentz and Paul Nugent (eds.): *Ethnicity in Ghana: The Limits of Invention*, pp. 204–25. London: Macmillan.

Bening, Raymond B. (1990): *A History of Education in Northern Ghana, 1907–1976*. Accra: Ghana University Press.

Dabire, Constantin Gbaane (1983): *Nisaal – L'homme comme relation*. PhD Thesis, Université Laval.

Delafosse, Maurice (1912): *Haut-Sénégal-Niger*. Tome I. Paris: Emil Larose.

Der, Benedict (1974): 'Church-state relations in Northern Ghana 1906–1940', *Transactions of the Historical Society of Ghana* 15: 41–61.

—— (1983): *Missionary Enterprise in Northern Ghana, 1906–1975: A Study in Impact*. PhD Thesis, University of Ghana.

Gandah, S.W.D.K. (1967/1993): *Gandah yir: The House of the Brave*. London: unpub. manuscript.

Girault, Louis (1959): 'Essai sur la religion des Dagara', *Bulletin de l'IFAN* 21, B 3–4: 329–56.

Goody, Jack (1956): *The Social Organisation of the LoWiili*. London: H.M. Stationery Office.

—— (1975): 'Religion, Social Change and the Sociology of Conversion', in: Jack Goody (ed.): *Changing Social Structure in Ghana*, pp. 91–106. London: International African Institute.

Hawkins, Sean (1996): 'Disguising chiefs and God as history: questions on the acephalousness of LoDagaa politics and religion', *Africa* 66: 207–47.

—— (1997): 'To pray or not to pray: politics, medicine, and conversion among the LoDagaa of Northern Ghana, 1929–1939', *Canadian Journal of African Studies* 31: 50–85.

—— (1998): 'The interpretation of Naangmin: missionaries ethnography, African theology and history among the LoDagaa', *Journal of Religion in Africa* 28: 32–61.

—— (2002): *Writing and Colonialism in Northern Ghana: The Encounter between the LoDagaa and 'the World on Paper'*. Toronto: University of Toronto Press.

Kpiebaya, Gregory (1991): *Dagaaba Traditional Marriage and Family Life*. Wa: Catholic Press.

Labouret, Henri (1931): *Les tribus du rameau Lobi*. Paris: L'Institut d'Ethnologie.

Lentz, Carola (1998): *Die Konstruktion von Ethnizität. Eine politische Geschichte Nord-West Ghanas, 1870–1990*. Köln: Köppe.

———— (1995): '"Unity for development': youth associations in north-western Ghana,' *Africa* 65: 395–429.

———— (1997): 'Creating ethnic identities in north-western Ghana', in Cora Govers and Hans Vermeulen (eds.): *The Politics of Ethnic Consciousness*, pp. 31–89. London: Macmillan.

———— (1998): 'The chief, the mines captain and the politician: legitimating power in northern Ghana', *Africa* 68: 46–67.

———— (2000a): '"Chieftaincy has come to stay." La chefferie dans les sociétés acéphales du Nord-Ouest Ghana', *Cahiers d'Etudes Africaines* 159: 593–613.

———— (2000b): 'Contested identities: the history of ethnicity in northwestern Ghana', in: Carola Lentz and Paul Nugent (eds): *Ethnicity in Ghana: The Limits of Invention*, pp. 137–61. London: Macmillan.

———— (2002): 'Contested boundaries: decentralisation and land conflicts in northwestern Ghana', *APAD Bulletin* 22: 7–26.

———— (2003): 'Stateless societies or chiefdoms? A debate among Dagara intellectuals', in: Franz Kröger and Barbara Meier (eds.): *Ghana's North: Research on Culture, Religion, and Politics of Societies in Transition*, pp. 129–59. Frankfurt a.M.: Peter Lang.

Lesourd, R.P. Jean (1938): *Un peuple en marche vers la lumière. Les Dagaris.* Soisson: Imp. de l'Argue.

McCoy, Remigius F. (1988): *Great Things Happen: Personal Memoir of the First Christian Missionary among the Dagaabas and Sissalas of Northwest Ghana.* Montreal: The Society of the Missionaries of Africa.

Meyer, Birgit (1999): *Translating the Devil: Religion and Modernity among the Ewe in Ghana.* Edinburgh: Edinburgh University Press.

Mukassa, Der (1987): *L'homme dans l'univers des Dagara. Essai d'anthropologie culturelle et religieuse Dagara.* Diébougou: unpub. manuscript.

Naameh, Philip (1986): *The Christianisation of the Dagara within the Horizon of the West European Experience.* Ph.D. Thesis, University of Münster.

Paternot, Marcel (1949): *Lumière sur la Volta. Chez les Dagari.* Lyon: Éditions de la Plus Grande France.

Peel, J.D.Y. (2000): *Religious Encounter and the Making of the Yoruba.* Bloomington: Indiana University Press.

Somé, Magloire (1993): *La christianisation de l'Ouest-Volta. De la révolution sociale au conflit culturel et à l'éveil politique, 1927–1960.* Thése de doctorat, Université de Paris IV.

———— (1996): 'Evangélisation et colonisation en Haute-Volta de 1900 à 1960', *Neue Zeitschrift für Missionswissenschaft/ Nouvelle Revue de science missionaire* 52: 81–103.

Somé, Roger (1991): 'La conception Dagara de Dieu en question', *Papers in Dagara Studies* I (3): 30–43.

Tauxier, Louis (1912): *Le noir du Soudan: pays Mossi et Gourounsi.* Paris: E. Larousse.

Tengan, Edward B. (1991): *The Land as Being and Cosmos: The Institution of the Earth Cult among the Sisala of Northwestern Ghana.* Frankfurt a.M.: Peter Lang.

Thomas, Roger (1975): 'Education in Northern Ghana, 1906–1940: a study in colonial paradox', *International Journal of African Historical Studies* 7: 427–67.

Wilks, Ivor (1989): *Wa and the Wala: Islam and Polity in Northwestern Ghana.* Cambridge: Cambridge University Press.

CHAPTER 20

A "Religious Encounter" in Amedzofe: Women and Change Through the Twentieth Century

Lynne Brydon

I have known John Peel since he hired me for my first job in Liverpool in 1977. At that time John had fairly recently returned from Nigeria and was working on the material that would subsequently become *Ijeshas and Nigerians*, but he also had other projects underway including the beginnings of a long term interest in the work of the Church Missionary Society. As a young lecturer I was sometimes invited to Sunday lunch and the rigorous family walks that followed them, during which John did not balk at discussing ideas he was working on with even the most junior of his departmental staff. I particularly remember "*Olaju*" and indigenous concepts of development (the indigenous term in Avatime [*siya*] for "civilization" is *aŋudradra*, literally, face- or visage-opening). Since then, of course, John's academic reputation has (deservedly) grown enormously, including the 2000 publication of *Religious encounter and the making of the Yoruba*.

But in all of John's work, from *Aladura* onward, there is little or no specific concern with either women or gender relationships, apart from the ways in which women / gender relationships were relevant to, impinged upon, the "real" and public lives and trials of Yoruba statesmen, male chiefs, churchmen and missionaries. This is certainly the case in *Ijeshas and Nigerians* (one need only glance through the index) where the public figures, the real actors, involved in the development and incorporation of states are all men. There is an emphasis in John's work on the "public" domain, in its western sense, peopled by men: any contrasting "domain," whether we refer to it as "private," "domestic," or anything else (where women might be) remains in the background, presumed to exist, but not elaborated, and since the male figures that appear in John's work are active in public domains, women are absent.

So, what I want to do here is to set out the ways in which indigenous women—men take a back seat here—became involved with the worlds outside of their village, initially through the influences of missionaries and colonial administrations. I do this at least partly in terms of my own career trajectory, beginning with the raw postgraduate, and also in terms of my growing historical and ethnographic knowledge of my "field"[1] over the years. I trace out ideas about women's lives and of women themselves through the twentieth century and try to resolve problems I had relating to gender "debates" from the 1970s onwards.

The "field" I am referring to is Avatime, a small ethnic group of seven villages, perhaps 15,000–20,000 people in all, in Ghana's Volta Region in the hills of the Togo Ranges, about twenty-five miles north of Ho, the regional capital, and about 150 miles northeast of Accra. The majority of the people in this area are Eυe, and while most Avatime speak Eυe, very few Eυe speak Avatime: the two languages are not closely related.

Avatime

When I first returned from ethnographic fieldwork in Amedzofe, one of the Avatime villages, it was 1974. "Second wave" feminist ideas had begun to disturb the waters of intellectual circles in the west, indeed, 1974 saw the publication of perhaps the most significant anthropological collection of the time, Rosaldo and Lamphere's *Woman, Culture and Society*. Marilyn Strathern had published *Women in Between* (1972), and I had come to realize from my fieldwork that both women and men were significant actors in the "social structure," the public domain of so-called "patrilineal" Avatime society, women much more so than my undergraduate reading had suggested.

"Structure" and Gender

Avatime is organized on an agnatic basis: each village is divided into a number of clans, and each clan further subdivided into a number of lineages trac-

---

1. I use this term deliberately here, as it is commonly used by the officials and missionaries from the North German Mission Society (*Norddeutsche Missionsgesellschaft*) who came to Avatime.

ing descent in the patri-line. Members of clans maintain that they are related, all lineages tracing descent (putatively)from a patrilineal forebear, but members of different clans within the villages do not necessarily claim any "original" relationship to one another: forebears of some clans are claimed to be brothers, but others are unrelated. Some of the classical examples of kin behavior and terminology that I had read about in ethnographies are also apparent: There are relatively easy relationships between grandparents and grandchildren, but those between parents and children are more formal; there are special kinds of behavior to be observed between mothers' brothers' and sisters' sons; and there are even some vague examples of matrilateral cross cousin marriage. But there are also specific behaviors and terminology associated with mothers' brothers' and sisters' daughters' relationships, not to mention special roles of women as adult female members of their natal patrilineal kin groups. Women are very obvious in both the public and private / domestic life of the villages. Just as there are male chiefs, there are also female chiefs; and where men, as elders, deliberate about the day to day affairs and running of the village, women also have public voices. Where there is any particular event to be announced and discussed, the gong-gong beater summons the villagers to a dawn meeting and women as well as men are included in the summons and expect to be heard.

When I was in the field for that first time I had not yet read Strathern, and Rosaldo and Lamphere had not been published. I came back and began to work on my material and I was struck over and over again by the prominence of women in my field notes and accounts of public events. Even in the rituals presided over by the local gods in which the presence of women of menstruating age is regarded as polluting, such women were significant by their absence: the harvesting rituals required the presence of pre-pubertal girls, and post-menopausal women were involved in the "first eating" rituals, but fecund women were denied any role for themselves. And while men could pass on "name," descent group membership, access to land to farm, to their offspring (male and female) when they died, when women died their lineage "sisters" came to distribute their property (mainly food stores, cloth, pots) throughout their (natal) lineage, to the senior male elder, and among themselves. Symbolically all signs of a woman's occupation of her adult household and kitchen were removed with the destruction and removal of the hearth(s) on which she had cooked and heated water.

But my reading and my peers were telling me that women were subordinated, from Marxist inspired ideas such as those of Karen Sacks (1974; 1979), to the "symbolist" perspectives of Sherry Ortner (1974). Even if women in "traditional" societies had had some kind of a voice, the effects of European colonization, capitalism, the impacts of world religions or whatever, had sti-fled women's voices, their political visibility and efficacy and legitimacy as public figures in their communities.[2] As an unconfident graduate student I was shunted into the conclusion that my fieldwork and field notes were totally biased and compromised, I had obviously over emphasized the significance of women both in formal structural terms and in day to day Avatime life.

Christianity

Avatime is in what was formerly German Togo,[3] and the missionaries who brought Christianity were from the tiny North German Mission Society (*Nord-deutsche Missionsgesellschaft*), based in Bremen. Meyer (1999) has written co-gently of the Pietist underpinnings of the Bremen Missionaries' beliefs, and the emphasis on the training of both the hands and the mind in the develop-ment of their "field." Simplifying grossly, the mission's ambition was to estab-lish among the Eʋe (and other local and, as they supposed, cognate) people, like Avatime, an idea of unity, a "*Volk*." They emphasized the importance of using the local language, and not only translated the Bible into Eʋe,[4] but also wrote hymns and schoolbooks. Although the Germans administered their colonies with harshness and strict military discipline in southern and eastern Africa, in Togo this violence seems to have been mitigated through the influ-ence of German (Hanseatic) merchants and their trading interests (Gann and Duignan, 1977). The Bremen Mission's own "Home Committee" contained representatives of a number of trading families, prominent among whom were the Vietors. The Vietors were active in the colonial project both at home and in Togo where, in the wake of German colonization, one Karl Vietor, the local representative of the family firm (Vietor and Son), aimed to "develop a capa-ble and morally superior peasant class among the natives...." (Röhrig, 1955:198). Several factors were involved in this planned development includ-ing Christianity, education and the acquisition and practice of craft skills. Christianity and education (in Eʋe) would instil both morality and rational-ity (in the general post-Enlightenment sense of these terms), leading to the

---

2. See, for example, Karen Sacks, 1974, 1979 and also the considerable literature fo-cussed on the Igbo 'Women's War' of 1929, for example, van Allen, 1976; Okonjo, 1976; Ifeka-Moller, 1975.

3. Later League of Nations Mandated Territory and, after the second World War, United Nations Trust Territory.

4. The Eʋe used, however, was the coastal dialect of the Anlo. The inland Eʋe dialect has distinct differences in both structure and accent.

formation and consolidation of a just and well-organized state, while craft skills would help local people develop their communities and economies, helping to render the state viable in the longer term.

The Bremen Mission founded a station and school in Amedzofe (the highest village) in 1889; and the Bremen seminary, primarily training teachers and catechists, was moved there in 1894. While there were non-Avatime Christians in the area when the station was established, the first Amedzofe Christians were baptised in October 1892. These were an Amedzofe man, his wife and three of their sons. An older daughter had begun to receive instruction in the Christian faith, but because she was already betrothed and her future husband objected to her potential conversion, the missionaries refused to baptise her. This early Amedzofe baptism was succeeded only by a slow trickle of local converts through the 1890s. But, by 1911, a pupil in the school wrote:

> In my home in Amedzowe there are no longer any idols. The word of God has shattered them all (Debrunner, 1965:137).

Conversion, therefore, in terms of local perceptions of numbers, seems to have been relatively successful in Amedzofe in the space of about twenty years.

Although Debrunner's quote is from a report published in the monthly newsletter of the Bremen Mission, and sent by the missionary, Emil Funke, stationed in Amedzofe, the intervening twenty years between the first local converts and Funke's school pupil's statement were not without difficulties for the missionaries in their *mission civilisatrice*, and a theme that occurs in the mission publications again and again is the intransigence and autonomy of the Amedzofe women.

Women and Change I: 1890–1910

The earliest mission reports from Amedzofe noted the economic independence of the women there.

> The early planting time is in the care chiefly of women. They usually choose grassy humus-rich places to make their farms. After the bush is cut it stays for a while usually until the rain, when it is planted. The produce belongs entirely to the women. They use it for their housekeeping. Whatever they have left over will be sold. With the proceeds they buy salt, soap and fish and sometimes trinkets. These earnings are easily enough to cover the different kinds of need. But they in no way forget their menfolk. They plant cotton and spin to get extra

earnings.[5] In many an Avatime town they make soap, in others the women are entirely taken up with trade, as for example, Dzokpe. There are (those) there…who are exclusively supported by trade…. (Spieth, MB, April, 1890: 36–8)[6]

And as part of a long article entitled *Afrikanisches Frauenleben* the Mission Sister Anna Knüsli wrote: "Her farm, her produce belong to her, she has her own cash-box. Her mat, her small belongings she has herself…." (MB, February, 1907 68(2): 10–11). Amedzofe women were (and are) neither beholden nor dependent upon men for their livelihoods.

But Amedzofe women's independent mindedness and raunchiness were also noted earlier by the missionaries. Missionary Seeger's Annual Report for 1890 is the first glimpse of Amedzofe's feisty women:

> The women seem to be very conservative*. Sometimes they have feasts lasting the day long and at which there is plenty of spirits (*Branntwein*). A total was not possible but it was over 100 women. These women for their most recent town feast for the dedication of a drum had bought 120 bottles and 3 demijohns of gin which were drunk in 3 days. They complained they were so drunk that they almost died. The next day they went with the same purpose to Vane. They made a ruling on the part of feasts that each women who wasn't among them should pay 4s 6d. The empty bottles still lie in rows and ranks in the market and proclaim to each stranger what the Amedzofe people have done. A particular desire for conversion can, for the meantime, not be found, least of all among the women.

> Already many a man who wants to send his child to school has experienced, as in so many others the case is, that not him, but his wife is master in the house. (Annual Report 1890:15)[7]

> (* Which I interpret here as meaning resistant to change)

Six years later Seeger remarks in the introduction to a long piece about the problems in the decline of paganism: "in Avatime the women have power over their men which is not known elsewhere." (MB, September, 1896: 66)

---

5. Women may plant cotton, harvest it and spin it, but it is men who weave in this area.

6. This is the same Spieth who wrote the standard early ethnographic work on the Eʋe, '*Die Ewe-Stämme*' (1906). He wrote extensively on Amedzofe and Avatime (published in the *Monatsblatt*, hereafter MB) after a period of about 6 weeks in Amedzofe in 1889.

7. My translation.

Seeger also noted that, "Each Avatime town has a queen something like the consort of the king but chosen...." (Annual report, 1890:15). Even that most prolific of Eʋe mission ethnographers, Jakob Spieth noted the importance and independence of women in Amedzofe:

> It is known that in Avatime there was a real queen for the women who was assisted by the women chiefs. In particular family matters the (male) chiefs may pronounce no decision without the agreement of the women's council. (Spieth, 1906: 65*)

The formal power and status of Avatime women are discussed again in 1899 in terms of the problems and processes of building a new and much larger chapel in Amedzofe with very little money:

> There [in Avatime] they are even further than the most advanced social democratic union with us: each village has alongside the town council of the male sex a similar one of the female sex and there is no important matter that goes 'through' without the approval of the women's council.

> One cannot but exert a gentle pressure on the pagan men and if it succeeds, win the women also. To ask costs nothing and in fact the Queen promised the help of her body of women and on the chosen day there appeared very early down there those belonging to the fair sex, from old women to the 2 year old child, and they brought stones to us.... (MB, June, 1899: 46–8 (Kirchbau und Kirchweihe in Amedzofe))

By 1902, although there had been considerable improvement in overall numbers, women still seemed more "conservative" than men, less willing to come to the church services than the men:

> In the Amedzofe congregation going to Church by pagans has increased significantly. In good weather the men's side is almost full to the last place and there are not many gaps on the women's side.' MB,October, 1902 13 (10): 88–9 Aus der Arbeit auf unseren Bergstationen (Schröder).

It is important to remember here that attendance at church services did not necessarily entail conversion. Although the missionaries commented frequently on women's independence and seemed, in many ways, to approve of their energies, they were not happy with the women's lives and their overall outlook on life, their "Weltanschauungen." Both Spieth and the mission sister, Anna Knüsli, felt that the underlying problems with respect to women derived

not from their lack of opportunity or economic or social equality and autonomy, but rather from their spiritual deprivation. Knüsli,[8] (1907), suggests that
although the practical lives of African women might not be much different
from the lives of contemporary rural peasant women in Germany, their inner
and spiritual lives were barren. Towards the end of her piece she writes at
length on the vices of African women, although she does admit that there is
a loyalty between mothers and daughters and between sisters. But, in particular, she mentions:

> ...their great touchiness and quarrelsomeness. A small thing is
> enough to set them off. Perhaps the neighbour's goat or lamb has
> come into the house through the open door, has drunk from the
> water pot or nibbled at a yam lying on the ground–the animal is
> thrown out with loud words. The other answers her in the same way.
> The first seeks to outdo her. From both sides flies a hail of insults—
> all bodily imperfections mentioned—this rubs off onto the children.
> (MB, February, 1907:11)

But whatever the Amedzofe women's apparent strengths, or missionaries' views
on what they perceived to be women's independence in Amedzofe society in
the late nineteenth century, by the beginning of the twentieth century missionaries' wives and later women missionaries (mission sisters) were providing
new role models for local young girls and women. By 1908 Amedzofe women
were already learning skills more appropriate to the new economy and society:

> ...Fr Härtter working among women and girls in Amedzofe...(ac-
> cording to the plan of Frau Bürgi)...organised a sewing afternoon for
> women... Fully 20 come, their babies on backs and the bigger chil-
> dren by the hand, who want to be introduced to the secrets of tailor-
> ing. (MB, October, 1908:10)

The missionaries' wives in Amedzofe also set up a day nursery[9] early in the
twentieth century where women could leave their small children for two or
three hours and go to farm. Very few girls went to the school, particularly
through the senior classes, and so the missionaries' wives instigated classes especially for girls and women. If a family wanted its child, boy or girl, to go to
school (with the concomitant aim of becoming a Christian), but was too poor
to pay, the missionaries' wives sometimes took them into their households as

---

8. Note here that Knüsli is writing generally of women in the Bremen Mission's area,
mainly Eʋe, but Avatime and other groups are included among them.

9. *Kindergarten: agbodzɔkpo* in Eʋe.

"housechildren" (*Hauskinder*). In exchange for domestic and agricultural services, the children would be taught literacy and practical skills as the missionaries and their wives deemed appropriate. All children were taught laundering and ironing, but there were gender differences in other tasks: girls learned sewing, mending and cooking, boys might begin to learn craft skills and work on the mission farm plots. All of the house children were expected to go to church services and to take instruction in Christianity with the goal of baptism, a fact that did influence congregation numbers, since the numbers of house children were often twenty to thirty.

So while the missionaries, then, might comment somewhat positively on Amedzofe women's independence on one hand, on the other, they feared for the inner spirituality, an emptiness threatening to lead to unrestrained violence and passion among them. Knüsli's comments (1907) with respect to the overall character of women, and particularly in their relations with men, indicate that she sees them as too strident and demanding. They seem to be unwilling to be submissive, diffident in the marital household, unwilling to strive for "peace" in the house. Moving ahead thirty years or so, they had yet to learn the proper values and virtues of "*Kinder, Küche, Kirche*," and that could only begin to come about through their conversion.

The First World War and its Aftermath

While a school pupil in 1911 in Amedzofe might write of the "success" of Christianity in the "struggle against paganism," that is, ridding the village of the "idols" of traditional religion, any vision of a smooth trajectory for the establishment and consolidation of Christianity in the village suffers a major hiccough with the outbreak of World War I.

While Togo might seem a very small and rather nugatory German colony, nevertheless the territory saw some of the first decisive battles of the war. The Germans had built an extremely powerful radio station at Kamina and, because of its significance for Atlantic shipping, when war was declared in early August 1914, British and French forces invaded the colony from the east and the west respectively. Togo fell to the allies on August 26, 1914. The Germans had no *Schutztruppe* based in the colony and called on civilians, including some of the missionaries to defend the station. No missionary was killed, but those who had fought were taken prisoner immediately.

After the fall of the German administration, the remaining missionaries were initially given permission to carry on their work under Allied auspices. The Bremen missionaries plodded on with no money or other support from

Bremen, but the last were finally removed from their posts in 1917. Fortunately for the mission, the mission station and seminary in Amedzofe were under the direction of a Swiss national, Ernst Bürgi, in 1914, and he, with the help of his wife and local pastors, catechists, teachers, and their wives, managed to maintain the bulk of the mission's work during the war.[10]

After the war and the division of responsibility for the former German colony between the British and the French, Bürgi too left, and the mission work was handed over to the Scottish Mission. The work of the mission underwent considerable changes; in particular the teaching was to be in English, and the British Administration wanted to keep a much closer watch over the mission schools' curriculum to ensure that it was in line with those approved in other parts of the Gold Coast Colony and Trans-Volta Togoland.[11] At first there could be no question of the Germans returning to their field. However, in September 1923, missionaries from Bremen were allowed back but had to agree to work under the direction of the Scottish Mission and their representative in Amedzofe, Rev. T.L. Beveridge.

While Bürgi's efforts to continue his work during the war had been based on the incorporation of a range of local people, only two Amedzofe men had any roles (as Presbyters or church elders) in the church at this time. In 1923 three young and educated men were chosen[12] to be church elders, and in 1926 the first Amedzofe man was ordained. It was not until 1933, at least twenty years after men had been similarly elevated, that the first (three) women were chosen to be, not church elders, but "Church Mothers."[13] Amedzofe consolidated its position, not so much as a centre of religion, but rather as a centre of educational excellence. New schools were built in the 1920s and Amedzofe had the only Senior School (teaching the higher "Standards"[14] of the basic ed-

---

10. This is a grossly compressed account. For more details see Debrunner, 1965, Gann and Duignan, 1977.

11. The bulk of this section draws on information from fieldnotes and from *Amedzofe E.P.Hame Ŋutinya 1889–1964* (Accra, 1964) and *Amedzofe E.P. Hame Ŋutinya 1889–1989* (Ho, 1989). Trans-Volta Togoland was the new formal name given to the parts of the former German colony which had come under British control after the partition.

12. Two of whom I knew when I first went to Amedzofe in 1973. Trans-Volta Togoland was the new formal name given to the parts of the former German colony which had come under British control after the partition.

13. The Eʋe term for church elders is *hamemega(wo)*, lit: 'congregation big men'. The equivalent term for women is *hamedada(wo)*, lit: 'congregation elder sisters', but it is usually translated into English as 'church mothers'.

14. Primary education consisted of three 'standards' at this time, each 'standard' lasted for two years. After completing Standard III, a pupil could go on to the Senior School for

ucation curriculum) in the former German territory now under British administration.

Through the 1920s the emphasis of the missionaries shifted. The drive to win converts to Christianity in Amedzofe seems to have receded into the background. The thrust of mission work and interaction with the villagers in the 1920s seems to have been on education and the consolidation of the congregation. In a sense, education subsumes conversion since it was assumed that any child who went to school would become Christian even if they had not already been baptised, but the educational emphasis suited the times. There had been labor migration from Togo to the Gold Coast throughout the German colony's history (much lamented by the Germans as the so-called "rush to Fante"). But with the change of administration and much more open links with the Gold Coast and its hinterland, there were new job opportunities open to people from the new Trans-Volta Togoland. Now, in addition to going to the Gold Coast as artisans, cocoa-caretakers and other manual workers, they could go and be civil servants or other bureaucrats, storekeepers, and even, after appropriate training, perhaps teachers.

Links with Bremen were maintained and expanded through the 1920s, and in 1931 Alexander Funke (Emil Funke's son) and his wife Luise arrived. The arrival of the second generation of Funkes in Amedzofe saw a brief flourishing of emphasis on work with women and girls.

Women and Change II: 1930 –

Mission personnel in Amedzofe in the early 1930s consisted of three mission sisters (including Luise Funke) and the Rev. Alexander Funke. While Alexander Funke's work oversaw a number of congregations and the mission field in its entirety, the mission sisters concentrated their work in Amedzofe. One of the women reestablished the dispensary that had existed for a few years in the early 1920s while the remaining two focused on education. In 1937 a domestic science block was built at the Senior School so that girl pupils could undertake practical work.

In 1932, however, Luise Funke began to work with the women of the village in new ways:

> The most significant were the training of mothers in child care, care
> for the sick and in First Aid. Added to these, she founded a school for

---

a further four years and take Standards IV through VII, each lasting one year. There was no formal secondary school in TVT until Mawuli School was opened in Ho in 1950.

the training of Kindergarten teachers and for a course in Domestic Science…for those girls that could not continue their school education up to the Middle (*Senior*) School level. But above all this, Mrs Luise Funke started a new movement in the congregation, from where it has since then spread to almost all the congregations in the E. P. Church, Ghana. This movement was the E. P. Church Womens' [*sic*] Bible Class. She started with a small group of devoted women in the congregation, teaching them Bible Reading and study, Christian home life, different domestic crafts: sewing, needlework, knitting [Textile and Fabrics of today]. She led them to sew and weave table cloths, covers for altars, pulpits and night-gowns for themselves. (Amedzofe, 1989:74)

The women's Bible Class took off throughout the former Bremen Mission field in a big way. There were conferences and meetings of members in various locations, and there were competitions for production of good work. Money from the sale of the women's work in Amedzofe allowed the women from Amedzofe's Bible Class to sponsor a catechist in one of the other congregations through the early and mid 1930s.

The promising and successful work with girls and women (the opening of two girls' schools, the Domestic Science block and the inauguration and consolidation of the women's Bible Class groups throughout the Church), however, received a setback with the outbreak of World War II. The Funkes had already left Amedzofe in February, 1939, but their place was taken by Rev. Dr. Voehringer and his wife from the American Evangelical Reformed Church. Nevertheless, with the declaration of war by the British, the remaining German missionaries in Amedzofe were taken away as prisoners of war and the loss of personnel and leadership was such that the two girls' schools (the school for the training of kindergarten teachers and the domestic science school) had to close immediately. Significant numbers of girls suddenly had to stop their schooling and a whole *tranche* of trainee nursery teachers found themselves without a course. The only girls whose education did not stop were those (relatively few) in the Senior (Middle) School. In 1943, four years after the departure of Luise Funke, the Amedzofe girls (in Standard VII) won the trophy for "Needlework and Dressmaking" for the whole of the Gold Coast. The women's Bible Class groups also continued under the auspices of local women (and still exist in very lively form up until the present).[15]

---

15. They are responsible for basic literacy, Bible study and interpretation and, in addition to various handicrafts, also give women the opportunity to act in morality plays and

More boys than girls went through the formal school system to Standard VII in the 1930s and '40s and there was more work (and a greater range of skills) available (and considered appropriate) for men than women in the embryonic economies of the Gold Coast / TVT. In any case ideas about women's lives and work within what we can call here a traditional Amedzofe world view revolved around adulthood, marriage and having children. Anything that a woman did in addition to this should be to enhance the lives and well-being of her children[16].

The "Subordination" of Amedzofe Women

Since the 1960s virtually all children, boys and girls, in Amedzofe have gone to school and the vast majority have completed the first cycle.[17] In the early 1970s, when I first went to Amedzofe, the number of non-Christians in the village could be counted on the fingers, certainly of two hands, if not one. Amedzofe continues, in the central Volta Region, as a beacon in both religious and educational terms. True, the village is no longer the site of the mission seminary (that had been removed to Peki long since), but there is a well-thought-of Teacher Training College there, founded in 1946, and both the Town Primary and the Demonstration Primary (attached to the Training College) schools attract students from surrounding villages as well as those from Amedzofe and from outside, children of Amedzofe parents working away elsewhere. Amedzofe people have evolved a range of strategies to cope with and outwit the vagaries of Ghana's intertwining with the global economy. But still in Ghana, as elsewhere in the capitalist periphery, the array of work and skills normally available to women is far narrower than that available to men: the gendering of now global labor markets, both formal and informal, favors men both in the range of work available and in the scales of remuneration[18].

Women, then, have a harder time than men in making a living in contemporary Ghana, and this applies to Amedzofe women as much as to any others. The array of work and training considered appropriate for all, except perhaps university-trained women, centres on skills that derive from western domes-

---

sing in choirs. Their organisation is now much more complex than originally so local village class leaders take part in meetings and training workshops and are encouraged to disseminate their work to others.

16. See Brydon, 1976, Chapter 5 for background here.

17. Standard VII, later Middle Form 4 and now Junior Secondary School.

18. For a discussion of contemporary gendering of the labour market in Ghana see MacEwen Scott, 1986; Brydon, 1992; Brydon and Legge, 1996.

tic/household training like that introduced by the missionaries' wives to their female house children: cleaning and laundry, sewing and cooking; caring for sick children, and early child care and training—such skills that were developed and enhanced by Luise Funke and the other mission sisters' work in the 1930s. What is considered to be appropriate work for women today derives not from any Amedzofe view of appropriate, but rather from western capitalist and largely Christian values. Perhaps inevitably, these ideas of appropriateness have become the dominant ideology in Ghana as elsewhere in the world.

Ideas about what constitutes appropriate or suitable skills for women are so strongly entrenched in world views of contemporary Ghanaians, including Amedzofe people, that even contemporary development projects for women tend to focus on the small scale commercialization of domestic skills: production and sale of cooked or processed food; food preservation and presentation; sewing. True, women have always sold what they produced (see above), and they continue to do so, but the money that they make by selling their own produce, whether grown or made, now covers a fraction of the needs it covered in the pre- and early colonial periods, when, as we saw above, some women did not even need to farm for their subsistence.

What has happened then to the "feisty" women of the 1890s who were "so drunk they nearly died"? What has happened to the women whose husbands discovered that "not him, but his wife is master in the house"? Have they succumbed, or been "succumbed," to the fate of women under capitalism everywhere? Their productive skills may be valued in the wider society (the Ghanaian state in this case), but do their reproductive skills, which made up so much more of their lives in the past, have no value? Reproductive work was highly valued in the wider Amedzofe society in the past, in the public as well as the domestic / private segments of the community. It was what women should do, and any extra that they could earn, in terms of money to buy consumer goods in the early colonial period, was welcomed. There was little, if any, divide between "production" and "reproduction."

Is the story of Amedzofe women's religious encounter, then, just another take on the translation of Christian and western capitalist values into a receptive periphery and the consequent downplaying of women's roles, status, whatever, in post-colonial times? Up to a point we can see that Christian and colonial recensions of domesticity in a changing and increasingly, first monetized, and then globalized, world order detracted from the obvious significance of women in Amedzofe society, as it was apparent to the missionaries in the early years of their work. Christian women in Amedzofe in the 1920s and '30s worked within the new rules and norms, and evolved strategies to become successful in the colonial/mission order in the early to mid-twentieth century. They made money to sponsor a catechist, the girls in the domestic science classes won trophies for their work. The women's Bible Class offered a new kind of order, network and hierarchy within which Christian women could work successfully, in the sense that they were successful, prominent, and respected in the eyes of the society and community of which they were a part.

By the 1970s when I went to begin my own encounter with Amedzofe, however, being prominent and respected within the community did not necessarily mean that women had the skills to be successful in the wider society of independent Ghana. Opportunities for the majority, having only basic education, were restricted to the narrow array of appropriate "women's work," and the labor market was already overcrowded, straining on the edge of Ghana's precipitate decline into near-bankruptcy (Brydon and Legge, 1996). Outside the community, women tended to struggle to make ends meet.[19]

Women who found life difficult outside of the village could choose to return there. As adult members of their lineages they had access to land on which to farm, even if they had no husband. They found shelter with relatives or built, minimally a single room with outside space for a hearth, for themselves. They had the basic requirements of life: food, water, shelter. Even the poorest women in Amedzofe managed to send their children to school and to clothe the children and themselves from whatever they managed to earn through either sales of farm produce or skills (perhaps sewing for other women, or cooking and selling breakfast porridge, or even hiring themselves out as farm laborers for others). Other family members, too, would sometimes help out. Within the villages women could be autonomous, independent, and highly respected. In the wider economy they were relegated to poorly paid jobs and little or no status: they were subordinated.

"Telling It Like It Is"

So my field notes were permeated with observations about women and farming, women and selling, women and families, both natal and procreated, and women and life crisis rituals. There were also copious sections on women's meetings and women's presence and voice in town meetings, and all this apart

---

19. In so short a space as this I can only note that from about the 1950s the norms relating to marriage and motherhood in Amedzofe had also undergone a major shift. From a situation where it was unthinkable for a woman to be left alone with no husband or husband's family to help in raising 'their' child in this patrilineal community, by the 1970s several women were on their own with children, whose fathers contributed little or nothing to their upbringing.

from women's significance in the church. I also knew that whenever there was a celebration for the town as it was represented by the (male) chiefs, and an animal was to be killed and palm wine and its distillate (*akpeteshie*) to be drunk, that a portion of the meat and the liquor had to be given to the women of the village. There was even an Avatime-wide celebration for the election of a new *tenu*, a (male) women's messenger, to which women (and some men) from all of the Avatime villages went and at which there was special drumming, dancing and singing of *tetieme* songs, that I heard in no other context.

Amedzofe women did not seem to me to be "subordinated," a term that I interpreted then to be saying that they were downtrodden, voiceless, invisible. Amedzofe women seemed to work hard with their husbands, if they had them, to provide a future for their children. Amedzofe men, too, seemed to work hard with their wives for their children. I tiptoed around the edge of trying to unravel patriliny and patriarchy, to make sense of Amedzofe women's lives in one chapter of my thesis and tried, not very successfully, to draw comparisons between Amedzofe women and their livelihoods and the strong and relatively autonomous matriarchs of the "matrifocal" families of the Caribbean. But the fulcrum of the thesis revolved around the ceremonies involved in, and the still-crucial significance of, the formal recognition of Amedzofe women's status as adults and as, therefore, women. I ended up by saying simply that it was important for women to be recognized as adults, and that, as adult women (*Ked'amidze'a*), they constituted an important category in Amedzofe society, and that Amedzofe people thought that women and men should work together for the good of their children. These points were a rather feeble conclusion given Marilyn Strathern's boldness in the face of the New Guinea ethnographies of the time, and the contributors to Rosaldo and Lamphere's materialist and structuralist / symbolist insights.

The book of the thesis was supposed to follow, and I spent several years preparing my manuscript, analyzing the ways that Amedzofe women had become subordinated under colonial rule, and the dominance of Christian values, in spite of the fact that my field notes were stuffed full of the deeds of women and the things that women said, the points that they made, and their obvious visibility in the community. The first attempt was destined never to be published, but John encouraged me to write it, and he read the finished manuscript. The problem was, he wrote, (and I paraphrase here), that it did not ring true. The key maxim for me, he said, was to move out from the hegemony of accepted theories, to have the courage of my convictions (and my field notes). " 'To thine own self be true,'" he said. It is a difficult maxim to follow, but it still creeps into my head whenever I waver over a point. So, here goes: today Amedzofe women are strong, powerful, important, in their own community: in their families, in the church and in the village. But, when they enter the worlds outside of their community there are problems, and they face the same obstacles and barriers to success and prosperity as other women in Ghana. They become "invisible," there are gender barriers to success in the workplace, and they are confined largely to the spheres of "women's work." The difference here, of course, is that women's work in the worlds outside of the village has so many negative trappings associated with it, within the village there are still ideological and institutional buttresses to confirm women as significant and powerful actors, reminiscent of a hundred years ago when "they and not their husbands...(were)...master(s) in the house." I could say that Amedzofe women are faced with the same dilemmas and problems as women in so many other parts of the world, from "First" through "Fifth", when they try to operate in the post-Enlightenment male constructed world of the hegemonic west, as filtered through to contemporary Ghana. They struggle to deal with, let alone overcome its ideological trappings, to get a fair deal, to start from a level playing field. But within their own culturally constructed communities they have adapted and shaped the west's hegemonic tentacles. They meet with discrimination in the worlds outside of the village, but their knowledge and sense of themselves as Avatime/Amedzofe women allows them to "cope". They at least know that they have a positive option of returning home, to have land, food, water and shelter, a life for their children, and, not only the support and demands of their kin, but also the respect and status associated with being an Amedzofe woman.

References

Amedzofe, 1964, *Amedzofe E.P. Hame Nutinya, 1889–1964*, Accra.

Amedzofe, 1989, *Amedzofe E.P. Hame Nutinya, 1889–1989*, Ho.

Brydon, Lynne, 1992, Ghanaian Women in the Migration Process, in *Gender and Migration in Developing Countries*, (ed) Sylvia Chant, Belhaven Press: 91–108.

Brydon, Lynne, 1976, *Status Ambiguity in Amedzofe: Women and Men in a Changing Patrilineal Society*, Unpublished PhD thesis, University of Cambridge.

Brydon, Lynne and Karen Legge, 1996, *Adjusting Society: The World Bank, the IMF and Ghana*, I.B. Tauris, London.

Debrunner, Hans W., 1965, *A church between colonial powers: a study of the church in Togo*, Lutterworth Press, London.

Gann, L.H. and Peter Duignan, 1977, *The Rulers of German Africa: 1884–1914*, University of Stanford Press, Stanford.

Ifeka-Moller, Caroline, 1975, Female Militancy and Colonial Revolt: The Women's War of 1929, Eastern Nigeria, in Shirley Ardener (ed), *Perceiving Women*, J.M. Dent and Sons, London: 127–158.

Meyer, Birgit, 1999, *Translating the Devil: Religion and Modernity among the Ewe of Ghana*, Edinburgh University Press for International African Institute, Edinburgh.

Okonjo, Kamene, 1976, The Dual-Sex Political system in Operation: Igo Women and Community Politics in Midwestern Nigeria, in Nancy Hafkin and Edna G Bay (eds), *Women in Africa*, Stanford University Press, Stanford: 45–58.

Ortner, Sherry B., 1974, Is Female to Male as Nature Is to Culture, in Rosaldo and Lamphere (eds) *op. cit.*: 67–88.

Peel, J.D.Y., 1968, *Aladura: a religious movement among the Yoruba*, Oxford University Press for IAI: London.

Peel, J.D.Y., 1978, '*Olaju*' a Yoruba concept of development, in *Journal of Development Studies*, 14: 139–65.

Peel, J.D.Y., 1983, *Ijeshas and Nigerians: The Incorporation of a Yoruba Kingdom, 1890s–1970s*, Cambridge University Press, Cambridge.

Peel, J.D.Y., 2000, *Religious encounter and the making of the Yoruba*, Indiana University Press, Bloomington.

Röhrig, E. W. (ed), 1955, *A History of the Vietor Family of Schwalenberg-Lippe*, private publication: no place of publication given.

Rosaldo Michelle Zimbalist and Louise Lamphere (eds), 1974, *Woman, Culture and Society*, Stanford University Press, Stanford.

Sacks, Karen, 1974, Engels Revisited: Women, the Organization of Production and Private Property, in Rosaldo and Lamphere (eds) *op. cit.*: 207–22.

Sacks, Karen B, 1979, *Sisters and Wives: The Past and Future of Sexual Equality*, Greenwood Press, Westport and London.

Scott, Alison MacEwen, 1986, Industrialization, Gender Segregation and Stratification Theory, in Rosemary Crompton and Michael Mann (eds), *Gender and Stratification*, Polity Press, Cambridge: 154–89.

Spieth, Jakob, 1906, *Die Ewe-Stämme: Material zur Kunde des Ewe-Volkes in Deutsch-Togo*, Dietrich Reimer, Berlin.

Strathern, Marilyn, 1972, *Women in Between: Female Roles in a Male World*, Seminar Press, London.

Van Allen, Judith, 1976, 'Aba Riots' or Igbo 'Women's War'? Ideology, Stratification, and the Invisibility of Women, in Hafkin and Bay (eds), *op. cit.*: 59–86.

Bremen Mission (Norddeutsche Missionsgesellschaft)

Monatsblätter, Monthly newsletters (dates given in text).

Jahresberichten, Yearly reports (dates in text).

CHAPTER 21

ANGLICANISM AND ASANTEHENE AGYEMAN PREMPEH

T.C. McCaskie

I

Much has been written about Christianity in the life of the thirteenth Asantehene Agyeman Prempeh (d. 1931).[1] The works deal with the subject from Agyeman Prempeh's point of view and, more broadly, from an Asante cultural perspective. They trace his thoughts on, and deliberations over, Anglican Christianity in his decades of political exile in the Gold Coast, Sierra Leone and Seychelles (1896–1924), and thereafter in his final years of repatriation in Asante (1924–31).[2] In this essay I offer a rather different perspective. I look at the issue in terms of Anglican Church history. Just what sort of Anglican was Agyeman Prempeh? I address this question by exploring the context of religious formation in the rather different Anglican Churches of Seychelles and Asante. I contend that Agyeman Prempeh's personal understanding of Anglicanism was shaped in Seychelles. I contend further that his view of Anglicanism in its social context was decisively refined in Asante, enabling him to search for ways and means by which workable compromises might be forged between Christian and Asante traditions.[3] Nowhere was this quest more apparent than in the unprecedented arrangements that attended Agyeman Prempeh's death and funeral rites in May 1931. He himself helped to plan what took place. To illus-

---

1. This paper is for John Peel, inspirational scholar and friend.
2. Boahen (1972; 1987; 2003); Akyeampong (1999; 2003).
3. The search continues today; see Sarpong (1996).

trate what Agyeman Prempeh sanctioned, I append to this essay the text of a hitherto overlooked account of his obsequies. This quite remarkable testimony was written by Rev. St. John Evans, Anglican Archdeacon of Accra, and a surprising – and surprised – leading actor in the events he describes.

Let me provide some contextual information for what is to follow. All retrospective accounts of Agyeman Prempeh's abduction, exile and return home (by himself as well as by others) privilege the heroic facts of his obdurate resistance and triumphant repatriation after nearly thirty years of detention outside Asante. Hindsight works to structure such narratives as an epic overcoming of adversity, but their linear accounts of a progress towards the satisfying closure of homecoming tend to gloss over paradoxes and contradictions. Admittedly, one *ex post facto* truth is that Agyeman Prempeh did survive to come home. But another truth, not widely discussed, is that he often despaired of doing so. Adversity, we might say, looked for long years as if it was not to be overcome. In this situation, the compromises Agyeman Prempeh arrived at with himself, to allay anxiety and maintain equilibrium through thirty years of detention by foreigners in alien lands, changed him in ways that sometimes made him a conflicted stranger to his own earlier understandings of himself. Destabilizations of this sort affected the Asantehene's relationship with everything, including Christianity. A consequence of this was that old and new values came into conflict in Agyeman Prempeh producing perturbed conversations within himself. This was not the either/or of equivocation, nor was it a simple dilemma. Agyeman Prempeh, I contend, truly lived in two worlds, and the compromises he constructed between them were intended to preserve the integrity of both. He intended to be an Asantehene and a Christian, and not a Christian Asantehene. I contend further that it was by means of this willed fission that he managed the issue of fusion and, in so doing, achieved a reconciliation with the jarring experiential discrepancies of his own unique personal history. I will labour these points no further here, except to ask that they be borne in mind throughout what follows.[4]

II

Agyeman Prempeh was born in 1872 and installed as Asantehene in 1888. He was seized and exiled by the British in 1896. He was detained, first at Elmina on the Gold Coast, then at Freetown in Sierra Leone, and from 1900 on Mahé, the largest island of the Seychelles archipelago in the Indian

---

4. This paragraph is a meditation on thirty-five years of conversation in Asante about Agyeman Prempeh.

Figure 21.1 - Agyeman Prempeh in exile at Elmina.

Ocean. In 1924, after nearly thirty years in exile, he was repatriated as the private Christian citizen Mr. Edward Prempeh. The British appointed him to head the reconstituted Kumase territorial division of Asante in 1926. They refused to reconfirm him in the office of Asantehene, although his people continued to think of him as such. He died of pernicious anaemia in May 1931.[5]

In January 1896 Agyeman Prempeh was an independent monarch in his palace in Kumase. A month later, he was an exiled prisoner in a British colonial jail in Elmina Castle. Neither he nor anyone taken with him, fellow captives, wives, servants, spoke English, or were equipped to grasp what habeas corpus was, or why it was suspended in their case. Apart from officials, the only people allowed any access to the Asantehene were clergy, who came to offer him comfort, point out the errors of his heathen ways, and set him on the path to Christian redemption. But even here, there were sectarian restrictions. In May 1896, James Kwabena of the Roman Catholic Society of African Missions at Cape Coast applied to see the Asantehene. The British turned him down because his father was Asante, and because as a member of a French mission and as an aide to the Vatican's local Apostolic Prefect he served two

---

5. McCaskie (2003); Boahen (2003); Akyeampong (2003); Tordoff (1960; 1965).

foreign powers and their alien Roman Catholic creed. In September, Rev. Jacob Anaman of the Wesleyan-Methodist Missionary Society (WMMS) in Anomabo also applied to see the Asantehene. Permission was granted because Anaman was known to the British in his role as a government interpreter, and because he belonged to an English and Protestant if dissenting church. Anaman spoke in Twi with Agyeman Prempeh on two occasions. He found the king disoriented and despondent. He warned him against the false witness of Catholicism. He advised him to start going to a Protestant church if and when opportunity arose. He told him the English king and all his servants, including those who ran Elmina prison, were Protestants. From all of this we can surmise that Agyeman Prempeh deduced three things: One, his British captors wanted him to embrace Christianity; two, this was bound up with their opinion of him and so affected his chances of release; three, Christianity was a divided house in which Protestantism was good and Catholicism bad.[6]

In December 1896 the British deported Agyeman Prempeh from the Gold Coast in case he became a focus for insurrection in Asante.[7] The Chief Justice himself went to tell the king that he and his party were being removed to Sierra Leone. Agyeman Prempeh pleaded not to be sent so far away from Asante. He was told he would never return home. Reportedly, the Asantehene "quailed when told of this definite end to his hopes." He proceeded "to call on every one of his savage deities to save him from the white man's power, and restore him to the bloody throne of his ancestors."[8] Imperial rhetoric aside, the depth of the crisis facing Agyeman Prempeh can be discerned in this outburst. He was being expelled from his own world and sent, frighteningly, across an unfamiliar ocean into the unknown. But was this also a crisis of belief? Certainly it unsettled his worldview, or at least that is what he told his kin in November 1924 (see below). He had appealed to all of Asante's otherworldly powers for help, but his pleading went unanswered. In January 1897 he and his party were shipped to Freetown.

Agyeman Prempeh spent three years (1897–1900) in Sierra Leone. This is the least well documented period of his exile, but it was manifestly a stressful

---

6. This account is based on PRAAD (Public Records and Archives Administration Department), Accra, ADM 11/1/624, 'Ashanti Political Prisoners 1916'; ADM 11/1/1478, 'Ashanti Political Prisoners 1887–1928'; ADM 11/1/1499, 'Ashanti Political Prisoners in the Seychelles'; ADM 11/1/1501, 'Ashanti Prisoners 1886–1898', 2 vols.; ADM 11/1/1905, 'King Prempeh 1908–1925.'

7. For Anglo-Asante relations at this time see Wilks (2000); McCaskie (2000).

8. PRAAD, Accra, ADM 11/1/1501, II, Chief Justice to Governor, dd. Victoriaborg, 2 December 1896; ADM 11/1/1478, Curran to Bristowe, dd. Elmina, 10 December 1896.

time of adjustment to the permanence of detention and exile. "We were brought here from Coomassie with nothing but the clothes we had on our body", he stated, "and with no money whatever." Materially and otherwise, this was a time of despair. Perhaps it was to counter this desolation that, in 1896, Agyeman Prempeh and his mother, Yaa Kyaa, began to attend Freetown's Anglican cathedral. Not everyone was convinced of their sincerity. Kofi Nti, appointed interpreter to the exiles by the British precisely because he held a grudge against Agyeman Prempeh, saw this churchgoing in purely instrumental terms. He advised that the Asantehene went to church only to advertise that he had "repented" of his former "wickedness", so that the British might relent and send him home. He added that the king had ordered his followers to have nothing to do with missions or schools. Others took a different view. The Colonial Chaplain A. Nicol was certain of the Asantehene's sincerity in "thirsting after" Christian salvation. He observed that "the King is struggling to gain the Blessed Truth in as much as it is in his power to do this with his few words of English and little by way of instruction or comfort." Nicol spoke no Twi, but with the help of an Asante boy he tried to "proclaim the good news to this unhappy Prince who begins to look most earnestly to his Redeemer."

There is no necessary contradiction between these views. The Asantehene's engagement with Anglican Christianity was born in desperate circumstances. It would be surprising if his motives did not include both Kofi Nti's political self-interest and Nicol's existential need. Two further points can be made. First, throughout the rest of his life the Asantehene encountered people (Asante as well as British) who thought his Anglicanism an expedient sham. Second, it should not be forgotten that Christian missionaries and churchmen had their own motives, worldly as well as spiritual, for wanting to believe that the monarch of an infamously bloody African kingdom had come to Christ. Somewhere in the middle of all this was the captive Asantehene, whose exotic celebrity was capable of accommodating a multitude of interested readings.[9]

In 1900–1901 there was a failed insurrection in Asante.[10] The British thought the Asantehene might inspire further trouble. They decided to re-

---

9. *Ibid.*, ADM 11/1/1501, II, Kofi Nti to Colonial Secretary (Accra), dd. Freetown, 13 September and 23 October 1897; Agyeman Prempeh to Governor (Sierra Leone), dd. Ascension Town, 27 October 1899; ADM 11/1/1499, Governor (Sierra Leone) to Governor (Gold Coast), dd. Freetown, 14 July 1899, encl. 'Mr. Nicol's Reports on the Ashanti Political Prisoners.'

10. See Arhin (2000); Boahen (2000; 2003a); Obeng (2000); Day (2000); Asirifi-Danquah (2002).

move him from West Africa to Seychelles in the Indian Ocean, a remote archipelago that hosted a succession of imperial prisoners.[11] In August 1900, Agyeman Prempeh and fifty-five fellow Asante, the contingent swollen by children born in exile, sailed from Freetown to Victoria on Mahé, the largest island in the Seychelles group. In June 1901, these detainees were joined by Yaa Asantewaa and fourteen other Asante leaders deported for their part in the 1900–1901 uprising. By the end of 1901, all of the Asante prisoners were living together at Le Rocher ("Ashanti Camp"), a sugar plantation estate near Victoria. They were lightly guarded, and had some freedom of movement, because escape was virtually impossible. Le Rocher was to be the Asantehene's home until 1924.[12]

III

Agyeman Prempeh landed in Seychelles on 11 September 1900. A scant twelve days later, on the 23rd, he was visited by Ven. H.D. Buswell of the Anglican Bishopric of Mauritius and Seychelles. Buswell was Archdeacon of Seychelles (1895–1912), but he administered Anglican affairs on Mahé by twice yearly visits from his parish in Mauritius, nine hundred and thirty-four nautical miles away. Informed of the impending arrival of the Asantehene, he made a special voyage to meet and talk with the exiled monarch and his party, "as soon as possible after their arrival." [13] Buswell was a very experienced missionary priest. He was an Evangelical, trained at Islington College by the Church Missionary Society (CMS) in the 1850s. He served as a CMS missionary in Sierra Leone, and then among the Tamil-speakers of southern India and Ceylon (Sri Lanka). In 1854, the Bishopric of Mauritius and Seychelles was created, and in 1866 Buswell was transferred to it. By 1900, Buswell had served two terms as chaplain to his bishop, and had been CMS Diocesan Secretary in the capital of Port Louis since 1877.

---

11. The series started with the Malaysian Sultan of Perak in the 1870s, and ended with the Greek Cypriot Archbishop Makarios in the 1950s. In 1900, the rulers of Buganda and Bunyoro were already held there.

12. NAS (National Archives of Seychelles), Victoria, C/SS/2, 'Political Exiles: Ashanti – Ex-King Prempeh and Others', 5 vols. and 2 supplementary folders, is the indispensable source for the period 1900–24. I thank H.J. McGaw, former Director NAS and Seychelles Museum Division, for copies of all these documents and for additional materials sent in response to queries arising from my research.

13. CMS (Church Missionary Society Archives), Birmingham, G2 MA/O (Mauritius), Annual Report by H.D. Buswell, dd. Port Louis, November 1900.

Buswell's lifelong vocation was to evangelize by bringing the gospel to the heathen.[14] He had this in mind when he rushed to Seychelles in 1900. On October 1, he set down his first impressions of Agyeman Prempeh:

> The Ashanti political prisoners arrived about a fortnight ago. I took an early opportunity of visiting them. King Prempeh expressed his readiness to hear 'good word.' It remains to be seen whether he was sincere in what he said.[15]

Throughout October and November more meetings took place, with the interpreter T.F. Korsah (a Fante from Saltpond, sent by the Gold Coast government for just this purpose) mediating between the Asantehene's Twi and Buswell's English. The latter soon came to believe that rapid strides were being made. "King Prempeh", he wrote in November:

> seems to look forward to my visits with pleasure. He certainly listens most attentively and by his questions and remarks I gather that he is trying, and not at all unsuccessfully, to take in what he hears. I find also that he talks about it afterwards. One day, when I was trying as simply as possible to illustrate the teaching of the Lord's Prayer he said, as it seemed to me, very feelingly, "I should like to give my heart to God", and that, as far as I can remember, without my using language to support such an expression. Three or four weeks ago, while speaking to him on the subject of prayer, I told him that prayer must be offered through Jesus Christ and that when we ask any favour of God it must be for Jesu's sake. I used illustrations such as I thought would make the matter plain to him and he seemed much interested. The next time I went his mother [Yaa Kyaa] came and seated herself by me. It was clear he had been telling her what I had said, for when I got up to leave, he said, "Explain to me again 'For Jesus Christ's sake.'" He was anxious that she should hear. The next week his father [Kwasi Gyambibi], brother [Agyeman Badu] and another old chief came to listen.[16]

Buswell was encouraged by the progress he had made. He returned to Mauritius, sure that "King Prempeh and his family have been the willing recipients of instruction in Christian truth."[17] Once in Port Louis, he per-

---

14. Peel (2000) on the Yoruba is the best and fullest account of CMS evangelism.

15. CMS, Birmingham, G2 MA/O (Mauritius), Buswell to Durrant, dd. Victoria, 1 October 1900.

16. *Ibid.*, Annual Report by H.D. Buswell, dd. Port Louis, November 1900.

17. *Ibid.*, Buswell to Durrant, dd. Port Louis, 28 November 1900.

suaded his bishop to send a local clergyman to Mahé, pending the appointment of a permanent chaplain to the Asante community. He also made arrangements for the civil chaplain in Victoria to meet regularly with Agyeman Prempeh for Bible reading, instruction, prayer and hymn singing. At the same time, and seemingly with the support of the Asantehene, he pressed the British administration in Seychelles to pay the interpreter Korsah an additional stipend to teach reading and writing in English to Agyeman Prempeh and his entourage, and to plan a similar educational provision for the ever increasing number of children in the Le Rocher community.[18] By February 1901 the civil chaplain was meeting regularly with the Asantehene, and shortly thereafter Korsah began English lessons. The Asantehene and his mother also began to attend services at St. Paul's Anglican cathedral in Victoria.[19]

Two immediate questions suggest themselves. Why did Buswell act with such speed in the matter of gaining access to the Asantehene, a decision that required him to make a sea voyage of nearly one thousand miles? And why did Buswell think Agyeman Prempeh such a prize? In his well informed, anecdotal history of Seychelles, Dr. J.T. Bradley, Chief Government Medical Officer in Victoria, and founding editor of the *Seychelles Clarion* newspaper, offered the blunt opinion that Buswell raced from Mauritius to Seychelles to prevent the local French-affiliated Catholic priesthood from getting to the Asantehene first.[20] This is credible. Anglicans in Mauritius and Seychelles were few in number. Indeed, the Anglican Church's record of conversions in the islands was disappointing, and for this it blamed the much-longer established and far-more-numerous Catholic priesthood's hold over the local population. The two denominations were bitter rivals, but historical circumstances decreed that Anglicanism remained far weaker than Catholicism in this region. It was this history, together with the dispositions of the clergymen who fostered Anglicanism in Mauritius and Seychelles, that gave a distinctive character and direction to the struggling Anglican Church there.[21]

---

18. See Adu Boahen, Akyeampong, Lawler, McCaskie and Wilks eds. (2003), Frontispiece, for a photograph of Agyeman Prempeh learning to read and write English.

19. NAS, Victoria, C/SS/2, I, Sweet-Escott to Colonial Secretary, dd. Victoria, 5 November 1901. Like Kofi Nti, Sweet-Escott thought Agyeman Prempeh's church attendance was politically motivated.

20. Bradley (1940), II, 304; for an astringent but insightful view of Bradley see Scarr (2000).

21. My history of Anglicanism in Mauritius and Seychelles is derived from Pascoe (1901); Stock (1916); Bradley (1940); Webb (1964); Hewitt (1977); Chung (1994); CMS, Birmingham G2 MA/O (Mauritius); PRO (Public Record Office), London, CO.167 and

France occupied Mauritius in 1715 and Seychelles in 1742,[22] but Britain acquired both in the 1810s, and its rule there was confirmed by treaty at the close of the Napoleonic wars. By then, the population of both territories was mostly descended from African slaves ruled over by a Franco-Creole plantation aristocracy. There was a long established French Catholic presence; in fact, nearly everyone was nominally Catholic, with due attention being paid to saints and holy days. But there was also widespread backsliding and animism. Under the articles of capitulation to Britain, Catholicism was guaranteed government protection and even, though most unusual, government funding. The British funded the building of a Catholic cathedral in Port Louis, and paid the stipends of both a French Catholic bishop and his establishment of priests. Until the 1850s, the Anglican presence was confined to a few under-resourced schools administered from the distant Bishoprics of Calcutta and Colombo.

In 1854 the Anglican Bishopric of Mauritius and Seychelles was created, and in 1856 the first CMS missionaries arrived in search of converts. In retrospect, it can be seen that the high watermark of the new diocese was reached under Bishop Royston (1872–90). He was a CMS Evangelical, and had been a missionary in southern India. He saw that Evangelical Anglicanism could not hope to compete with entrenched and hostile Catholicism, and that in any case it held limited appeal for a native population used to a more lax and easy-going religiosity. So he turned away from the indigenes, deciding instead to forge an Anglican Church from newly arriving economic immigrants from southern India. What he sought to create was an evangelical church in the "Three Selves" (self-supporting, self-governing, self-propagating) mold advocated by influential CMS Secretary Henry Venn. The engine of this was to be CMS missionaries supported (and in due course supplanted) by Tamil or Hindi speaking pastors trained for the job at the evangelical CMS college at Tinnevelly in India. Converts were organized into a Native Council, and church services were conducted in English and all the many other languages spoken by the congregation. Gospel reading and personal testimony to the saving grace of Christ were central to Bishop Royston's church. He had a distaste for anything that smacked of ritualism or Anglo-Catholicism, an antipathy that was much reinforced by his rebarbative dealings with the Catholic hierarchy in the islands. When he left in 1890, his Anglican Church numbered

---

CO.530 (Mauritius and Seychelles); and successive editions of *Crockford's Clerical Directory*.

22. France evicted the Dutch from Mauritius, but found Seychelles uninhabited.

about 2,000 souls. At that time, the combined population of Mauritius and Seychelles was some 375,000 people.[23]

If this was a modest start, then it was also a false dawn. Bishop Royston's policies meant further growth depended on a fluctuating and uncertain supply of immigrants. These first had to be converted from their natal religions to Anglicanism, and thereafter had to sustain their new minority faith in the face of RC hostility, temptations to backslide, and local varieties of syncretism. To make matters even more difficult, the CMS lacked the will or the resources to fight this battle. Mauritius and the dependent Seychelles was the smallest and most isolated part of the CMS's worldwide commitments. By 1900, when Buswell met the Asantehene, he was the ranking member of a CMS establishment that numbered only two other English clergymen in Mauritius. These were supported by only four Tamil-speaking pastors. Ten years after his departure, Royston's church had dwindled away. By this time too, Buswell had few illusions about the future of Anglicanism in the islands. Catholic "idolatry and indulgence" and the congenital "immorality" of the people, he wrote, had conspired to make of Mauritius and Seychelles "a bad ward in the great hospital that claims the Great Physician's care." This hygienic metaphor encapsulated the local CMS view of a people afflicted with a spiritual disease, but refusing to be cleansed by gospel evangelism. It was a losing battle, and in 1907 the hammer blow fell. The CMS in London resolved to send no more missionaries, and to wind down its operations. Buswell was sad but unsurprised, and set about helping to dismantle his life's work. In 1918 all CMS properties were gifted to the bishop and the mission withdrew. By 1931 less than one percent of the population of Mauritius and Seychelles was Anglican, and the backbone of the community was a mix of British, Indian, and Chinese residents brought up or converted in churches elsewhere.

Seychelles Anglicanism was the puny and neglected outpost of faraway Mauritius. It had a brief success on the small island of Praslin, but on Mahé it stuttered and sometimes lapsed altogether. The Anglican school in the ambitiously named Venn's Town, near Victoria, was chronically understaffed and underfunded. The Anglican Church itself was faced with the implacable hostility of French Capuchin priests, and the open contempt of *grands blancs*

---

23. A discussion of Venn's 'Three Selves' is in Sundkler and Steed (2000), 115–6. At the consecration of St. Paul's cathedral in Port Louis, so Royston recalled, the service was in English; morning prayers and psalms were in Bengali; hymns were in Hindustani (Hindi); one lesson was in Tamil, and the other in Bengali; the sermon combined English and French, with a Bengali translation; communion was administered in all these languages according to the recipient's vernacular.

Catholic oligarchs. By 1900, when Agyeman Prempeh arrived, no CMS personnel were resident in Seychelles. Mission and church affairs were dealt with on a daily basis by the government's civil chaplain, and twice a year, as noted, Archdeacon Buswell made the long sea journey from Port Louis to inspect buildings and audit accounts. Arguably, it was this sense of a failing missionary effort, thwarted for fifty years by Catholic intransigence and local indifference, that stirred Buswell to rush to Mahé in the hope of converting Agyeman Prempeh. In this, he was a true follower of Royston. Just like the Indians in Mauritius, the Asantehene was an immigrant.

To repeat, it is not the purpose of this essay to analyze how the Asantehene's conversations with himself led him to his decision to embrace Christianity. Equally, I am not concerned here to investigate that decision as an aspect of his ambiguous seduction (if ever he was so seduced) by the trappings of "modernity."[24] I am concerned, however, with Agyeman Prempeh's progress in the Anglican Church, and with what kind of church that was.

On May 29, 1904, the Asantehene, his mother and brother were baptised as Anglicans in St. Paul's Cathedral in Victoria by the Civil Chaplain of Seychelles, Rev. W.A. Johnson.[25] Buswell did not attend, but telegraphed his best wishes. The Asante took names associated with British royalty. Agyeman Prempeh was baptised Edward, after the reigning British King Edward VII. Reportedly, when Agyeman Prempeh was being courted by Anglican and Catholic priests in 1900 he asked, "What religion is the King of England?" On being told, he declared he preferred Anglicanism because "I am of opinion that all Kings should have the same religion."[26] This was prudent, but it also reflected Asante understandings of royalty. In Akan-Asante thinking, all dynasties composed a unitary caste. Solidarity between them was expressed in bonding rituals like the borrowing of names and cults. Be that as it may, Agyeman Prempeh's baptism coincided with the return home of his tutor Korsah. By then, the Asantehene was able to "read and write fair well", and could "do without interpreter."[27] After Korsah left, however, the king's education became sporadic. The bishopric in Port Louis said it had no money to pay a teacher,

---

24. Akyeampong (1999) is an insightful treatment of this theme, and it takes the evidence he uses as far as it will go.

25. For the date as given by Agyeman Prempeh, see Adu Boahen, Akyeampong, Lawler, McCaskie and Wilks eds. (2003), 176; but compare Boahen (2003), 28. Agyeman Prempeh's father Kwasi Gyambibi had already died on 1 August 1903.

26. Bradley (1940), II, 304.

27. PRAAD, Accra, ADM 11/1/1499, Korsah to Colonial Secretary (Gold Coast), dd. Saltpond, 4 July and 18 August 1904.

and the colonial government refused to defray the costs. Agyeman Prempeh came to depend on the English language skills of his son Frederick (Kwasi Gyambibi), who attended the government school in Victoria. It was Frederick who acted as scribe for his father. In 1907 he started to record an English transcription of Agyeman Prempeh's oral Twi memoir, *The History of Ashanti Kings and the whole country itself.* [28] There is some Christian phraseology in this text, but whether it originated with the father or the son is unclear.[29]

Once baptised, Agyeman Prempeh began to think of confirmation and the communion that would mark his full membership in the Anglican Church. The barrier here was polygamy, for three royal wives (two of whom were sent home in 1908) and a number of concubines were with him in his exile. Negotiations over this went backwards and forwards over the years, with the church recruiting government support to demand that the king contract a monogamous Christian marriage as a precondition of his confirmation. Agyeman Prempeh suffered much indecision over this, for multiple marriages were central to his royal status and political role.[30] In 1913 he moved to break the deadlock, having been told repeatedly to marry a woman who shared his Christian beliefs. Accordingly, he proposed to set aside his remaining wife and all others to marry one Abena Gyamfua, who had expressed a wish for Anglican baptism and confirmation.[31] But because the bride-to-be was of relatively humble status, Agyeman Prempeh wanted to be married in secret so as to present anyone at Le Rocher who opposed the union with a *fait accompli*. He insisted on being married in another colony "in which there is a Protestant Bishop" and clearly had Mauritius in mind. The British refused and reminded the Asantehene that he was a prisoner.[32] Agyeman Prempeh responded by repeating his request. He reasserted his wish to be confirmed, but set out the difficulties of reconciling the demands made of Asante royalty with those insisted upon by the Anglican Church.

28. Adu Boahen, Akyeampong, Lawler, McCaskie and Wilks eds. (2003).

29. I owe this point to Professor Adam Jones, University of Leipzig.

30. NAS, Victoria, C/SS/2, II, Minute Paper on Ashanti Political Prisoners, dd. Victoria, 3 February 1908; *ibid.*, V, Governor (Gold Coast) to Governor (Seychelles), dd. Atebubu, 7 February 1914 (encl. Agyeman Prempeh to Kwaku Fin and Ama Dusah, dd. Le Rocher, 3 November 1913); Governor (Seychelles) to Governor (Gold Coast), dd. Victoria, 14 April 1914.

31. Abena Gyamfua of Kwanwoma Aponsakwaa was younger sister of Afua Mansa, wife of the detained Ofinsohene Kwadwo Apea. Afua Mansa accompanied her husband into exile, and took Abena Gyamfua with her as a maidservant.

32. NAS, Victoria, C/SS/2, V, Governor's Minute, dd. Victoria, 27 June 1913.

The reason of my asking leave to go to other Colony to get married is that from the time I am here about 13 years ago, everyone in the Colony knows perfectly well that this said woman [Abena Gyamfua] is a maid servant to me, and it shall be awkward if I am seen here getting lawful marriage to her. But the reason of my getting married to her is that I have for several times applied to Archdeacon Newton and to the Bishop of Mauritius to confirm me and I was replied that I must get married to this said woman in question before I could be allowed to be confirmed; and as I am anxious to be confirmed and to follow my religion I prefer marry this woman Abina Ganfuah; and through this cause I asked a leave to go to another country where no one knows whether this woman is a maid servant to me or not. And after being getting married together, we shall also be confirmed and then return to Mahi together.[33]

The British repeated their refusal, and the matter was dropped.[34]

Let me sum up. In Seychelles, the Asantehene encountered an Anglican Church of a particular kind, and with a particular history. Evangelical in doctrine, and "low church" in forms of worship, it had an innate antagonism toward Anglican ritualism that was reinforced by its unhappy interactions with local Catholicism. It was a product of Venn's CMS, adapted to meet challenging conditions. As a mission church, it emphasised conversion as a personal encounter with God, and it insisted that revelation be supported by instruction, gospel study, prayer, and self-examination. If it set great store by behavioural rules, then it must be recalled that it saw itself as a besieged Anglican redoubt in a hostile environment. Accordingly, it required constant vigilance from its members in exercising self-discipline. As we have seen, however, the problem was that it lacked the resources in men and money to support its members in their struggle to live Christian lives. For long periods, Agyeman Prempeh was without pastoral care or instruction. This reached a miserable nadir when, in the space of a few weeks in 1917, the Asantehene lost his mother and brother. [35] He was in a desperate state after his mother Yaa

---

33. *Ibid.*, V, Edward Prempeh to Tonnet, dd. Le Rocher, 28 June 1913. 'Archdeacon Newton' was Rev. E.A. Newton, Civil Chaplain at Victoria (1909–14) and titular Archdeacon of Seychelles (1912–7).

34. Even today, the fact that Agyeman Prempeh contemplated marriage with a servant is not discussed openly in Asante; see the way in which this episode is glossed over in Boahen (1987), 149.

35. Yaa Kyaa died on 2 August and Agyeman Badu on 28 September 1917.

Kyaa's death. Then, his brother Agyeman Badu fell mortally ill, and Agyeman Prempeh unsuccessfully petitioned the British to send the exiles back to Sierra Leone, so that "my sole brother and two sisters at Kumassi" might come and see their "own brother" before he died. "I suppose", he entreated, "that it is God's will that he would not die here in an entire isolated land from his country and relatives." [36] Then, when Agyeman Badu did die at Le Rocher, his bereft brother had to manage this challenge to his Christian faith without help from his church. The Bishop of Mauritius had no one he could send. The aged Buswell offered to go, but the money was not forthcoming to pay for his passage. The civil chaplain was ill, but attended the burial to read the commital before going back to bed. A year later, Agyeman Prempeh appealed to go home, simply because he was now "very miserable." [37]

In 1920 the Bishop of Mauritius finally consented to confirm the Asantehene. He did this from "Christian charity", because "the Ex-King's behaviour is constant and he has given a solemn undertaking to marry." Agyeman Prempeh was duly confirmed on December 24, in St. Paul's Anglican Cathedral in Victoria. It seems that the Bishop acceded to government pressure in arriving at this decision. In both London and Victoria, it was felt that Agyeman Prempeh should be confirmed for political reasons, and most importantly because in the event of his repatriation, which was the object of a growing campaign in the Gold Coast, "he will be valuable to H.M. Govt. if it is known by the natives of Ashanti and the Colony that he has become a churchgoer under our care." [38]

Then, in 1924, the Asantehene was at last repatriated. A.C. Duncan-Johnstone, who escorted him from the Seychelles to Asante, described him as "a fervent Christian, Church of England", who thought "it had been his Destiny to be exiled and the Almighty had no doubt some purpose in decreeing it." He also said that "the Ex-King is an Anglican of the Low Church variety, inclined to fervour in all his observances, avid for the Gospel and keen to a fault on praying. He is the no nonsense sort of Christian – as far away it can be said from the Roman kind of Anglican as possible. He is to a high degree zealous." [39]

---

36. NAS, Victoria, C/SS/2, III, Edward Prempeh to Colonial Secretary (London), dd. Le Rocher, 6 August 1917.

37. *Ibid.*, Edward Prempeh to Fiennes, dd. Le Rocher, 22 October 1918.

38. *Ibid.*, supplementary folder II, Bishop of Mauritius to Governor (Seychelles), dd. Port Louis, 1 March 1920; Governor's Minutes, dd. Victoria, 27 August 1920 and 11 January 1921.

39. PRAAD, Accra, ADM 11/1/1905, Lt. Col. A.C. Duncan-Johnstone, 'A Report on the Repatriation of Ex-King Prempeh from the Seychelles to Ashanti, Sept. 12th to Nov. 11th 1924'; *ibid.*, ADM 11/1/1899, 'Nana Prempeh and Others 1924–1930', 2 vols., I, Duncan-Johnstone to Chief Commissioner (Asante), dd. Kumase, 4 August 1925.

The Anglican Church of Mauritius and Seychelles may have failed to provide Agyeman Prempeh with sustained pastoral care, but it was successful in stamping him with the Evangelical principles that ran through Venn's CMS, Royston's church, and Buswell's ministry. His Christianity made much of his own experience, being based on the idea of a life's journey from darkness into light, a progress enabled by the surrender of the self to the saving power of Jesus Christ. This was a simple and unadorned faith, literal in belief and muscular in expression. All this can be seen in a speech that Agyeman Prempeh delivered to the Kumase royal family less than three weeks after his return home.

> Nana Prempeh, for the first time since his arrival, had a spare evening on 28th November, when he called together the members of his family whom he had not seen for twenty eight years, a list of whom had been previously submitted to him. From the list he found that only a few of them had been baptised. He took the occasion to recount to them of the days when he reigned, and that although it was glorious and powerful, yet it was in darkness. He said that as they all knew, he kept 300 (Kramor) fetish priests as seers to divine what is going on in his kingdom, and to devise means for his safety. Besides these he had countless numbers of other fetishes to guide his person. All these charms were with him when he was taken into exile; they could not save him. In Seychelles where he had lived for 28 years these fetishes and seers were not there to render him service. He gave himself entirely to the Almighty God and became a Christian as he is today. It was God who had protected him all these years, and has been pleased to bring him again to his native land, the land of his forefathers to see his relatives. Therefore it is his express desire that every member of his family become a Christian. It is, he continued, by giving oneself to God and becoming a Christian that you are saved both here and hereafter.[40]

IV

Agyeman Prempeh quickly realized that the Anglican Church in Kumase differed from its Seychelles counterpart. In December 1924 Superintendent H. Webster of the long- established WMMS in Kumase invited "Mr. E. Prempeh" to a service of thanksgiving for his safe return home. Agyeman Prempeh

---

40. *The Gold Coast Independent* (Accra), 13 December 1924.

agreed to attend this Christian celebration, but on the day of the service he very suddenly begged off. The reason was a letter addressed to him by Fr. Peter, the priest in charge of St. Cyprian's Anglican church (now cathedral) in Kumase. This is what it said:

> My good friend, it has only just come to my notice and hearing that you have arranged to attend the Wesleyan Mission Service this Sunday evening to show your appreciation for the prayers their members have made for your repatriation. While I quite understand your motives for showing your gratitude in this way, yet as your priest I feel it only my duty to tell you that as a member of the Church it would be wrong for you to be present at any service of a dissenting mission, and that such a step might be misrepresented and exaggerated. [41]

Webster was incensed, accusing Fr. Peter of "priestly arrogance" and of "aping the Roman church in his ministry."

Anglicanism was a latecomer to the mission field in the Gold Coast and Asante.[42] In the eighteenth century, an initiative in Cape Coast simply collapsed. In the nineteenth century, the CMS declined to work on the Gold Coast, because a vigorous WMMS presence was established there from the 1830s onwards. But in 1905 the Society for the Propagation of the Gospel (SPG) commenced Anglican missionary work on the Gold Coast once again. The SPG found it hard going, even after N.T. Hamlyn was translated from Nigeria to the newly created Bishopric of Accra in 1909. Missionaries were few, internal conflicts were endemic, and the SPG could not meet the rising demand for teachers as well as pastors. In Asante, G.W. Morrison (with whom Agyeman Prempeh corresponded from Seychelles) was appointed the SPG's first permanent (but often absent) representative in 1913. He founded St. Cyprian's church (now cathedral) and St. Augustine's school (now college) in Kumase. But after he resigned in 1920, there was no Anglican missionary in Kumase for three years.

Under Bishop Hamlyn (1909–10), the Anglican Church's liturgy and forms of observance were like those described for Seychelles, and many SPG mis-

---

41. I thank Emeritus Professor William Tordoff, University of Manchester, for making a copy of this letter (Fr. Peter Harris to Nana Prempeh, dd. Kumase, 7 December 1924) available to me, and for copies of other documents relevant to this section of the paper. Tordoff consulted these materials in the National Archives of Ghana (now PRAAD), Kumase, in the 1960s. They have since been misplaced.

42. In this section, I acknowledge my debt to the excellent pioneering research of Jenkins (1974a; 1974b).

sionaries were "low church" Evangelicals.[43] But under Bishop O'Rorke (1913–24), and most particularly under his long-serving successor Bishop Aglionby, "low church" Evangelical precepts and practices gave way to an ever rising tide of Anglo-Catholic ritualism. This reflected the debates and divisions then going on within the Church in England. By 1920 in the Anglican Church in the Gold Coast and Asante, the Act of Communion was called and treated as the Mass; Sacrament was "reserved" in the Anglo-Catholic (and Roman) manner; confession was encouraged; incense, vestments, and the sacristan bell were all in use; pictures were placed on the walls over the altar; some churches had stations of the cross around the walls, and a large reredos with statues of saints. Increasingly too, the liturgy in use was the Eucharistic one in the Book of Common Prayer, which echoed the Catholic Tridentine Missal.[44]

In 1924 SPG missionaries were replaced by Anglican monks of the Order of St. Benedict (OSB) from Pershore Abbey in the English Midlands. [45] The revival of Anglican religious communities was a striking feature of Anglo-Catholicism, the initiative for it coming from Newman, Pusey, and others in the Oxford Movement in the 1840s. [46] Be that as it may, the creation of the Pershore Abbey community was slightly controversial. Its founders were originally members of Aelred Carlyle's Benedictine community on Caldey Island. In 1911 that community was censured by Anglican authorities for its use of openly Catholic Marian and extra-liturgical Eucharistic devotions. Rejecting this reproof, the Caldey majority submitted to Rome, while the tiny minority who elected to stay within the Anglican Church founded the Pershore community in 1913. In sum, OSB monks from Pershore Abbey were as close to Rome as it was possible to be and still remain within the Anglican Church. It was these men who took up the reins of missionary Anglicanism in the Gold Coast and Asante in 1924.

Fr. Peter (Harris) was from the OSB community at Pershore Abbey, and he was sent to take charge of Kumase just before Agyeman Prempeh's repatriation. He introduced to St. Cyprian's church the Roman Canon of the Mass in Latin, the Angelus, a side altar for the "reserved" Sacrament, plainsong,

---

43. Most members of the SPG were 'high church' ritualists, but there existed 'a gentleman's agreement', in Jenkins's phrase, to send only those of a 'low church' persuasion to the Evangelical diocese of Accra.

44. M.S. O'Rorke, *To English Priests with a Missionary Vocation*, Accra, 1920; Holdbrooke (1996).

45. I acknowledge here the kind assistance of Rt. Rev. Dom Basil Matthews OSB, Abbot of Elmore Abbey in Berkshire, successor house to Pershore.

46. Allchin (1958).

chants, genuflection, and incense. He was not insensitive to Asante cultural norms, but he saw these in terms of their potential use in advancing his mission. Thus, personally he appears to have shared the Catholic belief in the "real presence" of Christ in the communion wine, and their consequent preference for using white wine. But he learned of the real and symbolic significance of blood (*mogya*) in Asante life, and as a result the communion wine at St. Cyprian's was red. He also came to know that, in several Asante rituals, widespread use was made of strongly smelling herbs (*eme*), and he was well aware that incense triggered spiritual associations in the minds of his congregation. At one stage, he even borrowed a *kente* stole from the Kumase royals to add to his vestments. But it would be an error to think of Fr. Peter, or indeed of any of the other OSB personnel who came to join him in Asante, as being any sort of syncretists. The priest's task was to lead, and to enforce orthodoxy. Even today, Asante Anglicans say privately that the history of their church is one of *kyenkyensem* – being ruled over with severity.[47]

Fr. Peter, like Buswell before him, saw Agyeman Prempeh as a challenge and a prize, and one he intended to keep for himself. The Asantehene's appointment diaries show that he met with Fr. Peter at least once a week, and sometimes more often after he moved into the new Manhyia palace in 1926. At these meetings, Fr. Peter planned and directed the public religious life of his royal parishioner. Thus, he arranged the annual service of thanksgiving held to mark Agyeman Prempeh's return to Kumase on November 12, 1924.[48] It was he who persuaded the British of the importance of installing Agyeman Prempeh as head of the Kumase territorial division over the period November 10–15, 1926, coincident with the annual service for "Repatriation Day." He managed Aglionby's visit to Kumase in 1928, when the Bishop came to open the new buildings at St. Augustine's College, and to bless Kumase's refurbished royal cemeteries.[49] From 1926, Fr. Peter pressed the Asantehene to build a private royal chapel at his Manhyia residence. He drew up architectural plans, and contacted ecclesiastical furniture suppliers

---

47. See OMP (Old Manhyia Palace Archives), Kumase, Papers of the Asantehene Agyeman Prempeh (1888–1931), 'St. Cyprian's Parish Church', Fr. Peter to Agyeman Prempeh, dd. Kumase, 6 March, 13 September and 9 October 1925; 26 February 1926; 20 March and 20 May 1927; 6 January 1928; *ibid.*, Fr. Bernard to Agyeman Prempeh, 19 June 1928. Fr. Bernard was Dom Bernard Clements, a well known broadcaster and writer in England after his return from Asante; see Laing (1944).

48. *Ibid.*, 'Order of Procession and Service for the 5th Anniversary of Repatriation Day, 1929.'

49. *Ibid.*, 'Day Book: January–June 1928', entries for 20–23 April 1928.

in England. In the event, the British vetoed the scheme on the grounds of expense.[50]

Fr. Peter also guided Agyeman Prempeh's private religious life, talking with him so as to resolve problems, ease doubts, and strengthen faith. If this sounds like the behaviour of a Catholic priest, then so it was, at least in the sense that Fr. Peter often referred to himself as Agyeman Prempeh's "confessor."[51] We have some insight into what went on between the two of them. Thus, it is clear that the Asantehene was often perplexed by the problem of reconciling his Christian conscience with the performance of royal rituals and customary obligations. Fr. Peter proposed that the celebration of *adae*, festivals when offerings were made to the ancestors, should be modified and updated to include Christian worship and motifs. [52] This suggestion went to the heart of Asante tradition, and was sure to provoke outrage among many chiefs and people. Agyeman Prempeh wrestled with the problem and became agitated by it; so much so, in fact, that he talked about it to an astonished acting Chief Commissioner.

> I have never discussed religion with Prempeh as he has never broached the subject until last week, when I had him up to my bungalow for a private talk. He then expressed a wish that so soon as his Chapel is built at Menhyia he hoped to have a conference of the Kumasi chiefs and to suggest that the Adae Custom should cease. Presumably the idea is that Christian Ceremonies shall take its place. This matter was brought up quite gratuitously and I had no comments to make to him. In view of the antiquity and root that the Adae has, I was a little nonplussed at this somewhat naïve suggestion. Possibly Prempeh will enlarge on it at a later date.[53]

In the event, Agyeman Prempeh never raised the matter again with British officialdom. He prevaricated with Fr. Peter. The issue lapsed, perhaps because Fr. Peter became concerned with another and fundamental aspect of Asante tradition.

I have written elsewhere about the history of the Golden Stool (*sika dwa*) in this period.[54] This most sacred of objects was concealed from the British

---

50. *Ibid.*, 'Manhyia: Ground Plans and Building Drawings, 1925–51.'

51. *Ibid.*, Fr. Peter to Agyeman Prempeh, dd. Kumase, 29 March 1929.

52. *Ibid.*, 2 May 1926.

53. PRAAD, Accra, ADM 11/1/1906, 'Ex-King Prempeh 1926–1927', F.W. Applegate, Monthly Report on Ex-King Prempeh (June 1926), dd. Kumase, 3 July 1926.

54. McCaskie (2000).

throughout the Asantehene's exile. In 1921 its hiding place was discovered and its gold ornaments looted but the culprits were convicted and punished. It was given into Agyeman Prempeh's care on his return, and he spent a period of time, and much money, on restoring its gold appurtenances. Then, on June 17, 1928, the refurbished Golden Stool was carried in public procession through Kumase for the first time since 1896. Now that it was again in the public domain, Fr. Peter asked Agyeman Prempeh to remove it from the Manhyia palace and to place it, with appropriate security, in the nave of St. Cyprian's church in "a place of honour" below the high altar.[55] Agyeman Prempeh's response is unrecorded, but we may assume that he explained the history of the Golden Stool to Fr. Peter and offered reasons why it needed to be kept under guard in ritual seclusion. Fr. Peter changed tack. He proposed that on church holy days and festivals, the Golden Stool should be borne to St. Cyprian's with Agyeman Prempeh when he attended worship. This was agreed in principle. Then Fr. Peter went on to suggest that a gold plated replica of the stool, reduced in scale, should be installed in St. Cyprian's between the high altar and the pews reserved for the Kumase royal family. This was eventually done (although the replica was not as grand as was first proposed). There was considerable opposition to this development because, so it was said, the placing of the Golden Stool before and below the high altar symbolised the subservience of Asante to the Anglican Church.[56]

There can be no doubt that, in the 1920s, Agyeman Prempeh enjoyed a busier and much more intense Anglican Church life than he had in Seychelles. The circumstantial reasons for this have been outlined in this paper. It is clear too that the complex ritualism, display, and, we might say, the sheer textural depth of Asante Anglicanism echoed and resonated with the similarly formalised traditions and convoluted rites of historic Asante kingship. In both cases, sacrality and its meanings were performed. It was for such reasons, perhaps, that Anglicanism in Asante became associated with the Kumase dynasty, and is still often described as "the royal church." Twentieth-century Asante Anglicanism, which retained or even elaborated upon a number of the ritualistic precepts and practices implanted by the OSB, was and is a minority church. From the 1990s, its already limited mass appeal has been further eroded by the massive popularity of Pentecostalism in Ghana. [57] This has led to impassioned calls for drastic reform. In 1996 one friendly critic described the church

---

55. OMP, Kumase, Papers of the Asantehene Agyeman Prempeh (1888–1931), Fr. Peter to Agyeman Prempeh, dd. Kumase, 26 August 1928.

56. T.C. McCaskie, Interviews with I.K. Agyeman, dd. Kumase, 1979; 1983.

57. Gifford (2004); Jenkins (2002).

today as an institution in which Fr. Peter might still feel at home. The Anglican Church in Asante and throughout Ghana, he wrote, "is now more English than the English church in its buildings, clerical vestments, hymnology, chants and liturgy."[58] Its most high profile members remain the Kumase royal family. Be that as it may, let us now conclude by looking at Agyeman Prempeh's final interaction with the Anglican Church.

In 1929 the fifty-seven-year-old Agyeman Prempeh was diagnosed with incipient pernicious anaemia, then an incurable disease. This was confirmed in 1930, and the Asantehene, in ever increasing pain, spent the last year of his life pondering over and planning his funeral rites. Asante royal tradition had to be served, but Agyeman Prempeh wanted there to be a public indication of his continuing fealty to the Anglican Church. He persuaded his family to respect his wishes, and informed the British administration of his plans. The issue then became how, where, and to what extent was Anglican Christianity to be inserted into the customary obsequies for an Asante king? Frs. Martin and Bernard, the priests in charge at Kumase (Fr. Peter having gone on extended furlough in 1931), wanted a lying-in-state in St. Cyprian's the night before burial, a service in church the following day, a procession from church to burial place led by priests bearing a crucifix before them and accompanied by a choir, and a committal of the body with the full rites of the church. All this was agreed in principle by Agyeman Prempeh and the Kumase royal family. The crucial term here is, in principle. First, an Asantehene's funeral rites were not a series of controlled and static tableaux, but rather a dynamic, crowded, impassioned outpouring of emotion that ebbed and flowed around a succession of highly charged ritual happenings. Second, and for reasons that need not concern us here, there had been no full-scale funeral of a king in Kumase since that of Asantehene Kwaku Dua Panin in 1867. But that event, even if it could be recalled by the oldest palace officials, could hardly serve as a model for a funeral under British colonial rule. It was one of the bloodiest funerals in all of Asante history, with huge numbers of human sacrifices and passages of unrestrained violence.[59]

Agyeman Prempeh died between 5:00 and 6:30 A.M. on Tuesday, May 12, 1931. The body was laid in state in the specially prepared "golden room" (*sikadan*) in the Manhyia palace. At 10:00 A.M. Fr. Martin telephoned Acting Chief Commissioner Taylor and outlined the church's plans for the funeral. Taylor consulted the royal family, and was assured that Fr. Martin's plans had

---

58. Holdbrooke (1996), 7.
59. McCaskie (1989).

been agreed by the deceased. The British were anxious about public order, and wanted the funeral concluded as quickly as was consonant with Asante tradition. Accordingly, the funeral took place on Thursday, May 14. The official British report on proceedings reads as follows.

> The burial service had been arranged for the 14th at Saint Cyprian's Church, while the interment was to follow the same night at Bremang [the royal mausoleum]. About 4.00 p.m., an orderly and well-attended funeral procession wound its way from Manhyia to the Church, where the band of the Gold Coast regiment, at the request of the Royal Family, played before the service began. The ornate coffin, containing Nana Prempeh's body, was placed at the head of the aisle where the Amanhene of Juaben and Kokofu had their places. Father [Martin] Horsfield, the priest in charge, had seen the body placed in the coffin and had then accompanied it from Manhyia to the Church, and so was able to refute the ungenerous suggestion which was later made that the coffin was carried into the Church empty and that the deceased had already received his burial at Manhyia. Such a suggestion was not, however, likely to be taken seriously by the Ashantis themselves, since it was entirely at variance with custom.
>
> After the first part of the burial service had been read, the coffin was taken, in pouring rain, to Bantama [site of the precolonial royal mausoleum]. The funeral party rested there for some hours and proceeded later at night to Bremang where the interment took place.[60]

This rather arid report, however, is not the only account of these events. I close this paper by reproducing the text I mentioned in the opening paragraph. It was written by Rev. St. John Evans, Archdeacon of Accra, and the sometime Rector of St. Augustine's Anglican College in Kumase. It was published in *Golden Shore*, VI, 2, 1931, the magazine of the Anglican Diocesan Association of Accra. I include it because it is both unknown to scholarship and richly detailed. Beyond that, it speaks directly to the subject of this paper. It encapsulates, for a crucial historical moment and in a vividly immediate way, the compromise between Asante tradition and Anglican Christianity that was worked out in and through the life of Asantehene Agyeman Prempeh. It is a fitting capstone to what has been discussed above, and, in a wider frame, it is

---

60. PRAAD, Accra, ADM 11/1/1342, 'Funeral of Edward Prempeh, Ohene of Kumasi', E.A.T. Taylor to Colonial Secretary (Accra), encl. 'The Death and Funeral Custom of Nana Prempeh', dd. Kumase, 31 May 1931; for Bantama and Breman see Adu Boahen, Akyeampong, Lawler, McCaskie and Wilks eds. (2003), 182–91.

a document that records one aspect of Asante's transit from the nineteenth century into the twentieth.

The End of Prempeh

On May 12 all Ashanti was shaken by the news that its great chief "had gone to his village." Nana Prempeh had been in failing health for some time and on the previous Sunday, too ill to come to Mass, had been very sadly compelled to return to his palace at Menhia.

Prempeh's influence in Ashanti, since his return from exile in the Seychelles, had been exerted in a Christian direction. He was churchwarden and always attended his parish church, St. Cyprian's, Kumasi, in full State on Sundays. He made many gifts to the church, including a golden replica of the "Golden Stool" for use as an altar tabernacle, and he erected a large crucifix in the Royal burying place at Bantama. Last year his great wish was fulfilled when his son John, who had remained in the Seychelles and been ordained priest, returned to work among his own people in the Gold Coast.

Prempeh died at 5 o'clock on Tuesday morning, and the news was sent all over the town and beyond; at quite an early hour numerous boys from the northern territory could be seen hurrying out of Kumasi. There followed an exciting week. It was imperative to secure a Christian burial for Nana, in spite of the multitude of native funeral customs which were to take place. We communicated with the Royal Family and with certain of the important chiefs, and our proposals were very kindly received, though it was made clear that the presence in Kumasi of so many rather wild men from the bush was not likely to make matters easy.

We decided to go up to Menhia that night to sing hymns; by no means the least important reason was the hope that our efforts might do a little to check more horrible practices. The choir, a few church members, and the priests set out, somewhat apprehensive of what might be in store for them. When we reached the grounds we formed a procession, with the crucifix at its head, and entered the apartment where the body was lying in State. The body was in full ceremonial dress, with crown on head and jewelled sandals and gloves on feet and hands, and was placed on a gorgeously decorated bed at the far side of the room, with two fan-bearers standing before it. We took our places on benches and looked round to try to realize the amazing scene.

In the right-hand corner sat the Queen Mother, Nana's sister, surrounded by her women. In two annexes were parties of chiefs, members of the family and others, singing and crying. There were huge supplies of spirits at hand, and we felt a little nervous of the effect of these upon men already at the highest pitch of excitement. In our room were a number of Court Officers – heralds, drummers, horn blowers, executioners, and so on. The executioners looked especially terrifying in their leopard-skin hats, with a pouch containing three knives slung round their necks. These executioners stood immediately behind the chairs on which the priests were sitting. It was hard not to be continually casting surreptitious glances over one's shoulder.

After a few minutes we started a hymn. Africans can at least sing loudly, and we completely drowned all the other noises. After two or three more hymns we stopped for a rest. An executioner then came forward with a dagger in his outstretched hand and delivered a panegyric before his dead master, recounting many of his former exploits and glories, to the accompaniment of the shouts and cries of all the mourners. When we felt things were getting a little too excited and hysterical, we started another hymn. And so we went on till 5 o'clock in the morning. At one time we would be singing, at another various heathen customs would be taking place. Sometimes it would be a eulogy, at others a ceremonial dance of the most wonderful and at the same time vividly horrible nature. Frequently, too, the wonderful native drums would play – the great talking drums, the battery of small drums, the amazing Etwie drum which exactly reproduces the leopard's roar, and many others. And then there were the strange blarings of the horns. Nor must we forget the minstrels, who stood near our crucifer at the head of the bed, and from time to time chanted curious songs.

On Wednesday [61] the funeral took place. About 3.40 the great procession of chiefs from Menhia began to reach us. It was a magnificent sight to see so many gorgeous State umbrellas and other emblems of rule; the thick mass of golden-yellow cloths, the colour of mourning out here, was itself a real spectacle. We had a few policemen to assist us, but found that it was better to let the Ashantis do their own arranging of the mighty crowd. They did it with skill, if with a good deal of vigour.

Amid terrific shouting and a crowd of dancing and gesticulating attendants the Golden Stool arrived, carried by wild-looking men wear-

---

61. An error; the funeral occurred on Thursday, 14 May 1931.

ing grotesque head-dresses of gold with great golden horns. Attached to
the Stool were a number of bells, which jangled as it moved on its way.
They readily accepted our invitation to bring the Stool into the church,
and it was placed near the place where the coffin was to lie.

As soon as the Stool was in its place we saw the actual procession accompanying the corpse coming up the street. The huge brass coffin, covered with green silk, was borne by more than a dozen men, while on all
sides of it were heathen thurifers. The noise at this moment was inde-
scribable. The coffin was met at the door of the church by the four priests.
Fr. John Prempeh was with us by this time. After it had been sprinkled
with holy water it was carried to its place, and the first part of the Burial Service was solemnly sung and the absolutions given. There was a
terrific noise outside all the time, but the huge crowd in the church,
which included the Royal Family, Christian and heathen chiefs with
their followers, as well as representatives of the Government and members of our own congregation, was remarkably reverent and devout. At
the end of the service the coffin was carried out, while the band of the
Gold Coast Regiment played the Dead March.

Then began the procession to the royal mausoleum at Bantema, some
two miles distant. As we started rain began to fall. Crowds of the younger
Ashantis kept running ahead of us to knock people's hats off and to tear
their cloths down to the waist as a sign of mourning. This caused some
nasty scenes, but on the whole we reached Bantema without real trouble, though the occasional firing of muskets seemed to worry one more
as night came on.

On our arrival at Bantema it was pitch dark. We awaited the arrival of the coffin, and the four priests, together with two of the students from the college as servers, pushed their way behind it and followed it up to the gate. The coffin entered, together with certain
members of the Royal Family and certain grim officials. Our little party
followed, knowing full well that even to-day no white man other than
a priest (at least we hoped that the exception held good) would have
been allowed to go in and to come out alive. As soon as we entered the
enclosure the gate was locked behind us. We heard a great argument
going on at the gate, and the Rector of St. Augustine's, wondering
whether he and his friends were being discussed, asked a friendly
Ashanti to interpret. The interpretation was one that only brought a
very doubtful reassurance – "Some of the other chiefs and people want
to come in, and the gatekeepers say, 'You may come in if you wish, but
there is no return'."

At last we reached the inner room, where the coffin had been laid, and formed a little group around it, the only light being that given by our candles. Fr. (Martin) Horsfield read the committal. We all then fell on our knees in silent prayer, and to our amazement everyone in the room, executioners and all, did the same. For a full minute there was dead silence.

After saying "good-bye" to the Queen Mother and to James, Nana's son and secretary, who had been invaluable to us all the time, we came out, gathered the choir together, and marched home to the tune of "O valiant hearts", which the boys found the best thing for keeping up their spirits. All that remained for the Church to do was to arrange a solemn requiem, and this took place on the Tuesday of the following week.

Bibliography

Note: all primary sources are cited in full in the footnotes.

Adu Boahen, A., E. Akyeampong, N. Lawler, T.C. McCaskie and I. Wilks eds., 2003. *'The History of Ashanti Kings and the whole country itself' and Other Writings by Otumfuo, Nana Agyeman Prempeh I* (Oxford).

Akyeampong, E., 1999. 'Christianity, Modernity, and the Weight of Tradition in the Life of Asantehene Agyeman Prempeh I, c.1888–1931', *Africa*, 69, 2, 279–311.

——— 2003. 'Agyeman Prempeh's Return from Exile, 1924–1931', in Adu Boahen, Akyeampong, Lawler, McCaskie and Wilks eds., 43–55.

Allchin, A.M., 1958. *The Silent Rebellion: Anglican Religious Communities, 1845–1900* (London).

Arhin, K., 2000. 'The Role of Nana Yaa Asantewaa in the 1900 Asante War of Resistance', *Ghana Studies* vol. 3, 97–110.

Asirifi-Danquah, A., 2002. *Yaa Asantewaa: An African Queen who led an Army to fight the British* (Kumasi).

Boahen, A.A., 1972. 'Prempeh in Exile', *University of Ghana Institute of African Studies Research Review*, 8, 3, 3–20.

——— 1987. 'A Nation in Exile: The Asante on the Seychelles Islands, 1900–24', in E. Schildkrout ed., *The Golden Stool: Studies of the Asante Center and Periphery* (Washington, D.C.), 146–60.

——— 2003. 'Agyeman Prempeh in the Seychelles, 1900–1924', in Adu Boahen, Akyeampong, Lawler, McCaskie and Wilks eds., 21–41.

——— 2003a. *Yaa Asantewaa and the Asante-British War of 1900–1* (Oxford and Accra).

Bradley, J.T., 1940. *The History of Seychelles*, 2 vols. (Victoria, Seychelles).

Chung, R., 1994. 'The Anglican Church of Mauritius: the memory, the legacy and the vision', M.Phil. Dissertation (Birmingham University, U.K.).

Day, L., 2000. 'Long Live the Queen! The Yaa Asantewaa Centenary and the Politics of History', *Ghana Studies* vol. 3, 153–66.

Gifford, P., 2004. *Ghana's New Christianity: Pentecostalism in a Globalising African Economy* (London).

Hewitt, G., 1977. *The Problems of Success: A History of the Church Missionary Society 1910–1942: II, Asia, Overseas Partners* (London).

Holdbrooke, C.H., 1996. 'Inculturation and the Liturgy of the Anglican Church in Ghana', Postgraduate Diploma in Mission Studies Dissertation (Selly Oak Colleges, Birmingham, U.K.).

Jenkins, Philip, 2002. *The Next Christendom: The Coming of Global Christianity* (Oxford).

Jenkins, Paul, 1974a 'The Anglican Church in Ghana, 1905–1924 (I)', *Transactions of the Historical Society of Ghana*, 15, 1, 23–39.

———— 1974b 'The Anglican Church in Ghana, 1905–1924 (II)', *Transactions of the Historical Society of Ghana*, 15, 2, 177–200.

Laing, G.E.F. , 1944. *Dom Bernard Clements in Africa* (London).

McCaskie, T.C., 1989. 'Death and the *Asantehene*: A Historical Meditation', *Journal of African History*, 30, 3, 417–44.

———— 1999, 'The Golden Stool at the End of the Nineteenth Century: Setting the Record Straight', *Ghana Studies*, 3, 61–96.

———— 2003. 'Agyeman Prempeh before the Exile', in Adu Boahen, Akyeampong, Lawler, McCaskie and Wilks eds., 3–20.

Obeng, P., 2000. 'Yaa Asantewaa's War of Independence: Honoring and Ratifying an Historic Pledge', *Ghana Studies* vol. 3, 137–52.

Pascoe, C. F., 1901. *Two Hundred Years of the S.P.G.: an historical account of the Society for the Propagation of the Gospel in Foreign Parts, 1701–1900*, 2 vols. (London).

Peel, J.D.Y. , 2000. *Religious Encounter and the Making of the Yoruba* (Bloomington and Indianapolis, IN).

Sarpong, P., 1996. *Libation* (Accra).

Scarr, D., 2000. *Seychelles since 1770: History of a Slave and Post-Slavery Society* (London).

Stock, E., 1916. *The History of the Church Missionary Society*, 4 vols. (London).

Sundkler, B. and C. Steed, 2000. *A History of the Church in Africa* (Cambridge).

Tordoff, W., 1960. 'The exile and repatriation of Nana Prempeh I of Ashanti, 1896–1924', *Transactions of the Historical Society of Ghana*, 4, 2, 33–55.

———— 1965. *Ashanti under the Prempehs 1888–1935* (Oxford).

Webb, A.W.T., 1964. *Story of Seychelles* (Victoria, Seychelles).

Wilks, I., 'Asante at the End of the Nineteenth Century: Setting the Record Straight', *Ghana Studies*, 3, 13–59.

CHAPTER 22

Chiefdoms, Cantons, and Contentious Land: Mapping out a Mission Field in Twentieth-Century Colonial Cameroon

Guy Thomas

The label "Colonial Cameroon," like numerous other so-called colonized/colonial areas, could be considered a misnomer by the standards both of the modest numbers of European officials involved in governing the territory and of their impact on the everyday life of Africans over whom they claimed authority. Maps, however, convey quite a different impression of occupation and "possession", by color-coding areas under colonial influence in, say, green, red, yellow or blue, depending on which of the non-African powers they had been ascribed to. Paradoxically, this articulation of virtual colonial supremacy, both horizontal and vertical, provided the foundation for a real concept of dividing and ruling both people and space. Likewise, the shaded areas on decorative world mission maps of the nineteenth and early twentieth centuries provide some illustrative examples of how Christian missions and faith inscribed and contrasted their outreach with other world and local traditional religious systems.[1] But among the most telling manifestations

---

1. See, for instance, 'Weltkarte der Mission', lithographie de Engelmann père et fils, Mulhouse, printed in Basel: in der evangelischen Missions-Anstalt, 1845; the 'Missions-

of such juxtapositions, both within and beyond the realm of religious belief, to stress not merely visual but also mental maps, is the equation of mission station premises with a "white man's fence."[2]

That this must not be taken at face value is, among other much cherished insights, one of the merits that can be gleaned from J. D. Y. Peel's work on religious fermentation, encounter, contest and fusion among the Yoruba. To my understanding, the very essence of his research lies in a series of convincing attempts not simply at bestowing eloquent speech upon his African subjects but also at narrating their true ability to seize initiatives as architects of the world(s) they built around themselves and their communities, at distinct levels of society. As such, he acquaints us with a shift of paradigms, opening up a new depth and geography of interaction and impulse, where we find fundamental existential questions feeding into and off varied shadings of religious discourse. One of the intriguing aims linked to the broader theme of tracing such forms of interaction is to find out more about where they took place and how the locations were selected and demarcated.

Shifting the focus eastward from Yoruba land back to West-Central Africa, this essay investigates—in relation to missionary advance and church presence—how space was perceived, negotiated, reconfigured, and commonly subjected to the widespread predicament of access, use and ownership, and of notions of traditional overlordship, in the western region of present-day Anglophone Cameroon. Following two sections on chiefs, land, and cartography in Cameroon, bringing into focus both missionary and indigenous contributions to orientation and map-making, the emphasis is placed on a drawn-out dispute, from c. 1912–1937, over the plots of land allotted to the Basel Mission (BM) in Bali-Nyonga in the Cameroon Grassfields by the traditional ruler (*fon*) Fonyonga. At the core of the study lie both area maps as well as local site maps. I argue that maps represented an essential tool for the Basel missionaries to protect and consolidate their position and prerogatives at times of heightened pressure and adversity. Evidently, contests over land or land rights ultimately fell within the jurisdiction of the colonial magistracy and police, but this was frequently viewed by the BM's representatives as a last resort once all other negotiations had failed. Fonyonga, who was unwilling to com-

---

weltkarte', Lithographie von E. Kaufmann in Lahr, printed in Basel: Verlag der Missions-buchhandlung, 1891; the 'Missionskarte der Erde', designed by Dr. K. Heilmann, Königlicher Seminardirektor, printed in Gütersloh: Verlag von C. Bertelsmann, 4th ed., n.d. (presumably published at the beginning of the 20th century).

2. Jonas Dah. *Missionary Motivations and Methods. A Critical Examination of the Basel Mission in Cameroon, 1886–1914.* Basel: Basileia, 1983, 121.

ply with the BM's stance on territorial rights at first, eventually found himself confronting the limitations of his inherited power base, albeit not without laying down his own conditions with a view to reaching a satisfactory compromise and thereby maintaining well-established terms of concordance with European contingents. His target of an African-European *modus vivendi* mirrors a preceding history of skilful interaction, consent and functioning alliances during the reign of his father, Galega I, with several German expedition leaders to Cameroon's interior in the 1880s and 1890s. Galega's repute as an ingenious host goes back to his encounter with Eugen Zintgraff, reportedly the first German explorer—and European—to enter and cross the Cameroon Grassfields.[3]

The relevant sequences of Fonyonga's rule, as discussed below, open several windows on diplomatic manoeuvres between a mixed Swiss and German delegation on behalf of the BM's interests on the one side, and a high-ranking African counterpart together with his retinue on the other. As such, it points to the crux of distinguishing between—and perhaps to the incompatibility of—indigenous knowledge and customary forms of acquiring, allocating and demarcating land in the Cameroon Grassfields on the one hand, and alternative—here: missionary—concepts thereof on the other. An introductory discussion of maps in the context of missionary activity shall now throw light onto the background of the ensuing dissent.

Maps I: Cartography and the Construction of Information

A recent sampling of the map collection in the archives of the BM (now under mission 21) brings to the fore their potential as tools for a multipronged approach in historical studies.[4] First, they illuminate particular political, economic, and geostrategic interests that can be combined and compared by stacking individual sheets of maps and charts relating to a single geographical area in chronological order so as to build up multiple layers of information and orientation. Second, technical improvements, a growing abundance of descriptive features, and an increasingly diverse nomenclature

---

3. Shirley Ardener. *Eye-Witnesses to the Annexation of Cameroon, 1883–1887*. Buea: The Government Press, 1968.

4. Roger Schwegler. Ansätze möglicher Strukturierungen des historischen Kartenmaterials im Archiv von mission 21: Eine Analyse der Karten Kameruns und Indiens. Unpublished manuscript, Basel, August 2003.

in cartography illustrate varied strands of perception, designation and presentation of topography, boundaries, landmarks etc. Third, maps open up important leads for the analysis of settlement patterns, mobility, demographic trends and language clusters at large. Fourth, and most importantly in the present context, maps constitute the key to the basic documentation and examination of usufructuary and property models and rights. This brings to mind the fundamental question revolving around colonial territories as to what the occupation of land could imply in the selected African setting.

A general land alienation survey in 1938 shows that Victoria Division with its extensive coastal plantation systems bordering on the Atlantic Ocean, had lost about 34% (381.6 sq. miles) of a total 1,166 sq. miles, compared to 4% (157.44 sq. miles) of 4,162 sq. miles in Kumba Division, 0.009% (0.39 sq. miles) of 4,321 sq. miles in Mamfe Division (the three provinces comprising most of the Forest Area), and 0.005% (0.36 sq. miles) of 6,932 sq. miles in Bamenda Division (roughly synonymous with the Grassfields).[5] These contrasting figures reflect both the diverging extents of sequestration of land and regional differences in tenure and usufruct, as we will see below. The BM was already granted freehold titles on its existing plots in Buea and Victoria in 1897. The deeds of transfer were entered into the German *Grundbuch* (Land Register).[6] These plots did not result from expropriation. Meanwhile the situation in the Grassfields proved more complicated. Although non-African leasehold and freehold property in the Grassfields remained modest throughout the colonial experience, it was there that disputes between missionaries, both Catholic and Protestant, and traditional authorities over land and intrusion erupted most intensely.

Not only does Cameroon's checkered history of cartographic ventures mirror marked changes in the colonial experience under the German, British, and French systems, but also varied degrees of subtlety relative to respect for, and the ability to cope with, the linguistic and cultural diversity, and the plurality of indigenous political and social institutions. Pioneering German maps from the late 1880s to the early twentieth century focus principally on exploration and "discoveries", offering little detailed input about indigenous political and social institutions and organization. The chief concern during this period can be viewed as advancing the frontiers of foreign presence, which eventually resulted in the demarcation of a German sphere of territorial administration

---

5. Simon J. Epale. *Plantations and Development in Western Cameroon, 1885–1975. A Study in Agrarian Capitalism.* New York: Vantage Press, 1985, 96.

6. Edwin Ardener. *Kingdom on Mount Cameroon. Studies in the History of the Cameroon Coast,* 1500–1970. Oxford: Berghahn Books, 1996, 117–124.

Figure 22.1 - Heinrich Karl Dorsch. Copyright Basel Mission Archive; ref. QS-30.001.174.01).

shaped by large concessions under the control of leading German trading companies.[7] From about 1900–1914 the style and content of maps were gradually altered in the wake of a rising boom of cartography, beginning in the late nineteenth century, to include considerable ethnographic detail, travel routes, and logistics.[8] Similarly, later maps produced by the British during the League of Nations Mandate, and under UN Trusteeship, emphasized "tribal" boundaries in consonance with the constitution of Native Authority and Native Court areas under indirect rule.[9]

It is during the later German colonial period that the BM came to the fore with a range of cartographic endeavors, the most impressive being a sizeable map of West Cameroon produced by Heinrich Dorsch and published by the

---

7. Tilmann Renz. Bestand der historischen Karten in der Bibliothek der Basler Mission, e.g. no. 96090.

8. Tilmann Renz. Bestand der historischen Karten in der Bibliothek der Basler Mission, e.g. no. 96085.

9. Tilmann Renz. Bestand der historischen Karten in der Bibliothek der Basler Mission, e.g. nos. 96112, 96113 and 96118.

BM bookshop in 1908. The map depicts how the BM's presence and activity spread from the coast around the towns of Victoria and Douala towards the south, east, and subsequently into the Grassfields where it was launched in Bali-Nyonga in 1903.[10] Further, Dorsch offers an overview both of colonial government, military and customs posts, and scattered Basel, Baptist, and Catholic mission stations, supplemented with accurate ethnographic and geographical detail. Here we see the outcome of joint findings by missionaries and colonial agents under the influence of the renowned German cartographer Max Moisel.

Dorsch's cartographic exploit offers a row of insights into the larger and the smaller scales of the BM's mission field in Cameroon, the expeditions and social interaction involved in gathering relevant data, and the linkages between maps and missionary activity. Born in the German south-west province of Württemberg in 1871, Dorsch first trained to become a construction technician before joining the ranks of the BM in 1890. In 1896, having completed his studies at the mission seminary in Basel, he traveled to Cameroon where he was successively posted to the stations of Mangamba and Nyasoso in the Coastal and Forest Areas respectively before being transferred to Bali-Nyonga in November 1905.[11] Soon after Dorsch decided to undertake a tour of the "white patch", an expanse of largely unidentified land separating the older BM stations (Bethel, Bombe, Bonaku, Buea, Edea, Lobetal, Mangamba, Nyasoso, Sakbayeme, Victoria) in the coastal zone and Forest Area from its new stations (Bali-Nyonga and Foumban) in the Grassfields to the north. The aims of the trip were to reconnoitre more direct passages to link up the two portions of the mission field, to seek an opportunity to establish a mission station *en route* between the two regions, and to identify the southern boundaries of the Mungaka (Bali-Nyonga) speakers.[12] The entire trip took eighty-three days and involved a German official and two fellow missionaries as well as bearers, guides, sawyers, a group of BM schoolboys to perform choir songs, and Dorsch's house-boy, among all of whom Sona, a freed slave from the chiefdom of Banjoun, played a key role.[13]

Sona proved a reliable bearer, guide and interpreter who had acquired a wealth of contacts and geographical knowledge after passing 'through many

---

10. Tilmann Renz. Bestand der historischen Karten in der Bibliothek der Basler Mission, no. 98101.

11. BMCA (Basel Mission Cameroon Archive) Personal file (Pf 1327) of Heinrich Dorsch.

12. BMCA E-2,22, no. 242, Bericht einer Reise Heinrich Dorschs durch den "weissen Fleck". Bali, 5 July 1906, 7f.

13. Ibid., 22f.

Figure 22.2 - Returning from Bali, 1907. BMCA E-30.25.013: Gottlieb Freidrich Spellenberg. Copyright Basel Mission Archive; ref. QS-30.001.1174.01.

different hands' during his years as a slave. Much of the information gathered on the trip, along with a highly successful performance as an intermediary, was attributed to Sona who was apparently delighted at the chance to return home after many years. Dorsch affixed a sketch map of the routes they had traveled along to his extensive report, albeit not without regret that a new suitable connection between the northern and southern portions of the mission had yet to be found. All the same, the sketch map evolved over the next two years into one of the most noteworthy maps ever produced for the area composed of the contemporary North West and South West Provinces of Cameroon.[14]

Although Dorsch's trip in 1906 was not the first expedition into the "white patch", with two missionary parties including Friedrich Authenrieth in 1894–1895, and Jakob Keller, together with Ferdinand Ernst in 1904, having previously embarked on more narrowly defined ventures, he certainly achieved the widest, most detailed coverage of the region. Indeed, Dorsch himself had

---

14. Marcus Buess. 'Die Kartensammlung der Basler Mission', in *Die Kartographischen Sammlungen in der Schweiz. Reihe: Kartensammlung und Dokumentation, 2. Sonderreihe Bibliographica Cartographica*. Munich: Saur, 2005.

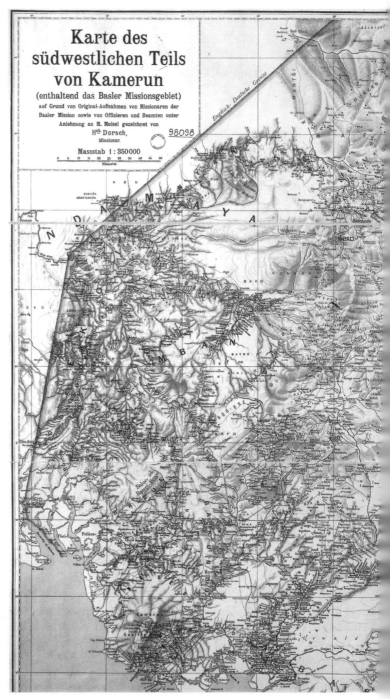

Figure 22.3 - Dorsch map of Cameroon, 1908. "Karte des südwestlichen Teils von Kamerun (enthaltend das Basler Missionsgebiet) auf Grund von Original-Aufnahmen von Missionaren der Basler Mission sowie von Offizieren und

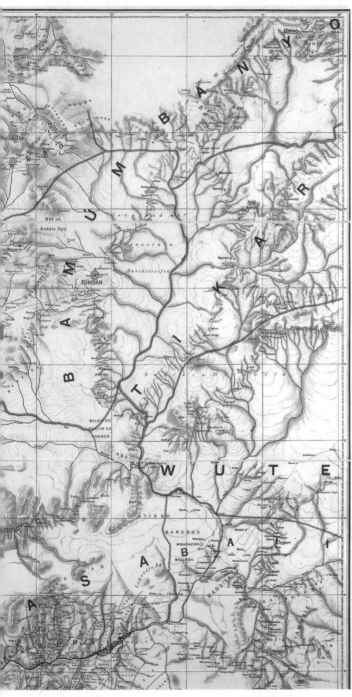

Beamten unter Anlehnung an M. Moisel gezeichnet von Heinrich Dorsch."
Basel: Verlag der Basler Missionsbuchhandlung in Basel, 1908. (Copyright
Basel Mission Archive).

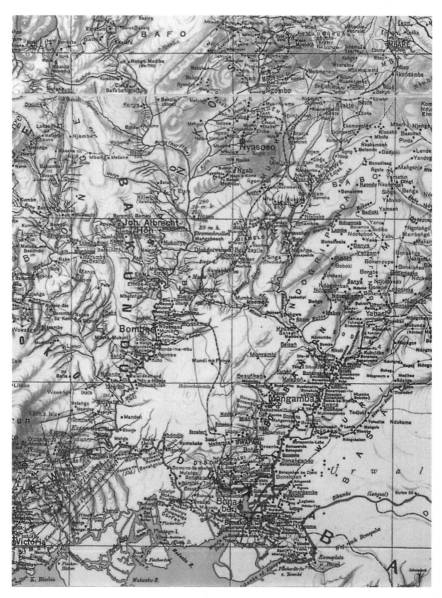

Figure 22.4 - Detail, Dorsch map of Cameroon, 1908. "Karte des südwestlichen Teils von Kamerun (enthaltend das Basler Missionsgebiet) auf Grund
von Original-Aufnahmen von Missionaren der Basler Mission sowie von Offizieren und Beamten unter Anlehnung an M. Moisel gezeichnet von Heinrich Dorsch." Basel: Verlag der Basler Missionsbuchhandlung in Basel, 1908.
(Copyright Basel Mission Archive).

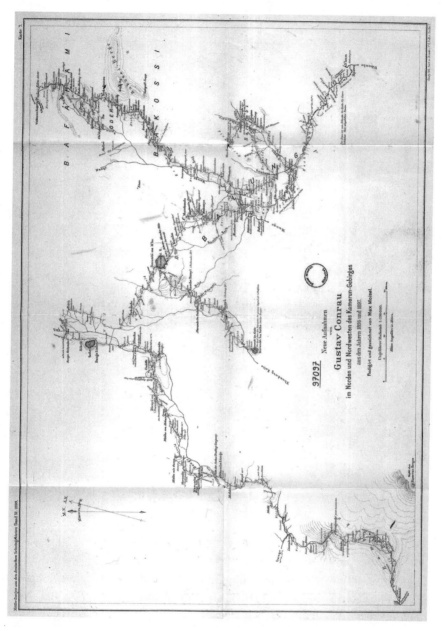

Figure 22.5 - Neue Aufnahmen von Gustav Conrau im Norden und Nordwesten des Kamerun-Gebirges aus den Jahren 1986 und 1897. Redigiert und gezeichnet von Max Moisel. Mittheilungen aus den deutschen Schutzgebieten, Bd. XI, 1898. (Copyright Basel Mission Archive).

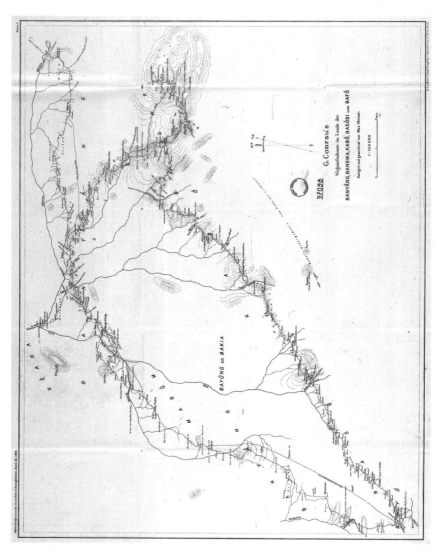

Figure 22.6 - G. Conrau's Wegeaufnahmen im Lande der Banyang, Bangwa, Kabo, Basosi und Bafo. Redigirt (sic) und gezeichnet von Max Moisel. Mittheilungen aus den deutschen Schutzgebieten, Bd. XI, 1898. (Copyright Basel Mission Archive).

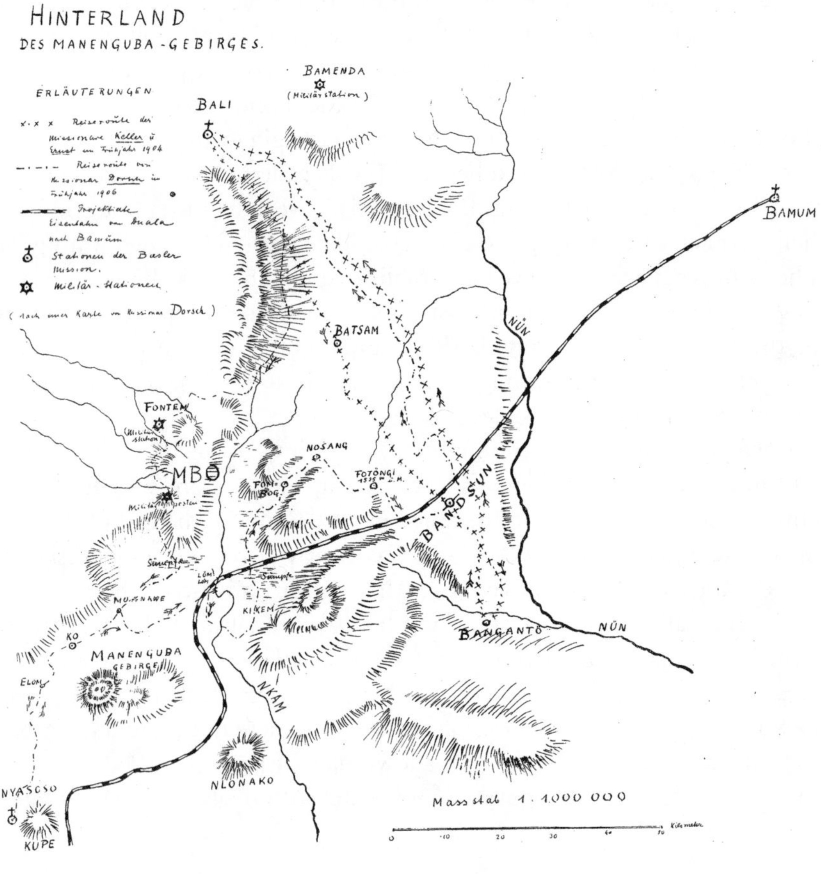

Figure 22.7 - Hinterland des Manenguba-Gebirges, in: Der Evangelische Heidenbote, December 1906(12), 93.

undertaken an initial trip in early 1902, and drew a fine sketch map of the Nkosi region based on a large-scale map attributed to Gustav Conrau, the first European to reach the Bangwa mountains in 1897, who touted trading contacts and laborers for the coastal plantations.[15] The main credit for Dorsch's efforts, save the maps themselves, accrues from his meticulous documentation which offers both a detailed run-down of the factors required to ascertain a successful undertaking as well as detailing problems involved in gathering useful information on geography and politics. Foremost among the latter is the question of language and, revulsively, the pronunciation and recording of place names. Notably, with this in mind, we begin to appreciate the role of guides like Sona. Not only did he and his colleagues display social skills that helped locate new target groups for evangelistic work, but they also employed their vernacular knowledge to the more complex end of delineating the spheres of language use as well as establishing possible links between related tongues. Here again Dorsch offers a vivid image of plurality when mentioning the various stop-overs on his 1906 tour and the importance of being able to count on each chief providing additional local guides with particular knowledge of the surrounding peoples and vernaculars.[16]

It would be useful at this juncture to delve into processes of indigenous map-making, though striking evidence remains rather scanty. To give an example, we can briefly turn to the kingdom of Bamum to the east of Bali-Nyonga, where *fon* (later Sultan) Njoya was clearly also involved in designing maps in the early twentieth century. Although his precise methods are not clear, his creative, inventive spirit and his palace scribes' skills are aptly exhibited in a drawing of the route from the royal palace in Foumban to an outlying farm. His own version shows a striking resemblance to a later European map of the same area, thus bearing witness to remarkable accuracy.[17] A parallel conclusion can be drawn from a town plan of Foumban produced by or under the instructions of Njoya around 1920.[18] Although such sources might

---

15. BMCA E-2,15, Heinrich Dorsch, First Quarterly Report, Nyasoso, 7 April 1902. On Gustav Conrau, see Elizabeth Dunstan. 'A Bangwa Account of early Encounters with the German Colonial Administration. Translation of a Text recorded by the Fon of Fontem', *Journal of the Historical Society of Nigeria*, Vol. III, No. 2. 1965.

16. Heinrich Dorsch. 'Reise durch den Weissen Fleck', *Der Evangelische Heidenbote*, December 1906(12), 92–95.

17. Bernhard Struck. 'König Nschoya von Bamum als Topograph', *Globus* 94, 1908, 206–209.

18. Alfred Schmitt. 'Ein Plan der Stadt Fumban, gezeichnet und beschriftet von einem Bamum-Mann', *Anthropos* 61, 1966, 529–542.

appear to be scarce, there is good reason to assume that variations of map-making could have featured prominently among other peoples in the Grass-fields, partially structured by their vernaculars and local cosmologies, and closely linked to specific rapports with their immediate and more extensive environments. In order to find out more about how concepts of map-making were cross-fertilized and spatial transformation was set in motion, we must take into account the reciprocal influence of German missionary and colonial cartographers' instructions and indigenous knowledge and methods of con-ceiving space. Dorsch, Sona and the other members of the expedition stand for a host of similarly joint efforts that were to define the internal and exter-nal contours of the mission field and establish the basis for use and spread of the two official mission/church languages of the BM in Cameroon, Duala in the Forest Area and Mungaka in the Grassfields.[19] We now turn to the inter-nal contours of the mission field and strategies of forging diplomatic ties with a view to enabling and securing the BM's presence. What Dorsch and his as-sistants assembled to produce the broader picture of West Cameroon will then be reduced to one portion and placed under the microscope of small-scale sketch maps.

The Spatial Concept of the Mission Field: Christian Advance and Patterns of Authority

The BM's enterprise in Cameroon was launched upon the arrival of the first four missionaries on December 23, 1886, two years after the Germans had signed a treaty with the Duala chiefs on July 12, 1884, and Otto von Bismarck's envoy Gustav Nachtigall had hoisted the *Reichsflagge* on the banks of the Wouri Estuary on July 14, 1884.[20] The BM's outreach from the coastal zone to the interior of German colonial *Kamerun* followed several different paths and occurred in a series of waves. The initial objective was to replace the Eng-lish Baptist Mission in concurrence with the general provision that 'A closer connection with Germany's colonial situation, and therewith to the German Reich, was created for the Basel Mission by the all-German Missions Confer-

---

19. See Guy Thomas. 'Why Do We Need the White Man's God? African Contributions and Responses to the Formation of a Christian Movement in Cameroon, 1914–1968.' Lon-don, Ph.D., 2002, 151ff.

20. Werner Keller. *The History of the Presbyterian Church in West Cameroon.* Victoria: Presbook, 1969, 8–13.

ence in Bremen held on October 27 and 28 1885.'[21] Accordingly, the first inherent logic for the newly arrived Basel missionaries was to start by moving into those areas where the Baptists already had a footing, and to rapidly man the two stations in Bethel (Douala) and Victoria. The second logic implied following the main axes of trading routes, expeditions, and local demands for missionary activity, which first led the BM contingent to Mangamba, Lobetal, and Edea to the east and south of the Wouri Estuary, later to Sakbayeme farther up the Sanaga River. The third logic was rooted in the necessity to form a web of mission stations between the colonial government headquarters in Buea and the adjacent hinterlands (Nyasoso, Bombe). Finally, the fourth logic was linked more broadly to a synchronized expansion of missionary frontiers within the sphere of German advance and influence, eventually sparking a missionary thrust toward and into the Grassfields from 1903 (Bali, Foumban, Bagam, Bana, Bandjoun, Bangwa).

However, the spatial concept of the mission field is not fully congruent with German precepts of political, economic, and military strategy and power. In effect, each mission station constituted the sacred and administrative capital of a small mission field in its own right, comprising scores of outstations. This in turn underpins the numerically dominant contributions of "native" agents—indigenous teacher-catechists, evangelists, elders, *Gemeindemütter* ("community/congregational mothers")—at the grassroots level of christianization in villages, hamlets, and compounds from a pioneering stage of the BM's agenda in Cameroon. Further, it cautions us to think carefully about dividing the mission field strictly along the political demarcations (provincial boundaries) of the Forest Area and the Grassfields as the itinerant clergy and sub-clergy in the ranks of the BM built bridges between the two zones, and some of the borderland peoples (Bakossi and Bangwa) partly bear shared cultural and political traits. Moreover, the decentralized pattern of the mission field unveils remarkable degrees to which indigenous codes of communication and interaction, as well as material cultures, were approximated and occasionally incorporated into evangelistic methods and practices, and into building styles (especially in mission church chapels).

The BM's spatial concept, then, is one of relatively widely distributed outposts, largely—with the exception of mission station compounds—small plots and a considerable infrastructure, all of which was to enhance a com-

---

21. Erik Halldén. *The Culture Policy of the Basel Mission in the Cameroons 1886–1905.* Lund: Berlingska Boktryckeriet, 1968, 28.

prehensive system of exchange, mutual support and organic growth, for, as Georg Tischhauser reported on the Bafut of the Grassfields in 1933, it was unacceptable 'that a congregation only sees to its own requirements; rather, it must engage in mission work, too, in order to survive. They [the congregations] must select an area as their own mission field and jointly support all new tasks in the area of Bafut.'[22] Tischhauser's critique invokes the object of early experiments with selfhood of the BM Church, the task of promoting "mission within the mission", inspiring a process of "missionisation through the missionised".

The concept of "mission within the mission" calls for further reflection on the formula for the processes of decentralizing and domesticating the BM's enterprise. *Out*-stations were set apart, just as the mission field comprised a distinct domain from the BM Home Board in Switzerland. The linkages between the mission field and the Home Board and between each mission station and the Principal of the mission field in Cameroon were based on a center-periphery model. This was reproduced at a third level, based on the necessity for evangelistic microcosms, local mission fields which constituted the "polis" of the BM Church, to be supervised by Cameroonian staff and coordinated through the European mission stations.[23] The concept of polis as used here is taken from Malcolm Ruel's observations on community structures among the Banyang. It is employed to throw light on the approximation of mission networks to local social organization. Ruel notes:

> The *etok* is a group of people who live together and who, by virtue of this fact, are, on the one hand, assumed to share an identity of interest in the regulation of their common affairs, and, on the other, are expected to observe the corporate authority of the group, as it is expressed collectively by those who represent them. This concept defines what I speak of as the Banyang 'political community'. An *etok* is a residential group organized to govern itself: one might speak of it as the 'polis' of Banyang political organization.[24]

---

22. BMCA E-5-1,1, Georg Tischhauser, Annual Report (extract), Bali, 1933. (Author's translation)

23. For an excellent in-depth analysis of the BM's centre-periphery model, see Jon Miller. *Missionary Zeal and Institutional Control. Organizational Contradictions in the Basel Mission on the Gold Coast, 1828–1917*. Grand Rapids, MI/Cambridge, UK: William B. Eerdmans Publishing Company, 2003, 81–121.

24. Malcolm Ruel. *Leopards and Leaders. Constitutional Politics among a Cross River People*. London: Tavistock Publications, 1969, 20.

To bring out the analogy with the BM's structures, Ruel's formulation could be rephrased by substituting "BM Church congregations" for the idea of Banyang "political communities". The BM congregations resembled integral components of the political communities among the Banyang in Mamfe Province, and were therefore partially incorporated into the web of indigenous social and political institutions. This occurred in varying degrees among the different peoples throughout the mission field.

The approximation of mission church structures to traditional socio-political contexts usually relied on approval by traditional rulers and/or councils. Working through such offices promised leverage for evangelization, for royal sanction granted open access to the populace. This approach prevailed in the highly centralized chieftaincies (*fondoms*) of the Grassfields.[25] As the cases of some Bakossi chiefs in the Forest Area disclose, it was also employed in communities whose clan leaders or district heads had gained wide recognition from the rank and file. By contrast, the BM had to revise this strategy where the institution of paramount chieftaincy carried less weight, notably among the "stateless" peoples of the Forest Area whose flat socio-political structures called for an alternative method. Due to 'the segmentary logic of the local patterns of organisation,' as ascribed for instance to the Bakweri of the Mount Cameroon region in Victoria Province, 'the whole native administrative machinery threatened to disintegrate.'[26] The colonial authorities sought to reinforce centralized chieftaincy in the Forest Area by installing district heads. This system was introduced by the Germans who selected Manga Williams as Paramount Chief of Victoria in 1908.[27]

Serious opportunities for evangelization commonly depended on invitations from chiefs. On no account could the BM establish itself permanently through claims to self-arrogated legitimacy or colonial support alone. The first missionary to reach Nyasoso in 1894, Friedrich Authenrieth, was astutely aware of this: 'He always knew that despite everything that he had to bring, on the human level he was still an invited guest in Nyasoso, not a master.'[28]

---

25. See Edward F. Lekunze. 'Chieftaincy and Christianity in Cameroon, 1886–1926: A Historical and Comparative Analysis of the Evangelistic strategy of the Basel Mission.' Chicago, Th.D., 1987, 89–153. For parallels with the BM in the Gold Coast, see for example the account of missionary encounters with Ofori Atta I in Richard Rathbone. *Murder and Politics in Colonial Ghana*. New Haven: Yale University Press, 1993, 21–42.

26. Peter Geschiere. 'Chiefs and Colonial Rule in Cameroon: Inventing Chieftaincy, French and British Style', *Africa*, 63(2), 1993, 161.

27. Edwin Ardener. *Coastal Bantu of the Cameroons*. London: International African Institute, 1956, 29.

28. Heinrich Balz. *Where the Faith has to Live. Studies in Bakossi Society and Religion. Part I: Living Together*. Basel: Basel Mission, 1984, 174.

Mutual co-operation was crucial, for instance when the BM appealed to the German Reichstag on behalf of the Bakweri against the expropriation of native land. In return, Chief Endeley Likenye offered the BM a large plot in the mid-1890s.[29] Thirty years later the European staff who resurrected the BM's enterprise confronted similar challenges of winning over African rulers and their retinues. Their path was intermittently lined with stumbling-blocks and pillars of support.

Misapprehension triggered by the expanding missionary enterprise most frequently revolved around land disputes, the more contested of which centred on chiefs' efforts to reclaim allotments of the rambling premises surrounding BM stations. Controversies prompted the BM to negotiate binding agreements with chiefs.[30] In 1927 Eduard Wunderli, the first European to return to the Grassfields once the BM had been reinstated in 1925, noted that colonial law prohibited whites from purchasing land. Difficulties arose because

> The whole village with all its farms belongs to the chief. This has frequently caused us problems when we build chapels. On one occasion the young chief of a village simply refused to grant the Christians permission to build, and there was nothing we could do about it when we approached the government. However, now we make sure that any land where a church is constructed is offered to the congregation as a gift to assure that it remains uncontested. The deed of gift is signed by the chief and recognised by the government. Consequently, our Christians enjoy a certain degree of protection.[31]

Wunderli's overview expounds a central feature of the vital negotiations involved in securing mission property in the Grassfields. It emphasizes the BM's double target of asserting the right of occupancy and of laying claims to ownership against the backdrop of customary land tenure and usufructuary rights. His account is characteristic of how the BM tried to fetter royal authority by introducing the procedure of issuing deeds of gift to safeguard the mission premises. This clearly upset traditional mechanisms of constraint associated with ways of obtaining access and rights to land in the Bamenda Grassfields, as elaborated by Elizabeth Chilver and Phyllis Kaberry:

---

29. Interview with Chief Samuel Moka Lifafa Endeley, Mokunda, Buea, 19 July 1999.

30. On overdue legislation, see BNA (Buea National Archives) Da/1928/1, no. 13/4/28, Bamenda Division, Quarterly Report Ending 1928, 3.

31. Eduard Wunderli. 'Widerstand des Heidentums in Kamerun', *Der Evangelische Heidenbote*, January 1927(1), 6. (Author's translation)

Throughout most of the Grassfields eminent domain in land is vested in the chief or village head as trustee of the community and the settlement of strangers requires his permission. *De facto* control over land is exercised by lineage or extended family heads and in some cases extends to trees planted by male dependents. The overlordship of a chief over land represents the territorial aspects of his authority over persons: in practice subjects were seldom dispossessed, except for crime or treason or for public purposes, such as the building of a new capital.[32]

The preponderance of overlordship in the Grassfields was widely contrasted by varied forms of community trusteeship in the coastal zone. Unlike the Grassfields, where traditional land tenure survived, the coastal peoples are considered to have experienced the 'wholesale loss of land and control' when the British arrived at the outbreak of the First World War.[33] This uneven process was linked to the plantation economy and its proximity to maritime transport routes.

Local controversies over missionary presence occasionally erupted into village affairs about whether to sanction or repel the missionary enterprise. They usually involved outstations such as that in Bamenka near Bapinyin in Bamenda Division. Adolf Vielhauer received a report in 1928 that a customs officer had ordered the construction of a "custom-house" on the land granted to the BM by the responsible village head. The local catechist-in-charge lodged the complaint, having unsuccessfully attempted to assert his right to use the space. His appeal was turned down by a sub-chief on the grounds that he had not sought permission to farm out the plot adjacent to the premises of the mission church.[34]

Earlier in 1922 Charles Frey had insisted that a series of incidents affecting the BM's work in Bali-Nyonga and its neighborhood were aggravated by political instability, giving rise to the widespread notion of a "Bali crisis" in mission circles. In Frey's view, 'Catechists have been caught up in the disputes be-

---

32. Elizabeth Chilver and Phyllis Kaberry. *Traditional Bamenda. The Precolonial History and Ethnography of the Bamenda Grassfields.* Buea: Government Printer, 1967, 38f.

33. Emmanuel Chiabi. *The Making of Modern Cameroon. A History of Substate Nationalism and Disparate Union, 1914–1961.* Lanham: University Press of America, 1997, 164f.

34. PCCCAL (Presbyterian Church in Cameroon Central Archives and Library) 556, Petition letter from Missionary Adolf Vielhauer to Ag. Div. Officer against custom-house or (sic) construction on Mission Plot, Bali, 16 May 1928.

35. Charles Frey. 'Aus unseren ehemaligen Gebieten. Kamerun', *Der Evangelische Heidenbote,* January 1922(1), 12. (Author's translation)

tween the Bali tribes whose discord has proven most disruptive.'[35] Jona Mbu, a Meta' BM catechist, was among the group who took on the *fon* of Bali-Nyonga. In a counteraction his house was burned down. Mbu took the matter to court but was soon compelled to withdraw the case and forced to leave Bali-Nyonga.[36] Mbu's case throws light on the ambiguous role of numerous teacher-catechists. They occasionally exacerbated traditional social control, as a dispute over the involvement of local BM agents in political affairs in Mamfe Division in the late 1920s stresses.[37] And by denying customary allegiance to village heads they had to reckon with severe measures such as expulsion or incarceration, a consequence highlighted both above and by the sentence of a catechist for assaulting the Chief of Abafum (in Mbembe) in 1927.[38]

Frequent struggles over the legitimacy of Christian affiliation underscore the extent to which numerous teacher-catechists were prepared to defend their title and responsibilities. They rallied support from missionaries and colonial authorities and backed congregations that were pressured by non-Christian elements and chiefs. In one instance the catechist of Bametchom/Bambütsom, a village under Bali-Nyonga's jurisdiction, successfully parried an attempt by a royal patrol in 1930 to dislodge the entire local Christian settlement.[39] By and large, Elias Cheng affirms,

> the catechists at that time [in the 1930s and 1940s] were very bold. They could stand. I remember the example of a catechist who stood for Christ in the Mbenka village which is part of our village [Wum]. He stood seriously, even for the community when they rose up against him, to the extent that he was chasing the chief of the village. He stood firm for the Gospel and was able to fight the encounter to show to the people that the church he was planting was the true Church and the god he had brought was more powerful than the local gods.[40]

---

36. Adolf Vielhauer. 'Unsere Bali-Christen', *Der Evangelische Heidenbote*, March 1926(3), 42. It is not clear why Mbu lost his case. Vielhauer insisted that Christians should endure, not fight such provocation.

37. Efforts to appease catechists and local authorities in Mamfe Division were geared to separate religion from politics. See BNA Ce/1929/1, no. 7/1930, Mamfe Division, Annual Report, 1929, 50–52.

38. BNA Da/1928/1, no. 13/4/1928, Bamenda Division, Quarterly Report ending March 1928, 14.

39. BMCA E-5-1,1, Adolf Vielhauer, Annual Report (extract), Bali, 1930; see also BNA Da/1927/1, Bamenda Division, Quarterly Report Ending 31 March 1927, 19, and Cb/1928/2, Bamenda Division, Annual Report, 1930, 56.

40. Interview with Elias Ngum Gbai Cheng, Bamenda, 19 April 1999.

Cheng goes further to explain how the catechist succeeded in convincing the villagers that the strength of Christians lay in a strong conviction for their cause. The ambivalent responses of such potentially vulnerable congregations, many of which comprised a mere handful of full members, buttressed the need for itinerant indigenous evangelists: Not only were they required for pastoral care and to motivate Christians to collect church contributions but also for their protection.[41]

Close collaboration with chiefs, as captured elsewhere by the missionary Wilhelm Zürcher in the 1930s, did not only lie at the heart of the BM's policy.[42] George Bender of the Baptist Mission advocated quite the same approach when venturing into new areas.[43] Chiefs' views on missionary activity were, to adopt Adrian Hastings' formula, principally 'a matter of political stratagem' for politics and religion were inseparable.[44]

In this light catholic teacher-catechists had allegedly come to pose a major threat to chiefs by the outbreak of the First World War.[45] A few years later, in 1917, the Divisional Officer (D.O.) of Bamenda Division felt that

> the opinion of chiefs is not altogether in favour of the re-establishment of Missions. Chiefs I have interviewed affirm and assure me emphatically that the German Missionaries undermined their authority and created many difficulties. These chiefs also inform me that since the German Missions were closed these difficulties have to a great extent disappeared and they are able to exercise a very much more efficient control over their "boys".[46]

The arrival of the Catholic Mill Hill missionaries in 1922 sparked further grievances between chiefs and Christians in Bamenda Division. 'On the one hand,' the D.O. deplored, 'one desires to rule indirectly through the Native Administration and therefore to uphold the prestige of the chiefs, and on the

---

41. Summary of miscellaneous correspondence from Cameroon: 'Die Nöte unserer Kamerun-Mission', *Der Evangelische Heidenbote*, October 1932(10), 147f.

42. See Wilhelm Zürcher. 'Das Christuszeugnis im Königsgehöft', *Der Evangelische Heidenbote*, July/August 1938(7/8), 100.

43. Lloyd Kwast. *The Discipling of West Cameroon: A Study of Baptist Growth*. Grand Rapids, MI: Eerdmans, 1971, 140.

44. Adrian Hastings. *The Church in Africa 1450–1950*. Oxford: Clarendon Press, 1994, 408.

45. Jonas Dah. *One Hundred Years: Roman Catholic Church in Cameroon*. Owerri: Nnamdi Printing Press, 1989, 14.

46. BNA (no shelf-mark), The D.O., Bamenda Division to the Resident, Bamenda, 8 September 1917.

other hand one must allow full scope for Christian Missionaries who it must be confessed have no love for Native Administration.'[47] The case of the Catholic catechist Michael Tinmeng reveals how the roles of mission agents became increasingly politicized as they eroded the authority of chiefs.[48] Yet, by 1928, discord between Catholics and the local authorities had subsided following Father Scully's disciplinary intervention, suggesting that Christians 'have ceased to try to claim a separate political existence under the leadership of a catechist.'[49] The uncompromising demands on Catholics to resolve their problems warned the BM to avoid power struggles. This lesson appears largely to have paid off in the late 1920s as recurring indications hinted at a peaceful coexistence between BM Christians, non-Christians, and Native Authorities.[50]

Maps II: The Instrumentality of Sketch Maps in Bali-Nyonga

The debate revolving around the BM plot in Bali-Nyonga features among the most protracted land disputes of its kind. It began in 1912, appeared to be resolved in 1913, but flared up again in 1937.[51] As I have stressed above, the objective of obtaining and possessing land was interlaced with the question of the BM being approved, thereby implicitly touching on the recognition and security of the mission's outstations in surrounding villages and other settlements.

I recall being told an anecdote about the establishment of the Basel Mission's first plot in the vicinity. It appears that Fonyonga, upon receiving the missionaries Ferdinand Ernst, Jakob Keller, and Eugen Schuler, and hearing their request to set up a station and open a school, rose from his stool, waved his arm in a sweeping gesture and concluded by pointing at a hill in the dis-

---

47. BNA Cb/1918/2, Annual Report, Bamenda Division, 1922, 21.

48. Jacqueline de Vries. *Catholic Mission, Colonial Government and Indigenous Response in Kom (Cameroon)*. Leiden: African Studies Centre, 1998, 34–51.

49. BNA Cb/1928/2, Annual Report, Bamenda Division, 1928, 40.

50. BNA Cb/1924/2, Quarterly Report Ending 31 March 1925, Bamenda Division, p. 29; BNA Da/1928/1, Quarterly Report Ending 30 September 1928, p. 13; BNA Da/1929/1, Quarterly Report Ending 30 June 1929, 10.

51. For a general overview, see PCCCAL 560, Adolf Vielhauer, Record on the Land Dispute between the Chief, Fonyonga, and the Basel Mission at Bali, Bafut, 29 November 1937; see also PCCCAL 562, Letter from the Missionary, BM Bali Station, to the D.O., Bamenda, 20 April 1928; and letter from the S.D.O., Bamenda Division, to Dr. Vielhauer of the BM Station Bali, 16 November 1937.

tance. Thus the hill was to become the designated site of the mission compound. It is unclear, however, whether it was understood that Fonyonga had intended to put the three visitors to the test by allocating a space that was inhabited by the spirits of the deceased. Such trials of examination through the exposure of strangers to forbidden or cursed parts of the ancestral lands also seem to have been common practice among Bali-Nyonga's neighbors, for instance in the settlements of Moghamo to the west.[52] Although the *fon* did show signs of adopting his father's approach to strategically advantageous alliances with preceding European contingents on the premise of expected benefits from their military strength and technological know-how, his support for a school was paired with ambiguity toward evangelism itself. And a varying degree of ambiguity prevailed over the next thirty-four years after the foundation of the mission station on May 17, 1903. The correlation between spatial transformation and the threat of waning traditional authority was to become the most contentious issue.

Turning to the formal negotiations for, and validation of, a mission plot, the allocation of c. 35 ha by Fonyonga comes across as having proceeded smoothly. The original deed of donation was signed on January 31, 1905 in two copies by both parties, comprising the *fon* on one side, and J. Keller of the Basel Mission in the presence of the witnesses F. Ernst and Rudolf Leimbacher on the other. A sketch map of the total area was affixed to the deed of donation.[53] Rather oddly, at first sight, a second deed of donation was issued just over a year later, on February 5, 1906. Yet it is in this deed that we can effectively begin to size up the crucial implications of the donation for the relationship between the *fon* and the Basel Mission in the years to follow, notably in the passage stating that

> The plot is undisputed property of the Bali-Chief Fo Nyonga. Other co-owners are not available. From henceforth the Bali-chief renounces all claims to the plot of land presented to the Mission. The legal effect of this transaction was especially stressed upon the chief.... No special conditions with regard to the utilization of the land were made to the Basel Mission Society as the whole land has already been used for mission purposes.[54]

It is worth adding that this renewed version of the deed of donation was witnessed and countersigned by Paymaster-Aspirant Lehmann, thus making

---

52. Interview with Daniel Gana Tita-Yebit, Mbengwi, 23 April 1999.
53. BMCA E-31.9,6, CI Bali, 2. Teil, Schenkungsurkunde, Bali, 31 January 1905.
54. BMCA E-31.9,6, CI Bali, 3. Teil, Transaction at Bali on 5 February 1906.

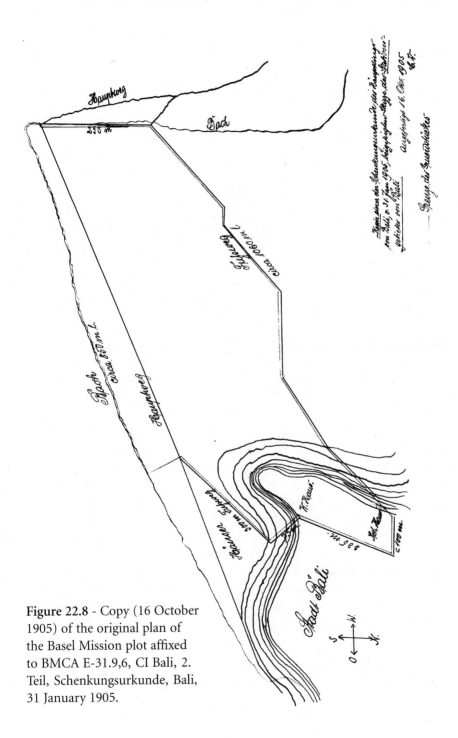

Figure 22.8 - Copy (16 October 1905) of the original plan of the Basel Mission plot affixed to BMCA E-31.9,6, CI Bali, 2. Teil, Schenkungsurkunde, Bali, 31 January 1905.

it an officially recognized and binding instrument in keeping with the laws of 1888/1896 concerning property in Cameroon.[55] The transactions in Bali-Nyonga present a unique case in that, according to a list of mission property in 1913, all the other plots occupied by the Basel Mission were acquired either through purchase, take-overs from the Baptist Missionary Society, or by way of exchange, with one single exception in Buea.[56] Admittedly, the Basel Mission declared to have offered the *fon* a gift ("return-present") which was considered commensurate with the value of the plot obtained in Bali-Nyonga, but the fact remains that the deal had been sealed as a donation.

Finally, a third agreement was issued in 1913, setting out the provisions for the *fon* of Bali-Nyonga to grant the Basel Mission a second plot for the construction of a church. An elder and eight other witnesses, possibly quarter-heads, were summoned to reaffirm the act. Three of them, an elder of Bandi and two *chindas* (retainers), Mbo and Mbiganga, put their mark on the deed under Fonyonga's, jointly with the signatures of Keller and Leimbacher of the BM, and of Paymaster-Aspirant Schmidt and a local interpreter, Boma.[57] Thus, the initial process of mapping out the terrain and compounds of the Basel Mission reached its conclusion shortly before all the European missionaries were withdrawn from Bali-Nyonga, and repatriated in 1915 following the outbreak of the First World War and the subsequent British-French invasion of Cameroon.

While the wave of Christian popularity and affiliation rose on the fringes of Bali-Nyonga, accounts of the internal situation unanimously reveal profound regret about the apparent decline of the former flagship of the BM. The reported state of deterioration is puzzling in view of the largely amicable relations between the *fon* and the BM from 1903–1914. Indeed, Fonyonga's new position and overtly hostile disposition towards the cause and acolytes of the mission require to be viewed within the wider context of his dwindling regional overlordship. During and after the war years, his neighbors, notably the Meta', staged several successful attempts at rebuffing the supremacy of Bali-Nyonga. Further, Bali-Nyonga appeared to be loosing its support base among the colonial authorities. The impact of the Meta' emancipation campaigns on the local mission community was ambivalent, as Charles Frey notes: 'Their leaders are mostly Christians. The British administration appears to express her sympathy for their endeavors. This purely political affair would not have to interest us in the least if the rupture were not cutting right through our

---

55. BMCA E-31,10, Gesetzgebung betr. Grundeigentum in Kamerun.
56. BMCA E-31,10, Grundbesitz der Basler Mission in Kamerun, Zusammenstellung von Generalkassier Nestele, 1913.
57. BMCA E-31.9,6, CI Bali, 4. Teil, Vertrag, Bali, 23 January 1913.

church.'[58] Frey's observation is critical to the interpretation of Christian advance into the distinct realms of centralized authority throughout the Grassfields. This advance, largely carried forward by Africans, could be seen as having revolutionized indigenous political mechanisms of social order and control in pursuit of the aim to establish a singular, unified kingdom of God. A visible side effect of the process is articulated in the contribution to the formation of a new map, free of boundaries, visible and invisible, constituting the mission field as a whole.

Such maps do indeed feature in several versions, most prominently in the published annual reports of the Basel Mission,[59] but they contrast the mission stations themselves which were once more occupied when Swiss and German missionaries were permitted to return to Cameroon from 1924/25 and to Bali-Nyonga in 1926. The model of the station compound was henceforth more or less maintained in line with the earlier agreements. The many station plans in particular appear to have continued radiating the aura of a "white man's fence", connoting seclusion in an imported and alienated insular cultural space. In reality, though, it is important to remember that the large mission buildings could not be erected without substantial contributions of an indigenous labor force. Leimbacher, for one, provides a good overview of his apprentices, among them sawyers who joined Dorsch's expedition with the aim of passing on their acquired skills in Nyasoso.[60] Moreover, the physical dividing line was equally conceived to offer shelter, protection and a refugee camp for defective, persecuted or otherwise marginalized members of society, either among the Bali-Nyonga proper or among immigrant Meta', Moghamo and other neighboring peoples residing in their midst.[61] Not surprisingly, Fonyonga abhorred the prospect of permitting such a "cultural asylum" to grow and unleash new forces of opposition from within his *fondom*, erode his vertical and horizontal supremacy, and degenerate into a most disadvantageous political stalemate. Consequently, he had taken it upon himself to farm out a southern section of the plot in the absence of the missionaries, which later brought the land question in its full breadth to a head.

---

58. BMCA E-4,7.122, C. Frey to W. Oettli, Foumban, 8 August 1921.

59. See for instance hundertunderster Jahresbericht der Evangelischen Missionsgesellschaft zu Basel, Basel, 1916, 88f.

60. E-31.6,1c, Rudolf Leimbacher. Bericht über den Stationsbau in Bali, Bali, 8 March 1905.

61. For a brief analysis of 'organisations allegedly in decline', see Jean-Pierre Warnier. 'Rebellion, Defection and the Position of Male Cadets: A Neglected Category', in Ian Fowler and David Zeitlyn (eds.). *African Crossroads: Intersections between History and Anthropology in Cameroon.* Oxford/Providence: Berghahn Book, 1996, 115–123.

Both the plans and sketch maps as well as a confluence of ditches which had been excavated to delineate the terrain of the Basel Mission plot did not deter Fonyonga from his counter-claims over the newly cultivated portion of land. Leimbacher's carefully designed and proportioned site plan of 1928 was intended to press the demands of the Basel Mission under the watchful eye of the Senior Divisional Officer in Bamenda. The two parties concurred once the original grant of 1906 was formally confirmed in 1929. But Fonyonga later re-iterated his bout to retrieve a section of the mission property in 1937 when the Government Surveyor, Arnold Kemavor, scrutinized the official Land Grant of 1906. It was M. D. W. Jeffreys, Senior District Officer at the time, who decided to assemble four missionaries, the *fon* and some twenty additional followers from Bali-Nyonga (who are not individually identified) to re-trace the boundary meticulously, from pillar to pillar, in order to fix the precise dimensions of the plot. Dr. Jeffreys finally succeeded in settling the dispute by fully reinstating the legal value of the original Land Grant of 1906.[62]

It was not only thanks to their accurate maps and good degree of familiarity with precepts of colonial law and order that the missionaries involved in the land dispute were able to stand their grounds and protect their own "canton". They also continued to rely on good relations with chiefs, quarter-heads and dignitaries to propel their cause. Therefore chiefdoms and chieftaincy retained their weight as instrumental political and social structures and institutions upon which to build a functioning missionary enterprise. All the same, maps and plans exerted a powerful force on the opportunities and ways for the Basel Mission to realize her legal and organizational objectives in spite of all odds, calculated acts of defiance and misapprehension, for they did not only represent a recognized guarantee but also the tools by means of which to establish the very foundation for enduring missionary and, more generally, religious encounters.

Although the preceding case revolving around maps and space highlights several differences between the two parties involved, a Swiss/German institution and a Grassfields ruler, it brings out at least one common trait shared by the two: They are both interconnected within larger socio-political frameworks made up of cantons in the broadest sense of the term. It has been suggested above that the Basel Mission's stations served as spiritual and administrative capitals of Christian cantons which in turn operated as dependent

---

62. PCCCAL/560, Land Matters, Basel Mission Bali (1929–1937). In the course of the 1930s several portions of the original plot of 35 hectares were exchanged 'in right title and interest' for 'the right of occupancy' in newly accessed parts of the Grassfields. See E-31.9,6, CI Bali, First Part, and E-31.9,8, Landakten Kamerun.

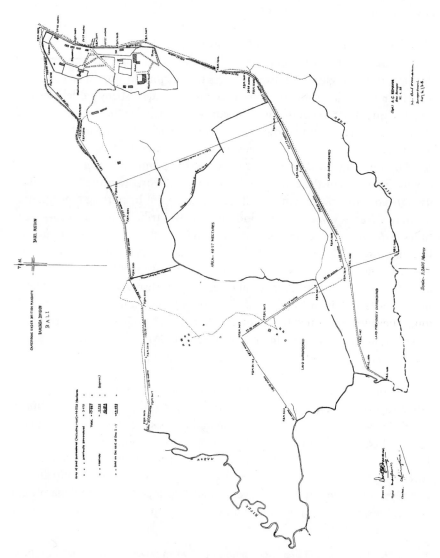

Figure 22.6 - BMCA E-31.9,6, CI Bali, 1. Teil, Certified plan of the Basel Mission plot signed by A. C. Kemavor, Government Surveyor, 21.1.1938.

organizational cells under the superstructure of the entire mission field. As for chiefdoms like Bali-Nyonga, they resemble a kind of canton by dint of their manifold rapports with each other through shifting power structures, diplomacy, conflict, trade, social and spiritual interaction, and exchange as well as, most importantly, variations of *cousinage sacré*,[63] entailing a reciprocal balance of power and responsibility.

Formally, then, the land dispute boils down to defining a canton within a canton (locating the mission close to the political hub of a prominent chiefdom). Another angle of the dispute refers to a custom we appear to have neglected for all too long: the *palaver*, a seemingly endless string of debates and negotiations about issues of common concern, much like the contest outlined above. One might wonder how the Basel missionaries coped with this quality of communication. Among the selection of responses to the question a comment by Wilhelm Zürcher in 1943 to one of the prominent *palaver* topics on language policies of the Basel Mission rather unfavorably brings the similarity of his origins to those of his subjects to the point by putting their quarrel down to a *Neger-Kantönligeist*, alluding to "petty" tribal—or cantonal—attitudes.[64] Yet on a more serious note, Zürcher touches on a theme that runs through the social and political history of missionary encounters in Anglophone Cameroon from its inception in the early twentieth century, the joint aim of the *fon* and the BM representatives to cultivate and expand a Mungaka-phone vernacular identity and language policy throughout the western Grassfields.[65] This plan was, at least partly, the result of preparing the terrain for Christian advance by carefully mapping out the BM's mission field.

* * *

Chiefdoms, cantons, and maps are corollaries to the overarching imperial target of fostering mutually recognized precepts and practices of legitimacy and authority to govern a larger system and all its key players in their (quasi-)colonial contours. In this wise, the European and indigenous staff and adherents of the BM came to adopt and partially or wholly assimilate certain features of imperial culture(s) with which they saw themselves compelled to comply. At the same time, they were caught up together in the dynamics of survival, aspiration, innovation, and reorientation at the grassroots of their

---

63. This term emerged in a conversation I had when travelling down the Niger River in 1995 with the former Director of the Institut des Hautes Etudes de Recherche Islamique - Ahmed Baba, Timbuktu, about the historical political, economic, social and spiritual relations between the Bamana, Bobo/Bwa, Bozo, Dogon, Fulani, Senufo, Songhai and Tuareg peoples in Mali. For a useful study along similar lines regarding the relations between the peoples/chiefdoms of the Cameroon Grassfields, see Paul N. Nkwi. *Traditional Diplomacy. A Study of Inter-Chiefdom Relations in the Western Grassfields, North West Province of Cameroon.* Yaounde: University of Yaounde, 1987.

64. BMCA E-5-2,15, Wilhelm Zürcher, Annual Report (1943), Bafut, 10 July 1944, 4.

65. Guy Thomas. Op. cit., 164–169.

host societies. The dual nature of their role lends them symbolic traits of a historic pendulum swaying between tradition and modernity, between colonizers and colonized, between the status of agents sent and employed by an institution based in a country without colonies—spurring social and religious change in direct contact with the missionized—and pawnship in the global clockwork of imperial culture(s).

Key to Abbreviations

BMCA   Basel Mission Cameroon Archive
BNA   Buea National Archives
PCCCAL Presbyterian Church in Cameroon Central Archives and Library

CHAPTER 23

RELIGION AND HEALING IN HAUSALAND

Murray Last

In his remarkable recent study, *Religious Encounter and the Making of the Yoruba*, John Peel in some pages (e.g. pp. 223, 232) examined the way Muslim scholars competed in the nineteenth century in the market for miracles— mainly miracles of healing and winning military victories. The Muslims, he suggests, dominated the market, having a better track-record in securing victories (given the success of the *jihad* further north), and being more ready to offer "magical" medicines which might at least defer death or even heal. In both fields Muslims offered intensely practical solutions which matched Yoruba interest in practical religion. The Christian missionaries from Europe weren't playing in the same league; miracle-working had not been, it seems, part of their training back home, let alone miracles on the battlefield. Machine-guns "worked miracles" there, not missionaries. He thus raises for me the question whether Yoruba cities were a special market for such Muslim purveyors of "practical magic" just when the market for such services in the Sokoto caliphate was being curtailed. Above all, it raises again the question of the role of religion in the work of healing (and in war). Over the last thirty years the rise of medical anthropology has tended to cause scholars interested in health to neglect the specifically religious dimension of illness and its treatment; before ca.1970, an anthropologist could say that the ethnography of illness and healing fell within "religion" as a sub-category of social anthropology—the best monographs on religion included the problems of suffering and evil, its diagnosis and alleviation.

So John Peel's fascinating work offers a reason for me as a medical anthropologist to re-examine briefly the role of specifically religious specialists in healing, in this case among nineteenth-century *malamai* in Hausaland—the colleagues of those proving so successful in Yorubaland at the time.

Healing in Islam and Christianity

The central point is that healing and suffering are not, I suggest, matters of prime importance within the Islamic tradition, despite the existence of a specific category of books on "*tibb al-nabi*" or "*al-tibb al-nabawi*," the medicine of the Prophet. There are well-known medical texts in both the Sunni and the Shi'a tradition of Islam—and these texts record the sayings and doings of the Prophet that relate to health; apart from predominantly practical recipes and prescriptions (mainly herbal), the most important topics are on prayer and on maintaining spiritual "health"—purely somatic suffering is downplayed.[1] Only in Shi'a spirituality does suffering play a large part, and that centers upon the martyrdom of Husayn at the battle of Karbala (680 AD). But West Africa has been wholly Sunni in its religious orientation (that is, until recently, when Iran became a focus of influence for some young Muslim radicals; but the Shi'ite concern for suffering was not what interested them). I am not suggesting that medicine in the Muslim world was not very important and well developed. As heirs to Greek, Persian and Indian medical expertise, Muslim doctors, dispensers, and surgeons could draw on a huge and expanding body of skills and technical knowledge; Muslims had hospitals and medical schools that Christians eventually learnt from.[2] But this medical professionalism was not specially imbued with religious meaning, however much the practitioners' daily lives might be built around their Muslim faith.

Ibn Khaldun, writing in his *Muqaddima* in 1377 AD, is quite explicit about the non-sacredness of Muslim medicine:

> The medicine mentioned in religious tradition is of the Bedouin type. It is in no way part of divine revelation. (Such medical matters) were merely part of Arab custom and happened to be mentioned in con-

---

1. For example, Ibn Qayyim al-Jawziyya, *Medicine of the Prophet* (tr. Penelope Johnstone), Cambridge: Islamic Texts Society, 1998; C. Elgood, "Tibb al-Nabbi or Medicine of the Prophet. Being a translation of two works of the same name," *Osiris* 14, 1962. A. Newman, (ed.) *Islamic Medical Wisdom: the Tibb al-A'imma* (tr. B. Ispahany), Qum: Ansariyan Publications 1379/2000–1. Sehban-ul-Hind, *Prophetic Medical Sciences* Delhi: Dini Book Depot, 15th edn., 1987. Umar Farouk Adamu, *Medicine in the Qur'an & Sunnah*, Sokoto: International Institute for Islamic Thought, 1422/2002.

2. On medicine in the early Muslim world: M. Ullman, *Islamic Medicine*, Edinburgh: Edinburgh University Press, 1978; Michael Dols, *Medieval Islamic Medicine: Ibn Ridwan's treatise "On the prevention of bodily ills in Egypt,"* Berkeley, CA: University of California Press, 1984. Contemporary practice in Britain is exemplified by Muhammad Salim Khan, *Islamic Medicine*, London Routledge & Kegan Paul, 1986.

nection with the circumstances of the Prophet, like other things that were customary in his generation. They were not mentioned in order to imply that that particular way of practising is stipulated by religious law. Muhammad was sent to teach us the religious law. He was not sent to teach us medicine or any other ordinary matter. None of the statements concerning medicine that occur in sound traditions should be considered as (having the force of) law. The only thing is that if that type of medicine is used for the sake of divine blessing and in true religious faith, it may be very useful. However that would have nothing to do with humoral medicine but be the result of true faith....[3]

The contrast with Christianity makes this still clearer. Muslims recognize that Jesus, as a Muslim prophet, was primarily a healer as well as an ascetic, a proto-sufi and non-violent, whereas the Prophet Muhammad was noted for his eloquence (and Moses for his magic).[4] In a list of 252 "miracle" stories about the Prophet Muhammad, only eighteen might be categorized as "medical" and eight of these were in the context of a military campaign (the Prophet's saliva was mentioned as the main source of healing), whereas some 40% of the Gospels' text is devoted to how Jesus healed the sick or raised the dead.[5] Jesus instructed his disciples to go out and heal (which they did), as did saints in subsequent centuries.[6] Shrines such as Lourdes even today attract the ill—including the present Pope; admittedly it is the Virgin Mary rather than Jesus who now figures as the mediator that brings about healing. Visions of her, reported to the Vatican, run to over three thousand a year whereas there are none of Jesus reported now. Similarly, in Yoruba Christianity today, healing is very much a Christian practice, with exorcism a speciality of many churches and their services. And not just in Nigeria, of course: Archibishop Milingo in Zambia was a notable healer (and exorcist) within the Catholic

3. Ibn Khaldun, *The Muqaddimah*, (tr. F. Rosenthal; ed. N.J. Dawood), London: Routledge & Kegan Paul, 1967, p. 387.

4. T. Khalidi, *The Muslim Jesus: sayings and stories in Islamic literature*. Cambridge MA: Harvard University Press, 2001, p. 137.

5. M.M. Inayat Ahmed, *The Authenticated Miracles of Mohammad*. New Delhi: Award Publishing House, 1982, pp. 68–75. On the Gospels, see John Wilkinson, *Health & Healing: studies in New Testament principles and practice*. Edinburgh: Handsel Press, 1980, p. 19.

6. H.C. Kee, *Medicine, Miracle & Magic in New Testament Times*. Cambridge: Cambridge University Press, 1986; S.L. Davies, *Jesus the Healer: possession, trance and the origins of Christianity*. London: SCM Press, 1995.

Church until he was retired by the Vatican.[7] One might suggest that many of today's Christians in Africa are closer to early Christian practice as expressed in the Gospels than is the hierarchy in Europe and in Africa where its white missionaries have built up clinics for biomedicine and are reluctant to perform rituals of exorcism or the laying-on of hands. Yet exorcism was a major element of Jesus's healing just as it is in many local churches in today's Africa. Jesus's miracles went further and even included resurrection from the dead; resurrection was the ultimate miracle, Jesus's own resurrection being the supreme example. (Muslim accounts of Jesus raising the dead include cases where he was shown the wrong grave and raises the wrong person — only to put him straight back in his grave.[8] The Prophet Muhammad did not raise from the dead, but there are three stories where, much later, a dead person is raised by the use of his name, and others'.[9]) Some early Christians rejected the notion of resurrecting the body in favor of the soul's resurrection, which is closer to the Muslim tradition.[10] Both downplay, even deny, any agony on the cross.

Core to the meaning of Jesus, however, for most Christians, is Jesus's own suffering; his crucifixion and its agony are displayed symbolically in most if not all churches. The cross hangs around the neck of many Christians. In short, the notion of transformative pain pervades Christian imagery; alleviating or helping others to bear pain is part of Christian work, whether through prayer or active intervention (in the form of doctors, hospitals, nursing). Monasteries took in patients where they could hear the daily round of offices; herbal gardens were developed for medicinal use.[11] The practice of monks' surgery was such that the Fourth Lateran Council in 1215 AD had eventually to forbid clerics from being polluted by blood, hence bringing to an end a tradition of monastic surgery and surgical scholarship and leaving the skill instead to the barbers. Not all blood was polluting: martyrs sought to have their

---

7. Gerrie Ter Haar, *Spirit of Africa: the healing ministry of Archbishop Milingo of Zambia*. London: Hurst & Co., 1992.

8. T. Khalidi, *The Muslim Jesus: sayings and stories in Islamic literature*. Cambridge MA: Harvard University Press, 2001, pp. 189, 206–7.

9. M.M. Inayat Ahmed, *The Authenticated Miracles of Mohammad*. New Delhi: Award Publishing House, 1982, pp. 75–6.

10. On Gnostic and Docetist views, see Joyce E. Salisbury, *The Blood of Martyrs*. London: Routledge, 2004, p. 137.

11. Rawcliffe, Carole. *Medicine for the soul: the life, death and resurrection of an English medieval hospital, St Giles's, Norwich, c. 1249–1550*. Stroud: Sutton, 1999, ch. IV. Roy Porter, "Religion and medicine," ch. 61 in W.F. Bynum, R. Porter (eds.) *Companion Encyclopaedia of the History of Medicine*. London: Routledge, 1993, pp. 1452–3.

blood spilled, preferably in public before a great crowd, and to endure an excruciating, slow death as witness to their faith.[12] There are, of course, martyrs in Islam too, but their deaths can be linked to their killing the non-Muslim enemy, whereas a Christian martyr may not kill in conjunction with his martyrdom (for orthodox Christians, even a military campaign was potentially polluting spiritually, which was not the case for the Western crusaders).[13] In short, martyrdom has different meanings; in Christianity, it reaffirms the sacredness of pain in a way alien to Sunni Muslims.

Institutionally, then, there was a place, both ideologically and physically, for suffering and its healing at the core of the Christian church in a way that there simply was not in Muslim religious institutions. The mosque was not a site for patients to lie until recovered; healing was not performed there—and there were, of course, no monasteries or monks in Islam. In North Africa and Egypt there are saints' shrines and therapeutic sites, and festivals are linked to them; prayers asking for intercession can be said there—but these were more popular and not professionally religious. Similarly, music in Muslim asylums was the solace of the sick, but it was not the music of the religious specialist (indeed non-military music is problematic for strict Muslims).[14] However none of this "popular Islam" has crossed the Sahara to any great extent; indeed other important North African institutions, such as hospitals, baths, gardens, or the establishment of a charitable *waqf* did not travel south into West Africa—care for the poor, the ill, the destitute traveler, or the pilgrim remained the concern of the lineage and the great political or mercantile houses.

My argument, then, is that pain, healing, and the patient are all sacralized in Christianity in a way that Muslims find alien. One might offer by way of explanation that, quite apart from the role model of Jesus as a healer, the very way early Christianity developed as a cult which was harshly persecuted for some three centuries dictated the religious meaning given to suffering, whereas the early success of the Muslim polity was largely free of persistent suffering (until the civil wars that killed Husayn); Muslim concern focused more on divine justice for all believers, in this world as well as in the next. It is a very different prime-mover. In the Nigerian context, the link between medicine and

---

12. Joyce E. Salisbury, *The Blood of Martyrs*. London: Routledge, 2004.

13. Mark C. Bartusis, *The Late Byzantine Army: arms and society, 1204–1453*, Philadelphia: University of Pennsylvania Press 1992, pp. 211–2; on war and religion more generally, see pp. 352–4. The key point is that being a soldier did not confer personal spiritual merit; the Muslim argument that it could was ridiculed by Byzantines.

14. On music, see M.W. Dols, *Majnun: the madman in medieval Islamic society* (ed. D. Immisch). Oxford: Clarendon Press, 1992, pp. 166–172.

Christianity has been emphasized by the European missions' deployment of hospitals, doctors and nurses — so much so that "health" is an occupation which Christians staff — to such an extent that recent converts to Islam, unable to get jobs in more properly Muslim sectors of employment, turn to the medical sector for getting work. In so far as employment is divided up denominationally, "health" counts as Christian.[15] This is not to say that Muslim doctors and nurses are not found in medicine; indeed Muslim women increasingly are moving into the field of gynaecology and obstetrics to offer their fellow Muslims a better, more appropriate service. Biomedicine may be "Western," even Christian, but as knowledge, it is (like all knowledge) Allah's and therefore appropriate for Muslims to acquire. For Muslims, medicine and its practice are primarily secular, not sacred. Yet problems with medicine remain.

Religion and Healing in Northern Nigeria

In Northern Nigeria, healing and illness were not always so secular in conception. "Traditional" Hausa medicine, in so far as illness is conceived of as "injury" — that is, from a source external to the patient or the household — focuses on the agents that can cause injury: spirits (*iskoki*) of various kinds, a soul (*kurwa*) of the dead, a specific non-human agent (*dodo*) that acts for witches, or protective cults that center upon a special being (e.g. *Mbagiro*).[16] These illness-causing agencies have to be "domesticated" so that they become protective in return for offerings to them. I would argue that this is not "worship" (and no fetish objects are involved, at least not today), but to a strict Muslim, who nonetheless recognizes the existence of jinn (*aljannu*), the attention paid to these subordinate, local beings is wrong. Spirit-possession (*bori*) is a lie, such people say vehemently — in marked contrast to the truth (*al-haqq*) of Islam. Furthermore, those who specialize in treating illness — the "witch" (*maye*), the medicine-man (*boka*), the organizer of spirit-possession séances (*mai bori*) — are cultivating a close acquaintance with such spirits and therefore are potentially compromising their faith (if, that is, they are Mus-

---

15. Richard Bruce pointed out the way occupations were identified with religious membership east of the Jos Plateau in his essay "Conversion among the Pyem," *Savanna*, vol.6 no. 2, December 1977, pp. 155–166. In an email to me he adds that 'traditional medicine' was seen as Islamic, in contrast to 'Christian' biomedicine.

16. This is based on data from my own fieldwork on Hausa medicine in southern Katsina, from 1970 to the present.

lim). Indeed, in the past I think it safe to say that most of such practitioners were not Muslim. A scholar (*malam*) who specialized in such skills—skills that included divination and numerology as well—was marginalized by the scholarly world. The most a "good" scholar or student (*almajiri*) could do was to write out texts from the Holy Qur'an for use in a charm (*laya*) or for drinking (*rubutu*)—as briefly I did as a young student when living with *almajirai*. We could also recite the appropriate prayers for the sick. A Muslim barber-surgeon (*wanzami*) does the circumcisions and says the relevant Muslim prayers, as would the bone-setter (*madori*) for any fracture. But much of this work (apart from bone-setting of course) is preventative rather than curative. It is ensuring that the body is protected and in the right state for good health (*lafiya*). Similarly, the role of the head of a household (*mai gida*) is to ensure the well-being of all those in the house. He does this by his own regular daily prayers, by the proper observance of annual rituals (such as the fast and the two festivals), by having the correct orientation, lay-out and site for the house; on occasions he can call in a scholar to add his formal prayers if necessary, he can give alms to the poor or even kill a ram. Persistent illness or a series of deaths within his household, however, call into question his control as a good Muslim over whatever spiritual attacks or social conflicts are bringing about the series of misfortunes: with illness being conceived as "injury," the *mai gida* should have erected and maintained defences enough to forestall injuries.

An important dimension of Islam is the way it sharply diminishes the powers attributed to spirits, and formally rejects the existence of witchcraft. Whereas for many Christians Satan is the source of illness, and it is sin that has brought on sickness (thus giving Satan—and sin—much greater, real power than he has in Islam), for Muslims Shaitan is just a trickster, almost a figure of fun, and never have I heard him mentioned in narratives of illness.[17] Instead, Allah is the source of everything, both health and harm. To complain of ill-health, then, is to lodge a complaint against Him—which is almost unthinkable. Illness is not necessarily due to "sin," since what Allah wishes is beyond our understanding; it may be wiser to treat your illness (or the death of your child) as a trial, testing your willingness to accept His will. Even overt mourning was restricted, in the house I lived in, to two days at most, and usually less for mourning a baby.

Nor is death a major ritual event. The dead are not buried in specifically sacred ground; the *mai gida* may well be buried in the private yard behind his

---

17. For an example of how Satan is depicted in a successful Christian healing ministry, see Arthur R.W. Nipper, *Why Some Fail to Receive Healing*, self-published; Dalbridge, Natal [ISBN 0620-06-107-3]; 6th impression, 1990.

room (or even in the room itself), while others, young and old, are put in the house's burial plot or the village / town one. A stranger can be buried in a field, his grave visible and left untilled. I have lived in houses where the bones of the dead were coming to the surface; it didn't bother anyone—nothing was done to re-cover them or remove them. Often, as a visitor inside a compound, I had no way of telling which patches of ground contained a grave and should not be disturbed yet. Kinsfolk are not meant to go to the burial ground to visit the graves of their dead which are, anyway, hard to locate after a while as there are (or, until quite recently, were) no inscribed grave-plaques to identify who was buried where. The local grave-digger will identify one for you, but whether he is correct is hard to say: as the stories about Jesus resurrecting the wrong corpse suggest, even He could get it wrong. I have, however, seen a young son pray at the (recent?) grave of his father; and the tombs of key notables (such as the radical politician Aminu Kano, or certain past "saints" [waliyyai]) are sites for prayerful visitors. Nor does burial require a religious specialist to officiate, though a scholar might be invited to be there, to say various prayers either at the house or at the graveside, or to say them at later rituals of commemoration (if they occur). I suggest that, for Muslims, faith so permeates everyday life that death does not "need" institutionalizing as it seems to do in Christianity. Death, like pain or healing, is inconspicuous; it is not separated out for special attention.

Healing and the Sokoto *Jihad*

The shift away from "traditional" medicine and its concern with spirits was a gradual process, and one that still continues. The almost austere approach to illness was part of the *jihad* program enunciated by the Sokoto scholars of the early nineteenth century. They were not primarily concerned, in the *jihad*, with converting "pagans"—they focused instead on the "bad" Muslims, the venal scholars and their bosses, the ruling classes (*masu sarauta*) whose own practice of Islam had been loose enough to allow non-Muslim behavior to be condoned in everyday Muslim Hausa society. The *amir al-mu'minin* Muhammad Bello wrote a number of books in Arabic on appropriate Muslim healing—mainly the correct use of prayers, but also some more "medical" texts derived from Middle-Eastern medicine.[18] He was, like his father and uncle,

18. Muhammad Bello's books on medicine include *Tibb al-Nabi, Tibb al-hayyin, 'Ujalat al-rakib fi'l-tibb al-sa'ib, Tanbih al-ikhwan 'ala adwiyat al-didan, al-Mawarid al-nabawiyya fi'l-masa'il al-tibbiyya, al-Qaul al-manthur fi bayan adwiya 'illat al-basur.* In addition, he

Figure 23.1 – Caliph entering Sokoto, 19th Century.

trying to make Muslim West Africa more like Muslim North Africa: they were "modernizing," updating the local Islam, to match the standards of the mainstream Muslim world. Though none of the three had ever visited, let alone stayed, in North Africa or the Middle East, they not only had classical texts to use but also many visitors—mainly returning pilgrims and North African merchants—to give them ideas about modern life abroad.

My argument is that in the Hausaland of the nineteenth century there was a conscious effort to de-sacralize both illness and healing, and to replace the "pagan" / religious dimensions of medicine with a practice rooted in prayer and in a knowledge of therapeutic herbs and minerals. This meant, of course, shifting the work of medicine from out of the hands of "pagans"—the *boka*, the *maye*, the *mai bori*—and into the hands of scholars who knew their Arabic well (medical terminology is difficult!) and had the classical texts to work from. It is possible that "bad" scholars, involved in the magic that was now disapproved of, simply left the main *jihadi* areas and went south to Yorubaland where their skills were still much appreciated. We simply do not know if there was such an exodus from, say, Sokoto, Kano, Katsina, or Zaria, or in-

---

wrote a lengthy, difficult letter to the Emir of Zaria advising him on his kidney disorder and what to do for it.

deed whether they converted to Islam instead; but to the new radical leadership it may have seemed, indeed may have been, easier to rid society of the practitioners than it was to stop the practice of old-style, "traditional" medicine. But, in reality, old-style therapies, even in these emirates, persisted albeit not in public. It was probably more common in some contexts than in others.

We should not forget that there was a huge slave component to nineteenth-century Hausa society. In the early part of the century it's probable that not many captives converted directly to Islam, or if they did, that there were not enough scholars to instruct them in the details of modern Islamic good practice—let alone to enforce it and punish any breaches. It seems that the ratio of slave to free in the 1820s could have been as high as 40:1—in which case slave culture was too large and disparate for the new state to police effectively. In addition, around this slave culture there was also the city-suburban world of travelers and transporters, of ordinary people on the move (especially in the four to five months of the non-farming dry season). Here we know (from the accounts of foreign visitors) there were all sorts of services available if not officially sanctioned.

The main site for continuing the old-style therapies, however, was probably inside the households of Muslims. One effect of the *jihad* seems to have been to accentuate whatever split there was between the world of men, centered outside the four walls of the house, and that of women, mainly inside the house. Slave women could move in and out, but with servants now, free women had no need in the daytime to leave the house, which was a large enough community in itself to be enjoyable. Privileged freeborn women often studied and taught the Qur'an; it was they who instructed the young in Islam. Some were more involved in Sufism. But there were also others with less education or indeed interest, especially in the country homesteads where such women were hugely outnumbered by slaves (who may have been ready to provide much-need remedies and succor for their owner's wives). With infant mortality rates at about fifty percent, much of these women's lives were dominated by the struggle against illness and death. In their despair they needed some way of combating illness and coping with suffering.

Domestic Therapies

We need to remember, epidemiologically, that in a Hausa community the bulk of illness and death in everyday life is experienced by children and by women. Men, once they have survived childhood illness and entered adulthood, have developed the immunity necessary to keep them relatively illness-free; only mental illness and accidents afflict them. An "epidemic," in local terms, is when even young men die of the disease; such an epidemic is communal, not domestic. Adult women, by contrast, are exposed to the infections passed round among the children they are caring for; above all, they are exposed to hazards of repeated pregnancy, childbirth and post-partum stresses. They have a certain immunity against common infections, but the very stress on the immune system posed by birthing compromises their health in a way men do not experience. Hence there is a very real demand for treatments that protect women and their children against disaster, that offer the women themselves solace or some solution when they are deeply depressed by loss. There are, in addition, the tensions within any large household— enmities, envy, jealousy, unhappiness—which only a very good senior wife and a wise head of house can ever control. How far such stresses might compromise an individual's immune system is not clear; in practice, an illness may have been brought on by so many possible causes. But I found, in my fieldwork, that the local households that were widely known to be "unhappy" tended to present more illness. The common vehicle for expressing or releasing such stresses was, and is still, the possession cult known as *bori*. So in this context it is scarcely surprising that women may resort to non-Islamic practices which their husbands overlook, or may even not know of (except, as a child, many a man must have seen his mother, her co-wives or their servants doing rituals he realized later were Islamically "wrong"). Given that neither traditional nor Muslim medicine was effective against acute infant infections, there were few proven therapies on offer. Treating the mother (through *bori*, for example), rather than her sick baby, has its own logic in times of despair.

It is therefore in this context, within the house, that illness regains some of its religious dimension that it has lost on men's side of society. It is not "syncretism," in the sense that Islamic and pagan elements are mixed into one; it is two systems running parallel, not interacting. The men sustain the house's well-being as a whole through their proper behavior as Muslims; women, who are believing Muslims too, ensure their children's well-being by including observances that may involve spirits (*iskoki*) as well as unorthodox charms and petty rituals. The variety in such practices, especially in pregnancy, can be huge: often they are little more than "good-luck" actions that multiply with every visitor's advice.

In short, the skewed incidence of illness affects the way in which illness can take on a religious dimension in a Hausa Muslim community. I am suggesting that men can afford to have a much more phlegmatic attitude to ill health generally; it is Allah who brings death, it is He who defers it—if He so wills. As a

Muslim, you do not pray for death not to come (as Christians do); you pray only that Allah's will be done, pray for what He knows is best for the Muslim community. Despite this, there remains a medical "marketplace." In a Muslim town, itinerant male healers may not have access to the household behind the house's walls. So some healers loudly call their wares in the street, and draw out such women as are allowed to leave the confines of the house. There they might buy the medicines offered. Otherwise, after dark, a woman could go out with a chaperone and visit a healer. Other therapies, such as private *bori,* take place within the privacy of the house; often it makes very little noise. No Muslim man need witness it (slaves or eunuchs do not count as adult men); no "police" can enter a house to investigate. In a formal sense, it has never occurred; its "paganness" is therefore not an affront to the morality of the *umma.* Privacy has cancelled the danger of its religious dimension. In recent years, however, with the rise of Muslim fundamentalism, especially among the young, young women are firmly rejecting the practice of *bori,* even inside the house. Households which once had *bori* as a potential solution to personal crises are now silent. I am not sure what will take the place of *bori* in such homes; at present nothing has that I have seen, though private prayer and reading the Holy Qur'an may have (yet I have not been there to witness it).

In Conclusion

I have argued here that in Muslim Northern Nigeria there has been a deliberate project to take the experience of illness out of the religious sphere. The project has not been entirely successful in that the distribution of illness and the existence of purdah have together made "public health" the responsibility of men while leaving "domestic health" to be the domain of women. Men's competence to ensure public health is challenged by periodic epidemics (just as periodic droughts call into question their control over the community's wellbeing), and these community-wide crises require a publicly religious response from the men in power. Otherwise, when a young man falls ill—for example, with a mental illness—he may well be taken to a healer living deep in the countryside and kept there, as in an asylum, until he recovers. I see such deep-rural healers as "the laundrymen" of the Hausa health system: they take in the "dirty washing" of Muslim society, "washing" that is too polluted or polluting for regular scholars (*malamai*) in urban areas to handle. In some cases, these healers are traditional non-Muslim Hausa. In short, for men, problematic illness that may involve spirits has been handed over to outsiders, just as the problematic ill health of women and children has been curtained off from publicly practiced Islam. However, as fewer and fewer non-Muslim healers continue to work (or have converted to Islam), this job passes to marginal *malamai*. Recently, a new technique of exorcism has been introduced from Saudi Arabia that utilizes Qur'anic verses whispered into the ear of the patient—a technique more legitimate for Muslims to use in town. It may fill the therapeutic gap.

In this context, biomedicine would have been suitably secular for a Muslim society were it not that it is suspected by some as being a vehicle for Western, Christian "plots." Recently (in 2004) there was strong resistance in Kano to the WHO's deployment of a polio vaccine on the grounds it contained substances introduced to make Muslim girls less fertile. Earlier, an unapproved medical trial by Pfizer had resulted in unexpected deaths, making all foreign medicaments problematic. As there are many fake medicines on sale over the counter of pharmacies, the "truth" of medical claims to cure is already suspect. But this general suspicion is nothing new. In the colonial period, people suspected hospitals were sites for Europeans to practice their brand of witchcraft, and the habitual use of post-mortems and autopsies only increased suspicions as the bodies returned for burial sometimes lacked some of their organs. The fact that many patients were taken to hospital only *in extremis* meant that many died there—so that there was real concern to retrieve the body immediately. In short, Christian countries' concern to export biomedicine to all parts of Africa is viewed by some more radical Muslims not as a charitable gesture but as self-interested and dangerous. When ill it is better, I have heard them say, not to buy or take medicines but to accept the will of Allah, and recover (or not) not in hospital but in the quiet of one's room. In this personal response, religion has perhaps returned to infuse the experience of illness in Muslim Hausa life. It is impressive to witness such calm in the face of distress.

Overall, then, I am suggesting that illness and its treatment have been cordoned off by Muslim men and kept out of the mainstream of their religious life; instead, treatment is left largely to others, often of lower status or even outside the Muslim community. By doing so, the Muslim *jama'a* remains unsullied, undisrupted. For illness, indeed all suffering, has the power to upset: it offers the severest challenge to men's abilities to run their households or their communities. The commonest suffering is loss—through children's deaths mainly, but also through famine or a trading catastrophe; the bitter despair in response to loss, to yet another loss, runs a jagged knife through the social fabric. By contrast, Christians seemed to have cordoned off suffering in rather a different way, by making it so exceptional an experience—and charity so central a virtue—that being imbued with the sacred they take precedence in the priorities of everyday life. In doing so, pain is magnified, victims are elevated in a way that, I think, many Muslims find puzzling if not distasteful. However, the Muslim scholars whom John Peel's missionaries met in the nineteenth century had found in Yorubaland a readier market for their skills; and as outsiders, they had that same "edge" over their local-born rivals that itinerant medicine men can exploit the world over. Even a lowly skill, "cordoned off," can have its advantages.

CHAPTER 24

"LISTEN WHILE I READ": PATRIOTIC CHRISTIANITY AMONG THE YOUNG GIKUYU

John Lonsdale[1]

Introduction

This chapter studies how the Kikuyu or, more properly, Gikuyu, people of central Kenya, faced up to what it meant to be native subjects and, in so doing, began to think themselves a people, with a patriotism worth questioning. Christian literacy helped to mold this intellectual, moral, and social process; and gives us the evidence with which to witness it, if from a partisan perspective. Literacy did not transform "the Gikuyu mind." The texts Christian "readers" created were recited to those who could not read for themselves; conversely, "readers" had to win trust among their kin and within an oral culture. The social premises of oral and literate debate were much the same; orators and writers both had much to argue about, to remember and to forget; there was a moral—and moralizing—continuity of debate between them.

1. A revision, with permission, of "'Listen While I Read": Orality, Literacy, and Christianity in the Young Kenyatta's Making of the Gikuyu' in L de la Gorgendière, K King & S Vaughan (eds), *Ethnicity in Africa: Roots, Meanings & Implications* (Center of African Studies, University of Edinburgh, 1996), 17–53. I thank seminars at London's SOAS, the University of Nairobi and Edinburgh's Center of African Studies for their comments and, in particular, Bruce Berman, Isabel Hofmeyr, John Iliffe, Greet Kershaw, Carola Lentz, Godfrey Muriuki, Derek Peterson, Marilyn Strathern, Lynn Thomas, Achim von Oppen and Richard Waller. Many of the issues discussed here are set in a longer time-span in Lonsdale 2002. I have learned most from Kershaw 1997, Peterson 2004, and from collaboration with Bruce Berman. Responsibility for error remains mine.

Nonetheless, print made a difference. Audiences enlarged; words gained a value of their own, unconnected to their author's status; there were new issues for Gikuyu to dispute. The literate ability to tell stories from a wider stock of reference—but which resonated with the rich oral archive—and to a wider audience than their elders could reach; the new democracy of the printed word that subverted the intimidating hierarchy of wealth and status which loomed behind all public speech; the magnetic, convergent, power of the vernacular press to create a larger market of ideas and images both new and old; the networks of mission schools and denominations which divided Gikuyu afresh (if sometimes along old fault lines of lineage), but which also, like the press, united them in one polemical arena; the Christian search for reconciliation with their kin and the wider society, by associating their cultural innovations with what they believed to be inherent in their native past; the sharper clash of generations and greater concern for the disciplines of gender that came with literacy and migrant labor—all these characteristics of the inter-war years in Gikuyuland suggest parallels with how the Yoruba had earlier made themselves in the course of their own religious encounters (Peel 2000).

Anybody, at any time in Gikuyu history, who wished to lead opinion faced an inherent difficulty in the way Gikuyu construed personal honor and moral responsibility. In a frontier society such as their own, male heads of households prized their own prickly autonomy above all. Wider "clan" or *mbari* settlements were always splitting on that issue; any joint enterprise had to guard against internal rivalries with costly and threatening oaths of commitment. This inheritance made any collective response to the humiliation of colonial subjection very problematic. How far political activists could claim social authority, how far it was acceptable for householders to submit to a coordinating leadership which was far removed from any face-to-face test of reputation, were (and remain) issues of great sensitivity. They made for deep moral distinctions between Gikuyu patriotism on the one hand and nationalism on the other. Patriotism found expression in concern for the future ability of Gikuyu to attain the civic virtue that men and women conventionally amassed in a successful passage through life. Gikuyu valued adult "self-mastery," or *wiathi*, above all, a disciplined achievement of household harmony and prosperity that allowed room for similar achievement by one's clients and sons (also, White 2004 a & b). Patriotism was exercised out of concern for the health of society, for "our personal relations with ourselves;" because of its concern with social obligation within small communities, and respect for personal honor, I have also called it "moral ethnicity." Ethnic nationalism or, preferably (since ethnic sovereignty was almost never sought), "political tribalism" was at odds with moral ethnicity. Patriotic moral ethnicity was, and is, necessarily self-critical; it stirs up internal argument. Nationalism or political tribalism places a premium on internal solidarity, in order to strengthen a community's hand in collective bargaining with others. The demands of external advocacy can only too easily silence principled doubts from within and below, too easily remove the responsibility of choice from where moral ethnicity insists it should rest, with householders whose civic virtue entitles them to exercise to the full that self-mastery, *wiathi*, which is the spirit of manhood.

The concept of "moral economy" has long served to remind us that negotiation of any economic relation, whether of labor or commerce, reflects the contracting parties' sense of personal identity and honor. Terms of trade need foundations in terms of trust, however unequal (von Oppen, 1993). The idea of "moral ethnicity" builds on this understanding, to suggest the growing boundedness—if also enlargement—of the discursive arenas within which in modern times people have renegotiated status in response to the social changes brought by alien rule, capitalism and invention of print-vernaculars. Moral precepts which had previously been largely implicit in face-to-face social action have become more explicit in political discourse, so that to debate old civic virtues in new times has been, in effect, to define ethnic identity (Lonsdale 1992: 268; 1994: 136–40). While Africans knew ethnic identities before colonial rule, they were one among many; under colonial rule ethnicity came for many people to be their principal focus of self-identity (cf. Alexander et al 2000: 9–10).

Like all Africa's peoples, Gikuyu were diverse of origin and tongue, with porous pre-colonial boundaries. Politically fragmented, they defined themselves in three potentially contradictory ways, by property, by moral community, and by public honor, none of which assumed common origin. Gikuyu saw themselves, first, as people who owned the land they had tamed by labor, *agikuyu* who knew how to farm where the *mukuyu* figtree grows: "the house of the digging stick." But the terms of labor caused dispute between genders, generations, clans, landed patrons, and landless clients. So Gikuyu also called themselves *mbari ya atiriri*, "the clan of I-say-to-you" (Cavicchi 1977: 14; Benson 1964: 18). This appellation set not so much a linguistic border (and Gikuyu dialects shaded off into peoples who nowadays repudiate Gikuyuness) as a permeably discursive or moral one, to include any audience within earshot who accepted for themselves the relevance of debate on the terms of trust appropriate to forest-clearing mixed farmers.

These first two elastic identities valued agrarian skill and political participation, as befitted a population of forest-clearing colonists in contiguous but mutually autonomous sub-clan settlements or *mbari*. The third identity focused on the crown of reputation, and with contradictory effects, both inclusive and exclusive. Gikuyu strove for self-mastering moral agency, *wiathi*. Circumcision started adolescent men and women on its upward path and, while the rite was the prime indicator of Gikuyuness, it was both open to all who could afford it, and formalized cultural diversity with its two forms, "Maasai" and "Gikuyu" or "*karing'a*," ("true"). One's home, proverbially, was the sternest test of this self-mastery and, hence, of civic virtue. "A man is judged by his household;...what he can do in the family he is expected to do on a larger scale [for] the community;" women too earned respect as "managing directors of the food supply" (Kenyatta 1938: 76, 315, 62). This third identity therefore, unlike the first two, differentiated some Gikuyu from others. Wealthier households dominated a net of patronage which absorbed dependent workers and herders. This patronage obeyed a theology of abundance which held that adults owed it to God and their ancestors to devote their inherited talents to making the wilderness flourish. Many Gikuyu could not meet this stern criterion of virtue. Since wealth proved industrious virtue, and poverty was the mark of delinquent sloth, to be rich was to be honored and after death remembered, while to be poor was to be despised and then forgotten (Lonsdale 1992: 332–50; Kershaw 1997).

None of these self-identities was in principle nor, so it seems, in the precolonial social imagination, associated with a single myth of ethnic origin. Gikuyu held different views of a plural past (Muriuki 1974: 37–61, 113–15; Lonsdale 2002: 216–30). These do not appear to have given way to a myth of monogenesis from Gikuyu and Muumbi—a tribal Abraham and Sarah—until the 1920s. That narrow self-image may have hovered as an ancestral projection of an ideal household; but this "tribal" image became concrete in the twentieth century by the interaction of an ethnically divisive exterior architecture of colonial rule with a unifying interior architecture of debate on civic virtue, the subject of this paper (cf., Lonsdale 1992: 330–2, 346–50). This new social imagination had contradictory effects. On the one hand the old parochial expectation was reinforced, that each household head should protect his kin's interests with their own resources. Yet, as Johnstone Kenyatta, one of the leading members of the new Christian generation, admitted, this meant that any attempt to create a wider Gikuyu authority in the name of a single ancestry was a moral affront to the self-mastery which each household owed to God and their more immediate ancestors (Kenyatta 1938: 174, 235, 310; Kershaw 1996: ch 6). During half a century of colonial rule, Gikuyu debate on civic virtue never solved this contradiction between their moral ethnicity's parochial, *mbari*-based, test of authority, and the collective leadership needed to resist external power or to compete for public resources, their political tribalism.

It has been objected that ethnic histories suppress those of class struggle (Marks 1994: 103); but in fact debates on moral ethnicity used an implicit language of class. Four new challenges to the daily negotiated custom of moral economy stirred the moral ethnicity debate; all carried connotations of social differentiation. They stemmed from the imposition of the colonial state, the alienation of labor from household production, the growth of wealth in property at the expense of wealth in people, and the emergence of wider fields of competition in autonomy between the sexes. State power, wielded by colonial chiefs and entirely unknown to pre-colonial Gikuyu, endowed some men with an authority that had no necessary base in household reputation and often denied that self-mastery to others. The penetration of capital enticed young men to "abscond" from household obedience by alienating their labor, exacerbating always-abrasive relations between generations. Rural capitalism also tempted patrons to value property above the non-kin clients who had helped to make land fruitful, and thus to repudiate old concepts of civic virtue. Gender relations, finally, became more volatile as the power that men gained by education, wages, and association with the state was contested by women in the markets of both country and town. In each case Gikuyu faced the realization, more appalling to men than to women, that land no longer meant people nor people land in a virtuous circle of moral responsibility between property and labor. The quasi-religious ties of labor, property, and reproduction were broken. While a new source of religious power, Christianity, seemed to legitimize such deplorable challenges to social obligation, its literacy also enlarged a Gikuyu discursive capacity to reconcile these fresh contradictions between terms of exchange and terms of trust. Literate migrant workers, especially, shared virtuous images of home with fellow Gikuyu whom they would never otherwise have met, strangers and yet intimates whose tongue they most easily understood in the polyglot social wilderness of town.[2]

What made Gikuyu—and others—debate the moral economy of identity was their desire, very nearly stated in these terms, to evade the social agony of class division. As elsewhere, young Christians often took the lead in one form of selfish disobedience, migrant wage-labor and, when married, pursued another, rural capitalism, even while sensing that such differentiations threatened to alienate a community other and larger than class. It is thus inherent in my argument that this larger, ethnic or national, identity may have entered the social imagination as a bounded entity only when its conventional

---

2. Cf. Lentz, 1994 a & b; Moodie 1994: 11–43 and the parable of the prodigal son, below. But see Giblin 2002 for objections to my equation of wilderness and town.

social bonds appeared to be on the brink of dissolution. The new premise of cultural unity transformed the constant debate on the moral economy of unequal obligation, to prevent new inequalities dividing people still further (Lonsdale 1992, 1994; cf. Lentz 1994 a: 166–7). Ethnic boundaries formed around these debates neither in obedience to primordial destiny nor by the instrumental will of individual actors, but because contingent social histories determined who would, or would not, heed the call of *atiriri*, "I say to you," at this time of social crisis. And the intimacy of Mau Mau violence in the 1950s shows, all too clearly, how little such social constructions of ethnic solidarity might in practice eliminate conflicts which intellectual discourse appeared to have resolved, especially that between local, landed, oral reputation, and the wider reach of print mastery (for intimate violence: Lonsdale 1994: 142–50; Anderson 2005; Elkins 2005).

This chapter examines an early episode in the construction of patriotism, at a time when Gikuyu elders sponsored literacy, and literates, in return, challenged oral authority by enlarging the range of moral discourse. But it was one thing for Kenyatta and his generation to create new audiences by reading aloud; it was quite another to turn the hybrid vigor of the print arena into a new level of legitimate power.

The Reconciler

The new Christian generation of Gikuyu is well represented by the young Johnstone Kenyatta. His public role rested on his ambivalent status. He was eldest son of a wealthy father, born to be a *muramati*, trustee to his *mbari* or clan. He was also a runaway orphan, and a *muthomi* or Christian "reader" who had lost much of his *mbari* status. His life was a search for the reconciliation of ambivalence by using his complementary skills of oratory and authorship. He was also an editor of genius. In 1928 he added to his office of secretary to the Kikuyu Central Association—the KCA being the young Christian party— that of founding editor of its monthly journal, *Muigwithania*.[3] No other title could more crisply state his double agenda, which was to resolve his personal ambiguities by advancing the general good.

Muigwithania is one of those many compound terms which reveal the intricacies of Gikuyu thought. Its root verb *igua* means to pay heed, to listen

---

3. Murray-Brown 1972: 109 argues that Kenyatta had little to do with *Muigwithania*. It is deposited, in the original and in translation by the Scots missionary linguist A. R. Barlow, in the Kenya National Archives (KNA): DC/MKS. 10B/13/1.

and obey. Harmony, *uiguano*, stems from it. Gikuyu clearly knew that unity depends on the forensic skill that sways an audience with a compelling story. So *muigwithania* is one who gets people to agree, a reconciler, and implicitly therefore, an elder of authority (Benson 1964: 183; Leakey 1977: 736).

In naming his journal *Muigwithania*, then, Kenyatta asserted the KCA's right to be heard (not read); and Gikuyu certainly stood in need of reconciliation. They were split in religious terms, between old and new practices and stories; politically, by narrow access to, and broad exclusion from, colonial state power; and in the cultural performance by which all societies transmit their values. The newly complex technology of the word, with literacy added to orality, was near the root of most controversy, not so much because print created a new Gikuyu "mind" (cf. Ong 1982), but because it enabled larger audiences to engage in debates old and new. Print's amplifying power threw existing parochial disunities into sharper relief, riven by clan and clientage, wealth and poverty. Yet Gikuyu faced new threats, to combat which they had to pay greater heed to each other and in wider circles of trust. As a proverb put it, "to be silent is to bear ill will towards one another, to talk is to love one another."[4] For meanwhile, outside this circle of Gikuyu discussion, Kenya's white settlers pressed for more African land and there were British plans to enlarge white numbers and power.

At this moment of extreme danger the KCA had to perform three tasks of reconciliation before they could represent the Gikuyu cause to others. They had to prove to elders that they were not traitors to ancestral religion; prove to fellow readers that political action would not alienate the main source of enlightenment, the missions; and, lastly, they had to appease official chiefs who, as its main source, shaped British knowledge of Gikuyu to their own advantage and to the disparagement of their rivals in the KCA. In all these differences KCA leaders did at least share two characteristics with their critics. With marriage and children, they were themselves mounting the virtuous ladder of male eldership; and they were prosperous, as leaders should be, in proof of ancestral approval. They could not be charged with the insane conceit of giving counsel in other men's homes while their own was going to ruin.[5]

Kenyatta, then, like his contemporaries, had to convert his moral failings as a reader, his Christian disobedience as a politician, and his insolence as a member of the literate opposition, from divisive grounds of scandal into agreed pillars of household authority which in the stateless Gikuyu world was

---

4. Quoted by Daudi G. Ndegwa, *Muigwithania* i, 12 (May 1929), 15.
5. Said to be a common saying by H. M. Gichuiri in *Ib.*, i, 6 (Oct 1928), 7.

the sole internal basis of external advocacy. He rose to the challenge with as-surance, proof of inner conviction. Ten years later he found another task of representation more difficult when writing *Facing Mount Kenya*; this time his case demanded silence and prevarication. This contrast between the two Keny-attas, authoritative mediator among fellow Gikuyu and their evasive advocate before the bar of imperial opinion, says much about the ambiguities of iden-tity, between the disputatious, patriotic, seriousness of moral ethnicity and political tribalism's nationalist demand for an adamantine unanimity.

In the 1920s readers were preoccupied by their first, religious task of rec-onciliation, which had to do with more than religion alone. They assured "un-lettered" elders, in a common axiom, that the river of baptism could not wash away Gikuyuness. But, writing from the northern, white-farming, Indian shopkeeping, township of Nanyuki—and his urban address is important to the argument—one Ndumo went on to urge fellow readers to heed their an-cestor Gikuyu. They must neither laugh at an ageing mother nor despise a pauper father lest, with his guts angrily knotted in a curse, he condemn them to poverty too. Readers who prospered, as *Muigwithania* expected them to, should not think themselves better than their people as, presumably, many of them did.[6] Print-discussion of religion thus led on naturally, in Ndumo's mind and not in his alone, to warnings against class formation, in the oral discourse of the moral economy of kinship obligation. The one new sanction that he quoted—a shared ancestry with one to whom God had given the land—de-noted an aspiration to moral ethnicity. Moreover, to illustrate the importance of Christian literacy in formulating that singular and sacred ethnogenesis, Ndumo's invocation of the ancestor Gikuyu was almost certainly dependent on his reading of a missionary-composed Gikuyu-language reading primer that, in 1924, began, "*Ngai* [God] gave the Gikuyu a good country that lacks neither food nor water nor forests...." (Peterson 2004: 97).

It may be that publication of the Gikuyu New Testament in 1926, two years before Muigwithania first appeared, had given to the general desire of *ath-omi*—to live at ease with their people—its precise formulation, namely, the effective mediation of social harmony. For the term *muigwithania* appears six times in the New Testament; and it carries in Gikuyu a weight lacking in the Swahili version's mere *mjumbe* or "messenger," that had been available from 1909 and which many Gikuyu could read. It is in guiding white missionaries' Bible translation that one first glimpses the intellectual gusto with which Gikuyu scholars squeezed meaning into words (Karanja 1993: ch 5; Peterson

---

6. *Ib.,* i, 4 (August 1928), 13. Cf, S. Karimu, 'The blessing of the ancestor', *Ib.,* 12.

2004). Inserting their own oral images into the book of the word, Gikuyu then appropriated Bible stories for their own use. Visualizing Christ as *muigwith-ania* between God and man (I Timothy 2: 5),[7] they read in their Bible that his new covenant fulfilled rather than betrayed the former cosmic contract agreed by Abraham and Moses (Galatians 3: 19–20; Hebrews 8: 6 and 9:15). Why, *athomi* clearly asked, could not their new faith similarly renew *Ngai*'s contract with Gikuyu and Muumbi?

How many *athomi* may have asked this question is suggested by the sales of sacred texts. The New Testament immediately went into a second printing and sold 20, 000 copies in two years. Each copy, one may reasonably estimate, will have had three readers. If so, the relation between Christ and *Ngai* may have concerned 60, 000 Gikuyu out of a population of one million. Here was Kenyatta's potential readership. His audience, those who heard *Muigwithania* read in public, or who borrowed it from friends, will have been much larger. A Nairobi subscriber complained that many people were not buying their own copies. They should remember that there were no free things.[8] Free riders, by implication the unpatriotic poor, had no right to debate moral ethnicity.

The KCA's cue for adopting the title *muigwithania* is recalled as having been the Letter to the Hebrews 12: 24.[9] This text portrays Jesus as both mediator and, at the same time, his own blood sacrifice, more eloquent than the sheep and goats offered by Cain's brother Abel—or by Gikuyu elders. Without sur-viving sermon notes I cannot prove but can imagine that missionaries used this text to draw contrasts and comparisons between the *Ngai* of the Old Gikuyu Testament and the Christian God whom whites had knowingly called *Ngai* also (Karanja 1993: 139–41; cf. Fadiman 1993: 233).

Kenyatta himself stressed the continuity from old to new religious practice, to prove not only the political expedience but also the moral admissibility of harmony or *uiguano* between them (cf Lonsdale 2002 a). In summary first, he and his fellow readers adopted, if implicitly, a three-stage argument of reli-gious reconciliation that began with repentance, experienced delight and is-sued in patriotic service. Their underlying premise was that the main threat to moral economy was urban employment, not their own Christianity as the elders thought. Their thesis then called on readers corrupted by town to re-

---

7. This is the only instance in the Swahili Bible in which 'mediator' was translated as *mpatanishi*, the nearest equivalent to *muigwithania*.

8. Karanja 1993: 175 for sales; Lonsdale 1992: 320–21, 322 and G. K. Ndegwa *Muig-withania* i, 4 (August 1928), 10, for reading aloud; J. M. Waggeni to *Ib.*, i, 12 (May 1929), 14, for the complaint.

9. Murray 1974: 100; also Gideon Mugo in *Muigwithania* i, 3 (July 1928), 10.

pent; took delight in finding that obedience created a community; and then turned the generational tables, finally, by claiming that loyal readers were better able than untutored elders to serve all true Gikuyu.

Few *athomi* had much trouble in making their peace with the unlettered majority. Many maintained proper social ties with clan—and age—mates. Some became the "trousered" clerks of clan litigation, so that their favorite simile compared spear and pen. Their mastery of writing, property's new-style defense, restored some of the youthful power they had lost in being disarmed.[10] Elders, in their turn, invested *mbari* labor, on *mbari* land, to build scores of "outschools" which, while nominally under white missionaries, were in fact run by Gikuyu teachers paid from *mbari* funds. This oral search for a literate presence within colonial state institutions bore fruit in the 1930s, when Christians numbered nearly one third of southern Gikuyu's clan trustees or *aramati* (Lonsdale 1992: 378). Kenyatta was by no means alone in his ambition.

But political and legal utility was not necessarily reconciliation. One forceful *muthomi*, George Kirongothi Ndegwa, put the problem thus:[11] He felt proud to be one of the new *irungu* ritual moiety, or generation, and, with them, hoped to "straighten" Gikuyu out of the disarray that was to be expected on the waning of ritual power of an outgoing generation, as now. But how could he, a prostitute, *maraya*, in his "mission clothes," presume to straighten society at some new feast of generational accession, an *ituika*? His answer was that the supposed dichotomy between generational pride and Christian shame was false, based only on appearances. Since *Ngai* was also the God of other races, one could be Christian, Muslim, or old believer and remain "original Gikuyu." Christianity did not have to mean corruption.

All who entered the press debate on how to reconcile the implicitly female harlotry of foreign ways with an implicitly male Gikuyu obedience condemned migrant labor's degradations. Readers found a wonderfully apt biblical image for promoting this first part of their case in the parable of the prodigal (Luke 15: 11–17). The story of the son who wasted his inheritance in high living among strangers, but for whom, on his returning home, a forgiving father killed a fattened calf, was the most often cited folktale, old or new. Paulo Karanja expounded its two-edged moral for young and old: "Those of us under authority should obey; those who give us orders should try to direct us with the wisdom—or unanswerable argument (*kihooto*)—of authority that

---

10. Of which they complained to Handley Hooper: Hooper to *Manchester Guardian*, early 1930 (reference stolen); more generally, Iliffe 1995: 236.

11. Ndegwa to *Muigwithania* i, 4 (August 1928), 10. Cf. Kenyatta's reassurance in *Ib.*, p. 5.

accords with leadership, knowing that we are all in the one path of Gikuyu nationality."[12] Kenyatta, a more typical prodigal than the high-minded Karanja, knew that reconciliation needed reciprocity. He and his stepfather "became reconciled," as the latter recalled it, only when the young man returned with cash and blanket after years of truancy from home, away at school (Delf 1961: 28).

The parable of the prodigal was intended to persuade readers of the virtues of tradition, but filial repentance proved to be only a preamble to a claim to a greater wisdom than their fathers. Readers could advance this final stage of their thesis only on behalf of a community that accepted a criterion of self-mastery other than *mbari* land management; and such a social project, wider than kin-based property yet defensive of it, was without precedent save, spasmodically, at times of war. Here lay the polemical importance of town. Readers compared the prodigal's shame with "the road of wilful ways" that led to Nairobi. Tempted by "spicy food" and selfishness, men "absconded" from home and adopted Swahili airs. Women who did likewise would no longer honor their fathers nor fear their husbands. Town thus destroyed the core of Gikuyu kinship and, with it, all notions of property. Yet migrant workers who failed to heed the call to return were deceiving themselves: however much they took new names or enjoyed urban life, they could not shed their black skin nor cease to be Gikuyu—just as the biblical prodigal was also spurned by his alien master.[13] So here again the argument of moral ethnicity first cited a threat to the face-to-face moral economy of kinship, and then transcended it in a wider social arena.

Readers thus argued that, as native subjects in a colonial world of unequal collective identities the only way to overcome others' disdain was to renovate the moral fiber of a wider communal, as much as filial, duty. And this community had to be newly conceived. The logic was simple, the truism of all conservative reform. Since town posed new moral dangers, Gikuyu needed new defenses. While conceding that they had led on the slippery path to town, *athomi* claimed that they alone could defend Gikuyu against the migrant's fate, which was to "peter out among the *chomba*," strangers. They had in mind the Muslim Swahili, Kenya's first townsfolk, although by now the term included

---

12. P. K. Karanja, 'Those who take counsel together do not come to destruction', *Ib.*, i, 4 (August 1928), 11; also P. O. Kiongo wa Kahiti to *Ib.*, 1, 10 (Feb–March 1929), 15; M. J. Muchikari, 'There the house of Muumbi died out', *Ib.*, i, 11 (April 1929), 9–10

13. The idea of "absconding" to town was also common in South Africa. See, Mayer 1961: 6–7; and Moodie 1994, whose analysis of migrants' maintenance of personal integrity between home and work parallels Gikuyu experience: Lonsdale 1992: 355–7, 360–1.

whites and would in later years refer only to them.[14] This new urban tempta-
tion to forget the moral economy of social obligation needed equally modern
antidotes, of which the first was a debate, which literacy alone made possible,
on the nature of ethnic responsibility. It followed, by "unanswerable argument," that readers were the truest Gikuyu. Enjoying in literacy the "authority that accords with leadership," they were not so much *maraya*, prostitutes,
as *mambere*, pioneers.[15]

In pondering the social reproduction of identity in modern times, *athomi*
started by noting that the Gikuyu world had enlarged beyond each clan settlement or ridge. Whether in household story-telling or in local public performance, the oral transmission of social values had ineluctably weakened
with the absence of migrant young adults in Nairobi or other places of employment. Literacy, on the other hand, widened the means of communication in parallel with this new economic mobility. School created a new, more
inclusive, community of thought for the new Gikuyu world of work, wider
than the oral bounds of *mbari*, age-set and locality.

But the sheer entrancement of writing what strangers would read was the
proof that this new community existed. That much is plain on *Muigwithania*'s
every page; to read it even today is to meet not a passive readership but an audience eager to answer back. Literacy made friends of strangers (cf. Ong 1982:
74). By encouraging his correspondents who felt ashamed of their literary failings, Kenyatta helped to domesticate the standardized print-vernacular which,
however stilted it seemed to many, alone made this discursive cohesion possible.[16] Journalism created an audience which delighted in its own existence,
readers who could see that there was indeed a Gikuyu people, themselves, and
which one could well imagine petering out among strangers—doubtless like
some of their friends. But literacy also turned an audience into scribes for a
community, controlling a medium of argument that gave them both a duty
and the power to save their fellows.

Kenyatta the newspaper editor had set out to reconcile Gikuyu as imagined
in biblical and folk stories and found, thanks to the correspondents who wrote
in from Nairobi and elsewhere, that they actually existed in the flesh. He was
finding a nation in words, a republic of letters both larger than each small
Gikuyu region, and yet delimited within a linguistic border (cf. Hofmeyr 1987;

---

14. Information from Godfrey Muriuki.

15. Petro Kigondu, "How we can bring on the country", *Muigwithania* i, 7 (Nov 1928),
7.

16. Editorial replies, *Ib.*, i, 4 (August 1928), 5. This argument has been clarified by discussion with Marilyn Strathern.

McNeill 1986: 40–1). Gikuyu had always been culturally plural. Now that their language was laminated too, and endowed with powers of both speech and print, they had, paradoxically, acquired the means to imagine an internal homogeneity. *Athomi* from all corners of Gikuyuland and beyond conversed with each other in print as if saying *atiriri agikuyu*, "I say to you Gikuyu," all at the same gathering. The question was, who else would recognize themselves in their audience and, having done so, pay heed?

Kenyatta in Committee

To know how readily others might accept the *athomi* community at its own valuation, one must take a closer look at the uses of their literacy. Kenyatta's report of a meeting held by the KCA's Kiambu branch gives marvelous insights.[17] Even his title, "matters discussed by the elders," was deliciously barbed. While it was not untrue, since KCA members had to be married, it was misleading: their age-grades were too junior to meet on their own authority. Kenyatta was making a point; the KCA might be readers, but they also carried weight. The meeting began with prayer, not a Gikuyu habit but a British ritual to initiate legislative sessions. Officials called the roll; one hundred were present; the KCA had not only acquired the state's addiction to numbers but wanted also to marshal a political team. Then Kenyatta, "standing, so that all might hear," read out his notes of two meetings KCA leaders had lately attended, one with a British commission of enquiry at no less a place than the governor's residence, the other with chiefs elsewhere. His members, he reported, were pleased to hear these discussions "just as they were spoken."

What are we to make of Kenyatta's remark, how much read into his members' pleasure? It is a key question. They appear to have enjoyed the greater accuracy, in their view, of speech set in script compared with that passed on by word of mouth (cf. Okonkwo, in Achebe 1963: 126). But that simple fact is a complex reflection. Like all cultures, Gikuyu culture was oral. The KCA branch enjoyed a performance at once literate and oral. Much has been made of the supposed gulf between oral, communally conformist minds, and literate, individually enquiring ones; yet literate cultures communicate mostly by social means and, conversely, oral artists or intellectuals can be shown to change style or content even when remaining obedient, like the busily scribbling composers

---

17. 'The matters discussed by the elders', *Ib.*, i, 8 (Dec 1928–Jan 1929), 8.

of orchestral music, to a classical tradition.[18] There is no need to postulate divergent "Gikuyu minds" to see what separated readers from unlettered elders. Differences in power structures, in rules for negotiating truth, in people's views on whether trust could transcend social distance, all these different ways of processing thought stood between them, but not different minds.

Oral leaders, *athamaki*, won authority by oral performances grounded in personal achievement; their maxim was "say and act." Words were only as pithy as property: "how can a man who is one goat speak to a man who is a hundred?" Yet, while their "unanswerable argument" was landed wealth, it also had to be rational: "a man not open to reason does not convince others."[19] So *athamaki* marshaled argument point by point, often with the dramatic aid of wooden batons, like material paragraphs, thrown with force upon the ground (Leakey 1977: 1000). Nonetheless, truth was always negotiable, to be tested face to face, between people of equally weighty repute, before equally substantial witnesses. When asked in 1920 about his part in an earlier land dispute, Paramount Chief Kinanjui replied, "Tell me who summoned me to give evidence[,] what I said depends on whose witness I was." The British judge, in dismissing his "accommodating nature," missed the sociological point that truth, like beauty, is in the historically conditioned eye of the beholder.[20]

Oral politics, clearly, was the politics of reputation. The question for the KCA was whether literacy compensated for the fact that, so early in their adult lives, they were "people who have no name," as all new generations had been called in the Gikuyu past, before their moral fiber had made itself known and given them a reputation.[21] Print might outdistance orality but was its grasp on authority equal to its social reach? Much depended on how far the British colonial administration's appreciation of the readers' bureaucratic skills outweighed their Gikuyu impudence.

Literacy made oral authority portable, transferable. For, to return to the KCA branch meeting, here was the upstart Kenyatta appropriating the weight of his seniors whom he made to speak by his own performance of their words. None who heard him could challenge his veracity; his own typescript was his

---

18. This section owes much both to Ong 1982's thesis on literacy's cognitive revolution and to his critics, Hofmeyr 1993, Vail and White 1991 and Peterson 2004

19. For wealth's authority, Kershaw 1972: 335. For reason, see chief Koinange's complaint against Kenyatta, in *Muigwithania* i, 10 (Feb–Mar 1929), 14.

20. Supreme Court case 4358/20, 17 November 1920, in *Kenya Land Commission Evidence Vol I* (Government Printer, Nairobi, 1933), 282. cf. Jack Goody 1977; Ong 1982: 96.

21. Ishmael Mungai, speaking for the KCA at a meeting with chiefs, early 1929, reported in *Muigwithania* i, 11 (April 1929), 2.

sole proof. Those he quoted were not present; they could not gainsay him either. Was it that unchallengeable power, so contrary to oral tests of truth, but so like the power of the state, that pleased the meeting? Literacy was clearly more than a discursive technology that was conveniently independent of seniority. And readers could convert this personal skill into public authority any time they read out *Muigwithania* or other texts in public. It is not surprising that chiefs, themselves used to oral tests, thought the KCA more dangerous than did British officials who had learned to economize on truth, in writing.

This contrast was nowhere more apparent than in April 1928, at a meeting which government called to calm conflict between chiefs and KCA. Many chiefs wanted the party banned, angered by its opposition and by its demand for membership fees that were properly due only to patrons privately wealthy enough to sway decision with words. Kenyatta, file of correspondence in hand, appealed to the provincial commissioner for understanding on the ground that, while the commissioner could check up KCA representations on file, the KCA had to face endless oral innuendo subject to no such check. He was also welcome to inspect the association's accounts, to verify that it spent money in the public interest. Proceedings became so heated that the provincial commissioner withdrew, telling the Gikuyu to reach consensus before he returned. When he did so he declared that he could see no reason to ban the KCA, for its officials were "clever (or knowledgeable) people, for they can write now, for formerly they had no wisdom."[22] Here was a remarkable appeal to literate identity from both sides of the racial divide. The external administrative architecture of tribal identity and the interior debate on moral ethnicity were met together in a correspondence file.

Kenyatta knew, however, that bureaucratic truth needed cautious negotiation if he were to retain British confidence. Writing could be scrutinized with more care than orations and could not be conveniently reworked in memory. At the Kiambu branch meeting he refused to take up a member's land grievance against one of the missions before seeing the file. Were the KCA to adopt a cause, he warned, "it behooves us to send only those things which will not make us ashamed later, for it is easy to write, but in answering about a matter one is not acquainted with, it is difficult to explain how the matter stands because one does not know about it"—unless one had read it up with a bureaucratic eye. Kenyatta, *muramati* and *muthomi*, clan trustee and reader, was showing at the start of his career a keen sense of their respective arts, oracy

---

22. Henry Mwangi Gichuiri's report of meeting between chiefs and KCA at Nyeri, 20 April 1928, in *Ib.*, i, 8 (Jan 1929) and i, 9 (Feb 1929).

and literacy, and of their respective place in politics, in convincing audiences internal and external.

The branch meeting had not yet exhausted the uses of literacy. Kenyatta dramatized its range in an announcement in which the first words epitomized the *athomi* appropriation of rhetorical authority: "Listen while I read to you about another black race, black as you, so that you may cease to think ill of yourselves on the ground that only you are having trouble regarding the land." He held up a pamphlet, probably from the West African Students Union, to show its photograph of Africans from the other side of the continent. The meeting thereupon resolved to start their own newspaper, to be subsidized by each *mbari*, so that "everybody may know how the country is advancing, and that the other races (or nations) may see our affairs in the same way as we see theirs." Print could represent locality before the world. Within months *Muigwithania* had a subscriber as far away as Paris, a Gikuyu domestic servant who was delighted to find in it "reliable things, not the things of a gossip but those of a sensible man (or elder)."[23]

There was something else that other nations had: memorials to past heroes. The Kiambu meeting resolved to mark each March 16th with discussion and prayer, the anniversary of the police killings of the pioneer nationalist Harry Thuku's supporters in Nairobi, in 1922. The calendar which thus formalized political memory was another product of imported education. Gikuyu chronology no longer depended on the succession of generations and age-sets, the periodicity of famine, the cycles of moon and seasons. Gikuyu had always known both linear and cyclical or restorative time. Here both were reinforced. The Nairobi deaths had marked an early stage of modern politics to which the KCA looked back; but they now looked forward too, in prayer but also with a photograph of their hero, to the exiled Thuku's return.[24]

The KCA's Kiambu meeting had, then, reveled in educated skills which, in adding to orality, subverted the authority of those who commanded oral performance alone. *Athomi* could both read and, by reading aloud, cause others to pay heed. The meeting received—and left—a record; it matched its bureaucratic procedure with the state's; got news from half a continent away and decided to make the KCA heard in return; knew how to raise the money to pay an Indian printer; and, finally, voted to make the memory of unantici-

---

23. John Gichung'wa, 'The voice of a Gikuyu who is in Europe', *Ib.*, i, 7 (Nov 1928), 10. Gichung'wa was to turn Queen's evidence against Kenyatta in 1953.

24. For Gikuyu time: Lonsdale 1995: 263–9. We cannot know if the KCA knew, when discussing 'Thuku day', that Princess Marie Louise was soon to unveil a war memorial to Kenya's African dead, 'the King's children', in Nairobi (*Muigwithania*, i, 4, Aug 1928).

pated butchery among suspect "Nairobi Gikuyu" into a monument to martyrdom, exemplary to Gikuyu as a whole. *Mbari* elders refused on principle to do anything on this scale. They wielded authority only over the land civilized by their *mbari* ancestors; to claim any wider authority except by loose affiliation with other landed elders was to provoke scandal (Kenyatta 1938: 235). Some, accordingly, were furious that anybody who did not lose a clan member in the Nairobi demonstration should presume to take up Thuku's cause.[25]

Nevertheless, for all the anger of parochial Gikuyu landowners, the *athomi* had imagined an ethnic political community; fixed it in time and space; given it a voice and a collective memory that was also a redemptive political narrative. A narrative of loss that contains some promise of restitution must be at the core of any nationalism; the Gikuyu, in a sense deeper than the *athomi* themselves perhaps realized, although they were insistent enough, had to be a literate—even a Christian—nation or they would be nothing in a British imperial world. We can trace that dawning realization in *Muigwithania's* pages.

Christianity and Memory

Enjoying their literate conduct of business, then, Kenyatta's generation were eager to put it to the service of their people, in their final transition from contrite prodigals to communal protectors. Their argument that in a racial order any political claim must rest on a modern ethnic identity was clearly self-interested, transforming Christian delinquency into a Gikuyu common weal. But it rested on solid evidence of the threats which faced all, but which only *athomi* could answer. With an easy and persuasive logic they converted their prodigal's plea for forgiveness into a claim to natural leadership, their reconciliation of internal division into external advocacy, and their religious marginality into representative cultural politics. And they argued all this out in print.

Charles Ng'undo, addressing *Muigwithania's* editor as one "who writes to the whole community," put best the *athomi* claim to be wiser than the elders. He asked the key question of modernity, how society can continue to transmit social knowledge and, with it, moral order. Deploring modern social laxity, he asked why youths knew neither their age-set nor clan, elders enjoyed no respect, and children did not know fathers. His answer was that the ritual which had once inscribed such knowledge on consciousness was in decay. But one could not do without festivals; there could be no self-knowledge nor cul

---

25. Chief Philip Karanja, at the Nyeri meeting, *Ib.*, i, 9 (Feb 1929), 11.

ture without them. "A man will not speak to his child or a child address his father for want of a sign." If the old festivals that imparted such incorporating signs could not survive new times then they must be reconstituted.

It was up to Christians to adapt more vital social rituals from a colonial culture which, however literate, was oral in its encounters with Africans (cf. Hofmeyr 1993). Ng'undo urged that tea replace beer as the beverage of culture. Tea-parties at times of circumcision would encourage parents and children to "recognize" each other and thank God. The white habit of celebrating birthdays might also mark clan and age-set membership. Quoting an old proverb to new effect, that, "ability to give advice on custom is not confined to old age," and, inserting Christianity into Gikuyu expectations of generational change, Ng'undo called on all to "wake up and turn over the fallowland of your brains," to think up new aids to social memory.[26]

Ng'undo's plea rested on the twin premise that modernity caused social amnesia and that only *athomi* had the gift of moral remembrance. While oral authority was losing its performative medium of cohesion, literate Christianity was both a culture of performance and an integral, and so durable, part of modernity's sacred code. The sacred was also political; biblical discourse stored a memory of resistance and liberation for a house of Israel that "spoke," literally from the pulpit and, by analogy, to the house of Muumbi. One can also see in *Muigwithania*'s constant citing of biblical references, without their narrative text (Luke 15: 11–17, rather than the prodigal's story) a lively reinvention of oral mnemonic formulae such as proverbs, which gave *athomi* the rhetorical comradeship which political confidence required (cf. Ong 1982: 41, 75). And there were good grounds for believing that print-religion protected against the modern loss of social memory. A mission school competition, after all, stimulated the first collection of Gikuyu proverbs (Barra 1939).

Kenyatta shared Ng'undo's hope for the conservative social role of mission education. On his arrival in London in 1929 he saw to it that the British knew that all thirty-one signatories to the KCA land petition he brought with him were both "pure Gikuyu" and yet Christian, and that he himself had learned English at his mission.[27] While that might be discounted as mere propaganda before a supposedly Christian imperial nation, the first letters he wrote back

---

26. 'One does not part from one's clan or circumcision guild' *Ib.*, i, 12 (May 1929), 5. (see also Peterson 2004: 97–8). Ng'undo could well have provided a premonitory text for Gellner 1983: 57–62, or Connerton 1989. Tea was so symbolic of respectability by the 1950s that 'taking tea' was a euphemism for taking a political oath.

27. *Manchester Guardian* interview with him on arrival in London, in *Muigwithania* i, 11 (April 1929), 4. In *Facing Mount Kenya* Kenyatta was silent on his mission education.

from Britain to *Muigwithania* and the audience who already knew him cannot be dismissed so lightly.

Kenyatta continued to commend the prodigal son's example. In postal sermons from London he reminded Gikuyu of their duty to the Almighty, in whom he united Gikuyu and Christian Gods, as Ndegwa had recently urged.[28] Warning migrant workers against "the wonders of other places, for after these attractions you will find only tears," he told them to return home "for Gikuyu, our father, has domestic sacrifices." Filial duty, again, was only a first step. Skilled workers living elsewhere must use their talents to improve Gikuyuland, just as educated English worked for their country. Kenyatta begged *athomi* not to dismiss their heritage as "'a matter of the past'; no, try to effect a change such as you see is in accord with things as they are today, for today's torments are not those of former times."[29] Town Gikuyu must not think ethnic identity irrelevant; if they neglected their history they would be left still further behind the strangers. They must rise as one and thatch (with new grass) the leaky roof of the house of custom—the most vividly collective of social practices and an echo of God's first command to Gikuyu—before the rains came.[30]

Kenyatta was the more convinced of the need to renovate custom when he saw modern British tradition at work.[31] Waiting six hours in the crowd to see the king and queen, he was deeply impressed, not least with the guardsmen who in their bearskins were like rows of sorghum in a Gikuyu field. Thrilled by the state opening of parliament, Kenyatta listed its lessons. Gikuyu must respect each other before others would respect them; use convincing arguments; choose good customs to preserve, equal to the traditions of other nations, and so make commemoration work as well for them as it did for the British. Had he known that the state opening had only recently been revived, to uphold authority in changing times (Cannadine 1983: 136), he might the more confidently have advised that, "since no day dawns like another, for many changes are coming, let us go with the tide."[32] For Kenyatta, as for his British rulers, it seemed best to ride the tide of change on conservative reforms that armed the future with memory.

---

28. To *Muigwithania* i, 11 (April 1929), 5–7; *ib*, i, 12 (May 1929), 8–10. His God was both *Mwene Nyaga*, "possessor of brightness", which missionaries had not adopted and *Ngai*, "divider of the inheritance", which they had.

29. To *Ib.*, i, 12 (May 1929), 10.

30. For his lyrical description of hut-building see, Kenyatta 1938: 76–84.

31. 'Seeing the King and his lady with one's eyes', *Muigwithania* ii, 2 (Jul–Aug 1929), 6–8.

32. To *Ib.*, i, 12 (May 1929), 10.

Kenyatta's friends did not need royal pomp to see the point of respecting the past; and his half-brother, James Muigai, agreed that, since all cultures were comparable, success in the wider world must rest on local pride. Muigai ridiculed those who thought Gikuyu custom foolish and yet enjoyed reading books in which others had written "their tales of long ago," like the Swahili edition of Aesop's fables. Since they could never cease to be Gikuyu it was ruinous to belittle tradition; outsiders would gladly follow their lead "in running down our affairs and custom, and will call us people of no importance because we do not possess good ways." And if it was modern to protect one's heritage, only *athomi* could do so. Household education around the cooking pots was dying out with the dispersion of families; "and then from what quarter shall we obtain those traditions that we seek so as to put them down *in order?*"[33]

Njuguna wa Karucha pointed out, further, that print fixed language when all else was changing; without a vernacular literacy their tongue was surely doomed. Literacy protected orality; linking internal order to a defense against otherness, he observed that many Gikuyu were starting to talk Swahili, a "foreign jargon" they once thought gibberish.[34] Swahilization, petering out among strangers, epitomized the urban threat. In an argument that made Christianity a natural defense in a mobile world, Gideon Mugo warned against adopting Muslim names. They made one a Swahili "stranger," and yet a subject people still. Christian names, by contrast, made Gikuyu "of the one clan [*muhiriga*] of Christianity," the equal of all.[35]

Kenyatta himself stimulated the search for a usable past with an editorial questionnaire on initiation, fertility and death—as if to confirm the thesis that nationalism is a secular religion which meets, as no other political doctrine dare claim, the human need for a community which outlives death. One colleague founded a history society; another likened Gikuyu interest in their past to the white habit of sending children "home" to school in Britain.[36] All this *athomi* desire for social rebirth in the shape of a morally responsible posterity showed a religious sense pleasing to any unlettered elder. But what best proved that Kenyatta and his friends retained a Gikuyu religious perspective that united spirit and matter was their call for industrious self-improvement.

---

33. James Muigai to *Ib.*, i, 8 (Dec 1928–Jan 1929), 15. Emphasis added.

34. S. Njuguna Karucha, 'Gikuyu time', *Ib.*, i, 6 (Oct 1928), 10. Cf. Anderson 1983: 47–8.

35. G. M. Kagika, 'Hold fast to tribal names', *Muigwithania* i, 7 (Nov 1928), 1.

36. 'Editor to the friends of *Muigwithania*', *Ib.*, i, 7 (Nov 1928), 4; Mockerie 1934: 64; G. Njeroge to *Muigwithania* i, 10 (Feb–March 1929), 13–14. For the thesis, Anderson 1983.

Like all remembered ancestors, *atiga iri na iriiri*, they wished to leave to their heirs both a morally disciplined upbringing and its due reward in property. That this was also an implicit discourse of legitimacy for an emergent rural capitalism added one more imaginative strand to the construction of moral ethnicity.[37]

Clan and School, Church and Nation

The only other area of reconciliation that can be dealt with here was between the KCA and those readers closer to the missions.[38] This was a political as much as a religious concern, to do with present power as well as visions of the future. Indeed, the KCA recognized that, without a base in oral institutions equivalent to *mbari*, literacy could never compete with oral culture, that discursive reach could not become political grasp. The KCA's calls for church support are all the more striking when one considers how strongly Gikuyu as a whole were then criticizing missionary failures in both education and political protection.

From London, Kenyatta expressed a widespread view that Gikuyu needed more than the missions could give. "If you want us to become...counsellors of our country, busy yourselves with EDUCATION. For knowledge is in the forefront here; it is as though knowledge were power; for here anyone without knowledge is of no consequence, and his voice will nowhere be heard, for power here consists of counsel led by EDUCATION. But do not think that the education I refer to is that which we are given a lick of; no, it is a methodical education to open out a man's head."[39]

Gikuyu were also becoming dismayed with failures in missionary political patronage. In one district KCA branches were, indeed, in violent conflict with the local Scottish mission, over its seemingly sinister use of school land and labor for agricultural training (but see Peterson 2004: 99–103). For their part, some missionaries opposed any KCA presence in church affairs. They felt that they had come to cure souls rather than mend grievances. Not all clergy took this conservative theological view; the Anglicans at Kahuhia, most liberal of

---

37. For ancestors, see, Benson 1964: 189, 447; Cavicchi 1977: 11; for the KCA's language of class, Lonsdale 1992: 376–97.

38. For fuller discussion of the KCA see, Lonsdale 1992: 371–401 and references there cited.

39. Kenyatta to *Muigwithania* i, 11 (April 1929), 6; for the context see, Anderson 1970: 116; Clough 1990: 80–3; Strayer 1978: 110–16; Tignor 1976: 255–61; Kershaw 1996: chapter 6.

stations, fostered a fusion between church growth and political activism (Clough 1990: 112–36; Strayer 1978: 119–33; Karanja 1993: 189–93). Readers were equally divided. There was a broad split between the spiritually and personally more dependent *athomi* who lived in the missions, and those whose Christianity was wholly Gikuyu, centered on *mbari* outschools. The KCA straddled both inner and outer circles of Christianity; it needed access to both the missions' educational resources and the outschools' organizational network, more loyal to *mbari* than to missions. It was dangerous to have one without the other. The embattled Scottish mission had all too easily split opinion, *mbari* school by *mbari* school, to raise up a "loyalist" opposition to the KCA.

Trying harder than others to unite Gikuyu, the KCA was all the more frustrated by Gikuyu divisions. It tried to ward off faction by selecting leaders from "metaclans" (*mihiriga*), known to be free from sorcery (Githige 1978: 119). But orally-linked and geographically dispersed *mihiriga* had no institutions to match the missions. A modern Gikuyu nation needed an outschool organization for its own outreach. So Kenyatta was alarmed when local KCA opposition to school agriculture gave the whole association a bad name. He ridiculed such "secret talk" by pointing out the missions had given his members what "little wisdom" they had. Would the KCA knowingly destroy the enclosure that protected their cattle from the hyena? His literary rhetoric was based on an oral proverb. Despite the rising dissatisfaction with missions he seemed happy that all, even mere listeners, should know his own view that they were essential to protect Gikuyu property from white settlers' greed.

But if Gikuyu were historically split into nine *mihiriga*, their outschools were also divided among half as many missions. Kenyatta had to cope with both old fears of witchcraft and this new sectarianism. One can sense anger, even despair, in his claim that the KCA sought "night and day for that which will cause all Gikuyu to attain unity, educated and uneducated, ceasing to ask each other, what Mission do *you* belong to? Or, you are not a reader. For if there could be an end of things like these the country of Gikuyu could go ahead in peace." One is bound to ask why he chose to cap his argument with the text, Galatians 6:2.[40] No reader, whatever their faith (or lack thereof), could object to the first clause of this Pauline injunction: "Bear ye one another's burdens." But it had a rider, "and so fulfill the law of Christ." Kenyatta could have easily selected some other scriptural or proverbial call to cooperation without invoking Christ as his authority. It seems that modernity's sacred code was, for the moment, a watchword for mustering Gikuyu political support.

---

40. 'A message from *Muigwithania*', *Muigwithania* i, 4 (Aug 1928), 3.

Gideon Mugo, faithful Anglican, KCA leader and contributor to *Muig-withania*, supported Kenyatta's appeal in an article "Setting forth what is right (or 'conclusive')."[41] He thought of Gikuyudom as a church, and agreed with Kenyatta that the missions were cattle-kraals, guardians of value in a now global environment. To his mind, everything overlapped. Gikuyuland itself was a church, but it was also part of a larger cattle-kraal, the worldwide church. Conversely, Christian Gikuyu were not a separate nation but only those who had heard the gospel first, with the implication that the rest would do so later. But Mugo's message of Gikuyu toleration and his vision of future unity depended on a radical change of heart from some of the missionaries.

Mugo's own Anglicans were exceptionally liberal, permitting active church membership to KCA officials. Most Protestant missionaries were theologically conservative, condemning politics as "worldly." But, Mugo answered in an impeccably incarnational argument, "We are all of us of the world." Had not Christ told his disciples to build the church here on earth "until He should take us to His home above?" In a delightful change of domestic image he concluded that "the people of the little digging stick" should agree, just as smoke mingled when rising from their cooking fires—at the very time of day, surely not coincidentally, in which elders told stories to the young. Some patriotic intellectuals found it impossible to imagine the reconciliation of their "country of Gikuyu" in even its most homely oral guise, without biblical intimations of literate church-building.[42]

Conclusion

By 1929, after a year of *Muigwithania*'s publication, Kenyatta and his contributors had worked out a project of harmony between literate modernity and the oral authority of elders. The prodigal's return made the readers' debate on Gikuyu memory an authentic basis for the future. Their patriotism owed much to their experience of migrant exile. Kenyatta and his generation, *irungu*, "straighteners," like other African patriots, persuaded themselves that Christian enlightenment was the best guide to oral authority in preserving ancestral ethnic virtue against the threat of social extinction. To share in the benefits of modernity without loss one needed modern skills; but more than that, Christianity seemed to many to be the best means to secure a united Gikuyu future (cf. Lentz 1994 b: 81–3; Peel 1993: 65–75).

---

41. G. H. M. Kagika to *Ib.*, ii, 1 (June 1929), 7–8.
42. However unwillingly, the works of Ngugi wa Thiong'o still make the same point.

Ten years later Kenyatta published his ethnographic polemic, *Facing Mount Kenya*. In large part this fulfilled *Muigwithania*'s project, which was to make Gikuyu modern by making modernity Gikuyu. He could never have imagined Gikuyu whole, as in his book, had he not first presided over his newspaper's discursive arena. In the book he more than met his brother Muigai's demand that *athomi*, as its guardians, write custom down in due order. And, from his viewpoint at the London School of Economics, Kenyatta continued in 1938 to claim that a knowledge of the outside world authorized one's leadership in internal "progressive movements." He still wanted wider access to a modern education, both to help his people "create a new culture which, though its roots are still in the soil, is yet modified to meet the pressure of modern conditions," and to enable them "to take part in world culture" (xix, 128, 317).[43] There could be no better précis of *Muigwithania*'s hybrid project.

In his book, nonetheless, Kenyatta faced—and at times evaded—dilemmas of change and continuity, modernity and identity for which, in *Muigwithania*'s pages, he had earlier shown little concern. In some respects, indeed, the author came close to repudiating the primary-schooled journalist's project, not directly but in the silent logic of his argument. One is tempted to say there were two Kenyattas, young modernizer and older conservative. The young journalist, "reader," and junior elder, argued to his own people that only change could guarantee continuity. The middle-aged student of anthropology and senior elder, writing for a British audience, no longer thought the harmony of modernity and tradition was quite so simple.

The young Kenyatta had been convinced that to ally with modernity was essential if Gikuyu were to survive modernity's ordeal. Unlettered elders could not resist, unaided, the socially intimate but physically distant delinquency of town. They had to reform custom to make it memorable in daily behavior. "To cope with modern torments" they must "go with the tide." And the communicative cohesion which reform required, he seems to have believed in the 1920s, could be found only in Christianity. Denominational division would not have otherwise have troubled him. Some readers also stressed the reforming cohesion of the new generation set, the *irungu*, membership of which caused no great offence to many of their missionary patrons.[44]

Yet in *Facing Mount Kenya* Kenyatta dismissed with scorn or in silence both approaches, Christian or generational, to the discursive cohesion needed for

---

43. Numbers in square brackets in this section refer to page numbers in Kenyatta 1938.

44. For missionary toleration of *irungu* see, Cagnolo 1933: 125; Ward 1976: 129; Strayer 1978: 82; Peterson 2004: 65–89; and conflict: McIntosh 1969: 408. No more than half the KCA's age-cohort will have been members of the eligible *irungu*.

reform. Why in 1938 he should have had doubts which neither he nor his colleagues had entertained in 1928 invites reflection on three possible influences on his changing thought: Kenya's intervening political history, his intellectual training in London, and his own estimate of his different audiences (also Lonsdale 2005).

While in *Muigwithania*'s pages the obedient prodigal became the informed guardian against social amnesia and delinquency, in *Facing Mount Kenya* Kenyatta got no further than the urgent need for youthful repentance from their willful ways. He belittled literates as mischief-makers whose ritual absences from their households destroyed harmony and prosperity; as people forgetful of, rather than recorders of, history; as bewildered souls "left floundering" between two worlds, rather than as influential opinion-formers who could reconcile them; as juniors between whom and their elders there was no prospect of reasoned debate [92, 105, 115, 120, 125, 134, 153, 250–52, 254]. To make this accusation stick, he was silent over both his own mission education and the threat of urban delinquency. He took the elders' view—and he was by now a senior elder himself—that mission schooling alone was to blame for the moral bewilderment of Gikuyu society.

More surprisingly, Kenyatta failed to exploit the native potential of generation sets to initiate progressive change. He had published that case in *Muigwithania*; his colleague in London, Parmenas Mukiri, had argued still more strongly; and to a British audience, the ability of successive pre-colonial generations to reform Gikuyu life (Mockerie 1934); and whites in Kenya admired the recent innovation whereby age sets had become school fundraising syndicates.[45] But Kenyatta—perhaps scandalized by how far Mukiri was prepared to go in renouncing Gikuyu practice in his search for enlightenment—allowed there to be only one generationally-based *revolution* in his book: the original, mythical revolt of property-owning Gikuyu democracy against the tyrant king Gikuyu. All other *matuika* since then had, in his view, served only to confirm those rules of obedient social harmony that had been established in the first (186–97).

Kenyatta's scorn for mission Christians—whose mutual goodwill had been the core of KCA organization—and his neglected opportunity to legitimize generationally inspired change, can in part be attributed to the Gikuyu experience since his departure for London in 1929. The "female circumcision" crisis of that year had cut the always fragile ties between the majority of outschool Christians and the minority of mission Christians who clung more closely to

---

45. Louis Leakey, 'Gikuyu age groups', (n. d., 1939): KNA, NM. 1/857.

their white patrons. The crisis was about social discipline and property, not about "culture" or sex. *Facing Mount Kenya* correctly linked clitoridectomy with the training of women to bring *wealth* to their family rather than with gender relations more generally. Kenyatta also focused the dispute between missions and Gikuyu on the question of control of access to *school*—which had everything to do with the defense of *mbari* property (111, 130–31). Ignorant missionaries, far from experiencing the change of heart for which Gideon Mugo had called, were now, in Kenyatta's view, "religious fanatics." No longer the cattle-kraals that protected Gikuyu wealth, their cultural imperialism threatened to destroy a civilization which rested on that kin-obedience to male elders which alone ensured social order and material accumulation.

Kenyatta espoused this patriarchal thesis all the more firmly as a way of replying to the Kenya Land Commission of 1932–34, sent by London to investigate the case, if any, for the return of white settler land to Africans. The white commissioners refused to accept the mass of Gikuyu *mbari* histories, often worked up by KCA members and on KCA-printed forms, as valid charters for the restitution of land. There was too much discrepancy between this written evidence and the publicly performed oral testimony by *mbari* spokesmen before the commission. So the disbelieving KLC had summed up the historical basis of Gikuyu land claims as mere "force and chicanery" (Lonsdale 1995). Kenyatta's book was an extended rebuttal of the commissioners' scepticism. But in promoting the authority of senior *mbari* land elders, his monograph also limited the conceptual space available for generational change and thus any legitimate unity of Gikuyu political purpose.

The circumcision crisis had divided Gikuyu modernizers, and discredited the KCA in British eyes. On the land issue, a few years later, the KCA had failed their people as a whole. These were good reasons for Kenyatta's ethnographic defense of the fragmented patriarchal authority of householder against both generational change and literacy's wider locutionary range. But it must also be asked how far his difficulty in allowing Gikuyu the moral legitimacy and institutional basis of debate, which he and his fellow *irungu* had enjoyed in *Muigwithania*, was due to the functionalist anthropology he learned from his tutor and friend Malinowski at the London School of Economics. Functionalism gave Kenyatta the cultural nationalist all the interconnected harmonies of a past golden age his heart could desire, and a withering critique of colonialism's destruction of the "spirit of manhood," and with it the Gikuyu capacity for moral choice. But his anthropology also deprived him of a program of reform. It made it difficult for him to argue that the Christian products of externally induced social change—and therefore functional decay—were able to guard a people's integrity. It also rendered the liberal solution he advocated to the divisive clitoridectomy crisis, namely "freedom of conscience," starkly inconsistent with his ethnography of Gikuyu as an "organic whole…controlled by an iron-bound code of duties" (131, 135, 271). Kenyatta no longer invited his audience to listen as he read out the news, but to read what he remembered from his elders in the past (cf. Berman 1996; Berman & Lonsdale 1998).

Indeed, Kenyatta the ethnographer came close to reinventing the archetypal "oral man," socially conformist, incapable of intellectual enquiry, that his journalism had so vigorously disproved. In his most closely reasoned chapter, on the differences between Gikuyu and western education, Kenyatta argued that the latter could never mould "the African" so as to both "make him fit in his community"—the Christian project of *uiguano*—and "establish good relations with the outside world" if it did not strengthen the ties of kin and age which were "the foundations of moral sentiments and the means of building up character." Most educationalists and moral philosophers would agree with this premise. But the task that Kenyatta set for formal education was impossible, since the "outside world" rested, he knew, on the mutual obligations of "economic, professional and religious associations" composed of individuals, not the clansmen of his internal world (122–3). Opening out one's head now looked to break up one's people.

If Kenyatta's acquired anthropology thus led him into a brick wall that divided the oral from the literate man, his modernizing project may also have been betrayed, finally, by his estimate of how to move his British audience. The young journalist had been herald to a cultural minority, boldly calling for the leadership that was their generation's due. His audience had been that minority; it had responded by debating the modern mix of moral ethnicity. The older ethnographer chose to speak for an innocent people whose harmony had been wrecked by British wrong. But the purity of cultural nationalism is all too easily pressed into the service of an intolerant political tribalism. Kenyatta came perilously close to that—if from an entirely reasonable calculation that the nobler he portrayed his people's past, and the more corrupt their present, the more his new pan-African and leftwing friends would champion them. It was a dangerous course to take. His friendliest reviewer, H. N. Brailsford (1938) of the Independent Labor Party, drew from his reading of *Facing Mount Kenya* the lesson that Gikuyu were now too far gone to save themselves. Their only hope lay in British anti-imperialism.

That was not what *Muigwithania* had so confidently proclaimed. Nor would it be accepted by a generation younger than Kenyatta's, who recovered their "spirit of manhood" by taking violent action. Yet these "Mau Mau" still failed in practice, as Kenyatta had failed in print, to resolve the conflict between the patriotic moral ethnicity of landed authority and the managerial nationalism of literacy that all too easily denied the individual's "spirit of manhood" and lent itself to the unchecked autocracy, even terror, of political tribalism (Lonsdale 1994: 142–50 and 2003: 60–69; Smith 1995).

References

Achebe, C. (1963) *No Longer at Ease*, Heinemann African Writers Series, London.

Alexander, J., McGregor, J., & Ranger, T (2000) *Violence and memory: One hundred years in the 'dark forests' of Matabeleland*, Currey, Heinemann, Philip, & Weaver: Oxford, Portsmouth NH, Cape Town, & Harare.

Anderson, B. (1983) *Imagined Communities*, Verso, London.

Anderson, D. M. (2005) *Histories of the hanged: Britain's dirty war in Kenya and the end of Empire*, Weidenfeld & Nicolson, London.

Anderson, J. (1970) *The Struggle for the School*, Longman, London.

Barra, G. (1939 [1987]) *1000 Gikuyu Proverbs*, Kenya Literature Bureau, Nairobi.

Benson, T. G. (1964) *Gikuyu-English Dictionary*, Oxford University Press.

Berman, B. J. (1996) 'Ethnography as politics, politics as ethnography: Kenyatta, Malinowski and the making of *Facing Mount Kenya*', *Canadian Journal of African Studies* 30, 3.

Berman, B & Lonsdale, J. (1998) 'The labors of *Muigwithania*: Jomo Kenyatta as author 1928–1945', *Research in African Literatures* 29.

Brailsford, H. N (1938) 'An African on African life', *New Statesman & Nation* (London, 17 September)

Cagnolo, C. (1933) *The AGikuyu*, Istituto Missioni Consolata, Nyeri.

Cannadine, D. (1983) 'The context, performance and meaning of ritual: the British monarchy and the "invention of tradition," c. 1820–1977', in E. Hobsbawm and T. Ranger (eds.), *The Invention of Tradition*, Cambridge University Press.

Cavicchi, E. (1977) *Problems of Change in Gikuyu Tribal Society*, EMI, Bologna.

Clough, M. S. (1990) *Fighting Two Sides: Kenyan Chiefs and Politicians, 1918–1940*, University Press of Colorado, Niwot.

Connerton, P. (1989) *How Societies Remember*, Cambridge University Press.

Delf, G. (1961) *Jomo Kenyatta*, Gollancz, London.

Elkins, C. M. (2005) *Britain's gulag: The brutal end of empire in Kenya*, Cape, London.

Fadiman, J. A. (1993) *When we Began there Were Witchmen*, University of California Press, Berkeley.

Gellner, E. (1983) *Nations and Nationalism*, Blackwell, Oxford.

Giblin, J. L (2002) 'History, imagination and remapping space in a small urban center: Makambako, Iringa region, Tanzania', in A. Burton (ed.), *The urban experience in Eastern Africa c. 1750–2000*, The British Institute in Eastern Africa: Nairobi & London.

Githige, R. M. (1978) 'The religious factor in Mau Mau, with particular reference to Mau Mau oaths', University of Nairobi MA dissertation.

Goody, J. (1977) *The Domestication of the Savage Mind*, Cambridge University Press.

Hofmeyr, I. (1987) 'Building a nation with words: Afrikaans language, literature and ethnic identity, 1902–1924', in S. Marks and S. Trapido (eds.), *The Politics of Race, Class & Nationalism in Twentieth Century South Africa*, Longman, London and New York.

Hofmeyr, I. (1993) *"We Spend Our Lives as a Tale that is Told": Oral Historical Narrative in a South African Chiefdom*, Heinemann, Portsmouth NH.

Iliffe, J. (1995) *Africans: a History of a Continent*, Cambridge University Press.

Karanja, J. K. (1993) 'The Growth of the African Anglican Church in Central Kenya, 1900–1945', University of Cambridge Ph.D. dissertation.

Kenyatta, J. (1938) *Facing Mount Kenya: the Tribal Life of the Gikuyu*, Secker and Warburg, London.

Kershaw, G. (1972) 'The land is the people', University of Chicago Ph.D. dissertation.

Kershaw, G. (1997) *Mau Mau from Below*, Currey, EAEP and Ohio University Press: Oxford, Nairobi, & Athens OH.

Leakey, L. S. B. (1977) *The Southern Gikuyu before 1903*, 3 vols, Academic Press, London and New York.

Lentz, C. (1994 a) 'Home, death and leadership: discourses of an educated elite from north-western Ghana', *Social Anthropology* Vol 2, No 2.

Lentz, C. (1994 b) '"They must be Dagaba first and any other thing second": the colonial and post-colonial creation of ethnic identities in north-western Ghana', *African Studies*, Vol 53, No 2.

Lonsdale, J. (1992) 'The moral economy of Mau Mau', in B. Berman & J. Lonsdale, *Unhappy Valley: conflict in Kenya and Africa*, Currey, London and Ohio University Press, Athens.

Lonsdale, J. (1994) 'Moral ethnicity and political tribalism', in P. Kaarshom and J Hultin (eds.), *Inventions and Boundaries: Historical and Anthropological Approaches to the Study of Ethnicity and Nationalism*, IDS, Roskilde University.

Lonsdale, J. (1995) 'The prayers of Waiyaki', in D. M. Anderson and D. H. Johnson (eds.), *Revealing Prophets: Prophecy in Eastern African History*, Currey, London.

Lonsdale, J (2002 a) 'Jomo Kenyatta, God, and modernity', in J-G. Deutsch, P. Probst & H. Schmidt (eds.), *African modernities*, Currey & Heinemann: Oxford & Portsmouth NH.

Lonsdale, J (2002 b) 'Contests of time: Kikuyu historiographies, old and new', in A. Harneit-Sievers (ed.), *A place in the world: New local historiographies from Africa and South-Asia*, Brill, Leiden & Boston.

Lonsdale, J (2003) 'Authority, gender, and violence: The war within Mau Mau's fight for land and freedom', in E. S. Atieno Odhiambo & J Lonsdale (eds), *Mau Mau & nationhood: Arms, authority and narration* (Currey, EAEP & Ohio University Press: Oxford, Nairobi and Athens OH)

Lonsdale, J (2005) 'Ornamental constitutionalism in Africa: Jomo Kenyatta and the two Queens', forthcoming in *Journal of Imperial and Commonwealth History*.

Marks, S. (1994) 'Black and white nationalisms in South Africa', in P. Kaarshom and J Hultin (eds.), *Inventions and Boundaries: Historical and Anthropological Approaches to the Study of Ethnicity and Nationalism*, IDS, Roskilde University.

Mayer, P. (1961) *Townsmen or Tribesmen*, Oxford University Press, Cape Town.

McIntosh, B. G. (1969) 'The Scottish mission in Kenya, 1891–1923', University of Edinburgh Ph.D. dissertation.

McNeill, W. H. (1986) *Polyethnicity and National Unity in World History*, University of Toronto Press, Toronto, Buffalo and London.

Mockerie, P. G. (1934) *An African Speaks for his People*, Hogarth, London.

Moodie, T. D. (1994)*Going for Gold: Men, Mines and Migration*, University of California Press, Berkeley and Los Angeles.

Muriuki, G. (1974) *A History of the Gikuyu 1500–1900*, Oxford University Press, Nairobi.

Murray, J. (1974) 'The Gikuyu female circumcision controversy, with special reference to the Church Missionary Society's sphere of influence', University of California, Los Angeles, Ph.D. dissertation.

Murray-Brown, J. (1972) *Kenyatta*, Allen and Unwin, London.

Smith, J. (1995) 'Eating words: the embodiment and deployment of literary potency by Mau Mau insurgents', University of Chicago MA dissertation in Anthropology.

Strayer, R. W. (1978) *The Making of Mission Communities in East Africa*, Heinemann, London.

Tignor, R. L. (1976) *The Colonial Transformation of Kenya, 1900 to 1939*, Princeton University Press.

Ong, W. J. (1982) *Orality and Literacy: the Technologizing of the Word*, Routledge, London and New York.

Peel, J. D. Y. (1993) 'The cultural work of Yoruba ethnogenesis', in T. Falola (ed.), *Pioneer, Patriot and Patriarch: Samuel Johnson and the Yoruba People*, African Studies Program, University of Wisonsin-Madison.

Peel, J. D. Y. (2000) *Religious encounter and the making of the Yoruba*, Indiana University Press, Bloomington & Indianapolis.

Peterson, D. (1995) '"A frugal peasantry"? Missionaries, Gikuyu *asomi* and the school in colonial Kenya', University of Minnesota Graduate Seminar paper.

Peterson, D. (2004) *Creative writing: Translation, bookkeeping, and the work of the imagination in colonial Kenya*, Heinemann, Portsmouth NH.

Vail, L. and White, L. (1991) *Power and the Praise Poem: Southern African Voices in History*, University Press of Virginia, Charlotteville and Currey, London.

von Oppen, A. (1993) *Terms of Trade and Terms of Trust: the History and Contexts of Pre-colonial Market Production around the Upper Zambezi and Kasai*, Studien zur Afrikanischen Geschichte Bd 6, LIT, Munster.

Ward, K. (1976) 'The development of Protestant Christianity in Kenya', University of Cambridge Ph.D. dissertation.

White, L (2004 a) 'Colonial states and civic virtues in Africa', *International Journal of African Historical Studies* 37, 1.

White, L (2004 b) 'Civic virtue, young men, and the family: Conscription in Rhodesia, 1974–1980', *Ibid.*

CHAPTER 25

THE HOLY TRINITY, OR
THE REDUCED MARX,
WEBER, DURKHEIM

Gavin Williams[1]

Karl Marx, Max Weber and Emile Durkheim are generally recognized as the founding fathers of sociology. This represents their work as of the past, laying foundations for subsequent scholars to build on. Few later sociologists, if any, can match each and all of their contributions to current historical understandings of societies in the past and the present. Their political priorities, intellectual foci, and explanatory strategies differ from one another and can be compared in order to contrast them. They can also be seen to complement one another.

Their work, like that of other great social scientists, is often vulgarized and misrepresented. This arises partly from the need to reduce complex ideas to simpler forms to make them more accessible, which will be true of my own account of their ideas. It arises also from a strong tendency among American and English scholars to assimilate their thinking to a dominant positivist and even utilitarian paradigm. Thus I will begin this essay with a discussion of mistaken identities. I then offer brief syntheses of the main themes and arguments of each thinker. From there, I will move to compare their views on four key issues for social and political theorists: capitalism; religion (Protestantism in particular); politics and the state; sociology and history. My own readings are necessarily selective.

---

1. I first learned about Marx, Weber and Durkheim from two professors of sociology at Durham University, John Rex and Philip Abrams. I owe much of my understanding of their work to Philip Corrigan and Derek Sayer, both Durham doctoral graduates. This paper is dedicated to John Peel for his critical and supportive guidance and in recognition of his varied and continuing intellectual achievements.

The greatness of these three authors is exemplified by the impossibility of arriving at an authoritative interpretation of their work. Their arguments and analyses are not always consistent and often in tension with one another. They shift their intellectual ground over time while sustaining important continuities. Hence, their writings are open to multiple readings, which continue to be renewed and extended. This enables us to appreciate their intellectual depth and deepens the significance of their writing. Their relevance for our times lies in their concern to make sense of a new and changing world. "All that is solid melts into air, all that is holy is profaned, and man is at last compelled to face with sober senses, his real conditions of life, and his relations with his kind."[2]

Of the three, I find myself in greatest sympathy with Weber, whose political ideas are furthest from my own. This may be because of his demand for sober reasoning and the duality of the callings of politics and science. The obligation of politicians to take responsibility for the consequences of their actions is too evidently met in the breach. The demand that scientists put intellectual integrity above all else is threatened by commercial priorities and by the organization of the academy itself. No universal ethical judgements seem able or likely to underpin our philosophies of science or politics. The formal rationalities of bureaucrats and markets, in unholy alliances with one another, displace the rational pursuit of substantive ends and human values. We are remaking our own "iron cage".[3]

Marx, Weber, Durkheim: Three Cases of Mistaken Identities?

Positivism has many, often inconsistent, meanings: the reduction of human action to utilitarian calculation; its determination by causal or evolutionary laws; inductive inference; the empirical testing of deductions from hypotheses, the application of science to the realization of moral values. They are found in different ways in Bentham, St. Simon, Comte and Spencer. These authors cross the line separating matters of fact from questions of value, crit-

---

2. Karl Marx and Friedrich Engels, *The Manifesto of the Communist Party* [1948], *Collected Works (CW)*, Lawrence & Wishart, London, 1975–2001, (vol.) 6, (item) 52, p. 487.

3. Max Weber, *The Protestant Ethic and the Spirit of Capitalism* [1905], George Allen & Unwin, 1905, ch. V, p. 181.

Figure 25.1 - Karl Marx.

ical to Popper's requirement that conjectures, in principle, be empirically fal-
sifiable,[4] and they tend to exclude human agency.

Marx, Weber and Durkheim each set out their methodologies in ways that
can be identified as positivist.[5] Their substantive research and analyses transcended positivist protocols. All three authors derive their methods from and
in response to the legacies of Immanuel Kant. They each all claimed to be scientists. This did not mean applying the protocols of the natural sciences to
the social world but rather that "the purpose of all science is to coordinate our
experiences into a logical framework."[6]

---

4. Karl Popper, "Science: conjectures and refutations" [1953] *Conjectures and Refutations: the growth of scientific knowledge*, 5th edition, Routledge, London, 1989, pp. 36–37,
53.

5. Karl Marx, "Preface" to *A Contribution to The Critique of Political Economy* [1859],
CW, 29, pp. 263–264 and Marx, *Capital*, I [1867/ 1873], Penguin, Harmondsworth, 1973
or "Preface to first German edition" and "Afterword to second German edition" or CW, 35;
Max Weber, *Economy and Society* [1920], University of California Press, 1978, (vol.) I,
(Part) 1, ch. 1, 1–2, pp. 4, 11–12; Emile Durkheim, *The Rules of Sociological Method* [1895]
and Selected Texts on Sociology and its Methods [1897–1917], ed. Steven Lukes, Macmillan,
1982, ch 2, p. 60 and "Preface to second edition" [1907], p. 35; ch 1–2.

6. Albert Einstein, *The Meaning of Relativity* [1922] London: Chapman and Hall, 1978,
p. 1.

Marx's claims to originality rest on his theories of historical materialism and of surplus value. The first has been taken to combine explanations of institutions as ultimately economic with an evolutionary theory of history, ensuring the realization of communism. The second is presented as building on Ricardo's labor theory of value. These theories are economistic, functionalist and evolutionist, allowing no scope for autonomous human agency. An alternative interpretation stresses Marx's application of the critical method to idealist philosophers, utopian socialists and classical economists and his commitment to human self-realization.

Weber identifies the work of Marx and Nietzsche as the key intellectual legacies of the age.[7] Weber has been criticized for his religious explanation for the rise of capitalism, and for defending technical rationality, modern bureaucracy and capitalist enterprise. His ideal-types of "rational action" identify the logical conditions for utilitarian calculation and economic efficiency.[8] His theories are allegedly idealist, determinist or positivist. He was a nationalist and a liberal and a critic of socialism. Explanations are always 'as if'. Weber's perspectives are always double-edged. Formal and instrumental rationality conflicts with the rational pursuit of substantive goals. The ascetic values of Protestantism have created a world in which "material goods have gained an inexorable power over the lives of men."[9]

Durkheim tells us to "treat social facts as things."[10] Parsons interprets him as solving Hobbes problem of order.[11] The individual is subordinated to the *conscience collective*. Social disorders, such as suicide, arise from inadequate integration into or regulation by society. Durkheim is accused of positivism, functionalism, and conservatism. But social agents construct social facts, the collective conscience, and the forms of moral regulation. A society predicated on contract and interest would be no society at all.[12] Durkheim asks: what forms of citizenship or solidarity are appropriate to a commercial society?

---

7. Bryan Turner, "Preface to the new edition", *From Max Weber: Essays in Sociology*, ed. H. H. Gerth and C. Wright Mills [1948], Routledge, London, 1991, p. 20.

8. Weber, *Economy and Society* I, 1, ch. 2, esp. 30, pp. 161–164.

9. Weber, *The Protestant Ethic*, ch. V, p. 181.

10. Emile Durkheim, *Rules of Sociological Method*, ch 2, p. 60 and "Preface to second edition" [1907], p. 35.

11. Talcott Parsons, *The Structure of Social Action: a study in social theory with special reference to a group of recent European writers*, Free Press, New York, 1968. vol. 1, p. 314.

12. Durkheim, *The Division of Labor in Society* [1893], The Free Press, New York, 1964, Book 1, ch. 7.

Marx: The Critical Method and Historical Materialism

In Marx's hands, the critical method identifies the social relations that make possible the economic phenomena of capitalism and their transcendence. Marx shares John Stuart Mill's commitment to human self-realization, but not Mill's analysis of the conditions which make this possible.[13] In 1843 Marx read Adam Smith and David Ricardo through the prism of Young Hegelian philosophy.[14] He rejects abstract idealism and Hegel's reconciliation of the claims of family, civil society and the constitutional state but recognizes that, unlike materialisms, idealism starts from human activity.[15]

Marx takes up Ludwig Feuerbach's critique of religion and of speculative philosophy: Man makes God in his own image and subordinates himself to his own creation.[16] As the secrets of religion are to be found in human activity, so the secrets of the state are to be found in civil society, and explained by political economy. Workers are alienated from the act of production, from the product of their labor, from other people and from their (human) species being.[17]

Between 1845 and 1859, Marx and Friedrich Engels outlined theories of class, state and ideology. They provided a template for interpreting the sweep of events and had to be squared with unanticipated outcomes, notably the failures of the bourgeois democratic revolutions of 1848 in France, Germany and Austria.[18] The ruling ideas are imposed by the ruling class and reflected relations of material domination.[19] Ruling classes are fractured. The state was al-

---

13. J. S. Mill, *On Liberty* [1859], *The Subjection of Women* [1869], *Three Essays*, introduction by Richard Wollheim, Oxford University Press, 1975.

14. Marx, *Economic and Philosophical Manuscripts* [1844], *CW*, 4, 12.

15. Marx, *Critique of Hegel's Philosophy of Law* [1843] and "Introduction" [1944], *CW*, 3, 1 & 7, esp. pp. 8, 175–176; "Theses on Feuerbach I" [1845], *CW*, 5, p. 3.

16. Ludwig Feuerbach, *The Essence of Christianity* [1841], Harper Torchbooks, New York, 1957; Marx, "Introduction", *CW* 7, 3, p. 175; "Theses on Feuerbach" *CW* 5, pp. 3–5; Marx and Engels, *The German Ideology* [1846], Part 1, "Ludwig Feuerbach", esp. p. 36.

17. Marx, "Estranged labour", *Economic and Philosophical Manuscripts* [1843], *CW* 3, 12, pp. 270–283.

18. Marx and Engels, *The Manifesto of the Communist Party* [1948], *CW* 6, 52; Marx, *Class Struggles in France* [1850] *CW* 10, 6; *The Eighteenth Brumaire of Louis Bonaparte* [1852] *CW* 12, 3; Engels, *Revolution and Counter-Revolution in Germany* [1851] *CW*, 11, 1.

19. Marx and Engels, *The German Ideology*, Part 1, *CW* 5. p. 59.

ways more than an instrument; it reconciled and protected the interests of property.

Theories of base and superstructure, forces and relations of production (productive capacities and productive relations) provide an appealing explanation of capitalist society and of the conditions of the working class, and how they can be transcended.[20] But it is hard to see how the legal form, contract, can be explained by economic relations which require it. Productive capacities are capacities of relations and can hardly exist independently of them.[21]

Capital begins with the commodity.[22] How is the commodity possible? If commodities, including labor-power, exchange at their value, how is profit possible? Why has an increase in the productive power of human labor not made work less onerous and workers relatively better off? Value in exchange is different from value in use. The first cannot be derived from the second. But it is only through exchange of commodities in the market that the value of our respective labor powers can be equated with one another.[23]

Marx distinguishes abstract from concrete labor, in parallel with his earlier analysis of alienation: concrete labor produces goods for use; abstract labor produces commodities for exchange.[24] Labor-power is able to produce more value than its reproduction cost; the difference is appropriated and reinvested by the capitalist.[25] Capitalist competition increases relative surplus value for all capitalists but not for each employer, who must resort to expanding or intensifying labor time to increase absolute surplus value.[26] Labor makes capital—and subordinates itself to it.[27] In *Capital*, Marx returns to the analysis of the alienation of labor.

The state seeks to ensure the conditions of and to constrain exploitation of labor in the interests of capitalists as a whole.[28] Manufacturing deskills workers and demands new skills. Capitalism requires the forceful separation of producers from the means of production. It makes possible the expansion of human productive capacities but prevents its free development. The working class, and humankind, can free itself only by overthrowing capitalism.[29]

---

20. Marx, "Preface" to *A Contribution to The Critique of Political Economy* [1859], CW, 29, pp. 263–264.

21. Marx, *The German Ideology*, Part 1, CW 5, p. 43.

22. Marx, *Capital*, I, ch. 1, p. 125 or CW, 35, p. 45.

23. Marx, *Capital*, I, ch. 1, p. 166 or CW, 35, pp. 84–85.

24. Marx, *Capital*, I, ch. 1, pp. 125–137 or CW, 35, pp. 45–56.

25. Marx, *Capital*, I, ch. 4–8, esp. ch. 7 or CW, 35.

26. Marx, *Capital*, I, ch. 10, 12 & 15 pp. 397–420 or CW, 35, pp. 517–543.

27. I owe this observation to Eluned Lewis.

28. Marx, *Capital*, I, ch. 10 or CW, 35.

29. Marx, *Capital*, I, ch. 26–32, esp. pp. 929–930 or CW, 35, esp. pp. 750–751.

Weber: Class, Power, and Politics

Max Weber applied the concepts of legal science to explaining the social world, thereby producing a distinct method and original analysis of the fate of the modern world, and Germany in particular. Central to both the substance and method of his analysis are notions of rationality.

We represent and interpret the world through selective ideal-typical representations of actors and of institutions and systems of belief. Explanations are partial and limited to historical contexts. They must be both meaningfully and causally adequate. Actors give meaning to their actions and respond to others. Weber distinguishes *Zweck* (purposive) from *Wert* (value) rationality and both from traditional and affective action.[30] *Wert* rationality refers to the choice of considered means to realise chosen ends. *Zweck* rationality refers to the pursuit of rational ends. How can ends be rational? Only if they can be defined and compared by a common measure: in the abstract, utility and in practice, money. Weber distinguishes formal rationality, the ordering of conduct and social institutions according to impersonal and calculable criteria, from substantive rationality.[31]

Weber disparages interpretations of history that insist on finding economic causes and treating other motives as accidents.[32] He explores the decisive significance of religious ethics for economic conduct.[33] His aim is not to substitute "for a one-sided materialistic a one-sided spiritualistic causal interpretation of history and culture".[34] Central to the modern world is the tendency towards the formal rationalization of all spheres of life. This has religious origins but extends to law, administration, architecture, science, music, and economy.[35]

The modern state, "a compulsory association which organizes domination"[36] is decisive for modern political life. It depends on the tripod of interests, legitimacy and force. Its legal-rational forms of administration distin-

---

30. Weber, *Economy and Society*, I, 1, ch. 1, 1–2, pp. 4–26.

31. Weber, *Economy and Society*, I, 1, ch. 1, 9, pp. 85–86.

32. Weber, "Objectivity in the social sciences" [1906] in Weber, *The Methodologies of the Social Sciences*, ed. E.A. Shils and H.A. Finch, Free Press, New York, 1949, pp. 68–71.

33. Weber, "The social psychology of world religions" [1915] *From Max Weber*, ch. XI; *Sociology of Religion* [1922], Beacon, Boston, 1991, esp. ch. XIII, XV, XVI and as *Economy and Society*, I, 2, ch. 6, esp. xii, xv.

34. Weber, *Protestant Ethic*, ch. V, p. 183.

35. Weber, *Economy and Society*, I, 2, ch. VI, esp. iii, viii, x (*The Sociology of Religion*, ch. IV, IX, XI); II, 2, ch. VII v–viii (in *Max Weber on Law in Economy and Society*, ed. E. Shils and M. Rheinstein, Harvard University Press, Cambridge MA, 1954); *The Rational and Social Foundations of Music*, ed. D. Martindale, Southern Illinois University Press, 1958.

36. Weber, "Politics as a vocation", *From Max Weber*, ch. IV, p. 82.

guish it from feudal or patrimonial rule.[37] Class, status [*Stand*] and party are analytically distinct but empirically related aspects of the "distribution of power within a community."[38] Weber defines class as "market relation," *Stände* as communities sharing a "social estimation of honor", a common "style of life" and "restricted social intercourse."[39] The Prussian Junkers were both a class of agrarian capitalists and a *Stand*, claiming political privileges and defending economic interests by virtue of their claims to honour.[40] Arguably, any class can form a basis for communal action only when its members share a common sense of their identity, when the class is also a *Stand*.

Capitalism, and the rationalization of conduct it entails, makes possible efficiency in production and administration, advances in science and procedural fairness. But "formal rationality…is always, in principle, in conflict with substantive rationality."[41] Means displace ends. What the Puritan did as a calling "we are forced to do."[42] Weber sees no political salvation: socialism offered only a bureaucratic administration of economic life.[43]

We must choose which "warring gods" we serve.[44] Politics can only be a "strong and slow boring of hard boards."[45] It entails a commitment, not to an "ethic of ultimate ends" but to an "ethic of responsibility [for consequences]" to the limit at which one can but stand and "do no other."[46] Sciences each have their presuppositions. Their truths are never final; they ask to be surpassed. Science rests on the "disenchantment of the world;" its virtue is "plain intellectual integrity;" "if ye will enquire, enquire ye: return come".[47] These are Weber's answers to his own requirement to address the legacies of Marx and Nietzsche.

---

37. Weber, *Economy and Society*, II, ch. XI–XIII; ch. XI "Bureaucracy" is *From Max Weber*, Ch. VII.

38. .

Weber, "Class, status, party", *From Max Weber*, VII, p. 181 or *Economy and Society*, II, 2, Ch. 11, 6, p. 927.

39. Weber, "Class, status, party", *From Max Weber*, VII, pp. 182, 186–187 or *Economy and Society*, II, pp. 928, 932.

40. Weber, "National character and the Junkers" *From Max Weber* ch. XV; "Class, status, party", *From Max Weber*, VII, pp. 190–191 or *Economy and Society*, II, pp. 935–936.

41. Weber, *Economy and Society*, I, 1, ch. 1, 9, p. 85.

42. Weber, *Protestant Ethic*, ch. V, p. 181.

43. Weber, "Socialism", Speech for the General Information of Austrian Officers in Vienna, 1918, *Max Weber: the Interpretation of Social Reality*, ed. J.E.T. Eldridge, Michael Joseph, London, 1970, Part 2 (C)

44. Weber, "Science as a vocation", *From Max Weber*, ch. V, p. 153.

45. Weber, "Politics as a vocation", p. 128.

46. Weber, "Politics as a vocation", pp. 120–127.

47. Weber, "Science as a vocation", pp. 155–156.

Durkheim: Social Solidarity

Durkheim can be represented as a conservative, as a liberal and as a socialist. The conservative addresses the problem of order by functional and holistic arguments. The liberal criticizes individualism to identify the conditions for people to live freely in society. The socialist explores the creation of social solidarities.

Durkheim was a rationalist but not a positivist. He instructs us to treat "social facts as things."[48] They are ways of acting, which are external, general, and constraining.[49] His central concern is always with "moral facts".[50] The examples vary: division of labor, legal rules, religious beliefs and rituals, social currents; rates of crime or suicide. They are not material but social. The shared "representations which form the network of social life"[51] arise from the ways individuals and groups relate to one another and to the whole society. Durkheim appears to conflate the different meanings of "normal" as average, as obligatory, and as desirable.[52] He gives centrality to the study of moral facts, and consequently also of their abnormal forms.[53]

"Why does the individual, while becoming more autonomous, depend more upon society?"[54] The function of the division of social labor is not simply the utility of exchange but establishing a social and moral order, rooted in a collective conscience, linked to but quite different from particular consciences (as Rousseau's general will is from particular wills[55]). Society moves from mechanical to organic solidarity, from repressive to regulative law.[56] Contra Spencer, free exchange, which rests on contract, cannot be the basis of any society.[57] "For

---

48. Durkheim, *Rules of Sociological Method*, ch. 2 p. 60, "Preface to second edition".

49. Durkheim, *Rules of Sociological Method*, ch 1. p. 59.

50. Durkheim, "The determination of moral facts" [1906] in *Sociology and Philosophy*, introduction by J. G. Peristiany, Free Press, New York, 1974, pp. 49–50.

51. Durkheim, "Individual and collective representations" [1898] in *Sociology and Philosophy*, p. 24.

52. Durkheim, *Division of Labor*, Book 3; *Rules of Sociological Method*, ch. 3.

53. Durkheim, *Division of Labor*, Book 3.

54. Durkheim, *Division of Labor*, "Preface to the first edition", p. 37.

55. Jean-Jacques Rousseau, *The Social Contract* [1752], *The Social Contract and the Discourses*, introduction by G. D. H. Cole, Everyman, London, 1993, Books 1–2, esp. pp. 192, 194, 203.

56. Durkheim, *Division of Labor*, Book 1.

57. J.D.Y. Peel, *Herbert Spencer: the Evolution of a Sociologist*, Heinemann, London, 1971; Durkheim, *Division of Labor*, Book 1, ch. 6–7.

if interest relates men, it is never for more than some few moments."[58] Non-contractual relations expand with contractual relations.[59]

Specialization of knowledge and production, routinization and globalization may produce an anomic division of labor lacking adequate regulation, or insufficient integration or a division imposed by force.[60] The progress of individual personality and the division of social labor depend on each other and on regulation defined by rules, nationally and across national boundaries. Every professional activity must have its own ethics.[61] Our present need is for an equivalent of medieval corporations, adapted to modern, international economic conditions[62]: "civil society" and "co-determination?"

Suicide exemplifies the above themes. Suicides are "external to the individual," indicated by relatively stable rates over time among populations, which should be studied comparatively; "societies cannot exist if there are only individuals."[63] The distinctions among egoistic, fatalistic and anomic suicide echo the abnormal forms of the division of labor. Egoistic and fatalistic suicide arises from insufficient and excessive integration respectively; anomic suicide from inadequate regulation. We cannot live without the constraints imposed by religion, family, community, and economic change. But if suicide increases with knowledge, knowledge is not its cause but its remedy.[64] Once the destruction of accepted opinions has commenced, intelligence is our only guide.

For Durkheim, society is real, and socially constructed. We study it from without, yet the forms of our knowledge are socially constructed. The work of the sociologist is not that of the politician. But it may open out our political perspectives.

Capitalism as Cultural Revolution

Marx, Weber and Durkheim each sought to identify the distinctive features of modern capitalist society and its implications for the fate of humanity. Cap-

---

58. Durkheim, *Division of Labor*, Book 1, ch. 7, p. 203.

59. Durkheim, *Division of Labor*, Book 1, ch. 7, p. 206.

60. Durkheim, *Division of Labor*, Book 3.

61. Durkheim, *Professional Ethics and Civic Morals* [1900], Routledge, London, 1992, p. 15.

62. Durkheim, *Division of Labor*, "Preface to the second edition" [1902]

63. Durkheim, *Suicide* [1897], Routledge and Kegan Paul, London, 1952, p. 38.

64. Durkheim, *Suicide*, pp. 168–169.

italism is necessarily more than an economic system: hence the need to study its social relations. These involve new forms of the division of social labor, of exchange, contract and property, of profit-making enterprises and economic conduct. Forms of law and state, as well as religious ideas and political ideologies, are prior conditions for the generalization of commodity relations. Capitalism combines individuation with new forms of association. It generates conflict between capital and labor.

Marx and Weber both define capitalism as the separation of producers from the means of production and produce remarkably similar definitions of its origins.[65] Marx starts from a critique of the classical labor theory of value and of limiting our conceptions of society to the "sphere of circulation...of Freedom, Equality, Property and Bentham."[66] Weber responded to the neo-classical abstraction of "economic rationality" from non-economic motives.[67] Interests and economic calculations matter but are insufficient to explain the economics of labor relations in agriculture or the politics of interests. Durkheim rejects the vision, or possibility, of a society based on contract and individualism.

Capitalism, says Marx, is a form of co-operative production, which makes possible the combination and direction of means of production and labor-power within the enterprise and between enterprises. The product of co-operative work appears to be attributable to, and is made possible by, capital.[68] Skills and scientific knowledge are detached from the producer, though more general capacities and education are demanded.[69] Workers become "an appendage of a machine."[70] The force of the state creates the class of free laborers.[71] As production expands so does a diversified reserve army of labor, sustained by poor relief and available to meet the demands of labor markets.[72]

Weber observes the age-old and diverse forms of capitalistic profit making, including "booty capitalism" and "unusual transactions with political bodies."[73] "Rational capital accounting" depends on free labor, free markets and

---

65. Marx, *Capital* I, part 8; Weber, *General Economic History*, part 4.
66. Marx, *Capital*, I, ch. 6, p. 280 or CW, 35, p. 186.
67. Weber, *Economy and Society*, I, 1, ch. 2, esp. 1–4.
68. Marx, *Capital*, I, ch. 13, 19 or CW, 35; *Capital* III [1894] Penguin, Harmondsworth, 1981, ch. 48, pp. 955–967 or CW, 37, pp. 803–805.
69. Marx, *Capital*, I, ch. 14–15, esp. pp. 482, 617–619 or CW, 35, esp. pp. 366, 481–491.
70. Marx, *Capital*, I, ch. 25, p. 799 or CW, 35, p. 639.
71. Marx, *Capital*, I, ch. 31, pp. 915–916 or CW, p. 739.
72. Marx, *Capital*, I, ch. 25, pp. 781–799 or CW, pp. 623–640.
73. Weber, *Economy and Society*, I, 1, ch. 2. 31, pp. 164–166.

impersonal calculations, thus on the institutions which makes this possible. They require coercion and the "whip of hunger" as well as double-entry book-keeping, scientific enquiry and its application, and calculable rational law and administration.[74] Weber's analysis of East Elbian agriculture explored the typical range of agrarian relations within and among estates and categories of workers, with different strategies for securing independence and livelihoods.[75] These are capitalist relations, not "feudal relics."[76]

Durkheim observes that the more dependent we are on one another, the greater the scope for individual autonomy. But our liberty requires regulation and thus the growth of the state. It is threatened by economic and social crises and by the separation of capital and labor and the forcible imposition of constraint. Science, like production, becomes specialized; the individual could become "an inert piece of machinery."[77] Hence the need for new forms of social integration to facilitate the moral regulation of society.

For Durkheim, as for Marx and Weber, the starting point of exchange and contract opens the way to an understanding of the complex historical conditions that make their existence possible. The study of capitalism is a study of cultural revolution.

The Spirit of Protestantism

Marx, Weber and Durkheim all recognize the affinity between the spirit of Protestantism and of capitalism. "Accumulate, accumulate. That is Moses and the prophets."[78] Weber identifies Protestantism as the most fitting form of religion for accumulating capital. The link involves changes in ideas and in the relations of individuals to society.

Marx starts out from Feuerbach: "*Man makes religion*". Society produces religion as the consciousness of an "inverted world". Religious distress expresses and protests against real distress.[79] Marx identifies the parallels between

74. *General Economic History* [1923] Collier, New York, 1961, part 4, pp. 207–209; *Economy and Society*, I, 1, ch. 20, 30.

75. Weber, "Developmental tendencies in the situation of East Elbian rural labourers" [1894] in *Reading Weber*, ed. Keith Tribe, Routledge, London, 1989, ch. 6.

76. Philip Corrigan, "Feudal relics or capitalist monuments: some notes in the sociology of unfree labour", *Sociology*, 11, 1977, and *Social Forms/ Human Capacities*, Routledge, London, 1990, ch. 2.

77. Durkheim, *Division of Labor*, Book 3, esp. p. 371.

78. Marx, *Capital* I, ch. 24, p. 742 or CW, p. 591.

79. Marx, "Introduction", to *The Critique of Hegel's Philosophy of Law*, CW 3, 7, p. 175.

religious ideas, political institutions and the forms of economic relations. The ways in which we provide our living explain why politics dominated the ancient world, Catholicism the middle ages, and material interests the present.[80] Marx sceptically observes the spirit of Protestantism at work in the building of prisons to furnish labor.[81] His critique of political economy strips away the mysteries of the commodity and capital to reveal that "Capital is a social relation…"[82]

Weber studies Protestantism's part in the expansion of the "spirit of capitalism." Luther emphasized the calling (*Beruf*, vocation) to act in the world.[83] The Calvinist doctrine of predestination had more radical political and economic implications. It carried the "elimination of magic as a means to salvation" to its rational conclusion, confronting individuals with "unprecedented inner loneliness."[84] Calvinists can do nothing to attain salvation but only attest, to themselves and others, of their election by their daily conduct. Protestantism led to accumulation of wealth, evidence of God's blessing on the righteous, encouraged sobriety and justified incentives for workers.[85]

The high religious traditions all reject magic to some extent. The promise of salavation requires prophets to give coherent meaning "both to human life and the world."[86] "The conceptions of a transcendental unitary god" poses the problem of theodicy: how to reconcile "his power with the imperfection of the world he has created and ruled over."[87] Calvinism offers one rational solution; the Hindu doctrine of *Karma* provides "the most complete formal solution of the problem."[88] Hinduism, Buddhism and Catholicism value ascetic ideals for the few but they do not define the norms for the whole society.[89] The inner-

80. Marx, *Capital* I, ch. 1, p. 176n35 or CW, 35, pp. 92–93n1.

81. Marx, *Capital* 1, ch. 27, p. 882n9 or CW, 35, p. 712n2.

82. Marx, *Capital* 1, ch. 33, p. 932; III, ch. 48, p. 953 or CW 35, p. 753; 37, p. 801.

83. Weber, *Protestant Ethic*, ch. III.

84. Weber, *Protestant Ethic*, ch. IV. A. pp. 114, 107.

85. Weber, *Protestant Ethic*, ch. II, V; "The Protestant sects and the spirit of capitalism" [1906] *From Max Weber*, ch. 12.

86. Weber, *The Sociology of Religion*, ch. 4, p. 59 or *Economy and Society*, I, 2, ch. 6, iii, p. 450.

87. Weber, *The Sociology of Religion*, ch. 4, p. 138–139 or *Economy and Society*, I, 2, ch. 6, p. 522.

88. Weber, *The Sociology of Religion*, ch. IX, p. 145 or *Economy and Society*, I, 2, ch. 6, p. 524.

89. Weber, *The Religion of India: the sociology of Hinduism and Buddhism* [1916–1920], Free Press, New York, 1858, esp. pp. 145–154.

worldly Confucian ethic of the literati adapts both to patrimonial rule and the cosmic order.[90] Protestantism takes asceticism into the world and has shaped a new capitalist order beyond its intentions, expectations or control.

Durkheim explains the higher suicide rates among Protestants than among Catholics or among Jews by their relative lack of common beliefs and practices and the spirit of free inquiry. Religious society, not doctrine, protects people.[91] If society is founded on a collective conscience, then we must find its foundations in religious life. Drawing on ethnographies of Australian peoples, Durkheim seeks out the "collective representations" by which we define and classify our societies and construct our forms of understanding.[92] Contrary to the ideas of the Enlightenment, he argued that religious beliefs are not illusory, nor are they privileged. The fundamental categories of thought are of religious origin; this is true of science, as it is true of magic, and also of moral and legal rules.[93] Religious experience is grounded not in the intuitions of the faithful but in society itself: religion is "in its image".[94] Consequently, the foundations of knowledge are not a priori presuppositions but collective representations.[95] "Social life embraces at once both representations and practices,"[96] the Kantian duality of scientific thought and moral reasoning is resolved by recognising their common origins in society itself.

Marx, Weber and Durkheim accept and criticize the assumptions of the Enlightenment. Marx looks to a new society to bury the old gods. Weber and Durkheim look for new sources of creativity to replace them.

The State as a Social Fact

Marx, Weber, and Durkheim are all concerned to find a source of political leadership to address the problems of capitalist society. "Every state is founded on force"[97] but also on its claims to legitimate authority and the support of powerful interests. It provides an essential framework of moral reg-

---

90. Weber, *The Religion in China* [1916–1920], Free Press, New York, 1858, Free Press, New York, 1951, ch V, VI, VIII.

91. Durkheim, *Suicide*, ch. 2, p. 170.

92. Durkheim, *Elementary Forms of Religious Life* [1912], George Allen and Unwin, London, 1964, esp. "Introduction".

93. Durkheim, *Elementary Forms*, pp. 417–419.

94. Durkheim, *Elementary Forms*, p. 421.

95. Durkheim, *Elementary Forms*, pp. 15–16, 431–447.

96. Durkheim, *Elementary Forms*, p. 456.

97. Leon Trotsky, cited Weber, "Politics as a vocation", p. 78.

ulation and is an instrument of class and other interests. They need access to the state, which shapes their political organization and alliances. The state reconciles and represents the particular interests as the interests of the whole society. It acts through its agents, who may use its policies and resources for their own ends.

"The executive of the *modern* State is but a committee for the management of the *common* affairs of the *whole* bourgeoisie."[98] Neither instrumental nor functionalist interpretations reflect these insights. The separation of the secular political state from civil society epitomizes political alienation. The bourgeoisie failed to carry through the 1848 political revolution. It was divided by it own conflicting interests and in conflict with a working class. It retreated behind to the "party of Order".[99] The peasantry is parochial and the bureaucracy self-interested. These are features of all capitalist states not just of France between 1848 and 1852. The state disciplines workers and also capitalists. Reflecting on the experience of the Paris Commune, Marx remarks that "the proletariat cannot lay hold on the ready-made state apparatus and wield it for their own purposes."[100]

Weber was committed to the power interests of the state and the social unification of the nation. The Junkers, bourgeoisie, Catholics and their parties were all unable to transcend their interests sufficiently to provide political leadership, as was socialism, with its bureaucratic impulses. Marxism has more to fear from the expansion of the Social Democratic Party than from bourgeois society. Modern bureaucracy provides the most technically efficient form of administration but constrains initiative.[101] Politics must find a material base in those who live "for politics" or, as party employees or machine politicians, "off politics".[102] Political action demands the acceptance of responsibility for the consequences of action.

As the division of labor progresses, so does the scope of the state. The state is a group of officials *sui generis* within which representations and acts of volition involving the collectivity are worked out."[103] It is separate from the rest of society and its claims over the individual: it "sets [moral individuality]

---

98. Marx and Engels, *Manifesto of the Communist Party*, CW 6, p. 486.

99. Marx, *Class Struggles in France CW* 10, 6; *The Eighteenth Brumaire CW* 12, 3.

100. Marx, "Second draft of *The Civil War in France*", 6. "The Commune" *CW*, 22, p. 533.

101. Weber, "Bureaucracy" *From Max Weber*, pp. 214–216; *Economy and Society*, pp. 973–980.

102. Weber, 'Politics as a vocation', pp. 84–87.

103. Durkheim, *Professional Ethics*.

free."[104] Democracy is not "the political form of a society governing itself," nor should it be. It "is a system based on reflection."[105] The moral regulation of society requires groups, with their own professional ethics, between the state and the individual, not least in the economic order. If each state promotes the moral life of its citizens, national and world patriotism will be aligned with rather than opposed to one another. State formation is a continuing process of "moral regulation."[106]

The state is a social fact. It is external to each of us, extends beyond its separate institutions and certainly constrains. But it is not a thing. It is an idea; the idea of the state is the collective misrepresentation of capitalist societies.[107]

Explaining Society, History, and the Future

Marx, Weber and Durkheim view society not from the end of history but from the middle. They reject individualist accounts of the origins of capitalism and share the conception of history as progressive change. But they each interpret its dynamics, direction, and fate differently. Each addresses the global problem of modernity.

Marx aims to found communism in empirical analysis rather than utopian speculation. His metaphors of base and superstructure and of the contradictions between productive forces and relations provide him with a theory of society and a motor of history. The bourgeoisie "creates a world after its own image."[108] So will the proletariat. Marx "treats the social movement as a process of natural history"[109] but also observes that Darwin kills off "'teleology' in the natural sciences."[110] Marx responds ambiguously when asked if Russia must follow the path of capitalism to arrive at socialism, but explicitly rejects any "supra-historical theory," which must necessarily stand outside his-

---

104. Durkheim, *Professional Ethics*, pp. 68–69.

105. Durkheim, *Professional Ethics*.

106. Philip Corrigan and Derek Sayer, *The Great Arch: State Formation as Moral Regulation*, Blackwells, 1985.

107. Philip Abrams, "Some notes on the difficulty of studying the state" [1977], *Journal of Historical Sociology*, I, 1988.

108. Marx and Engels, *Manifesto of the Communist Party*, CW 6, p. 488.

109. I.I. Kaufmann, cited Marx, "Afterword to the Second German edition" [1873] of *Capital* I, p.107 or *CW*, 35, p. 18.

110. Marx, Letter to Lasalle, 16 Jan. 1861, *CW*, 41, 146, p. 247.

tory.[111] Marx outlines the "original accumulation of capital" and proceeds to declaim the "expropriation of the expropriated" to realize freely the capacities of social labor.[112] The problems of why the denouement of capitalism should be realized and of putting communist politics into practice remained unresolved.

For Weber, rationalization is specific to the West and contingent on complex religious, economic and political developments. It redefined modes of thought and social institutions, and their relations. Commerce strengthened prebendalism in patrimonial states. In China, the interests of patrimonial rulers and the literati and the Confucian ethic precluded capitalist development.[113] Weber's account of the economic and political origins and nature of capitalism is similar to Marx's, but his view of the future is more sceptical and determinist. It develops within and is tied to the fate of the nation state and market economy. Rationalization appears inexorable.

Durkheim contests the explanation of the progress of the division of labor in "man's unceasing desire to increase happiness"[114] in favor of material and moral densities, which multiply relations among people. As the collective conscience extends and becomes more abstract and the idea of God more transcendent, law, morality, and civilization "more rational."[115] The division of labor may prove to be anomic or forced; hence the need for new forms of moral regulation, founded in justice and equity, which makes individual autonomy possible.

Positivists bridge the gap between fact and value by establishing general laws, which can be inform the realization of political goals. Evolutionary theories provide a handle on the future. For St. Simon and Comte, knowledge was power. For Marx, the point was to change the world,[116] opening the issue of the relation of intellectuals to the working class. Weber and Durkheim were concerned with politics/policy, and insisted that political action required coming to terms with modern society. Durkheim insisted that reflection and knowledge could enable us to direct social change. For Weber "the knowledge of causal *laws* is not the *end* of an investigation but only a *means*."[117] Generalizations rest on homologies, not analogies. They cannot be applied by pol-

---

111. Marx, Letter to *Otechestvenniye Zapiski* (ed. N.R. Michailokvski, Nov. 1877, *CW*, 24, 17, p. 201.

112. Marx, *Capital* 1, part 8, ch. 25–32 or CW, 35.

113. Weber, *Religion in China*, parts 1 and 2.

114. Durkheim, *Division of Labor*, Book 2, ch. 2, p. 233.

115. Durkheim, *Division of Labor*, Book 2, ch. 3, p. 290.

116. Marx, *Theses on Feuerbach*, XI, *CW*, 3, p. 5.

117. Weber, "Objectivity in social sciences", p. 80.

icy makers to prescribe answers to questions of policy. [118] And in their subject matter and preconceptions, "history and sociology are and always have been the same thing."[119]

---

118. Gavin Williams, Brian Williams and Roy Williams, "History and sociological explanation", *African Sociological Review*, 1, 2, 1998.

119. Philip Abrams, *Historical Sociology*, Open Books, Bath, 1982, p. x.

CHAPTER 26

AT THE *BARAZA*: SOCIALIZING AND INTELLECTUAL PRACTICE AT THE SWAHILI COAST

Kai Kresse[1]

Introduction

This essay seeks to portray and reflect upon an informal institution in the urban environment of Swahili neighborhoods, the *baraza*. Literally referring to the common stone bench built at the front of Swahili houses, a venue for meetings, *baraza* is also the name for the male groups of neighbors and friends that can be seen sitting together in the evenings, constituting a regular feature of street life. *Barazas*[2] historically have been significant venues of urban communication along the Swahili coast. Observing them may reveal the internal dynamics of social, political, and intellectual discourse. Yet despite their im-

---

1. I would like to thank J.D.Y. Peel for his advice on the wider research project to which this paper is related (Kresse 2002). Fieldwork in Mombasa was undertaken between August 1998 and September 1999, and supported by funds from the DAAD (HSP3) and SOAS. I am also most grateful to my friends and informants in Kibokoni, through whom I learned much (more than I could express here) during many *baraza* experiences. Different versions of this paper were presented at the Anthropology departments of Cornell University and Edinburgh University, in September and October 2003. I thank the organizers of both events for inviting me, and the audiences for their comments. In many ways this paper marks little more than a starting point, which can be followed up further ethnographically and theoretically. Yet I think that the contextualized research perspective I sketch out here may have some innovative and comparative value within the wider field of African Studies.

2. For the convenience of reading in an English-language text, I am creating a plural form adding an '–s' to the Swahili word.

portance in Swahili social life, hardly anything has been published on *barazas*. In this essay I describe socializing and intellectual practice in Swahili everyday life as it revolves around the *baraza*. But also, an argument is made for ethnographic and interdisciplinary research on philosophical discourse in Africa through a focus on the *baraza*, or similar institutions or venues for social debate. There are comparable settings elsewhere in Africa, which could be fruitfully discussed in comparison; the same applies to descriptions of relevant individuals and discursive fields, developed with historical, literary, or anthropological focus. Such comparative research would be particularly promising when conducted with an emphasis on the internal dynamics of regional discourses, the specificity of voices engaged in them, and the internal diversity of standpoints and arguments.

Taking these issues carefully into account, within a focus on specific events, forces the researcher to cover, and come to terms with, the "tiresome historicity" of their constitutive factors (Peel 1983: 15). J.D.Y. Peel's work has illustrated, among other things, the importance and merit of focusing on historical specifics in relation to texts, discourses, and events, as communicators and facilitators of social change. His work has also underlined the value of basing one's historical assessment of social processes on indigenous accounts in African languages (Peel 1983, 2000a), and he enforces the point that these sources should play a significant part in social portrayals, documentations, and reconstructions of African history, whether that of recent or earlier times. Peel also reminds us of the need to include in the envisaged audience those African subjects who are part of, or belong to, the regional narrative that is portrayed. They are major potential addressees whose judgment the social researcher should seek (cf. Peel 1983: ix). Having this in mind can also provide a writing focus assisting the researcher to keep anthropological and historical accounts compatible, so that interdisciplinary cross-references are facilitated within scholarship and, perhaps more importantly, that they may be drawn upon within the society concerned. This essay draws inspiration from these points pushed by Peel's work.[3]

---

3. Of course, in terms of region, there is a multitude of possible fields for comparative research between the Swahili and Yoruba contexts – such as religious encounters (in various forms), the history of city states, with sub-groups being shaped into a larger unity, tensions with other groups in a postcolonial nation state, and many more (for city-states, see e.g. Peel 2000b and Sinclair/Hakansson 2000). But these cannot be treated here, where my concern is to introduce the Swahili *baraza*, contextualize it within a perspective that focuses on the social dynamics of knowledge and is interested in philosophical discourse as social practice in everyday life.

The Swahili Context: Muslim Urban Communities and Islamic Debates

The Swahili coast has been part of the Muslim world for more than a millennium. Archaelogical evidence shows that Muslims have lived in this area since about 800 C.E., relatively soon after the emergence of Islam itself (Horton/Middleton 2000). Kiswahili, the Swahili language, emerged during the same period as a Bantu language (Nurse/Spear 1985). Local interpretations and practices of Islam have been central features in social life along the East African coast as far back as can be remembered. Maybe this is why the term "Swahili Islam" has often been used in academic accounts, implying—somewhat inadequately—a homogeneous and static religious understanding within the region. The term usually refers to the dominant local group of the twentieth century, belonging to the Shafii school of the Sunni Muslims, in which ancient Hadrami networks and *masharifu* families with Sufi orientation play a major role. Swahili urban communities have historically been city states. The ruling clans characterized themselves as of Arab or Persian ("Shirazi") ancestry, with reference to legends and genealogies. Thus Swahili society is something of a long-grown amalgam of people of different ethnic origins, from the African hinterland or the interior, or from the Indian Ocean region, through channels of trading, slavery, and serfdom. They were integrated into a society which nominally adhered to a strict hierarchical ideology of status and descent, but which nevertheless was rather open, as it was reliant on outsiders for various forms of labor and trade.[4]

One of the most interesting aspects to observe during fieldwork was the negotiation and debate about Islamic knowledge, which was observable in many instances of everyday life, about what should count as the correct Islamic way of doing things, and by what reasoning. There existed a discursive pluralism which could be explored in many directions. In Mombasa, as along the Swahili coast on the whole, there are competing interpretations and positions on this, linked to various local Muslim communities and active Islamic factions. Partly, these groups are of external origin and still funded from abroad. In this sense, East Africa, like other peripheral Muslim regions in the world, is something of a playing field for powerful Islamic interest groups from the Middle East (Saudi Arabia, Egypt, Kuwait, Pakistan, Iran, and others). But it would be wrong to assume that East African Muslims were simply passively used by

---

4. See e.g. Willis (1993).

those groups and their interests. The benefits are mutual, as personal careers as Islamic scholars are linked to factional affiliations. In this way, religious education, further studies, positions of employment, influence, and social prestige are secured.

There is, then, an ongoing power struggle in regard to the locally dominant understanding of "Islamic knowledge." For the last half century, this has been documented partly from within, in Kiswahili, through the publication of religious leaflets, pamphlets, and poetry. These reflect the dynamics of local critical discourse in the region, or what the philosopher Paulin Hountondji called "internal pluralism" (and marked as a starting-point for investigation on African philosophy):[5] a regionally and culturally rooted debate in which people with diverging standpoints seek to convince each other of the superiority of their arguments. Such debate is observable not only in printed publications, but also in everyday discourse—in speeches (*hotuba*) before the Friday prayers, in lectures by Islamic scholars during Ramadhan, or even during the daily discussions of news among friends and neighbors at their regular meeting points, the *baraza* benches in front of the houses. All of these instances can be followed as pathways for research into the local discursive dynamics on a wider scale.[6]

This essay follows one pathway, the *baraza* meetings of male groups of friends and neighbors. They take place in public street life, usually directly in front of houses or otherwise in local cafes or tea houses (*hoteli*). My main focus here is on the social dynamics of this discursive practice. As I introduce the *baraza* as a common social institution, and provide examples of the range of subjects and topics debated (as well as ways in which they are treated), I seek to make understandable some of the fascination that *baraza* venues hold for social research. During my fieldwork, I spent most of my evenings in my neighborhood in the Old Town of Mombasa sitting in at several *baraza* congregations where I was welcome; they were groups of older and younger men, neighbors, friends, and local intellectuals in slightly different settings. In the following, I will recount some observations on the *baraza* as a social and discursive setting that, through the way in which it creates opportunity for serious and open-ended discussion, also facilitates conversations of a philosophical nature (i.e., it may sometimes lead to them). Characterizing such instances, I will connect them to some reflections on what Kant's called the "worldly" conception of philosophy. In conclusion, I will briefly link these re-

---

5. Hountondji 1996: 165. (cf. the whole Chapter 6).
6. See Kresse (2002a) for an example of this, within a larger research framework.

flections to some recent works in African studies which can be read and discussed from a comparable angle.[7]

The main task here is to introduce the informal social institution of the *baraza* in everyday street life in Mombasa's Old Town. I will sketch out how the *baraza* gatherings work, and how "knowledge" plays a central role in the way that socializing takes place there. The transmission, exchange, negotiation, and questioning of knowledge is at the heart of social activity in these groups, and for research that is interested in documenting the living practice of Swahili philosophical discourse, the awareness about and reflection on *baraza* communication is a meaningful and important starting point.

Barazani, in Mombasa's Old Town

Swahili social life offers many public or semi-public opportunities for informal talks and discussions, especially for the men. In the Old Town of Mombasa, every evening groups of younger and older men meet up, sitting on wooden benches around a coffee seller in the street, or on the stone benches outside a house or mosque. They meet mostly according to age groups, preferably before sunset, that is before *magharibi*-prayers, or after the *isha*-prayers, at around 8 PM. This is a more or less regular daily practice of exchanging the news of the day (local, national, and global), discussing and interpreting them, and reflecting upon them, and also on other stories and issues that may be brought up. It is also, of course, recreational chatting. The locality of the meeting or the group of people gathered there, are called *baraza*.[8] Literally, *baraza* refers to a bench or verandah in front of a house, often (and originally) integrated into the outside wall. *Barazani* is the locative form of this noun, denoting the *baraza* as a place, and thus means "at the *baraza*." The *baraza* is the common and regular place provided for men, to rest and chat informally with neighbors and friends, without retreating into the privacy of the house. The *baraza* is a historical component of Swahili domestic architecture, and

---

7. This is part of a wider research project, an 'anthropology of philosophy'. Elsewhere I have outlined this in more detail vis-à-vis the African philosophical debate, and pursued systematically for the Swahili context (Kresse 2002a, 2002b).

8. The term *baraza* has also commonly come to be used for public political meetings and rallies all over Kenya (see e.g. Haugerud 1997). In Mombasa, this kind of use is rare but occurs for instance in the title of special public meetings or receptions. In Tanzania, due to its postcolonial history of socialism and a one-party state, *baraza*s often have an explicit political character, most prominently as the local meeting points for members of the CCM party.

also provides illustration of how space largely continues to be gendered, as the women, particularly those of high social status, have historically been confined to the area within the house. [9]

The *baraza* is an informal institution of practiced sociality in the neighborhood, expressing and reconfirming social ties between the male members of the families living in the street, or the town quarter (*mtaa*; pl.: *mitaa*) to which the street belongs; commonly families have lived in their *mtaa* for more than one generation. The quarters, *mitaa*, were historically constituted along the lines of clan and class, though this was never a totally closed system. Social status or occupation would determine the particular area of residence of an individual. A *mtaa* could be inhabited by established patrician trading families of high social status (*waungwana*), offspring of early influential refugee groups from along the coast, of lower class fishers or coconut tappers, or of former slave families (cf. Berg 1971). Each group was differently integrated into the urban society, creating the diverse internal character for which Swahili towns are well known. The *mitaa* were often at the heart of internal rivalries within Mombasa and other Swahili towns, similar to the historic rivalries between the city-states of the Swahili coast on a larger level. Expressions of these rivalries in popular culture, e.g. through the formation of dance and cultural associations or sport clubs, have been richly documented for the social history of the Swahili coast and Mombasa in particular (e.g. Ranger 1974, Kindy 1972, Strobel 1979, Fair 2001, Willis 1993). These accounts illustrate the complex internal vitality of Swahili city life, and up to now the alliances and groupings described play an important role in everyday life, even though *mitaa* are by no means homogeneous.

At *baraza* meetings, for instance, these factors play a role in the build-up of and the communication patterns within the *baraza*. *Barazas* are constituted through small peer groups, neighbors, relatives, age groups. Additional features such as common interests, religious affiliation, linguistic identity, and political views, play an important role as well. These variables determine the topics of conversation and the ways they are treated by the participants, usually about five to six people. Conflicting views and discussions arise soon, about any topic; and what is said and how it is said by the participating individuals provides us with much information about local knowledge, and knowledge about knowledge. We are provided with clues as to what is commonly shared social knowledge, what is contested, how and

---

9. That space inside the house is also often conceived of as the women's sphere. Female friends and neighbours usually visit each other, or meet up in groups, at their homes. This has been documented by various researchers, and here I will not follow this up further.

why, how individuals express their support or disapproval of certain assumptions, how discussions are led, and how the complex dynamics between individuals and social knowledge work. Viewed with an anthropological interest in "knowledge," *barazas* can be said to be all about knowledge, its contestation, and about intellectual practices and discursive strategies followed by individuals to defend or question claims to knowledge that have previously been made.

Meetings begin with exchanging opinions on the events of the day, and this sometimes leads to discussions or lively arguments on any conceivable topic. I was present at discussions on the existence of spirits (*pepo* or *majini*), on the permissibility of *dhikri* (Sufi invocations of God), on corruption, on national and global politics, on the interpretation of the Qur'an, and many others. Friends tell jokes and tease each other. The latest news and the newest gossip is passed around. Football results are discussed with vigor by young men who are more likely supporters of Manchester United, Bayern Munich, or Barcelona than of the local Mombasa Coast Stars. On days before and after big matches, lively discussions and serious arguments may go on for hours.

Baraza culture has been part of Mombasa and other Swahili towns for many centuries. Portuguese sources of the early sixteenth century already remarked that "nearly every house had a stone bench built out in front of it," making the narrow streets with up to three-storey-high houses feel even narrower (cf. Strandes 1961: 79). Though the basic communicative aspect of the *baraza* has persisted over time, its social function has changed, at least in two respects. Until the British takeover of political administration in 1895, it was part of the wider political system of Mombasa, in which each of the twelve hereditary sheikhs of the Twelve Tribes represented his area of influence. Each sheikh consulted and communicated with the elders of the *mitaa*, and these neighborhood representatives surely used their *barazas* for meetings at the level of local politics (Berg 1971). Only a few decades ago, some highly reputed *barazas* were still notable for their specific intellectual character and interest. As meeting points of knowledgeable elders (*wazee*), but open to a wider audience (i.e. those who were accepted to listen in), these were educational sites or even, in some respects, local "institutions" of higher learning.[10] Here, educational folk stories, fables, myths and legends were related and discussed. Moreover, the *baraza* was the setting of a competition of wit, as participants were challenged with riddles, spoken in poetic or other cryptic forms.

---

10. Sheikh Yahya Ali Omar, a Swahili intellectual living in London, likened such kind of *baraza* to a 'Swahili university'. Personal communication, July 2001.

Nowadays, there are hardly any exclusive intellectual or political *barazas* left. Even the informal *barazas* of today are somewhat exclusive, although in a different sense. They are friendly gatherings of people of the neighborhood, consisting of regular members and their friends who are invited to participate. They are not, by common understanding, open meetings where everyone is free or welcome to join in. This is naturally so, as a certain level of privacy and mutual trust is needed in order to freely carry on conversations across such a range of topics. The extent of openness can also be influenced by economic interests in some cases, as coffee-selling *barazas* or similar meetings in tea houses are open to new customers. But there is always a core of regulars, dominating the group dynamics, and determining topics and style of discussion.

We find, for example, a group of Swahili-speaking Shia Ithnashari Muslims, of Swahili, Indian, and Persian background, who have their regular meeting point in the café of a Bohra friend, to converse about daily events. Or, there are some young men meeting up with their friend Omari at "his" *baraza*. As a coffee seller who brews and sells his coffee at his particular spot in the street, Omari would set up two or three simple wooden benches for his customers every evening, serving coffee cheaply (two or three shillings)[11] so that his friends could afford to sip one on the side while the evening's topics would be opened up and followed around.

One evening I sat in on Omari's *baraza*, when the UEFA-Cup Champion's league games of the previous night had just been covered by the football specialists present (and they were a passionate lot about this). The mood changed when a small group of young men known to those present stopped by and joined the *baraza* to have a coffee. They were on their way to *maulidi* recitations at a mosque nearby, as the month of *maulidi* celebrations commemorating the birth of the Prophet, had already started. As they mentioned where they were going, one of the young men sitting asked them whether they didn't know that it wasn't right or proper for them as good Muslims to celebrate *maulidi*. At this point it wasn't clear whether the speaker might be teasing them, imitating local reformist activists who watch over the propriety of local Muslim practices. Locally denounced as "*Wahhabi*," these reformists attack practices which they see as *bid'a*—unduly innovative in relation to the paradigmatic life of the Prophet whose own behavior provides the path (*sunnah*) for all other Muslims to follow.[12] Once this young man had raised this ques-

---

11. At the time, one shilling was roughly worth 1pence of British currency.

12. Such reformist activism has become very influential during the 1990s, but has a longer dynamic history to it. I have discussed related aspects in more detail elsewhere (Kresse 2003).

tion, several others tried to respond immediately. One supported his stance, saying that yes, the older generation was simply wrong when claiming that *maulidi* was celebrated equally all over the Muslim world; he said these celebrations should be seen as a local aberration (which is what he had heard the imam say), and that local Muslims should find their way back to the proper path. Another disagreed and said no, the *maulidi* celebrations were indeed a proper and pious way to show one's love and respect for the Prophet. The ceremonies consisted in nothing but praise for the impeccable example of Prophet Muhammad, they were performed by people driven to emulate his doings, and furthermore, they brought the community together and reconfirmed its unity. But then another interjected critically, "What unity? Nowadays there is nothing but infighting and mutual attacks on this issue of *maulidi*. We don't have unity anymore. We only have a shouting match between two parties, and many of us don't know at all what is right anymore." Others agreed, nodding their heads, one saying that he envied his parents who (as he thought) lived during a time when this split had not yet dominated the Muslim community. By now, the small group on their way to the *maulidi* had finished coffee and gone on their way, while they left the *baraza* going on for much longer about this argument, reflecting crucial issues for Muslim identity in the Swahili region.[13] Now, this is not an example of intellectual discourse in any emphatic sense. Nevertheless it provides some illustration of common discursive dynamics and themes of discussion in the neighborhood.

During *baraza* talks, other serious issues may also be raised, most commonly in regard to politics or religious practice. Discussions that I attended centered around questions such as whether or not the mayor of Mombasa was right in stepping down, claiming that most of his councilors were being paid by a local tycoon, his biggest political foe, to undermine his policies. Or, they might have been about whether and why the Sufi practice of *dhikri* was *bid'a* (unduly innovative) or even *haramu* (sinful) according to Islamic judgments. Such discussions could be sparked off by remarks on a story that someone told (e.g. whether it was believable or not), and they could turn into long, heated arguments. This could be so for younger as well as for older age groups, though the older would usually have a more sober or humorous tone. Therefore, it can be said that the semi-private yet semi-public sphere of the *baraza* is also a delicate and ambiguous meeting point for conversation which can test the bonds of common interests and mutual trust that brought the group together. Thus, while friendships are developed and confirmed in *baraza* meet-

---

13. This is an edited account, emphasizing some of the typical features in the dispute.

ings, in some cases trust and friendship can also be broken up in relation to events taking place at a neighborhood *baraza*.

From my experience of the more serious, politically or religiously focused *baraza* discussions, two prototypical kinds of thinkers can be distinguished, separate from the rather quiet and receptive majority. They are firstly the intelligent, sharp-minded and fast-speaking agitator, and secondly the calm, reflective mediator. The first type is a talker who tries hard to get his listeners to support his views, to bring home an apparently "very clear" point, often in a populist manner, referring to a one-dimensional framework of reasons ("of course, the mayor was wrong because he gave in to corruption and bribery...," "*dhikri* is obviously *haramu* because it constitutes *shirk*..."). He is likely to associate himself with a "higher" standpoint of moral and religious integrity, and may well antagonize those in the group who do not show ready agreement with him. This ideological manner of speaking is commonly utilized in public religious speeches such as the *hotuba* (speech) before the Friday prayers. The second type, often the senior person around, is more interested in minimizing the differences within the group by pointing at a common basis of understanding, mediating controversies with an eye to something like a framework of general acceptability within the group. He shows a more reflective and questioning attitude, and is often at pains to point out the difficulty of a question or the reality of a problem, before volunteering his suggestions to solve it. He takes into account the possible validity of apparently conflicting claims, and weighs the extent to which they have to be taken seriously. This critical, reflexive way of formulating thoughts on a controversial or ambiguous issue, implies the responsibility of questioning oneself and the risk of making oneself vulnerable to others (by not readily subscribing to commonly accepted stereotypes of explanation or behavior) just as well as the possibility of mediating a conflict. Maybe because of this, thinkers of this second type are more rarely found, or, few people have the courage and self confidence to present themselves as such to an audience. But they are also much respected by a broader variety of people, even if only for their rhetorical mediating skills.

In any case, what a view on Swahili *baraza* culture shows is that reasoning, rhetoric, ideology, critical thinking, questioning and engaged debates in various fields, are acknowledged intellectual activities that are by no means the privileged resorts of intellectuals only. They are part of everyday street life in Mombasa. Everyone is a thinker, at least partly, and reflection upon knowledge and practice (or, various areas of knowledge and practices) that are usually taken for granted is part of many people's everyday life. In this way, the *baraza* hosts and enhances intellectual activity next to other social activities. Intellectual activity here is constituted in communication and social interaction among peers, in speech and oral skills, and mostly initiated situationally in relation to locally relevant events. People of the neighborhood, friends, peers, gather together in order to talk—and thereby to think—things over.

The Place of "Socializing Intellectual Practice"

The expressions "socializing" and "intellectual practice" used in the title of this essay can be joined together, to create a phrase that means to capture all the elements just mentioned. The Swahili *baraza* is, if you want, a historically grown and regionally distinct institution of "socializing intellectual practice." *Baraza* meetings cannot be properly understood without reference to the processes of dissemination and negotiation of knowledge that are going on from day to day, between people who know each other well. With this I mean that the intellectual character is a significant and crucial element of *baraza* communication, even if it is not always dominant, as simple chitchat, gossip, and the mutual exchange of news feature prominently as well. We can see the *baraza* as a common platform for Swahili men, regular people as well as qualified local intellectuals, to congregate together to reflect on their common problems of life. In an informal setting, within networks of usually long-standing and established social relationships, people exchange views and think things over, variously disagreeing and agreeing at different stages of the process. The *baraza* is an everyday venue which is constituted by individuals who perform a locally established practice of socializing in which testing and solidifying one's intellectual (and rhetorical) capacities in interaction with one's peers plays a central role.

As already stated, the *baraza* is often (though not exclusively) a meeting point between people of different intellectual levels or capacities: knowledge is passed on, disseminated, and created—but also questioned and challenged. In a (semi-)public sphere of Swahili street culture which again is dominated by sets of wider neighborhood and kin relationships, questions of proper behavior and issues of adequate principles of orientation in life are raised and followed. As a relevant and daily ongoing discourse internal to society, what concerns us all (in terms of the community, neighborhood, interest group, or kin) is put before the group to be negotiated or clarified, starting from everyday observations to more profound questions. Issues are raised, commented upon, discussed, agreed upon (or not), and set aside. This sort of discourse points at the parallel dimensions at work in such communications: next to "killing time" and simply relating to each other by verbal interaction, the potential of the *baraza* to help mediate conflict resolution should also be kept in mind. This may be distinct from the theoretically oriented, but possibly practically motivated, urge for clarification of the basic principles for orientation in life; the latter, again, may be called "philosophical," if philosophy is understood as the activity of reflecting on the basic fundamentals of one's thinking, knowing, and doing.[14]

Socializing with a concern for knowledge at the *baraza* may often bring with it a particular structure and a social order of discourse: there may be an implicit hierarchy within the group, which affects much of the communication. This hierarchy could run along the lines of social status, but also according to people's acknowledged status in relation to "knowledge" or "wisdom." There may be a seating order, a speaking order (who speaks when, why, and how), and rules of communication for any established *baraza* group (how one addresses others, puts forward opinions, arguments etc., and why) .[15] The *baraza* is a common social venue for the "negotiation of knowledge." Rather than supporting, or building up, particular schools of knowledge or knowledge systems, various (currently relevant) issues are brought up, commented upon, discussed, and then laid aside. If participants may push vehemently for their own viewpoint in discussion, *barazas* are not usually instrumented by individuals, even if they are socially powerful or dominant. As an informal institution in Swahili society, the *baraza* is a forum for communication and discussion, and decisively not accepted as a means to push certain substantive agendas or to achieve ideological dominance. Perhaps there is an implicit assumption in play about the participation of communicative actors: despite the variety of social factors that leads to the constitution of different *baraza* groups, these groups are principally never closed off, and it seemed to me that even if internal hierarchies could be discerned within the group, this did not oblige "weaker" participants to comply with the opinions of dominant patrons. In fact, disagreeing with other speakers at the *baraza* sometimes seems like a cherished moment for participants, acceptable to the others, and people often take up the chance to develop a counterargument. At the bottom of it all, we may then have a kind of general rule within *baraza* culture, stating that all participants have a principal right to talk and voice their concerns and opinions on any issue being discussed – despite existent internal hierarchies.

---

14. This definition of philosophy (taken from Schnädelbach 1988: 215) is useful for my purposes here. It offers a concise, accessible, and culturally widely applicable characterization, and can be situated in empirical contexts as a socialized, and socializing, human activity.

15. These may also be relevant factors for further investigation, for which the ethnography of speaking may provide valuable insight.

Links to a "Worldly" Conception of Philosophy

Thus in Swahili *baraza* discourse, "knowledge" is never completely given. It is constantly the object of dynamic discussion and negotiation; for each of these processes of discussion, knowledge can never be more than a given task, as something to be aimed for, something to be achieved, ultimately. The incompleteness of knowledge in *baraza* communication, the fact that knowledge is only ever a task in processes of discussion and analysis, provides us with the link to an age-old conception of philosophy which may still be of value for us when we seek to investigate philosophy as social practice (in African contexts or anywhere else). I refer to what Immanuel Kant long ago characterized as the "worldly" conception of philosophy (*Philosophie im Weltbegriff*). [16]

For Kant, this reflexive *Weltbegriff* stands for the original "basis" of the meaning of the term "philosophy." In contrast and overall in complementary position to the doctrinal "scholarly" conception of philosophy (*Philosophie im Schulbegriff*) signifying a system of knowledge, it refers to those fundamental areas of knowledge which are of "necessary interest to everyone."[17] It is here that genuinely creative philosophical work takes place, namely "philosophizing," where a "doctrine of wisdom" is formulated by the thinking individual. Worldly is used specifically to emphasize that here the knowledge specialist is not privileged over the common man: philosophical questions are principally of equal concern to all of us, and crucial innovative ideas are not necessarily initiated from within the scholarly realm. Unlike the historical scholarly knowledge, philosophizing in this sense cannot really be taught since it "can be learned only through practice and the use of one's own reason." This is why Kant concludes that philosophy, in the "true sense," is never a given (*gegeben*) but only ever given as a task (*aufgegeben*). Everyone may have something to contribute to the ongoing project of philosophy which at the bottom of it is concerned with questions of basic orientation in life that concern us all as human beings.

Following from this, there are two respects in which Kant's characterization of philosophy with its internal subdivision can be used to provide orientation for an anthropology of philosophy: first, the "scholarly" aspect may help

---

16. Kant develops his distinction between the *Weltbegriff* and the *Schulbegriff* of philosophy, which in their interrelationship covers philosophy as a whole, mainly in two different parts of his work, which I refer here: his *Critique of Pure Reason* (1930: 753–755; KrV B866–868) and *Logic* (1974: 25–30).

17. Kant 1990: 701; KrV B867, footnote.

to identify and study local schools of thought which are themselves socially and historically situated (and possibly institutionalized); second, the "worldly" aspect may assist to document and discuss critical and innovative ideas for orientation in life, as expressed by individual thinkers in their specific socio-historic contexts and in relation to their intellectual environments. Overall, the heart of philosophical activity is taken to lie in the potential of individuals as self-reliant, critical thinkers to deal creatively with fundamental questions of orientation, and to express and communicate their thoughts to others. As such, philosophy is open and potentially meaningful to all human beings, in all cultures and societies. [18]

Looking back, the Swahili *baraza* may be seen as an almost prototypical setting that provides a stage for the performance of philosophical discourse as social practice, along the lines of Kant's *Weltbegriff.* Within the respective social setting, philosophical discourse addresses fundamental questions common to the members of the human community, and anyone with a good point in reflecting on such issues may bring forward their contribution towards clarifying them. No one has, per se, a privileged access for succeeding in doing so, neither by social status nor by scholarly qualification. Such gathering points for discursive interaction and reflection on common problems may thus, over time, become recognized as informal institutions which are likely to assist in solving social problems, mediate and resolve conflicts within the neighborhood, and provide useful orientation for the community in times of political unrest, or economic dire straits. Perhaps this is one reason for the continuous existence and social relevance of *barazas* along the Swahili coast. [19]

Links to Research on African Practices of Philosophy

What we have seen here is a social setting, publicly accessible, yet with restricted participation, in which discussions and debates on a variety of issues

---

18. These considerations also show that the idea of an anthropological investigation into the forms and positions of philosophical discourse outside of the Western paradigm does not go against the grain of major schools of thought within the history of Western philosophy —even if, as has been pointed out, these did have a Eurocentric and sometimes even a racist bias (cf. Eze 1997a, 1997b). As systematic inquiry, it can be supported from there.

19. As stated above, *barazas* were already a distinct feature of Swahili towns since at least the fifteenth century (cf. Strandes 1961).

take place, social and political critiques are formulated, and customary standards of ritual practice and everyday behavior are questioned and even challenged. These are all critical discursive activities that play a role in constituting the social practice of philosophy, or philosophy as social practice. It is performed by individuals who express their critical thoughts to their peers through a common language. If philosophy consists of conscious efforts to orient oneself, reflecting on the basis of one's own thinking, knowing, and doing, this—while theoretically oriented—is still a particularly human practice embedded in specific social and cultural contexts that must be examined according to theme and investigated in relation to the respective thinking individual.

Drawing from Kant's characterization, we can gain both a rationale and a method for an anthropological approach to the investigation of philosophy within social life. Philosophy as a distinctly human activity of intellectual self-orientation is likely to occur in all cultures and societies. This insight can be employed for two central tasks of anthropological research on philosophical practice: the ethnographic aspect, i.e. the empirical observation of philosophy as a fundamentally reflexive and critical discursive practice in social life, and the theoretical evaluation of the observed socially and culturally specific forms of this practice in relation to a wider and potentially general understanding of philosophy.

This formal distinction is, in principle, applicable to any cultural context that human beings live in, in any part of the world. In Africa, just as anywhere else, we should be able to identify various institutionalized traditions of knowledge, schools of thought that teach historical "doctrines of skill" (the *Schulbegriff* of philosophy), and individual thinkers who develop their own creative "doctrines of wisdom" in regard to basic questions of human existence (the *Weltbegriff*). Approaching African philosophical discourse in this way, the Kantian distinction between worldly and scholarly aspects can help as a guideline in looking for and identifying philosophical practice in social life. Being formal, it can do this without predetermining any concrete form or shape that philosophical thought should take. It does not prescribe any content for a culturally specific practice of philosophizing, nor does it determine the concrete forms in which culturally specific philosophical thought can develop. It provides formal criteria with which to identify, contextualize, and understand philosophical discourse. Such a descriptive conception of philosophy enables us to approach existing institutionalized traditions ("systems") of knowledge in Africa, and since the historical knowledge of this realm can be taught and learned, it might also be publicly accessible or otherwise recordable by the philosophical field worker or the philosophically minded anthropologist.

Furthermore, individuals can be approached and their intellectual practice can be evaluated against its context: is it historically given knowledge or genuinely innovative? Is it critical or purely doctrinal? It is in the observation of the interaction between the two aspects of scholarly and worldly conceptions of philosophy that we can identify as a specific tradition of knowledge, and that we appreciate further attempts by individual thinkers to increase and improve knowledge and theory within that tradition? From a thorough description of the interaction between these two levels, then, we can work out an appropriate understanding of what one may call "philosophical discourses" within social dynamics, in Africa and elsewhere.

In this vein, using the Kantian distinction to situate specific thinkers or questions within schools or traditions of knowledge, Africanist research on philosophical traditions can link itself to existent studies. In particular, studies which have worked on local forms of "knowledge," local institutions of intellectual practice, and local conceptions of cosmologies in relation to social histories, questioning the validity of general Western categories such as "religion" and "politics," and working carefully on a depiction of the specific forms of indigenous traditions and their histories. To name some examples, in addition to Peel's (mentioned above), MacGaffey's work on religion and society in the lower Congo, or on prophets of indigenous Christian churches in the same area (1983, 1986), Janzen's work on Bantu "*ngoma*" institutions in Central- and South-East Africa (1992), or Johnson's work on Nuer prophets (1994), all achieve this. They portray and carefully work around the life histories of relevant intellectuals, and document their influence on regional social history. Brenner's historical biography of the West African Muslim sage Cerno Bokar also covers these aspects, and in addition provides translations of Bokar's spiritual discourses (1984). And Lambek's ethnography of a Comorian village, looking at the relation between knowledge and practice in local Islamic discourses, healing practices, and everyday life, integrates the portrayal of relevant individuals carefully into a wider picture of the social universe (1993).

Rereading and using such work will feed well into research on African philosophical traditions and intellectual histories. Furthermore, this kind of research also may open up fields of investigation for those working on African philosophy from a philosophical angle. The work of the few philosophers who in different ways embarked on fieldwork for their research on philosophy in Africa, Hallen (2001; and with Sodipo, 1986) and Oruka (1990/1), should also be mentioned. Coming from different backgrounds and with different methodological presuppositions, their research also sought the right balance between social discourse and individual thinkers and their ideas. Reconsidering African writers and thinkers, such as p'Bitek, Biko, Okri, or Ngugi, should also be an integral part of such interdisciplinary research efforts.[20] Finally, works on African languages and literary genres in their respective social dynamics, such as by Furniss for the Hausa (1996) and Barber (1991) for the Yoruba contexts, provide hallmarks for orientation. In conclusion, all these cases can be related to the *baraza* example presented here. They are all engaged with specific traditions and dynamics of knowledge in particular African contexts. They treat the ways in which local discourses of knowledge relate to theoretical conceptions, ideology, and everyday practice.

References

Barber, Karen 1991. *I could speak until tomorrow: oriki, women, and the past in a Yoruba town.* Edinburgh University Press.

Berg, Fred J. 1971: *Mombasa under the Busaidi sultanate: the city and its hinterlands in the nineteenth century.* PhD-thesis, University of Wisconsin.

Brenner, Louis 1984. West African Sufi. The religious heritage and spiritual search of Cerno Bokar Saalif Taal. London: Hurst.

Eze Emmanuel Ch. (ed) 1997a. 'Introduction', in idem (ed), *Postcolonial African philosophy: a critical reader.* Oxford: Blackwell.

Eze, Emmanuel Ch. (ed) 1997b. *Race and the enlightenment: a reader.* Oxford: Blackwell.

Fair, L. 2001. *Pastimes and politics: culture, community, and identity in post-abolition urban Zanzibar, 1890–1945.* Oxford: James Currey.

Furniss, Graham 1996. *Poetry, prose and popular culture in Hausa.* Edinburgh University Press.

Hallen, Barry 2001. *The good, the bad, and the beautiful.* Bloomington: Indiana University Press.

Haugerud, Angelique 1997 (1995): *The culture of politics in modern Kenya.* Cambridge: University Press.

Horton, Mark/ John Middleton 2000: *The Swahili. The social landscape of a mercantile society.* Oxford: Blackwell.

Hountondji, Paulin 1996 (1976). *African philosophy: myth and reality.* Bloomington: Indiana University Press.

Imbo, Samuel O. 2002. *Oral tradition as philosophy: Okot p'Bitek's legacy for African philosophy.* New York: Rowman & Littlefield.

---

20. On p'Bitek, for example see Imbo (2002) and Kresse (2002c).

Janzen, J. 1992. *Ngoma: discourses of healing in central Africa*. Berkeley: University of California Press.

Johnson, D.H. 1994. *Nuer prophets*. Oxford: Clarendon Press.

Kant, Immanuel 1990. *Kritik der reinen Vernunft* (edited by W. Weischedel). Frankfurt: Suhrkamp.

———— 1974. *Logic* (translated by R.S. Hartman and W. Schwarz). New York: Dover Publications.

Kindy, Hyder 1972: *Life and politics in Mombasa*. Nairobi: East African Publishing House.

Kresse, K. 2002a. *Approaching philosophical discourse in a Swahili context: knowledge, theory and intellectual practice in Old Town Mombasa, 1998–99*. PhD thesis, University of London.

———— 2002b. "Towards an anthropology of philosophies, in the African context", in G. Presbey et al. (eds), *Thought and practice in African Philosophy*. Nairobi: Konrad Adenauer Foundation, 29–46.

———— 2002c. "Towards a postcolonial synthesis in African philosophy – conceptual liberation and reconstructive self-evaluation in the work of Okot p'Bitek", in O. Oladipo (ed), *Issues in African Philosophy. Essays in honour of Kwasi Wiredu*. Ibadan: Hope Publishers, 215–232.

———— 2003. "'Swahili Enlightenment?' East African reformist discourse at the turning point: the example of Sheikh Muhammad Kasim Mazrui", *Journal of Religion in Africa* Vol. 33 (3), 279–309.

Lambek, Michael 1993. *Knowledge and practice in Mayotte*. Toronto University Press.

MacGaffey, Wyatt 1983. *Modern Kongo prophets*. Bloomington: Indiana University Press.

———— 1986. *Religion and society in central Africa*. Chicago University Press.

Nurse, Derek/Thomas Spear 1985: *The Swahili. Reconstructing the history and language of an African society, 800–1500*. Philadelphia: University of Pennsylvania Press.

Oruka, Henry Odera (ed) 1990/1. *Sage Philosophy*. Leiden: Brill/ Nairobi: ACTS Press.

Peel, J.D.Y. 1983. *Ijeshas and Nigerians*. Cambridge: Cambridge University Press.

———— 2000a. *Religious encounter and the making of the Yoruba*. Bloomington: Indiana University Press.

———— 2000b. 'Yoruba as a city-state culture', in M.H. Hansen (ed), *A comparative study of thirty city-state cultures*. Historisk-filosofiske Skrifter 21, Royal Danish Academy of Sciences and Letters.

Ranger, Terence 1974. *Dance and society in Eastern Africa, 1890–1970: the beni-ngoma*. London: Heinemann.

Schnädelbach, H. 1988. "Philosophie als Wissenschaft und als Aufklaerung", in W. Oelmueller (ed), *Philosophie und Wissenschaft*. Munich: Shoeningh, 206–220.

Sinclair, Paul/N.T. Hakansson 2000. 'The Swahili city-state culture', in M.H. Hansen (ed), *A comparative study of thirty city-state cultures*. Historiskfilosofiske Skrifter 21, Royal Danish Academy of Sciences and Letters.

Strandes, Justus 1961 (1899). *The Portuguese period in East Africa*. Nairobi: Kenya Literature Bureau.

Strobel, Margaret A. 1979. *Muslim women in Mombasa, Kenya, 1890–1975*. New Haven: Yale University Press

Willis, Justin 1993. *Mombasa, the Swahili, and the making of the Mijikenda*. Oxford: Clarendon Press.

INDEX

British civil law, 460, 462
British colonial, 43, 46, 142, 171, 224,
  363, 430, 432-433, 441, 443-444, 455,
  463, 491, 509, 520, 534, 576
British colonial administration, 576
British colonies, 400
British force, 181, 419
British Governor, 169, 575
British imperial world, 579
British laws, 170
British prohibition, 170
British Royal Anthropological Institute,
  29
British royalty, 395, 499
British rule, 195, 224, 235, 433, 439,
  443-444, 509, 534
British sociology, 30-31, 35-36, 97, 137
British tradition, 224, 510, 581, 586, 590
British West Africa, 137, 342
Broderick Hall, 347
Brooklyn, 73, 79
Brotherhood of Star and Cross, 310, 315,
  332, 336, 341, 359
Brown, David, 47-48, 54-55, 63-64, 74,
  76
Brydon, Lynne, 18, 33, 471, 487
Buddhism, 607
Buea, 519-520, 522, 532, 535-536, 542,
  547
Buea National Archives (BNA), 535, 547
Bugre, 372
Bugue, 372
Buguma, 344
Bunu Yoruba women, 143-144
Bureaucracy, 111, 312, 354, 598, 602,
  609
Burgess, Richard, 356-357
Burkina Faso, 280, 441-443
Burlet, Francisca, 47
Bush, George, 392, 396-397, 406
Buswell, H. D. (Ven.), 494
C&S coordinating council, 309
C&S movement, 256, 309, 327, 342
Cabildo de Lucumí, 48, 56
cabildo de nación, 49-50, 56
cabildos, 49-51, 53, 67, 76, 78-79
Cable News Network (CNN), 406
caboclo Bugue, 372

caboclos, 366, 368-370, 372-375, 381-383,
  385-387
Cabrera, Lydia, 66-67, 76-77
CAC Calendar,1965, 347
Cain, 571
Calabar, 235, 337-338, 414-415, 419-421,
  429, 432, 437-438
Caldey Island, 505
Calle Egido, 48
Calle San Nicolás, 48
Calvinism, 607
Calvinist doctrine, 607
Cameroon, 18, 178, 332, 517-524, 526,
  531-534, 536, 538-539, 542-543, 546-
  547
Cameroon Grassfields, 518-519, 531, 546
Canada, 441
Candomblé community, 60
candomblé de caboclo, 368
Candomblé house, 60
Candomblé terreiros, 59, 61
Canton, 544-546
Cape Coast, 460, 491, 504
Capital, 103-104, 106, 114, 173, 180,
  197, 213, 221-223, 327, 368, 472, 494,
  532, 536, 567, 597, 600, 605-607,
  610-611
Capitalism, 274, 304, 312, 331, 377, 474,
  484, 520, 565, 567, 583, 595-596,
  598-600, 602, 604-607, 610-611
Capitalist enterprise, 598
Capitalist market practices, 270
Capitalist states, 609
Capuchin priests, 498
Cardoso, Lourenço, 60
Caribbean, 73, 79, 81, 194, 322, 486
Carneiro, Edison, 60-61
Carr, Henry, 200
Carthage, 65
Caruru de Cosme e Damião, 372
Caruru meal, 372
Casement, Roger, 437, 439
Casey, 385, 388
Castellanos, Israel, 63, 76
Castro, Guillermo, 65
Catechumens, 446
Catholic, 47, 56-57, 59, 64, 72-73, 273,
  283, 290, 357-358, 366, 369-370, 374-